*Department of Commerce*

# Radio Stations of the United States

*Inktank publishing*

*Department of Commerce*

**Radio Stations of the United States**

*Inktank publishing, 2018*

*www.inktank-publishing.com*

*ISBN/EAN: 9783747768785*

DEPARTMENT OF COMMERCE

U. S. BUREAU OF NAVIGATION

# RADIO STATIONS OF THE UNITED STATES

EDITION JULY 1, 1913

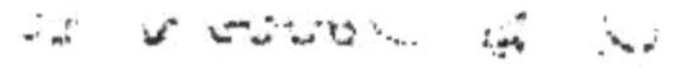

WASHINGTON
GOVERNMENT PRINTING OFFICE
1913

# CONTENTS.

## PART I.



## PART II.



DISTRICTS (HEADQUARTERS IN PARENTHESES).





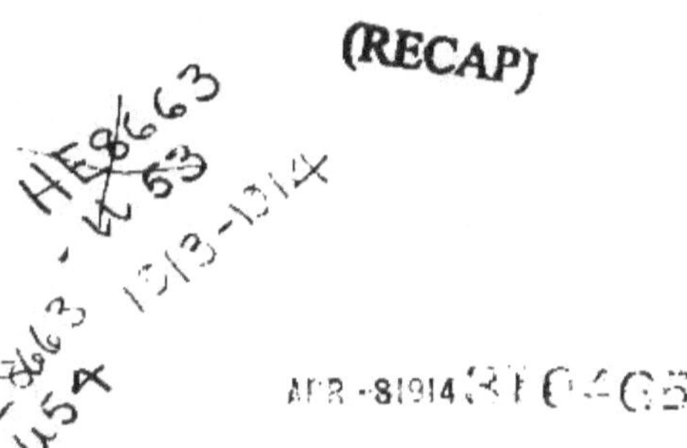

## NOTES.

Underscoring of normal wave lengths is indicated by the use of italics.

Government vessels showing "nature of service" to be PR, O, or PG, O, will accept or transmit paid messages for officers or members of crews.

Government vessels proceeding singly may relay messages to the coast upon request. The regular ship rate will apply.

### INTERNATIONAL ABBREVIATIONS USED IN THIS LIST.

Nature of service.—PG, general public; PR, limited public; P, Private (limited commercial); O, Government.

Hours of operation.—N, continuous; X, no regular hours.

Classification.—b, ship station; c, land station.

# RADIO STATIONS OF THE UNITED STATES.

## INTRODUCTION.

This list, including land and ship stations, is published in accordance with Section I of an act of Congress entitled "An act to regulate radio communication," approved August 13, 1912.

The following instructions concerning radio call letters are issued for the information of those concerned:

1. Section 7 of the act of August 13, 1912, to regulate radio communication provides:

Sec. 7. That a person, company, or corporation within the jurisdiction of the United States shall not knowingly utter or transmit, or cause to be uttered or transmitted, any false or fraudulent distress signal or call or false or fraudulent signal, call, or other radiogram of any kind. The penalty for so uttering or transmitting a false or fraudulent distress signal or call shall be a fine of not more than two thousand five hundred dollars or imprisonment for not more than five years, or both, in the discretion of the court, for each and every such offense, and the penalty for so uttering or transmitting, or causing to be uttered or transmitted, any other false or fraudulent signal, call, or other radiogram shall be a fine of not more than one thousand dollars or imprisonment for not more than two years, or both, in the discretion of the court, for each and every such offense.

2. The Service Regulations of the International Radiotelegraphic Conventions provide that the call letters of stations in the international system must each be formed of a group of three letters which shall be distinguishable from one another. The London International Radiotelegraphic Conference made a partial allotment of call letters among nations which signed the convention and the International Bureau at Berne, with the consent of such nations, has modified and added to this assignment of call letters by circular of April 23, 1913. The distribution of call letters among nations thus authorized is printed on the page following for the guidance of operators of all stations, ship and shore, of the United States.

A............All to Germany and protectorates.
B............All to Great Britain.
CAA to CMZ..Not yet assigned.
CNA to CNZ..Morocco.
COA to CPZ...Chile.
CQA to CQZ...Monaco.
CRA to CTZ...Portugal and colonies.
CUA to CUZ...Not yet assigned.
CVA to CVZ...Roumania.
CWA to CWZ..Uruguay.
CXA to CZZ...Not yet assigned.
D............All to Germany and protectorates.
EAA to EGZ..Spain and colonies.
EHA to EZZ..Not yet assigned.
F............All to France and colonies.
G............All to Great Britain.
HAA to HFZ..Austria-Hungary and Bosnia-Herzegovina.
HGA to HHZ..Siam.
HIA to HZZ..Not yet assigned.
I............All to Italy and colonies.
J............All to Japan and possessions.
KAA to KCZ..Germany and protectorates.
KDA to KZZ..United States.
LAA to LHZ..Norway.
LIA to LRZ...Argentine Republic.
LSA to LWZ..Not yet assigned.
LXA to LZZ..Bulgaria.
M............All to Great Britain.
N............All to the United States.
OAA to OFZ..Not yet assigned.
OGA to OMZ..Austria-Hungary and Bosnia-Herzegovina.
ONA to OTZ..Belgium and colonies.
OUA to OZZ..Denmark.
PAA to PIZ...Netherlands.
PJA to PJM...Curaçao (Dutch).
PJN to PJC...Surinam (Dutch).
PKA to PMZ..Dutch East Indies.
PNA to PZZ...Not yet assigned.
Q............Reserved for code abbreviations.
R............All to Russia.
SAA to SMZ...Sweden.
SNA to STZ...Brazil.
SUA to SUZ...Egypt.
SVA to SZZ...Greece.
TAA to TMZ..Turkey.
TNA to TZZ...Not yet assigned.
UAA to UMZ..France and colonies.
UNA to UZZ..Austria-Hungary and Bosnia-Herzegovina.
VAA to VGZ..Canada (British).
VHA to VKZ..Australian Federation (British).
VLA to VMZ..New Zealand (British).
VNA to VNZ..South African Union (British).
VOA to VOZ..Newfoundland (British).
VPA to VSZ...British colonies not autonomous.
VTA to VWZ..British India.
VXA to VZZ..Not yet assigned.
W............All to the United States.
XAA to XCZ..Mexico.
XDA to XZZ..Not yet assigned.
YAA to YZZ..Not yet assigned.
ZAA to ZZZ...Not yet assigned.

## PUBLIC-SERVICE STATIONS.

3. The call letters assigned to the United States are all combinations (676) beginning with the letter N and all (676) beginning with the letter W and all combinations (598) from KDA to KZZ, inclusive. The total number of international call letters assigned to the United States is thus 1,950 and these are reserved for Government stations and stations open to public and limited commercial service.

(*a*) All combinations beginning with the letter N are reserved for Government stations and in addition the combinations from WUA to WVZ and WXA to WZZ are reserved for stations of the Army of the United States.

(b) The combinations KDA to KZZ, with a few exceptions, are reserved for ship and coast stations on the Atlantic coast and Gulf of Mexico.

(c) The combinations beginning with W (except WUA to WVZ and WXA to WZZ as already indicated) are reserved, with a few exceptions, for ship and coast stations on the Pacific coast and on the Great Lakes.

### AMATEUR STATIONS.

4. The call letters for amateur stations in the United States will be awarded by radio inspectors, each for his own district, respectively, according to the following system:

(a) The call will consist of three items; number of radio district; followed by two letters of the alphabet. Thus, the call of all amateur stations in New England (which comprises the first district) will be the figure "one" in Continental Morse, followed by two letters; in California (in the sixth district) the figure "six" followed by two letters; in South Carolina the figure "four" followed by two letters; in Missouri the figure "nine" followed by two letters, etc. The letters X, Y, Z, must not be used as the first of the two letters.

The territory of each district is as follows:

1. Boston, Mass........Maine, New Hampshire, Vermont, Massachusetts, Rhode Island, Connecticut.
2. New York, N. Y.....New York (county of New York, Staten Island, Long Island, and counties on the Hudson River to and including Albany, Rensselaer, and Schenectady), and New Jersey (counties of Bergen, Passaic, Essex, Union, Middlesex, Monmouth, Hudson, and Ocean).
3. Baltimore, Md......New Jersey (all counties not included in second district), Pennsylvania (counties of Philadelphia, Delaware, all counties south of the Blue Mountains, and Franklin County), Delaware, Maryland, Virginia, District of Columbia.
4. Savannah, Ga.......North Carolina, South Carolina, Georgia, Florida, Porto Rico.
5. New Orleans, La...Alabama, Mississippi, Louisiana, Texas, Tennessee, Arkansas, Oklahoma, New Mexico.
6. San Francisco, Cal..California, Hawaii, Nevada, Utah, Arizona.
7. Seattle, Wash.......Oregon, Washington, Alaska, Idaho, Montana, Wyoming.
8. Cleveland, Ohio....New York (all counties not included in second district), Pennsylvania (all counties not included in third district), West Virginia, Ohio, Michigan (Lower Peninsula).
9. Chicago, Ill.........Indiana, Illinois, Wisconsin, Michigan (Upper Peninsula), Minnesota, Kentucky, Missouri, Kansas, Colorado, Iowa, Nebraska, South Dakota, North Dakota.

(*b*) The three items, a given figure first, followed by two letters of the alphabet, thus may be combined in 598 different calls, which will probably suffice for the amateur sending stations in most districts for some time to come.

(*c*) Radio inspectors will insert amateur station calls in station licenses according to this system, and will keep a permanent chart, of 598 squares, lettered with the alphabet from left to right and from top to bottom (A to W), inserting in the appropriate square the serial license number of the station to which the call letters were awarded. Within these limitations radio inspectors will use their discretion in the award of calls, avoiding, of course, duplications.

(*d*) When a station is abandoned and the license canceled, or if a license shall be forfeited for violation of law, the call assigned to it may be allotted to another station.

(*e*) If the entire 598 calls have been exhausted, radio inspectors will issue additional calls, consisting of the figure of the district followed by three letters. From such combinations should be excluded the combinations SOS and PRB, all three-letter combinations beginning with QR or QS, all combinations involving the repetition of the same letter three times, three-letter combinations beginning with K, N, W, X, Y, Z, and other combinations, which, for various reasons, international, national, local, or individual, may be objectionable. With such exclusions, over 10,000 calls will remain for each district.

### LIMITED COMMERCIAL STATIONS.

5. Calls for limited commercial land stations will be allotted by the Bureau of Navigation in a special manner to indicate, if practicable, the different radio districts over which such stations usually radiate messages, as well as to identify the stations.

### SPECIAL CLASSES OF STATIONS.

6. Calls for special classes of stations, such as experiment stations for the development of radio communication, technical and training school stations, and special amateur stations will be allotted by the Bureau of Navigation.

The call will consist of three items, the number of the radio district, followed by two letters of the alphabet. The first letter will be: X, for experiment stations; Y, technical and training schools; Z, special amateur stations.

Twenty-six different combinations for each class in each district, of course, are possible. If more should prove necessary for any class in any district, a third letter will be added to the call.

## RADIO STATIONS OF THE WORLD.

The International List of Radio Stations of the World, third edition, English, is adopted as the official list. This list will include the stations of the United States, excepting amateurs, and contain additional information, such as geographical location, normal range in nautical miles, radio system, and rates.

Persons desiring this list should communicate direct with the International Bureau of the Telegraphic Union (Radiotelegraphic Service), Berne, Switzerland. The price will be 60 cents per copy, not including postage. The rates of postage will be as follows: One copy, 24 cents; two copies, 32 cents; three copies, 48 cents. A subscription of 80 cents additional secures all supplements (postpaid) as issued from time to time until the next international list is published in the autumn of 1914. The stations of the United States will be printed in the first supplement.

Applications for the international list of call letters (stations of the world) should also be addressed to the International Bureau at Berne.

E. T. Chamberlain,
*Commissioner of Navigation.*

Approved:

Edwin F. Sweet,
*Assistant Secretary.*

# PART I.

## LAND RADIO STATIONS, ALPHABETICALLY BY NAMES OF STATIONS.

[This list includes commercial, special, Army, Navy, and all other land stations except restricted and general amateur. The special land stations are grouped at the end of this list.]

| Name. | Call signal. | Wave lengths. | Nature of service. | Hours of operation. | Station controlled by— |
|---|---|---|---|---|---|
| Annapolis, Md. | NAK | *600* | O | 8 a. m. to 10 p. m. | U. S. Navy. |
| Arlington, Radio, Va. | NAA | 2500 | O | N | U. S. Navy. |
| Ashtabula, Ohio | WSA | | | | Marconi Co.[1] |
| Astoria, Oreg. | KPC | 300, *600* | PG | N | Marconi Co. |
| Atlantic City, N. J. | WAX | | | | Marconi Co. |
| Avalon, Cal. | KPI | 300, *600* | PR | 7 a. m. to 8 p. m. | Marconi Co. |
| Balboa, Panama Canal Zone. | NPJ | 300, *600*, 1800 | PG | N | U. S. Navy. |
| Baltimore, Md. | WBS | 300, *600* | PG | N | Marconi Co. |
| Beaufort, N. C. | NAN | 300, *600* | PR | N | U. S. Navy. |
| Benton Harbor, Mich. | WBN | | | | Marconi Co. |
| Boston, Mass. | WCH | | | | National Electric Signaling Co. |
| Boston, Mass. | WBF | 300, *600* | PG | N | Marconi Co. |
| Boston, Mass. | NAD | 600, 1000 | O | N | U. S. Navy. |
| Bremerton, Wash. | NPC | 600 | O | N | U. S. Navy. |
| Brooklyn, N. Y. | WCG | | | | National Electric Signaling Co. |
| Buffalo, N. Y. | WBL | | | | Marconi Co. |
| Burnett Inlet, Alaska. | KIU | | | | Marconi Co. |
| Calumet, Mich. | WCM | | | | Marconi Co. |
| Cape Blanco, Oreg. | NPF | 300, *600* | PG | N | U. S. Navy. |
| Cape Cod, Mass. | NAE | 300, *600* | PR | N | U. S. Navy. |

[1] Marconi Wireless Telegraph Co. of America.

LAND RADIO STATIONS, ALPHABETICALLY BY NAMES OF STATIONS—Continued.

| Name. | Call signal. | Wave lengths. | Nature of service. | Hours of operation. | Station controlled by— |
|---|---|---|---|---|---|
| Cape Hatteras (Buxton), N. C. | WHA | 300, *600* | PG | N | Marconi Co. |
| Cape May, N. J | WCY | 300, *600* | PG | N | Marconi Co. |
| Cavite, P. I | NPO | *600* | O | N | U. S. Navy. |
| Charleston, S. C | NAG | 300, *600*, 1000, 1800. | PG, O. | N | U. S. Navy. |
| Chicago, Ill | WGO | 300, *600* | PG | 12.30 p.m. to 7 p. m., 8 p. m. to 11.30 p.m., 12.30 a.m. to 7 a. m., 8 a. m. to 11.30 a.m., when lake is open to navigation. | Marconi Co. |
| Chignic, Alaska | KHC | | | | Marconi Co. |
| Circle City, Alaska | WVA | | PG, O. | | U. S. Army. |
| Clarks Point, Alaska | KHG | | | | Marconi Co. |
| Cleveland, Ohio | WCX | 300, *600* | PG | N, Apr. 15 to Dec. 15. | Marconi Co. |
| Colon, Panama Canal Zone. | NAX | 300, *600*, 1800. | PG, O. | N | U. S. Navy. |
| Cordova, Alaska | NPA | 300, *600*, 1800. | PG | N | U. S. Navy. |
| Corregidor Island, P. I. | WVN | | O | | U. S. Army. |
| Cuyo, P. I | WVX | *600* | PG, O. | | U. S. Army. |
| Daley City, Cal | KHP | | | | Marconi Co. |
| Davao, P. I | WVO | *600* | PG, O. | | U. S. Army. |
| De Russey, T. H | WZG | | O | | U. S. Army. |
| Detroit, Mich | WDR | | | | Marconi Co. |
| Diamond Shoals Lightship (off Cape Hatteras, N. C.). | NLB | 300, *600* | PR | 8 a. m. to 10 p. m. | U. S. Navy. |
| Douglas, Ariz | KDC | 300, *600* | P | 10 a. m. to 11 a. m.; 4 p. m. to 5 p. m. | Copper Queen Consolidated Mining Co. |

LAND RADIO STATIONS, ALPHABETICALLY BY NAMES OF STATIONS—Continued.

| Name. | Call signal. | Wave lengths. | Nature of service. | Hours of operation. | Station controlled by— |
|---|---|---|---|---|---|
| Duluth, Minn. | WDM | 300, *600* | PG | Apr. 15 to Dec. 15: N, except from 6 a. m. to 7 a. m.; 12 noon to 1 p. m.; 6 p. m. to 7 p. m. Dec. 15 to Apr. 15: 7 a. m. to 7 p. m. except from 12 noon to 1 p. m. | Marconi Co. |
| Dutch Harbor, Alaska | NPR | 300, *600*, 1800 | PG | N | U. S. Navy. |
| El Paso, Tex | WEP | *2000*, 2500, 2900, 3500 | PR | 6 a. m. to 7 p. m. | Federal Telegraph Co. |
| Ensanada, P. R. | WPR | | | | Guanica Centrale. |
| Eureka, Cal | KPM | | | | Marconi Co. |
| Eureka, Cal | NPW | 300, *600*, 1000, 1800 | PG | N | U. S. Navy. |
| Fairbanks, Alaska | WVB | | PG, O. | | U. S. Army. |
| Farallons, Cal | NPI | 300, *600* | PR | N | U. S. Navy. |
| Fire Island, N. Y. | NAG | 300, *600* | PR | N | U. S. Navy. |
| Fort Andrews, Mass. | WUA | | O | | U. S. Army. |
| Fort Drum, P. I. | WVP | | O | | U. S. Army. |
| Fort Egbert, Alaska | WVC | | PG, O. | | U. S. Army. |
| Fort Frank, P. I. | WVL | | O | | U. S. Army. |
| Fort Gibbon, Alaska | WVD | | PG, O. | | U. S. Army. |
| Fort Hancock, N. J. | WUB | | O | | U. S. Army. |
| Fort H. G. Wright, N. Y. | WUC | | O | | U. S. Army. |
| Fort Hughes, P. I. | WVM | | O | | U. S. Army. |
| Fort Leavenworth, Kans. | WUD | | O | | U. S. Army. |

LAND RADIO STATIONS, ALPHABETICALLY BY NAMES OF STATIONS—Continued.

| Name. | Call signal. | Wave lengths. | Nature of service. | Hours of operation. | Station controlled by— |
|---|---|---|---|---|---|
| Fort Leavenworth, Kans. (Army Signal School). | WUV | .............. | O..... | ........... | U. S. Army. |
| Fort Levett, Me ..... | WUE | .............. | O..... | ........... | U. S. Army. |
| Fort Monroe, Va. .... | WUF | .............. | O..... | ........... | U. S. Army. |
| Fort Monroe, Va. (Coast Artillery School). | WUG | .............. | O..... | ........... | U. S. Army. |
| Fort Morgan, Ala..... | WFM | .............. | ...... | ........... | Marconi Co. |
| Fort Omaha, Nebr... | WUH | .............. | O..... | ........... | U. S. Army. |
| Fort Riley, Kans..... | WUI | .............. | O..... | ........... | U. S. Army. |
| Fort St. Michael, Alaska. | WVE | *600*, 1200..... | PG, O. | 9 a. m. to 9 p. m. | U. S. Army. |
| Fort Sam Houston, Tex. | WUJ | .............. | O..... | ........... | U. S. Army. |
| Fort Stevens, Oreg... | WUK | .............. | O..... | ........... | U. S. Army. |
| Fort Totten, N. Y.... | WUL | .............. | O..... | ........... | U. S. Army. |
| Fort Wm. McKinley, P. I. | WVQ | .............. | O..... | ........... | U. S. Army. |
| Fort Winfield Scott, Kans. | WUO | .............. | O..... | ........... | U. S. Army. |
| Fort Wint, P. I...... | WVR | .............. | O..... | ........... | U. S. Army. |
| Fort Wood, N. Y..... | WUM | .............. | O..... | ........... | U. S. Army. |
| Fort Worden, Wash.. | WUN | .............. | O..... | ........... | U. S. Army. |
| Fort Worth, Tex...... | WFF | *2000*, 2500, 2900, 3500 | PR.... | 6 a. m. to 6 p. m. | Federal Telegraph Co. |
| Frankfort, Mich...... | WFK | .............. | ...... | ........... | Marconi Co. |
| Friday Harbor, Wash. | KPD | 300, *600* ..... | PG.... | 7 a. m. to 2.30 a. m. | Marconi Co. |
| Frying Pan Shoals, N. C. (off Cape Fear). | NLC | 300, *600*...... | PR.... | 8 a. m. to 10 p. m. | U. S. Navy. |
| Galveston, Tex....... | WGV | .............. | ...... | ........... | Marconi Co. |
| Grand Haven, Mich.. | WGH | .............. | ...... | ........... | Marconi Co. |
| Grand Island, La..... | WGW | .............. | ...... | ........... | Marconi Co. |
| Grand Marais, Minn.. | WGM | .............. | ...... | ........... | Marconi Co. |
| Guam, Mariana (Ladrone) Islands, Pacific Ocean. | NPN | 300, *600*, 1800. | PG.... | N......... | U. S. Navy. |

LAND RADIO STATIONS, ALPHABETICALLY BY NAMES OF STATIONS—Continued.

| Name. | Call signal. | Wave lengths. | Nature of service. | Hours of operation. | Station controlled by— |
|---|---|---|---|---|---|
| Guantanamo Bay, Cuba. | NAW | 300, *600*, 1800. | PG | N | U. S. Navy. |
| Heeia Point, T. H. | KHX | | | | Federal Telegraph Co. |
| Honolulu, T. H. | NPM | 600 | O | N | U. S. Navy. |
| Isle Royal, Minn. | WRO | | | | Marconi Co. |
| Jacksonville, Fla. | WJX | 300, *600* | PG | N | Marconi Co. |
| Jolo, P. I. | WVS | *600* | PG, O. | | U. S. Army. |
| Jualin, Alaska | KJA | | | | Marconi Co. |
| Juneau, Alaska | KDU | | | | Marconi Co. |
| Jupiter, Fla. | NAQ | *300*, 600, 1800. | PG | N | U. S. Navy. |
| Kahuku, T. H. | KHK | | | | Mutual Telephone Co. (Ltd.). |
| Kake, Alaska | KIT | | | | Marconi Co. |
| Karluk, Alaska | KHA | | | | Marconi Co. |
| Kaunakakai, T. H. | KHO | | | | Mutual Telephone Co. (Ltd.). |
| Kawaihae, T. H | KHN | | | | Mutual Telephone Co. (Ltd.). |
| Ketchikan, Alaska | KPB | | | | Marconi Co. |
| Key West, Fla. | NAR | 300, *600*, 1000, 1800. | PG | N | U. S. Navy. |
| Kodiak, Alaska | NPS | 300, *600*, 1800. | PG | N | U. S. Navy. |
| Kogiung, Alaska | KHB | | | | Marconi Co. |
| Koko Head, T. H | KHJ | | | | Marconi Co. |
| Kotlik, Alaska | WVF | *600* | PG, O. | 9 a. m. to 9 p. m. during season of navigation only. | U. S. Army. |
| Lahaina, T. H. | KHL | | | | Mutual Telephone Co. (Ltd.). |
| Lihue, T. H | KHM | | | | Mutual Telephone Co. (Ltd.). |

LAND RADIO STATIONS, ALPHABETICALLY BY NAMES OF STATIONS—Continued.

| Name. | Call signal. | Wave lengths. | Nature of service. | Hours of operation. | Station controlled by— |
|---|---|---|---|---|---|
| Los Angeles, Cal. | KEX | 300, *600* | P | 9 a. m. to 5 p. m. | Marconi Co. |
| Ludington, Mich. | WLD | 300, *600* | PG | 7 a. m. to 6 p. m. 7 p. m. to 6 a. m. Apr. 15 to Dec. 15 only. | Marconi Co. |
| Mackinac Island, Mich. | WHQ | | | | Marconi Co. |
| Malabang, P. I. | WVT | *600* | PG, O. | | U. S. Army. |
| Manila, P. I. | WVU | | O | | U. S. Army. |
| Manistique, Mich. | WMX | | | | Marconi Co. |
| Manitowoc, Wis. | WMW | 300, *600* | PG | 8 a. m. to 11.30 a.m. 2.30 p. m. to 6 p. m. 7.30 p. m. to 9 p. m. | Marconi Co. |
| Mare Island, Cal. | NPH | 600, 1000 | O | N | U. S. Navy. |
| Marshfield, Ohio | KPX | 300, 435, *600* | PG | 8 a. m. to 6 p. m. | Marconi Co. |
| Milwaukee, Wis. | WME | 300, *600* | PG | 1.30 a. m. to 6 a. m. 7 a. m. to 12.30 p.m. 1.30 p. m. to 6 p. m. 7 p. m. to 12.30 a.m. | Marconi Co. |
| Mobile, Ala. | WMB | | | | Marconi Co. |
| Naknek, Alaska | KHT | | | | Marconi Co. |
| Nantucket Shoals Lightship (off Newport, R. I.). | NLA | 300, *600* | PR | 8 a. m. to 10 p. m. | U. S. Navy. |
| New London, Conn. | WLC | | | | T. A. Scott Co. (Inc.). |
| New Orleans, La. | WHK | | | | Marconi Co. |
| New Orleans, La. | NAT | 600, 1000 | PR | 8 a. m. to 10 p. m. | U. S. Navy. |
| Newport, R. I. | NAF | 600, 1000 | PR, O. | N | U. S. Navy. |
| Newton, Mass. | WLN | | | | Ralph C. Emery. |

LAND RADIO STATIONS, ALPHABETICALLY BY NAMES OF STATIONS—Continued.

| Name. | Call signal. | Wave lengths. | Nature of service. | Hours of operation. | Station controlled by— |
|---|---|---|---|---|---|
| New York, N. Y. | WNT | 300, *600* | PG | N | Atlantic Communication Co. |
| New York, N. Y. | WHB | 300, *600*, 1610. | PG | N | New York Herald Co. |
| New York, N. Y. | WHI | | | | Marconi Co. |
| New York, N. Y. | NAH | 600, 1000 | O | N | U. S. Navy. |
| Nome, Alaska | WVG | *600*, 1400 | PG, O | 9 a. m. to 9 p. m. | U. S. Army. |
| Norfolk, Va | NAM | 600, 1000 | O | N | U. S. Navy. |
| North Head, Wash | NPE | 300, *600*, 1000, 1800. | PG | N | U. S. Navy. |
| Nulato, Alaska | WVH | | PG, O | | U. S. Army. |
| Nushagak, Alaska | KHF | | | | Marconi Co. |
| Olongapo, P. I. | NPT | *600* | O | N | U. S. Navy. |
| Peking, China | NPP | 600 | O | N | U. S. Navy. |
| Pensacola, Fla | NAS | 300, *600*, 1800. | PG | N | U. S. Navy. |
| Petersburg, Alaska | WVI | *600* | PG, O. | 9 a. m. to 9 p. m. | U. S. Army. |
| Philadelphia, Pa | WHE | 300, *600*, 1610. | PG | N | Marconi Co. |
| Philadelphia, Pa | NAI | *600* | O | N | U. S. Navy. |
| Phoenix, Ariz | KHQ | | | | Federal Telegraph Co. |
| Point Arguello, Cal | NPK | 300, *600* | PG | N | U. S. Navy. |
| Port Arthur, Tex | WRU | | | | Marconi Co. |
| Portland, Me | NAB | 300, *600* | PR | 8 a. m. to 10 p. m. | U. S. Navy. |
| Porto Bello, Republic of Panama. | NAY | 300, *600* | O | X | U. S. Navy. |
| Portsmouth, N. H. | NAC | 600 | O | N | U. S. Navy. |
| Puerto Princesa, P. I. | WVV | *600* | PG, O | | U. S. Army. |
| Sagaponack, N. Y. | WSK | | | | Marconi Co. |
| St. Augustine, Fla | NAP | 300, *600* | PG | N | U. S. Navy |
| St. George, Pribilof Islands, Alaska. | NPY | 300 | O | X | U. S. Navy. |

LAND RADIO STATIONS, ALPHABETICALLY BY NAMES OF STATIONS—Continued.

| Name. | Call signal. | Wave lengths. | Nature of service. | Hours of operation. | Station controlled by— |
|---|---|---|---|---|---|
| St. Paul, Pribilof Islands, Alaska. | NPQ | 300, *600*, 1800. | PG | N | U. S. Navy. |
| San Diego, Cal | NPL | 300, *600*, 1000, 1800. | PG | N | U. S. Navy. |
| San Francisco, Cal | KPH | | | | Marconi Co. |
| San Juan, P. R | NAU | 300, *600*, 1800. | PG | N | U. S. Navy. |
| San Jose, P. I | WVY | *600* | PG, O. | | U. S. Army. |
| San Luis Obispo, Cal. | KDN | | | | Marconi Co. |
| San Pedro, Cal | KPJ | 300, *600* | PG | N | Marconi Co. |
| Sault Ste. Marie, Mich | WSI | | | | Marconi Co. |
| Savannah, Ga | WSV | 300, *600* | PG | N, except Mondays and Thursdays station closes at midnight. | Marconi Co. |
| Sayville, N. Y | WSL | 300, *600*, 1800, 2480, 2800, 2900, 3600, 4800. | PG | N | Atlantic Communication Co. |
| Sea Gate, N. Y | WSE | | | | Marconi Co. |
| Seattle, Wash | KPA | 300, *600* | PG | N | Marconi Co. |
| Siasconset, Mass | WSC | 300, *600* | PG | N | Marconi Co. |
| Sitka, Alaska | NPB | 300, *600*, 1800. | PG | N | U. S. Navy. |
| South Wellfleet, Mass. | WCC | 300, *600*, 2040. | PG | N | Marconi Co. |
| Tampa, Fla | WPD | | | | Marconi Co. |
| Tatoosh, Wash | NPD | 300, *600*, 1000. | PG | N | U. S. Navy. |
| Unalga, Alaska | NPV | 300, *600*, 1800. | PG | N | U. S. Navy. |
| Virginia Beach, Va | WSY | 300, *600* | PG | N | Marconi Co. |
| Washington, D. C. (Army Signal Corps Laboratory). | WUP | | O. | | U. S. Army. |
| Washington, D. C. (Bureau of Standards). | WUQ | | O. | | U. S. Army. |

2002°—13——2

LAND RADIO STATIONS, ALPHABETICALLY BY NAMES OF STATIONS—Continued.

| Name. | Call signal. | Wave lengths. | Nature of service. | Hours of operation. | Station controlled by— |
|---|---|---|---|---|---|
| Washington, D. C., (Navy Yard). | NAL | *600*.......... | O..... | N......... | U. S. Navy. |
| Wrangell, Alaska.... | WVJ | *600*.......... | PG, O | 9 a. m. to 9 p. m. | U. S. Army. |
| Zamboanga, P. I..... | WVW | *600*.......... | PG, O. | ........... | U. S. Army. |

SPECIAL LAND STATIONS.[1]

| Name. | Call signal. | Wave lengths. | Nature of service. | Hours of operation. | Station controlled by— |
|---|---|---|---|---|---|
| Ames, Iowa.......... | 9YI | .............. | ....... | ........... | Iowa State College of Agriculture & Mechanic Arts. |
| Amesbury, Mass..... | 1XA | *600*.......... | P...... | X........ | Wireless Specialty Apparatus Co. |
| Ann Arbor, Mich..... | 8XA | .............. | ....... | ........... | University of Michigan. |
| Atlanta, Ga.......... | 3ZH | *300*.......... | ....... | ........... | Georgia School of Technology. |
| Beloit, Wis.......... | 9XB | Variable...... | P...... | X........ | Beloit College. |
| Berkeley, Cal......... | 6XR | .............. | ....... | ........... | Frank Rieber. |
| Boston, Mass......... | 1XB | Variable...... | P...... | X........ | Wireless Specialty Apparatus Co. |
| Boston, Mass ........ | 1XH | .............. | ....... | ........... | Holtzer-Cabot Electric Co. |
| Cambridge, Mass..... | 1YH | Variable...... | P...... | X........ | Harvard University. |
| Cambridge, Mass..... | 1XP | 300, *550*, 600.. | P...... | X........ | George W. Pierce. |
| Chelsea, Mass........ | 1XC | .............. | ....... | ........... | Wm. J. Murdock Co. |
| Detroit, Mich........ | 8YD | 300, *400*, 600.. | P...... | 9 a. m. to 3 p. m.; 7 p. m. to 9 p. m. | Wm. J. Meisenheimer. |
| Grand Forks, N. Dak. | 9YN | *500*, variable to 730. | P...... | X........ | University of North Dakota. |
| Hyattsville, Md...... | 3XR | .............. | ....... | ........... | J. Harris Rogers. |
| Los Angeles, Cal..... | 6YL | .............. | ....... | ........... | High School. |

[1] See introduction, page 8.

LAND RADIO STATIONS, ALPHABETICALLY BY NAMES OF STATIONS—Continued.

| Name. | Call signal. | Wave lengths. | Nature of service. | Hours of operation. | Station controlled by— |
|---|---|---|---|---|---|
| New York, N. Y..... | 2YN | ............ | ...... | .......... | Alfred Norton Goldsmith (College of the City of New York). |
| Nutley, N. J........ | 2ZH | ............ | ...... | .......... | Arthur A. Hebert. |
| Philadelphia, Pa..... | 3XC | *480*.......... | P...... | X........ | Frank B. Chambers. |
| Philadelphia, Pa..... | 3XJ | *500*.......... | P...... | X........ | St. Joseph's College. |
| St. Davids, Pa....... | 3ZS | *450*.......... | P...... | X........ | Chas. H. Stewart. |
| St. Louis, Mo........ | 9YC | ............ | ...... | .......... | Christian Brothers College. |
| Washington, D. C.... | 3ZH | ............ | ...... | .......... | H. B. DeGroot. |

## SHIP RADIO STATIONS, ALPHABETICALLY BY NAMES OF VESSELS.

[This list includes all stations on merchant vessels, yachts, vessels of the Army, the Navy, and the Revenue-Cutter Service.]

| Name. | Call signal. | Wave lengths. | Nature of service. | Owner of vessel (line). | Station controlled by— |
|---|---|---|---|---|---|
| A. G. Lindsay | WNO | | | Pacific-American Fisheries | |
| Abarenda | NOB | 600 | PR, O | Government | U. S. Navy. |
| Acapulco | WWO | | | Pacific Mail S. S. Co. | Marconi Co.[1] |
| Acushnet | NRU | 300 | PG, O | Government | U. S. Revenue-Cutter Service. |
| Adams | KPN | 300, *600* | PG | Pennsylvania Nautical School | Marconi Co. |
| Adeline Smith | WHS | | | Inter-Ocean Transportation Co. | |
| Admiral Dewey | KUV | 300, *600* | PG | American Mail S. S. Co. | Marconi Co. |
| Admiral Farragut | WAF | | | Alaska-Pacific S. S. Co. | |
| Admiral Sampson | WAS | | | do. | |
| Admiral Schley | KUX | | | American Mail S. S. Co. | Marconi Co. |
| Advance | KMV | 300, *600* | PG | Panama R. R. Co. | Marconi Co. |
| Adventuress | KYV | | | John Borden | |
| Ajax | NBH | 600 | PR, O | Government | U. S. Navy. |
| Alabama | WFB | 300, *600* | PG | Goodrich Transit Co. | Marconi Co. |
| Alabama | KSX | | | Baltimore Steam Packet Co. | |
| Alabama | NBI | 600 | PR, O | Government | U. S. Navy. |

| | | | | | |
|---|---|---|---|---|---|
| Alameda | WAA | | | Alaska S. S. Co. | |
| Alamo | KEJ | 300, *600* | PG | Mallory S. S. Co. | Marconi Co. |
| Albany | NBJ | 600 | PR, O | Government | U. S. Navy. |
| Alert | NBL | 600 | PR, O | do | U. S. Navy. |
| Algonquin | KVG | 300, *600* | PG | Clyde S. S. Co. | Marconi Co. |
| Algonquin | NRA | 300, *600* | PG, O | Government | U. S. Revenue-Cutter Service. |
| Al-ki | WNK | | | H. C. Strong | |
| Alleghany | KQA | 300, *600* | PG | Merchants & Miners Transportation Co. | Marconi Co. |
| Allianca | KMA | 300, *600* | PG | Panama R. R. Co. | Marconi Co. |
| Alliance | WRV | | | North Pacific S. S. Co. | |
| Aloha | KYH | | | Arthur Curtiss James | |
| Alvina | WEY | | | Thomas F. Cole | |
| America | KNZ | | | Brooklyn & Manhattan Ferry Co. | |
| Ammen | NBP | 600 | PR, O | Government | U. S. Navy. |
| Ancon | KMS | 300, *600* | PG | Panama R. R. Co. | Marconi Co. |
| Androscoggin | NRD | 300, *600* | PG, O | Government | U. S. Revenue-Cutter Service. |
| Annapolis | NBR | 600 | PR, O | do | U. S. Navy. |
| Ann Arbor No. 3 | WDN | 300, *600* | PG | Ann Arbor R. R. Co. | Marconi Co. |

[1] Marconi Wireless Telegraph Co. of America.

SHIP RADIO STATIONS, ALPHABETICALLY BY NAMES OF VESSELS—Continued.

| Name. | Call signal. | Wave lengths. | Nature of service. | Owner of vessel (line). | Station controlled by— |
|---|---|---|---|---|---|
| Ann Arbor No. 4 | WDO | 300, *600* | PG | Ann Arbor R. R. Co. | Marconi Co. |
| Ann Arbor No. 5 | WDP | 300, *600* | PG | do | Marconi Co. |
| Antilles | KKA | 300, *600* | PG | Southern Pacific Co. | Marconi Co. |
| Apache | KVA | 300, *600* | PG | Clyde S. S. Co. | Marconi Co. |
| Apache | NRP | 300, *600* | PG, O | Government | U. S. Revenue-Cutter Service. |
| Arapahoe | KVB | 300, *600* | PG | Clyde S. S. Co. | Marconi Co. |
| Argyll | WTB | | | Union S. S. Co. (Union Oil Co.) | |
| Arizona | WFG | 300, *600* | PG | Goodrich Transit Co. | Marconi Co. |
| Arkansas | NBV | 600 | PR, O | Government | U. S. Navy. |
| Aroline | WRJ | | | Aroline S. S. Co. | Marconi Co. |
| Ashtabula | WEZ | 300, *600* | PG | Pennsylvania & Ontario Navigation Co. | Marconi Co. |
| Astral | KTO | | | Standard Oil Co. | |
| Asuncion | WTX | | | do | |
| Atalanta | KYA | | | George J. Gould | |
| Atlas | WTT | | | Standard Oil Co. | |
| Aztec | WWQ | | | Pacific Mail S. S. Co. | |

| | | | | | |
|---|---|---|---|---|---|
| Bailey | NCF | 600 | PR, O | Government | U. S. Navy. |
| Baltimore | NCH | 600 | PR, O | do | U. S. Navy. |
| Bayamon | KDX | | | Ocean Freight Line | |
| Bay State | KRE | | | Eastern S. S. Corporation | |
| Beale | NCL | 600 | PR, O | Government | U. S. Navy. |
| Bear | NRB | 300, *600* | PG, O | do | U. S. Revenue-Cutter Service. |
| Bear | WWD | | | San Francisco & Portland S. S. Co | Marconi Co. |
| Beaver | WWB | | | do | Marconi Co. |
| Belfast | KRD | 300, *600* | PG | Eastern S. S. Corporation | Marconi Co. |
| Berkshire | KQB | 300, *600* | PG | Merchants & Miners Transportation Co | Marconi Co. |
| Berlin | WRB | | | Alaska-Portland Packers' Association | |
| Bertha | WBR | | | Alaska Coast Co | |
| Birmingham | NCM | 600 | PR, O | Government | U. S. Navy. |
| Borinquen | KDW | 300, *600* | PG | Ocean Freight Line | Marconi Co. |
| Boston | KXA | | | New England S. S. Co | National Electric Signaling Co. |
| Brazos | KEZ | 300, *600* | PG | Mallory S. S. Co | Marconi Co. |
| Breakwater | WBK | | | Southern Pacific Co | |
| Brilliant | KTI | | | Standard Oil Co | |
| Brunswick | KOS | 300, *600* | PG | Gulf & Southern S. S. Co | Marconi Co. |

SHIP RADIO STATIONS, ALPHABETICALLY BY NAMES OF VESSELS—Continued.

| Name. | Call signal. | Wave lengths. | Nature of service. | Owner of vessel (line). | Station controlled by— |
| --- | --- | --- | --- | --- | --- |
| Brutus | NNA | 600 | PR, O | Government | U. S. Navy. |
| Buckman | WAB | | | Alaska-Pacific S. S. Co | Marconi Co. |
| Buffalo | NBU | 600 | PR, O | Government | U. S. Navy. |
| Buford | WXA | *600* | O | do | U. S. Army. |
| Bunker Hill | KJB | | | Eastern S. S. Corporation | |
| Burnside | WXR | *600* | O | Government | U. S. Army. |
| Burrows | NCV | 600 | PR, O | do | U. S. Navy. |
| Cabrillo | WBV | | | Wilmington Transportation Co | |
| Caesar | NCY | 600 | PR, O | Government | U. S. Navy. |
| California | NCZ | 600 | PR, O | do | U. S. Navy. |
| Calvin Austin | KRN | | | Eastern S. S. Corporation | |
| Camden | KRC | 300, *600* | PG | do | Marconi Co. |
| Camino | WQC | | | Western Steam Navigation Co | Marconi Co. |
| Cape Cod | KPW | | | George R. West | |
| Captain A. F. Lucas | WTV | | | Standard Oil Co | Marconi Co. |
| Captain Barrett | WYP | *300* | O | Government | U. S. Army. |
| Captain Chas. W. Rowell | WYI | *300* | O | do | U. S. Army. |

| | | | | | |
|---|---|---|---|---|---|
| Caracas | KDB | 300, *600* | PG | Atlantic & Carribean Steam Navigation Co. (Red D Line). | Marconi Co. |
| Carlos | WNC | | | Olson & Mahony | Marconi Co. |
| Carolina | WFE | | | Goodrich Transit Co | |
| Carolina | KGB | | | New York & Porto Rico S. S. Co | |
| Carolyn | KNF | | | A. H. Bull S. S. Co | |
| Cassandra | KYE | | | George J. Whalen | |
| Castine | NDA | 600 | PR, O | Government | U. S. Navy. |
| Catania | WTI | | | Coast Oil Transportation Co | |
| Celtic | NDB | 600 | PR, O | Government | U. S. Navy. |
| Centralia | WSN | | | Centralia Co. (Pollard S. S. Co.) | Marconi Co |
| Chalmette | KKC | 300, *600* | PG | Southern Pacific Co | Marconi Co. |
| Charleston | NFE | 600 | PR, O | Government | U. S. Navy. |
| Chattanooga | NGI | 600 | PR, O | do | U. S. Navy. |
| Chehalis | WSH | | | Sudden & Christenson | Marconi Co. |
| Cherokee | KVK | 300, *600* | PG | Clyde S. S. Co | Marconi Co. |
| Chester | NDG | 600 | PR, O | Government | U. S. Navy. |
| Chester W. Chapin | KXQ | | | New England S. S. Co | National Electric Signaling Co. |
| Cheyenne | NDH | 600 | PR, O | Government | U. S. Navy. |
| Chicago | WAC | | | Booth Fisheries Co | |

SHIP RADIO STATIONS, ALPHABETICALLY BY NAMES OF VESSELS—Continued.

| Name. | Call signal. | Wave lengths. | Nature of service. | Owner of vessel (line). | Station controlled by— |
|---|---|---|---|---|---|
| Chicago | WFI | | | Goodrich Transit Co | |
| Chicago | NDI | 600 | PR, O | Government | U. S. Navy. |
| China | WWA | | | Pacific Mail S. S. Co | |
| Chippewa | WBH | | | Tacoma-Seattle-Everett Route | |
| Christopher Columbus | WFJ | | | Goodrich Transit Co | |
| Cincinnati | NDL | 600 | PR, O | Government | U. S. Navy. |
| City of Alpena II | WEH | | | Detroit & Cleveland Navigation Co | |
| City of Atlanta | KFB | 300, *600* | PG | Ocean S. S. Co. (Savannah Line) | Marconi Co. |
| City of Augusta | KFJ | | | do | |
| City of Baltimore | KRY | | | Mercantile Trust & Deposit Co. (Chesapeake S. S. Co.). | |
| City of Bangor | KRH | | | Eastern S. S. Corporation | |
| City of Benton Harbor | WDV | | | Graham & Morton Transportation Co | |
| City of Buffalo | WFQ | 300, *600* | PG | Cleveland & Buffalo Transportation Co | Marconi Co. |
| City of Chicago | WDT | | | Graham & Morton Transportation Co | |
| City of Cleveland III | WEA | | | Detroit & Cleveland Navigation Co | Marconi Co. |
| City of Columbus | KFA | 300, *600* | PG | Ocean S. S. Co. (Savannah Line) | Marconi Co. |

| | | | | | |
|---|---|---|---|---|---|
| City of Detroit II | WEC | 300, 420, *600* | PG | Detroit & Cleveland Navigation Co. | Marconi Co. |
| City of Detroit III | WEF | 300, *600* | PG | do | Marconi Co. |
| City of Erie | WFP | 300, *600* | PG | Cleveland & Buffalo Transportation Co. | Marconi Co. |
| City of Everett | KTQ | | | Standard Oil Co. | |
| City of Grand Rapids | WDS | | | Graham & Morton Transportation Co. | |
| City of Lowell | KXB | | | New England S. S. Co. | National Electric Signaling Co. |
| City of Mackinac II | WEB | 300, *600* | | Detroit & Cleveland Navigation Co. | Marconi Co. |
| City of Macon | KFC | | | Ocean S. S. Co. (Savannah Line) | |
| City of Memphis | KFD | | | do | Marconi Co. |
| City of Montgomery | KFY | 300, *600* | PG | do | Marconi Co. |
| City of Norfolk | KRZ | | | Mercantile Trust & Deposit Co. (Chesapeake S. S. Co.). | |
| City of Panama | WWP | | | Pacific Mail S. S. Co. | |
| City of Para | WWF | | | do | |
| City of Puebla | WGQ | 300, *600* | PG | Pacific Coast Co. | Marconi Co. |
| City of Rockland | KRI | | | Eastern S. S. Corporation | |
| City of St. Ignace | WEG | | | Detroit & Cleveland Navigation Co | Marconi Co. |
| City of St. Louis | KFX | 300, *600* | PG | Ocean S. S. Co. (Savannah Line) | Marconi Co. |
| City of Savannah | KFK | 300, *600* | PG | do | Marconi Co. |
| City of Seattle | WGA | | | Pacific Coast Co. | |

SHIP RADIO STATIONS, ALPHABETICALLY BY NAMES OF VESSELS—Continued.

| Name. | Call signal. | Wave lengths. | Nature of service. | Owner of vessel (line). | Station controlled by— |
|---|---|---|---|---|---|
| City of South Haven | WDI | | | Chicago & South Haven S. S. Co. | |
| City of Sydney | WWG | | | Pacific Mail S. S. Co. | |
| City of Taunton | KXL | | | New England S. S. Co. | National Electric Signaling Co. |
| City of Topeka | WGY | | | Pacific Coast Co. | Marconi Co. |
| Cleveland | NDM | 600 | PR, O | Government | U. S. Navy. |
| Coamo | KGA | 300, *600* | PG | New York & Porto Rico S. S. Co. | Marconi Co. |
| Col. E. L. Drake | WTS | | | Standard Oil Co. | |
| Col. James M. Schoonmaker | WEQ | | | Shenango S. S. Co. | Marconi Co. |
| Colon | KMX | 300, *600* | PG | Panama R. R. Co. | Marconi Co. |
| Colorado | NDN | 600 | PR, O | Government | U. S. Navy. |
| Columbia | KRO | | | Chesapeake S. S. Co. | |
| Columbia | KYM | 300, 550 | P | J. Harvey Ladew | Owner. |
| Columbia | WPW | | | Port of Portland | |
| Columbia | WHC | | | Wilson Bros. & Co. | Marconi Co. |
| Comal | KEM | 300, *600* | PG | Mallory S. S. Co. | Marconi Co. |
| Comanche | KVC | 300, *600* | PG | Clyde S. S. Co. | Marconi Co |

| | | | | | |
|---|---|---|---|---|---|
| Commonwealth | KXC | | | New England S. S. Co | National Electric Signaling Co. |
| Comet | KTJ | | | Standard Oil Co | Marconi Co. |
| Comus | KKD | 300, *600* | PG | Southern Pacific Co | Marconi Co. |
| Concho | KEC | 300, *600* | PG | Mallory S. S. Co | Marconi Co. |
| Concord | KNC | | | Colonial Navigation Co | National Electric Signaling Co. |
| Congress | WGT | | | Pacific Coast S. S. Co | Marconi Co. |
| Connecticut | KXO | | | New England S. S. Co | |
| Connecticut | NDQ | 600 | PR, O | Government | U. S. Navy. |
| Cordova | WAR | | | Alaska S. S. Co | |
| Coronado | WSO | | | Coronado Co | |
| Corsair | KYC | | | J. Pierpont Morgan estate | |
| Corwin | WNN | | | Kotzebue Transportation & Trading Co | |
| Creole | KKR | 300, *600* | PG | Southern Pacific Co | Marconi Co. |
| Cretan | KQC | 300, *600* | PG | Merchants & Miners Transportation Co | Marconi Co. |
| Cristobal | KMD | 300, *600* | PG | Panama R. R. Co | Marconi Co. |
| Crook | WXB | *600* | O | Government | U. S. Army. |
| Cuba | KUC | 300, *600* | PG | Staples Transportation Co | Marconi Co. |
| Culgoa | NDU | 600 | PR, O | Government | U. S. Navy. |
| Curacao | WGK | | | Pacific Coast Co | |

SHIP RADIO STATIONS, ALPHABETICALLY BY NAMES OF VESSELS—Continued.

| Name. | Call signal. | Wave lengths. | Nature of service. | Owner of vessel (line). | Station controlled by— |
|---|---|---|---|---|---|
| Currier | KNU | | | Cuba Distilling Co | Marconi Co. |
| Cyclops | NDY | 600 | PR, O | Government | U. S. Navy. |
| Cyprus | KYD | | | Daniel C. Jackling | |
| Cyrus W. Field | WXS | *600* | O | Government | U. S. Army. |
| Dakotan | WKD | 300, *600* | PG | American-Hawaiian S. S. Co | Marconi Co. |
| Delaware | NEK | 600 | PR, O | Government | U. S. Navy. |
| Delaware Sun | KTW | | | Sun Co | |
| Delhi | WGD | | | Pacific Coast Co | |
| Denver | KED | 300, *600* | PG | Mallory S. S. Co | Marconi Co. |
| Denver | NEM | 600 | PR, O | Government | U. S. Navy. |
| Des Moines | NEN | 600 | PR, O | do | U. S. Navy. |
| Diamond Head | WNL | | | Tyee Co | |
| Dirigo | WAO | | | Alaska S. S. Co | |
| Dix | WXC | *600* | O | Government | U. S. Army. |
| Dixie | NEP | 600 | PR, O | do | U. S. Navy. |
| Dolphin | WAU | | | Alaska S. S. Co | |
| Dolphin | NEQ | 600 | PR, O | Government | U. S. Navy. |

| | | | | | |
|---|---|---|---|---|---|
| Dora | WAH | | | Alaska S. S. Co. | |
| Dorchester | KQD | 300, *600* | PG | Merchants & Miners Transportation Co. | Marconi Co. |
| Dorothy Bradford | KNA | | | Cape Cod S. S. Co., trustees | Marconi Co. |
| Drayton | NET | 600 | PR, O | Government | U. S. Navy. |
| E. G. Crosby | WEL | | | Crosby Transportation Co. | |
| E-1 | NXS | 600 | PR, O | Government | U. S. Navy. |
| E-2 | NXT | 600 | PR, O | do | U. S. Navy. |
| Eagle | NFC | 600 | PR, O | do | U. S. Navy. |
| Eastern States | WEE | 300, *600* | PG | Detroit & Buffalo S. S. Co. | Marconi Co. |
| Eastland | WFN | | | Eastland Navigation Co. | Marconi Co. |
| Edgar H. Vance | WQE | | | Nehalem S. S. Co. | |
| Edith | WAE | | | Alaska S. S. Co. | |
| El Alba | KKL | 300, *600* | PG | Southern Pacific Co. | Marconi Co. |
| Elcano | NFD | 600 | PR, O | Government | U. S. Navy. |
| El Cid | KKT | 300, *600* | PG | Southern Pacific Co. | Marconi Co. |
| El Dia | KKY | 300, *600* | PG | do | Marconi Co. |
| Elmer A. Keeler | KVU | | | Elmer A. Keeler | |
| El Mundo | KKU | 300, *600* | PG | Southern Pacific Co. | Marconi Co. |
| El Norte | KKN | | | do | |
| El Occidente | KKX | 300, *600* | PG | do | Marconi Co. |

SHIP RADIO STATIONS, ALPHABETICALLY BY NAMES OF VESSELS—Continued.

| Name. | Call signal. | Wave lengths. | Nature of service. | Owner of vessel (line). | Station controlled by— |
|---|---|---|---|---|---|
| El Oriente | KKV | 300, *600* | PG | Southern Pacific Co | Marconi Co. |
| El Rio | KKZ | 300, *600* | PG | do | Marconi Co. |
| Elsegundo | KTK | | | Standard Oil Co. | |
| El Siglo | KKS | 300, *600* | PG | Southern Pacific Co. | Marconi Co. |
| El Sol | KKB | 300, *600* | PG | do | Marconi Co. |
| El Sud | KKQ | 300, *600* | PG | do | Marconi Co. |
| El Valle | KKW | 300, *600* | PG | do | Marconi Co. |
| Emeline | KYU | | | Charles Sweeny | |
| Enterprise | WMN | | | Matson Navigation Co. | Marconi Co. |
| Eocene | KTM | | | Standard Oil Co. | |
| Erskine M. Phelps | WTA | | | William D. Sewall (Union Oil Co). | |
| Esperanza | KWZ | 300, *600* | PG | New York & Cuba Mail S. S. Co. (Ward Line). | Marconi Co. |
| Essex | KQE | 300, *600* | PG | Merchants & Miners Transportation Co. | Marconi Co. |
| Evelyn | KNE | | | A. H. Bull S. S. Co. | |
| Excelsior | KKO | 300, *600* | PG | Southern Pacific Co. | Marconi Co. |
| Explorer | NLI | 300, *600* | O | Government | U. S. Department of Commerce. |

| | | | | | |
|---|---|---|---|---|---|
| F. A. Kilburn | WRW | | | North Pacific S. S. Co | Marconi Co. |
| Falcon | WRK | | | Charles Nelson Co | Marconi Co. |
| Fanning | NFM | 600 | PR, O | Government | U. S. Navy. |
| Fifield | WRF | | | Fifield S. S. Co | Marconi Co. |
| Finland | KSF | | | International Mercantile Marine Co. (Red Star Line). | |
| Florence | KYF | | | Alphonse H. Alker | |
| Florida | KSY | | | Baltimore Steam Packet Co | |
| Florida | NFR | 600 | PR, O | Government | U. S. Navy. |
| Flusser | NFS | 600 | PR, O | do | U. S. Navy. |
| Forward | KPF | | | Yankee Salvage Association | |
| Francis H. Leggett | WSB | | | Hicks-Hauptman Transportation Co | |
| Frederick | KQF | 300, *600* | PG | Merchants & Miners Transportation Co | Marconi Co. |
| Frieda | KFF | 300, *600* | PG | Union Sulphur Co | Marconi Co. |
| Galveston | NGD | 600 | PR, O | Government | U. S. Navy. |
| General A. M. Randol | WYJ | *300* | O | do | U. S. Army. |
| General Harvey Brown | WYK | *300* | O | do | U. S. Army. |
| General Hubbard | WMT | | | Hubbard S. S. Co | |
| General R. B. Ayres | WYL | *300* | O | Government | U. S. Army. |
| General Robert Anderson | WYH | *300* | O | do | U. S. Army. |

Ship Radio Stations, Alphabetically by Names of Vessels—Continued.

| Name. | Call signal. | Wave lengths. | Nature of service. | Owner of vessel (line). | Station controlled by— |
|---|---|---|---|---|---|
| George W. Elder | WRT | | | North Pacific S. S. Co. | |
| George W. Fenwick | WNG | | | Fenwick S. S. Co. (California & Atlantic S. S. Co.). | |
| Georgia | WFA | | | Goodrich Transit Co. | |
| Georgia | NGF | 600 | PR, O | Government | U. S. Navy. |
| Georgian | WKG | | | American-Hawaiian S. S. Co. | Marconi Co. |
| Glacier | NGH | 600 | PR, O | Government | U. S. Navy. |
| Glory of the Seas | WBZ | | | Alaska Fish Co. | |
| Gloucester | KQG | 300, *600* | PG | Merchants & Miners Transportation Co. | Marconi Co. |
| Goldsborough | NGJ | 600 | PR, O | Government | U. S. Navy. |
| Goliah | WPG | | | Puget Sound Tug Boat Co. | |
| Governor | WGR | | | Pacific Coast Co. | Marconi Co. |
| Governor Cobb | KRB | 300, *600* | PG | Eastern S. S. Corporation | Marconi Co. |
| Governor Dingley | KRV | | | do | |
| Grace Dollar | WSF | | | Grace Dollar S. S. Co. | Marconi Co. |
| Grayson | KDV | | | Ocean Freight Line | |
| Grecian | KQR | 300, *600* | PG | Merchants & Miners Transportation Co. | Marconi Co. |

| | | | | | |
|---|---|---|---|---|---|
| Greenwood | WQG | | | Greenwood S. S. Co. | |
| Gresham | NRG | 300, *600*, 750 | PG, O | Government | U. S. Revenue-Cutter Service. |
| Guardian | WGZ | | | Central & South American Telegraph Co. | |
| Gulfoil | KTG | | | Gulf Refining Co. | |
| Hamilton | KOA | 300, *600* | PG | Old Dominion S. S. Co. | Marconi Co. |
| Hanalei | WHN | | | Independent S. S. Co. | Marconi Co. |
| Hannibal | NGU | 600 | PR, O | Government | U. S. Navy. |
| Harry Luckenbach | KDT | | | Edgar F. Luckenbach (Insular Line) | |
| Harvard | WRH | | | Metropolitan S. S. Co. (Pacific Steam Navigation Co.). | Marconi Co. |
| Havana | KWH | 300, *600* | PG | New York & Cuba Mail S. S. Co. (Ward Line). | Marconi Co. |
| Hector | NGX | 600 | PR, O | Government | U. S. Navy. |
| Helena | NGY | 600 | PR, O | do | U. S. Navy. |
| Henley | NHA | 600 | PR, O | do | U. S. Navy. |
| Henry T. Scott | WRA | | | California S. S. Co. | |
| Herman Frasch | KFH | | | Union Sulphur Co. | Marconi Co. |
| Hermosa | WBP | | | Wilmington Transportation Co. | |
| Hilonian | WMM | | | Matson Navigation Co. | |
| Holland | WDW | | | Graham & Morton Transportation Co. | |

SHIP RADIO STATIONS, ALPHABETICALLY BY NAMES OF VESSELS—Continued.

| Name. | Call signal. | Wave lengths. | Nature of service. | Owner of vessel (line). | Station controlled by— |
|---|---|---|---|---|---|
| Honolulan | WKH | | | American-Hawaiian S. S. Co. | |
| Hopkins | NHC | 600 | PR, O | Government | U. S. Navy. |
| Howard | KQH | 300, *600* | PG | Merchants & Miners Transportation Co. | Marconi Co. |
| Hull | NHE | 600 | PR, O | Government | U. S. Navy. |
| Humboldt | WHX | | | Humboldt S. S. Co. | |
| Huron | KVH | 300, *600* | PG | Clyde S. S. Co. | Marconi Co. |
| Hyades | WMK | | | Matson Navigation Co. | |
| I. D. Fletcher | KFI | | | Coast Transit Co. | |
| I. J. Merritt | KRQ | | | Merritt & Chapman Derrick & Wrecking Co. | |
| Idaho | NHN | 600 | PR, O | Government | U. S. Navy. |
| Illinois | WCZ | | | Northern Michigan Transportation Co. | Marconi Co. |
| Illinois | KTH | | | Texas S. S. Co. | |
| Illinois | NHO | 600 | PR, O | Government | U. S. Navy. |
| Indian | KQI | 300, *600* | PG | Merchants & Miners Transportation Co. | Marconi Co. |
| Indiana | WFC | 300, *600* | PG | Goodrich Transit Co. | Marconi Co. |
| Indiana | NHQ | 600 | PR, O | Government | U. S. Navy. |

| | | | | | |
|---|---|---|---|---|---|
| Iowa | WFD | 300, *600* | PG | Goodrich Transit Co | Marconi Co. |
| Iowa | NHT | 600 | PR, O | Government | U. S. Navy. |
| Iris | NHU | 600 | PR, O | do | U. S. Navy. |
| Iroquois | KVF | | | Clyde S. S. Co | |
| Iroquois | WBG | | | International S. S. Co | |
| Iroquois | NHV | 600 | PR, O | Government | U. S. Navy. |
| Itasca | KQU | 300, *600* | PG | Merchants & Miners Transportation Co | Marconi Co. |
| Itasca | NRI | 300, *600* | PG, O | Government | U. S. Revenue-Cutter Service. |
| J. A. Chanslor | WTK | | | Associated Oil Co | |
| J. B. Stetson | WRC | | | E. S. Hicks | Marconi Co. |
| J. M. Guffey | KTF | | | Gulf Refining Co | |
| James Fornance | WYM | *300* | O | Government | U. S. Army. |
| Jamestown | KOC | 300, *600* | PG | Old Dominion S. S. Co | Marconi Co. |
| Jarvis | NIB | 600 | PR, O | Government | U. S. Navy. |
| Jefferson | KOD | 300, *600* | PG | Old Dominion S. S. Co | Marconi Co. |
| Jefferson | WAJ | 300, *600* | PG | Alaska S. S. Co | Marconi Co. |
| Jenkins | NID | 600 | PR, O | Government | U. S. Navy. |
| John A. Hooper | WSJ | | | Sudden & Christenson (Inc) | Marconi Co. |
| Joseph Henry | WXT | *600* | O | Government | U. S. Army. |
| Joseph Pulitzer | WPZ | | | Port of Portland | |

SHIP RADIO STATIONS, ALPHABETICALLY BY NAMES OF VESSELS—Continued.

| Name. | Call signal. | Wave lengths. | Nature of service. | Owner of vessel (line). | Station controlled by— |
|---|---|---|---|---|---|
| Jouett | NIE | 600 | PR, O | Government | U. S. Navy. |
| Juniata | KQJ | 300, *600* | PG | Merchants & Miners Transportation Co. | Marconi Co. |
| Juniata | WCB | 300, *600* | PG | Erie & Western Transportation Co. (Anchor Line). | Marconi Co. |
| Kansan | WKK | | | American-Hawaiian S. S. Co. | |
| Kansas | NIO | 600 | PR, O | Government | U. S. Navy. |
| Kansas City | WWS | | | San Francisco & Portland S. S. Co. | |
| Karina | KYR | | | Robert E. Tod | |
| Kearsarge | NIP | 600 | PR, O | Government | U. S. Navy. |
| Kentucky | NIQ | 600 | PR, O | do | U. S. Navy. |
| Kershaw | KQK | 300, *600* | PG | Merchants & Miners Transportation Co. | Marconi Co. |
| Kilpatrick | WXD | *600* | O | Government | U. S. Army. |
| Kingfisher | WPK | | | New England Fish Co. | |
| Kismet | KYK | | | Raymond Hoagland | |
| Klamath | WSX | | | Klamath S. S. Co. | Marconi Co. |
| Korea | WWK | | | Pacific Mail S. S. Co. | Marconi Co. |
| Kroonland | KSH | | | International Mercantile Marine Co. (Red Star Line). | |

| | | | | | |
|---|---|---|---|---|---|
| Kukui | NLF | 300, *600* | O | Government | U. S. Department of Commerce. |
| Kvichak | WNS | | | Alaska Packers' Association | |
| Lakeland | WDL | | | Port Huron & Duluth S. S. Co | Marconi Co. |
| Lampasas | KEP | 300, *600* | PG | Mallory S. S. Co | Marconi Co. |
| Lamson | NIW | 600 | PR, O | Government | U. S. Navy. |
| Lansing | WTC | | | Union S. S. Co. (Union Oil Co.) | Marconi Co. |
| Larimer | KTA | | | Gulf Refining Co | |
| Latouche | WAI | | | Alaska S. S. Co | |
| Lawrence | NIY | 600 | PR, O | Government | U. S. Navy. |
| Lebanon | NIZ | 600 | PR, O | do | U. S. Navy. |
| Leelanaw | WNI | | | Leelanaw S. S. Co. (California & Atlantic S. S. Co.). | |
| Lenape | KVL | 300, *600* | PG | Clyde S. S. Co | Marconi Co. |
| Lewis Luckenbach | WNH | | | Edgar F. Luckenbach (California & Atlantic S. S. Co.). | |
| Lexington | KNB | 300, 450, 500, 550, *600*. | PG | Colonial Navigation Co | National Electric Signaling Co. |
| Lexington | KQL | | | Merchants & Miners Transportation Co | Marconi Co. |
| Ligonier | KTD | | | Gulf Refining Co | |
| Liscum | WXE | *600* | O | Government | U. S. Army. |
| Logan | WXF | *600* | O | do | U. S. Army. |

SHIP RADIO STATIONS, ALPHABETICALLY BY NAMES OF VESSELS—Continued.

| Name. | Call signal. | Wave lengths. | Nature of service. | Owner of vessel (line). | Station controlled by— |
|---|---|---|---|---|---|
| Louise | KRL | | | Tolchester Beach Improvement Co. | |
| Louisiana | NJB | 600 | PR, O | Government | U. S. Navy. |
| Lucy Neff | KNQ | | | C. L. Dimon | |
| Lurline | WML | | | Matson Navigation Co | Marconi Co. |
| Lydonia | WDY | | | W. A. Lydon | |
| Lyra | WNF | | | Edgar F. Luckenbach (Luckenbach S. S. Co.). | Marconi Co. |
| Lysistrata | KYL | | | James Gordon Bennett | |
| Macdonough | NJH | 600 | PR, O | do | U. S. Navy. |
| Mackinaw | WHW | | | Robert Dollar Co. | |
| Madison | KOG | 300, *600* | PG | Old Dominion S. S. Co | Marconi Co. |
| Maine | KXD | | | New England S. S. Co | National Electric Signaling Co. |
| Maine | NJL | 600 | PR, O | Government | U. S. Navy. |
| Major Thomas | WYO | *300* | O | do | U. S. Army. |
| Manchuria | WWE | | | Pacific Mail S. S. Co | |
| Manitou | WFW | | | Northern Michigan Transportation Co | Marconi Co. |
| Manning | NRN | 300, *600* | PG, O | Government | U. S. Revenue-Cutter Service. |

| | | | | | |
|---|---|---|---|---|---|
| Maracaibo | KDM | 300, *600* | PG | Atlantic & Caribbean Steam Navigation Co. (Red D Line). | Marconi Co. |
| Marietta | NJQ | 600 | PR, O | Government | U. S. Navy. |
| Mariposa | WHP | | | Alaska S. S. Co. | |
| Marquette & Bessemer No. 1 | WEW | | | Marquette & Bessemer Dock & Navigation Co. | Marconi Co. |
| Marquette & Bessemer No. 2 | WEX | | | do | Marconi Co. |
| Mars | NJR | 600 | PR, O | Government | U. S. Navy. |
| Mary Dodge | WMD | | | Alaska Investment & Developing Co. | |
| Maryland | NJS | 600 | PR, O | Government | U. S. Navy. |
| Mascotte | KOW | | | Peninsular & Occidental S. S. Co. | |
| Massachusetts | KJM | | | Eastern S. S. Corporation | |
| Massachusetts | NJT | 600 | PR, O | Government | U. S. Navy. |
| Maverick | WTW | | | Standard Oil Co. | |
| Mayflower | NJV | 600 | PR, O | Government | U. S. Navy. |
| Mayrant | NJU | 600 | PR, O | do | U. S. Navy. |
| McCall | NJW | 600 | PR, O | do | U. S. Navy. |
| McClellan | WXH | *600* | O | do | U. S. Army. |
| McCulloch | NRH | 300, *600* | PG, O | do | U. S. Revenue-Cutter Service. |
| Meade | WXG | *600* | O | do | U. S. Army. |

SHIP RADIO STATIONS, ALPHABETICALLY BY NAMES OF VESSELS—Continued.

| Name. | Call signal. | Wave lengths. | Nature of service. | Owner of vessel (line). | Station controlled by— |
|---|---|---|---|---|---|
| Merced | WSZ | | | C. R. McCormick Co. | |
| Merrimack | KQM | 300, *600* | PG | Merchants & Miners Transportation Co | Marconi Co. |
| Merritt | WXI | *600* | O | Government | U. S. Army. |
| Mexico | KWX | 300, *600* | PG | New York & Cuba Mail S. S. Co. (Ward Line). | Marconi Co. |
| Miami | KOZ | | | Peninsular & Occidental S. S. Co. | |
| Miami | NRQ | 300, *600*, 750 | PG, O | Government | U. S. Revenue-Cutter Service. |
| Michigan | NJZ | 600 | PR, O | do | U. S. Navy. |
| Millinocket | KNM | 300, *600* | PG | A. H. Bull S. S. Co. | Marconi Co. |
| Mills | KRR | | | Ogden Mills | |
| Minnesota | WEK | | | Crosby Transportation Co. | |
| Minnesota | WMI | | | Great Northern S. S. Co. | |
| Minnesota | NKD | 600 | PR, O | Government | U. S. Navy. |
| Minnesotan | WKM | 300, *600* | PG | American-Hawaiian S. S. Co. | Marconi Co. |
| Mississippi | NKE | 600 | PR, O | Government | U. S. Navy. |
| Missouri | WFX | | | Northern Michigan S. S. Co | |
| Missouri | NKF | 600 | PR, O | Government | U. S. Navy. |

| | | | | | |
|---|---|---|---|---|---|
| Mohawk | KVM | 300, *600* | PG | Clyde S. S. Co. | Marconi Co. |
| Mohawk | KXE | | | New England S. S. Co. | National Electric Signaling Co. |
| Mohawk | NRM | 300, *600* | PG, O | Government | U. S. Revenue-Cutter Service. |
| Mohegan | KXM | 300,450,500,550, *600*. | PG | New England S. S. Co. | National Electric Signaling Co. |
| Momus | KKM | 300, *600* | PG | Southern Pacific Co. | Marconi Co. |
| Monadnock | NKJ | 600 | PR, O | Government | U. S. Navy. |
| Monaghan | NKL | 600 | PR, O | do | U. S. Navy. |
| Mongolia | WWN | | | Pacific Mail S. S. Co. | |
| Monroe | KOM | 300, *600* | PG | Old Dominion S. S. Co. | Marconi Co. |
| Montana | NKM | 600 | PR, O | Government | U. S. Navy. |
| Montanan | WKN | | | American-Hawaiian S. S. Co. | |
| Montauk | KNT | | | Montauk S. S. Co. | |
| Monterey | KWY | 300, *600* | PG | New York & Cuba Mail S. S. Co. (Ward Line). | Marconi Co. |
| Monterey | NKN | 600 | PR, O | Government | U. S. Navy. |
| Montgomery | NKO | 600 | PR, O | do | U. S. Navy. |
| Morrill | NRC | *300* | PG, O | do | U. S. Revenue-Cutter Service. |
| Morro Castle | KWC | 300, *600* | PG | New York & Cuba Mail S. S. Co. (Ward Line). | Marconi Co. |

SHIP RADIO STATIONS, ALPHABETICALLY BY NAMES OF VESSELS—Continued.

| Name. | Call signal. | Wave lengths. | Nature of service. | Owner of vessel (line). | Station controlled by— |
|---|---|---|---|---|---|
| Multnomah | WMA | | | Chas. R. McCormick & Co. | |
| Nacoochee | KFP | | | Ocean S. S. Co. (Savannah Line) | Marconi Co. |
| Nann Smith | WBO | | | Inter-Ocean Transportation Co | |
| Nanshan | NNK | 600 | PR, O | Government | U. S. Navy. |
| Nantucket | KQN | 300, *600* | PG | Merchants & Miners Transportation Co. | Marconi Co. |
| Nashville | NKY | 600 | PR, O | Government | U. S. Navy. |
| Navajo | WNJ | | | Western Steam Navigation Co. (California & Atlantic S. S. Co.). | |
| Navajo | NKZ | 600 | PR, O | Government | U. S. Navy. |
| Nebraska | NMA | 600 | PR, O | do | U. S. Navy. |
| Nelson | KNL | 300, *600* | PG | Cuba Distilling Co. | Marconi Co. |
| Neptune | NMS | 600 | PR, O | Government | U. S. Navy. |
| Nero | NMB | 600 | PR, O | do | U. S. Navy. |
| New Hampshire | KXF | | | New England S. S. Co | National Electric Signaling Co. |
| New Hampshire | NME | 600 | PR, O | Government | U. S. Navy. |
| New Haven | KXN | 300, 450, 500, 550, *600*. | PG | New England S. S. Co | National Electric Signaling Co. |

| | | | | | |
|---|---|---|---|---|---|
| New Jersey | KNJ | | | United New York & Sandy Hook Pilots' Association. | |
| New Jersey | NMF | 600 | PR, O | Government | U. S. Navy. |
| New Orleans | KQV | 300, *600* | PG | Merchants & Miners Transportation Co. | Marconi Co. |
| New Orleans | NMG | 600 | PR, O | Government | U. S. Navy. |
| Newport | WWH | | | Pacific Mail S. S. Co. | |
| New York | KNK | | | United New York & Sandy Hook Pilots' Association. | |
| New York | KSN | | | International Mercantile Marine Co. (American Line). | |
| Niagara | KYN | | | Howard Gould | |
| Noma | KYO | | | Vincent Astor | |
| Nome City | WRN | | | Charles Nelson Co. | Marconi Co. |
| North American | WEN | | | Chicago, Duluth & Georgian Bay Transit Co. | Marconi Co. |
| North Carolina | NMN | 600 | PR, O | Government | U. S. Navy. |
| North Dakota | NMO | 600 | PR, O | do | U. S. Navy. |
| Northland | WNX | | | E. J. Dodge Co. | |
| North Land | WCN | | | Northern S. S. Co. | Marconi Co. |
| North Land | KJD | 300, *600* | PG | Eastern S. S. Corporation | Marconi Co. |
| North Star | KJS | 300, *600* | PG | do | Marconi Co. |
| Northwestern | WAN | 300, *600* | PG | Alaska S. S. Co. | Marconi Co. |

SHIP RADIO STATIONS, ALPHABETICALLY BY NAMES OF VESSELS—Continued.

| Name. | Call signal. | Wave lengths. | Nature of service. | Owner of vessel (line). | Station controlled by— |
|---|---|---|---|---|---|
| North Wind | KYB | *300* | P. | Charles Martin Clark | Owner. |
| Norwood | WSG | | | Sudden & Christenson (Inc.) | Marconi Co. |
| Nueces | KEH | 300, *600* | PG | Mallory S. S. Co. | Marconi Co. |
| Nushagak | WNE | | | Alaska Packers' Association | |
| Nyack | WEJ | | | Crosby Transportation Co. | |
| Octorara | W C D | | | Erie & Western Transportation Co. (Anchor Line). | Marconi Co. |
| Ohio | NMW | 600 | PR, O. | Government | U. S. Navy. |
| Oklahoma | KTB | | | Gulf Refining Co. | |
| Old Colony | KJO | | | Eastern S. S. Corporation | |
| Oleum | WTD | | | Fillmore Condit (Union Oil Co.) | |
| Oliver J. Olson | WNB | | | Olson & Mahony | |
| Olivette | KOV | | | Peninsular & Occidental S. S. Co. | Marconi Co. |
| Oneida | KYP | 300, 550, *600* | P. | E. C. Benedict | Owner. |
| Oneonta | WPX | | | Port of Portland | |
| Onondaga | NRO | 300, *600*, 750 | PG, O. | Government | U. S. Revenue-Cutter Service. |
| Ontario | KQO | 300, *600* | PG | Merchants & Miners Transportation Co. | Marconi Co. |

| | | | | | |
|---|---|---|---|---|---|
| Ontario | NTA | 600 | PR, O | Government | U. S. Navy. |
| Oregon | NMZ | 600 | PR, O | do | U. S. Navy. |
| Orion | NOC | 600 | PR, O | do | U. S. Navy. |
| Osceola | NOA | 600 | PR, O | do | U. S. Navy. |
| P. R. R. *707* | KPR | | | Pennsylvania R. R. Co | |
| Paducah | NOG | 600 | PR, O | Government | U. S. Navy. |
| Pamlico | NRR | *300* | PG, O | do | U. S. Revenue-Cutter Service. |
| Panama | KMH | 300, *600* | PG | Panama R. R. Co | Marconi Co. |
| Pan American | KUT | | | Texas S. S. Co | |
| Panther | NOJ | 600 | PR, O | Government | U. S. Navy. |
| Paraguay | KTT | | | Sun Co | |
| Paraiso | WRI | | | | |
| Parthian | KQP | 300, *600* | PG | Merchants & Miners Transportation Co | Marconi Co. |
| Patapsco | NOL | 600 | PR, O | Government | U. S. Navy. |
| Patterson | NLH | 300, *600* | O | do | U. S. Department of Commerce. |
| Patterson | NOK | 600 | PR, O | do | U. S. Navy. |
| Patuxent | NOM | 600 | PR, O | do | U. S. Navy. |
| Paulding | NON | 600 | PR, O | do | U. S. Navy. |
| Paul Jones | NOP | 600 | PR, O | do | U. S. Navy. |

SHIP RADIO STATIONS, ALPHABETICALLY BY NAMES OF VESSELS—Continued.

| Name. | Call signal. | Wave lengths. | Nature of service. | Owner of vessel (line). | Station controlled by— |
|---|---|---|---|---|---|
| Pennsylvania | WWI | | | Pacific Mail S. S. Co. | Marconi Co. |
| Peoria | NOW | 600 | PR, O | Government | U. S. Navy. |
| Pequonnock | KXP | | | New England S. S. Co. | National Electric Signaling Co. |
| Pere Marquette | WDA | 300, *600* | PR | Pere Marquette R. R. Co. | Marconi Co. |
| Pere Marquette 17 | WDC | 300, *600* | PG | do | Marconi Co. |
| Pere Marquette 18 | WDD | | | do | Marconi Co. |
| Pere Marquette 19 | WDB | 300, 345, *600* | PR | do | Marconi Co. |
| Pere Marquette 20 | WDE | | | do | Marconi Co. |
| Perfection | KTN | | | Standard Oil Co. | |
| Perkins | NOX | 600 | PR, O | Government | U. S. Navy. |
| Perry | NOY | 600 | PR, O | do | U. S. Navy. |
| Persian | KQX | | | Merchants & Miners Transportation Co. | Marconi Co. |
| Peru | WWJ | | | Pacific Mail S. S. Co. | |
| Petrel | NOZ | 600 | PR, O | Government | U. S. Navy. |
| Pettibone | KUP | | | | |
| Philadelphia | KDA | 300, *600* | PG | Atlantic & Caribbean Steam Navigation Co. (Red D Line). | Marconi Co. |

| | | | | | |
|---|---|---|---|---|---|
| Philadelphia | KSM | 300, *600* | PG | International Mercantile Marine Co. (American Line). | Marconi Co. |
| Pilgrim | KXG | | | New England S. S. Co | National Electric Signaling Co. |
| Pioneer | WPN | | | Puget Sound Tug Boat Co | |
| Pittsburgh | NOT | 600 | PR, O | Government | U. S. Navy. |
| Pleiades | WNP | | | Edgar F. Luckenbach | Marconi Co. |
| Plymouth | KXH | 300, 450, 500, 550, *600*. | PG | New England S. S. Co | National Electric Signaling Co. |
| Pompey | NQF | 600 | PR, O | Government | U. S. Navy. |
| Ponce | KGP | 300, *600* | PG | New York & Porto Rico S. S. Co | Marconi Co. |
| Portland | WNV | | | Portland Incorporated (California & Atlantic S. S. Co.). | |
| Potomac | NQK | 600 | PR, O | Government | U. S. Navy. |
| Powhatan | KQY | 300, *600* | PG | Merchants & Miners Transportation Co | Marconi Co. |
| Prairie | NQM | 600 | PR, O | Government | U. S. Navy. |
| Preble | N Q N | 600 | PR, O | do | U. S. Navy. |
| President | WGP | | | Pacific Coast Co | Marconi Co. |
| Preston | NQO | 600 | PR, O | Government | U. S. Navy. |
| Princess Anne | KOB | 300, *600* | PG | Old Dominion S. S. Co | Marconi Co. |
| Princeton | NQP | 600 | PR, O | Government | U. S. Navy. |
| Priscilla | KXI | | | New England S. S. Co | National Electric Signaling Co. |
| Prometheus | NQR | 600 | PR, O | Government | U. S. Navy. |

SHIP RADIO STATIONS, ALPHABETICALLY BY NAMES OF VESSELS—Continued.

| Name. | Call signal. | Wave lengths. | Nature of service. | Owner of vessel (line). | Station controlled by— |
|---|---|---|---|---|---|
| Proteus | KKP | 300, *600* | PG | Southern Pacific Co | Marconi Co. |
| Providence | KXJ | 300, 450, 500, 550, *600*. | PG | New England S. S. Co | National Electric Signaling Co. |
| Puritan | WDU | 300, *600* | PG | Graham & Morton Transportation Co | Marconi Co. |
| Puritan | KXK | | | New England S. S. Co | National Electric Signaling Co. |
| Quantico | KQQ | 300, *600* | PG | Merchants & Miners Transportation Co | Marconi Co. |
| Queen | WGX | | | Pacific Coast S. S. Co | Marconi Co. |
| Radiant | KTR | | | Standard Oil Co | |
| Rainbow | NTD | 600 | PR, O | Government | U. S. Navy. |
| Raleigh | NTE | 600 | PR, O | do | U. S. Navy. |
| Ransom B. Fuller | KRF | | | Eastern S. S. Corporation | |
| Rayo | KTL | | | Standard Oil Co | |
| Redondo | WBM | | | Inter-Ocean Transportation Co | |
| Reid | NTU | 600 | PR, O | Government | U. S. Navy. |
| Relay | KVZ | | | Mexican Telegraph Co | |
| Relief | KRJ | | | Merritt & Chapman Derrick & Wrecking Co. | |
| Reno | WYN | *300* | O | Government | U. S. Army. |

| | | | | | |
|---|---|---|---|---|---|
| Rescue | KRP | | | Merritt & Chapman Derrick & Wrecking Co. | |
| Reuce | WSR | | | Columbia River Packers' Association | |
| Rhode Island | NTX | 600 | PR, O | Government | U. S. Navy. |
| Richard Peck | KXR | | | New England S. S. Co | National Electric Signaling Co. |
| Richmond | WTR | | | Standard Oil Co | |
| Rio Grande | KEG | 300, *600* | PG | Mallory S. S. Co | Marconi Co. |
| Riverside | WRM | | | Charles Nelson Co | |
| Roanoke | WRR | | | North Pacific S. S. Co | Marconi Co. |
| Rochelle | WNR | | | | |
| Roe | NTZ | 600 | PR, O | Government | U. S. Navy. |
| Roma | WTE | | | Union S. S. Co. (Union Oil Co.) | |
| Rose City | WWR | | | San Francisco & Portland S. S. Co | Marconi Co. |
| S. O. Co. No. 91 | WTU | | | Standard Oil Co | |
| S. O. Co. No. 92 | KTY | | | do | |
| S. O. Co. No. 93 | WTY | | | do | |
| S. O. Co. No. 94 | KTP | | | do | |
| S. O. Co. No. 95 | WTZ | | | do | |
| S. V. Luckenbach | KDS | | | Edgar F. Luckenbach (Insular Line) | |
| Sabine | KEB | 300, *600* | PG | Mallory S. S. Co | Marconi Co |

SHIP RADIO STATIONS, ALPHABETICALLY BY NAMES OF VESSELS—Continued.

| Name. | Call signal. | Wave lengths. | Nature of service. | Owner of vessel (line). | Station controlled by— |
|---|---|---|---|---|---|
| St. Francis | WHH | | | Alaska Fisherman's Packing Co. | |
| St. Helens | WNY | | | E. J. Dodge Co. | |
| St. Louis | KSL | | | International Mercantile Marine Co. (American Line). | |
| St. Louis | NTF | 600 | PR, O. | Government | U. S. Navy. |
| St. Nicholas | WSS | | | Columbia River Packers' Association | |
| St. Paul | KSO | | | International Mercantile Marine Co. (American Line). | |
| Salem | NTP | 600 | PR, O. | Government | U. S. Navy. |
| San Francisco | NTQ | 600 | PR, O. | do | U. S. Navy. |
| San Jacinto | KES | 300, *600* | PG | Mallory S. S. Co. | Marconi Co. |
| San Jose | WWL | | | Pacific Mail S. S. Co. | |
| San Juan | KGJ | 300, *600* | PG | New York & Porto Rico S. S. Co. | Marconi Co. |
| San Juan | WWM | | | Pacific Mail S. S. Co. | Marconi Co. |
| San Marcos | KEK | 300, *600* | PG | Mallory S. S. Co. | Marconi Co. |
| San Ramon | WNW | | | E. J. Dodge Co. | Marconi Co. |
| Santa Ana | WAL | | | Alaska S. S. Co. | |
| Santa Clara | WRS | 300, *600* | PG | North Pacific S. S. Co. | Marconi Co. |

| | | | | | |
|---|---|---|---|---|---|
| Santa Cruz | WPA | | | Puget Sound Salvage Co. | |
| Santa Cruz | WBD | | | W. R. Grace & Co. | |
| Santa Maria | WTF | | | United S. S. Co. (Union Oil Co.) | |
| Santa Rita | WTG | | | do | |
| Santa Rosa | WGN | | | Pacific Coast Co. | |
| Saratoga | KWS | 300, *600* | PG | New York & Cuba Mail S. S. Co. (Ward Line). | Marconi Co. |
| Saratoga | NTR | 600 | PR, O | Government | U. S. Navy. |
| Savage | KRS | | | Consolidation Coal Co. | |
| Scorpion | NTT | 600 | PR, O | Government | U. S. Navy. |
| Sea Otter | KYS | | | Hugh L. Willoughby | |
| Seeandbee | WFS | 300, *600* | PG | Cleveland & Buffalo Transportation Co. | Marconi Co. |
| Seguranca | KWG | 300, *600* | PG | New York & Cuba Mail S. S. Co. (Ward Line). | Marconi Co. |
| Seminole | KVJ | 300, *600* | PG | Clyde S. S. Co. | Marconi Co. |
| Seminole | NRS | 300, *600* | PG, O | Government | U. S. Revenue-Cutter Service. |
| Senator | WGS | | | Pacific Coast Co. | |
| Senator Bailey | KGS | | | | |
| Seneca | NRE | 300, *600*, 750 | PG, O | Government | U. S. Revenue-Cutter Service. |
| Seward | WAV | | | Alaska S. S. Co. | |

SHIP RADIO STATIONS, ALPHABETICALLY BY NAMES OF VESSELS—Continued.

| Name. | Call signal. | Wave lengths. | Nature of service. | Owner of vessel (line). | Station controlled by— |
|---|---|---|---|---|---|
| Shenango | KTC | | | Gulf Refining Co. | |
| Shenango | WET | | | Shenango S. S. Co. | Marconi Co. |
| Sheridan | WXJ | *600* | O. | Government | U. S. Army. |
| Sherman | WXK | *600* | O. | do | U. S. Army. |
| Shinnecock | KNS | | | Montauk S. S. Co. | |
| Siberia | WWU | | | Pacific Mail S. S. Co. | Marconi Co. |
| Sierra | WHJ | | | Oceanic S. S. Co. | Marconi Co. |
| Smith | NSQ | 600 | PR, O. | Government | U. S. Navy. |
| Snohomish | NRF | *300* | PG, O. | do | U. S. Revenue-Cutter Service. |
| Socony | KTX | | | Standard Oil Co. | |
| Solace | NST | 600 | PR, O. | Government | U. S. Navy. |
| Somerset | KQS | 300, *600* | PG. | State Street Trust Co. (Merchants & Miners Transportation Co.). | Marconi Co. |
| Sonoma | WHM | | | Oceanic S. S. Co. | |
| Sonoma | NTG | 600 | PR, O. | Government | U. S. Navy. |
| South Carolina | NSW | 600 | PR, O. | do | U. S. Navy. |
| South Dakota | NSX | 600 | PR, O. | do | U. S. Navy. |

| | | | | | |
|---|---|---|---|---|---|
| Speedwell | WQS | | | A. F. Estabrook (Southern Oregon Transportation Co.). | |
| Spokane | WGE | | | Pacific Coast Co. | |
| Stanley Dollar | WSD | | | Dollar S. S. Line | |
| Starr | WPS | | | San Juan Fishing & Packing Co. | |
| State of California | WGL | 300, *600* | PG | Pacific Coast S. S. Co. | Marconi Co. |
| State of Ohio | WFR | | | Cleveland & Buffalo Transportation Co. | Marconi Co. |
| Sterrett | NTB | 600 | PR, O | Government | U. S. Navy. |
| Stewart | NTC | 600 | PR, O | do | U. S. Navy. |
| Stringham | NTI | 600 | PR, O | do | U. S. Navy. |
| Sumner | WXL | *600* | O | do | U. S. Army. |
| Sun | KTU | | | Sun Co | |
| Supply | NTK | 600 | PR, O | Government | U. S. Navy. |
| Suwannee | KQZ | 300, *600* | PG | State Street Trust Co. (Merchants & Miners Transportation Co.) | Marconi Co. |
| Sylph | NTL | 600 | PR, O | Government | U. S. Navy. |
| Tacoma | NUA | 600 | PR, O | do | U. S. Navy. |
| Tahoma | NRK | 300, *600* | PG, O | do | U. S. Revenue-Cutter Service. |
| Tallahassee | NUC | 600 | PR, O | do | U. S. Navy. |
| Tarragon | NZZ | *300* | O | do | U.S. Department of Commerce. |

SHIP RADIO STATIONS, ALPHABETICALLY BY NAMES OF VESSELS—Continued.

| Name. | Call signal. | Wave lengths. | Nature of service. | Owner of vessel (line). | Station controlled by— |
|---|---|---|---|---|---|
| Tasco | KFT | 300, 400, 480, *600*. | P | T. A. Scott Co. (Inc.) | Owner. |
| Tatoosh | WPE | | | Puget Sound Tug Boat Co. | |
| Tennessee | NUG | 600 | PR, O | Government. | U. S. Navy. |
| Terry | NUI | 600 | PR, O | do | U. S. Navy. |
| Theodore Roosevelt | WCT | | | Indiana Transportation Co. | |
| Thetis | NRT | 300, *600* | PG, O | Government. | U. S. Revenue-Cutter Service. |
| Thomas | WXM | *600* | O | do | U. S. Army. |
| Tionesta | WCA | | | Erie & Western Transportation Co. (Anchor Line). | Marconi Co. |
| Toledo | KTV | | | Sun Co. | |
| Tonopah | NUN | 600 | PR, O | Government. | U. S. Navy. |
| Topila | KKE | | | Southern Pacific Co. | |
| Trippe | NUG | 600 | PR, O | Government. | U. S. Navy. |
| Truxton | NUS | 600 | PR, O | do | U. S. Navy. |
| Tuscan | KQT | 300, *600* | PG | Merchants & Mineis Transportation Co. | Marconi Co. |

| | | | | | |
|---|---|---|---|---|---|
| Tuscarora | NRL | 300, *600* | PG, O | Government | U. S. Revenue-Cutter Service. |
| Tyee | WPC | | | Puget Sound Tug Boat Co. | |
| Tyee Junior | WPB | | | Tyee Co. | |
| Umatilla | WGU | | | Pacific Coast Co. | Marconi Co. |
| Unalga | NRX | 300, *600*, 800 | PG, O | Government | U. S. Revenue-Cutter Service. |
| Utah | NVE | 600 | PR, O | do | U. S. Navy. |
| Vanguard | WNZ | | | E. J. Dodge Co. | |
| Vanadis | KYT | | | C. K. G. Billings | |
| Venetia | WOV | | | J. D. Spreckels | |
| Ventura | WHL | | | Oceanic S. S. Co. | Marconi Co. |
| Vermont | NVK | 600 | PR, O | Government | U. S. Navy. |
| Vesta | KTS | | | Standard Oil Co. | |
| Vesuvius | NVM | 600 | PR, O | Government | U. S. Navy. |
| Vicksburg | NVN | 600 | PR, O | do | U. S. Navy. |
| Victoria | WAD | | | Alaska S. S. Co. | |
| Vigilancia | KWV | 300, *600* | PG | New York & Cuba Mail S. S. Co. (Ward Line). | Marconi Co. |
| Villalobos | NVP | 600 | PR, O | Government | U. S. Navy. |
| Virginia | KSZ | | | Baltimore Steam Packet Co. | |
| Virginia | WFH | | | Goodrich Transit Co. | Marconi Co. |

SHIP RADIO STATIONS, ALPHABETICALLY BY NAMES OF VESSELS—Continued.

| Name. | Call signal. | Wave lengths. | Nature of service. | Owner of vessel (line). | Station controlled by— |
|---|---|---|---|---|---|
| Virginia | NVR | 600 | PR, O | Government | U. S. Navy. |
| Vulcan | NVT | 600 | PR, O | do | U. S. Navy. |
| W. B. Flint | WHG | | | Astoria Savings Bank (Alaska Fisherman's Packing Co.). | |
| W. S. Porter | WTM | | | Associated Oil Co | |
| Wakiva | KYI | | | Lamon V. Harkness | |
| Walke | NWL | 600 | PR, O | Government | U. S. Navy. |
| Wallula | WPY | | | Port of Portland | |
| Wana | KYX | | | George C. Sherman | Marconi Co. |
| Warren | WXN | *600* | O | Government | U. S. Army. |
| Warrington | NWD | 600 | PR, O | do | U. S. Navy. |
| Warrior | KYW | | | Frederick William Vanderbilt | |
| Washington | NWE | 600 | PR, O | Government | U. S. Navy. |
| Washtenaw | WTH | | | Union S. S. Co. (Union Oil Co.) | |
| Watson | WAW | | | Alaska-Pacific S. S. Co | Marconi Co. |
| West Virginia | NWG | 600 | PR, O | Government | U. S. Navy. |
| Western States | WED | 300, *600* | PG | Detroit & Cleveland Navigation Co | Marconi Co. |

| | | | | | |
|---|---|---|---|---|---|
| Wheeling | NWH | 600 | PR, O | do | U. S. Navy. |
| Whipple | NWI | 600 | PR, O | do | U. S. Navy. |
| Whittier | WHT | | | Max Dyer (Union Oil Co.) | Marconi Co. |
| Wilhelmina | WMO | | | Matson Navigation Co. | Marconi Co. |
| Willamette | WSW | | | Willamette S. S. Co. | |
| William Chatham | WMC | | | Steamer William Chatham Co | Marconi Co. |
| Wm. F. Herrin | WTN | | | Associated Oil Co. | |
| William P. Snyder | WER | | | Shenango S. S. Co. | Marconi Co. |
| William P. Snyder, Jr. | WES | | | do | Marconi Co. |
| Wilmington | NWK | 600 | PR, O | Government | U. S. Navy. |
| Wilpen | WEU | | | Shenango S. S. Co. | |
| Windber | WND | | | Pacific-American Fisheries | |
| Windom | NRW | 300, *600* | PG, O | Government | U. S. Revenue-Cutter Service. |
| Winifred | KTE | | | Gulf Refining Co. | |
| Winona | NRV | 300, *600* | PG, O | Government | U. S. Revenue-Cutter Service. |
| Wisconsin | NWM | 600 | PR, O | do | U. S. Navy. |
| Woodbury | NRJ | 300, *600* | PG, O | do | U. S. Revenue-Cutter Service. |
| Wyandotte | KNW | | | Montauk S. S. Co. | |
| Wyoming | NWQ | 600 | PR, O | Government | U. S. Navy. |

SHIP RADIO STATIONS, ALPHABETICALLY BY NAMES OF VESSELS—Continued.

| Name. | Call signal. | Wave lengths. | Nature of service. | Owner of vessel (line). | Station controlled by— |
|---|---|---|---|---|---|
| Yale | WRY | | | Metropolitan S. S. Co. (Pacific Steam Navigation Co.). | Marconi Co. |
| Yamacraw | NRY | 300, *600* | PG, O | Government | U. S. Revenue-Cutter Service. |
| Yaquez | KDY | 300, *600* | PG | Ocean Freight Line | Marconi Co. |
| Yosemite | WQY | | | Yosemite S. S. Co. | Marconi Co. |
| Yucatan | WMY | | | North Pacific S. S. Co. | Marconi Co. |
| Yukon | WBQ | | | Alaska Coast Co. | |
| Zapora | WPQ | | | International Fisheries Co. | |
| Zealandia | KNR | | | C. L. Dimon | |
| Zulia | KDZ | 300, *600* | PG | Atlantic & Caribbean Steam Navigation Co. (Red D Line). | Marconi Co. |

## LAND AND SHIP RADIO STATIONS, ALPHABETICALLY BY CALL SIGNALS.

[This list includes all call signals which have been assigned to United States radio stations, except those of the generaland restricted amateur grades. Special stations are grouped at the end of this list. b—ship stations; c—land stations.]

| Call signal. | Name of station. | Classification. |
|---|---|---|
| KDA | Philadelphia | b |
| KDB | Caracas | b |
| KDC | Douglas, Ariz | c |
| KDD | | |
| KDE | | |
| KDF | | |
| KDG | | |
| KDH | | |
| KDI | | |
| KDJ | | |
| KDK | | |
| KDL | | |
| KDM | Maracaibo | b |
| KDN | San Lúis Obispo, Cal | c |
| KDO | | |
| KDP | | |
| KDQ | | |
| KDR | | |
| KDS | S. V. Luckenbach | b |
| KDT | Harry Luckenbach | b |
| KDU | Juneau, Alaska | c |
| KDV | Grayson | b |
| KDW | Borinquen | b |
| KDX | Bayamon | b |
| KDY | Yaquez | b |
| KDZ | Zulia | b |
| KEA | | |
| KEB | Sabine | b |
| KEC | Concho | b |
| KED | Denver | b |
| KEE | | |
| KEF | | |
| KEG | Rio Grande | b |
| KEH | Nueces | b |
| KEI | | |
| KEJ | Alamo | b |
| KEK | San Marcos | b |
| KEL | | |
| KEM | Comal | b |
| KEN | | |
| KEO | | |
| KEP | Lampasas | b |
| KEQ | | |
| KER | | |
| KES | San Jacinto | b |
| KET | | |
| KEU | | |
| KEV | | |
| KEW | | |
| KEX | Los Angeles, Cal | c |
| KEY | | |
| KEZ | Brazos | b |
| KFA | City of Columbus | b |
| KFB | City of Atlanta | b |
| KFC | City of Macon | b |
| KFD | City of Memphis | b |
| KFE | | |
| KFF | Frieda | b |
| KFG | | |
| KFH | Herman Frasch | b |
| KFI | I. D. Fletcher | b |
| KFJ | City of Augusta | b |
| KFK | City of Savannah | b |
| KFL | | |
| KFM | | |
| KFN | | |
| KFO | | |
| KFP | Nacoochee | b |
| KFQ | | |
| KFR | | |
| KFS | | |

LAND AND SHIP RADIO STATIONS, ALPHABETICALLY BY CALL SIGNALS—Continued.

| Call signal. | Name of station. | Classification. |
|---|---|---|
| KFT | Tasco | b |
| KFU | | |
| KFV | | |
| KFW | | |
| KFX | City of St. Louis | b |
| KFY | City of Montgomery | b |
| KFZ | | |
| KGA | Coamo | b |
| KGB | Carolina | b |
| KGC | | |
| KGD | | |
| KGE | | |
| KGF | | |
| KGG | | |
| KGH | | |
| KGI | | |
| KGJ | San Juan | b |
| KGK | | |
| KGL | | |
| KGM | | |
| KGN | | |
| KGO | | |
| KGP | Ponce | b |
| KGQ | | |
| KGR | | |
| KGS | Senator Bailey | b |
| KGT | | |
| KGU | | |
| KGV | | |
| KGW | | |
| KGX | | |
| KGY | | |
| KGZ | | |

| Call signal. | Name of station. | Classification. |
|---|---|---|
| KHA | Karluk, Alaska | c |
| KHB | Kogiung, Alaska | c |
| KHC | Chignic, Alaska | c |
| KHD | | |
| KHE | | |
| KHF | Nushagak, Alaska | c |
| KHG | Clarks Point, Alaska | c |
| KHH | | |
| KHI | | |
| KHJ | Koko Head, T. H. | c |
| KHK | Kahuku, T. H. | c |
| KHL | Lahaina, T. H. | c |
| KHM | Lihue, T. H. | c |
| KHN | Kawaihae, T. H. | c |
| KHO | Kaunakakai, T. H | c |
| KHP | Daley City, Cal. | c |
| KHQ | Phoenix, Ariz. | c |
| KHR | | |
| KHS | | |
| KHT | Naknek, Alaska | c |
| KHU | | |
| KHV | | |
| KHW | | |
| KHX | | |
| KHY | | |
| KHZ | | |
| KIA | | |
| KIB | | |
| KIC | | |
| KID | | |
| KIE | | |
| KIF | | |
| KIG | | |
| KIH | | |
| KII | | |
| KIJ | | |

LAND AND SHIP RADIO STATIONS, ALPHABETICALLY BY CALL SIGNALS—Continued.

| Call signal. | Name of station. | Classification. |
|---|---|---|
| KIK | | |
| KIL | | |
| KIM | | |
| KIN | | |
| KIO | | |
| KIP | | |
| KIQ | | |
| KIR | | |
| KIS | | |
| KIT | Kake, Alaska | c |
| KIU | Burnett Inlet, Alaska | c |
| KIV | | |
| KIW | | |
| KIX | | |
| KIY | | |
| KIZ | | |
| KJA | Jualin, Alaska | c |
| KJB | Bunker Hill | b |
| KJC | | |
| KJD | North Land | b |
| KJE | | |
| KJF | | |
| KJG | | |
| KJH | | |
| KJI | | |
| KJJ | | |
| KJK | | |
| KJL | | |
| KJM | Massachusetts | b |
| KJN | | |
| KJO | Old Colony | b |
| KJP | | |
| KJQ | | |
| KJR | | |
| KJS | North Star | b |
| KJT | | |
| KJU | | |
| KJV | | |
| KJW | | |
| KJX | | |
| KJY | | |
| KJZ | | |
| KKA | Antilles | b |
| KKB | El Sol | b |
| KKC | Chalmette | b |
| KKD | Comus | b |
| KKE | Topila | b |
| KKF | | |
| KKG | | |
| KKH | | |
| KKI | | |
| KKJ | | |
| KKK | | |
| KKL | El Alba | b |
| KKM | Momus | b |
| KKN | El Norte | b |
| KKO | Excelsior | b |
| KKP | Proteus | b |
| KKQ | El Sud | b |
| KKR | Creole | b |
| KKS | El Siglo | b |
| KKT | El Cid | b |
| KKU | El Mundo | b |
| KKV | El Oriente | b |
| KKW | El Valle | b |
| KKX | El Occidente | b |
| KKY | El Dia | b |
| KKZ | El Rio | b |
| KLA | | |
| KLB | | |
| KLC | | |
| KLD | | |
| KLE | | |

LAND AND SHIP RADIO STATIONS, ALPHABETICALLY BY CALL SIGNALS—Continued

| Call signal. | Name of station. | Classification. | Call signal. | Name of station. | Classification. |
|---|---|---|---|---|---|
| KLF | ........ | ...... | KML | ........ | ...... |
| KLG | ........ | ...... | KMM | ........ | ...... |
| KLH | ........ | ...... | KMN | ........ | ...... |
| KLI | ........ | ...... | KMO | ........ | ...... |
| KLJ | ........ | ...... | KMP | ........ | ...... |
| KLK | ........ | ...... | KMQ | ........ | ...... |
| KLL | ........ | ...... | KMR | ........ | ...... |
| KLM | ........ | ...... | KMS | Ancon.............. | b |
| KLN | ........ | ...... | KMT | ........ | ...... |
| KLO | ........ | ...... | KMU | ........ | ...... |
| KLP | ........ | ...... | KMV | Advance............ | b |
| KLQ | ........ | ...... | KMW | ........ | ...... |
| KLR | ........ | ...... | KMX | Colon............... | b |
| KLS | ........ | ...... | KMY | ........ | ...... |
| KLT | ........ | ...... | KMZ | ........ | ...... |
| KLU | ........ | ...... | KNA | Dorothy Bradford.... | b |
| KLV | ........ | ...... | KNB | Lexington........... | b |
| KLW | ........ | ...... | KNC | Concord............ | b |
| KLX | ........ | ...... | KND | ........ | ...... |
| KLY | ........ | ...... | KNE | Evelyn.............. | b |
| KLZ | ........ | ...... | KNF | Carolyn............. | b |
| KMA | Alliance............ | b | KNG | ........ | ...... |
| KMB | ........ | ...... | KNH | ........ | ...... |
| KMC | ........ | ...... | KNI | ........ | ...... |
| KMD | Cristobal........... | b | KNJ | New Jersey.......... | b |
| KME | ........ | ...... | KNK | New York........... | b |
| KMF | ........ | ...... | KNL | Nelson.............. | b |
| KMG | ........ | ...... | KNM | Millinocket.......... | b |
| KMH | Panama............. | b | KNN | ........ | ...... |
| KMI | ........ | ...... | KNO | ........ | ...... |
| KMJ | ........ | ...... | KNP | ........ | ...... |
| KMK | ........ | ...... | KNQ | Lucy Neff.......... | b |
| | | | KNR | Zealandia.......... | b |
| | | | KNS | Shinnecock......... | b |
| | | | KNT | Montauk............ | b |
| | | | KNU | Currier............. | b |
| | | | KNV | ........ | ...... |
| | | | KNW | Wyandotte.......... | b |

LAND AND SHIP RADIO STATIONS, ALPHABETICALLY BY CALL SIGNALS—Continued.

| Call signal. | Name of station. | Classification. |
|---|---|---|
| KNX | | |
| KNY | | |
| KNZ | America | b |
| KOA | Hamilton | b |
| KOB | Princess Anne | b |
| KOC | Jamestown | b |
| KOD | Jefferson | b |
| KOE | | |
| KOF | | |
| KOG | Madison | b |
| KOH | | |
| KOI | | |
| KOJ | | |
| KOK | | |
| KOL | | |
| KOM | Monroe | b |
| KON | | |
| KOO | | |
| KOP | | |
| KOQ | | |
| KOR | | |
| KOS | Brunswick | b |
| KOT | | |
| KOU | | |
| KOV | Olivette | b |
| KOW | Mascotte | b |
| KOX | | |
| KOY | | |
| KOZ | Miami | b |
| KPA | Seattle, Wash | c |
| KPB | Ketchikan, Alaska | c |
| KPC | Astoria, Oreg | c |
| KPD | Friday Harbor, Wash | c |
| KPE | | |
| KPF | Forward | b |
| KPG | | |
| KPH | San Francisco, Cal | c |
| KPI | Avalon, Cal | c |
| KPJ | San Pedro, Cal | c |
| KPK | | |
| KPL | | |
| KPM | Eureka, Cal | c |
| KPN | Adams | b |
| KPO | | |
| KPP | | |
| KPQ | | |
| KPR | P. R. R. 707 | b |
| KPS | | |
| KPT | | |
| KPU | | |
| KPV | | |
| KPW | Cape Cod | b |
| KPX | Marshfield, Ohio | c |
| KPY | | |
| KPZ | | |
| KQA | Alleghany | b |
| KQB | Berkshire | b |
| KQC | Cretan | b |
| KQD | Dorchester | b |
| KQE | Essex | b |
| KQF | Frederick | b |
| KQG | Gloucester | b |
| KQH | Howard | b |
| KQI | Indian | b |
| KQJ | Juniata | b |
| KQK | Kershaw | b |
| KQL | Lexington | b |
| KQM | Merrimack | b |
| KQN | Nantucket | b |
| KQO | Ontario | b |
| KQP | Parthian | b |
| KQQ | Quantico | b |
| KQR | Grecian | b |
| KQS | Somerset | b |
| KQT | Tuscan | b |
| KQU | Itasca | b |
| KQV | New Orleans | b |
| KQW | | |
| KQX | Persian | b |
| KQY | Powhatan | b |
| KQZ | Suwannee | b |

2002°—13——5

LAND AND SHIP RADIO STATIONS, ALPHABETICALLY BY CALL SIGNALS—Continued.

| Call signal. | Name of station. | Classification. | Call signal. | Name of station. | Classification. |
|---|---|---|---|---|---|
| KRA | ........................ | ...... | KSP | ........................ | ...... |
| KRB | Governor Cobb....... | b | KSQ | ........................ | ...... |
| KRC | Camden............. | b | KSR | ........................ | ...... |
| KRD | Belfast............. | b | KSS | ........................ | ...... |
| KRE | Bay State........... | b | KST | ........................ | ...... |
| KRF | Ransom B. Fuller.... | b | KSU | ........................ | ...... |
| KRG | ........................ | ...... | KSV | ........................ | ...... |
| KRH | City of Bangor....... | b | KSW | ........................ | ...... |
| KRI | City of Rockland.... | b | KSX | Alabama............. | b |
| KRJ | Relief.............. | b | KSY | Florida.............. | b |
| KRK | ........................ | ...... | KSZ | Virginia............. | b |
| KRL | Louise............. | b | KTA | Larimer.............. | b |
| KRM | ........................ | ...... | KTB | Oklahoma............ | b |
| KRN | Calvin Austin........ | b | KTC | Shenango............ | b |
| KRO | Columbia............ | b | KTD | Ligonier............. | b |
| KRP | Rescue.............. | b | KTE | Winifred............ | b |
| KRQ | I. J. Merritt......... | b | KTF | J. M. Guffey......... | b |
| KRR | Mills............... | b | KTG | Gulfoil............... | b |
| KRS | Savage.............. | b | KTH | Illinois............. | b |
| KRT | ........................ | ...... | KTI | Brilliant............. | b |
| KRU | ........................ | ...... | KTJ | Comet............... | b |
| KRV | Governor Dingley.... | b | KTK | Elsegundo........... | b |
| KRW | ........................ | ...... | KTL | Rayo............... | b |
| KRX | ........................ | ...... | KTM | Eocene.............. | b |
| KRY | City of Baltimore.... | b | KTN | Perfection........... | b |
| KRZ | City of Norfolk....... | b | KTO | Astral............... | b |
| KSA | ........................ | ...... | KTP | S. O. Co. No. 94...... | b |
| KSB | ........................ | ...... | KTQ | City of Everett....... | b |
| KSC | ........................ | ...... | KTR | Radiant.............. | b |
| KSD | ........................ | ...... | KTS | Vesta............... | b |
| KSE | ........................ | ...... | KTT | Paraguay............ | b |
| KSF | Finland............. | b | KTU | Sun................. | b |
| KSG | ........................ | ...... | KTV | Toledo.............. | b |
| KSH | Kroonland........... | b | KTW | Delaware Sun........ | b |
| KSI | ........................ | ...... | KTX | Socony.............. | b |
| KSJ | ........................ | ...... | KTY | S. O. Co. No. 92...... | b |
| KSK | ........................ | ...... | KTZ | ........................ | ...... |
| KSL | St. Louis............ | b | KUA | ........................ | ...... |
| KSM | Philadelphia......... | b | KUB | ........................ | ...... |
| KSN | New York........... | b | KUC | Cuba............... | b |
| KSO | St. Paul............. | b | KUD | ........................ | ...... |
| | | | KUE | ........................ | ...... |
| | | | KUF | ........................ | ...... |
| | | | KUG | ........................ | ...... |
| | | | KUH | ........................ | ...... |

LAND AND SHIP RADIO STATIONS, ALPHABETICALLY BY CALL SIGNALS—Continued.

| Call signal. | Name of station. | Classification. | Call signal. | Name of station. | Classification. |
|---|---|---|---|---|---|
| KUI | ........................ | ...... | KVS | ........................ | ...... |
| KUJ | ........................ | ...... | KVT | ........................ | ...... |
| KUK | ........................ | ...... | KVU | Elmer A. Keeler...... | b |
| KUL | ........................ | ...... | KVV | ........................ | ...... |
| KUM | ........................ | ...... | KVW | ........................ | ...... |
| KUN | ........................ | ...... | KVX | ........................ | ...... |
| KUO | ........................ | ...... | KVY | ........................ | ...... |
| KUP | Pettibone............ | b | KVZ | Relay................ | b |
| KUQ | ........................ | ...... | KWA | ........................ | ...... |
| KUR | ........................ | ...... | KWB | ........................ | ...... |
| KUS | ........................ | ...... | KWC | Morro Castle.......... | b |
| KUT | Pan American........ | b | KWD | ........................ | ...... |
| KUU | ........................ | ...... | KWE | ........................ | ...... |
| KUV | Admiral Dewey...... | b | KWF | ........................ | ...... |
| KUW | ........................ | ...... | KWG | Segurança............ | b |
| KUX | Admiral Schley...... | b | KWH | Havana............... | b |
| KUY | ........................ | ...... | KWI | ........................ | ...... |
| KUZ | ........................ | ...... | KWJ | ........................ | ...... |
| KVA | Apache.............. | b | KWK | ........................ | ...... |
| KVB | Arapahoe............ | b | KWL | ........................ | ...... |
| KVC | Comanche........... | b | KWM | ........................ | ...... |
| KVD | ........................ | ...... | KWN | ........................ | ...... |
| KVE | ........................ | ...... | KWO | ........................ | ...... |
| KVF | Iroquois............. | b | KWP | ........................ | ...... |
| KVG | Algonquin........... | b | KWQ | ........................ | ...... |
| KVH | Huron............... | b | KWR | ........................ | ...... |
| KVI | ........................ | ...... | KWS | Saratoga............. | b |
| KVJ | Seminole............ | b | KWT | ........................ | ...... |
| KVK | Cherokee............ | b | KWU | ........................ | ...... |
| KVL | Lenape.............. | b | KWV | Vigilancia............ | b |
| KVM | Mohawk............. | b | KWW | ........................ | ...... |
| KVN | ........................ | ...... | KWX | Mexico............... | b |
| KVO | ........................ | ...... | KWY | Monterey............ | b |
| KVP | ........................ | ...... | KWZ | Esperanza............ | b |
| KVQ | ........................ | ...... | | | |
| KVR | ........................ | ...... | | | |

LAND AND SHIP RADIO STATIONS, ALPHABETICALLY BY CALL SIGNALS—Continued.

| Call signal. | Name of station. | Classification. |
|---|---|---|
| KXA | Boston | b |
| KXB | City of Lowell | b |
| KXC | Commonwealth | b |
| KXD | Maine | b |
| KXE | Mohawk | b |
| KXF | New Hampshire | b |
| KXG | Pilgrim | b |
| KXH | Plymouth | b |
| KXI | Priscilla | b |
| KXJ | Providence | b |
| KXK | Puritan | b |
| KXL | City of Taunton | b |
| KXM | Mohegan | b |
| KXN | New Haven | b |
| KXO | Connecticut | b |
| KXP | Pequonnock | b |
| KXQ | Chester W. Chapin | b |
| KXR | Richard Peck | b |
| KXS | | |
| KXT | | |
| KXU | | |
| KXV | | |
| KXW | | |
| KXX | | |
| KXY | | |
| KXZ | | |
| KYA | Atalanta | b |
| KYB | North Wind | b |
| KYC | Corsair | b |
| KYD | Cyprus | b |
| KYE | Cassandra | b |
| KYF | Florence | b |
| KYG | | |
| KYH | Aloha | b |
| KYI | Alvina | b |
| KYJ | | |
| KYK | Kismet | b |
| KYL | Lysistrata | b |
| KYM | Columbia | b |
| KYN | Niagara | b |
| KYO | Noma | b |
| KYP | Oneida | b |
| KYQ | | |
| KYR | Karina | b |
| KYS | Sea Otter | b |
| KYT | Vanadis | b |
| KYU | Emeline | b |
| KYV | Adventuress | b |
| KYW | Warrior | b |
| KYX | Wana | b |
| KYY | | |
| KYZ | | |
| KZA | | |
| KZB | | |
| KZC | | |
| KZD | | |
| KZE | | |
| KZF | | |
| KZG | | |
| KZH | | |
| KZI | | |
| KZJ | | |
| KZK | | |
| KZL | | |
| KZM | | |
| KZN | | |
| KZO | | |
| KZP | | |
| KZQ | | |
| KZR | | |
| KZS | | |
| KZT | | |
| KZU | | |
| KZV | | |
| KZW | | |
| KZX | | |
| KZY | | |
| KZZ | | |
| NAA | Arlington, Radio, Va. | c |

LAND AND SHIP RADIO STATIONS, ALPHABETICALLY BY CALL SIGNALS—Continued.

| Call signal. | Name of station. | Classification. | Call signal. | Name of station. | Classification. |
|---|---|---|---|---|---|
| NAB | Portland, Me. | c | NBP | Ammen | b |
| NAC | Portsmouth, N. H. | c | NBQ | | |
| NAD | Boston, Mass. | c | NBR | Annapolis | b |
| NAE | Cape Cod, Mass. | c | NBS | | |
| NAF | Newport, R. I. | c | NBT | | |
| NAG | Fire Island, Long Island, N. Y. | c | NBU | Buffalo | b |
| NAH | New York (Brooklyn), N. Y. | c | NBV | Arkansas | b |
| NAI | Philadelphia, Pa. | c | NBW | | |
| NAJ | | | NBX | | |
| NAK | Annapolis, Md. | c | NBY | | |
| NAL | Washington, D. C. | c | NBZ | | |
| NAM | Norfolk, Va. | c | NCA | | |
| NAN | Beaufort, N. C. | c | NCB | | |
| NAO | Charleston, S. C. | c | NCC | | |
| NAP | St. Augustine, Fla. | c | NCD | | |
| NAQ | Jupiter, Fla. | c | NCE | | |
| NAR | Key West, Fla. | c | NCF | Bailey | b |
| NAS | Pensacola, Fla. | c | NCG | | |
| NAT | New Orleans, La. | c | NCH | Baltimore | b |
| NAU | San Juan, P. R. | c | NCI | | |
| NAV | | | NCJ | | |
| NAW | Guantanamo Bay, Cuba. | c | NCK | | |
| NAX | Colon, Panama Canal Zone. | c | NCL | Beale | b |
| NAY | Porto Bello, Republic of Panama. | c | NCM | Birmingham | b |
| NAZ | | | NCN | | |
| NBA | | | NCO | | |
| NBB | | | NCP | | |
| NBC | | | NCQ | | |
| NBD | | | NCR | | |
| NBE | | | NCS | | |
| NBF | | | NCT | | |
| NBG | | | NCU | | |
| NBH | Ajax | b | NCV | Burrows | b |
| NBI | Alabama | b | | | |
| NBJ | Albany | b | | | |
| NBK | | | | | |
| NBL | Alert | b | | | |
| NBM | | | | | |
| NBN | | | | | |
| NBO | | | | | |

LAND AND SHIP RADIO STATIONS, ALPHABETICALLY BY CALL SIGNALS—Continued.

| Call signal. | Name of station. | Classification. | Call signal. | Name of station. | Classification. |
|---|---|---|---|---|---|
| NCW | | | NEG | | |
| NCX | | | NEH | | |
| NCY | Caesar | b | NEI | | |
| NCZ | California | b | NEJ | | |
| NDA | Castine | b | NEK | Delaware | b |
| NDB | Celtic | b | NEL | | |
| NDC | | | NEM | Denver | b |
| NDD | | | NEN | Des Moines | b |
| NDE | | | NEO | | |
| NDF | | | NEP | Dixie | b |
| NDG | Chester | b | NEQ | Dolphin | b |
| NDH | Cheyenne | b | NER | | |
| NDI | Chicago | b | NES | | |
| NDJ | | | NET | Drayton | b |
| NDK | | | NEU | | |
| NDL | Cincinnati | b | NEV | | |
| NDM | Cleveland | b | NEW | | |
| NDN | Colorado | b | NEX | | |
| NDO | | | NEY | | |
| NDP | | | NEZ | | |
| NDQ | Connecticut | b | NFA | | |
| NDR | | | NFB | | |
| NDS | | | NFC | Eagle | b |
| NDT | | | NFD | Elcano | b |
| NDU | Culgoa | b | NFE | Charleston | b |
| NDV | | | NFF | | |
| NDW | | | NFG | | |
| NDX | | | NFH | | |
| NDY | Cyclops | b | NFI | | |
| NDZ | | | NFJ | | |
| NEA | | | NFK | | |
| NEB | | | NFL | | |
| NEC | | | NFM | Fanning | b |
| NED | | | NFN | | |
| NEE | | | | | |
| NEF | | | | | |

LAND AND SHIP RADIO STATIONS, ALPHABETICALLY BY CALL SIGNALS—Continued.

| Call signal. | Name of station. | Classification. |
|---|---|---|
| NFO | ........................ | ...... |
| NFP | ........................ | ...... |
| NFQ | ........................ | ...... |
| NFR | Florida............. | b |
| NFS | Flusser............. | b |
| NFT | ........................ | ...... |
| NFU | ........................ | ...... |
| NFV | ........................ | ...... |
| NFW | ........................ | ...... |
| NFX | ........................ | ...... |
| NFY | ........................ | ...... |
| NFZ | ........................ | ...... |
| NGA | ........................ | ...... |
| NGB | ........................ | ...... |
| NGC | ........................ | ...... |
| NGD | Galveston............ | b |
| NGE | ........................ | ...... |
| NGF | Georgia............. | b |
| NGG | ........................ | ...... |
| NGH | Glacier............... | b |
| NGI | Chattanooga.......... | b |
| NGJ | Goldsborough....... | b |
| NGK | ........................ | ...... |
| NGL | ........................ | ...... |
| NGM | ........................ | ...... |
| NGN | ........................ | ...... |
| NGO | ........................ | ...... |
| NGP | ........................ | ...... |
| NGQ | ........................ | ...... |
| NGR | ........................ | ...... |
| NGS | ........................ | ...... |
| NGT | ........................ | ...... |
| NGU | Hannibal............ | b |
| NGV | ........................ | ...... |
| NGW | ........................ | ...... |
| NGX | Hector............. | b |
| NGY | Helena.............. | b |
| NGZ | ........................ | ...... |
| NHA | Henley............ | b |
| NHB | ........................ | ...... |
| NHC | Hopkins........... | b |
| NHD | ........................ | ...... |
| NHE | Hull............... | b |
| NHF | ........................ | ...... |
| NHG | ........................ | ...... |
| NHH | ........................ | ...... |
| NHI | ........................ | ...... |
| NHJ | ........................ | ...... |
| NHK | ........................ | ...... |
| NHL | ........................ | ...... |
| NHM | ........................ | ...... |
| NHN | Idaho............... | b |
| NHO | Illinois.............. | b |
| NHP | ........................ | ...... |
| NHQ | Indiana............ | b |
| NHR | ........................ | ...... |
| NHS | ........................ | ...... |
| NHT | Iowa................ | b |
| NHU | Iris.................. | b |
| NHV | Iroquois............ | b |
| NHW | ........................ | ...... |
| NHX | ........................ | ...... |
| NHY | ........................ | ...... |
| NHZ | ........................ | ...... |
| NIA | ........................ | ...... |
| NIB | Jarvis............... | b |
| NIC | ........................ | ...... |
| NID | Jenkins............ | b |
| NIE | Jouett.............. | b |
| NIF | ........................ | ...... |

LAND AND SHIP RADIO STATIONS, ALPHABETICALLY BY CALL SIGNALS—Continued.

| Call signal. | Name of station. | Classification. | Call signal. | Name of station. | Classification. |
|---|---|---|---|---|---|
| NIG | | | NJO | | |
| NIH | | | NJP | | |
| NII | | | NJQ | Marietta | b |
| | | | NJR | Mars | b |
| NIJ | | | NJS | Maryland | b |
| | | | NJT | Massachusetts | b |
| NIK | | | NJU | Mayrant | b |
| | | | NJV | Mayflower | b |
| NIL | | | NJW | McCall | b |
| NIM | | | NJX | | |
| NIN | | | NJY | | |
| NIO | Kansas | b | NJZ | Michigan | b |
| NIP | Kearsarge | b | | | |
| NIQ | Kentucky | b | NKA | | |
| NIR | | | NKB | | |
| NIS | | | NKC | | |
| NIT | | | NKD | Minnesota | b |
| | | | NKE | Mississippi | b |
| NIU | | | NKF | Missouri | b |
| NIV | | | NKG | | |
| NIW | Lamson | b | NKH | | |
| NIX | | | NKI | | |
| NIY | Lawrence | b | NKJ | Monadnock | b |
| NIZ | Lebanon | b | | | |
| NJA | | | NKK | | |
| NJB | Louisiana | b | NKL | Monaghan | b |
| | | | NKM | Montana | b |
| NJC | | | NKN | Monterey | b |
| | | | NKO | Montgomery | b |
| NJD | | | NKP | | |
| NJE | | | NKQ | | |
| NJF | | | NKR | | |
| NJG | | | NKS | | |
| NJH | Macdonough | b | NKT | | |
| NJI | | | NKU | | |
| NJJ | | | NKV | | |
| NJK | | | NKW | | |
| NJL | Maine | b | | | |
| NJM | | | NKX | | |
| | | | NKY | Nashville | b |
| NJN | | | NKZ | Navajo | b |

LAND AND SHIP RADIO STATIONS, ALPHABETICALLY BY CALL SIGNALS—Continued.

| Call signal. | Name of station. | Classification. | Call signal. | Name of station. | Classification. |
|---|---|---|---|---|---|
| NLA | Nantucket Shoals Lightship, off Newport, R. I. | c | NME | New Hampshire | b |
| | | | NMF | New Jersey | b |
| | | | NMG | New Orleans | b |
| NLB | Diamond Shoals Lightship, off Cape Hatteras, N. C. | c | NMH | | |
| NLC | Frying Pan Shoals, N. C. | c | NMI | | |
| NLD | | | NMJ | | |
| NLE | | | NMK | | |
| NLF | | | NML | | |
| NLG | | | NMM | | |
| | | | NMN | North Carolina | b |
| NLH | | | NMO | North Dakota | b |
| NLI | | | NMP | | |
| NLJ | | | NMQ | | |
| NLK | | | NMR | | |
| | | | NMS | Neptune | b |
| NLL | | | NMT | | |
| NLM | | | NMU | | |
| NLN | | | NMV | | |
| NLO | | | NMW | Ohio | b |
| NLP | | | NMX | | |
| NLQ | | | NMY | | |
| NLR | | | NMZ | Oregon | b |
| | | | NNA | Brutus | b |
| NLS | | | NNB | | |
| NLT | | | NNC | | |
| NLU | | | NND | | |
| NLV | | | NNE | | |
| NLW | | | NNF | | |
| NLX | | | NNG | | |
| NLY | | | NNH | | |
| NLZ | | | NNI | | |
| NMA | Nebraska | b | | | |
| NMB | Nero | b | NNJ | | |
| NMC | | | NNK | Nanshan | b |
| NMD | | | NNL | | |

LAND AND SHIP RADIO STATIONS, ALPHABETICALLY BY CALL SIGNALS—Continued.

| Call signal. | Name of station. | Classification. |
|---|---|---|
| NNM | ........................ | ...... |
| NNN | ........................ | ...... |
| NNO | ........................ | ...... |
| NNP | ........................ | ...... |
| NNQ | ........................ | ...... |
| NNR | ........................ | ...... |
| NNS | ........................ | ...... |
| NNT | ........................ | ...... |
| NNU | ........................ | ...... |
| NNV | ........................ | ...... |
| NNW | ........................ | ...... |
| NNX | ........................ | ...... |
| NNY | ........................ | ...... |
| NNZ | ........................ | ...... |
| NOA | Osceola | b |
| NOB | Abarenda | b |
| NOC | Orion | b |
| NOD | ........................ | ...... |
| NOE | ........................ | ...... |
| NOF | ........................ | ...... |
| NOG | Paducah | b |
| NOH | ........................ | ...... |
| NOI | ........................ | ...... |
| NOJ | Panther | b |
| NOK | Patterson | b |
| NOL | Patapsco | b |
| NOM | Patuxent | b |
| NON | Paulding | b |
| NOO | ........................ | ...... |
| NOP | Paul Jones | b |
| NOQ | ........................ | ...... |
| NOR | ........................ | ...... |
| NOS | ........................ | ...... |
| NOT | Pittsburgh | b |
| NOU | ........................ | ...... |
| NOV | ........................ | ...... |
| NOW | Peoria | b |
| NOX | Perkins | b |
| NOY | Perry | b |
| NOZ | Petrel | b |
| NPA | Cordova, Alaska | c |
| NPB | Sitka, Alaska | c |
| NPC | Bremerton, Wash | c |
| NPD | Tatoosh, Wash | c |
| NPE | North Head, Wash | c |
| NPF | Cape Blanco, Oreg | c |
| NPG | ........................ | ...... |
| NPH | Mare Island, Cal | c |
| NPI | Farallons, Cal | c |
| NPJ | Balboa, Panama Canal Zone. | c |
| NPK | Point Arguello, Cal | c |
| NPL | San Diego, Cal | c |
| NPM | Honolulu, T. H | c |
| NPN | Guam, Marianas (Ladrones). | c |
| NPO | Cavite, P. I | c |
| NPP | Peking, China | c |
| NPQ | St. Paul, Pribilof Islands, Alaska. | c |
| NPR | Dutch Harbor, Alaska | c |
| NPS | Kodiak, Alaska | c |
| NPT | Olongapo, P. I | c |
| NPU | ........................ | ...... |
| NPV | Unalga, Alaska | c |
| NPW | Eureka, Cal | c |
| NPX | ........................ | ...... |
| NPY | St. George, Pribilof Islands, Alaska. | c |
| NPZ | ........................ | ...... |
| NQA | ........................ | ...... |
| NQB | ........................ | ...... |
| NQC | ........................ | ...... |
| NQD | ........................ | ...... |
| NQE | ........................ | ...... |
| NQF | Pompey | b |
| NQG | ........................ | ...... |
| NQH | ........................ | ...... |
| NQI | ........................ | ...... |
| NQJ | ........................ | ...... |

LAND AND SHIP RADIO STATIONS, ALPHABETICALLY BY CALL SIGNALS—Continued.

| Call signal. | Name of station. | Classification. | Call signal. | Name of station. | Classification. |
|---|---|---|---|---|---|
| NQK | Potomac | b | NSD | | |
| NQL | | | NSE | | |
| NQM | Prairie | b | NSF | | |
| NQN | Preble | b | | | |
| NQO | Preston | b | NSG | | |
| NQP | Princeton | b | | | |
| NQQ | | | NSH | | |
| NQR | Prometheus | b | NSI | | |
| NQS | | | NSJ | | |
| NQT | | | NSK | | |
| NQU | | | NSL | | |
| NQV | | | NSM | | |
| NQW | | | NSN | | |
| NQX | | | NSO | | |
| NQY | | | NSP | | |
| NQZ | | | NSQ | Smith | b |
| NRA | Algonquin | b | NSR | | |
| NRB | Bear | b | | | |
| NRC | Morrill | b | NSS | | |
| NRD | Androscoggin | b | | | |
| NRE | Seneca | b | NST | Solace | b |
| NRF | Snohomish | b | | | |
| NRG | Gresham | b | NSU | | |
| NRH | McCulloch | b | | | |
| NRI | Itasca | b | NSV | | |
| NRJ | Woodbury | b | | | |
| NRK | Tahoma | b | NSW | South Carolina | b |
| NRL | Tuscarora | b | NSX | South Dakota | b |
| NRM | Mohawk | b | NSY | | |
| NRN | Manning | b | | | |
| NRO | Onondaga | b | NSZ | | |
| NRP | Apache | b | | | |
| NRQ | Miami | b | NTA | Ontario | b |
| NRR | Pamlico | b | NTB | Sterrett | b |
| NRS | Seminole | b | NTC | Stewart | b |
| NRT | Thetis | b | NTD | Rainbow | b |
| NRU | Acushnet | b | NTE | Raleigh | b |
| NRV | Winona | b | NTF | St. Louis | b |
| NRW | Windom | b | NTG | Sonoma | b |
| NRX | Unalga | b | | | |
| NRY | Yamacraw | b | NTH | | |
| NRZ | | | NTI | Stringham | b |
| NSA | | | NTJ | | |
| NSB | | | NTK | Supply | b |
| | | | NTL | Sylph | b |
| NSC | | | NTM | | |

LAND AND SHIP RADIO STATIONS, ALPHABETICALLY BY CALL SIGNALS—Continued.

| Call signal. | Name of station. | Classification. | Call signal. | Name of station. | Classification. |
|---|---|---|---|---|---|
| NTN | ........................ | ...... | NUW | ........................ | ...... |
| NTO | ........................ | ...... | NUX | ........................ | ...... |
| NTP | Salem................ | b | NUY | ........................ | ...... |
| NTQ | San Francisco........ | b | | | |
| NTR | Saratoga............. | b | NUZ | ........................ | ...... |
| NTS | ........................ | ...... | NVA | ........................ | ...... |
| NTT | Scorpion............. | b | NVB | ........................ | ...... |
| NTU | Reid................. | b | NVC | ........................ | ...... |
| NTV | ........................ | ...... | NVD | ........................ | ...... |
| NTW | ........................ | ...... | NVE | Utah................. | b |
| NTX | Rhode Island......... | b | NVF | ........................ | ...... |
| NTY | ........................ | ...... | NVG | ........................ | ...... |
| NTZ | Roe.................. | b | NVH | ........................ | ...... |
| NUA | Tacoma............... | b | | | |
| NUB | ........................ | ...... | NVI | ........................ | ...... |
| NUC | Tallahassee.......... | b | NVJ | ........................ | ...... |
| NUD | ........................ | ...... | NVK | Vermont.............. | b |
| NUE | ........................ | ...... | NVL | ........................ | ...... |
| NUF | ........................ | ...... | NVM | Vesuvius............. | b |
| NUG | Tennessee............ | b | NVN | Vicksburg............ | b |
| NUH | ........................ | ...... | NVO | ........................ | ...... |
| NUI | Terry................ | b | NVP | Villalobos........... | b |
| NUJ | ........................ | ...... | NVQ | ........................ | ...... |
| NUK | ........................ | ...... | NVR | Virginia............. | b |
| NUL | ........................ | ...... | NVS | ........................ | ...... |
| NUM | ........................ | ...... | NVT | Vulcan............... | b |
| NUN | Tonopah.............. | b | NVU | ........................ | ...... |
| NUO | ........................ | ...... | NVV | ........................ | ...... |
| NUP | ........................ | ...... | NVW | ........................ | ...... |
| NUQ | Trippe............... | b | NVX | ........................ | ...... |
| NUR | ........................ | ...... | NVY | ........................ | ...... |
| NUS | Truxton.............. | b | NVZ | ........................ | ...... |
| NUT | ........................ | ...... | NWA | ........................ | ...... |
| NUU | ........................ | ...... | NWB | ........................ | ...... |
| NUV | ........................ | ...... | NWC | ........................ | ...... |

LAND AND SHIP RADIO STATIONS, ALPHABETICALLY BY CALL SIGNALS—Continued.

| Call signal. | Name of station. | Classification. | Call signal. | Name of station. | Classification. |
|---|---|---|---|---|---|
| NWD | Warrington | b | NXL | | |
| NWE | Washington | b | NXM | | |
| NWF | | | NXN | | |
| NWG | West Virginia | b | NXO | | |
| NWH | Wheeling | b | NXP | | |
| NWI | Whipple | b | NXQ | | |
| NWJ | | | NXR | | |
| NWK | Wilmington | b | NXS | E-1 | b |
| NWL | Walke | b | NXT | E-2 | b |
| NWM | Wisconsin | b | NXU | | |
| NWN | | | NXV | | |
| NWO | | | NXW | | |
| NWP | | | NXX | | |
| NWQ | Wyoming | b | NXY | | |
| NWR | | | NXZ | | |
| NWS | | | NYA | | |
| NWT | | | NYB | | |
| NWU | | | NYC | | |
| NWV | | | NYD | | |
| NWW | | | NYE | | |
| NWX | | | NYF | | |
| NWY | | | NYG | | |
| NWZ | | | NYH | | |
| NXA | | | NYI | | |
| NXB | | | NYJ | | |
| NXC | | | NYK | | |
| NXD | | | NYL | | |
| NXE | | | NYM | | |
| NXF | | | NYN | | |
| NXG | | | NYO | | |
| NXH | | | NYP | | |
| NXI | | | | | |
| NXJ | | | | | |
| NXK | | | | | |

LAND AND SHIP RADIO STATIONS, ALPHABETICALLY BY CALL SIGNALS—Continued.

| Call signal. | Name of station. | Classification. |
|---|---|---|
| NYQ | | |
| NYR | | |
| NYS | | |
| NYT | | |
| NYU | | |
| NYV | | |
| NYW | | |
| NYX | | |
| NYY | | |
| NYZ | | |
| NZA | | |
| NZB | | |
| NZC | | |
| NZD | | |
| NZE | | |
| NZF | | |
| NZG | | |
| NZH | | |
| NZI | | |
| NZJ | | |
| NZK | | |
| NZL | | |
| NZM | | |
| NZN | | |
| NZO | | |
| NZP | | |
| NZQ | | |
| NZR | | |
| NZS | | |
| NZT | | |
| NZU | | |
| NZV | | |
| NZW | | |
| NZX | | |
| NZY | | |
| NZZ | | |
| WAA | Alameda | b |
| WAB | Buckman | b |
| WAC | Chicago | b |
| WAD | Victoria | b |
| WAE | Edith | b |
| WAF | Admiral Farragut | b |
| WAG | | |
| WAH | Dora | b |
| WAI | Latouche | b |
| WAJ | Jefferson | b |
| WAK | | |
| WAL | Santa Ana | b |
| WAM | | |
| WAN | Northwestern | b |
| WAO | Dirigo | b |
| WAP | | |
| WAQ | | |
| WAR | Cordova | b |
| WAS | Admiral Sampson | b |
| WAT | | |
| WAU | Dolphin | b |
| WAV | Seward | b |
| WAW | Watson | b |
| WAX | Atlantic City, N. J. | c |
| WAY | | |
| WAZ | | |
| WBA | | |
| WBB | | |
| WBC | | |
| WBD | Santa Cruz | b |
| WBE | | |
| WBF | Boston, Mass. | c |
| WBG | Iroquois | b |
| WBH | Chippewa | b |
| WBI | | |

LAND AND SHIP RADIO STATIONS, ALPHABETICALLY BY CALL SIGNALS—Continued.

| Call signal. | Name of station. | Classification. | Call signal. | Name of station. | Classification. |
|---|---|---|---|---|---|
| WBJ | .......................... | ...... | WCW | .......................... | ...... |
| WBK | Breakwater........... | b | WCX | Cleveland, Ohio..... | c |
| WBL | Buffalo, N. Y........ | c | WCY | Cape May, N. J...... | c |
| WBM | Redondo............ | b | WCZ | Illinois............... | b |
| WBN | Benton Harbor, Mich. | c | WDA | Pere Marquette...... | b |
| WBO | Nann Smith.......... | b | WDB | Pere Marquette 19... | b |
| WBP | Hermosa............. | b | WDC | Pere Marquette 17... | b |
| WBQ | Yukon............... | b | WDD | Pere Marquette 18... | b |
| WBR | Bertha.............. | b | WDE | Pere Marquette 20... | b |
| WBS | Baltimore, Md....... | c | WDF | .......................... | ...... |
| WBT | .......................... | ...... | WDG | .......................... | ...... |
| WBU | .......................... | ...... | WDH | .......................... | ...... |
| WBV | Cabrillo............. | b | WDI | City of South Haven. | b |
| WBW | .......................... | ...... | WDJ | .......................... | ...... |
| WBX | .......................... | ...... | WDK | .......................... | ...... |
| WBY | .......................... | ...... | WDL | Lakeland............ | b |
| WBZ | Glory of the Seas..... | b | WDM | Duluth, Minn........ | c |
| WCA | Tionesta............. | b | WDN | Ann Arbor No. 3..... | b |
| WCB | Juniata.............. | b | WDO | Ann Arbor No. 4..... | b |
| WCC | South Wellfleet, Mass. | c | WDP | Ann Arbor No. 5..... | b |
| WCD | Octorara............. | b | WDQ | .......................... | ...... |
| WCE | .......................... | ...... | WDR | Detroit, Mich......... | c |
| WCF | .......................... | ...... | WDS | City of Grand Rapids. | b |
| | | | WDT | City of Chicago....... | b |
| WCG | Brooklyn, N. Y...... | c | WDU | Puritan.............. | b |
| WCH | Boston, Mass......... | c | WDV | City of Benton Harbor | b |
| | | | WDW | Holland............. | b |
| WCI | .......................... | ...... | WDX | .......................... | ...... |
| WCJ | .......................... | ...... | WDY | Lydonia............. | b |
| WCK | .......................... | ...... | WDZ | .......................... | ...... |
| WCL | .......................... | ...... | WEA | City of Cleveland III. | b |
| WCM | Calumet, Mich........ | c | WEB | City of Mackinac II.. | b |
| WCN | North Land.......... | b | WEC | City of Detroit II.... | b |
| | | | WED | Western States....... | b |
| WCO | .......................... | ...... | WEE | Eastern States....... | b |
| | | | WEF | City of Detroit III.... | b |
| WCP | .......................... | ...... | WEG | City of St. Ignace.... | b |
| | | | WEH | City of Alpina II..... | b |
| WCQ | .......................... | ...... | WEI | .......................... | ...... |
| WCR | .......................... | ...... | WEJ | Nyack............... | b |
| | | | WEK | Minnesota............ | b |
| WCS | .......................... | ...... | WEL | E. G. Crosby......... | b |
| WCT | Theodore Roosevelt.. | b | WEM | .......................... | ...... |
| WCU | .......................... | ...... | WEN | North American...... | b |
| WCV | .......................... | ...... | WEO | .......................... | ...... |

LAND AND SHIP RADIO STATIONS, ALPHABETICALLY BY CALL SIGNALS—Continued.

| Call signal. | Name of station. | Classification. | Call signal. | Name of station. | Classification. |
|---|---|---|---|---|---|
| WEP | El Paso, Texas | c | WGG | | |
| WEQ | Col. James M. Schoonmaker. | b | WGH | Grand Haven, Mich | c |
| WER | William P. Snyder | b | WGI | | |
| WES | William P. Snyder, Jr. | b | WGJ | | |
| WET | Shenango | b | WGK | Curaçao | b |
| WEU | Wilpen | b | WGL | State of California | b |
| WEV | | | WGM | Grand Marais, Minn | c |
| WEW | Marquette & Bessemer No. 1. | b | WGN | Santa Rosa | b |
| WEX | Marquette & Bessemer No. 2. | b | WGO | Chicago, Ill | c |
| WEY | Alvina | b | WGP | President | b |
| WEZ | Ashtabula | b | WGQ | City of Puebla | b |
| WFA | Georgia | b | WGR | Governor | b |
| WFB | Alabama | b | WGS | Senator | b |
| WFC | Indiana | b | WGT | Congress | b |
| WFD | Iowa | b | WGU | Umatilla | b |
| WFE | Carolina | b | WGV | Galveston, Texas | c |
| WFF | Fort Worth, Texas | c | WGW | Grand Island, La | c |
| WFG | Arizona | b | WGX | Queen | b |
| WFH | Virginia | b | WGY | City of Topeka | b |
| WFI | Chicago | b | WGZ | Guardian | b |
| WFJ | Christopher Columbus. | b | WHA | Cape Hatteras (Buxton), N. C. | c |
| WFK | Frankfort, Mich | c | WHB | New York, N. Y | c |
| WFL | | | WHC | Columbia | b |
| WFM | Fort Morgan, Ala | c | WHD | | |
| WFN | Eastland | b | WHE | Philadelphia, Pa | c |
| WFO | | | WHF | | |
| WFP | City of Erie | b | WHG | W. B. Flint | b |
| WFQ | City of Buffalo | b | WHH | St. Francis | b |
| WFR | State of Ohio | b | WHI | New York, N. Y | c |
| WFS | Seeandbee | b | WHJ | Sierra | b |
| WFT | | | WHK | New Orleans, La | c |
| WFU | | | WHL | Ventura | b |
| WFV | | | WHM | Sonoma | b |
| WFW | Manitou | b | WHN | Hanalei | b |
| WFX | Missouri | b | WHO | | |
| WFY | | | WHP | Mariposa | b |
| WFZ | | | WHQ | Mackinac Island, Mich. | c |
| WGA | City of Seattle | b | WHR | | |
| WGB | | | WHS | Adeline Smith | b |
| WGC | | | WHT | Whittier | b |
| WGD | Delhi | b | WHU | | |
| WGE | Spokane | b | WHV | | |
| WGF | | | WHW | Mackinaw | b |
| | | | WHX | Humboldt | b |
| | | | WHY | | |

LAND AND SHIP RADIO STATIONS, ALPHABETICALLY BY CALL SIGNALS—Continued.

| Call signal. | Name of station. | Classification. | Call signal. | Name of station. | Classification. |
|---|---|---|---|---|---|
| WHZ | ........................ | ...... | WJD | ........................ | ...... |
| WIA | ........................ | ...... | WJE | ........................ | ...... |
| WIB | ........................ | ...... | WJF | ........................ | ...... |
| WIC | ........................ | ...... | WJG | ........................ | ...... |
| WID | ........................ | ...... | WJH | ........................ | ...... |
| WIE | ........................ | ...... | WJI | ........................ | ...... |
| WIF | ........................ | ...... | WJJ | ........................ | ...... |
| WIG | ........................ | ...... | WJK | ........................ | ...... |
| WIH | ........................ | ...... | WJL | ........................ | ...... |
| WII | ........................ | ...... | WJM | ........................ | ...... |
| WIJ | ........................ | ...... | WJN | ........................ | ...... |
| WIK | ........................ | ...... | WJO | ........................ | ...... |
| WIL | ........................ | ...... | WJP | ........................ | ...... |
| WIM | ........................ | ...... | WJQ | ........................ | ...... |
| WIN | ........................ | ...... | WJR | ........................ | ...... |
| WIO | ........................ | ...... | WJS | ........................ | ...... |
| WIP | ........................ | ...... | WJT | ........................ | ...... |
| WIQ | ........................ | ...... | WJU | ........................ | ...... |
| WIR | ........................ | ...... | WJV | ........................ | ...... |
| WIS | ........................ | ...... | WJW | ........................ | ...... |
| WIT | ........................ | ...... | WJX | Jacksonville, Fla...... | c |
| WIU | ........................ | ...... | WJY | ........................ | ...... |
| WIV | ........................ | ...... | WJZ | ........................ | ...... |
| WIW | ........................ | ...... | WKA | ........................ | ...... |
| WIX | ........................ | ...... | WKB | ........................ | ...... |
| WIY | ........................ | ...... | WKC | ........................ | ...... |
| WIZ | ........................ | ...... | WKD | Dakotan.............. | b |
| WJA | ........................ | ...... | WKE | ........................ | ...... |
| WJB | ........................ | ...... | WKF | ........................ | ...... |
| WJC | ........................ | ...... | WKG | Georgian.............. | b |
| | | | WKH | Honolulan............ | b |

2002°—13——6

LAND AND SHIP RADIO STATIONS, ALPHABETICALLY BY CALL SIGNALS—Continued

| Call signal. | Name of station. | Classification. |
|---|---|---|
| WKI | | |
| WKJ | | |
| WKK | Kansan | b |
| WKL | | |
| WKM | Minnesotan | b |
| WKN | Montanan | b |
| WKO | | |
| WKP | | |
| WKQ | | |
| WKR | | |
| WKS | | |
| WKT | | |
| WKU | | |
| WKV | | |
| WKW | | |
| WKX | | |
| WKY | | |
| WKZ | | |
| WLA | | |
| WLB | | |
| WLC | New London, Conn. | c |
| WLD | Ludington, Mich. | c |
| WLE | | |
| WLF | | |
| WLG | | |
| WLH | | |
| WLI | | |
| WLJ | | |
| WLK | | |
| WLL | | |
| WLM | | |
| WLN | Newton, Mass. | c |
| WLO | | |
| WLP | | |
| WLQ | | |
| WLR | | |
| WLS | | |
| WLT | | |
| WLU | | |
| WLV | | |
| WLW | | |
| WLX | | |
| WLY | | |
| WLZ | | |
| WMA | Multnomah | b |
| WMB | Mobile, Ala. | c |
| WMC | William Chatham | b |
| WMD | Mary Dodge | b |
| WME | Milwaukee, Wis. | c |
| WMF | | |
| WMG | | |
| WMH | | |
| WMI | Minnesota | b |
| WMJ | | |
| WMK | Hyades | b |
| WML | Lurline | b |
| WMM | Hilonian | b |
| WMN | Enterprise | b |
| WMO | Wilhelmina | b |
| WMP | | |
| WMQ | | |
| WMR | | |
| WMS | | |
| WMT | General Hubbard | b |
| WMU | | |
| WMV | | |
| WMW | Manitowoc, Wis. | c |
| WMX | Manistique, Mich. | c |
| WMY | Yucatan | b |
| WMZ | | |

LAND AND SHIP RADIO STATIONS, ALPHABETICALLY BY CALL SIGNALS—Continued.

| Call signal. | Name of station. | Classification. |
|---|---|---|
| WNA | | |
| WNB | Oliver J. Olson | b |
| WNC | Carlos | b |
| WND | Windber | b |
| WNE | Nushagak | b |
| WNF | Lyra | b |
| WNG | George W. Fenwick | b |
| WNH | Lewis Luckenbach | b |
| WNI | Leelanaw | b |
| WNJ | Navajo | b |
| WNK | Al-ki | b |
| WNL | Diamond Head | b |
| WNM | | |
| WNN | Corwin | b |
| WNO | A. G. Lindsay | b |
| WNP | Pleiades | b |
| WNQ | | |
| WNR | Rochelle | b |
| WNS | Kvichak | b |
| WNT | New York, N. Y. | c |
| WNU | | |
| WNV | Portland | b |
| WNW | San Ramon | b |
| WNX | Northland | b |
| WNY | St. Helens | b |
| WNZ | Vanguard | b |
| WOA | | |
| WOB | | |
| WOC | | |
| WOD | | |
| WOE | | |
| WOF | | |
| WOG | | |
| WOH | | |
| WOI | | |
| WOJ | | |
| WOK | | |
| WOL | | |
| WOM | | |
| WON | | |
| WOO | | |
| WOP | | |
| WOQ | | |
| WOR | | |
| WOS | | |
| WOT | | |
| WOU | | |
| WOV | Venetia | b |
| WOW | | |
| WOX | | |
| WOY | | |
| WOZ | | |
| WPA | Santa Cruz | b |
| WPB | Tyee Junior | b |
| WPC | Tyee | b |
| WPD | Tampa, Fla. | c |
| WPE | Tatoosh | b |
| WPF | | |
| WPG | Goliah | b |
| WPH | | |
| WPI | | |
| WPJ | | |
| WPK | Kingfisher | b |
| WPL | | |
| WPM | | |
| WPN | Pioneer | b |
| WPO | | |
| WPP | | |
| WPQ | Zapora | b |
| WPR | Ensanada, Porto Rico | c |
| WPS | Starr | b |
| WPT | | |
| WPU | | |
| WPV | | |
| WPW | Columbia | b |
| WPX | Oneonta | b |

LAND AND SHIP RADIO STATIONS, ALPHABETICALLY BY CALL SIGNALS—Continued.

| Call signal. | Name of station. | Classification. |
|---|---|---|
| WPY | Wallula | b |
| WPZ | Joseph Pulitzer | b |
| WQA | | |
| WQB | | |
| WQC | Camino | b |
| WQD | | |
| WQE | Edgar H. Vance | b |
| WQF | | |
| WQG | Greenwood | b |
| WQH | | |
| WQI | | |
| WQJ | | |
| WQK | | |
| WQL | | |
| WQM | | |
| WQN | | |
| WQO | | |
| WQP | | |
| WQQ | | |
| WQR | | |
| WQS | Speedwell | b |
| WQT | | |
| WQU | | |
| WQV | | |
| WQW | | |
| WQX | | |
| WQY | Yosemite | b |
| WQZ | | |
| WRA | Henry T. Scott | b |
| WRB | Berlin | b |
| WRC | J. B. Stetson | b |
| WRD | | |
| WRE | | |
| WRF | Fifield | b |
| WRG | | |
| WRH | Harvard | b |
| WRI | Paraiso | b |
| WRJ | Aroline | b |
| WRK | Falcon | b |
| WRL | | |
| WRM | Riverside | b |
| WRN | Nome City | b |
| WRO | Isle Royal, Mich | c |
| WRP | | |
| WRQ | | |
| WRR | Roanoke | b |
| WRS | Santa Clara | b |
| WRT | George W. Elder | b |
| WRU | Port Arthur, Tex | c |
| WRV | Alliance | b |
| WRW | F. A. Kilburn | b |
| WRX | | |
| WRY | Yale | b |
| WRZ | | |
| WSA | Ashtabula, Ohio | c |
| WSB | Francis H. Leggett | b |
| WSC | Siasconset, Mass | c |
| WSD | Stanley Dollar | b |
| WSE | Seagate, N. Y | c |
| WSF | Grace Dollar | b |
| WSG | Norwood | b |
| WSH | Chehalis | b |
| WSI | Sault Ste. Marie, Mich. | c |
| WSJ | John A. Hooper | b |
| WSK | Sagaponack, N. Y | c |
| WSL | Sayville, Long Island, N. Y | c |
| WSM | | |
| WSN | Centralia | b |
| WSO | Coronado | b |
| WSP | | |
| WSQ | | |
| WSR | Reuce | b |
| WSS | St. Nicholas | b |
| WST | | |
| WSU | | |
| WSV | Savannah, Ga | c |
| WSW | Willamette | b |
| WSX | Klamath | b |
| WSY | Virginia Beach, Va | c |

LAND AND SHIP RADIO STATIONS, ALPHABETICALLY BY CALL SIGNALS—Continued.

| Call signal. | Name of station. | Classification. |
|---|---|---|
| WSZ | Merced | b |
| WTA | Erskine M. Phelps | b |
| WTB | Argyll | b |
| WTC | Lansing | b |
| WTD | Oleum | b |
| WTE | Roma | b |
| WTF | Santa Maria | b |
| WTG | Santa Rita | b |
| WTH | Washtenaw | b |
| WTI | Catania | b |
| WTJ | | |
| WTK | J. A. Chanslor | b |
| WTL | | |
| WTM | W. S. Porter | b |
| WTN | Wm. F. Herrin | b |
| WTO | | |
| WTP | | |
| WTQ | | |
| WTR | Richmond | b |
| WTS | Col. E. L. Drake | b |
| WTT | Atlas | b |
| WTU | S. O. Co. No. 91 | b |
| WTV | Captain A. F. Lucas | b |
| WTW | Maverick | b |
| WTX | Asuncion | b |
| WTY | S. O. Co. No. 93 | b |
| WTZ | S. O. Co. No. 95 | b |
| WUA | Fort Andrews, Mass. | c |
| WUB | Fort Hancock, N. J. | c |
| WUC | Fort H. G. Wright, New York, N. Y. | c |
| WUD | Fort Leavenworth, Kans. | c |
| WUE | Fort Lovett, Me. | c |
| WUF | Fort Monroe, Va. | c |
| WUG | Fort Monroe, Va. | c |
| WUH | Fort Omaha, Nebr. | c |
| WUI | Fort Riley, Kans. | c |
| WUJ | Fort Sam Houston, Tex. | c |
| WUK | Fort Stevens, Oreg. | c |
| WUL | Fort Totten, N. Y. | c |
| WUM | Fort Wood, N. Y. | c |
| WUN | Fort Worden, Wash. | c |
| WUO | Fort Winfield Scott, Cal. | c |
| WUP | Washington, D. C. | c |
| WUQ | Washington, D. C. | c |
| WUR | | |
| WUS | | |
| WUT | | |
| WUU | | |
| WUV | Fort Leavenworth, Kans. | c |
| WUW | | |
| WUX | | |
| WUY | | |
| WUZ | | |
| WVA | Circle City, Alaska | c |
| WVB | Fairbanks, Alaska | c |
| WVC | Fort Egbert, Alaska | c |
| WVD | Fort Gibbon, Alaska | c |
| WVE | Fort St. Michael, Alaska. | c |
| WVF | Kotlik, Alaska | c |
| WVG | Nome, Alaska | c |
| WVH | Nulato, Alaska | c |
| WVI | Petersburg, Alaska | c |
| WVJ | Wrangell, Alaska | c |
| WVK | | |
| WVL | Fort Frank, P. I. | c |
| WVM | Fort Hughes, P. I. | c |
| WVN | Corregidor Island, P. I. | c |
| WVO | Davao, P. I. | c |
| WVP | Fort Drum, P. I. | c |
| WVQ | Fort McKinley, P. I. | c |
| WVR | Fort Wint, P. I. | c |
| WVS | Jolo, P. I. | c |
| WVT | Malabang, P. I. | c |
| WVU | Manila, P. I. | c |
| WVV | Puerto Princesa, P. I. | c |
| WVW | Zamboanga, P. I. | c |
| WVX | Cuyo, P. I. | c |
| WVY | San Jose, P. I. | c |
| WVZ | | |
| WWA | China | b |
| WWB | Beaver | b |
| WWC | | |
| WWD | Bear | b |
| WWE | Manchuria | b |
| WWF | City of Para | b |
| WWG | City of Sydney | b |
| WWH | Newport | b |
| WWI | Pennsylvania | b |
| WWJ | Peru | b |
| WWK | Korea | b |
| WWL | San Jose | b |
| WWM | San Juan | b |
| WWN | Mongolia | b |

LAND AND SHIP RADIO STATIONS, ALPHABETICALLY BY CALL SIGNALS—Continued.

| Call signal. | Name of station. | Classification. | Call signal. | Name of station. | Classification. |
|---|---|---|---|---|---|
| WWO | Acapulco | b | WYD | | |
| WWP | City of Panama | b | WYE | | |
| WWQ | Aztec | b | WYF | | |
| WWR | Rose City | b | WYG | | |
| WWS | Kansas City | b | WYH | General Robert Anderson. | b |
| WWT | | | WYI | Captain Chas. W. Rowell. | b |
| WWU | Siberia | b | WYJ | General A.M. Randol. | b |
| WWV | | | WYK | General Harvey Brown. | b |
| WWW | | | WYL | General R. B. Ayres | b |
| WWX | | | WYM | James Fornance | b |
| WWY | | | WYN | Reno | b |
| WWZ | | | WYO | Major Thomas | b |
| WXA | Buford | b | WYP | Captain Barrett | b |
| WXB | Crook | b | WYQ | | |
| WXC | Dix | b | WYR | | |
| WXD | Kilpatrick | b | WYS | | |
| WXE | Liscum | b | WYT | | |
| WXF | Logan | b | WYU | | |
| WXG | Meade | b | WYV | | |
| WXH | McClellan | b | WYW | | |
| WXI | Merritt | b | WYX | | |
| WXJ | Sheridan | b | WYY | | |
| WXK | Sherman | b | WYZ | | |
| WXL | Sumner | b | WZA | | |
| WXM | Thomas | b | WZB | | |
| WXN | Warren | b | WZC | | |
| WXO | | | WZD | | |
| WXP | | | WZE | | |
| WXQ | | | WZF | | |
| WXR | Burnside | b | WZG | De Russey, T. H | c |
| WXS | Cyrus W. Field | b | WZH | | |
| WXT | Joseph Henry | b | WZI | | |
| WXU | | | WZJ | | |
| WXV | | | | | |
| WXW | | | | | |
| WXX | | | | | |
| WXY | | | | | |
| WXZ | | | | | |
| WYA | | | | | |
| WYB | | | | | |
| WYC | | | | | |

LAND AND SHIP RADIO STATIONS, ALPHABETICALLY BY CALL SIGNALS—Continued.

| Call signal. | Name of station. | Classification. | Call signal. | Name of station. | Classification. |
|---|---|---|---|---|---|
| WZK | ........................ | ...... | WZS | ........................ | ...... |
| WZL | ........................ | ...... | WZT | ........................ | ...... |
| WZM | ........................ | ...... | WZU | ........................ | ...... |
| WZN | ........................ | ...... | WZV | ........................ | ...... |
| WZO | ........................ | ...... | WZW | ........................ | ...... |
| WZP | ........................ | ...... | WZX | ........................ | ...... |
| WZQ | ........................ | ...... | WZY | ........................ | ...... |
| WZR | ........................ | ...... | WZZ | ........................ | ...... |

## SPECIAL STATIONS.[1]

[This list consists of stations of the experimental, technical and training school, and special amateur grades.]

| | | | | | |
|---|---|---|---|---|---|
| 1XA | Amesbury, Mass...... | c | 4XG | Atlanta, Ga........... | c |
| 1XB | Boston, Mass......... | c | 6XR | Berkeley, Cal........ | c |
| 1XP | Cambridge, Mass..... | c | 6YL | Los Angeles, Cal..... | c |
| 1YH | Cambridge, Mass..... | c | 8XA | Ann Arbor, Mich..... | c |
| 2YN | New York, N. Y..... | c | 8YD | Detroit, Mich........ | c |
| 2ZH | Nutley, N. J........ | c | 9XB | Beloit, Wis.......... | c |
| 3XC | Philadelphia, Pa..... | c | 9YC | St. Louis, Mo........ | c |
| 3XJ | Philadelphia, Pa..... | c | 9YI | Ames, Iowa.......... | c |
| 3XR | Hyattsville, Md...... | c | 9YN | Grand Forks, N. Dak. | c |
| 3ZS | St. Davids, Pa....... | c | | | |

[1] See introduction, page 8.

# PART II.

## AMATEUR RADIO STATIONS.

### FIRST DISTRICT.

[Headquarters: Customhouse, barge office, Long Wharf, Boston, Mass. The first district comprises the States of Maine, New Hampshire, Vermont, Massachusetts, Rhode Island, and Connecticut.]

ALPHABETICALLY BY OWNERS OF STATIONS.

| Call signal. | Owner of station. | Location of station. | Power. |
|---|---|---|---|
| | | | *Watts.* |
| 1HL | Affel, Herman A | 45 St. Botolph St., Boston, Mass | 100 |
| 1GM | Allen, J. Wyman | 236 Hale St., Beverly, Mass | 25 |
| 1HA | Allison, William H | 37 Plantation St., Worcester, Mass | 500 |
| 1KJ | Anderson, Arvid E | Shore St., Falmouth, Mass | 100 |
| 1HT | Anderson, James H | 132 White St., Belmont, Mass | 100 |
| 1UJ | Ashworth, Harry | 34 Heath St., Providence, R. I | 100 |
| 1CO | Atkins, Harry C | 57 Pine St., Franklin, N. H | 100 |
| 1UI | Bailey, William M | 57 Brownell St., Providence, R. I | 100 |
| 1IT | Barnes, Irving T | 377 Main St., Waltham, Mass | 100 |
| 1WB | Barnum, Roland B | 250 Sherman Ave., New Haven, Conn | 500 |
| 1WJ | Barrett, John H | 64 Lafayette Pl., Greenwich, Conn | 100 |
| 1UQ | Barth, Karl E | 229 Washington Ave., Providence, R. I | 1,000 |
| 1IY | Baxter, Horace M | 160 Foster St., Brighton, Mass | 100 |
| 1VL | Belknop, Edward L | 91 Vine St., Hartford, Conn | 100 |
| 1HY | Bennett, Lawrence S | 2 Lawrence St., Everett, Mass | 500 |
| 1IE | Bennett, William F., jr | 24 Spring St., Somerville, Mass | 100 |
| 1GU | Bernardin, L. A | 456 Haverhill St., Lawrence, Mass | 750 |
| 1GH | Bibber, Harold | 31 Beacon St., Gloucester, Mass | 100 |
| 1UL | Bigelow, Clinton A | 96 Whittier Ave., Providence, R. I | 100 |
| 1UG | Bigelow, Fred C., jr | 128 Main St., Lincoln, R. I. (P. O., Manville). | 1,000 |
| 1GB | Blount, Henry G | Hamilton, Mass | 539 |
| 1KO | Bowen, Harold C | 168 Belmont St., Fall River, Mass | 250 |
| 1HQ | Broadley, Harry R | 44 Wenham St., Boston, Mass | 100 |

AMATEUR RADIO STATIONS—FIRST DISTRICT—ALPHABETICALLY BY OWNERS OF STATIONS—Continued.

| Call signal. | Owner of station. | Location of station. | Power. |
|---|---|---|---|
| | | | *Watts.* |
| 1AI | Brown, Olin C. | 23 Ledgelawn Ave., Bar Harbor, Me. | 1,000 |
| 1AB | Brown, Philip T. | 36 Taylor St., Portland, Me. | 500 |
| 1JN | Bruce, Arthur O. | 30 York St., Cambridge, Mass. | 500 |
| 1UX | Budlong, Clifton O. | 73 Rear Fort Ave., Cranston, R. I. | 100 |
| 1WS | Buffett, Salathiel. | Quarry Ave., Saybrook, Conn. | 100 |
| 1HB | Burgess, Warren B. | 62 Fruit St., Worcester, Mass. | 100 |
| 1HI | Burke, Alan W. | 40 Pollock Ave., Pittsfield, Mass. | 100 |
| 1GL | Bush, Arthur W. | 80 Tower Hill St., Lawrence, Mass. | 1,000 |
| 1AM | Butler, Guy W. | 56 Center St., Oldtown, Me. | 250 |
| 1HD | Canfield, Donald T. | 1-34 R. F. D., Westboro, Mass. | 100 |
| 1BO | Canty, William R. | 36 Lincoln Ave., Rutland, Vt. | 500 |
| 1JT | Carlson, Arthur G. | 19 Mechanic St., North Easton, Mass. | 500 |
| 1GC | Chadwick, Gilbert L. | 19 Eleventh Ave., Haverhill, Mass. | 100 |
| 1CW | Chase, Robert McC. | 25 Russell St., Plymouth, N. H. | 1,000 |
| 1HC | Cheetham, Harry R. | 81 Avon St., Somerville, Mass. | 45 |
| 1JM | Cheever, Walter G. | 6 Aldersay St., Somerville, Mass. | 100 |
| 1IU | Church, Arthur E. | 3 Wellington Terrace, Brookline, Mass. | 100 |
| 1HG | Cogswell, George R. | 18 Garden St., Cambridge, Mass. | 250 |
| 1JD | Collins, Lovejoy. | 44 Carver Road, Newton Highlands, Mass. | 100 |
| 1CP | Conrad, Philip W. | 172 Elm St., Keene, N. H. | 250 |
| 1BM | Copps, John L. | 138 South Main St., Rutland, Vt. | 100 |
| 1UC | Creaser, Isaiah. | 22 Bond St., Providence, R. I. | 1,000 |
| 1HP | Cromack, N. G. N. | 8 Elm Lawn St., Dorchester, Mass. | 100 |
| 1WP | Cummings, Edward H. | Warwick, R. I. | 300 |
| 1JU | Dane, Francis W. | Main St., Hamilton, Mass. | 500 |
| 1GJ | Daniels, Richard M. | 25 Outlook Rd., Swampscott, Mass. | 500 |
| 1KD | David, Harold E. | 21A Belchertown Rd., Amherst, Mass. | 100 |
| 1WZ | Davis, Maurice E. | 217 Dover St., New Haven, Conn. | 100 |
| 1JP | Decker, Clarence. | Cottage St., Great Barrington, Mass. | 250 |
| 1JR | Delano, Edward C. | 64 School St., Fall River, Mass. | 500 |
| 1KE | De Mello, Edward. | 93 Sidney St., New Bedford, Mass. | 250 |

AMATEUR RADIO STATIONS—FIRST DISTRICT—ALPHABETICALLY BY OWNERS OF STATIONS—Continued.

| Call signal. | Owner of station. | Location of station. | Power. |
|---|---|---|---|
| | | | Watts. |
| 1HK | Denison, Horace W. | 60 Garland St., Chelsea, Mass. | 500 |
| 1BC | Dimick, Leon R. | 27 Cliff St., St. Johnsbury, Vt. | 100 |
| 1JA | Dimond, Fred A., jr. | 4 Purchase St., East Carver, Mass. | 100 |
| 1UR | Doherty, James E. | 22 Orms St., Providence, R. I. | 100 |
| 1UD | Donle, Harold P. | 18 Observatory Ave., Providence, R. I. | 300 |
| 1KH | Doten, H. B. | 7 South St., Plymouth, Mass. | 1,000 |
| 1UO | Doyle, John B. | 306 Thurber Ave., Providence, R. I. | 100 |
| 1HZ | Duncan, Harrie E. | 34 Foster St., Newtonville, Mass. | 250 |
| 1KL | Edson, Allan W. | 167 Pleasant St., Whitman, Mass. | 100 |
| 1WN | Edwin Bancroft Foote Boys' Club. | Chapel St., New Haven, Conn. | 1,000 |
| 1HR | Elliott, Thomas H., jr. | 41 Brighton Rd., Brookline, Mass. | 200 |
| 1GO | Estey, F. Clifford | 3 Goodell St., Salem, Mass. | 250 |
| 1IF | Eveleth, Harlan A. | 72 Gray St., Arlington, Mass. | 1,000 |
| 1AJ | Fabbri, Alessandro | Eden St., Bar Harbor, Me. | 1,000 |
| 1JC | Fairbanks, Robert D. | 21 Carver Rd., Newton Highlands, Mass. | 100 |
| 1IJ | Fassitt, Andrew J., jr. | 27 Walden St., Cambridge, Mass. | 250 |
| 1BA | Fitts, Harold W. | 2 Park St., Barre, Vt. | 100 |
| 1HN | Flood, J. F. J. | 160 D St., South Boston, Mass. | 250 |
| 1GF | Fowler, F. M. | 16 Shore Ave., Salem, Mass. | 500 |
| 1JK | Franke, Alfred A. | 15 Orchard St., Boston, Mass. | 100 |
| 1IH | Fuller, Clarence C. | 50 Hight St., Mansfield, Mass. | 100 |
| 1JL | Gahm, Sebastian, jr. | 113 Sheridan St., Jamaica Plain, Boston, Mass. | 100 |
| 1HF | Gardner, Chester R. | 11 Spring Hill Ter., Somerville, Mass. | 100 |
| 1VN | Green, Louis | 126 Central Ave., Waterbury, Conn. | 100 |
| 1GV | Gavill, Wilbur W. | Main St., West Chelmsford, Mass. | 100 |
| 1GW | Haddock, Charles C. | 57 Lathrop St., Beverly, Mass. | 250 |
| 1HM | Hammett, Herbert M. | 4 Blue Hill Ave., Roxbury, Mass. | 100 |
| 1UH | Handy, William R. | Lincoln, R. I. (P. O., Manville) | 100 |
| 1GS | Hardy, Wilbur H. | 778 Hale St., Beverly Farms, Mass. | 350 |
| 1UA | Hargraves, Harold T. | 733 Cranston St., Providence, R. I. | 100 |

AMATEUR RADIO STATIONS—FIRST DISTRICT—ALPHABETICALLY BY OWNERS OF STATIONS—Continued.

| Call signal. | Owner of station. | Location of station. | Power. |
|---|---|---|---|
| | | | *Watts.* |
| 1VO | Haskell, Shirley D. | Main St., Essex, Conn. | 250 |
| 1CY | Haselton, Page S. | Hudson, N. H. | 100 |
| 1JE | Hayward, Edward E., jr. | 4 Pembroke St., Newton, Mass. | 100 |
| 1UN | Henry, William E. | 162 Prairie Ave., Providence, R. I. | 500 |
| 1JY | Herland, John N. | 48 Brush Hill Rd., Mattapan, Mass. | 100 |
| 1VH | Hickmott, William J., jr. | 29 Summer St., Hartford, Conn. | 275 |
| 1GR | Hodges, Duncan. | Groton School, Groton, Mass. | 250 |
| 1AF | Hodgkins, Winfield C. | 54 Eagle Lake Rd., Eden, Bar Harbor, Me. | 100 |
| 1JQ | Hoffman, Frank E. | 33 High St., Springfield, Mass. | 250 |
| 1WY | Hoggson, Wallace. | Maber Ave., Greenwich, Conn. | 300 |
| 1UZ | Homer, Arthur B. | 270 Boulevard, Providence, R. I. | 100 |
| 1KC | Howe, Milton A. | 347 Mt. Vernon St., Fitchburg, Mass. | 500 |
| 1CR | Howe, Reginald. | 94 School St., Keene, N. H. | 100 |
| 1JH | Hubbard, Allen, jr. | 11 Montvale Crescent, Newton Center, Mass. | 250 |
| 1AG | Hutchins, Ray. | Oak St., Springvale, Me. | 100 |
| 1HJ | Hunt, Albert M. | 12 Madison Ave., Newtonville, Mass. | 100 |
| 1GP | James, Albert W. | 36 Union St., Manchester, Mass. | 100 |
| 1UE | Jette, George E. | 161 Summer St., Central Falls, R. I. | 500 |
| 1KP | Justice, Francis C. | 148 Tremont St., Newton, Mass. | 100 |
| 1ID | Kehoe, Francis. | 41 Walnut St., Boston, Mass. | 100 |
| 1AC | Kennedy, Chester A. | 199 High St., South Portland, Me. | 250 |
| 1GD | Lane, Frederick A. | 7 Madison Ave., Gloucester, Mass. | 250 |
| 1JZ | Lanvuette, Kenneth H. | 21 Houston Ave., Milton, Mass. | 100 |
| 1JI | Lawrence, Milford R. | Main St., Falmouth, Mass. | 500 |
| 1IS | Leach, George. | 513 Liberty St., Rockland, Mass. | 100 |
| 1HX | Leavitt, Elmer A. | 41 Forest Ave., Everett, Mass. | 250 |
| 1IP | Leland, Harold. | 34 Irving St., Somerville, Mass. | 100 |
| 1IR | Lewis, Minott W. | 44 Kidder Ave., West Somerville, Mass. | 100 |
| 1UY | Lippitt, Gorton T. | 111 Benevolent St., Providence, R. I. | 200 |
| 1JW | Long, John J. | 32 London St., Somerville, Mass. | 100 |

AMATEUR RADIO STATIONS—FIRST DISTRICT—ALPHABETICALLY BY OWNERS OF STATIONS—Continued.

| Call signal. | Owner of station. | Location of station. | Power. |
|---|---|---|---|
| | | | Watts. |
| 1GT | Loomis, Arthur T | 35 Graves Ave., Lynn, Mass | 250 |
| 1JB | Lord, Howland C | 40 Clyde St., Newtonville, Mass | 100 |
| 1KI | Loring, Wilfred B | Plympton, Mass | 175 |
| 1WU | Lucas, Orville | 172 Washington St., Wallingford, Conn | 100 |
| 1IQ | Luey, Donald | 44 West St., Worcester, Mass | 500 |
| 1HE | Lynde, Kenneth R | 20 Cloelia Terrace, Newtonville, Mass | 100 |
| 1KG | Manning, Ralph K | 232 Vine St., Everett, Mass | 250 |
| 1TM | Mason, Lion G | Halidon Hall, Newport, R. I | 500 |
| 1VM | McGuire, William C | 76 Madison St., Hartford, Conn | 100 |
| 1OM | McLane, Henry R | Union Ave., Laconia, N. H | 1,000 |
| 1KM | Meekin, William J | 34 Custer St., Rockland, Mass | 250 |
| 1HO | Merrill, Clark B | 3 Elm St., Dorchester, Mass | 200 |
| 1UM | Miller, Bernard H | 38 Doyle Ave., Providence, R. I | 250 |
| 1UV | Monahan, Edward M | 1033 Eddy St., Providence, R. I | 100 |
| 1GI | Morse, H. E | 108 Essex St., Swampscott, Mass | 300 |
| 1HW | Munroe, H. W. T | 38 Beacon St., Everett, Mass | 500 |
| 1CV | Nelson, Rufus L | 16 Oak St., Northfield, N. H | 500 |
| 1UW | Nilson, Arthur R | 11 Colfax St., Providence, R. I | 100 |
| 1IX | Ohlson, Olof | 472 Crafts St., Newton, Mass | 250 |
| 1CX | Parker, George H | Hudson, N. H | 100 |
| 1UB | Pease, Reginald M | 5 West Park St., Providence, R. I | 100 |
| 1KF | Pennypacker, Thos. R | Chatham, Mass | 90 |
| 1UF | Perkins, Leonard M | 28½ Warren St., Providence, R. I | 250 |
| 1WO | Post, Harold | 131 Derby Ave., New Haven, Conn | 100 |
| 1JS | Powers, Leonard S | 431 Plymouth St., Carver, Mass | 100 |
| 1JG | Pratt, Fearing | 120 Main St., Hingham, Mass | 250 |
| 1IO | Pratt, Walter | 28 Summitt St., Rockland, Mass | 100 |
| 1JV | Reuther, Henry | 15 Jewett St., Northampton, Mass | 250 |
| 1AR | Rich, Marion | Cedar Ave., Bar Harbor, Me | 250 |
| 1KB | Richards, W. T | 15 Follen St., Cambridge, Mass | 100 |
| 1HV | Ryan, James A | 43 Linwood St., Somerville, Mass | 100 |

AMATEUR RADIO STATIONS—FIRST DISTRICT—ALPHABETICALLY BY OWNERS OF STATIONS—Continued.

| Call signal. | Owner of station. | Location of station. | Power. |
|---|---|---|---|
| | | | *Watts.* |
| 1WX | Safranek, Jerry | 28 South St., South Norwalk, Conn | 15 |
| 1IZ | Saint James, Robert T. | 38 Avery Lane, Great Barrington, Mass | 1,000 |
| 1WT | Salzgeber, John W. | West Main St., Ivoryton, Conn | 100 |
| 1WR | Sawtelle, Donald F. | 122 Gilbert Ave., New Haven, Conn | 100 |
| IKS | Seabury, William H | 1056 Beacon St., Brookline, Mass | 250 |
| 1WQ | Seeley, Arthur P. | 55 Pearl St., New Haven, Conn | 25 |
| 1HS | Shattuck, Herbert | 1-A Lewis Place, Roxbury, Mass | 100 |
| 1BN | Shaw, Raymond H. | 10 East Washington St., Rutland, Vt | 12 |
| 1GN | Smith, Malcolm H. | 115 Prospect St., Gloucester, Mass | 250 |
| 1AD | Smith, Edward S. C. | 58 South St., Biddeford, Me | 100 |
| 1JF | Snow, Albert E. | 30 Cary Ave., Chelsea, Mass | 100 |
| 1GA | Snow, Harold C. | 41 Paradise Rd., Swampscott, Mass | 250 |
| 1JO | Snow, William B. | 11 Devon Rd., Newton Center, Mass | 100 |
| 1IV | Snyder, William E. | 36 Monument Ave., Charlestown, Mass | 100 |
| 1GK | Stanley, Lyman R. | 52 Burrill St., Swampscott, Mass | 500 |
| 1IB | Stanyan, Starr W. | 76 Boston Ave., West Bedford, Mass | 200 |
| 1AE | Sterling, George E. | 28 Pine St., Springvale, Me | 100 |
| 1KA | Stickney, H. E. | 25 Tufts Ave., Everett, Mass | 100 |
| 1AK | Tabbut, Arthur R. | 6 First South St., Bar Harbor, Me | 250 |
| 1US | Thorndike, Don C. | 303 Doric Ave., Cranston, R. I | 100 |
| 1UP | Trainor, Francis J. | 126 Summer St., Providence, R. I. (Classical High School). | 300 |
| 1UK | Tutin, Kenneth A. | 312 Blackstone St., Woonsocket, R. I | 100 |
| 1HU | Upton, Harry E. | 18 Jackson Ave., Everett, Mass | 400 |
| 1AH | Ward, Donald G. | 14 Orchard St., Portland, Me | 200 |
| 1GQ | Westbrook, Leon R. | 41 Eleventh St., Haverhill, Mass | 1,000 |
| 1GE | Wheeler, Fred L. | 23 Mt. Vernon St., Cliftondale, Mass | 100 |
| 1IW | Wilde, Phillips B. | Government St., Woods Hole, Mass | 100 |
| 1KN | Wilkinson, John E. | 35 Malvey St., Fall River, Mass | 250 |
| 1KW | Wood, James E. | 17 Main St., Fairhaven, Mass | 1,000 |
| 1AL | Wyer, Otis W. | 237 Forest St., Cumberland Mills, Me | 100 |

## Amateur Radio Stations—First District—Continued.

ALPHABETICALLY BY CALL SIGNALS.

| Call signal. | Owner of station. |
|---|---|
| 1AB | Brown, Philip T. |
| 1AC | Kennedy, Chester A. |
| 1AD | Smith, Edward S. C. |
| 1AE | Sterling, George E. |
| 1AF | Hodgkins, Winfield C. |
| 1AG | Hutchins, Ray. |
| 1AH | Ward, Donald G. |
| 1AI | Brown, Olin C. |
| 1AJ | Fabbri, Alessandro. |
| 1AK | Tabbut, Arthur R. |
| 1AL | Wyer, Otis W. |
| 1AM | Butler, Guy W. |
| 1AR | Rich, Marion. |
| 1BA | Fitts, Harold W. |
| 1BC | Dimick, Leon R. |
| 1BM | Coppe, John L. |
| 1BN | Shaw, Raymond H. |
| 1BO | Canty, William R. |
| 1CM | McLane, Henry R. |
| 1CO | Atkins, Harry C. |
| 1CP | Conrad, Philip W. |
| 1CR | Howe, Reginald. |
| 1CV | Nelson, Rufus L. |
| 1CW | Chase, Robert McC. |
| 1CX | Parker, George H. |
| 1CY | Haselton, Page S. |
| 1GA | Snow, Harold C. |
| 1GB | Blount, Henry G. |
| 1GC | Chadwick, Gilbert L. |
| 1GD | Lane, Frederick A. |
| 1GE | Wheeler, Fred L. |
| 1GF | Fowler, F. M. |
| 1GH | Bibber, Harold. |
| 1GI | Morse, H. E. |
| 1GJ | Daniels, Richard M. |
| 1GK | Stanley, Lyman R. |
| 1GL | Bush, Arthur W. |
| 1GM | Allen, J. Wyman. |
| 1GN | Smith, Malcolm H. |
| 1GO | Estey, F. Clifford. |
| 1GP | James, Albert W. |
| 1GQ | Westbrook, Leon R. |
| 1GR | Hodges, Duncan. |
| 1GS | Hardy, Wilbur H. |
| 1GT | Loomis, Arthur T. |
| 1GU | Bernardin, L. A. |
| 1GV | Gavill, Wilbur W. |
| 1GW | Haddock, Charles C. |
| 1HA | Allison, William H. |
| 1HB | Burgess, Warren B. |
| 1HC | Cheetham, Harry R. |
| 1HD | Canfield, Donald T. |
| 1HE | Lynde, Kenneth R. |
| 1HF | Gardner, Chester R. |
| 1HG | Cogswell, George R. |
| 1HI | Burke, Alan W. |
| 1HJ | Hunt, Albert M. |
| 1HK | Denison, Horace W. |
| 1HL | Affel, Herman A. |
| 1HM | Hammett, Herbert M. |
| 1HN | Flood, J. F. J. |
| 1HO | Merrill, Clark B. |
| 1HP | Cromack, N. G. N. |
| 1HQ | Broadley, Harry R. |
| 1HR | Elliott, Thomas H., jr. |
| 1HS | Shattuck, Herbert. |
| 1HT | Anderson, James H. |
| 1HU | Upton, Harry E. |
| 1HV | Ryan, James A. |
| 1HW | Munroe, H. W. T. |
| 1HX | Leavitt, Elmer A. |
| 1HY | Bennett, Lawrence S. |
| 1HZ | Duncan, Harrie E. |
| 1IB | Stanyan, Starr W. |
| 1ID | Kehoe, Francis. |
| 1IE | Bennett, William F., jr. |
| 1IF | Eveleth, Harlan A. |
| 1IH | Fuller, Clarence C. |
| 1IJ | Fassitt, Andrew J., jr. |
| 1IO | Pratt, Walter. |
| 1IP | Leland, Harold. |
| 1IQ | Luey, Donald. |
| 1IR | Lewis, Minott W. |
| 1IS | Leach, George. |
| 1IT | Barnes, Irving T. |
| 1IU | Church, Arthur E. |
| 1IV | Snyder, William E. |
| 1IW | Wilde, Phillips B. |
| 1IX | Ohlson, Olof. |
| 1IY | Baxter, Horace M. |
| 1IZ | Saint James, Robert T. |
| 1JA | Dimond, Fred A., jr. |
| 1JB | Lord, Howland C. |
| 1JC | Fairbanks, Robert D. |
| 1JD | Collins, Lovejoy. |
| 1JE | Hayward, Edward E., jr. |
| 1JF | Snow, Albert E. |
| 1JG | Pratt, Fearing. |
| 1JH | Hubbard, Allen, jr. |
| 1JI | Lawrence, Milford R. |
| 1JK | Franke, Alfred A. |
| 1JL | Gahm, Sebastian, jr. |
| 1JM | Cheever, Walter G. |
| 1JN | Bruce, Arthur O. |
| 1JO | Snow, William B. |
| 1JP | Decker, Clarence. |
| 1JQ | Hoffman, Frank E. |
| 1JR | Delano, Edward C. |
| 1JS | Powers, Leonard S. |
| 1JT | Carlson, Arthur G. |
| 1JU | Dane, Francis W. |
| 1JV | Reuther, Henry. |
| 1JW | Long, John J. |
| 1JY | Herland, John N. |
| 1JZ | Lanvuette, Kenneth H. |

AMATEUR RADIO STATIONS—FIRST DISTRICT—ALPHABETICALLY BY CALL SIGNALS—Continued.

| Call signal. | Owner of station. |
|---|---|
| 1KA | Stickney, H. E. |
| 1KB | Richards, W. T. |
| 1KC | Howe, Milton A. |
| 1KD | David, Harold E. |
| 1KE | De Mello, Edward. |
| 1KF | Pennypacker, Thomas R. |
| 1KG | Manning, Ralph K. |
| 1KH | Doten, H. B. |
| 1KI | Loring, Wilfred B. |
| 1KJ | Anderson, Arvid E. |
| 1KL | Edson, Allan W. |
| 1KM | Meekin, William J. |
| 1KN | Wilkinson, John E. |
| 1KO | Bowen, Harold C. |
| 1KP | Justice, Francis C. |
| 1KS | Seabury, William H. |
| 1KW | Wood, James E. |
| 1TM | Mason, Lion G. |
| 1UA | Hargraves, Harold T. |
| 1UB | Pease, Reginald M. |
| 1UC | Creaser, Isaiah. |
| 1UD | Donle, Harold P. |
| 1UE | Jette, George E. |
| 1UF | Perkins, Leonard M. |
| 1UG | Bigelow, Fred C., jr. |
| 1UH | Handy, William R. |
| 1UI | Bailey, William M. |
| 1UJ | Ashworth, Harry. |
| 1UK | Tutin, Kenneth A. |
| 1UL | Bigelow, Clinton A. |
| 1UM | Miller, Bernard H. |
| 1UN | Henry, William E. |
| 1UO | Doyle, John B. |
| 1UP | Trainor, Francis J. |
| 1UQ | Barth, Karl E. |
| 1UR | Doherty, James E. |
| 1US | Thorndike, Don C. |
| 1UV | Monahan, Edward M. |
| 1UW | Nilson, Arthur R. |
| 1UX | Budlong, Clifton O. |
| 1UY | Lippitt, Gorton T. |
| 1UZ | Homer, Arthur B. |
| 1VH | Hickmott, William J., jr. |
| 1VL | Belknop, Edward L. |
| 1VM | McGuire, William C. |
| 1VN | Green, Louis. |
| 1VO | Haskell, Shirley D. |
| 1WB | Barnum, Roland B. |
| 1WJ | Barrett, John H. |
| 1WN | Edwin Bancroft Foote Boys' Club. |
| 1WO | Post, Harold. |
| 1WP | Cummings, Edward H. |
| 1WQ | Seeley, Arthur P. |
| 1WR | Sawtelle, Donald F. |
| 1WS | Buffett, Salathiel. |
| 1WT | Salzgeber, John W. |
| 1WU | Lucas, Orville. |
| 1WX | Safranek, Jerry. |
| 1WY | Hoggson, Wallace. |
| 1WZ | Davis, Maurice E. |

## SECOND DISTRICT.

[Headquarters: Customhouse, New York, N. Y. The second district comprises the States of New York (county of New York, Staten Island, Long Island, and counties on the Hudson River to and including Schenectady, Albany, and Rensselaer) and New Jersey (counties of Bergen, Passaic, Essex, Union, Middlesex, Monmouth, Hudson, and Ocean).]

ALPHABETICALLY BY OWNERS OF STATIONS.

| Call signal. | Owner of station. | Location of station. | Power. |
|---|---|---|---|
| | | | *Watts.* |
| 2LX | Adelphi College | St. James and Clifton Pl., Brooklyn, N. Y. | 385 |
| 2AB | Anderson, Lloyd C. | New Milford, N. J. | 20 |
| 2MM | Apgar, Charles E. | 549 Carleton Rd., Westfield, N. J. | 450 |
| 2ME | Archibald, John O. | 51 Cedar St., Yonkers, N. Y. | 500 |
| 2BA | Ash, Harry M., jr. | 337 Twelfth Ave., Paterson, N. J. | 90 |
| 2BV | Ashmall, William E., jr. | 11 Pavonia Ave., Arlington, N. J. | 24 |
| 2MR | Atwater, Frank G., jr. | 1562 East Fifteenth St., Brooklyn, N. Y. | 24 |

AMATEUR RADIO STATIONS—SECOND DISTRICT—ALPHABETICALLY BY OWNERS OF STATIONS—Continued.

| Call signal. | Owner of station. | Location of station. | Power. |
|---|---|---|---|
| | | | Watts. |
| 2CI | Austin, Edward | 576 Pavonia Ave., Jersey City, N. J | 250 |
| 2ER | Backer, William | 51 Hamilton Terrace, New York, N. Y | 27[illegible] |
| 2LU | Baker, William N | 881 Montgomery St., Jersey City, N. J | 2[illegible] |
| 2GM | Ballard, J. Adams | 73 Macon St., Brooklyn, N. Y | 24 |
| 2BD | Banta, Theodore C | 76 Walnut St., Ridgewood, N. J | 1[illegible] |
| 2BT | Barrett, Howard A | 343 East One hundred and fifty-second St., New York, N. Y. | 550 |
| 2HW | Barrett, L. W | 44 Ellis Pl., Ossining, N. Y | 24 |
| 2LW | Bartel, J. F | Harts Island, N. Y | 5 |
| 2GB | Bartlett, Bernard W | 545 Westfield Ave., Westfield, N. J | 500 |
| 2LF | Bartlett, Charles H | 774 Jefferson Ave., Brooklyn, N. Y | 12 |
| 2CJ | Bathgate, Walter E | 102 High St., Passaic, N. J | 60 |
| 2GJ | Beard, Gerald A | 150 Overlook St., Mt. Vernon, N. Y | 250 |
| 2EJ | Bechtloff, Claude B | 106 Walnut St., Ridgewood, N. J | 500 |
| 2KJ | Beebe, Lloyd S | 1143 Albany St., Schenectady, N. Y | 500 |
| 2FV | Behnken, Henry J | 868 Fifty-fifth St., Brooklyn, N. Y | 24 |
| 2LQ | Belt, Charles B | 145 West Fifty-seventh St., New York, N. Y. | 100 |
| 2LL | Benedict, Alonzo R | Leptondale, N. Y | 45 |
| 2FU | Benzing, Herman | 619 Fulton St., Elizabeth, N. J | 30 |
| 2MS | Berri, Herbert | 497 East Seventeenth St., Brooklyn, N. Y. | 500 |
| 2LB | Bertine, Edwin K | 57 South Second Ave., Mt. Vernon, N. Y | 220 |
| 2IX | Bicak, Edward T | 357 East Seventy-second St., New York, N. Y. | 160 |
| 2FT | Bishop, Mortimer | 568 West One hundred and forty-ninth St., New York, N. Y. | 550 |
| 2CR | Blauvelt, William M | 198 Main St., Nyack, N. Y | 90 |
| 2CG | Blodgett, Harry C | 606 Meade St., New York, N. Y | 20 |
| 2GI | Bockelmann, Charles F. | 1679 Forty-second St., Brooklyn, N. Y | 45 |
| 2JD | Boeder, Arthur | 3443 Duncomb Ave., New York, N. Y | 1,000 |
| 2BX | Brick, Frank R | 43 West Forty-fourth St., Bayonne, N. J | 500 |
| 2JH | Brown, David S., 3d | 206 West Eighty-sixth St., New York, N. Y. | 500 |

AMATEUR RADIO STATIONS—SECOND DISTRICT—ALPHABETICALLY BY OWNERS OF STATIONS—Continued.

| Call signal. | Owner of station. | Location of station. | Power. |
|---|---|---|---|
| | | | *Watts.* |
| 2KD | Browne, Walram S. | 1565 East Twelfth St., Brooklyn, N. Y. | 500 |
| 2JL | Brownell, Charles E. | 230 Newark Ave., Bloomfield, N. J. | 36 |
| 2JS | Bruns, Henry H. | 249 Seventh St., Jersey City, N. J. | 50 |
| 2AU | Bryan, Chester W. | 79 Elm St., Montclair, N. J. | 8 |
| 2AF | Bryant, Marquis V. | 6 Highland Ave., Nyack, N. Y. | 130 |
| 2MH | Buchanan, William F. | 128 Market St., Perth Amboy, N. J. | 24 |
| 2AV | Buhlman, Charles F. | Mallisen Ave., Allendale, N. J. | 48 |
| 2CT | Bunn, Milo B. | 110 Rockland Ave., Yonkers, N. Y. | 250 |
| 2HK | Burrows, Henry P. | 1415 Fifty-fifth St., Brooklyn, N. Y. | 12 |
| 2ES | Campbell, Robert, jr. | 117 Marshall St., Elizabeth, N. J. | 130 |
| 2MN | Carrougher, Vivian A. | 805 Ocean Ave., Brooklyn, N. Y. | 3 |
| 2HR | Chandler, Arthur C. | 2141 Pacific St., Brooklyn, N. Y. | 72 |
| 2FE | Cheel, Harold W. | 35 Corsa Terrace, Ridgewood, N. J. | 495 |
| 2DS | Clark, LeRoy. | Chestnut St., Englewood, N. J. | 880 |
| 2FO | Clark, William C. | 91 Fourth Ave., Brooklyn, N. Y. | 500 |
| 2IJ | Cochran, Alexander. | 256 Sterling Pl., Brooklyn, N. Y. | 24 |
| 2DP | Coene, Edgar S. | 680 Beck St., New York, N. Y. | 370 |
| 2LO | Coffin, Russell S. | 1102 St. Johns Pl., Brooklyn, N. Y. | 24 |
| 2KN | Collison, Percy B. | 172 Maple St., Brooklyn, N. Y. | 500 |
| 2DR | Cooper, Telfer C. | 260 Garfield Ave., Jersey City, N. J. | 500 |
| 2HF | Coote, Charles W. | 240 Audubon Ave., New York, N. Y. | 550 |
| 2AQ | Corson, David N. | 51 Berkeley St., Newark, N. J. | 330 |
| 2LD | Cotter, William F. | 68 Oakland Ave., Jersey City, N. J. | 24 |
| 2JC | Cowan, Clarence. | 1455 Bedford Ave., Brooklyn, N. Y. | 18 |
| 2EM | Crosby, Ray C. | 24 One hundred and forty-eighth St., New York, N. Y. | 20 |
| 2DN | Cullen, Edward R. | 626 Forty-fifth St., Brooklyn, N. Y. | 54 |
| 2DI | Cyriax, Ernest. | 219 East Seventy-first St., New York, N. Y. | 30 |
| 2GG | Dahlgren, Berger. | 1652 Forty-first St., Brooklyn, N. Y. | 18 |
| 2AD | Dammers, Albert. | 145 Newell Ave., Rutherford, N. J. | 250 |
| 2KK | Day, Howard B. | 133 Harrison Ave., Westfield, N. J. | 815 |

2002°—13——7

AMATEUR RADIO STATIONS—SECOND DISTRICT—ALPHABETICALLY BY OWNERS OF STATIONS—Continued.

| Call signal. | Owner of station. | Location of station. | Power. |
|---|---|---|---|
| | | | *Watts.* |
| 2LK | De Baun, Harold J | 14 Maple St., Nyak, N. Y | 15 |
| 2JX | De Cortin, Gustav A | 16 Elm St., Mt. Vernon, N. Y | 2 |
| 2HH | Dederick, H. C | 46 North Fifth St., Hudson, N. Y | 100 |
| 2JR | Deitz, Burr V | Slingerlands, N. Y | 3[illegible] |
| 2CF | Demarest, Merritt | 82 Bentley St., Tottenville, N. Y | 2[illegible] |
| 2AS | De Yoe, Willard L | 689 Broadway St., Paterson, N. J | 2[illegible] |
| 2CN | Dickey, Edward T | 1649 Amsterdam Ave., New York, N. Y | 220 |
| 2CQ | Dilg, A. Norman | 147 Bentley St., Tottenville, N. Y | 30 |
| 2CH | Driggs, Louis L., jr | 199 Cedar Rd., New Rochelle, N. Y | 500 |
| 2EU | Droste, George T | 2132 Glebe Ave., New York, N. Y | 500 |
| 2IY | Dugan, Edward W | 631 Jersey Ave., Jersey City, N. J | 15 |
| 2GS | Dunn, Allison van V | 98 North Rockland Ave., Yonkers, N. Y | 36 |
| 2LM | Dunn, Laurence J | 769 Dawson St., New York, N. Y | 8 |
| 2AI | Eber, John G | 5505 Third Ave., Brooklyn, N. Y | 40 |
| 2GQ | Eckhardt, John | 53 Clifton Pl., Brooklyn, N. Y | 18 |
| 2JI | Eddy, L. E | 295 Hackensack Rd., Ridgefield Park, N. J. | 36 |
| 2AH | Edelman, Abraham | 782 Prospect Ave., New York, N. Y | 30 |
| 2KQ | Edwards, Harry M., jr | 314 Ridgewood Ave., Glen Ridge, N. J | 24 |
| 2DH | Eells, Wallace H | 632 East Fifteenth St., Brooklyn, N. Y | 200 |
| 2LE | Egolf, Richard S | 1052 Forty-first St., Brooklyn, N. Y | 24 |
| 2IQ | Elliott, Paul C | 162 East Sixty-sixth St., New York, N. Y | 250 |
| 2BU | Eltz, George J., jr | 441 West Forty-seventh St., New York, N. Y. | 500 |
| 2ET | England, George B | 917 St. Nicholas Ave., New York N. Y | 432 |
| 2EK | Fagan, James F | 143 West Ninety-fifth St., New York, N. Y | 660 |
| 2GX | Fallon, Harry A., jr | 555 West One hundred and forty-eighth St., New York, N. Y. | 48 |
| 2GD | Farquharson, John S | 540 West One hundred and fifty-eighth St., New York, N. Y. | 280 |
| 2AK | Ferris, Howard E | 665 Franklin Ave., Nutley, N. J | 24 |
| 2DD | Fitzgerald, Gordon P | 611 West One hundred and forty-first St., New York, N. Y. | 250 |

AMATEUR RADIO STATIONS—SECOND DISTRICT—ALPHABETICALLY BY OWNERS OF STATIONS—Continued.

| Call signal. | Owner of station. | Location of station. | Power. |
|---|---|---|---|
| | | | *Watts.* |
| 2AA | Flagg, John H | 316 Lookout Ave., Hackensack, N. J | 21 |
| 2IR | Foulke, J. Brion, jr | Carll Ave., Babylon, N. Y | 50 |
| 2KM | Francis, Charles | 1662 Seventieth St., Brooklyn, N. Y | 18 |
| 2IZ | Fraser, Frank | 352 Archer St., Freeport, N. Y | 350 |
| 2JN | Freeland, Wilbur W | 34 Baldwin Ave., Newark, N. J | 550 |
| 2JF | Frey, Anthony C | 370 East One hundred and fifty-third St., New York, N. Y. | 10 |
| 2KE | Frey, George | 155 West Eightieth St., New York, N. Y | 36 |
| 2GF | Gabrielson, Henry M | 230 Fifty-third St., Brooklyn, N. Y | 60 |
| 2LT | Galvin, Lee R | 193 Fairview Ave., Jersey City, N. J | 32 |
| 2DO | Gerrity, John J | 538 Ocean Ave., Jersey City, N. J | 330 |
| 2CL | Gildersleeve, Louis C | Mattituck, N. Y | 30 |
| 2AY | Gittelbauer, Frederick | 38 Vreeland St., East Rutherford, N. J | 500 |
| 2JU | Goette, C. J | 1256 Hatch Ave., Woodhaven, N. Y | 250 |
| 2BK | Green, Adoniram J | 73 Paterson St., Paterson, N. J | 120 |
| 2LP | Green, R. J | 1352 St. Nicholas Ave., New York, N. Y. | 18 |
| 2KL | Gregory, Arthur V | 197 High St., Perth Amboy, N. J | 250 |
| 2BN | Griswold, Edmund J | R. F. D., Slingerlands, N. Y | 30 |
| 2AT | Guild, Baldwin | 495 Mount Prospect Ave., Newark, N. J | 30 |
| 2AR | Hackmann, William J | 8 Bright St., Jersey City, N. J | 15 |
| 2HJ | Hadden, Walter | 1716 Albermarle Road, Brooklyn, N. Y | 440 |
| 2AM | Haesselbarth, Percy | 54 Catherine St., Nyack, N. Y | 36 |
| 2AW | Hall, Joseph H | 605 West One hundred and forty-first St., New York, N. Y | 50 |
| 2DW | Hallahan, John | 180 Market St., Perth Amboy, N. J | 60 |
| 2MA | Hallenbeck, Charles | 959 Fifty-fifth St., Brooklyn, N. Y | 24 |
| 2EV | Hallock, Charles S | Foot of Fifty-seventh St., Brooklyn, N. Y. | 500 |
| 2EW | Hamilton, Joseph E | 16 West Broadway, Port Chester, N. Y | 30 |
| 2FK | Hamilton, Ralph | 352 Willett Ave., Port Chester, N. Y | 30 |
| 2AE | Happe, William H | 566 West One hundred and sixty-second St., New York, N. Y. | 100 |
| 2FQ | Hardwick, Ambrose H | 2240 Oakwood Ave., Orange, N. J | 1,000 |

AMATEUR RADIO STATIONS—SECOND DISTRICT—ALPHABETICALLY BY OWNERS OF STATIONS—Continued.

| Call signal. | Owner of station. | Location of station. | Power |
|---|---|---|---|
| | | | Watts |
| 2FZ | Harris, Charles C | Elliot Pl., Freeport, N. Y | 50 |
| 2AC | Hart, Gifford R | 34 Douglas Road, Glen Ridge, N. J | 5 |
| 2FY | Hartman, Robert | 500 West One-hundred and seventy-seventh St., New York, N. Y. | 25 |
| 2DV | Hathaway, Harry C. B | 20 Erie Pl., Nutley, N. J | [illegible] |
| 2JM | Hebert, Arthur A | 27 Maple Pl., Nutley, N. J | [illegible] |
| 2BM | Heermance, Earle | 523 State St., Hudson, N. Y | [illegible] |
| 2FJ | Helwig, Herman F | 711 East Eighteenth St., Brooklyn, N. Y. | 25 |
| 2MU | Hengerer, Howard B | 180 Fort Washington Ave., New York, N. Y. | [illegible] |
| 2CW | Hersh, Harry H | 254 First Ave., Elizabeth, N. J | 550 |
| 2IU | Hickman, Cedric A | 604 First Ave., Asbury Park, N. J | 500 |
| 2DG | Higgs, Harry Y | 707 Vanderbilt Ave., Brooklyn, N. Y | 35 |
| 2GY | Hill, Cedric S | 156 Urban St., Mt. Vernon, N. Y | [illegible] |
| 2DK | Hill, William S | 332 Rector St., Perth Amboy, N. J | [illegible] |
| 2JW | Hofmann, Charles | 1627 First Ave., Brooklyn, N. Y | [illegible] |
| 2LY | Hoover, Raymond | 171 Ridgewood Ave., Newark, N. J | [illegible] |
| 2MF | Hoppock, Allen H | 215 Clark St., Westfield, N. J | 500 |
| 2HU | Hotchkiss, Grosvenor | 146 Halsey St., Brooklyn, N. Y | [illegible] |
| 2HI | Hotter, Walter J | 640 Seventy-fourth St., Brooklyn, N. Y | [illegible] |
| 2IK | Howe, David D | 23 Maple Pl., Nutley, N. J | [illegible] |
| 2II | Howell, Walter J | 135 Edgecombe Ave., New York, N. Y | [illegible] |
| 2GK | Hubbard, John W | 327 King St., Port Chester, N. Y | 55 |
| 2CM | Huebner, Curtis J | 35 Pierrepont Ave., Rutherford, N. J | [illegible] |
| 2EG | Hurd, John B | Telton Ave., Red Bank, N. J | [illegible] |
| 2BQ | Ingraham, Wallace | 91 Sterling Pl., New York, N. Y | [illegible] |
| 2GU | Inwright, John A | 400-A Fairmont Ave., Jersey City, N. J | [illegible] |
| 2EX | Jackson, Benjamin B | 188 Montrose Ave., Rutherford, N. J | [illegible] |
| 2KU | Jackson, Edward C | 52 Hillcrest Ave., Yonkers, N. Y | [illegible] |
| 2EE | Jacobs, Charles F | 279 Park Pl., Brooklyn, N. Y | [illegible] |
| 2FN | Jamison, Herbert L | 1108 Intervale Ave., New York, N. Y | [illegible] |
| 2AO | Jones, Robert O | 196 Newark Ave., Bloomfield, N. J | [illegible] |

AMATEUR RADIO STATIONS—SECOND DISTRICT—ALPHABETICALLY BY OWNERS OF STATIONS—Continued.

| Call signal. | Owner of station. | Location of station. | Power. |
|---|---|---|---|
| | | | *Watts.* |
| 2DC | Kahn, Walter A. | 136 Stuyvesant Pl., New York, N. Y. | 24 |
| 2BC | Kaltenbach, Henry J., jr. | 150 Alta Ave., Park Hill, Yonkers, N. Y. | 65 |
| 2BY | Keller, Julius F. | 36 Ocean Ave., Edgewater, N. Y. | 30 |
| 2GH | Kelting, Clarence A. | 1469 Fifty-third St., Brooklyn, N. Y. | 27 |
| 2BL | Kirch, George | 364 Seventy-fifth St., Brooklyn, N. Y. | 24 |
| 2FI | Kirkpatrick, Louis W. | 317 Sixth Ave., Newark, N. J. | 12 |
| 2BR | Krech, Karl G. | 316 Godwin Ave., Midland Park, N. J. | 495 |
| 2KA | Kroener, Christian | 115 Watchung Ave., Plainfield, N. J. | 36 |
| 2JT | Ladow, Arthur C. | 515 Munroe Ave., Asbury Park, N. J. | 500 |
| 2HX | Lane, David M. | 343 Ninth St., Jersey City, N. J. | 24 |
| 2KR | Lebowitz, Samuel | 270 Riverside Drive, New York, N. Y. | 450 |
| 2MT | Leeb, Henry L. | 166 Ralston Ave., South Orange, N. J. | 880 |
| 2FL | Lehmann, August, jr. | 1520 Fifty-sixth St., Brooklyn, N. Y. | 9 |
| 2CA | Leidecker, Morris | 40 St. Nicholas Pl., New York, N. Y. | 400 |
| 2IE | Lemmon, Walter S. | 319 West Ninety-fourth St., New York N. Y. | 420 |
| 2JV | Lent, Richard C. | 616 Forty-fifth St., Brooklyn, N. Y. | 36 |
| 2GV | Lindmark, Elmer S. | 4510 Sixth Ave., Brooklyn, N. Y. | 18 |
| 2IV | Lindsay, Russell | 189 William St., East Orange, N. J. | 30 |
| 2EB | Lowe, Graham von S. | 262 West Seventy-seventh St., New York, N. Y. | 300 |
| 2BZ | Lyman, C. Glenn | George and Cooper Sts., Babylon, N. Y. | 150 |
| 2HO | Lyons, William B. | North Broad St., Bloomfield, N. J. | 1000 |
| 2HT | Macartney, George E. | 473 Prospect Pl., Brooklyn, N. Y. | 36 |
| 2HQ | MacDonald, Howard B. | 171 Ravine Ave., Yonkers, N. Y. | 25 |
| 2AJ | Mahr, George W. | 297 Gordon St., Stapleton, N. Y. | 60 |
| 2FW | Macpherson, Claude V. | 557 West One hundred and forty-fourth St., New York, N. Y. | 440 |
| 2GL | Marshall, Richard E. | 238 Westchester Ave., Rye, N. Y. | 550 |
| 2HP | Mayhew, B. Alan, jr. | Laurel Ave., Tenafly, N. J. | 495 |
| 2IL | McClintock, George C. | 535 Charlton Rd., Westfield, N. J. | 250 |
| 2KP | McClure, Donald | 11 Rudd Ct., Glen Ridge, N. J. | 48 |

AMATEUR RADIO STATIONS—SECOND DISTRICT—ALPHABETICALLY BY OWNERS OF STATIONS—Continued.

| Call signal. | Owner of station. | Location of station. | Power. |
|---|---|---|---|
| | | | Watts. |
| 2HA | McCoy, Daniel | 45 Lee Ave., Yonkers, N. Y. | 1,00[illegible] |
| 2IC | McGiehan, Donald C | 1222 East Thirty-ninth St., Brooklyn, N. Y. | 1[illegible] |
| 2DF | McIntyre, Meybert A | 1127 Avenue G, Brooklyn, N. Y. | 25[illegible] |
| 2CC | McKey, Dixie | 265 Herbert St., Red Bank, N. J. | 3[illegible] |
| 2EY | McKinney, Fred J | 300 Glenwood Ave., Bloomfield, N. J. | 24 |
| 2LG | McLaughlin, Fred L | 2621 Eighth Ave., New York, N. Y. | 6 |
| 2KY | McLoughlin, Robert J | 105 Francisco Ave., Rutherford, N. J. | 190 |
| 2LI | Meacham, Fred'k C., jr | 236 Decatur St., Brooklyn, N. Y. | 72 |
| 2EP | Mead, George S. V | 12 Archer Ave., Mt. Vernon, N. Y. | 330 |
| 2FC | Meersseman, Julian A | Tottenville, N. Y. | 12 |
| 2IG | Merkt, T. B. J. | 780 Macon St., Brooklyn, N. Y. | 20 |
| 2JG | Merrihew, Randall W | Slingerlands, N. Y. | 85 |
| 2JQ | Merrill, Walter E | 121 East One hundred and third St., New York, N. Y. | 45 |
| 2EL | Meyer, William E | 181 West Sixty-third St., New York, N. Y. | 36 |
| 2LA | Miller, Frederick R | 42 John St., Englewood, N. J. | 24 |
| 2JK | Mitchell, Arthur M | 299 North Seventh St., Newark, N. J. | 36 |
| 2BI | Morgan, Waller V | 149 Urban St., Mt. Vernon, N. Y. | 56 |
| 2CO | Morrell, W. Frank | Broadway and First St., Keyport West, N. J. | 250 |
| 2MI | Morris, Earle S | 1192 Dean St., Brooklyn, N. Y. | 500 |
| 2LN | Morrison, Clifford P | 365 Warburton St., Yonkers, N. Y. | 60 |
| 2BG | Mowton, Edward M | 70 Hillcrest Ave., Yonkers, N. Y. | 50 |
| 2AG | Mulford, Harold C | 6 Weekes Ave., Oyster Bay., N. Y. | 90 |
| 2CE | Muns, Robert | 85 Lincoln Ave., Ridgewood, N. J. | 1,000 |
| 2JZ | Naylor, Walker | 156 Leffert Pl., Brooklyn, N. Y. | 12 |
| 2KX | Noble, Kendrick | 441 North Broadway, Yonkers, N. Y. | 300 |
| 2GT | Noller, Charles, jr | 240 East Fifty-sixth St., New York, N. Y. | 30 |
| 2HY | Noonan, Edward J | 5419 Fourth Ave., Brooklyn, N. Y. | 20 |
| 2HB | Northshield, L. E | 252 Ontario St., Albany, N. Y. | 616 |
| 2CK | O'Brien, Thomas | 7 Nassau Ave., Freeport, N. Y. | 500 |
| 2IB | Oliver, George E | 677 Boulevard, Bayonne, N. J. | 50 |

AMATEUR RADIO STATIONS—SECOND DISTRICT—ALPHABETICALLY BY OWNERS OF STATIONS—Continued.

| Call signal. | Owner of station. | Location of station. | Power. |
|---|---|---|---|
| | | | *Watts.* |
| 2HS | O'Mara, Edward F. | 425 West Fifty-sixth St., New York, N. Y. | 12 |
| 2MO | Ostman, Frederick B. | 33 Edwards St., Ridgewood, N. J. | 40 |
| 2DY | Palmer, Corydon | 48 West Fiftieth St., New York, N. Y. | 500 |
| 2CU | Palmland, Philip | 1144 St. Johns Pl., Brooklyn, N. Y. | 30 |
| 2FB | Pareis, Robert | 189 Marshall St., Elizabeth, N. J. | 12 |
| 2AZ | Pearl, Eugene S. | 307 Gregory Ave., Passaic, N. J. | 30 |
| 2MP | Pearsall, William E. | 226 Moffat St., Brooklyn, N. Y. | 30 |
| 2BS | Pearson, Herbert B. | 997 Sterling Pl., Brooklyn, N. Y. | 500 |
| 2CS | Pedersen, Guy O. | 2128 Hudson Bvd., Jersey City, N. J. | 200 |
| 2GO | Peltier, Paul D | 345 West Seventieth St., New York, N. Y. | 10 |
| 2MD | Pendleton, Harold A | 830-A Quincy St., Brooklyn, N. Y. | 6 |
| 2FM | Perkins, William P. | 35 Grant Ave., Yonkers, N. Y. | 24 |
| 2HG | Peters, Frank J. | Broad St., Bloomfield, N. J. | 715 |
| 2FA | Pfeifer, Clarence H. | 306 Prospect St., Ridgewood, N. J. | 250 |
| 2BP | Phipps, Donald A. | Oyster Bay, N. Y. | 165 |
| 2GZ | Plate, Fred W. | 91 Vanheyken St., Jersey City, N. J. | 36 |
| 2KW | Plummer, James A. | 340 Orient Way, Rutherford, N. J. | 36 |
| 2CZ | Poe, Vergil C. | 862 Sterling Pl., Brooklyn, N. Y. | 30 |
| 2DL | Price, Henry S. | 435 Clinton Ave., Brooklyn, N. Y. | 500 |
| 2CD | Prosser, Rogers D. | Chestnut St., Englewood, N. J. | 30 |
| 2EI | Quick, Henry C. | 471 Seventy-fifth St., Brooklyn, N. Y. | 500 |
| 2ML | Quinby, E. Jay | Aqueduct Ave. and Fordham Rd., New York, N. Y. | 250 |
| 2HC | Raque, Carl P. | 82 Booream Ave., Jersey City, N. J. | 350 |
| 2HZ | Reichfeld, Nicholas | 991 Union Ave., New York, N. Y. | 50 |
| 2ID | Reyle, Stanley | 42½ Van Reipen Ave., Jersey City, N. J. | 24 |
| 2IS | Ricketts, Percy E. | George St., Babylon, N. Y. | 55 |
| 2LC | Roberts, A. Perry | Tenafly Rd., Tenafly, N. J. | 50 |
| 2MC | Roberts, Irving J. | 66 East Baldwin St., Bloomfield, N. J. | 24 |
| 2IP | Robin, Rev. Fernard | Hawthorne, N. Y. | 1,000 |
| 2LJ | Rodenburg, Herman | 1626 Second Ave., New York, N. Y. | 20 |

AMATEUR RADIO STATIONS—SECOND DISTRICT—ALPHABETICALLY BY OWNERS OF STATIONS—Continued.

| Call signal. | Owner of station. | Location of station. | Power. |
|---|---|---|---|
| | | | Watts. |
| 2KV | Rogers, Lorlys A. | 200 West One hundred and thirteenth St., New York, N. Y. | 660 |
| 2IA | Royce, Winfred A. | 1329 Forty-ninth St., Brooklyn, N. Y. | 500 |
| 2JY | Rupert, S. E. G. | 107 Second St., Pelham, N. Y. | 1,040 |
| 2GP | Rutherford, T. Bruce. | 42 Hawthorne St., Brooklyn, N. Y. | 24 |
| 2DE | Ruttmann, Ferdinand. | 605 West One hundred and forty-first St., New York, N. Y. | 250 |
| 2DM | Sachs, Harold. | 701 Madison Ave., New York, N. Y. | 10 |
| 2HE | Sackett, Milton B. | River Edge, N. J. | 330 |
| 2HN | Sands, Walter H. | 178 Anchor Ave., Mt. Vernon, N. Y. | 230 |
| 2KT | Saulnier, Stanley G. | 299 Gates Ave., New York, N. Y. | 9 |
| 2LH | Sayres, Ralph A. | 4645 Central Ave., Richmond, N. Y. | 36 |
| 2JB | Schaefer, Charles L. | 201 Broadway, Port Richmond, N. Y. | 50 |
| 2IO | Scharrenbeck, George H. | 126 West First St., Mt. Vernon, N. Y. | 220 |
| 2EQ | Schedler, Herbert. | 328 Central Ave., Jersey City, N. J. | 300 |
| 2BF | Schell, Richard, jr. | 35 Grasmere Ave., Grasmere, N. Y. | 12 |
| 2BO | Schermerhorn, Howard F. | 2 Union St., Montclair, N. J. | 24 |
| 2HL | Schippel, August, jr. | 2321 First Ave., New York, N. Y. | 18 |
| 2DJ | Schlitz, Karl W. | 28 Jefferson St., New York, N. Y. | 36 |
| 2EO | Schneider, Alexander. | 326 East Sixty-ninth St., New York, N. Y. | 36 |
| 2CB | Schram, John, jr. | 21 Locust St., Brooklyn, N. Y. | 60 |
| 2BH | Schulte, Carl. | 75 East Franklin Ave., Ridgewood, N. J. | 60 |
| 2EZ | Schupp, Charles H. | Linden Ave., River Edge, N. J. | 250 |
| 2DQ | Schwarzkopf, Irving M. | 138 East Ninty-fifth St., New York, N. Y. | 500 |
| 2IN | Scofield, Robert W. | 87 Macon St., Brooklyn, N. Y. | 42 |
| 2BJ | Seaman, Chapman W. | School St., Oyster Bay, N. Y. | 150 |
| 2KF | Searing, Hudson R. | 532 Wales Ave., New York, N. Y. | 385 |
| 2AN | Sedlak, Conrad J. | 683 Main St., New Durham, N. J. | 33 |
| 2DX | Seyd, Ernest K. | 231 Park Pl., Brooklyn, N. Y. | 35 |
| 2DT | Shaw, Oswald M. | 73 East Eighty-eighth St., New York, N. Y. | 500 |
| 2KS | Shropshire, Lee R. | 9 Castle Hill, Palisades Park, N. J. | 25 |

AMATEUR RADIO STATIONS—SECOND DISTRICT—ALPHABETICALLY BY OWNERS OF STATIONS—Continued.

| Call signal. | Owner of station. | Location of station. | Power. |
|---|---|---|---|
| | | | *Watts.* |
| 2GR | Slagle, Edwin L. | 25 South Second Ave., Mt. Vernon, N. Y. | 18 |
| 2MK | Smith, Daniel W. | South St., Oyster Bay, N. Y. | 250 |
| 2AX | Smith, David S. | 684 Belgrove Drive, Arlington, N. J. | 128 |
| 2AP | Smith, Irving R. | 56 Park Pl., New Brighton, N. Y. | 25 |
| 2DU | Smith, Joseph T. | 427 West Fifty-ninth St., New York, N. Y. | 500 |
| 2JP | Smith, Julius J. R. | 807 Lincoln Pl., Brooklyn, N. Y. | 9 |
| 2JO | Smith, Nelson V. | Lawrence Ave., Lawrence, N. Y. | 250 |
| 2GW | Snowden, Fred. | R. F. D. 49, Schenectady, N. Y. | 675 |
| 2KH | Solberg, Walter | 620 Forty-sixth St., Brooklyn, N. Y. | 25 |
| 2GC | Sonn, Albert E. | 150 Second Ave., Newark, N. J. | 440 |
| 2IM | Spangenberg, Lester | 25 South Fourth St., Lakeview, N. J. | 800 |
| 2BB | Sphar, Clark H. | 281 Mortimer Ave., Rutherford, N. J. | 575 |
| 2FS | Stanley, Howard L. | Main St., Babylon, N. Y. | 96 |
| 2AL | Stanley, Walter N. | 654 Putnam Ave., Brooklyn, N. Y. | 30 |
| 2KO | Stone, Brownell | 1128 Bedford Ave., New York, N. Y. | 250 |
| 2JA | Story, Robert K., jr. | 212 Hancock St., Brooklyn, N. Y. | 12 |
| 2LV | Stutz, Ernest W. | 126 Bainbridge St., Brooklyn, N. Y. | 15 |
| 2LS | Summers, William F. | 216 Main St., Nyack, N. Y. | 40 |
| 2FG | Tannenbaum, Harold | 235 West One hundred and thirteenth St., New York, N. Y. | 20 |
| 2LR | Taussig, Charles W. | 36 West Eighty-fifth St., New York, N. Y. | 360 |
| 2IH | Tense, William F. | 48 Quincy St., Passaic, N. J. | 24 |
| 2EC | Thiede, Ferdinand C. | 486 Decatur St., Brooklyn, N. Y. | 24 |
| 2CY | Tilton, Ernest R. | Fort Totten, N. Y. | 250 |
| 2CP | Totten, Elmer E. | 92 Thirtieth St., Bayonne, N. J. | 12 |
| 2KB | Tyrrel, Randolph E. | 677 East Nineteenth St., Brooklyn, N. Y. | 250 |
| 2HD | Underwood, Kenneth C. | 269 Mount Prospect Ave., Newark, N. J. | 250 |
| 2KI | Uphoff, Leslie S. | 120 Avenue B, Schenectady, N. Y. | 500 |
| 2EN | Uzmann, J. George | 5120 Sixth Ave., Brooklyn, N. Y. | 10 |
| 2CX | Van Dyke, John | 155 West Eightieth St., New York, N. Y. | 120 |
| 2MG | Vaughan, George W., jr. | 48 South Ninth Ave., Mount Vernon, N. Y. | 225 |

AMATEUR RADIO STATIONS—SECOND DISTRICT—ALPHABETICALLY BY OWNERS OF STATIONS—Continued.

| Call signal. | Owner of station. | Location of station. | Power. |
|---|---|---|---|
| | | | Watts. |
| 2MB | Villar, Laurence G. | 522 West One-hundred-and-eighty-fifth St., New York, N. Y. | 6 |
| 2CV | Waibel, Walter W. | 111 Fabyan Pl., Newark, N. J. | 250 |
| 2DZ | Watters, John J. | Port Richmond, N. Y. | 500 |
| 2FR | Way, John D. | 214 West Ninety-second St., New York, N. Y. | 280 |
| 2JJ | Webb, James L., jr. | 1257 East Fortieth St., Brooklyn, N. Y. | 9 |
| 2MQ | Weber, Ernest A. | 285 South Second St., New York, N. Y. | 18 |
| 2KZ | Weden, Charles. | 97 Myrtle St., Bloomfield, N. J. | 12 |
| 2FH | Weiss, Jacob. | 5 Adams St., Port Washington, N. Y. | 1,000 |
| 2JE | Wendelstadt, Lucius F. | 8 Seymour St., Montclair, N. J. | 880 |
| 2IF | Werker, Charles A. | 475 Brock Ave., New York, N. Y. | 20 |
| 2KC | Werner, Charles M. | 252 Cambridge Ave., Jersey City, N. J. | 25 |
| 2GE | West, Thomas R. | 256 Grand Ave., Leonia, N. J. | 20 |
| 2GN | Westman, Alexander. | 121-7 East Fifty-eighth St., New York, N. Y. | 48 |
| 2BW | Whitson, John H. | Briarcliff Manor, N. Y. | 500 |
| 2FX | Wilhelm, Frederick. | 1623 First Ave., New York, N. Y. | 42 |
| 2EH | Wilmott, George B. | 1138 East Thirty-seventh St., New York, N. Y. | 100 |
| 2EA | Williams, Earl C. | 261 Madison St., Perth Amboy, N. J. | 300 |
| 2MJ | Williams, Roy D. | 801 Halsey St., Brooklyn, N. Y. | 24 |
| 2GA | Winn, Carll P. | 1515 Forty-eighth St., Brooklyn, N. Y. | 32 |
| 2ED | Winslow, Charles D. | 1985 Amsterdam Ave., New York, N. Y. | 250 |
| 2FP | Woerner, Charles A. | 247 Union St., Jersey City, N. J. | 30 |
| 2LZ | Woodrow, William. | 224 West One hundred and fortieth St., New York, N. Y. | 880 |
| 2IW | Worth, John B. | Madison St., Cresskill, N. J. | 30 |
| 2KG | Wriggins, Charles A. | 18 Rodwell Ave., Irvington, N. J. | 12 |
| 2BE | Yerbury, George S., jr. | 21 Irving Pl., Passaic, N. J. | 100 |
| 2IT | Young, Henry. | 179 Fourth St., Jersey City, N. J. | 12 |
| 2HV | Zeitz, Edwin. | 404 Ralph St., Brooklyn, N. Y. | 40 |
| 2DB | Zucker, Richard D. | 45 Clinton Pl., Mount Vernon, N. Y. | 250 |

AMATEUR RADIO STATIONS—SECOND DISTRICT—Continued.

ALPHABETICALLY BY CALL SIGNALS.

| Call signal. | Owner of station. | Call signal. | Owner of station. |
|---|---|---|---|
| 2AA | Flagg, John H. | 2CG | Blodgett, Harry C. |
| 2AB | Anderson, Lloyd C. | 2CH | Driggs, Louis L., jr. |
| 2AC | Hart, Gifford R. | 2CI | Austin, Edward. |
| 2AD | Dammers, Albert. | 2CJ | Bathgate, Walter E. |
| 2AE | Happe, William H. | 2CK | O'Brien, Thomas. |
| 2AF | Bryant, Marquis V. | 2CL | Gildersleeve, Louis C. |
| 2AG | Mulford, Harold C. | 2CM | Huebner, Curtis J. |
| 2AH | Edelman, Abraham. | 2CN | Dickey, Edward T. |
| 2AI | Eber, John G. | 2CO | Morrell, W. Frank. |
| 2AJ | Mahr, George W. | 2CP | Totten, Elmer E. |
| 2AK | Ferris, Howard E. | 2CQ | Dilg, A. Norman. |
| 2AL | Stanley, Walter N. | 2CR | Blauvelt, William M. |
| 2AM | Haeselbarth, Percy. | 2CS | Pedersen, Guy O. |
| 2AN | Sedlak, Conrad J. | 2CT | Bunn, Milo B. |
| 2AO | Jones, Robert O. | 2CU | Palmland, Philip. |
| 2AP | Smith, Irving R. | 2CV | Waibel, Walter W. |
| 2AQ | Corson, David N. | 2CW | Hersh, Harry H. |
| 2AR | Hackmann, William J. | 2CX | Van Dyke, John. |
| 2AS | De Yoe, Willard L. | 2CY | Tilton, Ernest R. |
| 2AT | Guild, Baldwin. | 2CZ | Poe, Vergil C. |
| 2AU | Bryan, Chester W. | | |
| 2AV | Buhlman, Charles F. | 2DB | Zucker, Richard D. |
| 2AW | Hall, Joseph H. | 2DC | Kahn, Walter A. |
| 2AX | Smith, David S. | 2DD | Fitzgerald, Gordon P. |
| 2AY | Gittelbauer, Frederick. | 2DE | Ruttmann, Ferdinand. |
| 2AZ | Pearl, Eugene S. | 2DF | McIntyre, Meybert A. |
| | | 2DG | Higgs, Harry Y. |
| 2BA | Ash, Harry M., jr. | 2DH | Eells, Wallace H. |
| 2BB | Spahr, Clark H. | 2DI | Cyriax, Ernest. |
| 2BC | Kaltenbach, Harry J., jr. | 2DJ | Schlitz, Karl W. |
| 2BD | Banta, Theodore C. | 2DK | Hill, William S. |
| 2BE | Yerbury, George S., jr. | 2DL | Price, Henry S. |
| 2BF | Schell, Richard, jr. | 2DM | Sachs, Harold. |
| 2BG | Mowton, Edward M. | 2DN | Cullen, Edward R. |
| 2BH | Schulte, Carl. | 2DO | Gerrity, John J. |
| 2BI | Morgan, Waller V. | 2DP | Coene, Edgar S. |
| 2BJ | Seaman, Chapman W. | 2DQ | Schwarzkopf, Irving M. |
| 2BK | Green, Adoniram J. | 2DR | Cooper, Telfer F. |
| 2BL | Kirch, George. | 2DS | Clark, Le Roy. |
| 2BM | Heermance, Earle. | 2DT | Shaw, Oswald M. |
| 2BN | Griswold, Edmund J. | 2DU | Smith, Joseph T. |
| 2BO | Schermerhorn, Howard F. | 2DV | Hathaway, Harry C. B. |
| 2BP | Phipps, Donald A. | 2DW | Hallahan, John. |
| 2BQ | Ingraham, Wallace. | 2DX | Seyd, Ernest K. |
| 2BR | Krech, Karl G. | 2DY | Palmer, Corydon. |
| 2BS | Pearson, Herbert B. | 2DZ | Watters, John J. |
| 2BT | Barrett, Howard A. | | |
| 2BU | Eltz, George J., jr. | 2EA | Williams, Earl C. |
| 2BV | Ashmall, William E., jr. | 2EB | Lowe, Graham von S. |
| 2BW | Whitson, John H. | 2EC | Thiede, Ferdinand C. |
| 2BX | Brick, Frank R. | 2ED | Winslow, Charles D. |
| 2BY | Keller, Julius F. | 2EE | Jacobs, Charles F. |
| 2BZ | Lyman, C. Glenn. | 2EG | Hurd, John B. |
| | | 2EH | Wilmott, George B. |
| 2CA | Leidecker, Morris. | 2EI | Quick, Henry C. |
| 2CB | Schram, John, jr. | 2EJ | Bechtlofft, Claude B. |
| 2CC | McKey, Dixie. | 2EK | Fagan, James F. |
| 2CD | Prosser, Rogers D. | 2EL | Meyer, William E. |
| 2CE | Muns, Robert. | 2EM | Crosby, Ray C. |
| 2CF | Demarest, Merritt. | 2EN | Uzmann, J. George. |

AMATEUR RADIO STATIONS—SECOND DISTRICT—ALPHABETICALLY BY CALL SIGNALS—Continued.

| Call signal. | Owner of station. | Call signal. | Owner of station. |
|---|---|---|---|
| 2EO | Schneider, Alexander. | 2GW | Snowden, Fred. |
| 2EP | Mead, George S. V. | 2GX | Fallon, Harry A., jr. |
| 2EQ | Schedler, Herbert. | 2GY | Hill, Cedric S. |
| 2ER | Backer, William. | 2GZ | Plate, Fred W. |
| 2ES | Campbell, Robert, jr. | | |
| 2ET | England, George B. | 2HA | McCoy, Daniel. |
| 2EU | Droste, George T. | 2HB | Northshield, L. E. |
| 2EV | Hallock, Charles S. | 2HC | Raque, Carl P. |
| 2EW | Hamilton, Joseph E. | 2HD | Underwood, Kenneth C. |
| 2EX | Jackson, Benjamin B. | 2HE | Sackett, Milton B. |
| 2EY | McKinney, Fred J. | 2HF | Coote, Charles W. |
| 2EZ | Schupp, Charles H. | 2HG | Peters, Frank J. |
| | | 2HH | Dederick, H. C. |
| 2FA | Pfeifer, Clarence H. | 2HI | Hotter, Walter J. |
| 2FB | Pareis, Robert. | 2HJ | Hadden, Walter. |
| 2FC | Meersseman, Julian A. | 2HK | Burrows, Henry P. |
| 2FE | Cheel, Harold W. | 2HL | Schippel, August, jr. |
| 2FG | Tannenbaum, Harold. | 2HN | Sands, Walter H. |
| 2FH | Weiss, Jacob. | 2HO | Lyons, William B. |
| 2FI | Kirkpatrick, Louis W. | 2HP | Mayhew, B. Alan, jr. |
| 2FJ | Helwig, Herman F. | 2HQ | MacDonald, Howard B. |
| 2FK | Hamilton, Ralph. | 2HR | Chandler, Arthur C. |
| 2FL | Lehmann, August, jr. | 2HS | O'Mara, Edward F. |
| 2FM | Perkins, William P. | 2HT | Macartney, George E. |
| 2FN | Jamison, Herbert L. | 2HU | Hotchkiss, Grosvenor. |
| 2FO | Clark, William C. | 2HV | Zeitz, Edwin. |
| 2FP | Woerner, Charles A. | 2HW | Barrett, L. W. |
| 2FQ | Hardwick, Ambrose H. | 2HX | Lane, David M. |
| 2FR | Way, John D. | 2HY | Noonan, Edward J. |
| 2FS | Stanley, Howard L. | 2HZ | Reichfeld, Nicholas. |
| 2FT | Bishop, Mortimer. | | |
| 2FU | Benzing, Herman. | 2IA | Royce, Winfred A. |
| 2FV | Behnken, Henry J. | 2IB | Oliver, George E. |
| 2FW | Macpherson, Claude V. | 2IC | McGiehan, Donald C. |
| 2FX | Wilhelm, Frederick. | 2ID | Reyle, Stanley. |
| 2FY | Hartman, Robert. | 2IE | Lemmon, Walter S. |
| 2FZ | Harris, Charles C. | 2IF | Werker, Charles A. |
| | | 2IG | Merkt, T. B. J. |
| 2GA | Winn, Carll P. | 2IH | Tense, William F. |
| 2GB | Bartlett, Bernard W. | 2II | Howell, Walter J. |
| 2GC | Sonn, Albert E. | 2IJ | Cochran, Alexander. |
| 2GD | Farquharson, John S. | 2IK | Howe, David D. |
| 2GE | West, Thomas R. | 2IL | McClintock, George C. |
| 2GF | Gabrielson, Henry M. | 2IM | Spangenberg, Lester. |
| 2GG | Dahlgren, Berger. | 2IN | Scofield, Robert W. |
| 2GH | Kelting, Clarence A. | 2IO | Scharrenbeck, George H. |
| 2GI | Bockelmann, Charles F. | 2IP | Robin, Rev. Fernand. |
| 2GJ | Beard, Gerald A. | 2IQ | Elliott, Paul C. |
| 2GK | Hubbard, John W. | 2IR | Foulke, J. Brion, jr. |
| 2GL | Marshall, Richard E. | 2IS | Ricketts, Percy E. |
| 2GM | Ballard, J. Adams. | 2IT | Young, Henry. |
| 2GN | Westman, Alexander. | 2IU | Hickman, Cedric A. |
| 2GO | Peltier, Paul D. | 2IV | Lindsay, Russell. |
| 2GP | Rutherford, T. Bruce. | 2IW | Worth, John B. |
| 2GQ | Eckhardt, John. | 2IX | Bicak, Edward T. |
| 2GR | Slagle, Edwin L. | 2IY | Dugan, Edward W. |
| 2GS | Dunn, Allison van V. | 2IZ | Frazer, Frank. |
| 2GT | Noller, Charles, jr. | | |
| 2GU | Inwright, John A. | 2JA | Story, Robert K., jr. |
| 2GV | Lindmark, Elmer S. | 2JB | Schaefer, Charles L. |

AMATEUR RADIO STATIONS—SECOND DISTRICT—ALPHABETICALLY BY CALL SIGNALS—Continued.

| Call signal. | Owner of station. | Call signal. | Owner of station. |
|---|---|---|---|
| 2JC | Cowan, Clarence. | 2KZ | Weden, Charles. |
| 2JD | Boeder, Arthur. | | |
| 2JE | Wendelstadt, Lucius F. | 2LA | Miller, Frederick R. |
| 2JF | Frey, Anthony C. | 2LB | Bertine, Edwin K. |
| 2JG | Merrihew, Randall W. | 2LC | Roberts, A. Perry. |
| 2JH | Brown, David S., 3d. | 2LD | Cotter, William F. |
| 2JI | Eddy, L. E. | 2LE | Egolf, Richard S. |
| 2JJ | Webb, James L., jr. | 2LF | Bartlett, Charles H. |
| 2JK | Mitchell, Arthur M. | 2LG | McLaughlin, Fred L. |
| 2JL | Brownell, Charles E. | 2LH | Sayres, Ralph A. |
| 2JM | Hebert, Arthur A. | 2LI | Meacham, Frederick C., jr. |
| 2JN | Freeland, Wilbur W. | 2LJ | Rodenburg, Herman. |
| 2JO | Smith, Nelson V. | 2LK | De Baun, Harold J. |
| 2JP | Smith, Julius J. R. | 2LL | Benedict, Alonzo R. |
| 2JQ | Merrill, Walter E. | 2LM | Dunn, Laurence J. |
| 2JR | Dietz, Burr V. | 2LN | Morrison, Clifford P. |
| 2JS | Bruns, Henry H. | 2LO | Coffin, Russell S. |
| 2JT | Ladow, Arthur C. | 2LP | Green, R. J. |
| 2JU | Goette, C. J. | 2LQ | Belt, Charles B. |
| 2JV | Lent, Richard C. | 2LR | Taussig, Charles W. |
| 2JW | Hofmann, Charles. | 2LS | Summers, W. F. |
| 2JX | De Cortin, Gustav A. | 2LT | Galvin, Lee R. |
| 2JY | Rupert, S. E. G. | 2LU | Baker, William N. |
| 2JZ | Naylor, Walker. | 2LV | Stutz, Ernest W. |
| | | 2LW | Bartel, J. F. |
| 2KA | Kroener, Christian. | 2LX | Adelphi College. |
| 2KB | Tyrrel, Randolph E. | 2LY | Hoover, Raymond. |
| 2KC | Werner, Charles M. | 2LZ | Woodrow, William. |
| 2KD | Browne, Walram S. | | |
| 2KE | Frey, George. | 2MA | Hallenbeck, Charles. |
| 2KF | Searing, Hudson R. | 2MB | Villar, Laurence G. |
| 2KG | Wriggins, Charles A. | 2MC | Roberts, Irving J. |
| 2KH | Solberg, Walter. | 2MD | Pendleton, Harold A. |
| 2KI | Uphoff, Leslie S. | 2ME | Archibald, John O. |
| 2KJ | Beebe, Lloyd S. | 2MF | Hoppock, Allen H. |
| 2KK | Day, Howard B. | 2MG | Vaughan, George W., jr. |
| 2KL | Gregory, Arthur V. | 2MH | Buchanan, William F. |
| 2KM | Francis, Charles. | 2MI | Morris, Earle S. |
| 2KN | Collison, Percy B. | 2MJ | Williams, Roy D. |
| 2KO | Stone, Brownell. | 2MK | Smith, Daniel W. |
| 2KP | McClure, Donald. | 2ML | Quinby, E. J. |
| 2KQ | Edwards, Harry M., jr. | 2MM | Apgar, Charles E. |
| 2KR | Lebowitz, Samuel. | 2MN | Carrougher, Vivian A. |
| 2KS | Shropshire, Lee R. | 2MO | Ostman, Frederick B. |
| 2KT | Saulnier, Stanley G. | 2MP | Pearsall, William E. |
| 2KU | Jackson, Edward C. | 2MQ | Weber, Ernest A. |
| 2KV | Rogers, Lorlys A. | 2MR | Atwater, Frank G., jr. |
| 2KW | Plummer, James A. | 2MS | Berri, Herbert. |
| 2KX | Noble, Kendrick. | 2MT | Leeb, Henry L. |
| 2KY | McLoughlin, Robert J. | 2MU | Hengerer, Howard B. |

AMATEUR RADIO STATIONS—Continued.

### THIRD DISTRICT.

[Headquarters: Customhouse, Baltimore, Md. The third district comprises the States of New Jersey (all counties not included in second district), Pennsylvania (counties of Philadelphia, Delaware, all counties south of the Blue Mountains, and Franklin County), Delaware, Maryland, Virginia, District of Columbia.]

ALPHABETICALLY BY OWNERS OF STATIONS.

| Call signal. | Owner of station. | Location of station. | Power. |
|---|---|---|---|
| | | | *Watts.* |
| 2EB | Adam, Francis J | 1240 North Broad St., Philadelphia, Pa | 440 |
| 3CA | Adelberger, Adrian J | West Wayne Ave., Wayne, Pa | 275 |
| 3CG | Adelberger, Francis | West Wayne Ave., Wayne, Pa | 250 |
| 3KE | Allen, Francis H | 171 West Broad St., Burlington, N. J | 200 |
| 3BM | Allen, George Y | Bernardsville, N. J | 312 |
| 3BD | Allen, Percival R | Haverford, Pa | 24 |
| 3IP | Anderson, Albert | 313 Chestnut St., Camden, N. J | 30 |
| 3BA | Anthony, William H | 807 West Somerset St., Philadelphia, Pa | 96 |
| 3AX | Arner, Oscar Q | 56 V St. NW., Washington, D. C | 24 |
| 3AA | Ashmore, John W | 3408 Hamilton St., Philadelphia, Pa | 16 |
| 3CN | Ashton, Leon W | 106 Washington Ave., Collingwood, N. J | 30 |
| 3JA | August, Earl W | 3748 North Delhi St., Philadelphia, Pa | 72 |
| 3BV | Bacon, Franklin F | 101 Mansion Ave., Haddonfield, N. J | 300 |
| 3EN | Bailey, Albert S | 31 Sixty-first St., Philadelphia, Pa | 120 |
| 3DU | Bauman, F. J | 160 Carson St., Philadelphia, Pa | 60 |
| 3AJ | Bausman, George H | 1228 North Broadway, Baltimore, Md | 75 |
| 3EM | Beaty, Lehman C | 109 East Ave., Hackettstown, N. J | 15 |
| 3JS | Beekley, Francis C | 116 North Lemon St., Media, Pa | 72 |
| 3JQ | Benson, Thomas W | 2839 Swanson St., Philadelphia, Pa | 36 |
| 3DC | Bergen, Donald M | 920 Riverside Ave., Trenton, N. J | 510 |
| 3JJ | Bergmann, Frederick J | 1310 Alleghany Ave., Philadelphia, Pa | 27 |
| 3BP | Blackwood, George E | 5346 Wayne Ave., Philadelphia, Pa | 60 |
| 3GF | Blankenship, Elliott E | 920 Fifth St. NW., Washington, D. C | 24 |
| 3AY | Blodgett, Charles L | 599 Rutherford Ave., Trenton, N. J | 330 |
| 3GN | Board of Public Education. | Lehigh Ave. and Eighth St., Philadelphia, Pa. | 490 |
| 3KH | Bowen, Albert | 2437 East Preston St., Baltimore, Md | 12 |
| 3HJ | Bradley, Horace E | 315 V St. NW., Washington, D. C | 36 |

AMATEUR RADIO STATIONS—THIRD DISTRICT—ALPHABETICALLY BY OWNERS OF STATIONS—Continued.

| Call signal. | Owner of station. | Location of station. | Power. |
|---|---|---|---|
| | | | Watts. |
| 3BO | Brady, John B | Somerset, Md | 220 |
| 3EV | Brannan, Julian L | 2632 Guilford Ave., Baltimore, Md | 100 |
| 3JW | Broadbelt, J. Edward, jr. | 16 Hamilton Ave., Hamilton, Md | 18 |
| 3JH | Brockman, F. C | 3 North Main St., Nazareth, Pa | 775 |
| 3BK | Brown, Merritt M | 2417 Sixteenth St., Philadelphia, Pa | 36 |
| 3BQ | Bugbee, Newton A | 565 Rutherford Ave., Trenton, N. J | 330 |
| 3CP | Bunting, George M., jr. | 315 Broad St., Chester, Pa | 500 |
| 3JI | Burdette, Aubrey W | Adam St., Rockville, Md | 1,000 |
| 3AB | Butterworth, Horace D | 6952 Marsden St., Philadelphia, Pa | 15 |
| 3CO | Campbell, James S | 1700 South Sixtieth St., Philadelphia, Pa. | 75 |
| 3BW | Campbell, John W | 1209 Twenty-fifth St., Philadelphia, Pa | 30 |
| 3BX | Carpenter, C. E., jr | 7417 Sprague St., Philadelphia, Pa | 250 |
| 3BG | Clark, Edwin T | 1244 Fitzgerald St., Philadelphia, Pa | 12 |
| 3CS | Cochran, A. Robb | 412 East Thirteenth St., Chester, Pa | 550 |
| 3II | Coin, Thornley | 5726 Delancy St., Philadelphia, Pa | 18 |
| 3CL | Coleman, Walter V | 2245 North Fifteenth St., Philadelphia, Pa. | 30 |
| 2AO | Collier, Wilbur H | 820 West Fayette St., Baltimore, Md | 170 |
| 3FZ | Conley, Charles B | 709 North Thirty-ninth St., Philadelphia, Pa. | 30 |
| 3IJ | Cooper, James W | 2043 North College Ave., Philadelphia, Pa. | 60 |
| 3FY | Core, Christopher W | 907 East Leigh St., Richmond, Va | 32 |
| 3JZ | Costella, Pietro | 4313 Baltimore Ave., Philadelphia, Pa | 92 |
| 3BU | Crosse, Alfred J | Cold Spring, N. J | 72 |
| 3BE | Critchlow, Samuel T | 2632 North Seventeenth St., Philadelphia, Pa. | 24 |
| 3BR | Crothers, Harry W | 3033 Susquehanna St., Philadelphia, Pa | 24 |
| 3FB | Darby, George B., jr | 1 Bala Ave., Bala, Pa | 550 |
| 3FA | Davis, Edwin | 3812 Eighth St. NW., Washington, D. C | 490 |
| 3BI | Deery, Walter J | 5928 Pine St., Philadelphia, Pa | 330 |
| 3FN | Deichmiller, Alvin | 1323 South Carey St., Baltimore, Md | 24 |

AMATEUR RADIO STATIONS—THIRD DISTRICT—ALPHABETICALLY BY OWNERS OF STATIONS—Continued.

| Call signal. | Owner of station. | Location of station. | Powe[r] |
|---|---|---|---|
| | | | Watts. |
| 3FF | Dempster, Warren J.... | 118 Cleveland St., Norwood, Pa......... | [illegible] |
| 3FR | Denston, E. Craig...... | 610 Poplar Grove, Baltimore, Md......... | [illegible] |
| 3JE | Dickerson, E. S., jr.... | 121 West Cedar Ave., Merchantville, N. J. | 24 |
| 3DJ | Diggins, Edward P. G.. | 1631 Eager St., Baltimore, Md........... | [illegible] |
| 3EZ | Donovan, Edgar R...... | 2847 North Seventh St., Philadelphia, Pa. | [illegible] |
| 3GE | Doolittle, Chas. M...... | West Chester Turnpike, Upper Darby, Pa. | 315 |
| 3FT | Dudley, DeWitt C...... | 3916 Market St., Philadelphia, Pa....... | 15 |
| 3HP | Duncan, Rodney P..... | 2039 North College Ave., Philadelphia, Pa. | 100 |
| 3FS | Durkee, Alfred C....... | 5052 Ludlow St., Philadelphia, Pa...... | 440 |
| 3AK | Duvall, Edward B...... | 20 East Madison St., Baltimore, Md.... | 250 |
| 3FO | E. I. DuPont De Nemours Powder Co. | Tenth and Market Sts., Wilmington, Del. | 445 |
| 3IH | Eisele, Edward, jr...... | 1116 Glenwood St., Philadelphia, Pa .... | 60 |
| 3FV | Edwards, Charles....... | 3345 Ella St., Philadelphia, Pa.......... | 15 |
| 3CR | Ellis, William G........ | 2204 North Fifteenth St., Philadelphia, Pa. | 270 |
| 3AW | Ely, Harry S........... | 215 South Washington St., Baltimore, Md. | 275 |
| 3DR | Eyster, James A........ | 317 Washington Ave., Haddonfield, N. J.. | 540 |
| 3HU | Falconi, Louis.......... | 617 Crawford St., Portsmouth, Va....... | 100 |
| 3HT | Falkenberg, August E.. | 512 Franklin Terrace, Baltimore, Md.... | 550 |
| 3CT | Farnham, Henry A..... | 313 V St. NE., Washington, D. C ........ | 250 |
| 3IZ | Faunce, B. Warren ..... | 26 Bala Ave., Bala, Pa.................. | 30 |
| 3GM | Fellows, J. Howard..... | 5504 Wisconsin Ave., Washington, D. C.. | 50 |
| 3JU | Fenimore, Robert S .... | 1327 West North Ave., Baltimore, Md... | 24 |
| 3CH | Ferris, Malcolm......... | 3409 Baring St., Philadelphia, Pa........ | 16 |
| 3HO | Fithian, William S., jr.. | 313 East Commerce St., Bridgeton, N. J.. | 550 |
| 3BH | Flather, Bryan S....... | 241 Fourteenth St. NE., Washington, D. C. | 15 |
| 3AL | Flentje, George F...... | 2023 Eastern Ave., Baltimore, Md....... | 12 |
| 3DN | France, A. Ward....... | 3544 Eighteenth St., Philadelphia, Pa... | 15 |
| 3GW | Frazier, George F....... | Janvier, N. J.......................... | 30 |

AMATEUR RADIO STATIONS—THIRD DISTRICT—ALPHABETICALLY BY OWNERS OF STATIONS—Continued.

| Call signal. | Owner of station. | Location of station. | Power. |
|---|---|---|---|
| | | | *Watts.* |
| 3JM | Freedom, Leon | Franklin and Fourteenth Sts., Baltimore, Md. | 440 |
| 3EL | Frick, Henry W. L. | 801 Aisquith St., Baltimore, Md | 330 |
| 3AE | Gaffney, James H | 1427 East Hoffman St., Baltimore, Md | 80 |
| 3AI | Garrett, Curtis L | 400 North Gilmore St., Baltimore, Md | 6 |
| 3CU | Gauss, Harry W | 221 Fifth St. SE., Washington, D. C | 32 |
| 3EC | Giffin, Sidney H | 2614 North Calvert St., Baltimore, Md | 200 |
| 3AZ | Gillingham, Geo. L., jr | 4508 Richmond St., Bridesburg, Pa | 440 |
| 3AR | Gilpin, Levering H | 2702 North Calvert St., Baltimore, Md | 770 |
| 3AV | Glashoff, H. Irving | 126 North East Ave., Baltimore, Md | 9 |
| 3IF | Godfrey, Earle | 145 St. Charles Pl., Atlantic City, N. J | 550 |
| 3FG | Godfrey, James M | Forty-ninth St. and Florence Ave., Philadelphia, Pa. | 75 |
| 3IB | Good, Horace D | 514 Kerper St., Reading, Pa | 24 |
| 3KB | Goodal, Alfred B | 518 Rhode Island Ave. NE., Washington, D. C. | 60 |
| 3JF | Gooding, Frederick R | 1517 Franklin St., Wilmington, Del | 40 |
| 3CB | Grant, Ulysses S | 28 Church St., Newton, N. J | 90 |
| 3KF | Green, Anthony J | 1112 South Lakewood St., Baltimore, Md. | 10 |
| 3IO | Groves, Fred G | 230 Earlham Terrace, Philadeplhia, Pa | 30 |
| 3JT | Hampson, George M | 231 Newington Ave., Baltimore, Md | 100 |
| 3JY | Hann, Charles B | Sudbrook Park, Baltimore, Md | 48 |
| 3HQ | Happold, Harold H | Union Ave., Bala, Pa | 600 |
| 3IU | Hart, Reginald L., II | 233 Beech Tree Lane, Wayne, Pa | 265 |
| 3FM | Hartley, Milton E | 635 E St. SE., Washington, D. C | 24 |
| 3ID | Hasenfus, Joseph F | 2328 North Fairhill St., Philadelphia, Pa | 75 |
| 3BN | Heisley, George E | 1114 Monroe St. NW., Washington, D. C | 42 |
| 3BJ | Henderson, Frank | 813 Highland Ave., Philadelphia, Pa | 275 |
| 3HM | Hickman, Paul | 1917 Green St., Philadelphia, Pa | 330 |
| 3JO | Hicks, A. Willet, jr | 3232 North Thirteenth St., Philadelphia, Pa. | 60 |
| 3JX | Hoagland, Donald | 43 Lake St., Bridgeton, N. J | 180 |

AMATEUR RADIO STATIONS—THIRD DISTRICT—ALPHABETICALLY BY OWNERS OF STATIONS—Continued.

| Call signal. | Owner of station. | Location of station. | Power. |
|---|---|---|---|
| | | | Watts |
| 3BT | Hoffman, W. Hollis | Cold Spring, N. J. | 1 |
| 3KK | Hofmann, George A. | Engle Ave., Burlington, N. J. | 3 |
| 3GD | Hofmeister, Charles P. | 2711 Calvert St., Baltimore, Md. | 1 |
| 3AQ | Hogan, Harold O. | 2630 Guilford Ave., Baltimore, Md. | 12 |
| 3GU | Hopkins, Robert E. | 2428 Nicholas St., Philadelphia, Pa. | 3 |
| 3CY | Hubbs, Edwin E. | 145 East Washington Lane, Philadelphia, Pa. | 13 |
| 3HZ | Huber, Charles E. | 509 Washington St., Wilmington, Del. | 24 |
| 3FJ | Huber, Francis M. | 1313 South Carey St., Baltimore, Md. | 4 |
| 3FW | Hunter, Edwin J. | 2429 East Cumberland St., Philadelphia, Pa. | 385 |
| 3FX | Hutchinson, Samuel J. | 209 White Horse Pike, Haddon Heights, N. J. | 440 |
| 3CJ | Imfield, Fred | 117 North Sixth St., Philadelphia, Pa. | 330 |
| 3IE | Jacobson, Bernard H. | Walnut Ave., near Edmondson, Baltimore, Md. | 550 |
| 3HW | James, Herman | 239 Kaighn Ave., Camden, N. J. | 15 |
| 3BL | Jaquett, Maurice J. | 3155 Carlisle St., Philadelphia, Pa. | 1 |
| 3CC | Jenkins, Russell L. | 6804 Dittman St., Philadelphia, Pa. | 450 |
| 3IG | Johnson, Earle K. | 127 North Carolina Ave., South, Atlantic City, N. J. | 150 |
| 3GG | Jones, Winters | 728 North Monroe St., Baltimore, Md. | 12 |
| 3CV | Kelley, George W., jr. | 1738 Sixteenth St., Philadelphia, Pa. | 27 |
| 3KC | Kendall, Raymond V. | 1813 Milton Ave., Baltimore, Md. | 2 |
| 3EP | Kennedy, Joseph H. | 2052 East Fletcher St., Philadelphia Pa. | 275 |
| 3JB | Knebel, Arthur | 414 East Allegheny Ave., Philadelphia, Pa. | 18 |
| 3GC | Knieriemen, Joseph | Atco, N. J. | 4 |
| 3IQ | Knoll, Lloyd M. | 3260 Chestnut St., Philadelphia, Pa. | 40 |
| 3JN | Korab, Harry E. | 418 West Clay St., Richmond, Va. | 490 |
| 3FQ | Krainer, James B. | Washington St., Laurel, Md. | 33 |
| 3BB | Kralovec, Dalibor | 3535 North Water St., Philadelphia, Pa. | 3 |
| 3HX | Kratz, Herman | 2001 West Pratt St., Baltimore, Md. | 17 |

AMATEUR RADIO STATIONS—THIRD DISTRICT—ALPHABETICALLY BY OWNERS OF STATIONS—Continued.

| Call signal. | Owner of station. | Location of station. | Power. |
|---|---|---|---|
| | | | *Watts.* |
| 3EI | Kumler, Kelvin C | Washington St., Kensington, Md | 330 |
| 3CF | Laager, Creston F | 4904 Thompson St., Philadelphia, Pa | 18 |
| 3GV | Laber, Joseph M | 2422 Gratz St., Philadelphia, Pa | 15 |
| 3GZ | Laird, J. Ira | 25 Strode Ave., Coatesville, Pa | 30 |
| 3CW | Lange, John R | 1938 Lemmon St., Baltimore, Md | 16 |
| 3ER | Larrimore, James F | 1814 Calvert St., Baltimore, Md | 550 |
| 3HD | Larzelere, Lindley E | 305 Beechwood St., Jenkintown, Pa | 12 |
| 3JV | Lehr, William | 3912 Maine Ave., Baltimore, Md | 36 |
| 3BZ | Leister, Fayette | Sixty-fifth and Jefferson Sts., Philadelphia, Pa. | 36 |
| 3DW | Lowery, Norman S | Second St., Laurel, Md | 45 |
| 3DI | Lowell, Percival D | 2838 Twenty-seventh St. NW., Washington, D. C. | 330 |
| 3DX | Lukens, Wilfred P | 527 Spring Mill Ave., Conshohocken, Pa | 605 |
| 3GH | MacDonald, Stuart | 209 North Fifty-third St., Philadelphia, Pa. | 330 |
| 3DM | MacFeeters, John | 1538 Gratz St., Philadelphia, Pa | 32 |
| 3EQ | Mackendrick, Robt. G | 211 Lenoir St., Wayne, Pa | 990 |
| 3GA | Magee, John W | 518 Apple St., West Conshohocken, Pa | 505 |
| 3ES | Martin, E. Linton | 315 Radcliffe St., Bristol, Pa | 64 |
| 3EO | Mater, Caleb R | Beverly Road, Burlington, N. J | 180 |
| 3DO | Maxson, Donald L | Baltimore St., Kensington, Md | 330 |
| 3GL | Meck, Michael | 1550 North Allison St., Philadelphia, Pa | 32 |
| 3IM | Mellon, Charles E | 116 Pennsylvania St., Coatesville, Pa | 400 |
| 3CD | Michaels, Herman L | 843 East Russell St., Philadelphia, Pa | 72 |
| 3DY | Miller, Frederick E | 3134 Rosewood St., Philadelphia, Pa | 18 |
| 3GQ | Miller, Kelly, jr | 430 College St. NW., Washington, D. C | 15 |
| 3IW | Mitchener, Harold G | 528 Swain St., Bristol, Pa | 18 |
| 3CK | Moody, Matthew C | 2509 South Sheridan St., Philadelphia, Pa. | 12 |
| 3EK | Moore, Daniel D | 2308 Charles St., Baltimore, Md | 15 |
| 3IC | Morris, Edward P | 3114 D St., Philadelphia, Pa | 36 |

AMATEUR RADIO STATIONS—THIRD DISTRICT—ALPHABETICALLY BY OWNERS OF STATIONS—Continued.

| Call signal. | Owner of station. | Location of station. | Pow |
|---|---|---|---|
| | | | Wa |
| 3DL | Muniz, Manuel E | 901 South Sixtieth St., Philadelphia, Pa | 33 |
| 3HS | Murray, Eugene M | Grays Lane, Haverford, Pa | 99 |
| 3HL | Nielson, Harold, jr | 8751 Frankford Ave., Holmesburg, Pa | [illegible] |
| 3KD | Noel, James F | 228 Second St. NE., Washington, D. C | [illegible] |
| 3GO | Norcross, Earl L | 216 Roberts Ave., Glenside, Pa | 36 |
| 3CI | Nordstrom, John W | Gallitzin, Pa | 33 |
| 3HE | Parks, Laurence W | 12 South Yewdell St., Philadelphia, Pa | [illegible] |
| 3DS | Parks, Walther A | 901 Lawrence St. NE., Washington, D. C | 9 |
| 3AT | Parsons, Harry S | 13 North Carey St., Baltimore, Md | [illegible] |
| 3AP | Patzschke, August | Old Harford Road, Hamilton, Md | 99 |
| 3GI | Pelham, Fred B | 603 Howard Pl. NW., Washington, D. C | [illegible] |
| 3DA | Peterson, Raymond E | 1602 South Frazier St., Philadelphia, Pa | 3 |
| 3IX | Philadelphia School of Wireless Telegraphy. | Park Building, Broad and Cherry Sts., Philadelphia, Pa. | 4 |
| 3AD | Phillips, William J | 1530 Orleans St., Baltimore, Md | 2 |
| 3HH | Place, Samuel W | 662 Stanbridge St., Norristown, Pa | 6 |
| 3EH | Powell, Edwin H | 1206 East Capitol St., Washington, D. C | [illegible] |
| 3ED | Price, Thompson | 1600 Edgmont Ave., Chester, Pa | 66 |
| 3EJ | Primrose, Donald L | 1701 Park Pl., Baltimore, Md | 44 |
| 3IA | Puff, Stephen F | 222 Wildwood Ave., Wildwood, N. J | [illegible] |
| 3FE | Rabl, Samuel | 419 Third St., Baltimore, Md | [illegible] |
| 3EF | Reiff, W. Norman | 916 Fayette St., Conshohocken, Pa | 4 |
| 3DK | Richardson, Thomas L | Curtis Bay, Quarantine, Md | [illegible] |
| 3HY | Richwien, Louis C | 2014 West Pratt St., Baltimore, Md | [illegible] |
| 3JC | Riley, Arthur J | 147 Bank St., Bridgeton, N. J | 3 |
| 3GX | Robinson, George C | 607 North Tenth St., Richmond, Va | [illegible] |
| 3KG | Rogers, Alfred K | 2313 North Charles St., Baltimore, Md | [illegible] |
| 3GB | Rohrich, George J | Bethesda, Md | [illegible] |
| 3FP | Satterthwaite, Frank W | 715 North Fifth St., Reading, Pa | 3 |
| 3EW | Scheffey, Ralph | 346 Lafayette St., Bristol, Pa | [illegible] |

AMATEUR RADIO STATIONS—THIRD DISTRICT—ALPHABETICALLY BY OWNERS OF STATIONS—Continued.

| Call signal. | Owner of station. | Location of station. | Power. |
|---|---|---|---|
| | | | *Watts.* |
| 3FK | Schleher, Paul H | 1912 North Marvine St., Philadelphia, Pa. | 32 |
| 3JG | Scholl, Warren | 179 Kalso St., Wissahickon, Pa | 54 |
| 3HN | Schuck, Leon H | 2441 North Eighth St., Philadelphia, Pa | 550 |
| 3AU | Schultz, Henry | 14 South Arlington Ave., Baltimore, Md | 275 |
| 3GT | Searle, William J., jr | 125 New St., Glenside, Pa | 72 |
| 3EU | Shelley, Cheston | 2612 Hampden St., Baltimore, Md | 40 |
| 3AC | Simon, Henry | 1234 Carroll St., Baltimore, Md | 80 |
| 3FD | Simon, Walter | 1234 Carroll St., Baltimore, Md | 80 |
| 3HV | Sithens, Edward | 3205 Susquehanna St., Philadelphia, Pa | 24 |
| 3DB | Smiley, Richard E | 402 North Thirty-second St., Philadelphia, Pa. | 12 |
| 3DQ | Smith, G. Victor | 300 Mill St., Bristol, Pa | 800 |
| 3DF | Smith, Randolph | 2647 North Calvert St., Baltimore Md | 330 |
| 3FH | Smith, Sewall P | Wyndcrest Ave., Catonsville, Md | 440 |
| 3HG | Smith, W. P | 5043 Summer St., Philadelphia, Pa | 18 |
| 3JR | Snow, Harold A | 4715 Wisconsin Ave., Washington, D. C | 30 |
| 3IK | Snyder, Harry H | Cold Spring, N. J | 60 |
| 3EG | Snyder, James R | 319 Vassar Ave., Swarthmore, Pa | 550 |
| 3GJ | Sorenson, Christian | 4400 Baltimore Ave., Philadelphia, Pa | 36 |
| 3DH | Stahl, Harry E., jr | 275 Bellevue Ave., Trenton, N. J | 14 |
| 3KI | Stanley, John S | Laurel, Md | 30 |
| 3BY | Statz, Henry M | 709 Euclid St. NW., Washington, D. C | 48 |
| 3GY | Staub, James | Sluice Road, Burlington Township, N. J | 60 |
| 3BC | Stephen, C. Chester | Laurel Springs, N. J | 72 |
| 3HI | Stepp, John W | 630 Morton St. NW., Washington, D. C | 80 |
| 3JP | Sterns, Morton W | 29 Main St., Bethlehem, Pa | 24 |
| 3HK. | Stokes, Josiah T | 15 West Stiles Ave., Collingwood, N. J | 24 |
| 3IT | Stritzel, Alfred H | 12 North Carolina Ave. South, Atlantic City, N. J. | 250 |
| 3AS | Stumptner, Albert G | Old Harford Rd., Hamilton, Md | 440 |
| 3DE | Tallman, Frank G., jr | 1102 Broome St., Wilmington, Del | 550 |

AMATEUR RADIO STATIONS—THIRD DISTRICT—ALPHABETICALLY BY OWNERS OF STATIONS—Continued.

| Call signal. | Owner of station. | Location of station. | Powe[illegible] |
|---|---|---|---|
| | | | Wts |
| 3HB | Taylor, S. L. McD. | 321 Mohawk Ave., Norwood, Pa. | [illegible] |
| 3BF | Teller, Leslie W. | 4012 Seventh St. NW., Washington, D. C. | 60[illegible] |
| 3HC | Thackeray, Samuel J. | 4232 Paul St., Philadelphia, Pa. | 1[illegible] |
| 3HR | Thornton, Earl H. | 131 East Durham St., Philadelphia, Pa. | 55[illegible] |
| 3CX | Toboldt, William K. | 2412 North Sixteenth St., Philadelphia, Pa. | 3[illegible] |
| 3IY | Tolbert, Warren | 7037 Hegerman St., Philadelphia, Pa. | 1[illegible] |
| 3AH | Triede, Carl L. | 2402 East Baltimore St., Baltimore, Md. | 31[illegible] |
| 3GK | Troth, Raymond H. | 3350 North Eighteenth St., Philadelphia, Pa. | 3[illegible] |
| 3DV | Uphoff, Frank B. | 3649 York Rd., Philadelphia, Pa. | 1[illegible] |
| 3CM | Van Horn, J. Clunn | 7 Rutledge St., Rutledge, Pa. | 1,00[illegible] |
| 3IN | Vogel, Charles E. | 1244 Taney St., Philadelphia, Pa. | 1[illegible] |
| 3EX | Vogts, Wade C. | Second St., Laurel, Md. | 5[illegible] |
| 3HF | Wakefield, C. Bishop | 33 West Spring St., Merchantville, N. J. | [illegible] |
| 3IR | Wallace, Lewis J. | 2728 Poplar St., Philadelphia, Pa. | 1[illegible] |
| 3AN | Walsh, Maurice L. | 819 West Lexington St., Baltimore, Md. | 1,00[illegible] |
| 3AG | Weant, Clarence H. | 1546 Aisquith St., Baltimore, Md. | 10[illegible] |
| 3IS | Weaver, Howard A. | 5545 Webster St., Philadelphia, Pa. | 2[illegible] |
| 3FC | Weik, Charles F. | 7148 Vandyke St., Philadelphia, Pa. | 1[illegible] |
| 3DT | Wells, William C., jr. | 124 South Thirty-sixth St., Philadelphia, Pa. | 49[illegible] |
| 3AF | West, William M. | 1407 North Central Ave., Baltimore, Md. | [illegible] |
| 3FI | Wever, John A. | 238 South Patterson Park Ave., Baltimore, Md. | 2[illegible] |
| 3CZ | Wheatley, Douglas N. | 405 Thirty-second St., Philadelphia, Pa. | 4[illegible] |
| 3DG | White, Norman P. | 19 General Greene Ave., Trenton, N. J. | 1[illegible] |
| 3FL | Wiler, William L. | 1735 Arch St., Philadelphia, Pa. | 1[illegible] |
| 3JK | Wilson, Edward C. | Park Ave. and Lauren St., Baltimore, Md. | 6[illegible] |
| 3AM | Wise, Leonard J. | 419 North Patterson Park Ave., Baltimore, Md. | [illegible] |

Amateur Radio Stations—Third District—Alphabetically by Owners of Stations—Continued.

| Call signal. | Owner of station. | Location of station. | Power. |
|---|---|---|---|
| | | | *Watts.* |
| 3HA | Wiseman, Luther B.... | 330 W St. NW., Washington, D. C...... | 16 |
| 3JD | Wolcott, Roger G....... | 224 Forty-first St., Norfolk, Va........... | 104 |
| 3BS | Wolff, William J........ | 2422 South Iseminger St., Philadelphia, Pa. | 24 |
| 3GR | Wood, Richard M....... | West Forty-first St., Baltimore, Md...... | 330 |
| 3DD | Work, Ashton G........ | 807 St. Charles Pl., Ocean City, N. J..... | 250 |
| 3KJ | Worrest, Howard A..... | 627 North Duke St., Lancaster, Pa...... | 45 |
| 3EA | Wright, Clifton P....... | 1525 North Eden St., Baltimore, Md..... | 84 |
| 3FU | Wunder, William F.... | 5801 Germantown St., Philadelphia, Pa.. | 80 |
| 3CQ | Yeager, George R....... | 718 American St., Philadelphia, Pa....... | 50 |
| 3EE | Zinn, Richard S........ | 3325 Spring Garden St., Philadelphia, Pa. | 40 |

ALPHABETICALLY BY CALL SIGNALS.

| Call signal. | Owner of station. | Call signal. | Owner of station. |
|---|---|---|---|
| 3AA | Ashmore, John W. | 3BD | Allen, Percival R. |
| 3AB | Butterworth, Horace D. | 3BE | Critchlow, Samuel T. |
| 3AC | Simon, Henry. | 3BF | Teller, Leslie W. |
| 3AD | Phillips, William J. | 3BG | Clark, Edwin T. |
| 3AE | Gaffney, James H. | 3BH | Flather, Bryan S. |
| 3AF | West, William M. | 3BI | Deery, Walter J. |
| 3AG | Weant, Clarence H. | 3BJ | Henderson, Frank. |
| 3AH | Triede, Carl L. | 3BK | Brown, Merritt M. |
| 3AI | Garrett, Curtis L. | 3BL | Jaquett, Maurice J. |
| 3AJ | Bausman, George H. | 3BM | Allen, George Y. |
| 3AK | Duvall, Edward B. | 3BN | Heisley, George E. |
| 3AL | Flentje, George F. | 3BO | Brady, John B. |
| 3AM | Wise, Leonard J. | 3BP | Blackwood, George E. |
| 3AN | Walsh, Maurice L. | 3BQ | Bugbee, Newton A. |
| 3AO | Collier, Wilbur H. | 3BR | Crothers, Harry W. |
| 3AP | Patzschke, August. | 3BS | Wolff, William J. |
| 3AQ | Hogan, Harold O. | 3BT | Hoffman, W. Hollis. |
| 3AR | Gilpin, Levering H. | 3BU | Cresse, Alfred J. |
| 3AS | Stumptner, Albert G. | 3BV | Bacon, Franklin F. |
| 3AT | Parsons, Harry S. | 3BW | Campbell, John W. |
| 3AU | Schultz, Henry. | 3BX | Carpenter, C. E., jr. |
| 3AV | Glashoff, H. Irving. | 3BY | Statz, Henry M. |
| 3AW | Ely, Harry S. | 3BZ | Leister, Fayette. |
| 3AX | Arner, Oscar Q. | | |
| 3AY | Blodgett, Charles L. | 3CA | Adelberger, Adrian J. |
| 3AZ | Gillingham, George L., jr. | 3CB | Grant, Ulysses S. |
| | | 3CC | Jenkins, Russell L. |
| 3BA | Anthony, Wm. H. | 3CD | Michaels, Herman L. |
| 3BB | Kralovec, Dalibor. | 3CF | Laager, Creston F. |
| 3BC | Stephen, C. Chester. | 3CG | Adelberger, Francis. |

AMATEUR RADIO STATIONS—THIRD DISTRICT—ALPHABETICALLY BY CALL SIGNALS—Continued.

| Call signal. | Owner of station. |
|---|---|
| 3CH | Ferris, Malcolm. |
| 3CI | Nordstrom, John W. |
| 3CJ | Imfield, Fred. |
| 3CK | Moody, Matthew C. |
| 3CL | Coleman, Walter V. |
| 3CM | Van Horn, J. Clunn. |
| 3CN | Ashton, Leon W. |
| 3CO | Campbell, James S. |
| 3CP | Bunting, George M., jr. |
| 3CQ | Yeager, George R. |
| 3CR | Ellis, William G. |
| 3CS | Cochran, A. Robb. |
| 3CT | Farnham, Henry A. |
| 3CU | Gauss, Harry W. |
| 3CV | Kelley, George W., jr. |
| 3CW | Lange, John R. |
| 3CX | Toboldt, William K. |
| 3CY | Hubbs, Edwin E. |
| 3CZ | Wheatley, Douglas M. |
| 3DA | Peterson, Raymond E. |
| 3DB | Smiley, Richard E. |
| 3DC | Bergen, Donald M. |
| 3DD | Work, Ashton G. |
| 3DE | Tallman, Frank G., jr. |
| 3DF | Smith, Randolph. |
| 3DG | White, Norman P. |
| 3DH | Stahl, Harry E., jr. |
| 3DI | Lowell, Percival D. |
| 3DJ | Diggins, Edward P. G. |
| 3DK | Richardson, Thomas L. |
| 3DL | Muniz, Manuel E. |
| 3DM | MacFeeters, John. |
| 3DN | France, A. Ward. |
| 3DO | Maxson, Donald L. |
| 3DQ | Smith, G. Victor. |
| 3DR | Eyster, James A. |
| 3DS | Parks, Walther A. |
| 3DT | Wells, William C., jr. |
| 3DU | Bauman, F. J. |
| 3DV | Uphoff, Frank B. |
| 3DW | Lowery, Norman S. |
| 3DX | Lukens, Wilfred P. |
| 3DY | Miller, Frederick E. |
| 3EA | Wright, Clifton P. |
| 3EB | Adam, Francis J. |
| 3EC | Giffin, Sidney H. |
| 3ED | Price, Thompson. |
| 3EE | Zinn, Richard S. |
| 3EF | Reiff, W. Norman. |
| 3EG | Snyder, James R. |
| 3EH | Powell, Edwin H. |
| 3EI | Kumler, Kelvin C. |
| 3EJ | Primrose, Donald L. |
| 3EK | Moore, Daniel D. |
| 3EL | Frick, H. W. L. |
| 3EM | Beaty, Lehman C. |
| 3EN | Bailey, Albert S. |
| 3EO | Mater, Caleb R. |
| 3EP | Kennedy, Joseph H. |
| 3EQ | Mackendrick, Robert G. |
| 3ER | Larrimore, James F. |
| 3ES | Martin, E. Linton. |
| 3EU | Shelley, Cheston. |
| 3EV | Brannan, Julian L. |
| 3EW | Scheffey, Ralph. |
| 3EX | Vogts, Wade C. |
| 3EZ | Donovan, Edgar R. |
| 3FA | Davis, Edwin. |
| 3FB | Darby, George B., jr. |
| 3FC | Weik, Charles F. |
| 3FD | Simon, Walter. |
| 3FE | Rabl, Samuel. |
| 3FF | Dempster, Warren J. |
| 3FG | Godfrey, James M. |
| 3FH | Smith, Sewall P. |
| 3FI | Wever, John A. |
| 3FJ | Huber, Francis M. |
| 3FK | Schleher, Paul H. |
| 3FL | Wiler, William L. |
| 3FM | Hartley, Milton E. |
| 3FN | Deichmiller, Alvin. |
| 3FO | E. I. DuPont DeNemours Powder Co. |
| 3FP | Satterthwaite, Frank W. |
| 3FQ | Krainer, James B. |
| 3FR | Denston, E. Craig. |
| 3FS | Durkee, Alfred C. |
| 3FT | Dudley, De Witt C. |
| 3FU | Wunder, William F. |
| 3FV | Edwards, Charles. |
| 3FW | Hunter, Edwin J. |
| 3FX | Hutchinson, Samuel J. |
| 3FY | Core, Christopher W. |
| 3FZ | Conley, Charles B. |
| 3GA | Magee, John W. |
| 3GB | Rohrich, George J. |
| 3GC | Knieriemen, Joseph. |
| 3GD | Hofmeister, Charles P. |
| 3GE | Doolittle, Charles M. |
| 3GF | Blankenship, Elliott E. |
| 3GG | Jones, Winters. |
| 3GH | MacDonald, Stuart. |
| 3GI | Pelham, Fred B. |
| 3GJ | Sorenson, Christian. |
| 3GK | Troth, Raymond H. |
| 3GL | Meck, Michael. |
| 3GM | Fellows, J. Howard. |
| 3GN | Board of Public Education, Philadelphia, Pa. |
| 3GO | Norcross, Earl L. |
| 3GQ | Miller, Kelly, jr. |
| 3GR | Wood, Richard M. |
| 3GT | Searle, William J., jr. |
| 3GU | Hopkins, Robert E. |
| 3GV | Laber, Joseph M. |
| 3GW | Frazier, George F. |
| 3GX | Robinson, George C. |
| 3GY | Staub, James. |
| 3GZ | Laird, J. Ira. |

AMATEUR RADIO STATIONS—THIRD DISTRICT—ALPHABETICALLY BY CALL SIGNALS—Continued.

| Call signal. | Owner of station. |
|---|---|
| 3HA | Wiseman, Luther B. |
| 3HB | Taylor, S. L. McD. |
| 3HC | Thackeray, Samuel J. |
| 3HD | Larzelere, Lindley E. |
| 3HE | Parks, Laurence W. |
| 3HF | Wakefield, C. Bishop. |
| 3HG | Smith, W. P. |
| 3HH | Place, Samuel W. |
| 3HI | Stepp, John W. |
| 3HJ | Bradley, Horace E. |
| 3HK | Stokes, Josiah T. |
| 3HL | Nielson, Harold, jr. |
| 3HM | Hickman, Paul. |
| 3HN | Schuck, Leon H. |
| 3HO | Fithian, William S., jr. |
| 3HP | Duncan, Rodney P. |
| 3HQ | Happold, Harold H. |
| 3HR | Thornton, Earl H. |
| 3HS | Murray, Eugene M. |
| 3HT | Falkenberg, August E. |
| 3HU | Falconi, Louis. |
| 3HV | Sithens, Edward. |
| 3HW | James, Herman. |
| 3HX | Kratz, Herman. |
| 3HY | Richwein, Louis C. |
| 3HZ | Huber, Charles E. |
| | |
| 3IA | Puff, Stephen F. |
| 3IB | Good, Horace D. |
| 3IC | Morris, Edward P. |
| 3ID | Hasenfus, Joseph F. |
| 3IE | Jacobson, Bernard H. |
| 3IF | Godfrey, Earle. |
| 3IG | Johnson, Earle K. |
| 3IH | Eisele, Edward, jr. |
| 3II | Coin, Thornley. |
| 3IJ | Cooper, James W. |
| 3IK | Snyder, Harry H. |
| 3IM | Mellon, Charles E. |
| 3IN | Vogel, Charles E. |
| 3IO | Groves, Fred G. |
| 3IP | Anderson, Albert. |
| 3IQ | Knoll, Lloyd M. |
| 3IR | Wallace, Lewis J. |
| 3IS | Weaver, Howard A. |
| 3IT | Stritzel, Alfred H. |
| 3IU | Hart, Reginald L., II. |
| 3IW | Mitchener, Harold G. |
| 3IX | Philadelphia School of Wireless Telegraphy. |
| 3IY | Tolbert, Warren. |
| 3IZ | Faunce, B. Warren. |
| | |
| 3JA | August, Earl W. |
| 3JB | Knebel, Arthur. |
| 3JC | Riley, Arthur J. |
| 3JD | Wolcott, Roger G. |
| 3JE | Dickerson, E. S., jr. |
| 3JF | Gooding, Frederick R. |
| 3JG | Scholl, Warren. |
| 3JH | Brockman, F. C. |
| 3JI | Burdette, Aubrey W. |
| 3JJ | Bergmann, Frederick J. |
| 3JK | Wilson, Edward C. |
| 3JM | Freedom, Leon. |
| 3JN | Korab, Harry E. |
| 3JO | Hicks, A. Willet, jr. |
| 3JP | Sterns, Morton W. |
| 3JQ | Benson, Thomas W. |
| 3JR | Snow, Harold A. |
| 3JS | Beekley, Francis C. |
| 3JT | Hampson, George M. |
| 3JU | Fenimore, Robert S. |
| 3JV | Lehr, William. |
| 3JW | Broadbelt, J. Edward, jr. |
| 3JX | Hoagland, Donald. |
| 3JY | Hann, Charles B. |
| 3JZ | Costella, Pietro. |
| | |
| 3KB | Goodal, Alfred B. |
| 3KC | Kendall, Raymond V. |
| 3KD | Noel, James F. |
| 3KE | Allen, Francis H. |
| 3KF | Green, Anthony J. |
| 3KG | Rogers, Alfred K. |
| 3KH | Bowen, Albert. |
| 3KI | Stanley, John S. |
| 3KJ | Worrest, Howard A. |
| 3KK | Hofmann, George A. |

## FOURTH DISTRICT.

[Headquarters: Customhouse, Savannah, Ga. The fourth district comprises the States of North Carolina, South Carolina, Georgia, Florida, and the Territory of Porto Rico.]

ALPHABETICALLY BY OWNERS OF STATIONS.

| Call signal. | Owner of station. | Location of station. | Power. |
|---|---|---|---|
| | | | *Watts.* |
| 4AN | Adams, George G. | 45 Whitaker St., Savannah, Ga. | 20 |
| 4AU | Avera, W. W. | Watkinsville, Ga. | 30 |
| 4AL | Bangs, Philip C. | 918 East Duffy St., Savannah, Ga. | 350 |

AMATEUR RADIO STATIONS—FOURTH DISTRICT—ALPHABETICALLY BY OWNERS OF STATIONS—Continued.

| Call signal. | Owner of station. | Location of station. | Power. |
|---|---|---|---|
| | | | Watts. |
| 4AA | Bradberry, Alfred S.... | 806 College Ave., Athens, Ga............ | 550 |
| 4AS | Brandon, Beverly A..... | 1408 Main St., Jacksonville, Fla.......... | 330 |
| 4AX | Cole, Raymond J...... | 1712 Silver St., Jacksonville, Fla........ | 250 |
| 4AW | Crevasse, Joe N........ | 1605 Boulevard St., Jacksonville, Fla.... | 165 |
| 4AZ | Dunk, Thomas R....... | 1424 Laura St., Jacksonville, Fla......... | 300 |
| 4AT | Ehle, Frank R......... | 1337 Liberty St., Jacksonville, Fla....... | 220 |
| 4AE | Flagg, John F.......... | 118 Forest St., Jacksonville, Fla......... | 900 |
| 4BE | Fowler, Carl A......... | S. N. S. Station, Athens, Ga............ | 125 |
| 4AB | Funk, Arthur.......... | 226 West Liberty St., Savannah, Ga...... | 300 |
| 4AH | Jarvis, Parkhill O....... | 26 Pollock St., Newbern, N. C........... | 120 |
| 4BA | Lewis, Claude A........ | 128 West Bay St., Savannah, Ga.......... | 575 |
| 4AR | Marbury, Ralph E..... | 26 Wesley St., Newnan, Ga............. | 500 |
| 4BC | Marx, Earl I........... | 1654 Main Street., Jacksonville, Fla..... | 300 |
| 4AG | Miller, Walter H........ | 402 West Oglethorpe St., Savannah, Ga... | 300 |
| 4AJ | Moore, Victor W....... | 147 Nacoochee Ave., Athens, Ga ........ | 250 |
| 4AY | Moseley, Charles V..... | 815 Mulberry St., Columbia, S. C....... | 20 |
| 4AP | Peer, Emmitt E......... | 419 West Duval St., Jacksonville, Fla ... | 800 |
| 4AI | Pope, Wilbur B........ | 197 Dearing St., Athens, Ga.............. | 594 |
| 4BB | Rankin, Robert G., jr... | 3 North Ninth St., Wilmington, N. C..... | 16 |
| 4BF | Rankin, Robert G., jr... | Chadbourn St., Wrightsville Beach, N. C. | 22 |
| 4AC | Rice, Elmer L......... | 1702 East Duval St., Jacksonville, Fla... | 880 |
| 4AM | Sebastian, Lawrence F.. | 224 Parker St., Jacksonville, Fla ....... | 10 |
| 4BD | Speight, Marshall C..... | 5 Johnson St., Newbern, N. C............ | 100 |
| 4BG | Stanton, Alvin G....... | 1031 Highway Ave., Jacksonville, Fla.... | 27 |
| 4AD | Steinhauser, Elmer..... | 19 West Gordon St., Savannah, Ga....... | 300 |
| 4AF | Stringfellow, Fred...... | East Main St., Gainesville, Fla.......... | 500 |
| 4AO | Swearingen, Thos. J., jr. | 403 Prariur Ave., Gainesville, Fla........ | 990 |
| 4AV | Treisback, Robert T.... | 2228 Riverside Ave., Jacksonville, Fla... | 500 |
| 4BA | White, Manning ....... | 128 West Bay St., Savannah, Ga........ | 575 |
| 4AK | Whiting, Charles T..... | R. F. D. No. 6, Gainesville, Fla......... | 770 |

## Amateur Radio Stations—Fourth District—Continued.

ALPHABETICALLY BY CALL SIGNALS.

| Call signal. | Owner of station. | Call signal. | Owner of station. |
|---|---|---|---|
| 4AA | Bradberry, Alfred S. | 4AS | Brandon, Beverly A. |
| 4AB | Funk, Arthur. | 4AT | Ehle, Frank R. |
| 4AC | Rice, Elmer L. | 4AU | Avera, W. W. |
| 4AD | Steinhauser, Elmer. | 4AV | Treisback, Robert T. |
| 4AE | Flagg, John F. | 4AW | Crevasse, Joe N. |
| 4AF | Stringfellow, Fred. | 4AX | Cole, Raymond J. |
| 4AG | Miller, Walter H. | 4AY | Moseley, Charles V. |
| 4AH | Jarvis, Parkhill O. | 4AZ | Dunk, Thomas R. |
| 4AI | Pope, Wilbur B. | | |
| 4AJ | Moore, Victor W. | 4BA | Lewis, Claude A., and White, Manning. |
| 4AK | Whiting, Charles T. | | |
| 4AL | Bangs, Philip C. | 4BB | Rankin, Robert G., jr. |
| 4AM | Sebastian, Lawrence F. | 4BC | Marx, Earl I. |
| 4AN | Adams, George G. | 4BD | Speight, Marshall C. |
| 4AO | Swearingen, Thos. J., jr. | 4BE | Fowler, Carl A. |
| 4AP | Peer, Emmitt E. | 4BF | Rankin, Robert G., jr. |
| 4AR | Marbury, Ralph E. | 4BG | Stanton, Alvin G. |

## FIFTH DISTRICT.

[Headquarters: Customhouse, New Orleans, La. The fifth district comprises the States of Alabama, Mississippi, Louisiana, Texas, Tennessee, Arkansas, Oklahoma, New Mexico.]

ALPHABETICALLY BY OWNERS OF STATIONS.

| Call signal. | Owner of station. | Location of station. | Power. |
|---|---|---|---|
| | | | *Watts.* |
| 5AJ | Albertson, Clarence E. | 416 Park Ave., Tupelo, Miss. | 500 |
| 5AS | Bastian, Royal R. | 5523 Saratoga St., New Orleans, La. | 400 |
| 5AR | Beynon, Eugene T. | 604 Artesian St., Corpus Christi, Tex. | 295 |
| 5AM | Brownell, Harold S. | 1512 Phelan St., Birmingham, Ala. | 500 |
| 5AC | Budwig, Gilbert G. | 1404 Seventeenth Ave., Birmingham, Ala. | 500 |
| 5AO | Buster, John A. | 316 Main St., Brenham, Tex. | 270 |
| 5AK | Daly, Thomas J. M. | Covington, Tenn. | 1,000 |
| 5AQ | Goldstein, Henry R. | 1819 Octavia St., New Orleans, La. | 75 |
| 5AE | Jones, Ralph | 1103 Gibson St., Muskogee, Okla. | 20 |
| 5AA | Knight, Eugene B. | 2501 Battery St., Little Rock, Ark. | 1,000 |
| 5AH | Martin, Ben W. | 438 Spring Hill Ave., Mobile, Ala. | 660 |
| 5AG | Martin, Stanley | 219 North K St., Muskogee, Okla. | 500 |
| 5AF | Meyer, William F. | 2610 Ringo St., Little Rock, Ark. | 150 |
| 5AI | Ratcliff, Fred | 1207 East Ninth St., Shawnee, Okla. | 21 |
| 5AL | Reboul, Theophile | 2106 Chartres St., New Orleans, La. | 150 |
| 5AD | Rorshach, Harold E. | 619 North E St., Muskogee, Okla. | 250 |

AMATEUR RADIO STATIONS—FIFTH DISTRICT—ALPHABETICALLY BY OWNERS OF STATIONS—Continued.

| Call signal. | Owner of station. | Location of station. | Power. |
|---|---|---|---|
| | | | Watts. |
| 5AB | Scalco, Joe R. | 1102 Eighth Ave., Birmingham, Ala. | 500 |
| 5AP | Thompson, Vance. | 267 Pasadena Pl., Memphis, Tenn. | 330 |
| 5AT | Vickers, Alwyn. | 508 Clayton St., Montgomery, Ala. | 12 |
| 5AN | Watkins, Will O. | 203 First Ave., Birmingham, Ala. | 500 |

ALPHABETICALLY BY CALL SIGNALS.

| Call signal. | Owner of station. | Call signal. | Owner of station. |
|---|---|---|---|
| 5AA | Knight, Eugene B. | 5AK | Daly, Thomas J. M. |
| 5AB | Scalco, Joe R. | 5AL | Reboul, Theophile. |
| 5AC | Budwig, Gilbert C. | 5AM | Brownell, Harold S. |
| 5AD | Rorshach, Harold E. | 5AN | Watkins, Will O. |
| 5AE | Jones, Ralph. | 5AO | Buster, John A. |
| 5AF | Meyer, William F. | 5AP | Thompson, Vance. |
| 5AG | Martin, Stanley. | 5AQ | Goldstein, Henry R. |
| 5AH | Martin, Ben W. | 5AR | Beynon, Eugene T. |
| 5AI | Ratcliff, Fred. | 5AS | Bastian, Royal R. |
| 5AJ | Albertson, Clarence E. | 5AT | Vickers, Alwyn. |

## SIXTH DISTRICT.

[Headquarters: Customhouse, San Francisco, Cal. The sixth district comprises the States of California, Nevada, Utah, Arizona, and the Territory of Hawaii.]

ALPHABETICALLY BY OWNERS OF STATIONS.

| Call signal. | Owner of station. | Location of station. | Power. |
|---|---|---|---|
| | | | Watts. |
| 6DS | Adams, Charles C. | 704 East Twenty-first St., Los Angeles, Cal. | 750 |
| 6LD | Anderlini, Louis. | 2012 Keith St., San Francisco, Cal. | 32 |
| 6WA | Anthes, William F., jr. | 230 South Seventh Street, San Jose, Cal. | 20 |
| 6DM | Archer, Robert. | 2912 South Flower St., Los Angeles, Cal. | 30 |
| 6FA | Arnberger, Frank, jr. | 3230 Garfield Ave., Alameda, Cal. | 1,000 |
| 6AA | Aster, Alvin K. | 1814 Alameda Ave., Alameda, Cal. | 500 |
| 6EG | Aten, Arthur B. | 62 Hurlbert St., Pasadena, Cal. | 200 |
| 6BQ | Baer, Charles M. | Cupertino, Cal. | 15 |
| 6MB | Baden, Merle L. | 2637½ Piedmont Ave., Berkeley, Cal. | 1,000 |
| 6ER | Bailey, Cecil. | R. F. D. No. 18, Los Altos, Cal. | 4 |
| 6BN | Ballerini, Melvin. | 419 Randolph St., Napa, Cal. | 50 |

AMATEUR RADIO STATIONS—SIXTH DISTRICT—ALPHABETICALLY BY OWNERS OF STATIONS—Continued.

| Call signal. | Owner of station. | Location of station. | Power. |
|---|---|---|---|
| | | | *Watts.* |
| 6BX | Barrett, Eldridge D | 720 Capp St., San Francisco, Cal | 7 |
| 6DN | Barry, Gilbert | 423 West Twenty-eighth St., Los Angeles, Cal. | 110 |
| 6BY | Barstow, William R | 514 Twenty-third St., Oakland, Cal | ...... |
| 6LB | Barton, Larry J | 19 Crystal Springs Road, San Mateo, Cal | 1,000 |
| 6JD | Battle, James W | 110 West Whiting St., Fullerton, Cal | 1,000 |
| 6BP | Bauer, Roy M | 402 South Jefferson St., Napa, Cal | 35 |
| 6DY | Beaman, David E | 1306 Peralta Ave., Berkeley, Cal | 250 |
| 6EJ | Bean, Arthur E | 1450 Washington St., San Francisco, Cal | 440 |
| 6AJ | Bean, James | 1775 Alameda Ave., San Jose, Cal | 40 |
| 6FU | Bergstrom, Bernard | Turlock, Cal | 1,000 |
| 6LX | Berlin, Latham | 1525 Chestnut St., Alameda, Cal | 495 |
| 6BJ | Berringer, Hall | 6 Arundel Road, Burlingame, Cal | 300 |
| 6WR | Bilger, Anson S | 407 Vernon St., Oakland, Cal | 550 |
| 6SB | Bisson, Charles S | 1734 Channing Way, Berkeley, Cal | 330 |
| 6EO | Blake, Albert W | 1055 Lincoln St., Pasadena, Cal | 60 |
| 6LA | Blockman, Lawrence G | 3260 First St., San Diego, Cal | 500 |
| 6WB | Booth, Wilber | 2229 Ashby Ave., Berkeley, Cal | 770 |
| 6GB | Bowlus, Glen H | Paxton Ave., San Francisco, Cal | 120 |
| 6PB | Bradley, Philip L | 523 Nineteenth Ave., San Francisco, Cal | 500 |
| 6AL | Brandis, Fred A | 214 West San Carlos St., San Jose, Cal | 30 |
| 6ND | Breck, F. B | 285 Mather St., Oakland, Cal | 550 |
| 6FV | Brockett, Charles | 248 Olive St., Los Angeles, Cal | 250 |
| 6JB | Brown, Julian T | 2604 East Second St., Los Angeles, Cal | 500 |
| 6DA | Brown, Ralph E | 837 East Twenty-second St., Los Angeles, Cal. | 250 |
| 6AP | Brown, Victor | 520 Second St., San Jose, Cal | 500 |
| 6RB | Brumter, Ralph | 1214 E St., San Diego, Cal | 218 |
| 6AM | Buckley, Ernest V | 327 Martin Ave., San Jose, Cal | 30 |
| 6FY | Buell, Clarence R | 732 Fifty-sixth St., Oakland, Cal | 110 |
| 6EC | Burnett, Walter | 408 Lake Shore Ave., Los Angeles, Cal | 350 |

AMATEUR RADIO STATIONS—SIXTH DISTRICT—ALPHABETICALLY BY OWNERS OF STATIONS—Continued.

| Call signal. | Owner of station. | Location of station. | Power. |
|---|---|---|---|
| | | | Watts. |
| 6DZ | Caldwell, Duncan K | 427 Crane Ave., Turlock, Cal | 330 |
| 6AC | Capwell, Cebert | Oakland Ave., Oakland, Cal | 270 |
| 6FC | Carey, Francis K | 2116 Thompson St., Los Angeles, Cal | 235 |
| 6AG | Chamberlain, Leon H | 553 Twenty-seventh St., Oakland, Cal | 550 |
| 6JZ | Charters, John E | 2606 East First St., Los Angeles, Cal | 250 |
| 6JC | Chase, John H | 1323 Lemon St., Riverside, Cal | 300 |
| 6EZ | Christie, Edwin | 1052 Cole St., San Francisco, Cal | ...... |
| 6AU | Clark, Paul | 898 South Eighth St., San Jose, Cal | 18 |
| 6DD | Clark, Victor M | 1336 East Colorado St., Pasadena, Cal | 600 |
| 6LC | Comins, Frank L | Main St., Niles, Cal | 500 |
| 6DI | Cookson, Howard A | 465 University Ave., Palo Alto, Cal | 1,000 |
| 6RC | Cook, Ralph | 1221 Oxford St., Berkeley, Cal | 357 |
| 6CY | Cooper, Charles P | 66 Linda Ave., Oakland, Cal | 330 |
| 6CA | Corby, Grant W | 1129 West Sixth St., Los Angeles, Cal | 330 |
| 6WC | Cornish, Warren D | 312 Central Ave., Pacific Grove, Cal | 25 |
| 6HC | Craig, Harold F | 696 Second St., San Pedro, Cal | 330 |
| 6FX | Cross, Fred M | 144 North Beaudry St., Los Angeles, Cal | 500 |
| 6DE | Curtis, Burbank | 832 Linden St., Long Beach, Cal | 250 |
| 6WI | Cusick, William | 2595 Folsom St., San Francisco, Cal | 250 |
| 6MD | Davids, Mark | 958 Grand View, Los Angeles, Cal | 275 |
| 6BS | Davidson, G. E | 419 Sixth St., Richmond, Cal | 250 |
| 6EP | Davis, Elwood | 876 Orange Grove, Pasadena, Cal | 500 |
| 6EF | Dawson, Percy | 133 Delacy St., Pasadena, Cal | 200 |
| 6FD | Deardorf, Francis H | Los Altos, Cal | 12 |
| 6AQ | De La Cruz, George | 706 San Carlos St., San Jose, Cal | 12 |
| 6EN | de Neuf, Emil A | 1538 Russell St., Berkeley, Cal | 30 |
| 6DW | De Wald, Alfred | Felton, Cal | 80 |
| 6HD | Dickow, Henry | 413 Twenty-sixth Ave., San Francisco, Cal. | 500 |
| 6HG | Dilberger, Harold A | 1015 Myrtle St., Oakland, Cal | 220 |
| 6KE | Dogan, Kenneth | 1115 Cole St., San Francisco, Cal | ...... |

AMATEUR RADIO STATIONS—SIXTH DISTRICT—ALPHABETICALLY BY OWNERS OF STATIONS—Continued.

| Call signal. | Owner of station. | Location of station. | Power. |
|---|---|---|---|
| | | | *Watts.* |
| 6AZ | Downing, Alan S | 2510 Fruitvale Ave., Oakland, Cal | 1,000 |
| 6LT | Downs, LaRoy | 108 Pasadena Ave., Pasadena, Cal | 275 |
| 6BV | Drake, Charles | 422 Twenty-second St., Richmond, Cal | 300 |
| 6KD | Dutton, Kingsley | 1447 Salem St., Glendale, Cal | 250 |
| 6HE | Eastling, Harvey | 2659 Folsom St., San Francisco, Cal | 50 |
| 6HY | Ebeling, Hyde S | 444 Delmas St., San Jose, Cal | 18 |
| 6GZ | Edgar, George P | Broadmoor Boulevard, San Leandro, Cal. | 500 |
| 6EK | Eiferle, Chrissie | 3018 Boulevard Ave., Fruitvale, Cal | 15 |
| 6DL | Espe, Oliver E | 4425 South Main St., Los Angeles, Cal | 500 |
| 6RE | Esplen, Elmer R | 425 Hawthorne St., Stockton, Cal | 1,000 |
| 6CZ | Everard, Charles E | 158 Bruce Ave., Pasadena, Cal | 400 |
| 6VF | Falk, Victor H | 64 South Tenth St., San Jose, Cal | 20 |
| 6FB | Farlinger, Ernest | 227 Second St., Richmond, Cal | 495 |
| 6GF | Farmer, Gordon | Haynes, Cal | 50 |
| 6IF | Farwell, Ivyn | 2230 Ninth St., Berkeley, Cal | 250 |
| 6FE | Felt, Clarence J | 1732 Channing Way, Berkeley, Cal | 330 |
| 6ET | Fenner, Paul R | 1338 Masonic Ave., San Francisco, Cal | 42 |
| 6HV | Ferrill, Herbert E | Bostonia, Cal | ..... |
| 6JU | Fisher, Jules | 2213 Carlton St., Berkeley, Cal | 385 |
| 6HF | Flenner, Harry | 1695 Granada St., San Diego, Cal | 500 |
| 6ED | Flinspach, J. Henry | 403 Citrus and Eighth Sts., Redlands, Cal. | 250 |
| 6FO | Fones, Robert | 832 Cleveland St., Oakland, Cal | 1,000 |
| 6WF | Ford, Walter B | 3653 Arnold St., San Diego, Cal | 500 |
| 6JF | Forsburg, Joe A | 1616 Josephine St., Berkeley, Cal | 250 |
| 6FK | Frank, Walter | 465 Eighteenth St., San Diego, Cal | 450 |
| 6FH | French, Donald K | 3027 Capp St., Fruitvale, Cal | 250 |
| 6RS | Frerichs, Roy | Byron, Cal | 1,000 |
| 6RF | Frier, Robert L | 1017 West Seventeenth St., Los Angeles, Cal. | 250 |
| 6BK | Frost, William H | 473 Minor Ave, San Jose, Cal | 20 |

AMATEUR RADIO STATIONS—SIXTH DISTRICT—ALPHABETICALLY BY OWNERS OF STATIONS—Continued.

| Call signal. | Owner of station. | Location of station. | Power. |
|---|---|---|---|
| | | | Watts. |
| 6CX | Frank, Carl G | 1345 Northside Ave., Berkeley, Cal | 250 |
| 6GA | Garratt, Edward D | 1308 Crown Hill St., Los Angeles, Cal | 300 |
| 6JW | Gastman, Henry | 2530 Eunice St., Berkeley, Cal | 990 |
| 6GE | Gerlach, William G | 512 Crofton Ave., Oakland, Cal | 470 |
| 6LG | Gianini, Leo G | 535 Fifth Ave., San Francisco, Cal | 60 |
| 6GG | Gildersleeve, Given | 506 Calistoga Ave., Napa, Cal | 50 |
| 6PG | Gillmore, Purcell | 375 Fair Oaks St., Pasadena, Cal | 200 |
| 6MG | Glindemann, Melvern | 825 Fillmore St., San Francisco, Cal | 495 |
| 6BM | Godwin, Merle H | 19 Grigsby Ct., Napa, Cal | 300 |
| 6GO | Goss, William | 516½ Bath St., Santa Barbara, Cal | 500 |
| 6FG | Granger, Floyd | 305 Phelps St., Redwood, Cal | ...... |
| 6EE | Griffin, Clyde S | Stevison, Cal | ...... |
| 6DH | Grimes, W. Frank | 103 Pasadena St., Pasadena, Cal | 495 |
| 6DP | Grundell, Herbert | 285 Eleventh St., San Pedro, Cal | 2 |
| 6LR | Guenther, Leo H | 309 West Ortega St., Santa Barbara, Cal | 500 |
| 6AN | Guidotti, W. F | 745 West San Fernando St., San Jose, Cal | 115 |
| 6GU | Gurnette, Bernard A | 51 Beaver St., San Francisco, Cal | 330 |
| 6EH | Hall, Edward | 1721 Grove St., Berkeley, Cal | ...... |
| 6TH | Hall, Thomas C | 1278 Market St., San Francisco, Cal | 500 |
| 6MH | Hamilton, Martin E | 821 North Brown St., Napa, Cal | 250 |
| 6VP | Hancock, Hadys D | Venice Pier, Venice, Cal | 1,000 |
| 6FL | Haneuf, Forrest E | 153 Water St., Santa Cruz, Cal | 250 |
| 6CQ | Hanson, Earl C | 2534 Fourth Ave., Los Angeles, Cal | 330 |
| 6RH | Hare, Ralph M | 74 Castro St., San Francisco, Cal | 95 |
| 6CG | Harty, Courtenay E | 1944 Bonsallo Ave., Los Angeles, Cal | 220 |
| 6CH | Haun, John K | 152 East Thirty-sixth St., Los Angeles, Cal. | 330 |
| 6HN | Heinz, Albert | 127 North F St., San Mateo, Cal | 330 |
| 6WD | Hemsley, Will | 430 Twentieth St., San Diego, Cal | 450 |
| 6DB | Henry, Ralph E | 1031 South Bonnie Brae St., Los Angeles, Cal. | 200 |

AMATEUR RADIO STATIONS—SIXTH DISTRICT—ALPHABETICALLY BY OWNERS OF STATIONS—Continued.

| Call signal. | Owner of station. | Location of station. | Power. |
|---|---|---|---|
| | | | *Watts.* |
| 6DC | Hibbard, Charles H., jr. | 156 Bellefontaine St., Pasadena, Cal. | 900 |
| 6WH | Hill, William F. | 2348 G St., San Diego, Cal. | 500 |
| 6CC | Hilleary, Frank J. | 2600 East Second St., Los Angeles, Cal. | 400 |
| 6HZ | Hoffman, Harold | 625 Forest Ave., Pacific Grove, Cal. | ...... |
| 6HH | Hollingsworth, Dale | 804 Beaver St., Santa Rosa, Cal. | ...... |
| 6DQ | Holmes, Joseph J. | 135 Ripley Ave., Richmond, Cal. | 250 |
| 6BU | Hosmer, Merritt R. | San Carlos, Cal. | 25 |
| 6LH | Hunt, Lloyd F. | Fir St., Inglewood, Cal. | 770 |
| 6BW | Hyde, Stanley E. | 403½ South Bonnie Brae St., Los Angeles, Cal. | 330 |
| 6IR | Irey, Earl R. | 3667 Third St., San Diego, Cal. | 250 |
| 6LI | Isaacs, Louis R. | 1200 Regent St., Alameda, Cal. | 1,000 |
| 6JA | Janes, Charles V | 38 Jupiter St., San Francisco, Cal | 32 |
| 6JJ | Jessup, John H. | 2620 Cedar St., Berkeley, Cal. | 250 |
| 6JO | Johnson, Clarence N. | 730 Julian Ave., San Diego, Cal. | 500 |
| 6MJ | Jones, Myron A. | 4190 Forty-first St., San Diego, Cal. | 500 |
| 6RJ | Jones, Russell B. | 1041 Stanyan St., San Francisco, Cal. | 250 |
| 6BL | Kather, Karl E. | 104 Wilson St., Napa, Cal. | 250 |
| 6RK | Kerns, Roy | 229 Russell St., Berkeley, Cal. | 250 |
| 6AH | Kessell, James H. | 551 Willis Ave., San Jose, Cal. | 20 |
| 6CE | Kilto, Carl | 506 Fremont Ave., Los Angeles, Cal. | 400 |
| 6KK | Kincaid, Kenneth | 1604 South Hope St., Los Angeles, Cal. | 250 |
| 6EX | King, William E. | 80 Elgin Park, San Francisco, Cal. | 250 |
| 6CK | Kinsel, Charles M. | 396 Oakland Ave., Oakland, Cal. | 550 |
| 6KI | Kispert, Charles H. | 1748 Quesada Ave., San Francisco, Cal. | ...... |
| 6JK | Klemgard, James G. | 947 Cedar Ave., Long Beach, Cal. | 345 |
| 6AT | Knowles, Raymond | 496 North Fifth St., San Jose, Cal. | 120 |
| 6WK | Koerber, Walter A. | 1099 North Wilson Ave., Los Angeles, Cal. | 660 |
| 6HK | Krauter, Howard R. | 850 West Twenty-third Pl., Los Angeles, Cal. | 1,000 |
| 6PK | Kyes, Percy L. | 617 Eucalyptus Ave., Riverside, Cal. | 500 |

2002°—13——9

AMATEUR RADIO STATIONS—SIXTH DISTRICT—ALPHABETICALLY BY OWNERS OF STATIONS—Continued.

| Call signal. | Owner of station. | Location of station. | Power. |
|---|---|---|---|
| | | | Watts. |
| 6HW | La Barre, Harold J | 64 Colorado St., Pasadena, Cal | 280 |
| 6KL | Laird, Kenneth V | 105 Parkside Drive, Berkeley, Cal | 700 |
| 6CW | Lares, Herman | 1333 East Fifty-seventh St., Los Angeles, Cal. | 50 |
| 6SL | Leach, Stanley P | 2049 Tenth Ave., Oakland, Cal | 495 |
| 6EL | Le Fevre, Eugene | 243 Boniview Ave., San Francisco, Cal | 100 |
| 6WL | Leland, Wallace H | 912 Indian Rock Ave., Berkeley, Cal | 250 |
| 6HL | Linhoff, Harold R | 416 Winona St., Pasadena, Cal | 250 |
| 6LO | Lory, C. S | 3839 Seventh St., San Diego, Cal | 25 |
| 6CP | Lowe, William E | 1300 Garfield Ave., South Pasadena, Cal | 500 |
| 6SF | Mack, Franklin | 541 Pine Ave., Pacific Grove, Cal | 500 |
| 6MX | Magill, Clyde | East Sixth St., Ontario, Cal | 200 |
| 6MN | Maher, Edward T | 3409 Grove St., Oakland, Cal | 250 |
| 6EQ | Maher, Zacheus J | 2211 Hayes St., San Francisco, Cal | 476 |
| 6BR | Manassee, Mervyn H | 618 Franklin St., Napa, Cal | 30 |
| 6HM | Mansfelt, Harold | 2590 Pine St., San Francisco, Cal | ..... |
| 6EM | Marlin, Evan M | Capitola Ave., Capitola, Cal | ..... |
| 6LM | Martinelli, Lloyd | 1512 Shrader St., San Francisco, Cal | 50 |
| 6CU | Maskey, Franklin | 822 East Thirty-third St., Los Angeles, Cal | 30 |
| 6BO | Mattoon, Stanley F | San Carlos, Cal | 30 |
| 6MA | Max, Charles A | Morrill Road, San Jose, Cal | 500 |
| 6CF | McClatchy, Keith | Hawthorne and Ivy Sts., Inglewood, Cal | 1,000 |
| 6PJ | McDonald, Byron C | 85 El Molino St., Pasadena, Cal | 1,000 |
| 6MC | McGown, Dudley B | 1247 Forty-seventh Ave., San Francisco, Cal. | 500 |
| 6HJ | McIntosh, Harold St. J | 249 Bixel St., Los Angeles, Cal | 500 |
| 6MM | McKay, Malcolm | 1635 Grant St., Berkeley, Cal | 50 |
| 6RM | McLaughlin, Richard A | 420 Ffith Ave., San Francisco, Cal | 50 |
| 6FM | McNabb, Floyd R | 1886 Harmon St., Berkeley, Cal | 380 |
| 6GM | McPhail, Graham H | 3 Marin St., San Rafael, Cal | ..... |
| 6MR | McRoberts, Lewis H | 3960 Elm St., San Diego, Cal | 50 |

MATEUR RADIO STATIONS—SIXTH DISTRICT—ALPHABETICALLY BY OWNERS OF STATIONS—Continued.

| ll signal. | Owner of station. | Location of station. | Power. |
|---|---|---|---|
| | | | *Watts.* |
| 6EV | Medaris, Eddie | 334 Pasadena Ave., Pasadena, Cal | 60 |
| 6DJ | Merritt, Lawrence G | 252 Clinton St., Pasadena, Cal | 600 |
| 6JM | Michaels, Joe E | 327 Seventh St., Richmond, Cal | 50 |
| 6MI | Mirsky, Sylvian L | 1834 McAllister St., San Francisco, Cal | 500 |
| 6BE | Mitchell, John C | Mark West, Cal | 42 |
| 6AV | Mocker, De Forest | Capitola, Cal | 30 |
| 6AI | Mooers, Ernest | 155 Ninth St., San Jose, Cal | 1,000 |
| 6BI | Moore, Ezra | 108 Eleventh St., Redlands, Cal | 500 |
| 6MO | Moore, Paul | 116 Berkeley Way, Whittier, Cal | 500 |
| 6FN | Morris, Fred W | 1106 El Molino St., Los Angeles, Cal | 330 |
| 6WM | Morse, Willard A | 416 East Seventh St., Oakland, Cal | 500 |
| 6MU | Murray, Donald W | 70 Eureka St., Pasadena, Cal | 120 |
| 6NN | Nelson, Cyril B | 205 North St., Woodland, Cal | 385 |
| 6NE | Newbould, C. Percy | 351 Twenty-sixth St., San Diego, Cal | ...... |
| 6HQ | Newton, Henry G | Fifth St. and Bay Boulevard, Coronado, Cal. | 80 |
| 6KN | Nicholson, Knox W | 721 Seventeenth St., Oakland, Cal | ...... |
| 6NI | Nilli, Emil | 34 Hester St., San Jose, Cal | 60 |
| 6HA | Niver, Henry A | 618 East Center St., Anaheim, Cal | 660 |
| 6RN | Norton, Russell | 825 First St., Napa, Cal | ...... |
| 6AW | Nosler, Claud E | 228 University St., Healdsburg, Cal | 500 |
| 6BC | Oldham, William G., jr. | 720 Mendocino St., Santa Rosa, Cal | 125 |
| 6HO | Olschefsky, Henry H | 283 Ney St., San Francisco, Cal | 80 |
| 6BZ | O'Neill, Frank M. J | 1423 Oxford St., Berkeley, Cal | 1,000 |
| 6OT | Otto, Harry F | 437 East Main St., Stockton, Cal | 1,000 |
| 6OY | Oyarzo, Ben | 343 Forty-ninth St., Oakland, Cal | 220 |
| 6HP | Pampinella, Harold | 1755 Hayes St., San Francisco, Cal | 50 |
| 6GK | Parkin, Miss Gladys K | 22 Terradillo Ave., San Rafael, Cal | ...... |
| 6PA | Pattison, Alexander | 3881 Telegraph Ave., Oakland, Cal | 15 |
| 6DG | Patton, Nelson | 194 North El Molino Ave., Pasadena, Cal | 330 |
| 6SP | Peck, Sherman | 1033 Cole St., San Francisco, Cal | 20 |

AMATEUR RADIO STATIONS—SIXTH DISTRICT—ALPHABETICALLY BY OWNERS OF STATIONS—Continued.

| Call signal. | Owner of station. | Location of station. | Power. |
|---|---|---|---|
| | | | Watts. |
| 6FP | Peterson, Frank E. | 2815 Virginia St., Berkeley, Cal. | 250 |
| 6CD | Peterson, Walter | 2177 West Twenty-ninth Pl., Los Angeles, Cal. | 440 |
| 6AE | Pinard, Vivian E. | 505 San Salvador St., San Jose, Cal. | 20 |
| 6RP | Pittman, Rey F. | 1001 North Pacific St., Glendale, Cal. | 1,000 |
| 6AO | Portal, Emile | 142 Vine St., San Jose, Cal. | 32 |
| 6GP | Post, George W. | 715½ Lyon St., San Francisco, Cal. | 15 |
| 6CR | Potter, Lee R. | Maple and Spadra Sts., Fullerton, Cal. | 990 |
| 6BF | Powell, Meade W. | Cole Building, Warren, Ariz. | 263 |
| 6PR | Preston, Alva W. | Euclid Ave., Garden Grove, Cal. | ...... |
| 6DV | Prosser, Norman | Linda Vista Road, R. F. D. No. 2, Pasadena, Cal. | 990 |
| 6EB | Richardson, Charles, jr. | 406 West Twenty-eighth Pl., Los Angeles, Cal. | 20 |
| 6EB | Richardson, Charles, jr. | 929 West Fiftieth Pl., Los Angeles, Cal. | 330 |
| 6RI | Richman, Clinton | 541 West Commonwealth St., Fullerton, Cal. | 1,000 |
| 6DU | Rigby, Townsend J., jr. | 2910 South Flower St., Los Angeles, Cal. | 250 |
| 6FR | Rodgers, Frank | 82 Echo St., Oakland, Cal. | ...... |
| 6NK | Roehrig, Russell S. | 501 Oakland Ave., Pasadena, Cal. | 500 |
| 6BT | Rogers, Henry J. | Vacaville, Cal. | 30 |
| 6BD | Rogers, Stuart De Witt | 312 Orange St., Santa Rosa, Cal. | 200 |
| 6GN | Rose, George E. | 105 Grattan St., San Francisco, Cal. | 250 |
| 6RO | Roussin, Cecil | 364 Lincoln St., Pasadena, Cal. | ...... |
| 6HR | Royden, Herbert N., jr. | 311 Ellsworth Ave., San Mateo, Cal. | 1,000 |
| 6GR | Rucker, George A. | 2639 Grant St., Berkeley, Cal. | 500 |
| 6EU | Rumble, Ernest | 114 G St., Napa, Cal. | 250 |
| 6DR | Sandham, Bert E. | 1122 West Fifty-fifth St., Los Angeles, Cal. | 300 |
| 6IS | Sawyer, Irving W. | Capitola, Cal. | ...... |
| 6HS | Schade, Henry | 15 Bennington St., San Francisco, Cal. | 180 |
| 6ES | Schaefer, Carl | 3118 Stillson Ave., Sacramento, Cal. | 550 |

AMATEUR RADIO STATIONS—SIXTH DISTRICT—ALPHABETICALLY BY OWNERS OF STATIONS—Continued.

| Call signal. | Owner of station. | Location of station. | Power. |
|---|---|---|---|
| | | | *Watts.* |
| 6OS | Scheidemantel, Oscar A. | 823 East Twenty-eighth St., Los Angeles, Cal. | 550 |
| 6TS | Schneider, Tony | 424 Twentieth Ave., San Francisco, Cal. | 24 |
| 6WS | Schneider, William P. | 2716 Twenty-second St., Fruitvale, Cal. | 15 |
| 6SC | Schroder, Harold | 666 Fifty-third St., Oakland, Cal. | 250 |
| 6EA | Seefred, Howard C. and Lyndon F. | 339 Fremont Ave., Los Angeles, Cal. | 250 |
| 6CT | Seidel, William E. | 2717 Brighton Ave., Los Angeles, Cal. | 500 |
| 6SH | Shippam, Cecil H. | 3939 I St., San Diego, Cal. | 330 |
| 6FS | Short, Frank A. | 846 Walnut St., Riverside, Cal. | 187 |
| 6JS | Silvershield, Bernhard J | 832 West Ninety-second St., Los Angeles, Cal. | 36 |
| 6AX | Simney, Albert | 300 Joaquin Ave., San Leandro, Cal. | 275 |
| 6SK | Skaale, Arthur J. | Martinez St., Berkeley, Cal. | 250 |
| 6LS | Smelser, Laurel J. | 318 Second St., Napa, Cal. | 500 |
| 6SM | Smith, Hazel P. | 138 Wilshire St., Fullerton, Cal. | 250 |
| 6NC | Smith, Norman E. | 115 I Ave., Coronado, Cal. | 15 |
| 6AS | Soules, Ernest H. | 75 Bush St., San Jose, Cal. | 18 |
| 6OJ | Spencer, Oscar J. | 35 Douglass St., San Francisco, Cal. | 90 |
| 6JR | Stauffer, John | 601 Broderick St., San Francisco, Cal. | 250 |
| 6BB | Stevens, Russell | 617 Johnson St., Healdsburg, Cal. | 300 |
| 6CN | Stock, Reinhold F. | 397 Walnut St., Anaheim, Cal. | 400 |
| 6CO | Storm, Hans O. | 707 West Broadway, Anaheim, Cal. | 495 |
| 6CJ | Stowe, Theodore E. | Forty-first Ave., Capitola, Cal. | 60 |
| 6DO | Strader, William F. | 1021 Tenth St., Sacramento, Cal. | 456 |
| 6GH | Stricker, George H., jr. | 1411 Oxford St., Berkeley, Cal. | 500 |
| 6WG | Strong, William | 721 Petaluma St., San Rafael, Cal. | 1,000 |
| 6SN | Sunderland, Arthur G. | 92 Mary St., Pasadena, Cal. | 990 |
| 6SU | Sutherland, C. | 2334 Ninety-fourth Ave., Oakland, Cal. | 990 |
| 6GS | Swartout, Glenn | 1044 Seventy-seventh St., Los Angeles, Cal. | 500 |

AMATEUR RADIO STATIONS—SIXTH DISTRICT—ALPHABETICALLY BY OWNERS OF STATIONS—Continued.

| Call signal. | Owner of station. | Location of station. | Power. |
|---|---|---|---|
| | | | Watts. |
| 6CV | Swinnerton, Kenneth | 1242 West Fifty-first St., Los Angeles, Cal. | 275 |
| 6HX | Taylor, Howard L. | 394 Fifteenth St., San Pedro, Cal. | 330 |
| 6HT | Thayer, Halsey | 2123 Oak St., Los Angeles, Cal. | 440 |
| 6GT | Timmermann, Gustave | 256 California Ave., San Francisco, Cal. | 160 |
| 6TT | Tournat, Thomas | Garden Grove, Cal. | 250 |
| 6AY | Tuggy, Arthur W. | 1289 Lemon St., Riverside, Cal. | 1,000 |
| 6DT | Underwood, Ernest G. | Commercial St., Inglewood, Cal. | 30 |
| 6HU | Unger, Harry J. | 228 Grattan St., San Francisco, Cal. | 50 |
| 6AB | Valentine, Philip C. | 246 Perry St., Oakland, Cal. | 425 |
| 6GL | Van Auken, George L. | McKee and Jackson Sts., San Jose, Cal. | ...... |
| 6GV | Van Wagner, George | 22 Franklin St., Santa Cruz, Cal. | 990 |
| 6SV | Verney, Stanley S. | 406 Grand Boulevard, San Mateo, Cal. | 216 |
| 6KV | Vesper, Karl C. | 1339 Bay St., Alameda, Cal. | 250 |
| 6DF | Vogeley, Herbert H. | 341 Chestnut St., Long Beach, Cal. | 20 |
| 6BA | Wadsworth, Claude E. | 468 Matheson St., Healdsburg, Cal. | 250 |
| 6CL | Walters, Clarence | 4326 Grand Ave., Los Angeles, Cal. | 350 |
| 6RR | Waterman, Russell R. | 4561 Thirty-eighth St., San Diego, Cal. | 80 |
| 6QW | Waters, John E. | 2002 North Broadway, Santa Ana, Cal. | 1,000 |
| 6WW | Webb, Walter R. | 700 East Forty-seventh St., Los Angeles, Cal. | 50 |
| 6CS | Webber, Franklin | 632 North Bunkerhill St., Los Angeles, Cal. | 450 |
| 6CI | Weber, Anton | 252 West Forty-third St., Los Angeles, Cal. | 350 |
| 6WE | Weddell, Clarence C. | 553 Willis Ave., San Jose, Cal. | 1,000 |
| 6RW | Weisbrod, Raymond H. | 2213 West Fifteenth St., Los Angeles, Cal. | 250 |
| 6OW | Welling, Orville E. | 582 Fifty-eighth St., Oakland, Cal. | 500 |
| 6JE | Welsh, John E. | 55 Eureka St., Pasadena, Cal. | 60 |
| 6EY | Werner, Edward A. | 2313 Ninth St., West Berkeley, Cal. | 1,000 |
| 6GW | Werner, George W., jr. | 3039 Adeline St., Berkeley, Cal. | 250 |
| 6DK | Westcott, Lawrence M. | Eber St., Ocean Beach, Cal. | 50 |
| 6DX | Wheelock, Charles D. | 1235 Lemon St., Los Angeles, Cal. | 65 |

AMATEUR RADIO STATIONS—SIXTH DISTRICT—ALPHABETICALLY BY OWNERS OF STATIONS—Continued.

| Call signal. | Owner of station. | Location of station. | Power. |
|---|---|---|---|
| | | | Watts. |
| 6AF | White, Clarence E. | 3024 Blossom St., Fruitvale, Cal. | 1,000 |
| 6FT | Wiese, Fred T. | 4174 Seventeenth St., San Francisco, Cal. | 500 |
| 6WV | Williams, Creah | 228 East San Carlos St., San Jose, Cal. | 30 |
| 6GX | Williams, George F. | 2700 High St., Oakland, Cal. | 1,000 |
| 6BH | Williamson, Harry | 724 East State St., Redlands, Cal. | 30 |
| 6FW | Wisner, Fred L. | 1352 Thirtieth St., San Diego, Cal. | 50 |
| 6AK | Wright, John W. | 657 Asbury St., San Jose, Cal. | 30 |
| 6EI | Young, Bert C. | 1401 West Ninth St., Los Angeles, Cal. | 550 |
| 6EW | Zahniser, Charles L. | 320 Lexington St., Rust, Cal. | ...... |

ALPHABETICALLY BY CALL SIGNALS.

| Call signal. | Owner of station. |
|---|---|
| 6AA | Aster, Alvin K. |
| 6AB | Valentine, Philip C. |
| 6AC | Capwell, Cebert. |
| 6AE | Pinard, Vivian E. |
| 6AF | White, Clarence E. |
| 6AG | Chamberlain, Leon H. |
| 6AH | Kessell, James H. |
| 6AI | Mooers, Ernest. |
| 6AJ | Bean, James. |
| 6AK | Wright, John W. |
| 6AL | Brandis, Fred A. |
| 6AM | Buckley, Ernest V. |
| 6AN | Guidotti, W. F. |
| 6AO | Portal, Emile. |
| 6AP | Brown, Victor. |
| 6AQ | De La Cruz, George. |
| 6AS | Soules, Ernest H. |
| 6AT | Knowles, Raymond. |
| 6AU | Clark, Paul. |
| 6AV | Mocker, De Forest. |
| 6AW | Nosler, Claud E. |
| 6AX | Simney, Albert. |
| 6AY | Tuggy, Arthur W. |
| 6AZ | Downing, Alan S. |
| 6BA | Wadsworth, Claude E. |
| 6BB | Stevens, Russell. |
| 6BC | Oldham, William G., jr. |
| 6BD | Rogers, Stuart De Witt. |
| 6BE | Mitchell, John C. |
| 6BF | Powell, Meade W. |
| 6BH | Williamson, Harry. |
| 6BI | Moore, Ezra. |
| 6BJ | Berringer, Hall. |
| 6BK | Frost, William H. |
| 6BL | Kather, Karl E. |
| 6BM | Godwin, Merle H. |
| 6BN | Ballerini, Melvin. |
| 6BO | Mattoon, Stanley F. |
| 6BP | Bauer, Roy M. |
| 6BQ | Baer, Charles M. |
| 6BR | Manassee, Mervyn H. |
| 6BS | Davidson, G. E. |
| 6BT | Rogers, Henry J. |
| 6BU | Hosmer, Merritt R. |
| 6BV | Drake, Charles. |
| 6BW | Hyde, Stanley E. |
| 6BX | Barrett, Eldridge D. |
| 6BY | Barstow, William R. |
| 6BZ | O'Neill, Frank M. J. |
| 6CA | Corby, Grant W. |
| 6CC | Hilleary, Frank J. |
| 6CD | Peterson, Walter. |
| 6CE | Kilto, Carl. |
| 6CF | McClatchy, Keith. |
| 6CG | Harty, Courtenay E. |
| 6CH | Haun, John K. |
| 6CI | Weber, Anton. |
| 6CJ | Stowe, Theodore E. |
| 6CK | Kinsel, Charles M. |
| 6CL | Walters, Clarence. |
| 6CN | Stock, Reinhold F. |
| 6CO | Storm, Hans O. |
| 6CP | Lowe, William E. |
| 6CQ | Hanson, Earl C. |
| 6CR | Potter, Lee R. |
| 6CS | Webber, Franklin. |
| 6CT | Seidel, William E. |
| 6CU | Maskey, Franklin. |

AMATEUR RADIO STATIONS—SIXTH DISTRICT—ALPHABETICALLY BY CALL SIGNALS—Continued.

| Call signal. | Owner of station. | Call signal. | Owner of station. |
|---|---|---|---|
| 6CV | Swinnerton, Kenneth. | 6FA | Amberger, Frank, jr. |
| 6CW | Lares, Herman. | 6FB | Farlinger, Ernest. |
| 6CX | Frunk, Carl G. | 6FC | Carey, Francis K. |
| 6CY | Cooper, Charles P. | 6FD | Deardorf, Francis H. |
| 6CZ | Everard, Charles E. | 6FE | Felt, Clarence J. |
| | | 6FG | Granger, Floyd. |
| 6DA | Brown, Ralph E. | 6FH | French, Donald K. |
| 6DB | Henry, Ralph E. | 6FK | Frank, Walter. |
| 6DC | Hibbard, Charles H., jr. | 6FL | Haneuf, Forrest E. |
| 6DD | Clark, Victor M. | 6FM | McNabb, Floyd R. |
| 6DE | Curtis, Burbank. | 6FN | Morris, Fred W. |
| 6DF | Vogeley, Herbert H. | 6FO | Fones, Robert. |
| 6DG | Patton, Nelson. | 6FP | Peterson, Frank E. |
| 6DH | Grimes, W. Frank. | 6FR | Rodgers, Frank. |
| 6DI | Cookson, Howard A. | 6FS | Short, Frank A. |
| 6DJ | Merritt, Lawrence G. | 6FT | Wiese, Fred T. |
| 6DK | Westcott, Lawrence M. | 6FU | Bergstrom, Bernard. |
| 6DL | Espe, Oliver E. | 6FV | Brockett, Charles. |
| 6DM | Archer, Robert. | 6FW | Wisner, Fred L. |
| 6DN | Barry, Gilbert. | 6FX | Cross, Fred M. |
| 6DO | Strader, William F. | 6FY | Buell, Clarence R. |
| 6DP | Grundell, Herbert. | | |
| 6DQ | Holmes, Joseph J. | 6GA | Garratt, Edward D. |
| 6DR | Sandham, Bert E. | 6GB | Bowlus, Glen H. |
| 6DS | Adams, Charles C. | 6GE | Gerlach, William G. |
| 6DT | Underwood, Ernest G. | 6GF | Farmer, Gordon. |
| 6DU | Rigby, Townsend J., jr. | 6GG | Gildersleeve, Given. |
| 6DV | Prosser, Norman. | 6GH | Stricker, George H., jr. |
| 6DW | De Wald, Alfred. | 6GK | Parkin, Miss Gladys K. |
| 6DX | Wheelock, Charles D. | 6GL | Van Auken, George L. |
| 6DY | Beaman, David E. | 6GM | McPhail, Graham H. |
| 6DZ | Caldwell, Duncan K. | 6GN | Rose, George E. |
| | | 6GO | Goss, William. |
| 6EA | Seefred, Howard C. and Lyndon F. | 6GP | Post, George W. |
| | | 6GR | Rucker, George A. |
| 6EB | Richardson, Charles, jr. | 6GS | Swartout, Glenn. |
| 6EC | Burnett, Walter. | 6GT | Timmermann, Gustave. |
| 6ED | Flinspach, J. Henry. | 6GU | Gurnette, Bernard A. |
| 6EE | Griffin, Clyde S. | 6GV | Van Wagner, George. |
| 6EF | Dawson, Percy. | 6GW | Werner, George W., jr. |
| 6EG | Aten, Arthur B. | 6GX | Williams, George F. |
| 6EH | Hall, Edward. | 6GZ | Edgar, George P. |
| 6EI | Young, Bert C. | | |
| 6EJ | Bean, Arthur E. | 6HA | Niver, Henry A. |
| 6EK | Eiferle, Chrissie. | 6HC | Craig, Harold F. |
| 6EL | Le Fevre, Eugene. | 6HD | Dickow, Henry. |
| 6EM | Marlin, Evan M. | 6HE | Eastling, Harvey. |
| 6EN | de Neuf, Emil A. | 6HF | Flenner, Harry. |
| 6EO | Blake, Albert W. | 6HG | Dilberger, Harold A. |
| 6EP | Davis, Elwood. | 6HH | Hollingsworth, Dale. |
| 6EQ | Maher, Zacheus J. | 6HJ | McIntosh, Harold St. J. |
| 6ER | Bailey, Cecil. | 6HK | Krauter, Howard R. |
| 6ES | Schaefer, Carl. | 6HL | Linhoff, Harold R. |
| 6ET | Fenner, Paul R. | 6HM | Mansfelt, Harold. |
| 6EU | Rumble, Ernest. | 6HN | Heinz, Albert. |
| 6EV | Medaris, Eddie. | 6HO | Olschefsky, Henry H. |
| 6EW | Zahniser, Charles L. | 6HP | Pampinella, Harold. |
| 6EX | King, William F. | 6HQ | Newton, Henry G. |
| 6EY | Werner, Edward A. | 6HR | Royden, Herbert N., jr. |
| 6EZ | Christie, Edwin. | 6HS | Schade, Henry. |

AMATEUR RADIO STATIONS—SIXTH DISTRICT—ALPHABETICALLY BY CALL SIGNALS—Continued.

| Call signal. | Owner of station. | Call signal. | Owner of station. |
|---|---|---|---|
| 6HT | Thayer, Halsey. | 6MO | Moore, Paul. |
| 6HU | Unger, Harry J. | 6MR | McRoberts, Lewis H. |
| 6HV | Ferrill, Herbert E. | 6MU | Murray, Donald W. |
| 6HW | La Barre, Harold J. | 6MX | Magill, Clyde. |
| 6HX | Taylor, Howard L. | | |
| 6HY | Ebeling, Hyde S. | 6NC | Smith, Norman E. |
| 6HZ | Hoffman, Harold. | 6ND | Breck, F. B. |
| | | 6NE | Newbould, C. Percy. |
| 6IF | Farwell, Ivyn. | 6NI | Nilli, Emil. |
| 6IR | Irey, Earl R. | 6NK | Roehrig, Russell S. |
| 6IS | Sawyer, Irving W. | 6NN | Nelson, Cyril B. |
| | | | |
| 6JA | Janes, Charles V. | 6OJ | Spencer, Oscar J. |
| 6JB | Brown, Julian T. | 6OS | Scheidemantel, Oscar A. |
| 6JC | Chase, John H. | 6OT | Otto, Harry F. |
| 6JD | Battle, James W. | 6OW | Welling, Orville E. |
| 6JE | Welsh, John E. | 6OY | Oyarzo, Ben. |
| 6JF | Forsburg, Joe A. | | |
| 6JJ | Jessup, John H. | 6PA | Pattison, Alexander. |
| 6JK | Klemgard, James G. | 6PB | Bradley, Philip L. |
| 6JM | Michaels, Joe E. | 6PG | Gillmore, Purcell. |
| 6JO | Johnson, Clarence N. | 6PJ | McDonald, Byron C. |
| 6JR | Stauffer, John. | 6PK | Kyes, Percy L. |
| 6JS | Silvershield, Bernhard J. | 6PR | Preston, Alva W. |
| 6JU | Fisher, Jules. | | |
| 6JW | Gastman, Henry. | 6QW | Waters, John E. |
| 6JZ | Charters, John E. | | |
| | | 6RB | Brumter, Ralph. |
| 6KD | Dutton, Kingsley. | 6RC | Cook, Ralph. |
| 6KE | Dogan, Kenneth. | 6RE | Esplen, Elmer R. |
| 6KI | Kispert, Charles H. | 6RF | Frier, Robert L. |
| 6KK | Kincaid, Kenneth. | 6RH | Hare, Ralph M. |
| 6KL | Laird, Kenneth V. | 6RI | Richman, Clinton. |
| 6KN | Nicholson, Knox W. | 6RJ | Jones, Russell B. |
| 6KV | Vesper, Karl C. | 6RK | Kerns, Roy. |
| | | 6RM | McLaughlin, Richard A. |
| 6LA | Blockman, Lawrence G. | 6RN | Norton, Russell. |
| 6LB | Barton, Larry J. | 6RO | Roussin, Cecil. |
| 6LC | Comins, Frank L. | 6RP | Pittman, Roy F. |
| 6LD | Anderlini, Louis. | 6RR | Waterman, Russell R. |
| 6LG | Gianini, Leo G. | 6RS | Frerichs, Roy. |
| 6LH | Hunt, Lloyd F. | 6RW | Weisbrod, Raymond H. |
| 6LI | Isaacs, Louis R. | | |
| 6LM | Martinelli, Lloyd. | 6SB | Bisson, Charles S. |
| 6LO | Lory, C. S. | 6SC | Schroder, Harold. |
| 6LR | Guenther, Leo H. | 6SF | Mack, Franklin. |
| 6LS | Smelser, Laurel J. | 6SH | Shippam, Cecil H. |
| 6LT | Downs, LaRoy. | 6SK | Skaale, Arthur J. |
| 6LX | Berlin, Latham. | 6SL | Leach, Stanley P. |
| | | 6SM | Smith, Hazel P. |
| 6MA | Max, Charles A. | 6SN | Sunderland, Arthur G. |
| 6MB | Baden, Merle L. | 6SP | Peck, Sherman. |
| 6MC | McGown, Dudley B. | 6SU | Sutherland, C. |
| 6MD | Davids, Mark. | 6SV | Verney, Stanley S. |
| 6MG | Glindemann, Melvern. | | |
| 6MH | Hamilton, Martin E. | 6TH | Hall, Thomas C. |
| 6MI | Mirsky, Sylvian L. | 6TS | Schneider, Tony. |
| 6MJ | Jones, Myron A. | 6TT | Tournat, Thomas. |
| 6MM | McKay, Malcolm. | | |
| 6MN | Maher, Edward T. | 6VF | Falk, Victor H. |
| | | 6VP | Hancock, Hadys D. |

AMATEUR RADIO STATIONS—SIXTH DISTRICT—ALPHABETICALLY BY CALL SIGNALS—Continued.

| Call signal. | Owner of station. | Call signal. | Owner of station. |
|---|---|---|---|
| 6WA | Anthes, William F., jr. | 6WI | Cusick, William. |
| 6WB | Booth, Wilber. | 6WK | Koerber, Walter A. |
| 6WC | Cornish, Warren D. | 6WL | Leland, Wallace H. |
| 6WD | Hemsley, Will. | 6WM | Morse, Willard A. |
| 6WE | Weddell, Clarence C. | 6WR | Bigler, Anson S. |
| 6WF | Ford, Walter B. | 6WS | Schneider, William P. |
| 6WG | Strong, William. | 6WV | Williams, Creah. |
| 6WH | Hill, William F. | 6WW | Webb, Walter R. |

## SEVENTH DISTRICT.

[Headquarters: Customhouse, Seattle, Wash. The seventh district comprises the States of Oregon, Washington, Idaho, Montana, Wyoming, and the Territory of Alaska.]

ALPHABETICALLY BY OWNERS OF STATIONS.

| Call signal. | Owner of station. | Location of station. | Power. |
|---|---|---|---|
| | | | Watts. |
| 7AB | Anderson, Alfred S. | 1253 Grand St., Astoria, Oreg. | ...... |
| 7CB | Bennett, Cecil H. | Rainier, Oreg. | 500 |
| 7JB | Blanchet, James J. | 5263 East Sixty-ninth St., Portland, Oreg. | 22[illegible] |
| 7GB | Butterfield, George H. | 815 Kearney St., Portland, Oreg. | 30[illegible] |
| 7JC | Colesworthy, Joseph B. | 112 East High St., Pendleton, Oreg. | 1,000 |
| 7FC | Colt, Fayette E. | 637 Pearson St., Walla Walla, Wash. | 220 |
| 7LC | Connell, Lorne L. | Cherry St., Sumas, Wash. | 250 |
| 7AC | Dailey, Arthur C. | 3915 Colby St., Everett, Wash. | 550 |
| 7HD | Davis, Hubert A. | 1904 Canoe Pl., Seattle, Wash. | 500 |
| 7AD | Douglas, Alfred E. | 804 E and Eighth Sts., Grants Pass, Oreg. | 1,000 |
| 7ME | Elliott, Morton W. | 635 Atlantic St., Dillon, Mont. | 250 |
| 7CF | Farrar, Clyde | 311 Wimer St., Ashland, Oreg. | ...... |
| 7JF | Folen, Jonas H. | 1021 Mississippi Ave., Portland, Oreg. | 775 |
| 7MG | Gable, Martin | Fifth and Nelson Sts., Sedro Woolley, Wash. | 300 |
| 7CG | Gillespie, Charles R. | Kalama, Wash. | 75 |
| 7WG | Goetchius, Walter L. | Eighth and Sycamore Sts., Pullman, Wash. | 840 |
| 7RO | Grant, Robert E. | 1317 Fort St., Boise, Idaho. | 500 |
| 7TH | Hakanson, Thor | 126 West Forty-ninth St., Seattle, Wash. | ...... |
| 7AL | Hansen, Arnold | Sumas, Wash. | 900 |

AMATEUR RADIO STATIONS—SEVENTH DISTRICT—ALPHABETICALLY BY OWNERS OF STATIONS—Continued.

| Call signal. | Owner of station. | Location of station. | Power. |
|---|---|---|---|
| | | | *Watts.* |
| 7CH | Hansen, Carl L. | 5415 Sixth Ave. NW., Seattle, Wash. | 495 |
| 7GC | Henny, George C. | 530 Heights Terrace, Portland, Oreg. | 32 |
| 7GH | Hess, George F. | 1604 Van Buren St., Corvallis, Oreg. | 330 |
| 7JH | Holt, John M., jr. | 749 Grand Ave., Astoria, Oreg. | 500 |
| 7DJ | John, D. Morris. | 745 North Ninth St., Corvallis, Oreg. | ...... |
| 7GJ | Johnson, Gale H. | 124 Queen Ann Ave., Seattle, Wash. | 620 |
| 7JJ | Johnson, Joseph E. | 2716 Grand St., Everett, Wash. | 495 |
| 7HJ | Jones, Henry L. | 1111 East Cherry St., Seattle, Wash. | 250 |
| 7PK | Kemp, Philip. | 1747 West Fifty-eighth St., Seattle, Wash. | 250 |
| 7AK | Koester, Alpha M. | North Powder, Oreg. | 450 |
| 7EL | La Pine, Earl. | 4217 Second Ave. NW., Seattle, Wash. | 55 |
| 7FW | Lee, Emery H. I. | 1412 Summit Ave., Seattle, Wash. | 550 |
| 7LL | Lennard, Lloyd P. | 1035 East Harrison St., Portland, Oreg. | 250 |
| 7WL | Lester, Warren C. | Warrenton, Oreg. | 1,000 |
| 7EH | Lynch, Edward H. | 2527 Baker St., Astoria, Oreg. | ...... |
| 7AM | Meehan, Andrew. | Sumas, Wash. | 480 |
| 7JO | Methven, John H. | Ronald-by-Roslyn, Wash. | 12 |
| 7MH | Middlekauff, Mark H. | North Twenty-seventh St., Corvallis, Oreg. | ...... |
| 7DM | Minkler, Darrell. | 240 C St., Ashland, Oreg. | 495 |
| 7MI | Minter, John W. | 610 East Nineteenth St., Cheyenne, Wyo. | 1,000 |
| 7WM | Moses, William. | Ronald, Wash. | 12 |
| 7JM | McIlhain, John A., jr. | 118 Nob Hill Ave., Seattle, Wash. | 350 |
| 7LN | Nagle, Leo W. | 1109 Washington St., Vancouver, Wash. | 1,000 |
| 7IN | Nelson, Ivan L. | 1003 North Twelfth St., Boise, Idaho. | 495 |
| 7SN | Norman, Stacy W. | 137 North Seventy-ninth St., Seattle, Wash. | 500 |
| 7IO | O'Donoughue, Ivan. | 355 Almond St., Ashland, Oreg. | 50 |
| 7EP | Peterson, Edward T. | 718 East Ash St., Portland, Oreg. | 90 |
| 7HP | Pyle, Howard S. | 3311 South Thirty-seventh Ave., Seattle, Wash. | ...... |
| 7PR | Robinson, Philip F. | 890 Clackamas St., Portland, Oreg. | 110 |

AMATEUR RADIO STATIONS—SEVENTH DISTRICT—ALPHABETICALLY BY OWNERS OF STATIONS—Continued.

| Call signal. | Owner of station. | Location of station. | Pow |
|---|---|---|---|
| | | | Wat |
| 7WR | Rogers, Wilber L. | 2304 Monroe St., Corvallis, Oreg. | .... |
| 7LR | Ross, Lindsley W. | 590 Main St., Portland, Oreg. | 50 |
| 7ES | Schurch, Edward C. | Deer Lodge, Mont. | 1,00 |
| 7AA | Skyles, Theron G. | 522 Eleventh St., Astoria, Oreg. | 7 |
| 7HS | Slocum, Herbert R. | 47 East Ninth St. South, Portland, Oreg. | 30 |
| 7VS | Small, Vincent. | 2322 Wetmore St., Everett, Wash. | 95 |
| 7WS | Sparrow, William I. | 932 West Sixty-third St., Seattle, Wash. | 55 |
| 7CA | Spork, Carl. | 2418 Pine St., Everett, Wash. | ..... |
| 7GG | Stamey, Grady G. | Second Ave., Sumas, Wash. | 45 |
| 7GS | Sturley, G. W. F., jr. | Vancouver Barracks, Vancouver, Wash. | 18 |
| 7CS | Suyder, Claude E. | Fort Flagler, Wash. | 55 |
| 7GW | Wilson, George D. | 1022 Heron St., Aberdeen, Wash. | 500 |
| 7JW | Wilson, John C. | 295 North Twenty-fourth St., Portland, Oreg. | 50 |
| 7HW | Winningham, Harold. | 3701 North Eighteenth St., Tacoma, Wash. | ..... |

ALPHABETICALLY BY CALL SIGNALS.

| Call signal. | Owner of station. |
|---|---|
| 7AA | Skyles, Theron G. |
| 7AB | Anderson, Alfred S. |
| 7AC | Dailey, Arthur C. |
| 7AD | Douglas, Alfred E. |
| 7AK | Koester, Alpha M. |
| 7AL | Hansen, Arnold. |
| 7AM | Meehan, Andrew. |
| 7CA | Spork, Carl. |
| 7CB | Bennett, Cecil H. |
| 7CF | Farrar, Clyde. |
| 7CG | Gillespie, Charles R. |
| 7CH | Hansen, Carl L. |
| 7CS | Suyder, Claude E. |
| 7DJ | John, D. Morris. |
| 7DM | Minkler, Darrell. |
| 7EH | Lynch, Edward H. |
| 7EL | La Pine, Earl. |
| 7EP | Peterson, Edward T. |
| 7ES | Schurch, Edward C. |
| 7FC | Colt, Fayette E. |
| 7FW | Lee, Emery H. I. |
| 7GB | Butterfield, George H. |
| 7GC | Henny, George C. |
| 7GG | Stamey, Grady G. |
| 7GH | Hess, George F. |
| 7GJ | Johnson, Gale H. |
| 7GS | Sturley, G. W. F., jr. |
| 7GW | Wilson, George D. |
| 7HD | Davis, Hubert A. |
| 7HJ | Jones, Henry L. |
| 7HP | Pyle, Howard S. |
| 7HS | Slocum, Herbert R. |
| 7HW | Winningham, Harold. |
| 7IN | Nelson, Ivan L. |
| 7IO | O'Donoughue, Ivan. |
| 7JB | Blanchet, James J. |
| 7JC | Colesworthy, Joseph B. |
| 7JF | Folen, Jonas H. |

[AM]ATEUR RADIO STATIONS—SEVENTH DISTRICT—ALPHABETICALLY BY CALL SIGNALS—Continued.

| [Call] signal. | Owner of station. | Call signal. | Owner of station. |
|---|---|---|---|
| [7]JH | Holt, John M., jr. | 7PK | Kemp, Philip. |
| [7]JJ | Johnson, Joseph E. | 7PR | Robinson, Philip F. |
| [7]JM | McIhain, John A., jr. | | |
| [7]JO | Methven, John H. | 7RO | Grant, Robert E. |
| [7]JW | Wilson, John C. | | |
| | | 7SN | Norman, Stacy W. |
| [7]LC | Connell, Lorne L. | | |
| [7]LL | Lennard, Lloyd P. | 7TH | Hakanson, Thor. |
| [7]LN | Nagle, Leo W. | | |
| [7]LR | Ross, Lindsley W. | 7VS | Small, Vincent. |
| | | 7WG | Goetchius, Walter L. |
| 7ME | Elliott, Morton W. | 7WL | Lester, Warren C. |
| 7MG | Gable, Martin. | 7WM | Moses, William. |
| 7MH | Middlekauff, Mark H. | 7WR | Rogers, Wilber L. |
| 7MI | Minter, John W. | 7WS | Sparrow, William I. |

## EIGHTH DISTRICT.

[H]eadquarters: Customhouse, Cleveland, Ohio. The eighth district comprises the States of New York [(]all counties not included in second district), Pennsylvania (all counties not included in third district), West Virginia, Ohio, Michigan (Lower Peninsula).]

ALPHABETICALLY BY OWNERS OF STATIONS.

| [Ca]ll signal. | Owner of station. | Location of station. | Power. |
|---|---|---|---|
| | | | *Watts.* |
| 8CE | Adler, Jerome | 5550 Avondale Ave., Pittsburgh, Pa. | 275 |
| 8BU | Allonier, Howard R. | 1045 Sunset Ave., Cincinnati, Ohio | 550 |
| 8AA | Anderson, Sidney E. | 1320 Fourteenth St., Detroit, Mich. | 250 |
| 8CJ | Andrews, William S. | 907 Mellon St., Pittsburgh, Pa. | 250 |
| 8DW | Apger, Charles O. | 520 Sixteenth St., Detroit, Mich. | 20 |
| 8JL | Appleton, Francis W. | 12 Kanada St., Detroit, Mich. | 220 |
| 8CP | Baker, Norman E. | 638 Junction Ave., Detroit, Mich. | 12 |
| 8DI | Barton, Charles E. | 155 Harmon Ave., Detroit, Mich. | 250 |
| 8AC | Becelaere, Lawrence | 400 Dix Ave., Detroit, Mich. | 250 |
| 8AE | Berndt, William F. | 608 Clark Ave., Detroit, Mich. | 27 |
| 8CQ | Brede, Erwin F. | 55 Melbourne Ave., Detroit, Mich. | 220 |
| 8DG | Bremer, Edmund | 301 Forest Ave., Detroit, Mich. | 182 |
| 8AD | Broome, Donald | 100 Grand Ave., Mt. Clements, Mich. | 770 |
| 8DM | Bruns, Carl H. | 1316 Ontario St., Toledo, Ohio | 30 |
| 8ED | Carver, Alfred J. | 4 Warring Ave., Buffalo, N. Y. | 20 |
| 8AJ | Claugh, Bert E. | 186 North Washington Ave., Battle Creek, Mich. | 1,000 |

AMATEUR RADIO STATIONS—EIGHTH DISTRICT—ALPHABETICALLY BY OWNERS OF STATIONS—Continued.

| Call signal. | Owner of station. | Location of station. | Power. |
|---|---|---|---|
| | | | Watts. |
| 8DV | Cobb, Rupert | 17 East Alexandrine Ave., Detroit, Mich. | 50 |
| 8EE | Coleman, Clarence E | 47 Yale St., Buffalo, N, Y | 770 |
| 8CR | Cook, Wilbur E | 552 Ferdinand Ave., Detroit, Mich | 24 |
| 8AM | Cornell, Merle H | Lake St., Ripley, N. Y | 150 |
| 8AN | Davis, Frank | 73 Dakota Ave., Columbus, Ohio | 1,000 |
| 8AP | Dorsch, George | 1338 Walnut St., Cincinnati, Ohio | 550 |
| 8EF | Dorst, Edward | 39 Eaton St., Buffalo, N. Y | 18 |
| 8DU | Downing, Harry E | 2308 East Fifty-seventh St., Cleveland, Ohio. | 20 |
| 8EC | Dunn, Frank L | 23 West Eleventh St., Erie, Pa | 1,000 |
| 8AR | Ela, Edward C | 1320 Woodland Ave., Pittsburgh, Pa | 270 |
| 8AS | Feightner, Amos E | 715 South Broadway, Lima, Ohio | 220 |
| 8DB | Fellows, Bernard D | 67 Park St., Pontiac, Mich | 150 |
| 8AT | France, William | 829 Western St., Pittsburgh, Pa | 500 |
| 8AU | Frost, Harry E | 1048 Genesee St., Buffalo, N. Y | 990 |
| 8AV | Fullwood, William R | 1017 Pollock Ave., New Castle, Pa | 500 |
| 8BV | Gale, Roy H | 1806 Brewster St., Cleveland, Ohio | 50 |
| 8EG | Gebhard, Louis A | 1127 Ellicott St., Buffalo, N. Y | 550 |
| 8AX | Gentzsch, Leonard H | 109 Northampton St., Buffalo, N. Y | 200 |
| 8AY | Grosse, Frederick W | 1326 Walnut St., Cincinnati, Ohio | 500 |
| 8EH | Grove, Nelson B | 242 Ashland Ave., Buffalo, N. Y | 60 |
| 8AZ | Hansen, Edmund H | Dier St., Plymouth, Mich | 950 |
| 8BW | Herman, Harold | 2237 Frances Lane, Cincinnati, Ohio | 35 |
| 8BB | Higbee, Glenn A | 1047 Monroe Ave., Detroit, Mich | 250 |
| 8BD | Hoch, Ellery T | R. F. D. No. 33, Barberton, Ohio | 48 |
| 8DR | Holmes, Charles E | 310 Brown St., Grand Rapids, Mich | 490 |
| 8BC | Holt, Nelson E | 185 Congress St., Buffalo, N. Y | 825 |
| 8JN | Howes, Stanley L | 515 Eleanor St., Kalamazoo, Mich | 550 |
| 8CS | Howland, Dean W | 1081 Cass Ave., Detroit Mich | 330 |
| 8BX | Hubbell, Aaron W | 3458 Hallwood Pl., Cincinnati, Ohio | 600 |
| 8CF | Hull, Guy McC | 123 South Whitfield St., Pittsburgh, Pa | 50 |

AMATEUR RADIO STATIONS—EIGHTH DISTRICT—ALPHABETICALLY BY OWNERS OF STATIONS—Continued.

| Call signal. | Owner of station. | Location of station. | Power. |
|---|---|---|---|
| | | | *Watts.* |
| 8CG | Hull, Ralph | 5819 Rural St., Pittsburgh, Pa | 550 |
| 8BF | Jarvis, Roy B | 647 Main St., Wheeling, W. Va | 250 |
| 8BG | Kastenberg, Paul | 298 Hurlbut Ave., Detroit, Mich | 30 |
| 8CC | Kesel, George | 2704 Wylie Ave., Pittsburgh, Pa | 440 |
| 8DN | Knappen, Bert | 4 Trankla Ave., Grand Rapids, Mich | 12 |
| 8EJ | Kolb, Edwin H | 18 Camp St., Buffalo, N. Y | 660 |
| 8CT | Kreinbring, Walter F | 924 Forest Ave., Detroit, Mich | 36 |
| 8BI | Kroeger, Gustav | 1837 Clarion Ave., Cincinnati, Ohio | 330 |
| 8EK | Kumpf, Elmer H | 26 Wohlers Ave., Buffalo, N. Y | 675 |
| 8DP | Lane, John C | Broad St., Holly, Mich | 275 |
| 8EL | Langenbach, Leo | 186 Riley St., Buffalo, N. Y | 30 |
| 8BK | Lapp, E. Robert | 5520 Baywood St., Pittsburgh, Pa | 240 |
| 8BL | Leyh, Edward L | 10 Overhill St., Pittsburgh, Pa | 60 |
| 8BE | Lippert, John P | 41 Stanwood Road, East Cleveland, Ohio | 275 |
| 8JO | Little, Donald G | 415 Woodward Ave., Kalamazoo, Mich | 805 |
| 8CZ | London, Henry | 267 Palmer St., Grand Rapids, Mich | 90 |
| 8BN | Lovejoy, Julian | 3325 Perkins Ave., Cincinnati, Ohio | 40 |
| 8BM | Lueschen, C. D. G | 110 Roehrer Ave., Buffalo, N. Y | 15 |
| 8BO | Lyons, Henry E | Main and Cemetery Sts., Ripley, N. Y | 60 |
| 8EA | Mack, Clifford J | 49 McGovern Ave., Ashtabula, Ohio | 770 |
| 8BQ | Menges, William E | 6428 Aurelia St., Pittsburgh, Pa | 275 |
| 8BR | Miner, Simeon | 2253 East Jefferson Ave., Detroit, Mich | 21 |
| 8BS | Mogridge, Clarence J | 463 Sixteenth St., Detroit, Mich | 1,000 |
| 8DS | Moynahan, Roy D | 355 East Warren Ave., Detroit, Mich | 400 |
| 8EB | Munsell, Robert S | 191 Center St., Ashtabula, Ohio | 330 |
| 8EM | Murphy, John V | 98 St. James Pl., Buffalo, N. Y | 24 |
| 8BT | Ogle, Harry B | 2530 East Boulevard, Cleveland, Ohio | 375 |
| 8DF | Orrell, Robert W | 87 Frederick Ave., Detroit, Mich | 500 |
| 8CW | Osborn, Burr K | 59 Delaware Ave., Detroit, Mich | 960 |
| 8DY | Pancoast, Donald F | 107 Prospect St., Ashtabula, Ohio | 1,000 |

AMATEUR RADIO STATIONS—EIGHTH DISTRICT—ALPHABETICALLY BY OWNERS OF STATIONS—Continued.

| Call signal. | Owner of station. | Location of station. | Power. |
|---|---|---|---|
| | | | Watts. |
| 8CH | Paul, James T. | 628 North Euclid Ave., Pittsburgh, Pa. | 80 |
| 8DJ | Phillips, Glenn | 380 Dix Ave., Detroit, Mich. | 16 |
| 8CX | Phippeny, Forrest J. | R. F. D. No. 4, Battle Creek, Mich. | 30 |
| 8DX | Porter, Harry T. | 714 Main St., Conneaut, Ohio | 900 |
| 8DA | Rathbun, Hugh T. | 112 Colfax St. NE., Grand Rapids, Mich. | 50 |
| 8DC | Reb, Frank | 1635 Gratiot Ave., Detroit, Mich. | 990 |
| 8CI | Richards, Theodore D. | 934 West North Ave., Pittsburgh, Pa. | 605 |
| 8DT | Rogers, Grant | 1297 West One hundred and fourteenth St., Cleveland, Ohio. | 525 |
| 8CD | Sachs, Gus | 1522 Center St., Pittsburgh, Pa. | 275 |
| 8JM | Saunders, Norman W. | 21 Bushey St., Detroit, Mich. | 220 |
| 8BY | Schwindt, Herman J. | 3517 Bevis Ave., Cincinnati, Ohio | 66 |
| 8EN | Shepard, Charles A. | 186 Grant St., Buffalo, N. Y. | 12 |
| 8CN | Sheppard, Hamilton W. | 6420 Darlington Road, Pittsburgh, Pa. | 250 |
| 8CO | Sherrill, Alvin C. | 816 North Euclid Ave., Pittsburgh, Pa. | 440 |
| 8BZ | Shumard, Asbury | 5609 Tompkins Ave., Cincinnati, Ohio | 680 |
| 8DL | Sisson, William A. | 1024 Erie St., Toledo, Ohio | 30 |
| 8CU | Smith, Arthur R. | 721 Hubbard Ave., Detroit, Mich. | 250 |
| 8CL | Smith, G. C. | 335 Atwood St., Pittsburgh, Pa. | 250 |
| 8CV | Smith, Lewis A. | 55 Brandon Ave., Detroit, Mich. | 35 |
| 8CK | Smith, Roland C. | 5814 Hays St., Pittsburgh, Pa. | 302 |
| 8EO | Stickney, Richard W. | 94 Normal Ave., Buffalo, N. Y. | 25 |
| 8CA | Stueve, Everett S. | 3540 Wabash Ave., Cincinnati, Ohio | 330 |
| 8CB | Thiessen, H. F. W. | 161 East McMicken Ave., Cincinnati, Ohio. | 590 |
| 8CM | Thorn, Thomas H. | 1217 Chislett St., Pittsburgh, Pa. | 225 |
| 8DK | Whitmoyer, Ralph | 190 Frederick Ave., Detroit, Mich. | 190 |
| 8DZ | Williams, Homer | 28 Auburn Ave., Ashtabula, Ohio | 12 |
| 8DQ | Wood, Corlan E. | Walnut St., Allegan, Mich. | 550 |
| 8DO | Wright, Claude B. | 822 Michigan St., Petoskey, Mich. | 250 |

Amateur Radio Stations—Eighth District—Continued.

ALPHABETICALLY BY CALL SIGNALS.

| Call signal. | Owner of station. | Call signal. | Owner of station. |
|---|---|---|---|
| 8AA | Anderson, Sidney E. | 8CP | Baker, Norman E. |
| 8AC | Becelaere, Lawrence. | 8CQ | Brede, Erwin F. |
| 8AD | Broome, Donald. | 8CR | Cook, Wilbur E. |
| 8AE | Berndt, William F. | 8CS | Howland, Dean W. |
| 8AJ | Claugh, Bert E. | 8CT | Kreinbring, Walter F. |
| 8AM | Cornell, Merle H. | 8CU | Smith, Arthur R. |
| 8AN | Davis, Frank. | 8CV | Smith, Lewis A. |
| 8AP | Dorsch, George. | 8CW | Osborn, Burr K. |
| 8AR | Ela, Edward C. | 8CX | Phippeny, Forrest J. |
| 8AS | Feightner, Amos E. | 8CZ | London, Henry. |
| 8AT | France, William. | | |
| 8AU | Frost, Harry E. | 8DA | Rathbun, Hugh T. |
| 8AV | Fullwood, William R. | 8DB | Fellows, Bernard D. |
| 8AX | Gentzsch, Leonard H. | 8DC | Reb, Frank. |
| 8AY | Grosse, Frederick W. | 8DF | Orrell, Robert W. |
| 8AZ | Hansen, Edmund H. | 8DG | Bremer, Edmund. |
| | | 8DI | Barton, Charles E. |
| 8BB | Higbee, Glenn A. | 8DJ | Phillips, Glenn. |
| 8BC | Holt, Nelson E. | 8DK | Whitmoyer, Ralph. |
| 8BD | Hoch, Ellery T. | 8DL | Sisson, William A. |
| 8BE | Lippert, John P. | 8DM | Bruns, Carl H. |
| 8BF | Jarvis, Roy. | 8DN | Knappen, Bert. |
| 8BG | Kastenberg, Paul. | 8DO | Wright, Claude B. |
| 8BI | Kroeger, Gustav. | 8DP | Lane, John C. |
| 8BK | Lapp, Robert E. | 8DQ | Wood, Corlan C. |
| 8BL | Leyh, Edward L. | 8DR | Holmes, Charles E. |
| 8BM | Lueschen, C. D. G. | 8DS | Moynahan, Roy D. |
| 8BN | Lovejoy, Julian. | 8DT | Rogers, Grant. |
| 8BO | Lyons, Henry E. | 8DU | Downing, Harry E. |
| 8BQ | Menges, William E. | 8DV | Cobb, Rupert. |
| 8BR | Miner, Simeon. | 8DW | Apger, Charles O. |
| 8BS | Mogridge, Clarence J. | 8DX | Porter, Harry T. |
| 8BT | Ogle, Harry B. | 8DY | Pancoast, Donald F. |
| 8BU | Allonier, Howard R. | 8DZ | Williams, Homer. |
| 8BV | Gale, Roy H. | | |
| 8BW | Herman, Harold. | 8EA | Mack, Clifford J. |
| 8BX | Hubbell, Aaron W. | 8EB | Munsell, Robert S. |
| 8BY | Schwindt, Herman J. | 8EC | Dunn, Frank L. |
| 8BZ | Shumard, Asbury. | 8ED | Carver, Alfred J. |
| | | 8EE | Coleman, Clarence E. |
| 8CA | Stueve, Everett S. | 8EF | Dorst, Edward. |
| 8CB | Thiessen, H. F. W. | 8EG | Gebhard, Louis A. |
| 8CC | Kesel, George. | 8EH | Grove, Nelson B. |
| 8CD | Sachs, Gus. | 8EJ | Kolb, Edwin H. |
| 8CE | Adler, Jerome. | 8EK | Kumpf, Elmer H. |
| 8CF | Hull, Guy McC. | 8EL | Langenbach, Leo. |
| 8CG | Hull, Ralph. | 8EM | Murphy, John V. |
| 8CH | Paul, James T. | 8EN | Shepard, Charles A. |
| 8CI | Richards, Theodore D. | 8EO | Stickney, Richard W. |
| 8CJ | Andrews, William S. | | |
| 8CK | Smith, Roland C. | 8JL | Appleton, Francis W. |
| 8CL | Smith, G. C. | 8JM | Saunders, Norman W. |
| 8CM | Thorn, Thomas H. | 8JN | Howes, Stanley L. |
| 8CN | Sheppard, Hamilton W. | 8JO | Little, Donald G. |
| 8CO | Sherrill, Alvin C. | | |

2002°—13——10

AMATEUR RADIO STATIONS—Continued.

## NINTH DISTRICT.

[Headquarters: Customhouse, Chicago, Ill. The ninth district comprises the States of Indiana, Illinois, Wisconsin, Michigan (Upper Peninsula), Minnesota, Kentucky, Missouri, Kansas, Colorado, Iowa, Nebraska, South Dakota, North Dakota.]

ALPHABETICALLY BY OWNERS OF STATIONS.

| Call signal. | Owner of station. | Location of station. | Power. |
|---|---|---|---|
| | | | *Watts.* |
| 9AS | Billister, Earl D | 2610 Dupont Ave., Minneapolis, Minn | 1,000 |
| 9AD | Bryant, Stanley C | 2439 Mozart St., Chicago, Ill | 150 |
| 9AI | Cutting, Irving E | 3611 Galena St., Milwaukee, Wis | 700 |
| 9AM | Foster, Edwin J | 925 Winchester St., Milwaukee, Wis | 750 |
| 9AB | Groskopf, William L | 4816 West Berteau Ave., Chicago, Ill | 250 |
| 9AE | Gundlach, Waldo L | 1837 Pratt Ave., Chicago, Ill | 20 |
| 9AV | Hamel, Walter H | 1006 South Fourteenth St., Lafayette, Ind. | |
| 9AR | Hines, Gene | 1209 West Twenty-fifth St., Minneapolis, Minn. | 250 |
| 9AF | Hollister, Harold A | 370 Eighteenth Ave., Milwaukee, Wis | |
| 9AA | Klentz, Clarence | 3809 Vincennes Ave., Chicago, Ill | 500 |
| 9AK | Kottler, C. F | 1035 Second St., Milwaukee, Wis | |
| 9AO | Lipman, Theodore E | 136 Grand Ave., Belair, Wis | 1,000 |
| 9AG | Marx, Gustav A | 334½ Fifteenth St., Milwaukee, Wis | |
| 9AP | Morgan, Hiram | Morgan Farm, R. F. D. No. 30, near Beloit, Wis. | 1,000 |
| 9AC | McGuffage, William J | 4418 Wabash Ave., Chicago, Ill | 500 |
| 9AQ | Riner, John A | High School, Beloit, Wis | 1,000 |
| 9AL | Schroeder, William | 647 Washington St., Milwaukee, Wis | |
| 9AJ | Siegel, R. C | 478 Potter Ave., Milwaukee, Wis | 800 |
| 9AT | Stetson, Donald T | 2162 Carrol Ave., St. Paul, Minn | 400 |
| 9AU | Taylor, Thomas J | 1846 Lincoln Ave., St. Paul, Minn | 280 |
| 9AH | Thomas, Carroll W | 266 Seventeenth St., Milwaukee, Wis | 12 |
| 9AN | Willett, Charles J | 425 Clement Ave., Milwaukee, Wis | 440 |

AMATEUR RADIO STATIONS—NINTH DISTRICT—Continued.

ALPHABETICALLY BY CALL SIGNALS.

| Owner of station. | Call signal. | Owner of station. |
|---|---|---|
| ɜntz, Clarence. | 9AL | Schroeder, William. |
| ɔskopf, William L | 9AM | Foster, Edwin J. |
| Gufiage, William J. | 9AN | Willett, Charles J. |
| ɪant, Stanley C. | 9AO | Lipman, Theodore E. |
| ndlach, Waldo L. | 9AP | Morgan, Hiram. |
| llister, Harold A | 9AQ | Riner, John A. |
| rx, Gustav A. | 9AR | Hines, Gene. |
| ɔmas, Carroll W. | 9AS | Billister, Earl D. |
| tting, Irving E. | 9AT | Stetson, Donald T. |
| gel, R. C. | 9AU | Taylor, Thomas J. |
| ttler, C. F. | 9AV | Hamel, Walter H. |

O

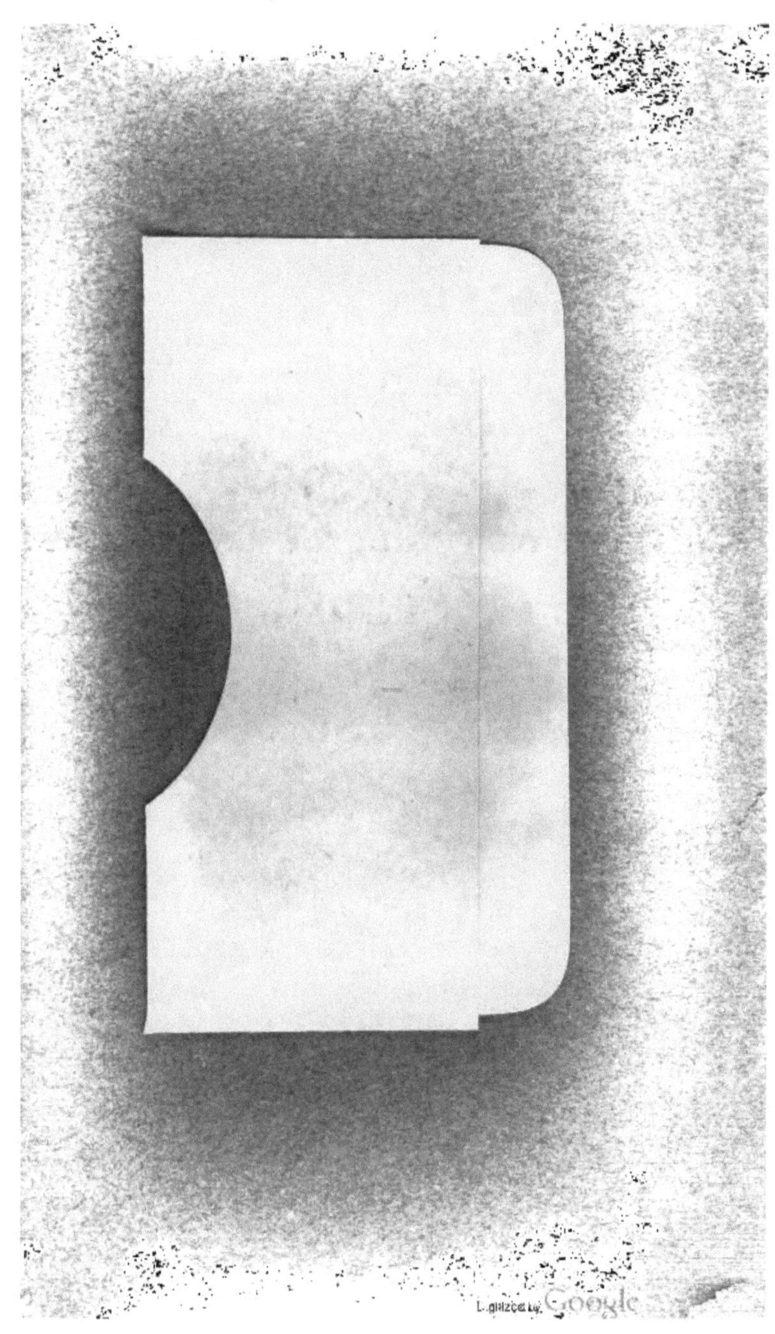

DEPARTMENT OF COMMERCE
U.S. BUREAU OF NAVIGATION
RADIO SERVICE

# RADIO STATIONS OF THE UNITED STATES

EDITION JULY 1, 1914

WASHINGTON
GOVERNMENT PRINTING OFFICE
1914

ADDITIONAL COPIES

OF THIS PUBLICATION MAY BE PROCURED FROM
THE SUPERINTENDENT OF DOCUMENTS,
GOVERNMENT PRINTING OFFICE,
WASHINGTON, D. C.
AT
15 CENTS PER COPY

---

SUPPLEMENTS WILL BE ISSUED QUARTERLY, AND THE LIST REVISED ANNUALLY AS OF JULY 1. THE SUPPLEMENTS WILL CONTAIN INFORMATION CONCERNING GOVERNMENT, COMMERCIAL, AND SPECIAL STATIONS ONLY. INFORMATION REGARDING AMATEUR STATIONS WILL APPEAR ONLY IN THE ANNUAL EDITION OF RADIO STATIONS.

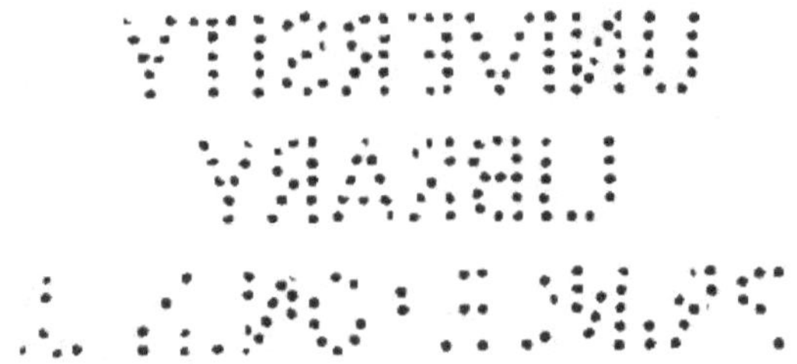

# CONTENTS.

## PART I.



## PART II.

## NOTES.

Underscoring of normal wave lengths is indicated by the use of italics.

Government vessels showing "nature of service" to be PG will accept c paid messages for officers or members of crews.

Government vessels proceeding singly may relay messages to the coast upc The regular ship rate will apply.

### INTERNATIONAL ABBREVIATIONS USED IN THIS LIST.

Nature of service:

- PG=General public.
- PR=Limited public.
- P=Private (limited commercial and special).
- O=Government business exclusively.

Hours of operation:

- N=Continuous service.
- X=No regular hours.

Classification:

- b=Ship station.
- c=Land station.

### OTHER ABBREVIATIONS.

Assn.=Association.

Corp.=Corporation.

Nav. =Navigation.

Transp.=Transportation.

Marconi Co.=Marconi Wireless Telegraph Co. of America.

U. S. R. C. S.=United States Revenue-Cutter Service.

D., L. & W. R. R. Co.=Delaware, Lackawanna & Western Railroad Co.

# RADIO STATIONS OF THE UNITED STATES.

## INTRODUCTION.

This list, including land and ship stations, is published in accordance ith Section I of an act of Congress entitled "An act to regulate radio ommunication," approved August 13, 1912.

The following instructions concerning radio call letters are issued r the information of those concerned:

1. Section 7 of the act of August 13, 1912, to regulate radio communication provides:

Sec. 7. That a person, company, or corporation within the juridiction of the nited States shall not knowingly utter or transmit, or cause to be uttered or transitted, any false or fraudulent distress signal or call or false or fraudulent signal, call, r other radiogram of any kind. The penalty for so uttering or transmitting a false or audulent distress signal or call shall be a fine of not more than two thousand five undred dollars or imprisonment for not more than five years, or both, in the discreon of the court, for each and every such offense, and the penalty for so uttering or ansmitting, or causing to be uttered or transmitted, any other false or fraudulent gnal, call, or other radiogram shall be a fine of not more than one thousand dollars or nprisonment for not more than two years, or both, in the discretion of the court, for ch and every such offense.

2. The Service Regulations of the International Radiotelegraphic onventions provide that the call letters of stations in the internaional system must each be formed of a group of three letters which hall be distinguishable from one another. The London Interational Radiotelegraphic Conference made a partial allotment of all letters among nations which signed the convention and the Interational Bureau at Berne, with the consent of such nations, has modied and added to this assignment of call letters by circular of April , 1914. The distribution of call letters among nations thus authored is printed below for the guidance of operators of all stations ship and shore) of the United States.

.............All to Germany and protectorates.
.............All to Great Britain.
AA to CEZ..Chile.
FA to CMZ..Not yet assigned.
NA to CNZ..Morocco.
OA to COZ..Not yet assigned.
PA to CPZ...Bolivia.
QA to CQZ...Monaco.
CRA to CTZ...Portugal and colonies.
CUA to CUZ..Not yet assigned.
CVA to CVZ...Roumania.
CWA to CWZ..Uruguay.
CXA to CZZ...Not yet assigned.
D.............All to Germany and protectorates.
EAA to EGZ..Spain and colonies.
EHA to EZZ..Not yet assigned.

F.............All to France and colonies.
G.............All to Great Britain.
HAA to HFZ..Austria-Hungary and Bosnia-Herzegovina.
HGA to HHZ..Siam.
HIA to HIZ..Dominican Republic.
HJA to HKZ..Colombia (Republic).
HLA to HZZ..Not yet assigned.
I.............All to Italy and colonies.
J.............All to Japan and possessions.
KAA to KCZ..Germany and protectorates.
KDA to KZZ..United States.
LAA to LHZ..Norway.
LIA to LRZ..Argentine Republic.
LSA to LWZ..Not yet assigned.
LXA to LZZ..Bulgaria.
M.............All to Great Britain.
N.............All to the United States.
OAA to OFZ..Not yet assigned.
OGA to OMZ..Austria-Hungary and Bosnia-Herzegovina.
ONA to OTZ...Belgium and colonies.
OUA to OZZ..Denmark.
PAA to PIZ...Netherlands.
PJA to PJM...Curaçao (Dutch).
PJN to PJZ....Surinam (Dutch).
PKA to PMZ..Dutch East Indies.
PNA to PZZ...Brazil.
Q.............Reserved for code abbreviations.
R.............All to Russia.
SAA to SMZ...Sweden.
SNA to STZ...Brazil.
SUA to SUZ...Egypt.
SVA to SZZ...Greece.
TAA to TMZ...Turkey.
TNA to TZZ...Not yet assigned.
UAA to UMZ..France and colonies.
UNA to UZZ..Austria-Hungary and Bosnia-Herzegovina.
VAA to VGZ..Canada (British).
VHA to VKZ..Australian Federation (British).
VLA to VMZ..New Zealand (British).
VNA to VNZ..South African Union (British).
VOA to VOZ..Newfoundland (British).
VPA to VSZ...British colonies not autonomous.
VTA to VWZ..British India.
VXA to VZZ..Great Britain.
W.............All to the United States.
XAA to XDZ..Mexico.
XEA to XZZ..Not yet assigned.
YAA to YZZ..Not yet assigned.
ZAA to ZZZ...Not yet assigned.

## PUBLIC-SERVICE STATIONS.

3. The call letters assigned to the United States are all combinations (676) beginning with the letter N and all (676) beginning with the letter W, and all combinations (598) from KDA to KZZ, inclusive. The total number of international call letters assigned to the United States is thus 1,950, and these are reserved for Government stations and stations open to public and limited commercial service.

(*a*) All combinations beginning with the letter N are reserved for Government stations and in addition the combinations from WUA to WVZ and WXA to WZZ are reserved for stations of the Army of the United States.

(*b*) The combinations KDA to KZZ, with a few exceptions, are reserved for ship stations on the Atlantic and Gulf of Mexico and for land stations on the Pacific coast.

(*c*) The combinations beginning with W (except WUA to WVZ and WXA to WZZ as already indicated) are reserved, with a few exceptions, for ship stations on the Pacific and the Great Lakes and for land stations on the Atlantic and Gulf coasts and in the Great Lakes region.

### AMATEUR STATIONS.

4. The call letters for amateur stations in the United States will be awarded by radio inspectors, each for his own district, according to the following system:

(*a*) The call will consist of three items—the number of the radio district, followed by two letters of the alphabet. Thus, the call of all amateur stations in New England (which comprises the first district) will be the figure "one" in Continental Morse, followed by two letters; in California (in the sixth district) the figure "six" followed by two letters; in South Carolina the figure "four" followed by two letters; in Missouri the figure "nine" followed by two letters, etc. The letters X, Y, Z, must not be used as the first of the two letters.

The territory of each district is as follows:

1. BOSTON, MASS........Maine, New Hampshire, Vermont, Massachusetts, Rhode Island, Connecticut.
2. NEW YORK, N. Y.....New York (county of New York, Staten Island, Long Island, and counties on the Hudson River to and including Albany, Rensselaer, and Schenectady), and New Jersey (counties of Bergen, Passaic, Essex, Union, Middlesex, Monmouth, Hudson, and Ocean).
3. BALTIMORE, MD......New Jersey (all counties not included in second district), Pennsylvania (counties of Philadelphia, Delaware, all counties south of the Blue Mountains, and Franklin County), Delaware, Maryland, Virginia, District of Columbia.
4. SAVANNAH, GA........North Carolina, South Carolina, Georgia, Florida, Porto Rico.
5. NEW ORLEANS, LA....Alabama, Mississippi, Louisiana, Texas, Tennessee, Arkansas, Oklahoma, New Mexico.
6. SAN FRANCISCO, CAL..California, Hawaii, Nevada, Utah, Arizona.
7. SEATTLE, WASH.......Oregon, Washington, Alaska, Idaho, Montana, Wyoming.
8. CLEVELAND, OHIO.....New York (all counties not included in second district), Pennsylvania (all counties not included in third district), West Virginia, Ohio, Michigan (Lower Peninsula).
9. CHICAGO, ILL.........Indiana, Illinois, Wisconsin, Michigan (Upper Peninsula), Minnesota, Kentucky, Missouri, Kansas, Colorado, Iowa, Nebraska, South Dakota, North Dakota.

(*b*) The three items—a given figure first, followed by two letters of the alphabet—thus may be combined in 598 different calls, which will probably suffice for the amateur sending stations in most districts for some time to come.

(*c*) Radio inspectors will insert amateur station calls in station licenses according to this system, and will keep a permanent chart of 598 squares, lettered with the alphabet from left to right and from top to bottom (A to W), inserting in the appropriate square the serial license number and name of owner of the station to which the call letters were awarded. Within these limitations radio inspectors will use their discretion in the award of calls, avoiding, of course, duplications.

(*d*) When a station is abandoned and the license canceled, or if a license shall be forfeited for violation of law, the call assigned to it may be allotted to another station.

(*e*) If the entire 598 calls have been exhausted, radio inspectors will issue additional calls, consisting of the figure of the district followed by three letters. From such combinations should be excluded the combinations SOS and PRB, all three-letter combinations beginning with QR or QS, all combinations involving the repetition of the same letter three times, three-letter combinations beginning with K, N, W, X, Y, Z, and other combinations, which, for various reasons, international, national, local, or individual, may be objectionable. With such exclusions, over 10,000 calls will remain for each district.

### LIMITED COMMERCIAL STATIONS.

5. Calls for limited commercial land stations will be allotted by the Bureau of Navigation.

### SPECIAL CLASSES OF STATIONS.

6. Calls for special classes of stations, such as experiment stations for the development of radio communications, technical and training school stations, and special amateur stations will be allotted by the Bureau of Navigation.

The call will consist of three items—the number of the radio district, followed by two letters of the alphabet. The first letter will be: X, for experiment stations; Y, technical and training schools; Z, special amateur stations.

Twenty-six different combinations for each class in each district, of course, are possible. If more should prove necessary for any class in any district, a third letter will be added to the call.

### RADIO STATIONS OF THE WORLD.

The International List of Radio Stations of the World (edition in English) can be procured from the International Bureau of the Telegraphic Union (Radiotelegraphic Service), Berne, Switzerland.

In addition to the information contained in the pamphlet of the United States stations, published by the Bureau of Navigation, the international list shows geographical locations, normal ranges in nautical miles, radio systems, and rates.

The international list includes the Government and commercial land and ship stations of the United States. The list is divided into three parts. The first part contains a list of ship stations, grouped by countries and arranged alphabetically; the second part contains a list of land stations arranged in the same manner; and the third part contains tables of land line and cable charges from coast radio stations to inland and various other points. In computing the total word rate applicable to a radiogram from a ship station to an inland point, or vice versa, the three rates must be added. The rates in the international list are given in francs, but may be converted into dollars and cents by multiplying by five. Supplements to the international list will be issued monthly, and will contain new stations and tables of alterations. A copy of the international list should be in every land and ship station open to commercial business as the official tariff book.

The International Alphabetical List of Call Letters (stations of the world) is also issued by the International Bureau at Berne, and supplements will be issued monthly.

Neither the international list nor the supplements will contain a list of amateur stations.

Inquiries as to the subscription prices of these lists should be made direct to the Berne bureau at the address given above. Remittances to Berne should be made by international postal money orders.

E. T. Chamberlain,
*Commissioner of Navigation.*

Approved:
William C. Redfield,
*Secretary.*

# PART I.

## LAND RADIO STATIONS, ALPHABETICALLY BY NAMES OF STATIONS.

[This list includes commercial, special, Army, Navy, and all other land stations except restricted and general amateur. The special land stations are grouped at the end of this list.]

| Station. | Call signal. | Wave lengths. | Serv-ice. | Hours of operation. | Station controlled by— |
|---|---|---|---|---|---|
| Annapolis, Md....... | NAK | .............. | O | 8 a. m. to 10 p. m. | U. S. Navy. |
| Arlington, Radio, Va. | NAA | .............. | O | N | U. S. Navy. |
| Ashtabula, Ohio...... | WSA | 300, *600* | PG | 6.30 a. m. to 6 p. m. | Marconi Co. |
| Astoria, Oreg......... | KPC | 300, *600* | PG | N | Marconi Co. |
| Avalon, Cal.......... | KPI | 300, *600* | PR | 7 a. m. to 8 p. m. | Marconi Co. |
| Balboa, Panama...... | NPJ | 600 | PG | N | U. S. Navy. |
| Baltimore, Md....... | WBS | 300, 550, *600* | PG | 6 a. m. to midnight. | Marconi Co. |
| Beaufort, N. C....... | NAN | .............. | O | N | U. S. Navy. |
| Belmar, N. J......... | WII | .............. | .... | ........... | Marconi Co. |
| Benton Harbor, Mich. | WBN | .............. | .... | ........... | Marconi Co. |
| Binghamton, N. Y... | WBT | 1610 | PR | X | D., L. & W. R. R. Co. |
| Bolinas, Cal.......... | KET | .............. | .... | ........... | Marconi Co. |
| Boston, Mass......... | WCH | 300, *600*, 1610, 2000, 2400, 2800 | P | X | Nat. Elec. Signaling Co. |
| Boston, Mass......... | WBF | 300, *600* | PG | N | Marconi Co. |
| Boston, Mass......... | NAD | .............. | O | N | U. S. Navy. |
| Bremerton, Wash. *See* Puget Sound. | | | | | |
| Brooklyn, N. Y..... | WCG | 300, *600*, 1610, 2000, 2400, 2800 | PR | 4 a. m. to 9 p. m. | Nat. Elec. Signaling Co. |
| Buffalo, N. Y........ | WBL | 300, *600* | PG | ........... | Marconi Co. |
| Burrwood, La....... | WBW | .............. | .... | ........... | Tropical Radio Telegraph Co. |
| Calumet, Mich....... | WCM | .............. | .... | ........... | Marconi Co. |

LAND RADIO STATIONS, ALPHABETICALLY BY NAMES OF STATIONS—Continued.

| Station. | Call signal. | Wave lengths. | Service. | Hours of operation. | Station controlled by— |
|---|---|---|---|---|---|
| Cape Blanco, Oreg. | NPF | 600 | PG | N | U. S. Navy. |
| Cape Cod, Mass. | NAE | ............ | O | N | U. S. Navy. |
| Cape Hatteras (Buxton), N. C. | WHA | 300, *600* | PG | N | Marconi Co. |
| Cape May, N. J. | WCY | 300, *600* | PG | N | Marconi Co. |
| Cavite, P. I. | NPO | ............ | O | N | U. S. Navy. |
| Charleston, S. C. | NAO | 600 | PG | N | U. S. Navy. |
| Chicago, Ill. | WGO | 300, *600* | PG | 12.30 p. m. to 7 p. m.; 8 p. m. to 11.30 p.m.; 12.30 a.m. to 7 a. m.; 8 a. m. to 11.30 a.m.; when lake is open to navigation. | Marconi Co. |
| Chignik, Alaska | KHC | ............ | .... | ........... | Marconi Co. |
| Circle City, Alaska | WVA | *600*, 1400 | O | ........... | U. S. Army. |
| Clarks Point, Alaska | KHG | ............ | .... | ........... | Marconi Co. |
| Cleveland, Ohio | WCX | 300, *600* | PG | ........... | Marconi Co. |
| Colon, Panama | NAX | 600 | PG | N | U. S. Navy. |
| Cordova, Alaska | NPA | 600 | PG | N | U. S. Navy. |
| Corregidor Isld., P. I. *See* Fort Mills. | | | | | |
| Cuyo, P. I. | WVX | *600*, 1200 | PG | 7 a. m. to 6.15 p. m. | Insular Govt., Philippine Islds. |
| Daly City, Cal. *See* Hillcrest. | | | | | |
| Davao, Mindanao Isld., P. I. | WVO | 600, *1200* | PG | 7 a. m. to 6 p. m. | U. S. Army. |
| Detroit, Mich. | WDR | 300, *600* | PG | 7 a. m. to 11.30 a. m.; 12.30 p. m. to 6.00 p. m.; 7 p. m. to 11 p. m.; midnight to 6 a.m. | Marconi Co. |

LAND RADIO STATIONS, ALPHABETICALLY BY NAMES OF STATIONS—Continued.

| Station. | Call signal. | Wave lengths. | Service. | Hours of operation. | Station controlled by— |
|---|---|---|---|---|---|
| Diamond Shoals Lightship (off Cape Hatteras, N. C.). | NLB | .............. | O | 6 a. m. to 10 p. m. | U. S. Navy. |
| D., L. & W. R. R. limited train. | WBI | .............. | .... | .......... | D., L. & W. R. R. Co. |
| Douglas, Ariz......... | KDC | 300, *600* | P | 10 a. m. to 11 a. m.; 4 p. m. to 5 p. m. | Copper Queen Consolidated Mining Co. |
| Dover, N. J.......... | WBX | .............. | .... | .......... | D., L. & W. R. R. Co. |
| Duluth, Minn........ | WDM | 300, *600* | PG | Apr. 15 to Dec. 15: N, except from 6 a. m. to 7 a. m.; 12 noon to 1 p. m.; 6 p. m. to 7 p. m. Dec. 15 to Apr. 15: 7 a. m. to 7 p. m., except from 12 noon to 1 p. m. | Marconi Co. |
| Dutch Harbor, Alaska | NPR | 600 | PG | N | U. S. Navy. |
| East San Pedro, Cal.. | KPJ | 300, 500, *600* | PR<br>PG | N | Marconi Co. |
| Ellamar, Alaska...... | KIS | .............. | .... | .......... | Marconi Co. |
| El Paso, Tex........ | WEP | *2000*, 2500, 2900, 3500 | PR | 6 a. m. to 7 p. m. | Federal Telegraph Co. |
| Ensenada, P. R...... | WPR | .............. | .... | .......... | Guanica Centrale. |
| Eureka, Cal......... | KPM | .............. | .... | .......... | Marconi Co. |
| Eureka, Cal......... | NPW | 600 | PG | N | U. S. Navy. |
| Fairbanks, Alaska... | WVB | *600*, 1400 | PG | .......... | U. S. Army. |
| Farallons, Cal....... | NPI | .............. | O | N | U. S. Navy. |
| Fire Island, N. Y.... | NAG | .............. | O | N | U. S. Navy. |
| Fort Andrews, Mass.. | WUA | .............. | O | .......... | U. S. Army. |

LAND RADIO STATIONS, ALPHABETICALLY BY NAMES OF STATIONS—Continued.

| Station. | Call signal. | Wave lengths. | Service. | Hours of operation. | Station controlled by— |
|---|---|---|---|---|---|
| Fort De Russy, Hawaii. | WZG | ............. | O | ........... | U. S. Army. |
| Fort Drum, El Fraile Isld., Manila Bay, P. I. | WVP | ............. | O | ........... | U. S. Army. |
| Fort Egbert, Eagle, Alaska. | WVC | *600*, 1400 | O | ........... | U. S. Army. |
| Fort Frank, Carabao Isld., Manila Bay, P. I. | WVL | ............. | O | ........... | U. S. Army. |
| Fort Gibbon, Tanana, Alaska. | WVD | *1600*, 2000 | O | ........... | U. S. Army. |
| Fort Hancock, N. J. . | WUB | ............. | O | ........... | U. S. Army. |
| Fort H. G. Wright, N. Y. | WUC | ............. | O | ........... | U. S. Army. |
| Fort Hughes, Caballo Isld., Manila Bay, P. I. | WVM | ............. | O | ........... | U. S. Army. |
| Fort Leavenworth, Kans. | WUD | *1800* | O | ........... | U. S. Army. |
| Fort Leavenworth, Kans. (Army Signal School). | WUV | ............. | O | ........... | U. S. Army. |
| Fort Levett, Me...... | WUE | ............. | O | ........... | U. S. Army. |
| Fort Mills, Corregidor Isld., Manila Harbor, P. I. | WVN | ............. | O | ........... | U. S. Army. |
| Fort Monroe, Va..... | WUF | ............. | O | ........... | U. S. Army. |
| Fort Monroe, Va. (Coast Artillery School). | WUG | ............. | O | ........... | U. S. Army. |
| Fort Morgan, Ala..... | WFM | ............. | .... | ........... | Marconi Co. |
| Fort Omaha, Nebr... | WUH | *1600* | O | ........... | U. S. Army. |
| Fort Riley, Kans..... | WUI | *1200* | O | ........... | U. S. Army. |
| Fort Sam Houston, Tex. | WUJ | *650* | O | ........... | U. S. Army. |
| Fort Shafter, Honolulu, Hawaii. | WZH | *300* | O | ........... | U. S. Army. |
| Fort Stevens, Oreg... | WUK | ............. | O | ........... | U. S. Army. |

LAND RADIO STATIONS, ALPHABETICALLY BY NAMES OF STATIONS—Continued.

| Station. | Call signal. | Wave lengths. | Service. | Hours of operation. | Station controlled by— |
|---|---|---|---|---|---|
| Fort St. Michael, St. Michael Isld., Alaska. | WVE | *600*, 1200 | PG | 9 a. m. to 9 p. m. | U. S. Army. |
| Fort Terry, N. Y.... | WUW | 1200 | O | .......... | U. S. Army. |
| Fort Totten, N. Y.... | WUL | .............. | O | .......... | U. S. Army. |
| Fort Winfield Scott, Cal. | WUO | .............. | O | .......... | U. S. Army. |
| Fort Wint, Grand Isld., Manila Bay, P. I. | WVR | .............. | O | .......... | U. S. Army. |
| Fort Wm. McKinley, Luzon Isld., P. I. | WVQ | *600* | O | .......... | U. S. Army. |
| Fort Wood, N. Y..... | WUM | .............. | O | .......... | U. S. Army. |
| Fort Worden, Wash.. | WUN | .............. | O | .......... | U. S. Army. |
| Fort Worth, Tex..... | WFF | *2000*, 2500, 2900, 3500 | PR | 6 a. m. to 6 p. m. | Federal Telegraph Co. |
| Frankfort, Mich...... | WFK | 300, *600* | .... | .......... | Marconi Co. |
| Friday Harbor, Wash. | KPD | 300, *600* | PG | 7 a. m. to 2.30 a. m. | Marconi Co. |
| Frying Pan Shoals Lightship (off Cape Fear, N. C.) | NLC | .............. | O | 6 a. m. to 10 p. m. | U. S. Navy. |
| Galveston, Tex....... | WGV | 300, *600* | PG | 7 a. m. to 11 p. m. | Marconi Co. |
| Grand Haven, Mich.. | WGH | 300, *600* | PR | .......... | Marconi Co. |
| Grand Marais, Minn.. | WGM | 300, *600* | PR | .......... | Marconi Co. |
| Guam, Marianne Islds., Pacific Ocean. | NPN | 600 | PG | N | U. S. Navy. |
| Guantanamo Bay, Cuba. | NAW | 600 | PG | N | U. S. Navy. |
| Hatteras, N. C. *See* Cape Hatteras. | | | | | |
| Heeia Point, Hawaii.. | KHX | 300, *600*, 3000, 3500, 5500, 8000, 10000, 12000 | PR | N | Federal Telegraph Co. |
| Hillcrest, Cal....... | KPH | 300, *600* | PG | N | Marconi Co. |
| Hoboken, N. J....... | WBU | .............. | .... | .......... | D., L. & W. R. R. Co. |

LAND RADIO STATIONS, ALPHABETICALLY BY NAMES OF STATIONS—Continued.

| Station. | Call signal. | Wave lengths. | Service. | Hours of operation. | Station controlled by— |
|---|---|---|---|---|---|
| Hollister (near), Cal.. | KGH | 300, *600*, 1700 | PR | X | George Hewlett (Inc.). |
| Honolulu, Hawaii.... | NPM | .............. | O | N | U. S. Navy. |
| Isle Royal, Mich..... | WRO | 300, *600* | ..... | ........... | Marconi Co. |
| Jacksonville, Fla..... | WJX | 300, *600* | PG | 5.30 a. m. to midnight. | Marconi Co. |
| Jolo, Jolo Isld., P. I... | WVS | *600* | PG | 7 a. m. to 5.15 p. m. | Insular Govt., Philippine Islds. |
| Jualin, Alaska ....... | KJA | .............. | ..... | ........... | Marconi Co. |
| Juneau, Alaska....... | KDU | .............. | ..... | ........... | Marconi Co. |
| Jupiter, Fla.......... | NAQ | 600 | PG | N | U. S. Navy. |
| Kahuku, Hawaii..... | KIE | .............. | ..... | ........... | Marconi Co. |
| Kahuku, Hawaii..... | KHK | .............. | ..... | ........... | Mutual Telephone Co. (Ltd.). |
| Karluk, Alaska....... | KHA | .............. | ..... | ........... | Marconi Co. |
| Kaunakakai, Hawaii . | KHO | *300*, 450 | PR | X | Mutual Telephone Co. (Ltd.). |
| Kawaihae, Hawaii.... | KHN | 300, *600* | ..... | ........... | Mutual Telephone Co. (Ltd.). |
| Ketchikan, Alaska... | KPB | .............. | ..... | ........... | Marconi Co. |
| Key West, Fla....... | NAR | 600 | PG | N | U. S. Navy. |
| Kodiak, Alaska...... | NPS | 600 | PG | N | U. S. Navy. |
| Kogiung, Alaska..... | KHB | .............. | ..... | ........... | Marconi Co. |
| Koko Head, Hawaii.. | KHJ | .............. | ..... | ........... | Marconi Co. |
| Koko Head, Hawaii.. | KIE | .............. | ..... | ........... | Marconi Co. |
| Kotlik, Alaska....... | WVF | *600* | PG | 9 a. m. to 9 p. m. during season of navigation only. | U. S. Army. |
| "Lackawanna Limited." *See* D., L. & W. R. R. limited train. | | | | | |
| Lahaina, Hawaii... | KHL | 300, *600* | PG | ........... | Mutual Telephone Co. (Ltd.). |

LAND RADIO STATIONS, ALPHABETICALLY BY NAMES OF STATIONS—Continued.

| Station. | Call signal. | Wave lengths. | Service. | Hours of operation. | Station controlled by— |
|---|---|---|---|---|---|
| Lihue, Hawaii | KHM | 300, *600* | PG | ........ | Mutual Telephone Co. (Ltd.). |
| Los Angeles, Cal | KEX | 300, *600* | P | 9 a. m. to 5 p. m. | Marconi Co. |
| Los Angeles, Cal | KLS | ........ | ........ | ........ | Federal Telegraph Co. |
| Ludington, Mich | WLD | 300, *600* | PG | 7 a. m. to 6 p. m.; 7 p. m. to 6 a.m. Apr. 15 to Dec. 15 only. | Marconi Co. |
| Mackinac Island, Mich. | WHQ | ........ | ........ | ........ | Marconi Co. |
| Malabang, Mindanao Isld., P. I. | WVT | 600, *1200* | PG | 7 a. m. to 7.30 p. m. | Insular Govt., Philippine Islds. |
| Manila, P. I | WVU | *600* | O | ........ | U. S. Army. |
| Manistique, Mich | WMX | ........ | ........ | ........ | Marconi Co. |
| Manitowoc, Wis | WMW | 300, *600* | PG | 8 a. m. to 11.30 a.m.; 2.30 p. m. to 6 p. m.; 7.30 p. m. to 9 p. m. | Marconi Co. |
| Mare Island, Cal | NPH | ........ | O | N | U. S. Navy. |
| Marshall, Cal. *See* Bolinas, Cal. | | | | | |
| Marshfield, Oreg | KPX | 300, 435, *600* | PG | 8 a. m. to 6 p. m. | Marconi Co. |
| Miami, Fla | WST | 300, *600*, 1800 | PG | N | Marconi Co. |
| Milwaukee, Wis | WME | 300, *600* | PG | 1.30 a. m. to 6 a. m.; 7 a. m. to 12.30 p.m.; 1.30 p. m. to 6 p. m.; 7 p. m. to 12.30 a.m. | Marconi Co. |
| Mobile, Ala | WMB | 300, *600* | PG | 7 a. m. to 9 a. m.; 10 a. m. to noon; 2 p. m. to 6 p. m. | Marconi Co. |
| Naknek, Alaska | KHT | ........ | ........ | ........ | Marconi Co. |
| Nantucket Shoals Lightship (off Newport, R. I.). | NLA | ........ | O | 4 a. m. to midnight | U. S. Navy. |

LAND RADIO STATIONS, ALPHABETICALLY BY NAMES OF STATIONS—Continued.

| Station. | Call signal. | Wave lengths. | Service. | Hours of operation. | Station controlled by— |
|---|---|---|---|---|---|
| New Brunswick, N. J. *See* Belmar, N. J. | | | | | |
| New London, Conn. | NRZ | 300, *600* | [1]O | X | U. S. R. C. S. |
| New London, Conn. | WLC | 300, 510, *600*, 1610, 1700, 1800, 1900, 2000. | PG | 8 p. m. to 4. a. m. | T. A. Scott Co. (Inc.). |
| New Orleans, La.... | NAT | .............. | O | 8 a. m. to 10 p. m. | U. S. Navy. |
| New Orleans, La.... | WHK | 300, *600* | PG | 7 a. m. to 11 p. m. | Marconi Co. |
| New Orleans, La.... | WNU | .............. | .... | ........... | Tropical Radio Telegraph Co. |
| Newport, R. I....... | NAF | .............. | O | N | U. S. Navy. |
| Newport, R. I....... | WCI | 300, 400, 500, *600*. | PG | 7 p. m. to 5 a. m. | Nat. Elec. Signaling Co. |
| Newton, Mass....... | WLN | 300, *600*, 1650, 2000. | PR | X | Ralph C. Emery. |
| New York, N. Y..... | NAH | .............. | O | N | U. S. Navy. |
| New York, N. Y..... | WHB | 300, *600*, 1610 | PG | N | N. Y. Herald Co. |
| New York, N. Y..... | WHD | .............. | .... | ........... | N. Y. City Fire Dept. |
| New York, N. Y..... | WHI | 300, *600* | PG | N | Marconi Co. |
| New York, N. Y..... | WNT | 300, *600*, 1800 | PG | N | Atlantic Communication Co. |
| Nome, Alaska........ | WVG | *600*, 2000 | PG | 9 a. m. to 9 p. m. | U. S. Army. |
| Norfolk, Va......... | NAM | .............. | O | N | U. S. Navy. |
| North Head, Wash... | NPE | 600 | PG | N | U. S. Navy. |
| Nulato, Alaska...... | WVH | *2000* | O | ........... | U. S. Army. |
| Nushagak, Alaska.... | KHF | .............. | .... | ........... | Marconi Co. |
| Olongapo, P. I....... | NPT | .............. | O | N | U. S. Navy. |
| Peking, China....... | NPP | .............. | O | N | U. S. Navy. |
| Pensacola, Fla....... | NAS | 600 | PG | N | U. S. Navy. |
| Petersburg, Alaska... | WVI | 600 | PG | 9 a. m. to 9 p. m. | U. S. Army. |

[1] This station will accept general public service in emergencies, when open.

54773°—14——2

LAND RADIO STATIONS, ALPHABETICALLY BY NAMES OF STATIONS—Continued.

| Station. | Call signal. | Wave lengths. | Service. | Hours of operation. | Station controlled by— |
|---|---|---|---|---|---|
| Philadelphia, Pa. | WHE | 300, *600*, 1610 | PG | N | Marconi Co. |
| Philadelphia, Pa. | NAI | | O | N | U. S. Navy. |
| Phoenix, Ariz. | KHQ | | | | Federal Telegraph Co. |
| Point Arguello, Cal. | NPK | 600 | PG | N | U. S. Navy. |
| Port Arthur, Tex. | WRU | 300, *600* | PG | 6.30 a.m. to 7.30 a.m.; 9.30 a.m. to 10.30 a.m; 2.30 p.m. to 3.30 p.m.; 4.30 p.m. to 5.30 p.m.; 7 p.m. to 8 p.m. | Marconi Co. |
| Portland, Me. | NAB | | O | 8 a. m. to 10 p. m. | U. S. Navy. |
| Portsmouth, N. H. | NAC | | O | N | U. S. Navy. |
| Puerto Princesa, Paragua, P. I. | WVV | *600*, 1200 | PG | 7 a. m. to 6 p. m. | Insular Govt., Philippine Islds. |
| Puget Sound, Wash. | NPC | | O | N | U. S. Navy. |
| River Rouge, Mich. *See* Detroit, Mich. | | | | | |
| Sagaponack, N. Y. | WSK | 300, *600* | PG | N | Marconi Co. |
| San Diego, Cal. | KSD | | | | Federal Telegraph Co. |
| San Diego, Cal. | NPL | 600 | PG | N | U. S. Navy. |
| San Francisco, Cal. | KFS | 300, *600*, 3000, 3500, 3700, 3800 | PR | N | Federal Telegraph Co. |
| San Francisco, Cal. *See* Hillcrest. | | | | | Marconi Co. |
| San Jose, Mindoro Isld., P. I. | WVY | *600* | PG | 7 a. m. to 6.15 p. m. | Insular Govt., Philippine Islds. |
| San Juan, P. R. | NAU | 600 | PG | N | U. S. Navy. |
| San Luis Obispo, Cal. | KDN | 300, *600* | PG | 8.30 a. m. to noon; 1.30 p.m. to 5 p.m.; 7.30 p.m. to 10 p.m. | Marconi Co. |
| San Pedro, Cal. *See* East San Pedro. | | | | | |
| Sault Ste. Marie, Mich. | WSI | | | | Marconi Co. |

LAND RADIO STATIONS, ALPHABETICALLY BY NAMES OF STATIONS—Continued.

| Station. | Call signal. | Wave lengths. | Service. | Hours of operation. | Station controlled by— |
|---|---|---|---|---|---|
| Savannah, Ga........ | WSV | 300, *600* | PG | 6 a. m. to midnight. | Marconi Co. |
| Sayville, N. Y....... | WSL | 300, *600*, 2740 | PG | N | Atlantic Communication Co. |
| Sayville, N. Y....... | WSL | *2480*, 2740, 3600, 4800, 8000. | PR | X | Atlantic Communication Co. |
| Scranton, Pa......... | WTP | .............. | .... | .......... | D., L. & W. R. R. Co. |
| Sea Gate, N. Y....... | WSE | 300, *600* | PG | N | Marconi Co. |
| Seattle, Wash........ | KPA | 300, *600* | PG | N | Marconi Co. |
| Siasconset, Mass..... | WSC | 300, *600* | PG | N | Marconi Co. |
| Sitka, Alaska......... | NPB | 600 | PG | N | U. S. Navy. |
| South San Francisco, Cal. | KSS | 300, *600*, 3000, 3500, 5000, 8000, 10000, 12000. | PR | N | Federal Telegraph Co. |
| South Wellfleet, Mass. | WCC | 300, *600*, 2040 | PG | N | Marconi Co. |
| St. Augustine, Fla... | NAP | 600 | PG | N | U. S. Navy. |
| St. George, Pribilof Islds., Alaska. | NPY | 600 | O | X | U. S. Navy. |
| St. Paul, Pribilof Islds., Alaska. | NPQ | 600 | PG | N | U. S. Navy. |
| Tampa, Fla........... | WPD | 300, *600* | PG | June 1 to Sept. 30: 7 a. m. to 10 a. m.; noon to 3 p. m; 6 p. m. to 8 p. m. Oct. 1 to May 31: 7 a. m. to 1 a. m. | Marconi Co. |
| Tatoosh, Wash....... | NPD | 600 | PG | N | U. S. Navy. |
| Tuckerton, N. J...... | WGG | .............. | .... | .......... | |
| Tutuila, Samoa...... | NPU | 600 | PG | .......... | U. S. Navy. |
| Unalga, Alaska...... | NPV | 600 | PG | N | U. S. Navy. |
| Virginia Beach, Va... | WSY | 300, *600* | PG | N | Marconi Co. |
| Washington, D. C. (Navy Yard). | NAL | .............. | O | N | U. S. Navy. |
| Washington, D. C. (U. S. Capitol). | NZY | 250, 650, 1000 | O | X | Supt. U. S. Capitol Building and Grounds. |

LAND RADIO STATIONS, ALPHABETICALLY BY NAMES OF STATIONS—Continued.

| Station. | Call signal. | Wave lengths. | Service. | Hours of operation. | Station controlled by— |
|---|---|---|---|---|---|
| Washington, D. C. (Army Signal Corps Laboratory). | WUP | .............. | O | ........... | U. S. Army. |
| Washington, D. C. (Bureau of Standards). | WUQ | .............. | O | ........... | U. S. Army. |
| Wrangell, Alaska..... | WVJ | 300, *600* | PG | 9 a. m. to 9 p. m. | U. S. Army. |
| Zamboango, Mindanao Isld., P. I. | WVW | 600, *1200* | PG | 7 a. m. to 7.30 p.m. | Insular Govt., Philippine Islds. |

SPECIAL STATIONS, ALPHABETICALLY BY NAMES OF STATIONS.

[Variable wave lengths authorized for experimental purposes are indicated by an asterisk (*).]

| Station. | Call signal. | Wave lengths. | Service. | Hours of operation. | Station controlled by— |
|---|---|---|---|---|---|
| Alameda, Cal........ | 6XS | 300, *600** | P | X | Hugh R. Sprado. |
| Ames, Iowa.......... | 9YI | *300** | P | X | Iowa State College of Agriculture and Mechanic Arts. |
| Amesbury, Mass...... | 1XA | 300, *600** | P | X | Wireless Specialty Apparatus Co. |
| Ann Arbor, Mich..... | 8XA | 450, 600 | P | X | University of Michigan. |
| Atlanta, Ga......... | 4XG | *300** | P | X | Georgia School of Technology. |
| Beloit, Wis.......... | 9XB | (*) | P | X | Beloit College. |
| Berkeley, Cal........ | 6XB | 200–3000* | P | X | University of California. |
| Berkeley, Cal........ | 6XR | 300, 600* | P | X | Frank Rieber. |
| Boston, Mass......... | 1XB | 300, 600* | P | X | Wireless Specialty Apparatus Co. |
| Boston, Mass......... | 1XH | 300, 400, 600* | P | X | Holtzer-Cabot Electric Co. |
| Cambridge, Mass.... | 1XP | 300, 550, 600 | P | X | George W. Pierce. |
| Cambridge, Mass.... | 1YH | 300, 550, *600** | P | X | Harvard University. |
| Charleston, S. C..... | 4YC | 300, *600* | P | X | "The Citadel" (S. C. Military Academy). |
| Chelsea, Mass....... | 1XC | 300, 600, 700* | P | X | Wm. J. Murdock Co. |
| Columbia University, N. Y. City. | 2XM | *600*, 1845, 2220, 2630 | P | X | John H. Morecroft. |

LAND RADIO STATIONS, ALPHABETICALLY BY NAMES OF STATIONS—Continued.

SPECIAL STATIONS, ALPHABETICALLY BY NAMES OF STATIONS—Continued.

| Station. | Call signal. | Wave lengths. | Serv-ice. | Hours of operation. | Station controlled by— |
|---|---|---|---|---|---|
| Detroit, Mich. | 8YD | 300, 400, 600 | P | 9 a. m. to 3 p. m.; 7 p. m. to 9 p. m. | Wm. J. Meisenheimer. |
| Friendship Heights, D. C. | 3ZF | 200, *250* | P | X | John V. Pursell. |
| Gloucester, Mass. | 1XI | ... | ... | ... | John Hays Hammond, jr. |
| Grand Forks, N. Dak. | 9YN | *500–730** | P | X | University of North Dakota. |
| Hyattsville, Md. | 3XR | 300, *400*, 600* | P | X | J. Harris Rogers. |
| Kansas City, Mo.[1] | 9XH | (*) | P | X | Harry D. Betz. |
| Key West, Fla. | 4XA | 200, *600* | P | X | George W. Almour. |
| Los Angeles, Cal. | 6XL | 300, 485, 510, 600* | P | X | Y. M. C. A. |
| Los Angeles, Cal. | 6YL | ... | P | X | High School. |
| Memphis, Tenn. | 5XC | *482*, 500, 550, 600 | P | X | Christian Brothers College. |
| Memphis, Tenn. | 5ZD | 600 | P | X | C. B. De La Hunt. |
| Minneapolis, Minn. | 9ZE | *200** | P | X | Philip E. Edelman. |
| New Bedford, Mass. | 1ZO | 200, 300* | P | X | Lester I. Jenkins. |
| New York, N. Y. | 2XH | 300, *600*, 800* | P | X | Walter G. Hudson. |
| New York, N. Y. | 2XN | 300, *600** | P | X | Alfred N. Goldsmith (College of the City of New York). |
| New York, N. Y. *See* Columbia University. | 2XM | | | | |
| Nutley, N. J. | 2ZH | 200,300,450,600 | P | X | Arthur A. Hebert. |
| Oakland, Cal. | 6XC | 300, 550, *600** | P | X | Lewis M. Clement. |
| Oakland, Cal. | 6YE | 300, 500, *600* | P | X | Ellery W. Stone. |
| Oakland, Cal. | 6XT | 300, *600*, 800* | P | X | Howard H. Tremble. |
| Philadelphia, Pa. | 3XC | 300, 480, 600* | P | X | Frank B. Chambers. |
| Philadelphia, Pa. | 3XJ | 300, 500, 600 | P | X | St. Joseph's College. |
| Pittsfield, Mass. | 1XG | *600** | P | X | General Electric Co. |

[1] Portable station.

LAND RADIO STATIONS, ALPHABETICALLY BY NAMES OF STATIONS—Continued.

SPECIAL STATIONS, ALPHABETICALLY BY NAMES OF STATIONS—Continued.

| Station. | Call signal. | Wave lengths. | Service. | Hours of operation. | Station controlled by— |
|---|---|---|---|---|---|
| Quarantine, Curtis Bay, Md. | 3ZR | 300, *600* | P | Sunrise to sunset and until 10 p. m. | Thomas L. Richardson. |
| Riverdale, Md. | 3ZD | | | | Frank A. DeGroot. |
| San Diego, Cal. | 6YS | 300, 500, *600* | P | X | Southern Electrical Co. |
| San Francisco, Cal. | 6XA | 300, *600** | P | X | Howard G. Aylsworth. |
| San Francisco, Cal. | 6XH | *600** | P | X | Wm. W. Hanscom. |
| Savannah, Ga. | 4XL | 300, 460, 560, *600** | P | X | Claude A. Lewis and Manning White. |
| Slingerlands, N. Y. | 2XD | 200, 400, 500, *900*, 2000, 5000 | P | X | Burr V. Deitz. |
| St. Davids, Pa. | 3ZS | 300, *450*, 600 | P | X | Chas. H. Stewart. |
| St. Louis, Mo. | 9YC | | P | | Christian Brothers College. |
| Steamship "Tyler" | 2XT | | P | X | D. G. McCaa. |
| Summit, N. J. | 2XW | *600** | P | X | Frank N Waterman. |
| Takoma Park, Md. | 3XB | 300, 450, 500, *600*, 800, 900, 1100 | P | X | Bliss Electrical School. |
| Valparaiso, Ind. | 9XD | 300, *600** | P | X | Dodge's Institute of Telegraphy. |
| Washington, D. C. | 3ZH | | P | | H. B. DeGroot. |
| Watchaug Pond, R. I. | 1XW | | | | Ralph C. Watrous. |

## SHIP RADIO STATIONS, ALPHABETICALLY BY NAMES OF VESSELS.

[This list includes stations on merchant vessels, yachts, vessels of the Army, the Navy, and the Revenue-Cutter Service.]

| Vessel. | Call signal. | Wave lengths. | Service. | Owner of vessel (line). | Station controlled by— |
|---|---|---|---|---|---|
| Abarenda | NOB | 600 | PG | Government | U. S. Navy. |
| Acushnet | NRU | 300 | PG | do | U. S. R. C. S. |
| Adeline Smith | WHS | | | Inter-Ocean Transp. Co. | |

SHIP RADIO STATIONS, ALPHABETICALLY BY NAMES OF VESSELS—Continued.

| Vessel. | Call signal. | Wave lengths. | Service. | Owner of vessel (line). | Station controlled by— |
|---|---|---|---|---|---|
| Admiral Dewey | WAY | 300, *600* | PG | Pacific-Alaska Nav. Co. | Marconi Co. |
| Admiral Evans | WAB | 300, *600* | PG | Alaska-Pacific S. S. Co. | Marconi Co. |
| Admiral Farragut | WAF | | | Pacific-Alaska Nav. Co. | |
| Admiral Sampson | WAS | 300, *600* | PG | Alaska-Pacific S. S. Co. | Marconi Co. |
| Admiral Schley | WAZ | 300, *600* | PG | Pacific-Alaska Nav. Co. | Marconi Co. |
| Admiral Watson | WAW | 300, *600* | PG | Alaska-Pacific S. S. Co. | Marconi Co. |
| Advance | KMV | 300, *600* | PG | Panama R. R. Co. | Atlantic Communication Co. |
| Adventuress | KYV | | | John Borden | |
| A. G. Lindsay | WNO | | | Pacific-American Fisheries. | |
| Ajax | NBH | 300, *600* | PG | Government | U. S. Navy. |
| Alabama | WFB | 300, *600* | PG | Goodrich Transit Co. | Marconi Co. |
| Alabama | KSX | 300, *600* | PG | Baltimore Steam Packet Co. | Marconi Co. |
| Alabama | NBI | 300, *600* | PG | Government | U. S. Navy. |
| Alameda | WAA | 300, *600* | PG | Alaska S. S. Co. | Marconi Co. |
| Alamo | KEJ | 300, *600* | PG | Mallory S. S. Co. | Marconi Co. |
| Alaskan | WKA | 300, *600* | PG | American-Hawaiian S.S. Co. | Atlantic Communication Co. |
| Albany | NBJ | 300, *600* | PG | Government | U. S. Navy. |
| Albatross | NQY | 300, *600* | PG | ....do | U. S. Navy. |
| Alert | NBL | 300, *600* | PG | ....do | U. S. Navy. |
| Algonquin | KVG | 300, *600* | PG | Clyde S. S. Co. | Marconi Co. |
| Algonquin | NRA | 300, *600* | PG | Government | U. S. R. C. S. |
| Al-Ki | WNK | 300, *600* | PG | H. C. Strong | Marconi Co. |
| Aliança | KMA | 300, *600* | PG | Panama R. R. Co. | Marconi Co. |
| Alliance | WRV | | | Cal. & Oreg. Coast S. S. Co. | |
| Aloha | KYH | | | Arthur Curtiss James | |
| Alvina | WEY | | | Thomas F. Cole | |
| America | KNZ | | | Brooklyn & Manhattan Ferry Co. | |

SHIP RADIO STATIONS, ALPHABETICALLY BY NAMES OF VESSELS—Continued.

| Vessel. | Call signal. | Wave lengths. | Service. | Owner of vessel (line). | Station controlled by— |
|---|---|---|---|---|---|
| American | WKF | 300, 600 | PG | American-Hawaiian S.S. Co. | Atlantic Communication Co. |
| Ammen | NBP | 300, 600 | PG | Government | U. S. Navy. |
| Amphitrite | NHG | 300, 600 | .... | ....do |  |
| Ancon | KMS | 300, 600 | PG | Panama R. R. Co | Atlantic Communication Co. |
| Androscoggin | NRD | 300, 600 | PG | Government | U. S. R. C. S. |
| Annapolis | NBR | 300, 600 | PG | ....do | U. S. Navy. |
| Ann Arbor No. 3 | WDN | 300, 600 | PG | Ann Arbor R. R. Co | Marconi Co. |
| Ann Arbor No. 4 | WDO | 300, 600 | PG | ....do | Marconi Co. |
| Ann Arbor No. 5 | WDP | 300, 600 | PG | ....do | Marconi Co. |
| Antilles | KKA | 300, 600 | PG | Southern Pacific Co | Marconi Co. |
| Apache | KVA | 300, 600 | PG | Clyde S. S. Co | Marconi Co. |
| Apache | NRP | 300, 600 | PG | Government | U. S. R. C. S. |
| Arapahoe | KVB | 300, 600 | PG | Clyde S. S. Co | Marconi Co. |
| Arethusa | NBU | 300, 600 | PG | Government | U. S. Navy. |
| Argyll | WTB | ........ | .... | Union S. S. Co. (Union Oil Co.). |  |
| Arizona | WFG | 300, 600 | PG | Goodrich Transit Co | Marconi Co. |
| Arizonan | WKB | 300, 600 | PG | American-Hawaiian S.S. Co. | Atlantic Communication Co. |
| Arkansas | NBV | 300, 600 | PG | Government | U. S. Navy. |
| Aroline | WRJ | 300, 600 | PG | Aroline S. S. Co | Marconi Co. |
| Ashtabula | WEZ | 300, 600 | PG | Pennsylvania & Ontario Nav. Co. | Marconi Co. |
| Asuncion | WTX | ........ | .... | Associated Oil Co |  |
| Atalanta | KYA | ........ | .... | George J. Gould |  |
| Atlantic City | KMN | ........ | .... | Atlantic City Transp. Co. | Marconi Co. |
| Atlas | WTT | 300, 600 | PG | Standard Oil Co | Marconi Co. |
| Aylwin | NIH | 300, 600 | PG | Government | U. S. Navy. |
| Aztec | WWQ | 300, 600 | PG | Pacific Mail S. S. Co | Marconi Co. |

SHIP RADIO STATIONS, ALPHABETICALLY BY NAMES OF VESSELS—Continued.

| Vessel. | Call signal. | Wave lengths. | Service. | Owner of vessel (line). | Station controlled by— |
|---|---|---|---|---|---|
| Bache | NLK | 300, 400 600 | ..... | Government | U. S. Dept. of Commerce. |
| Bailey | NCF | 300, 600 | PG | .....do | U. S. Navy. |
| Bainbridge | NIA | 300, 600 | PG | .....do | U. S. Navy. |
| Balch | NII | 300, 600 | PG | .....do | U. S. Navy. |
| Baltimore | NCH | 300, 600 | PG | .....do | U. S. Navy. |
| Bayamon | KDX | ........ | ..... | A. H. Bull S. S. Co | |
| Bay State | KRE | 300, 600 | PG | Eastern S. S. Corp | Marconi Co. |
| Beale | NCL | 300, 600 | PG | Government | U. S. Navy |
| Bear | NRB | 300, 600 | PG | .....do | U. S. R. C. S. |
| Bear | WWD | 300, 600 | PG | San Francisco & Portland S. S. Co. | Marconi Co. |
| Beaver | WWB | 300, 600 | PG | .....do | Marconi Co. |
| Belfast | KRD | 300, 600 | PG | Eastern S. S. Corp | Marconi Co. |
| Beluga | WLB | ........ | ..... | American Deep Sea Exploration Co. | Marconi Co. |
| Benham | NIJ | 300, 600 | PG | Government | U. S. Navy. |
| Berkshire | KQB | 300, 600 | PG | Merchants & Miners Transp. Co. | Marconi Co. |
| Berlin | WRB | ........ | ..... | Alaska-Portland Packers' Assn. | |
| Bertha | WBR | ........ | ..... | Alaska Coast Co | |
| Beverly | KND | 300, 600 | ..... | Colonial Nav. Co | |
| Birmingham | NCN | 300, 600 | PG | Government | U. S. Navy. |
| Borinquen | KDW | 300, 600 | PG | Ocean Freight Line (Inc.). | Marconi Co. |
| Boston | KXA | 300, 450, 500, 550, 600 | PG | New England S. S. Co | Nat. Elec. Signaling Co. |
| Brazos | KEZ | 300, 600 | PG | Mallory S. S. Co | Marconi Co. |
| Breakwater | WBK | ........ | ..... | Southern Pacific Co | |
| Brilliant | KTI | 300, 600 | PG | Standard Oil Co | Marconi Co. |
| Brooklyn | NFA | 300, 600 | PG | Government | U. S. Navy. |
| Brunswick | KOS | 300, 600 | PG | Gulf & Southern S. S. Co. | Marconi Co. |
| Prutus | NNA | 300, 600 | PG | Government | U. S. Navy. |

SHIP RADIO STATIONS, ALPHABETICALLY BY NAMES OF VESSELS—Continued.

| Vessel. | Call signal. | Wave lengths. | Service. | Owner of vessel (line). | Station controlled by— |
|---|---|---|---|---|---|
| Buffalo | NCU | 300, *600* | PG | Government | U. S. Navy. |
| Buford | WXA | 600 | PG | ....do | U. S. Army. |
| Bunker Hill | KJB | | | Eastern S. S. Corp | |
| Burnside | WXR | 600 | O | Government | U. S. Army. |
| Burrows | NCV | 300, *600* | PG | ....do | U. S. Navy. |
| Cabrillo | WBV | 300, 500, *600* | PG | Wilmington Transp. Co. | Marconi Co. |
| Caesar | NCY | 300, *600* | PG | Government | U. S. Navy. |
| California | KYQ | | | Mrs. Clara B. Stocker | |
| California | NCZ | 300, *600* | PG | Government | U. S. Navy. |
| Californian | WKC | 300, *600* | PG | American-Hawaiian S.S. Co. | |
| Calvin Austin | KRN | 300, *600* | PG | Eastern S. S. Corp | Marconi Co. |
| Camden | KRC | 300, *600* | PG | ....do | Marconi Co. |
| Camino | WQC | 300, *600* | PG | Western Steam Nav. Co. | Marconi Co. |
| Cape Cod | KPW | | | George R. West | |
| Captain A. F. Lucas. | WTV | 300, *600* | PG | Standard Oil Co. of Cal. | Marconi Co. |
| Captain A. M. Wetherill. | WYT | 300 | O | Government | U. S. Army. |
| Captain Barrett | WYP | 300 | O | ....do | U. S. Army. |
| Captain Chas. W. Rowell. | WYI | 300 | O | ....do | U. S. Army. |
| Captain James Fornance. | WYM | 300 | O | ....do | U. S. Army. |
| Caracas | KDB | 300, *600* | PG | Atlantic & Carribean Steam Nav. Co. (Red D Line). | Marconi Co. |
| Carlos | WNC | 300, *600* | PG | Olson & Mahony S. S. Co. | Marconi Co. |
| Carolina | WFE | 300, *600* | PG | Goodrich Transit Co | Marconi Co. |
| Carolina | KGB | | | New York & Porto Rico S. S. Co. | Marconi Co. |
| Carolyn | KNF | | | A. H. Bull S. S. Co | |
| Cassandra | KYE | | | George J. Whelan | |

SHIP RADIO STATIONS, ALPHABETICALLY BY NAMES OF VESSELS—Continued.

| Vessel. | Call signal. | Wave lengths. | Service. | Owner of vessel (line). | Station controlled by— |
|---|---|---|---|---|---|
| Cassin | NIK | 300, *600* | PG | Government | U. S. Navy. |
| Castine | NDA | 300, *600* | PG | Government | U. S. Navy. |
| Catania | WTI | | | Coast Oil Transp. Co. | |
| Celilo | WMF | 300, *600* | | Charles R. McCormick & Co. (Inc.). | Marconi Co. |
| Celtic | NDB | 300, *600* | PG | Government | U. S. Navy. |
| Centralia | WSN | 300, *600* | PG | Centralia Co. | Marconi Co. |
| Chalmette | KKC | 300, *600* | PG | Southern Pacific Co. | Marconi Co. |
| Charleston | NFE | 300, *600* | PG | Government | U. S. Navy. |
| Chattanooga | NGI | 300, *600* | PG | do | U. S. Navy. |
| Cherokee | KVK | 300, *600* | PG | Clyde S. S. Co. | Marconi Co. |
| Chester | NDG | 600 | PG | Government | U. S. Navy. |
| Chester W. Chapin | KXQ | 300, 450, 500, 550, *600* | PG | New England S. S. Co. | Nat. Elec. Signaling Co. |
| Cheyenne | NDH | 300, *600* | PG | Government | U. S. Navy. |
| Chicago | WAC | | | Booth Fisheries Co. | |
| Chicago | WFI | | | Goodrich Transit Co. | |
| Chicago | NDI | 300, *600* | PG | Government | U. S. Navy. |
| China | WWA | | | Pacific Mail S. S. Co. | |
| Chippewa | WBH | | | Puget Sound Nav. Co. | |
| Christopher Columbus. | WFJ | 300, *600* | PG | Goodrich Transit Co. | Marconi Co. |
| Cincinnati | NDL | 300, *600* | PG | Government | U. S. Navy. |
| City of Alpena II. | WEH | 300, *600* | PG | Detroit & Cleveland Nav. Co. | Marconi Co. |
| City of Annapolis. | KSW | 300, *600* | PG | Chesapeake S. S. Co. | Marconi Co. |
| City of Atlanta | KFB | 300, *600* | PG | Ocean S. S. Co. (Savannah Line). | Marconi Co. |
| City of Augusta | KFJ | 300, *600* | PG | do | Marconi Co. |
| City of Baltimore. | KRY | 300, *600* | PG | Mercantile Trust & Deposit Co. (Chesapeake S. S. Co.). | Marconi Co. |
| City of Bangor | KRH | | | Eastern S. S. Corp. | |

SHIP RADIO STATIONS, ALPHABETICALLY BY NAMES OF VESSELS—Continued.

| Vessel. | Call signal. | Wave lengths. | Service. | Owner of vessel (line). | Station controlled by— |
|---|---|---|---|---|---|
| City of Benton Harbor. | WDV | 300, *600* | PG | Graham & Morton Transp. Co. | Marconi Co. |
| City of Buffalo.... | WFQ | 300, *600* | PG | Cleveland & Buffalo Transit Co. | Marconi Co. |
| City of Chicago.... | WDT | 300, *600* | PG | Graham & Morton Transp. Co. | Marconi Co. |
| City of Cleveland III. | WEA | 300, *600* | PG | Detroit & Cleveland Nav. Co. | Marconi Co. |
| City of Columbus.. | KFA | 300, *600* | PG | Ocean S. S. Co. (Savannah Line). | Marconi Co. |
| City of Detroit II.. | WEC | 300, *600* | PG | Detroit & Cleveland Nav. Co. | Marconi Co. |
| City of Detroit III. | WEF | 300, *600* | PG | .....do................. | Marconi Co. |
| City of Erie....... | WFP | 300, *600* | PG | Cleveland & Buffalo Transit Co. | Marconi Co. |
| City of Everett... | KTQ | ......... | ..... | Standard Oil Co........ | |
| City of Grand Rapids. | WDS | 300, *600* | PG | Graham & Morton Transp. Co. | Marconi Co. |
| City of Lowell.... | KXB | 300, 450, 500, 550, *600* | PG | New England S. S. Co... | Nat. Elec. Signaling Co. |
| City of Mackinac II. | WEB | 300, *600* | PG | Detroit & Cleveland Nav. Co. | Marconi Co. |
| City of Macon..... | KFC | 300, *600* | PG | Ocean S. S. Co. (Savannah Line). | Marconi Co. |
| City of Memphis.. | KFD | 300, *600* | PG | .....do................. | Marconi Co. |
| City of Montgomery. | KFY | 300, *600* | PG | .....do................. | Marconi Co. |
| City of Norfolk.... | KRZ | 300, *600* | PG | Mercantile Trust & Deposit Co. (Chesapeake S. S. Co.). | Marconi Co. |
| City of Panama... | WWP | ......... | ..... | Pacific Mail S. S. Co.... | |
| City of Para....... | WWF | 300, *600* | PG | .....do................. | Marconi Co. |
| City of Puebla.... | WGQ | 300, *600* | PG | Pacific Coast Co........ | Marconi Co. |
| City of Richmond. | KSV | 300, *600* | PG | Mercantile Trust & Deposit Co. (Chesapeake S. S. Co.). | Marconi Co. |
| City of Rockland.. | KRI | 300, *600* | PG | Eastern S. S. Corp...... | Marconi Co. |
| City of St. Ignace. | WEG | 300, *600* | PG | Detroit & Cleveland Nav. Co. | Marconi Co. |

SHIP RADIO STATIONS, ALPHABETICALLY BY NAMES OF VESSELS—Continued.

| Vessel. | Call signal. | Wave lengths. | Service. | Owner of vessel (line). | Station controlled by— |
|---|---|---|---|---|---|
| City of St. Louis.. | KFX | 300, *600* | PG | Ocean S. S. Co. (Savannah Line). | Marconi Co. |
| City of Savannah.. | KFK | 300, *600* | PG | .....do.................. | Marconi Co. |
| City of Seattle.... | WGA | .......... | ..... | Pacific Coast Co......... | Marconi Co. |
| City of South Haven. | WDI | .......... | ..... | Chicago & South Haven S. S. Co. | |
| City of Sydney.... | WWG | 300, *600* | PG | Pacific Mail S. S. Co.... | Marconi Co. |
| City of Taunton... | KXL | 300, 450, 500, 550, *600* | PG | New England S. S. Co.. | Nat. Elec. Signaling Co. |
| City of Topeka.... | WGY | 300, *600* | PG | Pacific Coast Co......... | Marconi Co. |
| Cleveland......... | NDM | 300, *600* | PG | Government............. | U. S. Navy. |
| Coamo............ | KGA | 300, *600* | PG | New York & Porto Rico S. S. Co. | Marconi Co. |
| Col. E. L. Drake.. | WTS | .......... | ..... | Standard Oil Co........ | |
| Col. James M. Schoonmaker. | WEQ | 300, *600* | PG | Shenango S. S. Co...... | Marconi Co. |
| Colon............. | KMX | 300, *600* | PG | Panama R. R. Co....... | Atlantic Communication Co. |
| Colorado........... | KEA | .......... | ..... | Mallory S. S. Co........ | |
| Colorado........... | NDN | 300, *600* | PG | Government............. | U. S. Navy. |
| Columbia......... | KRO | .......... | ..... | Chesapeake S. S. Co..... | |
| Columbia......... | KYM | *300*, 550 | P | J. Harvey Ladew....... | Owner of vessel. |
| Columbia......... | NGA | 300, *600* | PG | Government........... | U. S. Navy. |
| Columbia......... | WPW | .......... | ..... | Port of Portland....... | |
| Columbia......... | WHC | 300, *600* | PG | J. H. Wilson........... | Marconi Co. |
| Columbian........ | WKS | 300, *600* | PG | American-Hawaiian S.S. Co. | Atlantic Communication Co. |
| Comal............ | KEM | 300, *600* | PG | Mallory S. S. Co........ | Marconi Co. |
| Comanche........ | KVC | 300, *600* | PG | Clyde S. S. Co......... | Marconi Co. |
| Comet............ | KTJ | 300, *600* | PG | Standard Oil Co........ | Marconi Co. |
| Commonwealth... | KXC | 300, 450, 500, 550, *600* | PG | New England S. S. Co.. | Nat. Elec. Signaling Co. |

SHIP RADIO STATIONS, ALPHABETICALLY BY NAMES OF VESSELS—Continued.

| Vessel. | Call signal. | Wave lengths. | Service. | Owner of vessel (line). | Station controlled by— |
|---|---|---|---|---|---|
| Comus | KKD | 300, *600* | PG | Southern Pacific Co | Marconi Co. |
| Concho | KEC | 300, *600* | PG | Mallory S. S. Co | Marconi Co. |
| Concord | KNC | 300, 450, 500, 550, *600* | PG | Colonial Nav. Co | Nat. Elec. Signaling Co. |
| Congress | WGT | 300, *600* | PG | Pacific Coast Co | Marconi Co. |
| Connecticut | NDQ | 300, *600* | PG | Government | U. S. Navy. |
| Cordova | WAR | 300, *600* | PG | Alaska S. S Co | Marconi Co. |
| Coronado | WSO | | | Coronado Co | |
| Corsair | KYC | | | J. P. Morgan estate | |
| Corwin | WNN | | | Kotzebue Transp. & Trading Co. | |
| Creole | KKR | 300, *600* | PG | Southern Pacific Co | Marconi Co. |
| Cretan | KQC | 300, *600* | PG | Merchants & Miners Transp. Co. | Marconi Co. |
| Cristobal | KMD | 300, *600* | PG | Panama R. R. Co | Atlantic Communication Co. |
| Crook | WXB | 600 | PG | Government | U. S. Army. |
| Culgoa | NDU | 300, *600* | PG | .....do | U. S. Navy. |
| Cummings | NIL | 300, *600* | PG | .....do | U. S. Navy. |
| Currier | KNU | 300, *600* | PG | Cuba Distilling Co | Marconi Co. |
| Cushing | NIM | 300, *600* | PG | Government | U. S. Navy. |
| C. W. Morse | KMO | 300, *600* | | McAllister Bros | Marconi Co. |
| Cyclops | NDY | 300, *600* | PG | Government | U. S. Navy. |
| Cyprus | KYD | | | Daniel C. Jackling | |
| Dakotan | WKD | 300, *600* | PG | American-Hawaiian S. S. Co. | Marconi Co. |
| Damara | WNM | | | Edgar F. Luckenbach | |
| Decatur | NJC | 300, *600* | PG | Government | U. S. Navy. |
| Delaware | NEK | 300, *600* | PG | .....do | U. S. Navy. |
| Delaware Sun | KTW | 300, *600* | PG | Sun Co | Marconi Co. |
| Delhi | WGD | | | Pacific Coast Co | |
| Denver | KED | 300, *600* | PG | Mallory S. S. Co | Marconi Co. |

SHIP RADIO STATIONS, ALPHABETICALLY BY NAMES OF VESSELS—Continued.

| Vessel. | Call signal. | Wave lengths. | Service. | Owner of vessel (line). | Station controlled by— |
|---|---|---|---|---|---|
| Denver | NEM | 300, *600* | PG | Government | U. S. Navy. |
| Des Moines | NEN | 300, *600* | PG | .....do | U. S. Navy. |
| Diamond Head | WNL | | | Tyee Co | |
| Dirigo | WAO | | | Alaska S. S. Co | |
| Dix | WXC | 600 | PG | Government | U. S. Army. |
| Dixie | NEP | 300, *600* | PG | .....do | U. S. Navy. |
| Dolphin | WAU | | | Alaska S. S. Co | Marconi Co. |
| Dolphin | NEQ | 300, *600* | PG | Government | U. S. Navy. |
| Dora | WAH | | | Alaska S. S. Co | |
| Dorchester | KQD | 300, *600* | PG | Merchants & Miners Transp. Co. | Marconi Co. |
| Dorothy Bradford | KNA | 300, *600* | PG | Cape Cod S. S. Co., trustees. | Marconi Co. |
| Downes | NIN | 300, *600* | PG | Government | U. S. Navy. |
| Drayton | NET | 300, *600* | PG | .....do | U. S. Navy. |
| Dubuque | NEU | 300, *600* | | .....do | |
| Duncan | NIR | 300, *600* | PG | .....do | U. S. Navy. |
| E-1 | NXS | 300, *600* | PG | .....do | U. S. Navy. |
| E-2 | NXT | 300, *600* | PG | .....do | U. S. Navy. |
| Eagle | NFC | 300, *600* | PG | .....do | U. S. Navy. |
| Eastern States | WEE | 300, *600* | PG | Detroit & Cleveland Nav. Co. | Marconi Co. |
| Eastland | WFN | 300, *600* | PG | St. Joseph-Chicago S. S. Co. | Marconi Co. |
| Edgar H. Vance | WQE | | | Nehalem S. S. Co | |
| E. G. Crosby | WEL | | | Crosby Transp. Co | |
| Edith | WAE | | | Alaska S. S. Co | |
| El Alba | KKL | 300, *600* | PG | Southern Pacific Co | Marconi Co. |
| Elcano | NFD | 300, *600* | PG | Government | U. S. Navy. |
| El Cid | KKT | 300, *600* | PG | Southern Pacific Co | Marconi Co. |
| El Dia | KKY | 300, *600* | PG | .....do | Marconi Co. |
| Elmer A. Keeler | KVU | | | Elmer A. Keeler | |

SHIP RADIO STATIONS, ALPHABETICALLY BY NAMES OF VESSELS—Continued.

| Vessel. | Call signal. | Wave lengths. | Service. | Owner of vessel (line). | Station controlled by— |
|---|---|---|---|---|---|
| El Mundo | KKU | 300, 600 | PG | Southern Pacific Co | Marconi Co. |
| El Norte | KKN | | | do | |
| El Occidente | KKX | 300, 600 | PG | do | Marconi Co. |
| El Oriente | KKV | 300, 600 | PG | do | Marconi Co. |
| El Rio | KKZ | 300, 600 | PG | do | Marconi Co. |
| El Segundo | WTQ | | | Standard Oil Co | |
| El Siglo | KKS | 300, 600 | PG | Southern Pacific Co | Marconi Co. |
| El Sol | KKB | 300, 600 | PG | do | Marconi Co. |
| El Sud | KKQ | 300, 600 | PG | do | Marconi Co. |
| El Valle | KKW | 300, 600 | PG | do | Marconi Co. |
| Enterprise | WMN | 300, 600 | PG | Matson Nav. Co | Marconi Co. |
| Eocene | KTM | | | Standard Oil Co | Owner of vessel. |
| Erskine M. Phelps | WTA | | | William D. Sewall (Union Oil Co.). | |
| Esperanza | KWZ | 300, 600 | PG | N. Y. & Cuba Mail S. S. Co. (Ward Line). | Marconi Co. |
| Essex | KQE | 300, 600 | PG | Merchants & Miners Transp. Co. | Marconi Co. |
| Evelyn | KNE | | | A. H. Bull S. S. Co | |
| Excelsior | KKO | 300, 600 | PG | Southern Pacific Co | Marconi Co. |
| Explorer | NLI | 300, 600 | O | Government | U. S. Dept. of Commerce. |
| F-1 | NXU | 300. 600 | PG | do | U. S. Navy. |
| F-2 | NXV | 300, 600 | PG | do | U. S. Navy. |
| F-3 | NXW | 300, 600 | PG | do | U. S. Navy. |
| F-4 | NXX | 300, 600 | PG | do | U. S. Navy. |
| F. A. Kilburn | WRW | 300, 600 | PG | North Pacific S. S. Co. | Marconi Co. |
| Falcon | WRK | 300, 600 | PG | Charles Nelson Co | Marconi Co. |
| Fanning | NFM | 300, 600 | PG | Government | U. S. Navy. |
| Farragut | NVS | 300, 600 | PG | do | U. S. Navy. |
| Favorite | WCF | 300, 600 | PG | Great Lakes Towing Co. | Marconi Co. |
| Fifield | WRF | 300, 600 | PG | Fifield S. S. Co | Marconi Co. |

SHIP RADIO STATIONS, ALPHABETICALLY BY NAMES OF VESSELS—Continued.

| Vessel. | Call signal. | Wave lengths. | Service. | Owner of vessel (line). | Station controlled by— |
|---|---|---|---|---|---|
| Finland | KSF | | | International Mercantile Marine Co. (Red Star Line). | Marconi Co. |
| Florence | KYF | | | Alphonse H. Alker | |
| Florida | KSY | 300, *600* | PG | Baltimore Steam Packet Co. | Marconi Co. |
| Florida | KUS | | | The Texas Co | Marconi Co. |
| Florida | NFR | 300, *600* | PG | Government | U. S. Navy. |
| Flusser | NFS | 300, *600* | PG | do | U. S. Navy. |
| Forward | KPF | | | Yankee Salvage Assn | Marconi Co. |
| Frank H. Buck | WTO | 300, *600* | | Associated Oil Co | |
| Frieda | KFF | 300, *600* | PG | Union Sulphur Co | Marconi Co. |
| G-1 | NXY | 300, *600* | PG | Government | U. S. Navy. |
| G-2 | NXZ | 300, *600* | PG | do | U. S. Navy. |
| G-3 | NYA | 300, *600* | PG | do | U. S. Navy. |
| G-4 | NYB | 300, *600* | PG | do | U. S. Navy. |
| Galveston | NGD | 300, *600* | PG | do | U. S. Navy. |
| General A. M. Randol. | WYJ | 300 | O | do | U. S. Army. |
| General E. O. C. Ord. | WYF | 400, *600* | O | do | U. S. Army. |
| General Harvey Brown. | WYK | 300 | O | do | U. S. Army. |
| General Henry J. Hunt. | WYD | 400 | O | do | U. S. Army. |
| General Henry Knox. | WYE | 400 | O | do | U. S. Army. |
| General Hubbard. | WMT | | | Hubbard S. S. Co | |
| General R. B. Ayres. | WYL | 300 | O | Government | U. S. Army. |
| General Robert Anderson. | WYH | 300 | O | do | U. S. Army. |
| General Royal T. Frank. | WYA | 300 | O | do | U. S. Army. |

54773°—14——3

SHIP RADIO STATIONS, ALPHABETICALLY BY NAMES OF VESSELS—Continued.

| Vessel. | Call signal. | Wave lengths. | Service. | Owner of vessel (line). | Station controlled by— |
|---|---|---|---|---|---|
| General S. N. Mills. | WYB | 300, 600 | O | Government | U. S. Army. |
| Genl. Pettibone | KUP | 300, 600 | | Guyton & Co | Marconi Co. |
| Geo. W. Elder | WRT | | | North Pacific S. S. Co. | |
| George W. Fenwick. | WNG | | | Fenwick S. S. Co. (California & Atlantic S. S. Co.). | |
| Georgia | WFA | | | Goodrich Transit Co | |
| Georgia | NGF | 300, 600 | PG | Government | U. S. Navy. |
| Georgian | WKG | 300, 600 | PG | American-Hawaiian S.S. Co. | Marconi Co. |
| Glacier | NGH | 600 | PG | Government | U. S. Navy. |
| Glory of the Seas. | WBZ | | | Glacier Fisheries Co | |
| Gloucester | KQG | 300, 600 | PG | Merchants & Miners Transp. Co. | Marconi Co. |
| Gloucester | NSL | 300, 600 | | Government | |
| Goldsborough | NGJ | 300, 600 | PG | do | U. S. Navy. |
| Goliah | WPG | | | Puget Sound Tug Boat Co. | |
| Governor | WGR | 300, 600 | PG | Pacific Coast Co | Marconi Co. |
| Governor Cobb | KRB | 300, 600 | PG | Eastern S. S. Corp | Marconi Co. |
| Governor Dingley. | KRV | 300, 600 | PG | do | Marconi Co. |
| Grace Dollar | WSF | 300, 600 | PG | Grace Dollar S. S. Co | Marconi Co. |
| Grayson | KDV | | | Ocean Freight Line (Inc.) | |
| Grecian | KQR | 300, 600 | PG | Merchants & Miners Transp. Co. | Marconi Co. |
| Greenwood | WQG | | | Greenwood S. S. Co | |
| Gresham | NRG | 300, 600, 750 | PG | Government | U. S. R. C. S. |
| Guardian | WGZ | 300, 600 | PG | Central & South American Telegraph Co. | Owner of vessel. |
| Gulfoil | KTG | 300, 600 | PG | Gulf Refining Co | Marconi Co. |
| H-1 | NYC | 300, 600 | PG | Government | U. S. Navy. |
| H-2 | NYD | 300, 600 | PG | do | U. S. Navy. |
| H-3 | NYE | 300, 600 | PG | do | U. S. Navy. |

SHIP RADIO STATIONS, ALPHABETICALLY BY NAMES OF VESSELS—Continued.

| Vessel. | Call signal. | Wave lengths. | Service. | Owner of vessel (line). | Station controlled by— |
|---|---|---|---|---|---|
| Hamilton | KOA | 300, *600* | PG | Old Dominion S. S. Co. | Marconi Co. |
| Hanalei | WHN | 300, *600* | PG | Independent S. S. Co. | Marconi Co. |
| Hancock | NHI | 300, *600* | PG | Government | U. S. Navy. |
| Hannibal | NGU | 300, *600* | PG | do | U. S. Navy. |
| Harvard | WRH | 300, *600* | PG | Metropolitan S. S. Co. (Pacific Steam Nav. Co.). | |
| Havana | KWH | 300, *600* | PG | N. Y. & Cuba Mail S. S. Co. (Ward Line). | Marconi Co. |
| Hawaiian | WKU | 300, *600* | PG | American-Hawaiian S. S. Co. | |
| Hector | NGX | 300, *600* | PG | Government | U. S. Navy. |
| Helena | NGY | 300, *600* | PG | do | U. S. Navy. |
| Henley | NHA | 300, *600* | PG | do | U. S. Navy. |
| Henry T. Scott | WRA | | | California S. S. Co. | |
| Herman Frasch | KFH | 300, *600* | PG | Union Sulphur Co. | |
| Hermosa | WBP | | | Wilmington Transp. Co. | |
| Hilonian | WMM | 300, *600* | PG | Matson Nav. Co. | Marconi Co. |
| Holland | WDW | 300, *600* | PG | Graham & Morton Transp. Co. | Marconi Co. |
| Honolulan | WKH | 300, *600* | PG | American-Hawaiian S. S. Co. | Marconi Co. |
| Hopkins | NHC | 300, *600* | PG | Government | U. S. Navy. |
| Howard | KQH | 300, *600* | PG | Merchants & Miners Transp. Co. | Marconi Co. |
| Hull | NHE | 300, *600* | PG | Government | U. S. Navy. |
| Humboldt | WHX | | | Humboldt S. S. Co. | Marconi Co. |
| Huron | KVH | 300, *600* | PG | Clyde S. S. Co. | Marconi Co. |
| Hyades | WMK | | | Matson Nav. Co. | |
| Iaqua | WLI | 300, *600* | PG | John A. McGregor | Marconi Co. |
| I. D. Fletcher | KFI | | | Coast Transit Co. | |
| I. J. Merritt | KRQ | | | Merritt & Chapman Derrick & Wrecking Co. | |
| Illinois | WCZ | 300, *600* | PG | Northern Michigan Transp. Co. | Marconi Co. |

SHIP RADIO STATIONS, ALPHABETICALLY BY NAMES OF VESSELS—Continued.

| Vessel. | Call signal. | Wave lengths. | Service. | Owner of vessel (line). | Station controlled by— |
|---|---|---|---|---|---|
| Illinois | KTH | | | Texas S. S. Co | |
| Illinois | NHO | 300, *600* | PG | Government | U. S. Navy. |
| Independent | WPI | | | Weiding & Independent Fisheries Co. | |
| Indian | KQI | 300, *600* | PG | Merchants & Miners Transp. Co. | Marconi Co. |
| Indiana | WFC | 300, *600* | PG | Goodrich Transit Co | Marconi Co. |
| Indiana | NHQ | 300, *600* | PG | Government | U. S. Navy. |
| Iowa | WFD | 300, *600* | PG | Goodrich Transit Co | Marconi Co. |
| Iowa | NHT | 600 | PG | Government | U. S. Navy. |
| Iowan | WKJ | 300, *600* | PG | American-Hawaiian S.S. Co. | Atlantic Communication Co. |
| Iris | NHU | 300, *600* | PG | Government | U. S. Navy. |
| Iroquois | KVF | | | Clyde S. S. Co | |
| Iroquois | WBG | | | Puget Sound Nav. Co | |
| Iroquois | NHV | 300, *600* | PG | Government | U. S. Navy. |
| Isla de Luzon | NQJ | 300, *600* | | do | |
| Isthmian | WKI | 300, *600* | PG | American-Hawaiian S. S. Co. | Atlantic Communication Co. |
| Itasca | NRI | 300, *600* | PG | Government | U. S. R. C. S. |
| J. A. Chanslor | WTK | | | Associated Oil Co | |
| James Duane | KIJ | | | New York City | N. Y. City Fire Dept. |
| Jamestown | KOC | 300, *600* | PG | Old Dominion S. S. Co | Marconi Co. |
| Jarvis | NIB | 300, *600* | PG | Government | U. S. Navy. |
| Jason | NNB | 300, *600* | PG | do | U. S. Navy. |
| J. B. Stetson | WRC | 300, *600* | PG | Hicks-Hauptman Nav. Co. | Marconi Co. |
| Jefferson | KOD | 300, *600* | PG | Old Dominion S. S. Co | Marconi Co. |
| Jefferson | WAJ | 300, *600* | PG | Alaska S. S. Co | Marconi Co. |
| Jenkins | NID | 300, *600* | PG | Government | U. S. Navy. |
| J. M. Guffey | KTF | 300, *600* | PG | Gulf Refining Co | Marconi Co. |

SHIP RADIO STATIONS, ALPHABETICALLY BY NAMES OF VESSELS—Continued.

| Vessel. | Call signal. | Wave lengths. | Service. | Owner of vessel (line). | Station controlled by— |
|---|---|---|---|---|---|
| John A. Hooper... | WSJ | 300, *600* | PG | Sudden & Christenson (Inc.). | Marconi Co. |
| John D. Archbold. | KTK | 300, *600* | ..... | Standard Oil Co........ | Marconi Co. |
| Joseph Henry.... | WXT | 600 | O | Government........... | U. S. Army. |
| Joseph Pulitzer.... | WPZ | ........... | ..... | Port of Portland......... | |
| Jouett............ | NIE | 300, *600* | PG | Government........... | U. S. Navy. |
| Juniata........... | KQJ | 300, *600* | PG | Merchants & Miners Transp. Co. | Marconi Co. |
| Juniata........... | WCB | 300, *600* | PG | Erie & Western Transp. Co. (Anchor Line). | Marconi Co. |
| Jupiter............ | NNC | 300, *600* | PG | Government........... | U. S. Navy. |
| Justin............ | NNJ | 300, *600* | PG | .....do................ | U. S. Navy. |
| K-1.............. | NYF | 300, *600* | PG | .....do................ | U. S. Navy. |
| K-2.............. | NYG | 300, *600* | PG | .....do................ | U. S. Navy. |
| K-3.............. | NYH | 300, *600* | PG | .....do................ | U. S. Navy. |
| K-4.............. | NYI | 300, *600* | PG | .....do................ | U. S. Navy. |
| K-5.............. | NYJ | 300, *600* | PG | .....do................ | U. S. Navy. |
| K-6.............. | NYK | 300, *600* | PG | .....do................ | U. S. Navy. |
| K-7.............. | NYL | 300, *600* | PG | .....do................ | U. S. Navy. |
| K-8.............. | NYM | 300, *600* | PG | .....do................ | U. S. Navy. |
| Kansan........... | WKK | ........... | ..... | American-Hawaiian S. S. Co. | |
| Kansas........... | NIO | 300, *600* | PG | Government........... | U. S. Navy. |
| Kansas City....... | WWS | ........... | ..... | San Francisco & Portland S. S. Co. | |
| Karina .......... | KYR | ........... | ..... | Theodore P. Burgess.... | |
| Kearsarge......... | NIP | 300, *600* | PG | Government........... | U. S. Navy. |
| Kentuckian....... | WKE | 300, *600* | PG | American-Hawaiian S.S. Co. | |
| Kentucky......... | NIQ | 300, *600* | PG | Government........... | U. S. Navy. |
| Kershaw.......... | KQK | 300, *600* | PG | Merchants & Miners Transp. Co. | Marconi Co. |
| Kilpatrick........ | WXD | 600 | PG | Government........... | U. S. Army. |
| Kingfisher........ | WPK | ........... | ..... | New England Fish Co... | |

SHIP RADIO STATIONS, ALPHABETICALLY BY NAMES OF VESSELS—Continued.

| Vessel. | Call signal. | Wave lengths. | Service. | Owner of vessel (line). | Station controlled by— |
|---|---|---|---|---|---|
| Kismet | KYK | | | Bob Myers Babcock | |
| Klamath | WSX | 300, *600* | PG | Klamath S. S. Co | Marconi Co. |
| Korea | WWK | 300, *600* | PG | Pacific Mail S. S. Co | Marconi Co. |
| Kroonland | KSH | | | International Mercantile Marine Co. (Red Star Line). | Marconi Co. |
| Kukui | NLF | 300, *600* | O | Government | U. S. Dept. of Commerce. |
| Kvichak | WNS | | | Alaska Packers' Assn | |
| Lakeland | WDL | 300, *600* | PG | Port Huron & Duluth S. S. Co. | Marconi Co. |
| Lakeport | WDJ | | | do | Marconi Co. |
| Lakewood | WDK | | | do | Marconi Co. |
| Lampasas | KEP | 300, *600* | PG | Mallory S. S. Co | Marconi Co. |
| Lamson | NIW | 300, *600* | PG | Government | U. S. Navy. |
| Lansing | WTC | 300, *600* | PG | Union S. S. Co. (Union Oil Co.). | Marconi Co. |
| Larimer | KTA | 300, *600* | PG | Gulf Refining Co | Marconi Co. |
| Latouche | WAI | | | Alaska S. S. Co | Marconi Co. |
| Lawrence | NIY | 300, *600* | PG | Government | U. S. Navy |
| Lebanon | NIZ | 300, *600* | PG | do | U. S. Navy. |
| Leelanaw | WNI | | | Leelanaw S. S. Co. (California & Atlantic S. S. Co.). | Marconi Co. |
| Lenape | KVL | 300, *600* | PG | Clyde S. S. Co | Marconi Co. |
| Leonidas | NNH | 300, *600* | PG | Government | U. S. Navy. |
| Lewis Luckenbach | WNH | | | Edgar F. Luckenbach (California & Atlantic S. S. Co.). | |
| Lexington | KNB | 300, 450, 500, 550, *600*. | PG | Colonial Nav. Co | Nat. Elec. Signaling Co. |
| Lexington | KQL | 300, *600* | PG | Merchants & Miners Transp. Co. | Marconi Co. |
| Ligonier | KTD | | | Gulf Refining Co | |
| Liscum | WXE | 600 | PG | Government | U. S. Army. |
| Logan | WXF | 600 | PG | do | U. S. Army. |

SHIP RADIO STATIONS, ALPHABETICALLY BY NAMES OF VESSELS—Continued.

| Vessel. | Call signal. | Wave lengths. | Service. | Owner of vessel (line). | Station controlled by— |
|---|---|---|---|---|---|
| Louise | KRL | | | Tolchester Beach Improvement Co. | |
| Louisiana | NJB | 300, *600* | PG | Government | U. S. Navy. |
| Lucy Neff | KNQ | | | C. L. Dimon | |
| Lundin power lifeboat. | KVX | | | Welin Marine Equipment Co. | |
| Lurline | WML | 300, *600* | PG | Matson Nav. Co | Marconi Co. |
| Lydonia | WDY | | | W. A. Lydon | |
| Lyra | WNF | 300, *600* | PG | Edgar F. Luckenbach (Luckenbach S. S. Co.). | Marconi Co. |
| Lysistrata | KYL | | | James G. Bennett | |
| Macdonough | NJH | 300, *600* | PG | Government | U. S. Navy. |
| Machias | NQL | 300, *600* | PG | .....do | U. S. Navy. |
| Mackinaw | WHW | | | Mackinaw Co | Marconi Co. |
| Madison | KOG | 300, *600* | PG | Old Dominion S. S. Co | Marconi Co. |
| Maine | KME | | | Charles Clark & Co | Marconi Co. |
| Maine | KXD | 300, 450, 500, 550, *600* | PG | New England S. S. Co | Nat. Elec. Signaling Co. |
| Maine | NJL | 300, *600* | PG | Government | U. S. Navy. |
| Major Evan Thomas. | WYO | 300 | O | .....do | U. S. Army. |
| Major Samuel Ringgold. | WYC | 300 | O | .....do | U. S. Army. |
| Manchuria | WWE | 300, *600* | PG | Pacific Mail S. S. Co | Marconi Co. |
| Manitou | WFW | 300, *600* | PG | Northern Michigan Transp. Co. | Marconi Co. |
| Manning | NRN | 300, *600* | PG | Government | U. S. R. C. S. |
| Manoa | WMQ | 300, *600* | PG | Matson Nav. Co | Marconi Co. |
| Maracaibo | KDM | 300, *600* | PG | Atlantic & Caribbean Steam Nav. Co. (Red D Line). | Marconi Co. |
| Marietta | NJQ | 300, *600* | PG | Government | U. S. Navy. |
| Mariposa | WHP | | | Alaska S. S. Co | Marconi Co. |
| Marquette & Bessemer No. 1. | WEW | 300, *600* | PG | Marquette & Bessemer Dock & Nav. Co. | Marconi Co. |

SHIP RADIO STATIONS, ALPHABETICALLY BY NAMES OF VESSELS—Continued.

| Vessel. | Call signal. | Wave lengths. | Service. | Owner of vessel (line). | Station controlled by— |
|---|---|---|---|---|---|
| Marquette & Bessemer No. 2. | WEX | 300, *600* | PG | Marquette & Bessemer Dock & Nav. Co. | Marconi Co. |
| Mars | NJR | 300, *600* | PG | Government | U. S. Navy. |
| Marblehead | NGK | 300, *600* | | do | |
| Maryland | NJS | 300, *600* | PG | do | U. S. Navy. |
| Mascotte | KOW | | | Peninsular & Occidental S. S. Co. | |
| Massachusetts | KJM | 300, *600* | PG | Eastern S. S. Corp | |
| Massachusetts | NJT | 300, *600* | PG | Government | U. S. Navy. |
| Matsonia | WMP | 300, *600* | PG | Matson Nav. Co. | Marconi Co. |
| Maverick | WTW | | | Standard Oil Co. | |
| Mayflower | NJV | 300, *600* | PG | Government | U. S. Navy. |
| Mayrant | NJU | 300, *600* | PG | do | U. S. Navy. |
| McCall | NJW | 300, *600* | PG | do | U. S. Navy. |
| McClellan | WXH | 600 | PG | do | U. S. Army. |
| McCulloch | NRH | 300, *600* | PG | do | U. S. R. C. S. |
| McDougal | NIT | 300, *600* | PG | do | U. S. Navy. |
| Meade | WXG | 600 | PG | do | U. S. Army. |
| Merrimack | KQM | 300, *600* | PG | Merchants & Miners Transp. Co. | Marconi Co. |
| Merritt | WXI | 600 | PG | Government | U. S. Army. |
| Mexican | WKL | 300, *600* | PG | American-Hawaiian S. S. Co. | Atlantic Communication Co. |
| Mexico | KWX | 300, *600* | PG | N. Y. & Cuba Mail S. S. Co. (Ward Line). | Marconi Co. |
| Miami | KOZ | | | Peninsular & Occidental S. S. Co. | |
| Miami | NRQ | 300, *600*, 750 | PG | Government | U. S. R. C. S. |
| Michigan | NJZ | 300, *600* | PG | do | U. S. Navy. |
| Millinocket | KNM | 300, *600* | PG | A. H. Bull S. S. Co. | Marconi Co. |
| Mills | KRR | | | Ogden Mills | |
| Milwaukee | NFB | 300, *600* | PG | Government | U. S. Navy. |
| Minneapolis | NGB | 300, *600* | PG | do | U. S. Navy. |

SHIP RADIO STATIONS, ALPHABETICALLY BY NAMES OF VESSELS—Continued.

| Vessel. | Call signal. | Wave lengths. | Service. | Owner of vessel (line). | Station controlled by— |
|---|---|---|---|---|---|
| Minnesota.......... | WEK | 300, *600* | PG | Crosby Transp. Co...... | Marconi Co. |
| Minnesota.......... | WMI | .......... | ..... | Great Northern S. S. Co. | Marconi Co. |
| Minnesota.......... | NKD | 300, *600* | PG | Government............ | U. S. Navy. |
| Minnesotan........ | WKM | 300, *600* | PG | American-Hawaiian S. S. Co. | Marconi Co. |
| Missouri........... | WFX | 300, *600* | PG | Northern Michigan Transp. Co. | Marconi Co. |
| Missouri........... | NKF | 300, *600* | PG | Government............ | U. S. Navy. |
| Missourian........ | WKX | 300, *600* | PG | American-Hawaiian S.S. Co. | |
| Mohawk.......... | KVM | 300, *600* | PG | Clyde S. S. Co......... | Marconi Co. |
| Mohawk.......... | KXE | 300, 450, 500, 550, *600* | PG | New England S. S. Co.. | Nat. Elec. Signaling Co. |
| Mohawk.......... | KYU | 300 | P | Ralph E. Barry........ | Owner of vessel. |
| Mohawk.......... | NVM | 300, *600* | PG | Government............ | U. S. R. C. S. |
| Mohegan.......... | KXM | 300, 450, 500, 550, *600*. | PG | New England S. S. Co.. | Nat. Elec. Signaling Co. |
| Momus............ | KKM | 300, *600* | PG | Southern Pacific Co..... | Marconi Co. |
| Monadnock....... | NHD | 300, *600* | PG | Government............ | U. S. Navy. |
| Monaghan......... | NKL | 300, *600* | PG | .....do.................. | U. S. Navy. |
| Mongolia.......... | WWN | 300, *600* | PG | Pacific Mail S. S. Co.... | Marconi Co. |
| Monocacy......... | NQQ | 300, *600* | PG | Government............ | U. S. Navy. |
| Montana.......... | NKM | 300, *600* | PG | .....do.................. | U. S. Navy. |
| Montanan......... | WKN | .......... | ..... | American-Hawaiian S.S. Co. | |
| Montauk.......... | KNT | .......... | ..... | Montauk Steamboat Co. | |
| Monterey......... | KWY | 300, *600* | PG | N. Y. & Cuba Mail S. S. Co. (Ward Line). | Marconi Co. |
| Monterey......... | NKN | 300, *600* | PG | Government............ | U. S. Navy. |
| Montgomery...... | NKO | 300, *600* | PG | .....do.................. | U. S. Navy. |
| Morrill........... | NRC | 300 | PG | .....do.................. | U. S. R. C. S. |
| Morro Castle...... | KWC | 300, *600* | PG | N. Y. & Cuba Mail S. S. Co. (Ward Line). | Marconi Co. |

SHIP RADIO STATIONS, ALPHABETICALLY BY NAMES OF VESSELS—Continued.

| Vessel. | Call signal. | Wave lengths. | Service. | Owner of vessel (line). | Station controlled by— |
|---|---|---|---|---|---|
| Multnomah | WMA | .......... | ..... | Multnomah S. S. Co | |
| Nacoochee | KFP | 300, *600* | PG | Ocean S. S. Co. (Savannah Line). | Marconi Co. |
| Nann Smith | WBO | 300, *600* | PG | Inter-Ocean Transp. Co | Marconi Co. |
| Nanshan | NNK | 300, *600* | PG | Government | U. S. Navy. |
| Nantucket | KQN | 300, *600* | PG | Merchants & Miners Transp. Co. | Marconi Co. |
| Nashville | NKY | 300, *600* | PG | Government | U. S. Navy. |
| Navajo | WNJ | .......... | ..... | Western Steam Nav. Co. (California & Atlantic S. S. Co.). | |
| Navajo | NKZ | 300, *600* | PG | Government | U. S. Navy. |
| Navesink | WXU | 400–800 (*600*) | O | .....do | U. S. Army. |
| Nebraska | NMA | 300, *600* | PG | .....do | U. S. Navy. |
| Nebraskan | WKY | 300, *600* | PG | American-Hawaiian S. S. Co. | Atlantic Communication Co. |
| Nelson | KNL | 300, *600* | PG | Cuba Distilling Co | Marconi Co. |
| Neptune | NMS | 300, *600* | PG | Government | U. S. Navy. |
| Nereus | NNF | 300, *600* | PG | .....do | U. S. Navy. |
| Nero | NMB | 300, *600* | PG | .....do | U. S. Navy. |
| Nevadan | WKZ | 300, *600* | PG | American-Hawaiian S. S. Co. | Atlantic Communication Co. |
| New Hampshire | KXF | 300, 450, 500, 550, *600* | PG | New England S. S. Co | Nat. Elec. Signaling Co. |
| New Hampshire | NME | 300, *600* | PG | Government | U. S. Navy. |
| New Haven | KXN | 300, 450, 500, 550, *600*. | PG | New England S. S. Co | Nat. Elec. Signaling Co. |
| New Jersey | KNJ | .......... | ..... | United N. Y. & Sandy Hook Pilots' Assn. | |
| New Jersey | NMF | 300, *600* | PG | Government | U. S. Navy. |
| New Orleans | NMG | 300, *600* | PG | .....do | U. S. Navy. |
| Newport | NMH | 300, *600* | PG | .....do | U. S. Navy. |
| Newport | WWH | 300, *600* | PG | Pacific Mail S. S. Co | Marconi Co. |

SHIP RADIO STATIONS, ALPHABETICALLY BY NAMES OF VESSELS—Continued.

| Vessel. | Call signal. | Wave lengths. | Service. | Owner of vessel (line). | Station controlled by— |
|---|---|---|---|---|---|
| New York........ | KNK | .......... | ..... | United N. Y. & Sandy Hook Pilots' Assn. | |
| New York........ | KSN | .......... | ..... | International Mercantile Marine Co. (American Line). | |
| New York........ | NCC | 300, *600* | PG | Government.......... | U. S. Navy. |
| Niagara.......... | KYN | .......... | ..... | Howard Gould........ | |
| Nicholson....... | NIU | 300, *600* | PG | Government.......... | U. S. Navy. |
| Noma........... | KYO | .......... | ..... | Vincent Astor......... | |
| Nome City....... | WRN | 300, *600* | PG | Charles Nelson Co...... | Marconi Co. |
| North American.. | WEN | 300, *600* | PG | Chicago, Duluth & Georgian Bay S. S. Co. | Marconi Co. |
| North Carolina.... | NMN | 300, *600* | PG | Government.......... | U. S. Navy. |
| North Dakota..... | NMO | 300, *600* | PG | .....do.............. | U. S. Navy. |
| Northland........ | WNX | .......... | ..... | E. J. Dodge Co........ | |
| North Land...... | WCN | 300, *600* | PG | Northern S. S. Co...... | Marconi Co. |
| North Land....... | KJD | 300, *600* | PG | Eastern S. S. Corp...... | Marconi Co. |
| North Star....... | KJS | 300, *600* | PG | .....do.............. | Marconi Co. |
| North Star....... | KYZ | .......... | ..... | Cornelius Vanderbilt.... | |
| North Star....... | WHR | .......... | ..... | Alaska Fishermen's Packing Co. | Marconi Co. |
| Northwestern..... | WAN | 300, *600* | PG | Alaska S. S. Co........ | Marconi Co. |
| North Wind....... | KYB | 300 | P | Charles Martin Clark.... | Owner of vessel. |
| Norwood......... | WSG | 300, *600* | PG | Sudden & Christenson (Inc.). | Marconi Co. |
| Nueces........... | KEH | 300, *600* | PG | Mallory S. S. Co........ | Marconi Co. |
| Nushagak........ | WNE | ........ | ..... | Alaska Packers' Assn... | |
| Nyack........... | WEJ | .......... | ..... | Crosby Transp. Co..... | |
| O'Brien.......... | NIV | 300, *600* | PG | Government.......... | U. S. Navy. |
| Octorara......... | WCD | 300, *600* | PG | Erie & Western Transp. Co. (Anchor Line). | Marconi Co. |
| Ohio............. | NMW | 300, *600* | PG | Government.......... | U. S. Navy. |
| Ohioan........... | WKQ | 300, *600* | PG | American-Hawaiian S.S. Co. | |

SHIP RADIO STATIONS, ALPHABETICALLY BY NAMES OF VESSELS—Continued.

| Vessel. | Call signal. | Wave lengths. | Service. | Owner of vessel (line). | Station controlled by— |
|---|---|---|---|---|---|
| Old Colony | KJO | | | Eastern S. S. Corp. | |
| Oleum | WTD | | | Fillmore Condit (Union Oil Co.). | |
| Oliver J. Olson | WNB | 300, *600* | PG | Steamer California Co. | Marconi Co. |
| Olivette | KOV | 300, *600* | PG | Peninsular & Occidental S. S. Co. | Marconi Co. |
| Oneida | KYP | 300, 550, *600* | P | E. C. Benedict | Owner of vessel. |
| Oneonta | WPX | | | Port of Portland | |
| Onondaga | NRO | 300, *600*, 750 | PG | Government | U. S. R. C. S. |
| Ontario | KQO | 300, *600* | PG | Merchants & Miners Transp. Co. | Marconi Co. |
| Ontario | NTA | 300, *600* | PG | Government | U. S. Navy. |
| Oregon | NMZ | 300, *600* | PG | do | U. S. Navy. |
| Oregonian | WKO | 300, *600* | PG | American-Hawaiian S.S. Co. | |
| Orion | NOC | 300, *600* | PG | Government | U. S. Navy. |
| Osceola | NOA | 300, *600* | PG | do | U. S. Navy. |
| Ossabaw | KEO | | | Atlantic, Gulf & West Indies S. S. Lines. | |
| Ozark | NHH | 300, *600* | PG | Government | U. S. Navy. |
| Paducah | NOG | 300, *600* | PG | do | U. S. Navy. |
| Palos | NQS | 300, *600* | PG | do | U. S. Navy. |
| Pamlico | NRR | 300 | PG | do | U. S. R. C. S. |
| Pampanga | NQT | 300, *600* | PG | do | U. S. Navy. |
| Panama | KMH | 300, *600* | PG | Panama R. R. Co. | Atlantic Communication Co. |
| Panaman | WKR | 300, *600* | PG | American-Hawaiian S.S. Co. | |
| Pan American | KUT | | | Texas S. S. Co. | |
| Panther | NOJ | 300, *600* | PG | Government | U. S. Navy. |
| Paraguay | KTT | | | Sun Co. | Marconi Co. |
| Paraiso | WRI | 300, *600* | PG | Craig Shipbuilding Co. | Marconi Co. |

SHIP RADIO STATIONS, ALPHABETICALLY BY NAMES OF VESSELS—Continued.

| Vessel. | Call signal. | Wave lengths. | Service. | Owner of vessel (line). | Station controlled by— |
|---|---|---|---|---|---|
| Parker | NIX | 300, 600 | PG | Government | U. S. Navy. |
| Parthian | KQP | 300, 600 | PG | Merchants & Miners Transp. Co. | Marconi Co. |
| Patapsco | NOL | 600 | PG | Government | U. S. Navy. |
| Pathfinder | NLJ | | | do | U. S. Dept. of Commerce. |
| Patterson | NLH | 300, 600 | O | do | U. S. Dept. of Commerce. |
| Patterson | NOK | 300, 600 | PG | do | U. S. Navy. |
| Patuxent | NOM | 300, 600 | PG | do | U. S. Navy. |
| Paulding | NON | 300, 600 | PG | do | U. S. Navy. |
| Paul Jones | NOP | 300, 600 | PG | do | U. S. Navy. |
| Pennsylvania | WWI | 300, 600 | PG | Pacific Mail S. S. Co | Marconi Co. |
| Pennsylvanian | WKP | 300, 600 | PG | American-Hawaiian S.S. Co. | |
| Peoria | NOW | 300, 600 | PG | Government | U. S. Navy. |
| Pequonnock | KXP | 300, 450, 500, 550, 600. | PG | New England S. S. Co. | Nat. Elec. Signaling Co. |
| Pere Marquette | WDA | 300, 600 | PG | Pere Marquette R. R. Co | Marconi Co. |
| Pere Marquette 17 | WDC | 300, 600 | PG | do | Marconi Co. |
| Pere Marquette 18 | WDD | 300, 600 | PG | do | Marconi Co. |
| Pere Marquette 19 | WDB | 300, 345, 600. | PG | do | Marconi Co. |
| Pere Marquette 20 | WDE | 300, 375, 600. | PG | do | Marconi Co. |
| Perfection | KTN | | | Standard Oil Co | |
| Perkins | NOX | 300, 600 | PG | Government | U. S. Navy. |
| Perry | NOY | 300, 600 | PG | do | U. S. Navy. |
| Persian | KQX | 300, 600 | PG | Merchants & Miners Transp. Co. | Marconi Co. |
| Peru | WWJ | 300, 600 | PG | Pacific Mail S. S. Co | Marconi Co. |
| Petrel | NOZ | 300, 600 | PG | Government | U. S. Navy. |
| Philadelphia | KDA | 300, 600 | PG | Atlantic & Caribbean Steam Nav. Co. (Red D Line). | Marconi Co. |

SHIP RADIO STATIONS, ALPHABETICALLY BY NAMES OF VESSELS—Continued.

| Vessel. | Call signal. | Wave lengths. | Service. | Owner of vessel (line). | Station controlled by— |
|---|---|---|---|---|---|
| Philadelphia...... | KSM | 300, *600* | PG | International Mercantile Marine Co. (American Line). | Marconi Co. |
| Pilgrim.......... | KXG | 300, 450, 500, 550, *600*. | PG | New England S. S. Co.. | Nat. Elec. Signaling Co. |
| Pilot Boy......... | KPL | 300, *600* | ..... | Texas & Gulf S. S. Co.. | Marconi Co. |
| Pioneer.......... | WPN | .......... | ..... | Puget Sound Tug Boat Co. | |
| Pittsburgh....... | NOT | 300, *600* | PG | Government.......... | U. S. Navy. |
| Pleiades.......... | WNP | 300, *600* | PG | Edgar F. Luckenbach.. | Marconi Co. |
| Plymouth........ | KXH | 300, 450, 500, 550, *600*. | PG | New England S. S. Co... | Nat. Elec. Signaling Co. |
| Pompey......... | NQF | 300, *600* | PG | Government.......... | U. S. Navy. |
| Ponce........... | KGP | 300, *600* | PG | New York & Porto Rico S. S. Co. | Marconi Co. |
| Portland......... | WNV | 300, *600* | PG | Nyno Line........... | Marconi Co. |
| Potomac.......... | NQK | 300, *600* | PG | Government.......... | U. S. Navy. |
| Powhatan......... | KQY | 300, *600* | PG | Merchants & Miners Transp. Co. | Marconi Co. |
| Prairie........... | NQM | 300, *600* | PG | Government.......... | U. S. Navy. |
| Preble........... | NQN | 300, *600* | PG | .....do............... | U. S. Navy. |
| President........ | WGP | 300, *600* | PG | Pacific Coast Co........ | Marconi Co. |
| Preston........... | NQO | 300, *600* | PG | Government.......... | U. S. Navy. |
| Princess Anne.... | KOB | 300, *600* | PG | Old Dominion S. S. Co.. | Marconi Co. |
| Princeton........ | NQP | 300, *600* | PG | Government.......... | U. S. Navy. |
| Priscilla......... | KXI | 300, 450, 500, 550, *600*. | PG | New England S. S. Co... | Nat. Elec. Signaling Co. |
| Prometheus....... | NQR | 300, *600* | PG | Government.......... | U. S. Navy. |
| Proteus........... | KKP | 300, *600* | PG | Southern Pacific Co..... | Marconi Co. |
| Proteus........... | NNG | 300, *600* | PG | Government.......... | U. S. Navy. |
| Providence....... | KXJ | 300, 450 500, 550 *600* | PG | New England S. S. Co... | Nat. Elec. Signaling Co. |
| P. R. R. Barge 707. | KPR | .......... | ..... | Pennsylvania R. R. Co.. | |

SHIP RADIO STATIONS, ALPHABETICALLY BY NAMES OF VESSELS—Continued.

| Vessel. | Call signal. | Wave lengths. | Service. | Owner of vessel (line). | Station controlled by— |
|---|---|---|---|---|---|
| Puritan | WDU | 300, *600* | PG | Graham & Morton Transp. Co. | Marconi Co. |
| Puritan | KXK | 300, 450 500, 550 *600* | PG | New England S. S. Co | Nat. Elec. Signaling Co. |
| Quantico | KQQ | 300, *600* | PG | Merchants & Miners Transp. Co. | Marconi Co. |
| Queen | WGX | 300, *600* | PG | Pacific Coast S. S. Co | Marconi Co. |
| Radiant | KTR | 300, *600* | PG | Standard Oil Co | Marconi. Co |
| Rainbow | NTD | 300, *600* | PG | Government | U. S. Navy. |
| Raleigh | NTE | 300, *600* | PG | .....do | U. S. Navy. |
| Ranger | NFU | 300, *600* | PG | .....do | U. S. Navy. |
| Ransom B. Fuller. | KRF | 300, *600* | PG | Eastern S. S. Corp | Marconi Co. |
| Rayo | KTL | | | Standard Oil Co | |
| Redondo | WBM | 300, *600* | PG | Inter-Ocean Transp. Co. | Marconi Co. |
| Reid | NTU | 300, *600* | PG | Government | U. S. Navy. |
| Relay | KVZ | 300, *600* | PR | Mexican Telegraph Co | Owner of vessel. |
| Relief | KRJ | | | Merritt & Chapman Derrick & Wrecking Co. | |
| Relief Lightship 66 or 85. | NLD | 300, *600* | O | Government | U. S. Navy. |
| Relief Lightship 71 or 72. | NLE | 300, *600* | O | .....do | U. S. Navy. |
| Relief Lightship 94 or 53. | NLG | 300, *600* | O | .....do | U. S. Navy. |
| Reno | WYN | 300 | O | .....do | U. S. Army. |
| Rescue | KRP | | | Merritt & Chapman Derrick & Wrecking Co. | |
| Reuce | WSR | | | Columbia River Packers' Assn. | |
| Rhode Island | NTX | 300, *600* | PG | Government | U. S. Navy. |
| Richard Peck | KXR | 300, 450, 500, 550, *600* | PG | New England S. S. Co | Nat. Elec. Signaling Co. |
| Richmond | WTR | 300, *600* | PG | Standard Oil Co | Marconi Co. |
| Rio Grande | KEG | 300, *600* | PG | Mallory S. S. Co | Marconi Co. |
| Riverside | WRM | | | Charles Nelson Co | |

SHIP RADIO STATIONS, ALPHABETICALLY BY NAMES OF VESSELS—Continued.

| Vessel. | Call signal. | Wave lengths. | Service. | Owner of vessel (line). | Station controlled by— |
|---|---|---|---|---|---|
| Roanoke | WRR | 300, *600* | PG | North Pacific S. S. Co | Marconi Co. |
| Rochelle | WNR | | | Pacific S. S. Co | |
| Roe | NTZ | 300, *600* | PG | Government | U. S. Navy. |
| Roma | WTE | | | Union S. S. Co. (Union Oil Co.) | |
| Rose City | WWR | 300, *600* | PG | San Francisco & Portland S. S. Co. | Marconi Co. |
| Sabine | KEB | 300, *600* | PG | Mallory S. S. Co | Marconi Co. |
| Sacramento | NQV | 300, *600* | PG | Government | U. S. Navy. |
| Salem | NTP | 300, *600* | PG | Government | U. S. Navy. |
| Samson | WOS | | | Columbia Construction Co. | Marconi Co. |
| San Francisco | NTQ | 300, *600* | PG | Government | U. S. Navy. |
| San Jacinto | KES | 300, *600* | PG | Mallory S. S. Co | Marconi Co. |
| San Jose | WWL | 300, *600* | PG | Pacific Mail S. S. Co | Marconi Co. |
| San Juan | KGJ | 300, *600* | PG | New York & Porto Rico S. S. Co. | Marconi Co. |
| San Juan | WWM | 300, *600* | PG | Pacific Mail S. S. Co | Marconi Co. |
| San Marcos | KEK | 300, *600* | PG | Mallory S. S. Co | Marconi Co. |
| San Ramon | WNW | 300, *600* | PG | E. J. Dodge Co | Marconi Co. |
| Santa Ana | WAL | | | Alaska S. S. Co | |
| Santa Catalina | WBC | | | Atlantic & Pacific S. S. Co. (Grace Line). | Marconi Co. |
| Santa Cecilia | WBB | | | do | Marconi Co. |
| Santa Clara | WBA | 300, *600* | PG | do | Marconi Co. |
| Santa Clara | WRS | 300, *600* | PG | North Pacific S. S. Co | Marconi Co. |
| Santa Cruz | WPA | | | Puget Sound Salvage Co. | |
| Santa Cruz | WBD | | | Atlantic & Pacific S. S. Co. (Grace Line). | |
| Santa Maria | WTF | 300, *600* | PG | United S. S. Co. (Union Oil Co.). | Marconi Co. |
| Santa Rita | WTG | | | do | |
| Santa Rosa | WGN | | | Pacific Coast Co | |
| Saratoga | KWS | 300, *600* | PG | N. Y. & Cuba Mail S. S. Co. (Ward Line). | Marconi Co. |

SHIP RADIO STATIONS, ALPHABETICALLY BY NAMES OF VESSELS—Continued.

| Vessel. | Call signal. | Wave lengths. | Service. | Owner of vessel (line). | Station controlled by— |
|---|---|---|---|---|---|
| Saratoga.......... | NTR | 300, *600* | PG | Government.......... | U. S. Navy. |
| Satellite.......... | KPS | 300, *600* | ..... | Alfred S. Sorensen & Sons. | |
| Satilla............ | KEN | ........... | ..... | Atlantic, Gulf & West Indies S. S. Lines. | |
| Saturn............ | NNM | 300, *600* | PG | Government.......... | U. S. Navy. |
| Savage............ | KRS | ........... | ..... | Consolidation Coal Co... | |
| Sayonara.......... | KYJ | ........... | ..... | A. J. Drexel.......... | Owner of vessel. |
| Scorpion.......... | NTT | 300, *600* | PG | Government.......... | U. S. Navy. |
| Sea Otter.......... | KYS | ........... | ..... | Hugh L. Willoughby.... | |
| Seeandbee........ | WFS | 300, *600* | PG | Cleveland & Buffalo Transit Co. | Marconi Co. |
| Seguranca......... | KWG | 300, *600* | PG | N. Y. & Cuba Mail S. S. Co. (Ward Line). | Marconi Co. |
| Seminole......... | KVJ | 300, *600* | PG | Clyde S. S. Co......... | Marconi Co. |
| Seminole......... | NRS | 300, *600* | PG | Government.......... | U. S. R. C. S. |
| Senator........... | WGS | ........... | ..... | Pacific Coast Co......... | Marconi Co. |
| Senator Bailey.... | KGS | 300, *600* | PG | Steele Towing & Wrecking Co. | Marconi Co. |
| Seneca............ | NRE | 300, *600*, 750 | PG | Government.......... | U.S. R. C. S. |
| Seward........... | WAV | ........... | ..... | Alaska S. S. Co......... | |
| Sheboygan........ | WFL | ........... | ..... | Goodrich Transit Co.... | Marconi Co. |
| Shenango.......... | KTC | 300, *600* | PG | Gulf Refining Co....... | Marconi Co. |
| Shenango.. .. .... | WET | 300, *600* | PG | Shenango S. S. Co...... | Marconi Co. |
| Sheridan.......... | WXJ | 600 | PG | Government.......... | U. S. Army. |
| Sherman.......... | WXK | 600 | PG | .....do................ | U. S. Army. |
| Shinnecock....... | KNS | ........... | ..... | Montauk S. S. Co....... | |
| Sialia............ | WFY | ........... | ..... | J. K. Stewart........... | |
| Siberia........... | WWU | 300, *600* | PG | Pacific Mail S. S. Co.... | Marconi Co. |
| Sierra............ | WHJ | 300, *600* | PG | Oceanic S. S. Co........ | Marconi Co. |
| Smith............. | NSQ | 300, *600* | PG | Government.......... | U. S. Navy. |

54773°—14——4

SHIP RADIO STATIONS, ALPHABETICALLY BY NAMES OF VESSELS—Continued.

| Vessel. | Call signal. | Wave lengths. | Service. | Owner of vessel (line). | Station controlled by— |
|---|---|---|---|---|---|
| Snohomish | NRF | 300 | PG | Government | U. S. R. C. S. |
| Socony | KTX | | | Standard Oil Co. | |
| Solace | NST | 300, 600 | PG | Government | U. S. Navy. |
| Somerset | KQS | 300, *600* | PG | State Street Trust Co. (Merchants & Miners Transp. Co.). | Marconi Co. |
| Sonoma | WHM | 300, *600* | PG | Oceanic S. S. Co. | Marconi Co. |
| Sonoma | NTG | 300, *600* | PG | Government | U. S. Navy. |
| Sotoyomo | NUX | 300, *600* | PG | do | U. S. Navy. |
| South American | WEO | 300, *600* | PG | Chicago, Duluth & Georgian Bay S. S. Co. | Marconi Co. |
| South American | KVW | 300, *600* | PG | The Texas Co. | Marconi Co. |
| South Carolina | NSW | 300, *600* | PG | Government | U. S. Navy. |
| South Dakota | NSX | 300, *600* | PG | do | U. S. Navy. |
| Speedwell | WQS | 300, *600* | PG | A. F. Estabrook (Sou. Oreg. Transp. Co.). | Marconi Co. |
| Spokane | WGE | | | Pacific Coast Co. | Marconi Co. |
| S. O. Co. No. 91 | WTU | | | Standard Oil Co. | |
| S. O. Co. No. 92 | KTY | | | do | |
| S. O. Co. No. 93 | WTY | | | do | |
| S. O. Co. No. 94 | KTP | | | do | |
| S. O. Co. No. 95 | WTZ | | | do | |
| St. Frances | WHH | | | Libby, McNeill & Libby | |
| St. Helens | WNY | | | E. J. Dodge Co. | Marconi Co. |
| St. Louis | KSL | | | International Mercantile Marine Co. (American Line). | |
| St. Louis | NTF | 300, *600* | PG | Government | U. S. Navy. |
| St. Nicholas | WSS | | | Columbia River Packers' Assn. | |
| St. Paul | KSO | | | International Mercantile Marine Co. (American Line). | |
| Stanley Dollar | WSD | | | Dollar S. S. Line | |
| Starr | WPS | | | San Juan Fishing & Packing Co. | |

SHIP RADIO STATIONS, ALPHABETICALLY BY NAMES OF VESSELS—Continued.

| Vessel. | Call signal. | Wave lengths. | Service. | Owner of vessel (line). | Station controlled by— |
|---|---|---|---|---|---|
| State of Ohio...... | WFR | 300, *600* | PG | Cleveland & Buffalo Transp. Co. | Marconi Co. |
| Sterrett.......... | NTB | 300, *600* | PG | Government........... | U. S. Navy. |
| Stewart.......... | NTC | 300, *600* | PG | .....do................ | U. S. Navy. |
| Stranger ......... | NSR | 300, *600* | ..... | .....do................ | |
| Sumner........... | WXL | 600 | PG | .....do................ | U. S. Army. |
| Sun.............. | KTU | 300, *600* | PG | Sun Co................ | Marconi Co. |
| Supply........... | NTK | 300, *600* | PG | Government........... | U. S. Navy. |
| Suwannee......... | KQZ | 300, *600* | PG | State Street Trust Co. (Merchants & Miners Transp. Co.). | Marconi Co. |
| Sylph............ | NTL | 300, *600* | PG | Government........... | U. S. Navy. |
| Tacoma........... | NUA | 300, *600* | PG | .....do................ | U. S. Navy. |
| Tahoma........... | NRK | 300, *600* | PG | .....do................ | U. S. R. C. S. |
| Tallahassee....... | NUC | 300, *600* | PG | .....do................ | U. S. Navy. |
| Tarragon.......... | NZZ | 200, 300, 450, *600*. | O | .....do................ | U. S. Dept. of Commerce. |
| Tasco............ | KFT | 300, 400, 480, *600*. | P | T. A. Scott Co. (Inc.)... | Owner of vessel. |
| Tatoosh........... | WPE | ........... | ..... | Puget Sound Tug Boat Co. | |
| Tennessee......... | NUG | 300, *600* | PG | Government........... | U. S. Navy. |
| Terry............ | NUI | 300, *600* | PG | .....do................ | U. S. Navy. |
| Texan............ | WKT | 300, *600* | PG | American-Hawaiian S.S. Co. | |
| Texas............ | NCD | 300, *600* | PG | Government........... | U. S. Navy. |
| The Harvester.... | WCR | 300, *600* | ..... | Wisconsin Steel Co...... | Marconi Co. |
| Theodore Roosevelt. | WCT | 300, *600* | PG | Indiana Transp. Co..... | Marconi. |
| Thetis........... | NRT | 300, *600* | PG | Government........... | U. S. R. C. S. |
| Thomas........... | WXM | 600 | PG | .....do................ | U. S. Army. |
| Tionesta......... | WCA | 300, *600* | PG | Erie & Western Transp. Co. (Anchor Line). | Marconi Co. |
| Toledo........... | KTV | ........... | ..... | Sun Co................ | |
| Tonopah......... | NUN | 300, *600* | PG | Government........... | U. S. Navy. |

SHIP RADIO STATIONS, ALPHABETICALLY BY NAMES OF VESSELS—Continued.

| Vessel. | Call signal. | Wave lengths. | Service. | Owner of vessel (line). | Station controlled by— |
|---|---|---|---|---|---|
| Topila | KKE | 300, *600* | PG | Southern Pacific Co | Marconi Co. |
| Trippe | NUQ | 300, *600* | PG | Government | U. S. Navy. |
| Truxton | NUS | 300, *600* | PG | do | U. S. Navy. |
| Tuscan | KQT | 300, *600* | PG | Merchants & Miners Transp. Co. | Marconi Co. |
| Tuscarora | NRL | 300, *600* | PG | Government | U. S. R. C. S. |
| Tyee | WPC | | | Puget Sound Tug Boat Co. | |
| Tyee Junior | WPB | | | Tyee Co | |
| Umatilla | WGU | 300, *600* | PG | Pacific Coast Co | Marconi Co. |
| Unalga | NRX | 300, *600*, 800. | PG | Government | U. S. R. C. S. |
| Uncas | NVF | 300, *600* | PG | do | U. S. Navy. |
| United States | WIT | | | Indiana Transp. Co | |
| Utah | NVE | 300, *600* | PG | Government | U. S. Navy. |
| Vanadis | KYT | | | C. K. G. Billings | |
| Venetia | WOV | | | J. D. Spreckels | |
| Ventura | WHL | 300, *600* | PG | Oceanic S. S. Co | Marconi Co. |
| Vermont | NVK | 300, *600* | PG | Government | U. S. Navy. |
| Vesta | KTS | | | Standard Oil Co | |
| Vestal | NMC | 300, *600* | PG | Government | U. S. Navy. |
| Vesuvius | NVM | 300, *600* | PG | do | U. S. Navy. |
| Vicksburg | NVN | 300, *600* | PG | do | U. S. Navy. |
| Victoria | WAD | | | Alaska S. S. Co | Marconi Co. |
| Vigilancia | KWV | 300, *600* | PG | N. Y. & Cuba Mail S. S. Co. (Ward Line). | Marconi Co. |
| Villalobos | NVP | 300, *600* | PG | Government | U. S. Navy. |
| Virginia | KSZ | 300, *600* | PG | Baltimore Steam Packet Co. | Marconi Co. |
| Virginia | WFH | 300, *600* | PG | Goodrich Transit Co | Marconi Co. |
| Virginia | NVR | 300, *600* | PG | Government | U. S. Navy. |
| Virginian | WKV | 300, *600* | PG | American-Hawaiian S. S. Co. | Atlantic Communication Co. |

Ship Radio Stations, Alphabetically by Names of Vessels—Continued.

| Vessel. | Call signal. | Wave lengths. | Service. | Owner of vessel (line). | Station controlled by— |
|---|---|---|---|---|---|
| Vixen | NSU | 300, 600 | | Government | |
| Vulcan | NVT | 300, 600 | PG | ....do | U. S. Navy. |
| Wakiva | WLA | | | E. L. Doheny | |
| Wakiva | KYI | | | Lamon V. Harkness | |
| Walke | NWL | 300, 600 | PG | Government | U. S. Navy. |
| Wallula | WPY | | | Port of Portland | |
| Wana | KYX | 300, 600 | P | George C. Sherman | Marconi Co. |
| Warren | WXN | 600 | PG | Government | U. S. Army. |
| Warrington | NWD | 300, 600 | PG | ....do | U. S. Navy. |
| Warrior | KYW | | | F. W. Vanderbilt | |
| Washington | NWE | 300, 600 | PG | Government | U. S. Navy. |
| Washingtonian | WKW | 300, 600 | PG | American-Hawaiian S.S. Co. | |
| Washtenaw | WTH | 300, 600 | PG | Union S. S. Co. (Union Oil Co.). | Marconi Co. |
| Wasp | NSV | 300, 600 | PG | Government | U. S. Navy. |
| W. B. Flint | WHG | | | Libby, McNeill & Libby. | |
| W. B. Keene | KWK | 300, 600 | | Hilton Dodge Transp. Co. | Marconi Co. |
| West Virginia | NWG | 300, 600 | PG | Government | U. S. Navy. |
| Western States | WED | 300, 600 | PG | Detroit & Cleveland Nav. Co. | Marconi Co. |
| Wheeling | NWH | 300, 600 | PG | Government | U. S. Navy. |
| Whipple | NWI | 300, 600 | PG | ....do | U. S. Navy. |
| Whittier | WHT | 300, 600 | PG | Max Dyer (Union Oil Co.). | Marconi Co. |
| Wild Duck | KYG | | | Paul E. De Fere | Marconi Co. |
| Wilhelmina | WMO | 300, 600 | PG | Matson Nav. Co | Marconi Co. |
| Willamette | WSW | | | Willamette S. S. Co | |
| William Chatham | WMC | 300, 600 | PG | William Chatham Co. (Inc.). | Marconi Co. |
| Wm. F. Herrin | WTN | 300, 600 | PG | Associated Oil Co | Marconi Co. |
| William P. Snyder | WER | 300, 600 | PG | Shenango S. S. Co | Marconi Co. |
| William P. Snyder, Jr. | WES | 300, 600 | PG | ....do | Marconi Co. |

SHIP RADIO STATIONS, ALPHABETICALLY BY NAMES OF VESSELS—Continued.

| Vessel. | Call signal. | Wave lengths. | Service. | Owner of vessel (line). | Station controlled by— |
|---|---|---|---|---|---|
| Wilmington | NWK | 300, *600* | PG | Government | U. S. Navy. |
| Wilpen | WEU | | | Shenango S. S. Co | |
| Windber | WND | | | Pacific-American Fisheries. | |
| Windom | NRW | 300, *600* | PG | Government | U. S. R. C. S. |
| Winifred | KTE | 300, *600* | PG | Gulf Refining Co | Marconi Co. |
| Winona | NRV | 300, *600* | PG | Government | U. S. R. C. S. |
| Winslow | NJA | 300, *600* | PG | do | U. S. Navy. |
| Wisconsin | NWM | 300, *600* | PG | do | U. S. Navy. |
| Woodbury | NRJ | 300, *600* | PG | do | U. S. R. C. S. |
| Worden | NWP | 300, *600* | PG | do | U. S. Navy. |
| W. S. Porter | WTM | | | Associated Oil Co | |
| Wyandotte | KNW | | | Montauk S. S. Co | |
| Wyoming | NWQ | 600 | PG | Government | U. S. Navy. |
| Yaguez | KDY | 300, *600* | PG | Ocean Freight Line (Inc.). | Marconi Co. |
| Yale | WRY | 300, *600* | PG | Metropolitan S. S. Co. (Pacific Steam Nav. Co.). | |
| Yamacraw | NRY | 300, *600* | PG | Government | U. S. R. C. S. |
| Yankton | NSK | 300, *600* | PG | do | U. S. Navy. |
| Yorktown | NQX | 300, *600* | PG | Government | U. S. Navy. |
| Yosemite | WQY | 300, *600* | PG | Yosemite S. S. Co | Marconi Co. |
| Yucatan | WMY | 300, *600* | PG | North Pacific S. S. Co. | Marconi Co. |
| Zapora | WPQ | | | International Fisheries Co. | |
| Zealandia | KNR | | | C. L. Dimon | |
| Zulia | KDZ | 300, *600* | PG | Atlantic & Caribbean Steam Nav. Co. (Red D Line). | Marconi Co. |

## LAND AND SHIP RADIO STATIONS, ALPHABETICALLY BY CALL SIGNALS.

[This list includes all call signals which have been assigned to United States radio stations, except amateur and certain "special" stations. b=ship station; c=land station.]

| Call signal. | Station. |
|---|---|
| KDA | Philadelphia.....b |
| KDB | Caracas.....b |
| KDC | Douglas, Ariz.....c |
| KDD | ..... |
| KDE | ..... |
| KDF | ..... |
| KDG | ..... |
| KDH | ..... |
| KDI | ..... |
| KDJ | ..... |
| KDK | ..... |
| KDL | ..... |
| KDM | Maracaibo.....b |
| KDN | San Luis Obispo, Cal.....c |
| KDO | ..... |
| KDP | ..... |
| KDQ | ..... |
| KDR | ..... |
| KDS | ..... |
| KDT | ..... |
| KDU | Juneau, Alaska.....c |
| KDV | Grayson.....b |
| KDW | Borinquen.....b |
| KDX | Bayamon.....b |
| KDY | Yaguez.....b |
| KDZ | Zulia.....b |
| KEA | Colorado.....b |
| KEB | Sabine.....b |
| KEC | Concho.....b |
| KED | Denver.....b |
| KEE | ..... |
| KEF | ..... |
| KEG | Rio Grande.....b |
| KEH | Nueces.....b |
| KEI | ..... |
| KEJ | Alamo.....b |
| KEK | San Marcos.....b |
| KEL | ..... |
| KEM | Comal.....b |
| KEN | Satilla.....b |
| KEO | Ossabaw.....b |
| KEP | Lampasas.....b |
| KEQ | ..... |
| KER | ..... |
| KES | San Jacinto.....b |
| KET | Bolinas, Cal.....c |
| KEU | ..... |
| KEV | ..... |
| KEW | ..... |
| KEX | Los Angeles, Cal.....c |
| KEY | ..... |
| KEZ | Brazos.....b |
| KFA | City of Columbus.....b |
| KFB | City of Atlanta.....b |
| KFC | City of Macon.....b |
| KFD | City of Memphis.....b |
| KFE | ..... |
| KFF | Frieda.....b |
| KFG | ..... |
| KFH | Herman Frasch.....b |
| KFI | I. D. Fletcher.....b |
| KFJ | City of Augusta.....b |
| KFK | City of Savannah.....b |
| KFL | ..... |
| KFM | ..... |
| KFN | ..... |
| KFO | ..... |
| KFP | Nacoochee.....b |
| KFQ | ..... |
| KFR | ..... |
| KFS | San Francisco, Cal.....c |
| KFT | Tasco.....b |
| KFU | ..... |
| KFV | ..... |

LAND AND SHIP RADIO STATIONS, ALPHABETICALLY BY CALL SIGNALS—Continued.

| Call signal. | Station. | Call signal. | Station. |
|---|---|---|---|
| KFW | .............................. | KHH | .............................. |
| KFX | City of St. Louis............b | KHI | .............................. |
| KFY | City of Montgomery..........b | KHJ | Koko Head, Hawaii..........c |
| KFZ | .............................. | KHK | Kahuku, Hawaii..............c |
| KGA | Coamo.......................b | KHL | Lahaina, Hawaii.............c |
| KGB | Carolina.....................b | KHM | Lihue, Hawaii................c |
| | | KHN | Kawaihae, Hawaii...........c |
| KGC | .............................. | KHO | Kaunakakai, Hawaii........c |
| KGD | .............................. | KHP | .............................. |
| | | KHQ | Phoenix, Ariz................c |
| KGE | .............................. | KHR | .............................. |
| KGF | .............................. | KHS | .............................. |
| KGG | .............................. | KHT | Naknek, Alaska..............c |
| KGH | Hollister, Cal................c | KHU | .............................. |
| KGI | .............................. | | |
| KGJ | San Juan.....................b | KHV | .............................. |
| KGK | .............................. | KHW | .............................. |
| | | KHX | Heeia Point, Hawaii.........c |
| KGL | .............................. | KHY | .............................. |
| KGM | .............................. | KHZ | .............................. |
| KGN | .............................. | KIA | .............................. |
| KGO | .............................. | | |
| KGP | Ponce.......................b | KIB | .............................. |
| KGQ | .............................. | KIC | .............................. |
| KGR | .............................. | KID | .............................. |
| KGS | Senator Bailey..............b | KIE | Koko Head, Hawaii.........c |
| KGT | .............................. | KIF | .............................. |
| KGU | .............................. | KIG | .............................. |
| KGV | .............................. | KIH | .............................. |
| KGW | .............................. | KII | .............................. |
| KGX | .............................. | KIJ | James Duane................b |
| KGY | .............................. | KIK | .............................. |
| KGZ | .............................. | KIL | .............................. |
| KHA | Karluk, Alaska...............c | | |
| KHB | Kogiung, Alaska.............c | KIM | .............................. |
| KHC | Chignik, Alaska..............c | KIN | .............................. |
| KHD | .............................. | KIO | .............................. |
| KHE | .............................. | KIP | .............................. |
| KHF | Nushagak, Alaska............c | | |
| KHG | Clarks Point, Alaska........c | KIQ | .............................. |

LAND AND SHIP RADIO STATIONS, ALPHABETICALLY BY CALL SIGNALS—Continued.

| Call signal. | Station. |
|---|---|
| KIR | |
| KIS | Ellamar, Alaska....c |
| KIT | |
| KIU | |
| KIV | |
| KIW | |
| KIX | |
| KIY | |
| KIZ | |
| KJA | Jualin, Alaska....c |
| KJB | Bunker Hill....b |
| KJC | |
| KJD | North Land....b |
| KJE | |
| KJF | |
| KJG | |
| KJH | |
| KJI | |
| KJJ | |
| KJK | |
| KJL | |
| KJM | Massachusetts....b |
| KJN | |
| KJO | Old Colony....b |
| KJP | |
| KJQ | |
| KJR | |
| KJS | North Star....b |
| KJT | |
| KJU | |
| KJV | |
| KJW | |
| KJX | |
| KJY | |
| KJZ | |
| KKA | Antilles....b |
| KKB | El Sol....b |
| KKC | Chalmette....b |
| KKD | Comus....b |
| KKE | Topila....b |
| KKF | |
| KKG | |
| KKH | |
| KKI | |
| KKJ | |
| KKK | |
| KKL | El Alba....b |
| KKM | Momus....b |
| KKN | El Norte....b |
| KKO | Excelsior....b |
| KKP | Proteus....b |
| KKQ | El Sud....b |
| KKR | Creole....b |
| KKS | El Siglo....b |
| KKT | El Cid....b |
| KKU | El Mundo....b |
| KKV | El Oriente....b |
| KKW | El Valle....b |
| KKX | El Occidente....b |
| KKY | El Dia....b |
| KKZ | El Rio....b |
| KLA | |
| KLB | |
| KLC | |
| KLD | |
| KLE | |
| KLF | |
| KLG | |
| KLH | |
| KLI | |
| KLJ | |
| KLK | |
| KLL | |
| KLM | |

LAND AND SHIP RADIO STATIONS, ALPHABETICALLY BY CALL SIGNALS—Continued.

| Call signal. | Station. |
|---|---|
| KLN | |
| KLO | |
| KLP | |
| KLQ | |
| KLR | |
| KLS | Los Angeles, Cal. c |
| KLT | |
| KLU | |
| KLV | |
| KLW | |
| KLX | |
| KLY | |
| KLZ | |
| KMA | Alliança b |
| KMB | |
| KMC | |
| KMD | Cristobal b |
| KME | Maine b |
| KMF | |
| KMG | |
| KMH | Panama b |
| KMI | |
| KMJ | |
| KMK | |
| KML | |
| KMM | |
| KMN | Atlantic City b |
| KMO | C. W. Morse b |
| KMP | |
| KMQ | |
| KMR | |
| KMS | Ancon b |
| KMT | |
| KMU | |
| KMV | Advance b |
| KMW | |
| KMX | Colon b |
| KMY | |
| KMZ | |
| KNA | Dorothy Bradford b |
| KNB | Lexington b |
| KNC | Concord b |
| KND | Beverly b |
| KNE | Evelyn b |
| KNF | Carolyn b |
| KNG | |
| KNH | |
| KNI | |
| KNJ | New Jersey b |
| KNK | New York b |
| KNL | Nelson b |
| KNM | Millinocket b |
| KNN | |
| KNO | |
| KNP | |
| KNQ | Lucy Neff b |
| KNR | Zealandia b |
| KNS | Shinnecock b |
| KNT | Montauk b |
| KNU | Currier b |
| KNV | |
| KNW | Wyandotte b |
| KNX | |
| KNY | |
| KNZ | America b |
| KOA | Hamilton b |
| KOB | Princess Anne b |
| KOC | Jamestown b |
| KOD | Jefferson b |
| KOE | |
| KOF | |
| KOG | Madison b |
| KOH | |
| KOI | |
| KOJ | |
| KOK | |

LAND AND SHIP RADIO STATIONS, ALPHABETICALLY BY CALL SIGNALS—Continued.

| Call signal. | Station. | Call signal. | Station. |
|---|---|---|---|
| KOL | ........ | KPY | ........ |
| KOM | ........ | KPZ | ........ |
| KON | ........ | KQA | ........ |
| | | KQB | Berkshire........b |
| KOO | ........ | KQC | Cretan........b |
| | | KQD | Dorchester........b |
| KOP | ........ | KQE | Essex........b |
| KOQ | ........ | KQF | ........ |
| | | KQG | Gloucester........b |
| | | KQH | Howard........b |
| KOR | ........ | KQI | Indian........b |
| KOS | Brunswick........b | KQJ | Juniata........b |
| | | KQK | Kershaw........b |
| KOT | ........ | KQL | Lexington........b |
| | | KQM | Merrimack........b |
| KOU | ........ | KQN | Nantucket........b |
| KOV | Olivette........b | KQO | Ontario........b |
| KOW | Mascotte........b | KQP | Parthian........b |
| | | KQQ | Quantico........b |
| KOX | ........ | KQR | Grecian........b |
| | | KQS | Somerset........b |
| KOY | ........ | KQT | Tuscan........b |
| KOZ | Miami........b | | |
| KPA | Seattle, Wash........c | KQU | ........ |
| KPB | Ketchikan, Alaska........c | | |
| KPC | Astoria, Oreg........c | KQV | ........ |
| KPD | Friday Harbor, Wash........c | | |
| | | KQW | ........ |
| KPE | ........ | KQX | Persian........b |
| KPF | Forward........b | KQY | Powhatan........b |
| | | KQZ | Suwannee........b |
| KPG | ........ | | |
| | | KRA | ........ |
| KPH | Hillcrest, Cal........c | KRB | Governor Cobb........b |
| KPI | Avalon, Cal........c | KRC | Camden........b |
| KPJ | East San Pedro, Cal........c | KRD | Belfast........b |
| | | KRE | Bay State........b |
| KPK | ........ | KRF | Ransom B. Fuller........b |
| KPL | Pilot Boy........b | KRG | ........ |
| KPM | Eureka, Cal........c | KRH | City of Bangor........b |
| | | KRI | City of Rockland........b |
| KPN | ........ | KRJ | Relief........b |
| KPO | ........ | KRK | ........ |
| | | KRL | Louise........b |
| KPP | ........ | | |
| | | KRM | ........ |
| KPQ | ........ | KRN | Calvin Austin........b |
| KPR | P. R. R. Barge 707........b | KRO | Columbia........b |
| KPS | Satellite........b | KRP | Rescue........b |
| | | KRQ | I. J. Merritt........b |
| KPT | ........ | KRR | Mills........b |
| | | KRS | Savage........b |
| KPU | ........ | | |
| | | KRT | ........ |
| KPV | ........ | | |
| KPW | Cape Cod........b | KRU | ........ |
| KPX | Marshfield, Oreg........c | KRV | Governor Dingley........b |

LAND AND SHIP RADIO STATIONS, ALPHABETICALLY BY CALL SIGNALS—Continued.

| Call signal. | Station. |
|---|---|
| KRW | |
| KRX | |
| KRY | City of Baltimore b |
| KRZ | City of Norfolk b |
| KSA | |
| KSB | |
| KSC | |
| KSD | San Diego, Cal. c |
| KSE | |
| KSF | Finland b |
| KSG | |
| KSH | Kroonland b |
| KSI | |
| KSJ | |
| KSK | |
| KSL | St. Louis b |
| KSM | Philadelphia b |
| KSN | New York b |
| KSO | St. Paul b |
| KSP | |
| KSQ | |
| KSR | |
| KSS | South San Francisco, Cal. c |
| KST | |
| KSU | |
| KSV | City of Richmond b |
| KSW | City of Annapolis b |
| KSX | Alabama b |
| KSY | Florida b |
| KSZ | Virginia b |
| KTA | Larimer b |
| KTB | |
| KTC | Shenango b |
| KTD | Ligonier b |
| KTE | Winifred b |
| KTF | J. M. Guffey b |
| KTG | Gulfoil b |
| KTH | Illinois b |
| KTI | Brilliant b |
| KTJ | Comet b |
| KTK | John D. Archbold b |
| KTL | Rayo b |
| KTM | Eocene b |
| KTN | Perfection b |
| KTO | |
| KTP | S. O. Co. No. 94 b |
| KTQ | City of Everett b |
| KTR | Radiant b |
| KTS | Vesta b |
| KTT | Paraguay b |
| KTU | Sun b |
| KTV | Toledo b |
| KTW | Delaware Sun b |
| KTX | Socony b |
| KTY | S. O. Co. No. 92 b |
| KTZ | |
| KUA | |
| KUB | |
| KUC | |
| KUD | |
| KUE | |
| KUF | |
| KUG | |
| KUH | |
| KUI | |
| KUJ | |
| KUK | |
| KUL | |
| KUM | |
| KUN | |
| KUO | |
| KUP | Pettibone b |
| KUQ | |
| KUR | |
| KUS | Florida b |
| KUT | Pan American b |
| KUU | |
| KUV | |
| KUW | |
| KUX | |

LAND AND SHIP RADIO STATIONS, ALPHABETICALLY BY CALL SIGNALS—Continued.

| Call signal. | Station. | Call signal. | Station. |
|---|---|---|---|
| KUY | .......... | KWG | Seguranca..........b |
| KUZ | .......... | KWH | Havana..........b |
| KVA | Apache..........b | KWI | .......... |
| KVB | Arapahoe..........b | KWJ | .......... |
| KVC | Comanche..........b | KWK | W. B. Keene..........b |
| KVD | .......... | KWL | .......... |
| KVE | .......... | KWM | .......... |
| KVF | Iroquois..........b | KWN | .......... |
| KVG | Algonquin..........b | KWO | .......... |
| KVH | Huron..........b | KWP | .......... |
| KVI | .......... | KWQ | .......... |
| KVJ | Seminole..........b | KWR | .......... |
| KVK | Cherokee..........b | KWS | Saratoga..........b |
| KVL | Lenape..........b | KWT | .......... |
| KVM | Mohawk..........b | KWU | .......... |
| KVN | .......... | KWV | Vigilancia..........b |
| KVO | .......... | KWW | .......... |
| KVP | .......... | KWX | Mexico..........b |
| KVQ | .......... | KWY | Monterey..........b |
| KVR | .......... | KWZ | Esperanza..........b |
| KVS | .......... | KXA | Boston..........b |
| KVT | .......... | KXB | City of Lowell..........b |
| KVU | Elmer A. Keeler..........b | KXC | Commonwealth..........b |
| KVV | .......... | KXD | Maine..........b |
| KVW | South American..........b | KXE | Mohawk..........b |
| KVX | Lundin power lifeboat..........b | KXF | New Hampshire..........b |
| KVY | .......... | KXG | Pilgrim..........b |
| KVZ | Relay..........b | KXH | Plymouth..........b |
| KWA | .......... | KXI | Priscilla..........b |
| KWB | .......... | KXJ | Providence..........b |
| KWC | Morro Castle..........b | KXK | Puritan..........b |
| KWD | .......... | KXL | City of Taunton..........b |
| KWE | .......... | KXM | Mohegan..........b |
| KWF | .......... | KXN | New Haven..........b |
| | | KXO | .......... |
| | | KXP | Pequonnock..........b |
| | | KXQ | Chester W. Chapin..........b |
| | | KXR | Richard Peck..........b |
| | | KXS | .......... |
| | | KXT | .......... |

LAND AND SHIP RADIO STATIONS, ALPHABETICALLY BY CALL SIGNALS—Continued.

| Call signal. | Station. |
|---|---|
| KXU | ........ |
| KXV | ........ |
| KXW | ........ |
| KXX | ........ |
| KXY | ........ |
| KXZ | ........ |
| KYA | Atalanta........b |
| KYB | North Wind........b |
| KYC | Corsair........b |
| KYD | Cyprus........b |
| KYE | Cassandra........b |
| KYF | Florence........b |
| KYG | Wild Duck........b |
| KYH | Aloha........b |
| KYI | Wakiva........b |
| KYJ | Sayonara........b |
| KYK | Kismet........b |
| KYL | Lysistrata........b |
| KYM | Columbia........b |
| KYN | Niagara........b |
| KYO | Noma........b |
| KYP | Oneida........b |
| KYQ | California........b |
| KYR | Karina........b |
| KYS | Sea Otter........b |
| KYT | Vanadis........b |
| KYU | Mohawk........b |
| KYV | Adventuress........b |
| KYW | Warrior........b |
| KYX | Wana........b |
| KYY | ........ |
| KYZ | North Star........b |
| KZA | ........ |
| KZB | ........ |
| KZC | ........ |
| KZD | ........ |
| KZE | ........ |
| KZF | ........ |
| KZG | ........ |
| KZH | ........ |
| KZI | ........ |
| KZJ | ........ |
| KZK | ........ |
| KZL | ........ |
| KZM | ........ |
| KZN | ........ |
| KZO | ........ |
| KZP | ........ |
| KZQ | ........ |
| KZR | ........ |
| KZS | ........ |
| KZT | ........ |
| KZU | ........ |
| KZV | ........ |
| KZW | ........ |
| KZX | ........ |
| KZY | ........ |
| KZZ | ........ |
| NAA | Arlington, Radio, Va........c |
| NAB | Portland, Me........c |
| NAC | Portsmouth, N. H........c |
| NAD | Boston, Mass........c |
| NAE | Cape Cod, Mass........c |
| NAF | Newport, R. I........c |
| NAG | Fire Island, Long Island, N.Y.c |
| NAH | New York (Brooklyn), N. Y..c |
| NAI | Philadelphia, Pa........c |
| NAJ | ........ |
| NAK | Annapolis, Md........c |
| NAL | Washington, D. C........c |
| NAM | Norfolk, Va........c |
| NAN | Beaufort, N. C........c |
| NAO | Charleston, S. C........c |
| NAP | St. Augustine, Fla........c |
| NAQ | Jupiter, Fla........c |
| NAR | Key West, Fla........c |
| NAS | Pensacola, Fla........c |
| NAT | New Orleans, La........c |
| NAU | San Juan, P. R........c |
| NAV | ........ |
| NAW | Guantanamo Bay, Cuba.....c |
| NAX | Colon, Panama........c |
| NAY | ........ |
| NAZ | ........ |

LAND AND SHIP RADIO STATIONS, ALPHABETICALLY BY CALL SIGNALS—Continued.

| Call signal. | Station. |
|---|---|
| NBA | |
| NBB | |
| NBC | |
| NBD | |
| NBE | |
| NBF | |
| NBG | |
| NBH | Ajax.....b |
| NBI | Alabama.....b |
| NBJ | Albany.....b |
| NBK | |
| NBL | Alert.....b |
| NBM | |
| NBN | |
| NBO | |
| NBP | Ammen.....b |
| NBQ | |
| NBR | Annapolis.....b |
| NBS | |
| NBT | |
| NBU | Arethusa.....b |
| NBV | Arkansas.....b |
| NBW | |
| NBX | |
| NBY | |
| NBZ | |
| NCA | |
| NCB | |
| NCC | New York.....b |
| NCD | Texas.....b |
| NCE | |
| NCF | Bailey.....b |
| NCG | |
| NCH | Baltimore.....b |
| NCI | |
| NCJ | |
| NCK | |
| NCL | Beale.....b |
| NCM | |
| NCN | Birmingham.....b |
| NCO | |
| NCP | |
| NCQ | |
| NCR | |
| NCS | |
| NCT | |
| NCU | Buffalo.....b |
| NCV | Burrows.....b |
| NCW | |
| NCX | |
| NCY | Caesar.....b |
| NCZ | California.....b |
| NDA | Castine.....b |
| NDB | Celtic.....b |
| NDC | |
| NDD | |
| NDE | |
| NDF | |
| NDG | Chester..... |
| NDH | Cheyenne.....b |
| NDI | Chicago.....b |
| NDJ | |
| NDK | |
| NDL | Cincinnati.....b |
| NDM | Cleveland.....b |
| NDN | Colorado.....b |
| NDO | |
| NDP | |
| NDQ | Connecticut.....b |
| NDR | |
| NDS | |
| NDT | |
| NDU | Culgoa.....b |
| NDV | |

LAND AND SHIP RADIO STATIONS, ALPHABETICALLY BY CALL SIGNALS—Continued.

| Call signal. | Station. | Call signal. | Station. |
|---|---|---|---|
| NDW | | NFH | |
| NDX | | NFI | |
| NDY | Cyclops.....b | NFJ | |
| NDZ | | NFK | |
| NEA | | NFL | |
| NEB | | NFM | Fanning.....b |
| NEC | | NFN | |
| NED | | NFO | |
| NEE | | NFP | |
| NEF | | NFQ | |
| NEG | | NFR | Florida.....b |
| NEH | | NFS | Flusser.....b |
| NEI | | NFT | |
| NEJ | | NFU | Ranger.....b |
| NEK | Delaware.....b | NFV | |
| NEL | | NFW | |
| NEM | Denver.....b | NFX | |
| NEN | Des Moines.....b | NFY | |
| NEO | | NFZ | |
| NEP | Dixie.....b | NGA | Columbia.....b |
| NEQ | Dolphin.....b | NGB | Minneapolis.....b |
| NER | | NGC | |
| NES | | NGD | Galveston.....b |
| NET | Drayton.....b | NGE | |
| NEU | Dubuque.....b | NGF | Georgia.....b |
| NEV | | NGG | |
| NEW | | NGH | Glacier.....b |
| NEX | | NGI | Chattanooga.....b |
| NEY | | NGJ | Goldsborough.....b |
| NEZ | | NGK | Marblehead.....b |
| NFA | Brooklyn.....b | NGL | |
| NFB | Milwaukee.....b | NGM | |
| NFC | Eagle.....b | NGN | |
| NFD | Elcano.....b | NGO | |
| NFE | Charleston.....b | NGP | |
| NFF | | NGQ | |
| NFG | | NGR | |

LAND AND SHIP RADIO STATIONS, ALPHABETICALLY BY CALL SIGNALS—Continued.

| Call signal. | Station. |
|---|---|
| NGS | |
| NGT | |
| NGU | Hannibal b |
| NGV | |
| NGW | |
| NGX | Hector b |
| NGY | Helena b |
| NGZ | |
| NHA | Henley b |
| NHB | |
| NHC | Hopkins b |
| NHD | Monadnock b |
| NHE | Hull b |
| NHF | |
| NHG | Amphitrite b |
| NHH | Ozark b |
| NHI | Hancock b |
| NHJ | |
| NHK | |
| NHL | |
| NHM | |
| NHN | |
| NHO | Illinois b |
| NHP | |
| NHQ | Indiana b |
| NHR | |
| NHS | |
| NHT | Iowa b |
| NHU | Iris b |
| NHV | Iroquois b |
| NHW | |
| NHX | |
| NHY | |
| NHZ | |
| NIA | Bainbridge b |
| NIB | Jarvis b |
| NIC | |
| NID | Jenkins b |
| NIE | Jouett b |
| NIF | |
| NIG | |
| NIH | Aylwin b |
| NII | Balch b |
| NIJ | Benham b |
| NIK | Cassin b |
| NIL | Cummings b |
| NIM | Cushing b |
| NIN | Downes b |
| NIO | Kansas b |
| NIP | Kearsarge b |
| NIQ | Kentucky b |
| NIR | Duncan b |
| NIS | |
| NIT | McDougal b |
| NIU | Nicholson b |
| NIV | O'Brien b |
| NIW | Lamson b |
| NIX | Parker b |
| NIY | Lawrence b |
| NIZ | Lebanon b |
| NJA | Winslow b |
| NJB | Louisiana b |
| NJC | Decatur b |
| NJD | |
| NJE | |
| NJF | |
| NJG | |
| NJH | Macdonough b |
| NJI | |
| NJJ | |
| NJK | |
| NJL | Maine b |
| NJM | |
| NJN | |
| NJO | |
| NJP | |
| NJQ | Marietta b |
| NJR | Mars b |
| NJS | Maryland b |
| NJT | Massachusetts b |
| NJU | Mayrant b |
| NJV | Mayflower b |
| NJW | McCall b |
| NJX | |
| NJY | |
| NJZ | Michigan b |

54773°—14——5

LAND AND SHIP RADIO STATIONS, ALPHABETICALLY BY CALL SIGNALS—Continued.

| Call signal. | Station. | Call signal. | Station. |
|---|---|---|---|
| NKA | .......... | NLP | .......... |
| NKB | .......... | NLQ | .......... |
| NKC | .......... | NLR | .......... |
| NKD | Minnesota..........b | NLS | .......... |
| NKE | .......... | NLT | .......... |
| NKF | Missouri..........b | NLU | .......... |
| NKG | .......... | NLV | .......... |
| NKH | .......... | NLW | .......... |
| NKI | .......... | NLX | .......... |
| NKJ | .......... | NLY | .......... |
| NKK | .......... | NLZ | .......... |
| NKL | Monaghan..........b | NMA | Nebraska..........b |
| NKM | Montana..........b | NMB | Nero..........b |
| NKN | Monterey..........b | NMC | Vestal..........b |
| NKO | Montgomery..........b | NMD | .......... |
| NKP | .......... | NME | New Hampshire..........b |
| NKQ | .......... | NMF | New Jersey..........b |
| NKR | .......... | NMG | New Orleans..........b |
| NKS | .......... | NMH | Newport..........b |
| NKT | .......... | NMI | .......... |
| NKU | .......... | NMJ | .......... |
| NKV | .......... | NMK | .......... |
| NKW | .......... | NML | .......... |
| NKX | .......... | NMM | .......... |
| NKY | Nashville..........b | NMN | North Carolina..........b |
| NKZ | Navajo..........b | NMO | North Dakota..........b |
| NLA | Nantucket Shoals Lightship..c | NMP | .......... |
| NLB | Diamond Shoals Lightship...c | NMQ | .......... |
| NLC | Frying Pan Shoals Lightship..c | NMR | .......... |
| NLD | Relief Lightship 66 or 85....b | NMS | Neptune..........b |
| NLE | Relief Lightship 71 or 72.....b | NMT | .......... |
| NLF | Kukui..........b | NMU | .......... |
| NLG | Relief lightship 94 or 53.....b | NMV | .......... |
| NLH | Patterson..........b | NMW | Ohio..........b |
| NLI | Explorer..........b | NMX | .......... |
| NLJ | Pathfinder..........b | NMY | .......... |
| NLK | Bache..........b | NMZ | Oregon..........b |
| NLL | .......... | | |
| NLM | .......... | | |
| NLN | .......... | | |
| NLO | .......... | | |

LAND AND SHIP RADIO STATIONS, ALPHABETICALLY BY CALL SIGNALS—Continued.

| Call signal. | Station. |
|---|---|
| NNA | Brutus........b |
| NNB | Jason........b |
| NNC | Jupiter........b |
| NND | ........ |
| NNE | ........ |
| NNF | Nereus........b |
| NNG | Proteus........b |
| NNH | Leonidas........b |
| NNI | ........ |
| NNJ | Justin........b |
| NNK | Nanshan........b |
| NNL | ........ |
| NNM | Saturn........b |
| NNN | ........ |
| NNO | ........ |
| NNP | ........ |
| NNQ | ........ |
| NNR | ........ |
| NNS | ........ |
| NNT | ........ |
| NNU | ........ |
| NNV | ........ |
| NNW | ........ |
| NNX | ........ |
| NNY | ........ |
| NNZ | ........ |
| NOA | Osceola........b |
| NOB | Abarenda........b |
| NOC | Orion........b |
| NOD | ........ |
| NOE | ........ |
| NOF | ........ |
| NOG | Paducah........b |
| NOH | ........ |
| NOI | ........ |
| NOJ | Panther........b |
| NOK | Patterson........b |
| NOL | Patapsco........b |
| NOM | Patuxent........b |
| NON | Paulding........b |
| NOO | ........ |
| NOP | Paul Jones........b |
| NOQ | ........ |
| NOR | ........ |
| NOS | ........ |
| NOT | Pittsburgh........b |
| NOU | ........ |
| NOV | ........ |
| NOW | Peoria........b |
| NOX | Perkins........b |
| NOY | Perry........b |
| NOZ | Petrel........b |
| NPA | Cordova, Alaska........c |
| NPB | Sitka, Alaska........c |
| NPC | Puget Sound, Wash........c |
| NPD | Tatoosh, Wash........c |
| NPE | North Head, Wash........c |
| NPF | Cape Blanco, Oreg........c |
| NPG | ........ |
| NPH | Mare Island, Cal........c |
| NPI | Farallons, Cal........c |
| NPJ | Balboa, Panama........c |
| NPK | Point Arguello, Cal........c |
| NPL | San Diego, Cal........c |
| NPM | Honolulu, Hawaii........c |
| NPN | Guam, Marianne Islds........c |
| NPO | Cavite, P. I........c |
| NPP | Peking, China........c |
| NPQ | St. Paul, Pribilof Islds., Alaska.c |
| NPR | Dutch Harbor, Alaska........c |
| NPS | Kodiak, Alaska........c |
| NPT | Olongapo, P. I........c |
| NPU | Tutuila, Samoa........c |
| NPV | Unalga, Alaska........c |
| NPW | Eureka, Cal........c |
| NPX | ........ |
| NPY | St. George, Pribilof Islds., Alaska........c |
| NPZ | ........ |
| NQA | ........ |
| NQB | ........ |
| NQC | ........ |
| NQD | ........ |

LAND AND SHIP RADIO STATIONS, ALPHABETICALLY BY CALL SIGNALS—Continued.

| Call signal. | Station. | Call signal. | Station. |
|---|---|---|---|
| NQE | ........................ | NSC | ........................ |
| NQF | Pompey..................b | NSD | ........................ |
| NQG | ........................ | NSE | ........................ |
| NQH | ........................ | NSF | ........................ |
| NQI | ........................ | NSG | ........................ |
| NQJ | Isla de Luzon...........b | NSH | ........................ |
| NQK | Potomac.................b | NSI | ........................ |
| NQL | Machias.................b | NSJ | ........................ |
| NQM | Prairie.................b | NSK | Yankton.................b |
| NQN | Preble..................b | NSL | Gloucester..............b |
| NQO | Preston.................b | NSM | ........................ |
| NQP | Princeton...............b | NSN | ........................ |
| NQQ | Monocacy................b | NSO | ........................ |
| NQR | Prometheus..............b | NSP | ........................ |
| NQS | Palos...................b | NSQ | Smith...................b |
| NQT | Pampanga................b | NSR | ........................ |
| NQU | ........................ | NSS | ........................ |
| NQV | Sacramento..............b | NST | Solace..................b |
| NQW | ........................ | NSU | ........................ |
| NQX | Yorktown................b | NSV | Wasp....................b |
| NQY | Albatross...............b | NSW | South Carolina..........b |
| NQZ | ........................ | NSX | South Dakota............b |
| NRA | Algonquin...............b | NSY | ........................ |
| NRB | Bear....................b | NSZ | ........................ |
| NRC | Morrill.................b | NTA | Ontario................. |
| NRD | Androscoggin............b | NTB | Sterrett................b |
| NRE | Seneca..................b | NTC | Stewart.................b |
| NRF | Snohomish...............b | NTD | Rainbow.................b |
| NRG | Gresham.................b | NTE | Raleigh.................b |
| NRH | McCulloch...............b | NTF | St. Louis...............b |
| NRI | Itasca..................b | NTG | Sonoma..................b |
| NRJ | Woodbury................b | NTH | ........................ |
| NRK | Tahoma..................b | NTI | ........................ |
| NRL | Tuscarora...............b | NTJ | ........................ |
| NRM | Mohawk..................b | NTK | Supply..................b |
| NRN | Manning.................b | NTL | Sylph...................b |
| NRO | Onondaga................b | NTM | ........................ |
| NRP | Apache..................b | | |
| NRQ | Miami...................b | | |
| NRR | Pamlico.................b | | |
| NRS | Seminole................b | | |
| NRT | Thetis..................b | | |
| NRU | Acushnet................b | | |
| NRV | Winona..................b | | |
| NRW | Windom..................b | | |
| NRX | Unalga..................b | | |
| NRY | Yamacraw................b | | |
| NRZ | [1]New London, Conn.....c | | |
| NSA | ........................ | | |
| NSB | ........................ | | |

[1] This station will accept general public service in emergencies, when open.

LAND AND SHIP RADIO STATIONS, ALPHABETICALLY BY CALL SIGNALS—Continued.

| Call signal. | Station. |
|---|---|
| NTN | |
| NTO | |
| NTP | Salem..........b |
| NTQ | San Francisco..........b |
| NTR | Saratoga..........b |
| NTS | |
| NTT | Scorpion..........b |
| NTU | Reid..........b |
| NTV | |
| NTW | |
| NTX | Rhode Island..........b |
| NTY | |
| NTZ | Roe..........b |
| NUA | Tacoma..........b |
| NUB | |
| NUC | Tallahassee..........b |
| NUD | |
| NUE | |
| NUF | |
| NUG | Tennessee..........b |
| NUH | |
| NUI | Terry..........b |
| NUJ | |
| NUK | |
| NUL | |
| NUM | |
| NUN | Tonapah..........b |
| NUO | |
| NUP | |
| NUQ | Trippe..........b |
| NUR | |
| NUS | Truxton..........b |
| NUT | |
| NUU | |
| NUV | |
| NUW | |
| NUX | Sotoyomo..........b |
| NUY | |
| NUZ | |
| NVA | Farragut..........b |
| NVB | |
| NVC | |
| NVD | |
| NVE | Utah..........b |
| NVF | Uncas..........b |
| NVG | |
| NVH | |
| NVI | |
| NVJ | |
| NVK | Vermont..........b |
| NVL | |
| NVM | Vesuvius..........b |
| NVN | Vicksburg..........b |
| NVO | |
| NVP | Villalobos..........b |
| NVQ | |
| NVR | Virginia..........b |
| NVS | |
| NVT | Vulcan..........b |
| NVU | |
| NVV | |
| NVW | |
| NVX | |
| NVY | |
| NVZ | |
| NWA | |
| NWB | |
| NWC | |
| NWD | Warrington..........b |
| NWE | Washington..........b |
| NWF | |
| NWG | West Virginia..........b |
| NWH | Wheeling..........b |
| NWI | Whipple..........b |

LAND AND SHIP RADIO STATIONS, ALPHABETICALLY BY CALL SIGNALS—Continued.

| Call signal | Station. |
|---|---|
| NWJ | |
| NWK | Wilmington b |
| NWL | Walke b |
| NWM | Wisconsin b |
| NWN | |
| NWO | |
| NWP | Worden b |
| NWQ | Wyoming b |
| NWR | |
| NWS | |
| NWT | |
| NWU | |
| NWV | |
| NWW | |
| NWX | |
| NWY | |
| NWZ | |
| NXA | |
| NXB | |
| NXC | |
| NXD | |
| NXE | |
| NXF | |
| NXG | |
| NXH | |
| NXI | |
| NXJ | |
| NXK | |
| NXL | |
| NXM | |
| NXN | |
| NXO | |
| NXP | |
| NXQ | |
| NXR | |
| NXS | E-1 b |
| NXT | E-2 b |
| NXU | F-1 b |
| NXV | F-2 b |
| NXW | F-3 b |
| NXX | F-4 b |
| NXY | G-1 b |
| NXZ | G-2 b |
| NYA | G-3 b |
| NYB | G-4 b |
| NYC | H-1 b |
| NYD | H-2 b |
| NYE | H-3 b |
| NYF | K-1 b |
| NYG | K-2 b |
| NYH | K-3 b |
| NYI | K-4 b |
| NYJ | K-5 b |
| NYK | K-6 b |
| NYL | K-7 b |
| NYM | K-8 b |
| NYN | |
| NYO | |
| NYP | |
| NYQ | |
| NYR | |
| NYS | |
| NYT | |
| NYU | |
| NYV | |
| NYW | |
| NYX | |
| NYY | |
| NYZ | |
| NZA | |
| NZB | |
| NZC | |
| NZD | |
| NZE | |

LAND AND SHIP RADIO STATIONS, ALPHABETICALLY BY CALL SIGNALS—Continued.

| Call signal. | Station. |
|---|---|
| NZF | |
| NZG | |
| NZH | |
| NZI | |
| NZJ | |
| NZK | |
| NZL | |
| NZM | |
| NZN | |
| NZO | |
| NZP | |
| NZQ | |
| NZR | |
| NZS | |
| NZT | |
| NZU | |
| NZV | |
| NZW | |
| NZX | |
| NZY | Washington, D. C. . . . . c |
| NZZ | Tarragon . . . . . b |
| WAA | Alameda . . . . . b |
| WAB | Admiral Evans . . . . . b |
| WAC | Chicago . . . . . b |
| WAD | Victoria . . . . . b |
| WAE | Edith . . . . . b |
| WAF | Admiral Farragut . . . . . b |
| WAG | |
| WAH | Dora . . . . . b |
| WAI | Latouche . . . . . b |
| WAJ | Jefferson . . . . . b |
| WAK | |
| WAL | Santa Ana . . . . . b |
| WAM | |
| WAN | Northwestern . . . . . b |
| WAO | Dirigo . . . . . b |
| WAP | |
| WAQ | |
| WAR | Cordova . . . . . b |
| WAS | Admiral Sampson . . . . . b |
| WAT | |
| WAU | Dolphin . . . . . b |
| WAV | Seward . . . . . b |
| WAW | Admiral Watson . . . . . b |
| WAX | |
| WAY | Admiral Dewey . . . . . b |
| WAZ | Admiral Schley . . . . . b |
| WBA | Santa Clara . . . . . b |
| WBB | Santa Cecilia . . . . . b |
| WBC | Santa Catalina . . . . . b |
| WBD | Santa Cruz . . . . . b |
| WBE | |
| WBF | Boston, Mass . . . . . c |
| WBG | Iroquois . . . . . b |
| WBH | Chippewa . . . . . b |
| WBI | D., L. & W. R. R. limited train . . . . . c |
| WBJ | |
| WBK | Breakwater . . . . . b |
| WBL | Buffalo, N. Y . . . . . c |
| WBM | Redondo . . . . . b |
| WBN | Benton Harbor, Mich . . . . . c |
| WBO | Nann Smith . . . . . b |
| WBP | Hermosa . . . . . b |
| WBQ | |
| WBR | Bertha . . . . . b |
| WBS | Baltimore, Md . . . . . c |
| WBT | Binghamton, N. Y . . . . . c |
| WBU | Hoboken, N. J . . . . . c |
| WBV | Cabrillo . . . . . b |
| WBW | Burrwood, La . . . . . c |
| WBX | Dover, N. J . . . . . c |
| WBY | |
| WBZ | Glory of the Seas . . . . . b |
| WCA | Tionesta . . . . . b |
| WCB | Juniata . . . . . b |
| WCC | South Wellfleet, Mass . . . . . c |
| WCD | Octorara . . . . . b |
| WCE | |
| WCF | Favorite . . . . . b |
| WCG | Brooklyn, N. Y . . . . . c |
| WCH | Boston, Mass . . . . . c |
| WCI | Newport, R. I . . . . . c |
| WCJ | |
| WCK | |

LAND AND SHIP RADIO STATIONS, ALPHABETICALLY BY CALL SIGNALS—Continued.

| Call signal. | Station. | Call signal. | Station. |
|---|---|---|---|
| WCL | ............................ | WEG | City of St. Ignace...........b |
| WCM | Calumet, Mich..............c | WEH | City of Alpena II...........b |
| WCN | North Land.................b | WEI | ............................ |
| WCO | ............................ | WEJ | Nyack.....................b |
| WCP | ............................ | WEK | Minnesota..................b |
| WCQ | ............................ | WEL | E. G. Crosby...............b |
| WCR | The Harvester..............b | WEM | ............................ |
| WCS | ............................ | WEN | North American............b |
| WCT | Theodore Roosevelt..........b | WEO | South American............b |
| WCU | ............................ | WEP | El Paso, Tex................c |
| WCV | ............................ | WEQ | Col. James M. Schoonmaker..b |
| WCW | ............................ | WER | William P. Snyder..........b |
| WCX | Cleveland, Ohio............c | WES | William P. Snyder, Jr.......b |
| WCY | Cape May, N. J.............c | WET | Shenango..................b |
| WCZ | Illinois....................b | WEU | Wilpen....................b |
| WDA | Pere Marquette.............b | WEV | ............................ |
| WDB | Pere Marquette 19..........b | WEW | Marquette & Bessemer No. 1.b |
| WDC | Pere Marquette 17..........b | WEX | Marquette & Bessemer No. 2.b |
| WDD | Pere Marquette 18..........b | WEY | Alvina....................b |
| WDE | Pere Marquette 20..........b | WEZ | Ashtabula..................b |
| WDF | ............................ | WFA | Georgia....................b |
| WDG | ............................ | WFB | Alabama...................b |
| WDH | ............................ | WFC | Indiana....................b |
| WDI | City of South Haven........b | WFD | Iowa.......................b |
| WDJ | Lakeport...................b | WFE | Carolina...................b |
| WDK | Lakewood...................b | WFF | Fort Worth, Tex............c |
| WDL | Lakeland...................b | WFG | Arizona....................b |
| WDM | Duluth, Minn...............c | WFH | Virginia...................b |
| WDN | Ann Arbor No. 3............b | WFI | Chicago....................b |
| WDO | Ann Arbor No. 4............b | WFJ | Christopher Columbus........b |
| WDP | Ann Arbor No. 5............b | WFK | Frankfort, Mich.............c |
| WDQ | ............................ | WFL | Sheboygan..................b |
| WDR | Detroit, Mich...............c | WFM | Fort Morgan. Ala............c |
| WDS | City of Grand Rapids........b | WFN | Eastland...................b |
| WDT | City of Chicago............b | WFO | ............................ |
| WDU | Puritan....................b | WFP | City of Erie................b |
| WDV | City of Benton Harbor.......b | WFQ | City of Buffalo.............b |
| WDW | Holland....................b | WFR | State of Ohio...............b |
| WDX | ............................ | WFS | Seeandbee..................b |
| WDY | Lydonia....................b | WFT | ............................ |
| WDZ | ............................ | WFU | ............................ |
| WEA | City of Cleveland III........b | WFV | ............................ |
| WEB | City of Mackinac II.........b | WFW | Manitou....................b |
| WEC | City of Detroit II...........b | WFX | Missouri...................b |
| WED | Western States.............b | WFY | Sialia.....................b |
| WEE | Eastern States.............b | WFZ | ............................ |
| WEF | City of Detroit III..........b | WGA | City of Seattle..............b |
| | | WGB | ............................ |
| | | WGC | ............................ |
| | | WGD | Delhi......................b |
| | | WGE | Spokane....................b |

LAND AND SHIP RADIO STATIONS, ALPHABETICALLY BY CALL SIGNALS—Continued.

| Call signal. | Station. |
|---|---|
| WGF | |
| WGG | Tuckerton, N. J. . . . c |
| WGH | Grand Haven, Mich. . . . c |
| WGI | |
| WGJ | |
| WGK | |
| WGL | |
| WGM | Grand Marais, Minn. . . . c |
| WGN | Santa Rosa. . . . b |
| WGO | Chicago, Ill. . . . c |
| WGP | President. . . . b |
| WGQ | City of Puebla. . . . b |
| WGR | Governor. . . . b |
| WGS | Senator. . . . b |
| WGT | Congress. . . . b |
| WGU | Umatilla. . . . b |
| WGV | Galveston, Tex. . . . c |
| WGW | |
| WGX | Queen. . . . b |
| WGY | City of Topeka. . . . b |
| WGZ | Guardian. . . . b |
| WHA | Cape Hatteras (Buxton), N. C. c |
| WHB | New York, N. Y. . . . c |
| WHC | Columbia. . . . b |
| WHD | New York, N. Y. . . . c |
| WHE | Philadelphia, Pa. . . . c |
| WHF | |
| WHG | W. B. Flint. . . . b |
| WHH | St. Frances. . . . b |
| WHI | New York, N. Y. . . . c |
| WHJ | Sierra. . . . b |
| WHK | New Orleans, La. . . . c |
| WHL | Ventura. . . . b |
| WHM | Sonoma. . . . b |
| WHN | Hanalei. . . . b |
| WHO | |
| WHP | Mariposa. . . . b |
| WHQ | Mackinac Island, Mich. . . . c |
| WHR | North Star. . . . b |
| WHS | Adeline Smith. . . . b |
| WHT | Whittier. . . . b |
| WHU | |
| WHV | |
| WHW | Mackinaw. . . . b |
| WHX | Humboldt. . . . b |
| WHY | |
| WHZ | |
| WIA | |
| WIB | |
| WIC | |
| WID | |
| WIE | |
| WIF | |
| WIG | |
| WIH | |
| WII | Belmar, N. J. . . . c |
| WIJ | |
| WIK | |
| WIL | |
| WIM | |
| WIN | |
| WIO | |
| WIP | |
| WIQ | |
| WIR | |
| WIS | |
| WIT | United States. . . . b |
| WIU | |
| WIV | |
| WIW | |
| WIX | |
| WIY | |
| WIZ | |
| WJA | |
| WJB | |
| WJC | |
| WJD | |
| WJE | |
| WJF | |

LAND AND SHIP RADIO STATIONS, ALPHABETICALLY BY CALL SIGNALS—Continued.

| Call signal. | Station. |
|---|---|
| WJG | |
| WJH | |
| WJI | |
| WJJ | |
| WJK | |
| WJL | |
| WJM | |
| WJN | |
| WJO | |
| WJP | |
| WJQ | |
| WJR | |
| WJS | |
| WJT | |
| WJU | |
| WJV | |
| WJW | Hoboken, N. J. … c |
| WJX | Jacksonville, Fla … c |
| WJY | |
| WJZ | |
| WKA | Alaskan … b |
| WKB | Arizonan … b |
| WKC | Californian … b |
| WKD | Dakotan … b |
| WKE | Kentuckian … b |
| WKF | American … b |
| WKG | Georgian … b |
| WKH | Honolulan … b |
| WKI | Isthmian … b |
| WKJ | Iowan … b |
| WKK | Kansan … b |
| WKL | Mexican … b |
| WKM | Minnesotan … b |
| WKN | Montanan … b |
| WKO | Oregonian … b |
| WKP | Pennsylvanian … b |
| WKQ | Ohioan … b |
| WKR | Panaman … b |
| WKS | Columbian … b |
| WKT | Texan … b |
| WKU | Hawaiian … b |
| WKV | Virginian … b |
| WKW | Washingtonian … b |
| WKX | Missourian … b |
| WKY | Nebraskan … b |
| WKZ | Nevadan … b |
| WLA | Wakiva … b |
| WLB | Beluga … b |
| WLC | New London, Conn … c |
| WLD | Ludington, Mich … c |
| WLE | |
| WLF | |
| WLG | |
| WLH | |
| WLI | Iaqua … b |
| WLJ | |
| WLK | |
| WLL | |
| WLM | |
| WLN | Newton, Mass … c |
| WLO | |
| WLP | |
| WLQ | |
| WLR | |
| WLS | |
| WLT | |
| WLU | |
| WLV | |
| WLW | |
| WLX | |
| WLY | |
| WLZ | |
| WMA | Multnomah … b |
| WMB | Mobile, Ala … c |
| WMC | William Chatham … b |
| WMD | |
| WME | Milwaukee, Wis … c |
| WMF | Celilo … b |
| WMG | |
| WMH | |
| WMI | Minnesota … b |

LAND AND SHIP RADIO STATIONS, ALPHABETICALLY BY CALL SIGNALS—Continued.

| Call signal. | Station. | Call signal. | Station. |
|---|---|---|---|
| WMJ | .................................. | WOF | .................................. |
| WMK | Hyades....................b | WOG | .................................. |
| WML | Lurline....................b | WOH | .................................. |
| WMM | Hilonian....................b | WOI | .................................. |
| WMN | Enterprise....................b | WOJ | .................................. |
| WMO | Wilhelmina....................b | WOK | .................................. |
| WMP | Matsonia....................b | WOL | .................................. |
| WMQ | Manoa....................b | WOM | .................................. |
| WMR | .................................. | WON | .................................. |
| WMS | .................................. | WOO | .................................. |
| WMT | General Hubbard............ b | WOP | .................................. |
| WMU | .................................. | WOQ | .................................. |
| WMV | .................................. | WOR | .................................. |
| WMW | Manitowoc, Wis...............c | WOS | Samson....................b |
| WMX | Manistique, Mich.............c | WOT | .................................. |
| WMY | Yucatan....................c | WOU | .................................. |
| WMZ | .................................. | WOV | Venetia....................b |
| WNA | .................................. | WOW | .................................. |
| WNB | Oliver J. Olson..............b | WOX | .................................. |
| WNC | Carlos....................b | WOY | .................................. |
| WND | Windber....................b | WOZ | .................................. |
| WNE | Nushagak....................b | WPA | Santa Cruz..................b |
| WNF | Lyra....................b | WPB | Tyee Junior................b |
| WNG | George W. Fenwick..........b | WPC | Tyee....................b |
| WNH | Lewis Luckenbach..........b | WPD | Tampa, Fla..................c |
| WNI | Leelanaw....................b | WPE | Tatoosh....................b |
| WNJ | Navajo....................b | WPF | .................................. |
| WNK | Al-Ki....................b | WPG | Goliah....................b |
| WNL | Diamond Head..............b | WPH | .................................. |
| WNM | Damara....................b | WPI | Independent................b |
| WNN | Corwin....................b | WPJ | .................................. |
| WNO | A. G. Lindsay...............b | WPK | Kingfisher..................b |
| WNP | Pleiades....................b | WPL | .................................. |
| WNQ | .................................. | WPM | .................................. |
| WNR | Rochelle....................b | WPN | Pioneer....................b |
| WNS | Kvichak....................b | | |
| WNT | New York, N. Y.............c | | |
| WNU | New Orleans, La.............c | | |
| WNV | Portland....................b | | |
| WNW | San Ramon..................b | | |
| WNX | Northland....................b | | |
| WNY | St. Helens....................b | | |
| WNZ | .................................. | | |
| WOA | .................................. | | |
| WOB | .................................. | | |
| WOC | .................................. | | |
| WOD | .................................. | | |
| WOE | .................................. | | |

LAND AND SHIP RADIO STATIONS, ALPHABETICALLY BY CALL SIGNALS—Continued.

| Call signal. | Station. |
|---|---|
| WPO | ...... |
| WPP | ...... |
| WPQ | Zapora......b |
| WPR | Ensenada, P. R......c |
| WPS | Starr......b |
| WPT | ...... |
| WPU | ...... |
| WPV | ...... |
| WPW | Columbia......b |
| WPX | Oneonta......b |
| WPY | Wallula......b |
| WPZ | Joseph Pulitzer......b |
| WQA | ...... |
| WQB | ...... |
| WQC | Camino......b |
| WQD | ...... |
| WQE | Edgar H. Vance......b |
| WQF | ...... |
| WQG | Greenwood......b |
| WQH | ...... |
| WQI | ...... |
| WQJ | ...... |
| WQK | ...... |
| WQL | ...... |
| WQM | ...... |
| WQN | ...... |
| WQO | ...... |
| WQP | ...... |
| WQQ | ...... |
| WQR | ...... |
| WQS | Speedwell......b |
| WQT | ...... |
| WQU | ...... |
| WQV | ...... |
| WQW | ...... |
| WQX | ...... |
| WQY | Yosemite......b |
| WQZ | ...... |
| WRA | Henry T. Scott......b |
| WRB | Berlin......b |
| WRC | J. B. Stetson......b |
| WRD | ...... |
| WRE | ...... |
| WRF | Fifield......b |
| WRG | ...... |
| WRH | Harvard......b |
| WRI | Paraiso......b |
| WRJ | Aroline......b |
| WRK | Falcon......b |
| WRL | ...... |
| WRM | Riverside......b |
| WRN | Nome City......b |
| WRO | Isle Royal, Mich......c |
| WRP | ...... |
| WRQ | ...... |
| WRR | Roanoke......b |
| WRS | Santa Clara......b |
| WRT | Geo. W. Elder......b |
| WRU | Port Arthur, Tex......c |
| WRV | Alliance......b |
| WRW | F. A. Kilburn......b |
| WRX | ...... |
| WRY | Yale......b |
| WRZ | ...... |
| WSA | Ashtabula, Ohio......c |
| WSB | ...... |
| WSC | Siasconset, Mass......c |
| WSD | Stanley Dollar......b |
| WSE | Seagate, N. Y......c |
| WSF | Grace Dollar......b |
| WSG | Norwood......b |
| WSH | ...... |
| WSI | Sault Ste. Marie, Mich......c |
| WSJ | John A. Hooper......b |
| WSK | Sagaponack, N. Y......c |
| WSL | Sayville, Long Island, N. Y..c |
| WSM | ...... |
| WSN | Centralia......b |
| WSO | Coronado......b |
| WSP | ...... |
| WSQ | ...... |
| WSR | Reuce......b |
| WSS | St. Nicholas......b |
| WST | Miami, Fla......c |

LAND AND SHIP RADIO STATIONS, ALPHABETICALLY BY CALL SIGNALS—Continued.

| Call signal. | Station. |
|---|---|
| WSU | |
| WSV | Savannah, Ga. c |
| WSW | Willamette. b |
| WSX | Klamath. b |
| WSY | Virginia Beach, Va. c |
| WSZ | |
| WTA | Erskine M. Phelps. b |
| WTB | Argyll. b |
| WTC | Lansing. b |
| WTD | Oleum. b |
| WTE | Roma. b |
| WTF | Santa Maria. b |
| WTG | Santa Rita. b |
| WTH | Washtenaw. b |
| WTI | Catania. b |
| WTJ | |
| WTK | J. A. Chanslor. b |
| WTL | |
| WTM | W. S. Porter. b |
| WTN | Wm. F. Herrin. b |
| WTO | Frank H. Buck. b |
| WTP | Scranton, Pa. c |
| WTQ | El Segundo. b |
| WTR | Richmond. b |
| WTS | Col. E. L. Drake. b |
| WTT | Atlas. b |
| WTU | S. O. Co. No. 91. b |
| WTV | Captain A. F. Lucas. b |
| WTW | Maverick. b |
| WTX | Asuncion. b |
| WTY | S. O. Co. No. 93. b |
| WTZ | S. O. Co. No. 95. b |
| WUA | Fort Andrews, Mass. c |
| WUB | Fort Hancock, N. J. c |
| WUC | Fort H. G. Wright, N. Y. c |
| WUD | Fort Leavenworth, Kans. c |
| WUE | Fort Levett, Me. c |
| WUF | Fort Monroe, Va. c |
| WUG | Fort Monroe, Va. c |
| WUH | Fort Omaha, Nebr. c |
| WUI | Fort Riley, Kans. c |
| WUJ | Fort Sam Houston, Tex. c |
| WUK | Fort Stevens, Oreg. c |
| WUL | Fort Totten, N. Y. c |
| WUM | Fort Wood, N. Y. c |
| WUN | Fort Worden, Wash. c |
| WUO | Fort Winfield Scott, Cal. c |
| WUP | Washington, D. C. c |
| WUQ | Washington, D. C. c |
| WUR | |
| WUS | |
| WUT | |
| WUU | |
| WUV | Fort Leavenworth, Kans. c |
| WUW | Fort Terry, N. Y. c |
| WUX | |
| WUY | |
| WUZ | |
| WVA | Circle City, Alaska. c |
| WVB | Fairbanks, Alaska. c |
| WVC | Fort Egbert, Alaska. c |
| WVD | Fort Gibbon, Alaska. c |
| WVE | Fort St. Michael, Alaska. c |
| WVF | Kotlik, Alaska. c |
| WVG | Nome, Alaska. c |
| WVH | Nulato, Alaska. c |
| WVI | Petersburg, Alaska. c |
| WVJ | Wrangell, Alaska. c |
| WVK | |
| WVL | Fort Frank, P. I. c |
| WVM | Fort Hughes, P. I. c |
| WVN | Fort Mills, P. I. c |
| WVO | Davao, P. I. c |
| WVP | Fort Drum, P. I. c |
| WVQ | Fort Wm. McKinley, P. I. c |
| WVR | Fort Wint, P. I. c |
| WVS | Jolo, P. I. c |
| WVT | Malabang, P. I. c |
| WVU | Manila, P. I. c |
| WVV | Puerto Princesa, P. I. c |
| WVW | Zamboanga, P. I. c |
| WVX | Cuyo, P. I. c |
| WVY | San Jose, P. I. c |
| WVZ | |
| WWA | China. b |
| WWB | Beaver. b |
| WWC | |
| WWD | Bear. b |
| WWE | Manchuria. b |
| WWF | City of Para. b |
| WWG | City of Sydney. b |
| WWH | Newport. b |
| WWI | Pennsylvania. b |
| WWJ | Peru. b |
| WWK | Korea. b |
| WWL | San Jose. b |
| WWM | San Juan. b |
| WWN | Mongolia. b |
| WWO | |
| WWP | City of Panama. b |
| WWQ | Aztec. b |
| WWR | Rose City. b |
| WWS | Kansas City. b |
| WWT | |
| WWU | Siberia. b |
| WWV | |
| WWW | |

LAND AND SHIP RADIO STATIONS, ALPHABETICALLY BY CALL SIGNALS—Continued.

| Call signal. | Station. |
|---|---|
| WWX | ........................... |
| WWY | ........................... |
| WWZ | ........................... |
| WXA | Buford.........................b |
| WXB | Crook..........................b |
| WXC | Dix.............................b |
| WXD | Kilpatrick.....................b |
| WXE | Liscum........................b |
| WXF | Logan..........................b |
| WXG | Meade..........................b |
| WXH | McClellan.....................b |
| WXI | Merritt........................b |
| WXJ | Sheridan......................b |
| WXK | Sherman.......................b |
| WXL | Sumner........................b |
| WXM | Thomas........................b |
| WXN | Warren........................b |
| WXO | ........................... |
| WXP | ........................... |
| WXQ | ........................... |
| WXR | Burnside......................b |
| WXS | ........................... |
| WXT | Joseph Henry.................b |
| WXU | Navesink......................b |
| WXV | ........................... |
| WXW | ........................... |
| WXX | ........................... |
| WXY | ........................... |
| WXZ | ........................... |
| WYA | General Royal T. Frank......b |
| WYB | General S. N. Mills..........b |
| WYC | Major Samuel Ringgold.......b |
| WYD | General Henry T. Hunt.......b |
| WYE | General Henry Knox.........b |
| WYF | General E. O. C. Ord.........b |
| WYG | ........................... |
| WYH | General Robert Anderson....b |
| WYI | Captain Chas. W. Rowell.....b |
| WYJ | General A. M. Randol.........b |
| WYK | General Harvey Brown........b |
| WYL | General R. B. Ayres..........b |
| WYM | Captain James Fornance....b. |
| WYN | Reno............................b |
| WYO | Major Evan Thomas..........b |
| WYP | Captain Barrett...............b |
| WYQ | ........................... |
| WYR | ........................... |
| WYS | ........................... |
| WYT | Captain A. M. Wetherill......b |
| WYU | ........................... |
| WYV | ........................... |
| WYW | ........................... |
| WYX | ........................... |
| WYY | ........................... |
| WYZ | ........................... |
| WZA | ........................... |
| WZB | ........................... |
| WZC | ........................... |
| WZD | ........................... |
| WZE | ........................... |
| WZF | ........................... |
| WZG | Fort De Russey, Hawaii......c |
| WZH | Fort Shafter, Hawaii.........c |
| WZI | ........................... |
| WZJ | ........................... |
| WZK | ........................... |
| WZL | ........................... |
| WZM | ........................... |
| WZN | ........................... |
| WZO | ........................... |
| WZP | ........................... |
| WZQ | ........................... |
| WZR | ........................... |
| WZS | ........................... |
| WZT | ........................... |
| WZU | ........................... |
| WZV | ........................... |
| WZW | ........................... |
| WZX | ........................... |
| WZY | ........................... |
| WZZ | ........................... |

## SPECIAL STATIONS, GROUPED BY DISTRICTS.

### FIRST DISTRICT.

| | |
|---|---|
| 1XA | Amesbury, Mass. |
| 1XB | Boston, Mass. |
| 1XC | Chelsea, Mass. |
| 1XG | Pittsfield, Mass. |
| 1XH | Boston, Mass. |
| 1XI | Gloucester, Mass. |
| 1XP | Cambridge, Mass. |
| 1XW | Watchaug Pond, R. I. |
| 1YH | Cambridge, Mass. |
| 1ZO | New Bedford, Mass. |

### SECOND DISTRICT.

| | |
|---|---|
| 2XD | Slingerlands, N. Y. |
| 2XH | New York, N. Y. |
| 2XM | Columbia University, New York, N. Y. |
| 2XN | New York, N. Y. |
| 2XT | Steamship "Tyler." |
| 2XW | Summit, N. J. |
| 2ZH | Nutley, N. J. |

### THIRD DISTRICT.

| | |
|---|---|
| 3XB | Takoma Park, Md. |
| 3XC | Philadelphia, Pa. |
| 3XJ | Philadelphia, Pa. |
| 3XR | Hyattsville, Md. |
| 3ZD | Riverdale, Md. |
| 3ZF | Friendship Heights, D. C. |
| 3ZH | Washington, D. C |
| 3ZR | Quarantine, Md. |
| 3ZS | St. Davids, Pa. |

### FOURTH DISTRICT.

| | |
|---|---|
| 4XA | Key West, Fla. |
| 4XG | Atlanta, Ga. |
| 4XL | Savannah, Ga. |
| 4YC | Charleston, S. C. |

### FIFTH DISTRICT.

| | |
|---|---|
| 5XC | Memphis, Tenn. |
| 5ZD | Memphis, Tenn. |

### SIXTH DISTRICT.

| | |
|---|---|
| 6XA | San Francisco, Cal. |
| 6XB | Berkeley, Cal. |
| 6XC | Oakland, Cal. |
| 6XH | San Francisco, Cal. |
| 6XL | Los Angeles, Cal. |
| 6XR | Berkeley, Cal. |
| 6XS | Alameda, Cal. |
| 6XT | Oakland, Cal. |
| 6YE | Oakland, Cal. |
| 6YL | Los Angeles, Cal. |
| 6YS | San Diego, Cal. |

### EIGHTH DISTRICT.

| | |
|---|---|
| 8XA | Ann Arbor, Mich. |
| 8YD | Detroit, Mich. |

### NINTH DISTRICT.

| | |
|---|---|
| 9XB | Beloit, Wis. |
| 9XD | Valparaiso, Ind. |
| 9XH | Kansas City, Mo. |
| 9YC | St. Louis, Mo. |
| 9YI | Ames, Iowa. |
| 9YN | Grand Forks, N. Dak. |
| 9ZE | Minneapolis, Minn. |

# PART II.

## AMATEUR RADIO STATIONS.

### FIRST DISTRICT.

[Headquarters: Customhouse, barge office, Long Wharf, Boston, Mass. The first district comprises the States of Maine, New Hampshire, Vermont, Massachusetts, Rhode Island, and Connecticut.]

ALPHABETICALLY BY OWNERS OF STATIONS.

| Call signal. | Owner of station. | Location of station. | Power. |
|---|---|---|---|
| | | | Watts. |
| 1TC | Aerogram Club of Newport. | 16 John St., Newport, R. I. | 350 |
| 1HL | Affel, Herman A. | 45 St. Botolph St., Boston, Mass. | 100 |
| 1GM | Allen, J. Wyman | 236 Hale St., Beverly, Mass. | 250 |
| 1HA | Allison, William H. | 37 Plantation St., Worcester, Mass. | 500 |
| 1KJ | Anderson, Arvid E. | Shore St., Falmouth, Mass. | 100 |
| 1HT | Anderson, James H. | 132 White St., Belmont, Mass. | 100 |
| 1NA | Andonegui, Lane | 1010 Mass. Ave., Cambridge, Mass. | 250 |
| 1ME | Angell, Otis P. | 20 Trowbridge St., Cambridge, Mass. | 500 |
| 1MA | Anthony, Harvey M. | Harvard University, Cambridge, Mass. | 250 |
| 1KQ | Armstrong, James B. | 15 Bradford Rd., Newton Highlands, Mass. | 50 |
| 1UJ | Ashworth, Harry | 34 Heath St., Providence, R. I. | 100 |
| 1CO | Atkins, Harry C. | 57 Pine St., Franklin, N. H. | 100 |
| 1OZ | Baer, Louis F. | 3 Washburn St., East Weymouth, Mass. | 100 |
| 1WE | Baldwin, James P. | 66 Forest St., New Britain, Conn. | 250 |
| 1VK | Barnes, Howard M. | 12 Hawkins St., New Britain, Conn. | 250 |
| 1IT | Barnes, Irving T. | 377 Main St., Waltham, Mass. | 100 |
| 1WB | Barnum, Roland B. | 250 Sherman Ave., New Haven, Conn. | 500 |
| 1WJ | Barrett, John H. | 64 Lafayette Pl., Greenwich, Conn. | 100 |
| 1UQ | Barth, Karl E. | 229 Washington Ave., Providence, R. I. | 1,000 |
| 1KX | Batcheller, Arthur | 199 Sherley Ave., Revere, Mass. | 150 |
| 1IY | Baxter, Horace M. | 160 Foster St., Brighton, Mass. | 100 |
| 1MC | Baylies, Milton A. | 111 Grinnell St., New Bedford, Mass. | 500 |
| 1TR | Bazinet, Wilfred J. | 1667 Westminster St., Providence, R. I. | 250 |
| 1CZ | Bean, Harold W. | 82 S. Main St., Penacook, N. H. | 1,000 |
| 1PB | Bean, John E., jr. | Church St., Merrimac, Mass. | 60 |
| 1PA | Beckman, Carl W. | 243 Arnold St., New Bedford, Mass. | 250 |
| 1NF | Beecher, George E. | 416 Allen St., Springfield, Mass. | 100 |
| 1VL | Belknap, Edward L. | 91 Vine St., Hartford, Conn. | 100 |
| 1ND | Bellis, Clifford B. | 9 Brown St., Waltham, Mass. | 200 |
| 1HY | Bennett, Lawrence S. | 2 Lawrence St., Everett, Mass. | 500 |
| 1IE | Bennett, William F., jr. | 24 Spring St., Somerville, Mass. | 100 |
| 1KT | Benoit, Walter R. | 73 Independent St., New Bedford, Mass. | 100 |
| 1GU | Bernardin, Leo A. | 456 Haverhill St., Lawrence, Mass. | 750 |
| 1LF | Beverly High School | 16 Essex St., Beverly, Mass. | 500 |
| 1GH | Bibber, Harold W. | 31 Beacon St., Gloucester, Mass. | 1,000 |
| 1UL | Bigelow, Clinton A. | 96 Whittier Ave., Providence, R. I. | 100 |
| 1UG | Bigelow, Fred C. | 123 Chapel St., Saylesville, R. I. | 1,000 |
| 1KY | Bishop, Leon W. | 18 Irving St., Boston, Mass. | 40 |
| 1QK | Black, William R. | 32 Jefferson St., Newton, Mass. | 50 |
| 1NB | Blanchard, Ralph N. | 73 Jenkins Ave., Whitman, Mass. | 100 |
| 1WV | Blanke, Donald C. | Old Church Rd., Greenwich, Conn. | 250 |
| 1GB | Blount, Henry G. | Hamilton, Mass. | 539 |
| 1LB | Blume, Carl T. | 8 Upham St., Revere, Mass. | 45 |
| 1KR | Borden, Howard G. | 710 Rock St., Fall River, Mass. | 500 |
| 1MB | Boudette, Clayton M. | 194 Elm St., Everett, Mass. | 500 |

AMATEUR RADIO STATIONS—FIRST DISTRICT—ALPHABETICALLY BY OWNERS OF STATIONS—Continued.

| Call signal. | Owner of station. | Location of station. | Power. |
|---|---|---|---|
| | | | Watts. |
| 1LC | Bowen, Arthur N | 34 Apthorp St., Revere, Mass | 250 |
| 1KU | Bowen, Earl H | 459 Madison St., Fall River, Mass | 250 |
| 1KO | Bowen, Harold C | 168 Belmont Ave., Fall River, Mass | 250 |
| 1OR | Boyden, Laurance E | 44 Cypress Pl., Brookline, Mass | 100 |
| 1TK | Branigan, Hugh S. C | 310 Prairie Ave., Providence, R. I | 100 |
| 1PN | Briggs, Ralph E | 100 West St., Whitman, Mass | 250 |
| 1HQ | Broadley, Harry R | 44 Wenham St., Boston, Mass | 48 |
| 1AI | Brown, Olin C | 23 Ledgelawn Ave., Bar Harbor, Me | 1,000 |
| 1AB | Brown, Philip T | 36 Taylor St., Portland, Me | 500 |
| 1JN | Bruce, Arthur O | 30 York St., Cambridge, Mass | 500 |
| 1QE | Bruce, Edmond | 1010 Massachusetts Ave., Cambridge, Mass | 250 |
| 1UX | Budlong, Clifton O | Cranston, R. I | 100 |
| 1WA | Bueb, John J., jr | 12 Maher Ave., Greenwich, Conn | 100 |
| 1WS | Buffett, Salathiel | Quarry Ave., Saybrook, Conn | 100 |
| 1MJ | Burdett, Roland E | 559 Main St., Wakefield, Mass | 1,000 |
| 1HB | Burgess, Warren B | 62 Fruit St., Worcester, Mass | 6 |
| 1HI | Burke, Alan W | 40 Pollock Ave., Pittsfield, Mass | 750 |
| 1GL | Bush, Arthur W | 80 Tower Hill St., Lawrence, Mass | 1,000 |
| 1AM | Butler, Guy W | 239 Center St., Oldtown, Me | 160 |
| 1MU | Byers, John R | 154 Lowell Ave., Newtonville, Mass | 200 |
| 1MV | Caldwell, George W | 52 Cherry St., Lynn, Mass | 500 |
| 1NU | Campbell, Harold G | 86 Kenwood St., Dorchester, Mass | 100 |
| 1HD | Canfield, Donald T | R. F. D., Westboro, Mass | 100 |
| 1BO | Canty, William R | 36 Lincoln Ave., Rutland, Vt | 500 |
| 1JT | Carlson, Arthur G | 19 Mechanic St., North Easton, Mass | 500 |
| 1GC | Chadwick, Gilbert L | 19 11th Ave., Haverhill, Mass | 27 |
| 1CW | Chase, Robert McC | 25 Russell St., Plymouth, N. H | 798 |
| 1HC | Cheetham, Harry R | 81 Avon St., Somerville, Mass | 45 |
| 1JM | Cheever, Walter G | 6 Aldersey St., Somerville, Mass | 25 |
| 1IU | Church, Arthur E | 3 Wellington Ter., Brookline, Mass | 90 |
| 1AQ | Claflin, Harold M | 160 College Ave., Waterville, Me | 750 |
| 1PT | Clayton, Henry C | 1422 Washington St., Canton, Mass | 100 |
| 1HG | Cogswell, George R | 18 Garden St., Cambridge, Mass | 250 |
| 1NE | Coleman, Benj. B. B | 193 Clapp St., Milton, Mass | 200 |
| 1WC | Coleman, William F | 177 Wethersfield Ave., Hartford, Conn | 100 |
| 1JD | Collins, Lovejoy | 44 Carver Rd., Newton Highlands, Mass | 100 |
| 1IM | Conner, George W | 72 Medford St., Malden, Mass | 250 |
| 1CP | Conrad, Philip W | 172 Elm St., Keene, N. H | 250 |
| 1OS | Copland, H. Depew | 42 Huron Ave., Cambridge, Mass | 100 |
| 1BM | Copps, John L | 138 S. Main St., Rutland, Vt | 100 |
| 1LG | Corey, Frank J | 41 Sycamore St., Somerville, Mass | 160 |
| 1LE | Corney, Chester A | 815 E. 4th St., South Boston, Mass | 250 |
| 1VJ | Cowles, George R | 181 Thomas St., West Haven, Conn | 25 |
| 1UC | Creaser, Isaiah | 641 Plainfield St., Providence, R. I | 1,000 |
| 1HP | Cromack, N. G. N | 8 Elm Lawn St., Dorchester, Mass | 100 |
| 1PW | Crosby, Carlton | 173 Davis Ave., Brookline, Mass | 30 |
| 1WP | Cummings, Edward H | Warwick, R. I | 300 |
| 1NL | Curtis, Samuel, jr | 3 Myrick St., Allston, Mass | 75 |
| 1IK | Dallin, Edwin B | 69 Oakland Ave., Arlington Heights, Mass | 250 |
| 1JU | Dane, Francis W | Main St., Hamilton, Mass | 500 |
| 1QZ | Danehy, Edward J | 21 Sargent St., Cambridge, Mass | 100 |
| 1GJ | Daniels, Richard M | 25 Outlook Rd., Swampscott, Mass | 500 |
| 1KD | David, Harold E | 21-A Belchertown Rd., Amherst, Mass | 100 |
| 1AX | Davies, Orel E | 301 Main St., Rockland, Me | 250 |
| 1WZ | Davis, Maurice E | 217 Dover St., New Haven, Conn | 50 |
| 1IL | Dean, Samuel W | 4 Eliot Rd., Lexington, Mass | 1,000 |
| 1JP | Decker, Clarence | Housatonic, Mass | 250 |
| 1JR | Delano, Edward C | 64 School St., Fall River, Mass | 500 |
| 1HK | Denison, Horace W | 60 Garland St., Chelsea, Mass | 500 |

54773°—14——6

AMATEUR RADIO STATIONS—FIRST DISTRICT—ALPHABETICALLY BY OWNERS OF STATIONS—Continued.

| Call signal. | Owner of station. | Location of station. | Power. |
|---|---|---|---|
| | | | Watts. |
| 1LH | Dickson, William E. | 59 Hamden Circle, Quincy, Mass. | 250 |
| 1BC | Dimick, Leon R. | 27 Cliff St., St. Johnsbury, Vt. | 100 |
| 1JA | Dimond, Fred A., jr. | 4 Purchase St., East Carver, Mass. | 100 |
| 1UR | Doherty, James E. | 22 Orms St., Providence, R. I. | 100 |
| 1UD | Donle, Harold P. | 18 Observatory Ave., Providence, R. I. | 300 |
| 1LO | Donovan, Arthur B. | 49 Bigelow Ave., Rockland, Mass. | 250 |
| 1UO | Doyle, John B. | 306 Thurber Ave., Providence, R. I. | 12 |
| 1PC | Drake, Ervin T., jr. | 40 Holyoke House, Cambridge, Mass. | 30 |
| 1HZ | Duncan, Harrie E. | 34 Foster St., Newtonville, Mass. | 500 |
| 1LI | Eales, Malcolm A. L. | 4 Chestnut Park, Melrose, Mass. | 250 |
| 1QG | Edmester, Earle C. | 23 Beacon St., Everett, Mass. | 250 |
| 1KL | Edson, Allan W. | 167 Pleasant St., Whitman, Mass. | 250 |
| 1WN | Edwin Bancroft Foote Boys' Club. | Chapel St., New Haven, Conn. | 1,000 |
| 1NC | Ekwall, George O. | "The Standish," Waltham, Mass. | 100 |
| 1OF | Eldredge, Clarence R. | 41 Lawrence St., Wakefield, Mass. | 500 |
| 1AZ | Elkins, Ben T. | Robbins Rd., Belfast, Me. | 100 |
| 1HR | Elliott, Thomas H., jr. | 41 Brington Rd., Brookline, Mass. | 500 |
| 1GO | Estey, F. Clifford | 3 Goodell St., Salem, Mass. | 250 |
| 1AJ | Fabbri, Alessandro | Eden St., Bar Harbor, Me. | 1,000 |
| 1JC | Fairbanks, Robert D. | 21 Carver Rd., Newton Highlands, Mass. | 100 |
| 1IJ | Fassitt, Andrew J., jr. | 27 Walden St., Cambridge, Mass. | 1,000 |
| 1PU | Fearing, Sumner E. | 36 Water St., East Weymouth, Mass. | ..... |
| 1KZ | Fiske, John | 114 Brattle St., Cambridge, Mass. | 50 |
| 1LJ | Fitch, Conover | 321 Hammond St., Newton, Mass. | 500 |
| 1BA | Fitts, Harold W. | 2 Park St., Barre, Vt. | 100 |
| 1OH | Flanders, Fred F. | 9 Norway St., Boston, Mass. | 275 |
| 1TL | Flint, Carl O. | R. F. D. No. 1, Union, Me. | 550 |
| 1HN | Flood, J. Frank J. | 160 D St., South Boston, Mass. | 250 |
| 1OG | Florence, William E., jr. | 79 Salem St., Reading, Mass. | 250 |
| 1PV | Folsom, Rolfe A. | 76 Rockland Ave., Malden, Mass. | 75 |
| 1GF | Fowler, F. Malcolm | 16 Shore Ave., Salem, Mass. | 500 |
| 1JK | Franke, Alfred A. | 15 Orchard St., Jamaica Plain, Mass. | 100 |
| 1IH | Fuller, Clarence C. | 50 High St., Mansfield, Mass. | 500 |
| 1JL | Gahm, Sebastian, jr. | 113 Sheridan St., Jamaica Plain, Mass. | 100 |
| 1HF | Gardner, Chester R. | 11 Spring Hill Ter., Somerville, Mass. | 100 |
| 1GV | Gavill, Wilbur W. | West Chelmsford, Mass. | 210 |
| 1NR | Gerrish, Kenneth B. | 170 Summer St., Malden, Mass. | 100 |
| 1NQ | Getchell, Melvin D. | 127 Monument St., West Medford, Mass. | 100 |
| 1VN | Green, Louis S. | 126 Central Ave., Waterbury, Conn. | 100 |
| 1GW | Haddock, Charles C. | 57 Lathrop St., Beverly, Mass. | 250 |
| 1TV | Hale, Edward E. | 92 Hallick Ave., Riverside, R. I. | 100 |
| 1NS | Hamilton, Edward P. | 69 Canton Ave., Milton, Mass. | 100 |
| 1HM | Hammett, Herbert M. | 4 Blue Hill Ave., Roxbury, Mass. | 500 |
| 1UH | Handy, William R. | Lincoln, R. I. | 100 |
| 1AW | Harden, Edward F. | South Brewer, Me. | 250 |
| 1GS | Hardy, Wilbur H. | 778 Hale St., Beverly Farms, Mass. | 250 |
| 1UA | Hargraves, Harold T. | 733 Cranston St., Providence, R. I. | 100 |
| 1CY | Haselton, Page S. | R. F. D. No. 3, Hudson, N. H. | 100 |
| 1VO | Haskell, Shirley D. | Main St., Essex, Conn. | 250 |
| 1LK | Haskins, Frederic C. | 220 Lexington St., Belmont, Mass. | 250 |
| 1AY | Hatch, James F. | 86 Elm St., Portland, Me. | 250 |
| 1MX | Hathaway, Francis R. | Salem, Mass. | 250 |
| 1JE | Hayward, Edward E., jr. | 4 Pembroke St., Newton, Mass. | 100 |
| 1OT | Heap, Sheldon S. | 132 Atlantic St., Atlantic, Mass. | 100 |
| 1UN | Henry, William E. | 162 Prairie Ave., Providence, R. I. | 500 |
| 1JY | Herland, John N. | 48 Brush Hill Rd., Mattapan, Mass. | 15 |
| 1MH | Herrick, Sumner E. | 7 Birch Hill Ave., Wakefield, Mass. | 250 |
| 1QV | Heyman, Harry | 15 Congress St., Springfield, Mass. | 100 |
| 1VH | Hickmott, William J., jr. | 29 Sumner St., Hartford, Conn. | 275 |

AMATEUR RADIO STATIONS—FIRST DISTRICT—ALPHABETICALLY BY OWNERS OF STATIONS—Continued.

| Call signal. | Owner of station. | Location of station. | Power. |
|---|---|---|---|
| | | | *Watts.* |
| 1OC | Hill, Harold F. | 788 Massachusetts Ave., Cambridge, Mass. | 12 |
| 1OL | Hinman, George W. | 198 Russell St., Worcester, Mass. | 12 |
| 1PE | Hitchcock, Frederick J. | 14 Burrough St., Danvers, Mass. | 100 |
| 1TF | Hodges, Duncan | Cloyne School, Newport, R. I. | 500 |
| 1AF | Hodgkins, Winfield C. | 54 Eagle Lake Rd., Bar Harbor, Me. | 100 |
| 1JQ | Hoffman, Frank E. | 33 High St., Springfield, Mass. | 250 |
| 1WY | Hoggson, Wallace | Maher Ave., Greenwich, Conn. | 500 |
| 1UZ | Homer, Arthur B. | 270 Blackstone Blvd., Providence, R. I. | 12 |
| 1TI | Horgan, T. Francis | 239 Broadway, Newport, R. I. | 250 |
| 1VQ | Horsfall, George W. | Unionville, Conn. | 100 |
| 1OJ | Howard, Charles S. | Townsend, Mass. | 500 |
| 1KC | Howe, Milton A. | 347 Mt. Vernon St., Fitchburg, Mass. | 500 |
| 1CR | Howe, Reginald | 94 School St., Keene, N. H. | 100 |
| 1JH | Hubbard, Allen, jr. | 11 Montvale Crescent, Newton Center, Mass. | 250 |
| 1WL | Hubbard, George F. | 267 Milbank Ave., Greenwich, Conn. | 250 |
| 1HJ | Hunt, Albert M. | 12 Madison Ave., Newtonville, Mass. | 100 |
| 1KV | Hurley, Albert V. | 16 Oakland Ave., Everett, Mass. | 250 |
| 1AG | Hutchins, Ray | Oak St., Springvale, Me. | 24 |
| 1GP | James, Albert W. | 36 Union St., Manchester, Mass. | 100 |
| 1NK | Jennings, Charles E., jr. | 28 Wrentham St., Dorchester, Mass. | 100 |
| 1VR | Jennings, John W. | West Redding, Conn. | 100 |
| 1TP | Jensen, Leonard C. | 17 Mt. Vernon St., Providence, R. I. | 100 |
| 1PF | Jerauld, Dorrance G. | Harwich, Mass. | 100 |
| 1UE | Jette, George E. | 161 Summer St., Central Falls, R. I. | 500 |
| 1TJ | Johnson, Alexander R. | 371 Sayles St., Providence, R. I. | 100 |
| 1PG | Johnson, David E. | 25 Glen St., Worcester, Mass. | 30 |
| 1MK | Johnson, Thurston A. | 123 Winthrop St., Winthrop, Mass. | 250 |
| 1PH | Jones, R. Warren | 218 Pleasant St., Brockton, Mass. | 100 |
| 1KP | Justice, Francis C. | 148 Tremont St., Newton, Mass. | 100 |
| 1ID | Kehoe, Francis | 41 Walnut St., Boston, Mass. | 250 |
| 1IC | Keller, Adrian C. | 36 Grand View Ave., Medford, Mass. | 250 |
| 1AC | Kennedy, Chester A. | 199 High St., South Portland, Me. | 250 |
| 1OA | Kenison, Arthur C. | 45 Parker St., Lexington, Mass. | 1,000 |
| 1NP | Kiley, John T. | 11 Morton St., Somerville, Mass. | 10 |
| 1OB | Kilton, James A., jr. | 96 Browne St., Brookline, Mass. | 250 |
| 1LM | King, Alexander R. | 27 Brantwood Rd., Arlington, Mass. | 250 |
| 1LP | Knight, Hugh C. | 132 Melrose St., Melrose Highlands, Mass. | 200 |
| 1PI | Knight, Maurice E. | 3 Edwin St., Boston, Mass. | 30 |
| 1IN | Lamson, Horatio W. | 10 Oakland Ave., Arlington Heights, Mass. | 500 |
| 1GD | Lane, Frederic A. | 7 Madison Ave., Gloucester, Mass. | 250 |
| 1VC | Langevin, Carl C. | 44 Sumner St., Hartford, Conn. | 100 |
| 1JZ | Lanvuette, Kenneth H. | 21 Houston Ave., Milton, Mass. | 18 |
| 1AT | Lawford, Arthur H. | 292 Main St., Bar Harbor, Me. | 250 |
| 1JI | Lawrence, Milford R. | Main St., Falmouth, Mass. | 500 |
| 1IS | Leach, George F. | 513 Liberty St., Rockland, Mass. | 100 |
| 1HX | Leavitt, Elmer A. | 41 Forest Ave., Everett, Mass. | 500 |
| 1IP | Leland, Harold B. | 34 Irving St., Somerville, Mass. | 100 |
| 1NZ | Leutz, Charles R. | 34 Wyman St., Jamaica Plain, Mass. | 100 |
| 1VA | Lewis, George B. | North Haven, Conn. | 100 |
| 1IR | Lewis, Minott W. | 44 Kidder Ave., West Somerville, Mass. | 330 |
| 1MW | Linn, Harold W. | 107 Alden St., Whitman, Mass. | 250 |
| 1QY | Linsert, Henry | 124 Goden St., Belmont, Mass. | 20 |
| 1UY | Lippitt, Gorton T. | 111 Benevolent St., Providence, R. I. | 200 |
| 1PK | Loheed, William J., jr. | 12 Clifton Ave., Campello, Mass. | .... |
| 1JW | Long, John J. | 32 London St., Somerville, Mass. | 100 |
| 1GT | Loomis, Arthur T. | 35 Graves Ave., Lynn, Mass. | 250 |
| 1JB | Lord, Howland C. | 40 Clyde St., Newtonville, Mass. | 100 |
| 1KI | Loring, Wilfred B. | Plympton, Mass. | 175 |
| 1NY | Lovis, Donald B. | 26 Adelaide St., Jamaica Plain, Mass. | 100 |

AMATEUR RADIO STATIONS—FIRST DISTRICT—ALPHABETICALLY BY OWNERS OF STATIONS—Continued.

| Call signal. | Owner of station. | Location of station. | Power. |
|---|---|---|---|
| | | | Watts. |
| 1WU | Lucas, Orville | 172 Washington St., Wallingford, Conn | 100 |
| 1IQ | Luey, Donald | 44 West St., Worcester, Mass | 500 |
| 1NT | Lynch, John P | 25 Speedwell St., Boston, Mass | 10 |
| 1HE | Lynde, Kenneth R | 20 Cloelia Ter., Newtonville, Mass | 100 |
| 1ML | Lyon, William H | Maple St., East Lexington, Mass | 1,000 |
| 1OK | Mackenzie, Roy G | 102 High St., Danvers, Mass | 600 |
| 1TN | Mahoney, Charles J | 18 Pond Ave., Newport, R. I | 100 |
| 1TG | Manchester, Arthur W | 31 Newport Ave., Newport, R. I | 100 |
| 1KG | Manning, Ralph K | 232 Vine St., Everett, Mass | 250 |
| 1TH | Manuel, Lloyd | 106 2d St., Newport, R. I | 500 |
| 1NG | Marshall, Stanley | 1 Hobart St., Danvers, Mass | 250 |
| 1VF | Mascare, Fred A | 15 Cassidy Park, Greenwich, Conn | 500 |
| 1TM | Mason, Lion G | Halidon Hall, Newport, R. I | 500 |
| 1NV | Mathews, Lloyd F | 40 Ibbetson St., Somerville, Mass | 16 |
| 1WH | Maxim, Hiram P | 550 Prospect Ave., Hartford, Conn | 375 |
| 1NW | McDermott, Joseph H | Belmont, Mass | 200 |
| 1VM | McGuire, William C | 76 Madison St., Hartford, Conn | 100 |
| 1CM | McLane, Henry R | 342 Union Ave., Laconia, N. H | 1,00 |
| 1VD | McPartland, Frank J | 35 Holmes St., Orange, Conn | 100 |
| 1WF | McSweeney, Lawrence P | 6 Wethersfield Ave., Hartford, Conn | 100 |
| 1TQ | Medbery, Chester H | 156 Hanover St., Providence, R. I | 100 |
| 1KM | Meekin, William J | 34 Custer St., Rockland, Mass | 250 |
| 1QH | Melvin, Arthur W | R. F. D. No. 1, Chelmsford, Mass | 250 |
| 1HO | Merrill, Clark B | 3 Elm St., Dorchester, Mass | 200 |
| 1MI | Merrill, Donald F | 282 Buckminster Rd., Brookline, Mass | 250 |
| 1OD | Miller, Alden W | 16 Chestnut St., Medford, Mass | 20 |
| 1UM | Miller, Bernard H | 38 Doyle Ave., Providence, R. I | 250 |
| 1UV | Monahan, Edward M | 1033 Eddy St., Providence, R. I | 100 |
| 1WK | Moore, David L | Farmington, Conn | 250 |
| 1GI | Morse, Harold E | 108 Essex St., Swampscott, Mass | 300 |
| 1LY | Moulton, Albert B | 26 Monadnock Rd., Worcester, Mass | 500 |
| 1HW | Munroe, Henry W. T | 38 Beacon St., Everett, Mass | 500 |
| 1LZ | Murphy, Dudley B | 176 Highland Ave., Winchester, Mass | 1,00 |
| 1PX | Murphy, Harry J | Florence, Mass | 100 |
| 1AU | Nash, Arthur F | 277 Spring St., Portland, Me | 500 |
| 1QF | Nash, Paul | 64 Fairmont Ave., Newton, Mass | 15 |
| 1CV | Nelson, Rufus L | 16 Oak St., Northfield, N. H | 500 |
| 1TO | Newton, Raymond C | 292 California Ave., Providence, R. I | 25 |
| 1LN | Newton Technical High School. | Newton, Mass | 250 |
| 1UW | Nilson, Arthur R | 11 Colfax St., Providence, R. I | 100 |
| 1AP | Norton, Edward L | 26 Grove St., Rockland, Me | 750 |
| 1QL | Noyes, Russell | 33 Washington Park, Newtonville, Mass | 100 |
| 1QA | Nyquist, Norman A | 107 Chestnut Ave., Jamaica Plain, Mass | 100 |
| 1QJ | O'Brine, Daniel | 152 Bridge St., Manchester, Mass | 100 |
| 1IX | Ohlson, Olof | 472 Crafts St., Newton, Mass | 250 |
| 1MO | Ostrander, Freeman K., jr | 215 White St., Springfield, Mass | 250 |
| 1PL | Oudin, C. Folger | Marblehead Neck, Mass | 250 |
| 1CX | Parker, George H | Hudson, N. H | 100 |
| 1IG | Patten, Ernest L. O | 11 Holmes St., Malden, Mass | 500 |
| 1OM | Payson, Gilbert R., jr | 545 Belmont St., Belmont, Mass | 100 |
| 1UB | Pease, Reginald M | 5 W. Park St., Providence, R. I | 100 |
| 1MN | Pennell, Leon | 69 N. Main St., Brockton, Mass | 330 |
| 1KF | Pennypacker, Thomas R | Chatham, Mass | 100 |
| 1UF | Perkins, Leonard M | 335 Public St., Providence, R. I | 250 |
| 1LQ | Perry, Willard H | Thompsons Isld., Boston Harbor, Mass | 250 |
| 1OE | Porter, Ralph H | 7 Randal St., Salem, Mass | 250 |
| 1WO | Post, Harold D | 131 Derby Ave., New Haven, Conn | 100 |
| 1JS | Powers, Leonard S | 431 Plymouth St., Carver, Mass | 100 |
| 1JG. | Pratt, Fearing | 120 Main St., Hingham, Mass | 250 |

AMATEUR RADIO STATIONS—FIRST DISTRICT—ALPHABETICALLY BY OWNERS OF STATIONS—Continued.

| Call signal. | Owner of station. | Location of station. | Power. |
|---|---|---|---|
| | | | *Watts.* |
| 1AN | Pratt, Rhama W | Longfellow St., Westbrook, Me | 250 |
| 1IO | Pratt, Walter | 28 Summit St., Rockland, Mass | 100 |
| 1QM | Proulx, George H | 147 Pemberton St., Cambridge, Mass | 100 |
| 1PY | Pulley, Lester A | 33 Porter St., Melrose, Mass | 500 |
| 1MP | Pursell, Clarence V | 1257 Morton St., Dorchester, Mass | 250 |
| 1PZ | Ranlett, Frederick J., jr. | 351 Central St., Auburndale, Mass | 100 |
| 1LR | Rawson, Homer E | 83 Brattle St., Cambridge, Mass | 500 |
| 1ON | Readio, George U | 58 Pearl St., Springfield, Mass | 1,000 |
| 1CQ | Reed, Coleman C | 672 Marlboro St., Keene, N. H | 100 |
| 1PO | Reed, Leslie S | 61 Chestnut St., New Bedford, Mass | 100 |
| 1BD | Reed, Sherman A | 19 Dunbar St., Keene, N. H | 500 |
| 1LA | Remington, Kenneth F. | 747 High St., Fall River, Mass | 500 |
| 1JV | Reuther, Henry R | 15 Jewett St., Northampton, Mass | 250 |
| 1AR | Rich, Marion | Cedar Ave., Bar Harbor, Me | 250 |
| 1PR | Richards, Fred J | 1060 Saratoga St., East Boston, Mass | 100 |
| 1KB | Richards, William T | 15 Follen St., Cambridge, Mass | 100 |
| 1IA | Richmond, Harold B | 12 George St., Medford, Mass | 250 |
| 1AS | Rocheleau, William H | 71 Church St., Westbrook, Me | 250 |
| 1WI | Rockefeller, Godfrey S | Lake Ave., Greenwich, Conn | 500 |
| 1MR | Roddin, Thomas | 17 Bartlett Rd., Waverly, Mass | 250 |
| 1PQ | Rogers, Wallace B | 368 N. Main St., Natick, Mass | 100 |
| 1LS | Runey, Leon C | 49 Fairmont St., Belmont, Mass | 250 |
| 1HV | Ryan, James A | 13 Knowlton St., Somerville, Mass | 100 |
| 1OU | Ryer, Edwin D | 29 Gorham Ave., Brookline, Mass | 100 |
| 1MS | Sabin, G. C | 29 S. East St., Amherst, Mass | 1,000 |
| 1WX | Safranek, Jerry | 28 South St., South Norwalk, Conn | 15 |
| 1WT | Salzgeber, John W | W. Main St., Ivoryton, Conn | 100 |
| 1TS | Sampson, Ross D | 627 Elmwood Ave., Providence, R. I | 365 |
| 1QB | Saunders, George B | 52 Francis St., Boston, Mass | 100 |
| 1WR | Sawtelle, Donald F | 122 Gilbert Ave., New Haven, Conn | 100 |
| 1LT | Scott, Ralph A | 952 Franklin St., Melrose Highlands, Mass. | 250 |
| 1KS | Seabury, William H | 1056 Beacon St., Brookline, Mass | 250 |
| 1WQ | Seeley, Arthur P | 55 Pearl St., New Haven, Conn | 100 |
| 1OP | Sharpe, Floyd H | 260 Tinkham Ave., New Bedford, Mass | 250 |
| 1HS | Shattuck, Herbert | 1-A Lewis Pl., Roxbury, Mass | 100 |
| 1BN | Shaw, Raymond H | 10 E. Washington St., Rutland, Vt | 100 |
| 1AB | Sherman, Calvin A | 80 Camden St., Rockland, Me | 20 |
| 1VI | Slawson, Spencer W | Brookside Drive, Greenwich, Conn | 100 |
| 1AD | Smith, Edward S. C | 58 South St., Biddeford, Me | 100 |
| 1GN | Smith, Malcolm H | 115 Prospect St., Gloucester, Mass | 250 |
| 1JF | Snow, Albert E | 30 Cary Ave., Chelsea, Mass | 500 |
| 1GA | Snow, Harold C | 41 Paradise Rd., Swampscott, Mass | 250 |
| 1JO | Snow, William B | 11 Devon Rd., Newton Center, Mass | 100 |
| 1IV | Snyder, William E | 36 Monument Ave., Charlestown, Mass | 100 |
| 1WM | Soules, Norman E | 244 Hickory St., Norwich, Conn | 500 |
| 1OV | Southwick, Francis B | 176 Waban Ave., Waban, Mass | 45 |
| 1QX | Spaulding, Ralph H | 14 Alberta Ter., Cambridge, Mass | 100 |
| 1MY | Spear, G. Dana | 32 Common St., Walpole, Mass | 750 |
| 1AO | Sprague, Philip L | 18 Brewer St., South Brewer, Me | 250 |
| 1IZ | St. James, Robert T | 38 Avery Lane, Great Barrington, Mass | 1,000 |
| 1QI | St. James, Vincent | 258 1st St., Pittsfield, Mass | 550 |
| 1OW | Stackhouse, Walter T | 755 Winthrop Ave., Revere, Mass | 100 |
| 1TU | Stackpole, Nelson B | 725 Mineral Spring Ave., Pawtucket, R.I. | 250 |
| 1GK | Stanley, Lyman R | 52 Burrill St., Swampscott, Mass | 500 |
| 1IB | Stanyan, Starr W | 76 Boston Ave., West Medford, Mass | 200 |
| 1NM | Starkweather, John B | 17 Gibson Rd., Newtonville, Mass | 75 |
| 1AE | Sterling, George E | 28 Paine St., Springvale, Me | 100 |
| 1KA | Stickney, H. E | 25 Tufts Ave., Everett, Mass | 15 |
| 1OQ | Struthers, Francis W | Townsend, Mass | 200 |
| 1AK | Tabbut, Arthur R | 6 South St., Bar Harbor, Me | 250 |

AMATEUR RADIO STATIONS—FIRST DISTRICT—ALPHABETICALLY BY OWNERS OF STATIONS—Continued.

| Call signal. | Owner of station. | Location of station. | Power. |
|---|---|---|---|
| | | | Watts. |
| 1OX | Tarr, Mellville S | 45 Parker St., Chelsea, Mass | 100 |
| 1LU | Taylor, Frank J | 15 Orrin St., Cambridge, Mass | 250 |
| 1QD | Therrien, Arthur J | 37 Barrett St., Lynn, Mass | 20 |
| 1US | Thorndike, Don C | 303 Doric Ave., Cranston, R. I | 100 |
| 1TD | Tilley, Henry H., jr | 5 Dartmouth St., Newport, R. I | 100 |
| 1UP | Trainor, Francis J | 126 Summer St., Providence, R. I (Classical High School). | 300 |
| 1LV | Tufts, J. Warren | 11 Clarendon Ave., West Somerville, Mass. | 250 |
| 1VG | Tucker, George W | East Granby, Conn | 250 |
| 1UK | Tutin, Kenneth A | 312 Blackstone St., Woonsocket, R. I | 100 |
| 1WD | Tuska, Clarence D | 136 Oakland Ter., Hartford, Conn | 100 |
| 1MT | Tyler, Samuel F | 28 Sargent St., Newton, Mass | 25 |
| 1HU | Upton, Harry E | 18 Jackson Ave., Everett, Mass | 400 |
| 1LW | Van Brocklin, William S. | 51 Oakland Rd., Brookline, Mass | 100 |
| 1NO | Varnum, George E | 47 Decatur St., Charlestown, Mass | 100 |
| 1QC | Wadsworth, Arthur G | Eastham, Mass | 100 |
| 1VE | Walker, Alva S | 69 Dearfield Drive, Greenwich, Conn | 250 |
| 1AH | Ward, Donald G | 14 Orchard St., Portland, Me | 200 |
| 1NX | Ward, Talbot | 68 Oak St., Boston, Mass | 440 |
| 1TW | Watrous, Ralph C | 20 Diman Pl., Providence, R. I | 100 |
| 1VP | Weimann, Alfred F | 101 Cliff St., Shelton, Conn | 100 |
| 1GQ | Westbrook, Leon R | 41 11th Ave., Haverhill, Mass | 30 |
| 1GE | Wheeler, Fred L | 23 Mt. Vernon St., Cliftondale, Mass | 100 |
| 1MZ | White, Dallas E | Boston Rd., Billerica, Mass | 500 |
| 1BE | White, Earle B | R. F. D. No. 6, Belfast, Me | 100 |
| 1QW | White, Thomas C | 53 Perkins Ave., Malden, Mass | 20 |
| 1PD | Whittier, Ellerton W | 63 Terrace Ave., Winthrop, Mass | 250 |
| 1IW | Wilde, Phillips B | Government St., Woods Hole, Mass | 100 |
| 1KN | Wilkinson, John E | 35 Malvey Ave., Fall River, Mass | 250 |
| 1PM | Wireless Society, Massachusetts Institute of Technology. | Stanhope St., and Trinity Pl., Boston, Mass. | 500 |
| 1VW | Woodward, Raymond W. | 14 Tremont St., Hartford, Conn | 125 |
| 1PS | Zahn, Edward G | 6 Atherton Pl., Roxbury, Mass | 12 |
| 1MD | Ziegler, Alfred A., jr | 36 Greenough Ave., Jamaica Plain, Mass | 250 |
| 1OY | Zwinge, Conrad J | 776 Winthrop Ave., Revere, Mass | 250 |

ALPHABETICALLY BY CALL SIGNALS.

| Call signal. | Owner of station. | Call signal. | Owner of station. |
|---|---|---|---|
| 1AB | Brown, Philip T. | 1AR | Rich, Marion. |
| 1AC | Kennedy, Chester A. | 1AS | Rocheleau, William H. |
| 1AD | Smith, Edward S. C. | 1AT | Lawford, Arthur H. |
| 1AE | Sterling, George E. | 1AU | Nash, Arthur F. |
| 1AF | Hodgkins, Winfield C. | 1AV | Sherman, Calvin A. |
| 1AG | Hutchins, Ray. | 1AW | Harden, Edward F. |
| 1AH | Ward, Donald G. | 1AX | Davies, Orel E. |
| 1AI | Brown, Olin C. | 1AY | Hatch, James F. |
| 1AJ | Fabbri, Alessandro. | 1AZ | Elkins, Ben T. |
| 1AK | Tabbut, Arthur R. | | |
| 1AM | Butler, Guy W. | 1BA | Fitts, Harold W. |
| 1AN | Pratt, Rhama W. | 1BC | Dimick, Leon R. |
| 1AO | Sprague, Philip L. | 1BD | Reed, Sherman A. |
| 1AP | Norton, Edward L. | 1BE | White, Earle B. |
| 1AQ | Claflin, Harold M. | 1BM | Coppe, John L. |

AMATEUR RADIO STATIONS—FIRST DISTRICT—ALPHABETICALLY BY CALL SIGNALS—Continued.

| Call signal. | Owner of station. | Call signal. | Owner of station. |
|---|---|---|---|
| 1BN | Shaw, Raymond H. | 1HY | Bennett, Lawrence S. |
| 1BO | Canty, William R. | 1HZ | Duncan, Harrie E. |
| 1CM | McLane, Henry R. | 1IA | Richmond, Harold B. |
| 1CO | Atkins, Harry C. | 1IB | Stanyan, Starr W. |
| 1CP | Conrad, Philip W. | 1IC | Keller, Adrian C. |
| 1CQ | Reed, Coleman C. | 1ID | Kehoe, Francis. |
| 1CR | Howe, Reginald. | 1IE | Bennett, William F., jr. |
| 1CV | Nelson, Rufus L. | 1IG | Patten, Ernest L. O. |
| 1CW | Chase, Robert McC. | 1IH | Fuller, Clarence C. |
| 1CX | Parker, George H. | 1IJ | Fassitt, Andrew J., jr. |
| 1CY | Haselton, Page S. | 1IK | Dallin, Edwin B. |
| 1CZ | Bean, Harold W. | 1IL | Dean, Samuel W. |
| | | 1IM | Conner, George W. |
| 1GA | Snow, Harold C. | 1IN | Lamson, Horatio W. |
| 1GB | Blount, Henry G. | 1IO | Pratt, Walter. |
| 1GC | Chadwick, Gilbert L. | 1IP | Leland, Harold B. |
| 1GD | Lane, Frederic A. | 1IQ | Luey, Donald. |
| 1GE | Wheeler, Fred L. | 1IR | Lewis, Minot W. |
| 1GF | Fowler, F. Malcolm. | 1IS | Leach, George F. |
| 1GH | Bibber, Harold. | 1IT | Barnes, Irving T. |
| 1GI | Morse, Harold E. | 1IU | Church, Arthur E. |
| 1GJ | Daniels, Richard M. | 1IV | Snyder, William E. |
| 1GK | Stanley, Lyman R. | 1IW | Wilde, Phillips B. |
| 1GL | Bush, Arthur W. | 1IX | Ohlson, Olof. |
| 1GM | Allen, J. Wyman. | 1IY | Baxter, Horace M. |
| 1GN | Smith, Malcolm H. | 1IZ | St. James, Robert T. |
| 1GO | Estey, F. Clifford. | | |
| 1GP | James, Albert W. | 1JA | Dimond, Fred A., jr. |
| 1GQ | Westbrook, Leon R. | 1JB | Lord, Howland C. |
| 1GS | Hardy, Wilbur H. | 1JC | Fairbanks, Robert D. |
| 1GT | Loomis, Arthur T. | 1JD | Collins, Lovejoy. |
| 1GU | Bernardin, Leo A. | 1JE | Hayward, Edward E., jr. |
| 1GV | Gavill, Wilbur W. | 1JF | Snow, Albert E. |
| 1GW | Haddock, Charles C. | 1JG | Pratt, Fearing. |
| | | 1JH | Hubbard, Allen, jr. |
| | | 1JI | Lawrence, Milford R. |
| 1HA | Allison, William H. | 1JK | Franke, Alfred A. |
| 1HB | Burgess, Warren B. | 1JL | Gahm, Sebastian, jr. |
| 1HC | Cheetham, Harry R. | 1JM | Cheever, Walter G. |
| 1HD | Canfield, Donald T. | 1JN | Bruce, Arthur O. |
| 1HE | Lynde, Kenneth R. | 1JO | Snow, William B. |
| 1HF | Gardner, Chester R. | 1JP | Decker, Clarence. |
| 1HG | Cogswell, George R. | 1JQ | Hoffman, Frank E. |
| 1HI | Burke, Alan W. | 1JR | Delano, Edward C. |
| 1HJ | Hunt, Albert M. | 1JS | Powers, Leonard S. |
| 1HK | Denison, Horace W. | 1JT | Carlson, Arthur G. |
| 1HL | Affel, Herman A. | 1JU | Dane, Francis W. |
| 1HM | Hammett, Herbert M. | 1JV | Reuther, Henry R. |
| 1HN | Flood, J. Frank J. | 1JW | Long, John J. |
| 1HO | Merrill, Clark B. | 1JY | Herland, John N. |
| 1HP | Cromack, N. G. N. | 1JZ | Lanvuette, Kenneth H. |
| 1HQ | Broadley, Harry R. | | |
| 1HR | Elliott, Thomas H., jr. | 1KA | Stickney, H. E. |
| 1HS | Shattuck, Herbert. | 1KB | Richards, William T. |
| 1HT | Anderson, James H. | 1KC | Howe, Milton A. |
| 1HU | Upton, Harry E. | 1KD | David, Harold E. |
| 1HV | Ryan, James A. | 1KF | Pennypacker, Thomas R. |
| 1HW | Munroe, Henry W. T. | 1KG | Manning, Ralph K. |
| 1HX | Leavitt, Elmer A. | 1KI | Loring, Wilfred B. |

AMATEUR RADIO STATIONS—FIRST DISTRICT—ALPHABETICALLY BY CALL SIGNALS—Continued.

| Call signal. | Owner of station. | Call signal. | Owner of station. |
|---|---|---|---|
| 1KJ | Anderson, Arvid E. | 1MY | Spear, G. Dana. |
| 1KL | Edson, Allan W. | 1MZ | White, Dallas E. |
| 1KM | Meekin, William J. | | |
| 1KN | Wilkinson, John E. | 1NA | Andonegui, Lane. |
| 1KO | Bowen, Harold C. | 1NB | Blanchard, Ralph N. |
| 1KP | Justice, Francis C. | 1NC | Ekwall, George O. |
| 1KQ | Armstrong, James B. | 1ND | Bellis, Clifford B. |
| 1KR | Borden, Howard G. | 1NE | Coleman, Benjamin B. B. |
| 1KS | Seabury, William H. | 1NF | Beecher, George E. |
| 1KT | Benoit, Walter R. | 1NG | Marshall, Stanley. |
| 1KU | Bowen, Earl H. | 1NK | Jennings, Charles E., jr. |
| 1KV | Hurley, Albert V. | 1NL | Curtis, Samuel, jr. |
| 1KX | Batcheller, Arthur. | 1NM | Starkweather, John B. |
| 1KY | Bishop, Leon W. | 1NO | Varnum, George E. |
| 1KZ | Fiske, John. | 1NP | Kiley, John T. |
| | | 1NQ | Getchell, Melvin D. |
| 1LA | Remington, Kenneth F. | 1NR | Gerrish, Kenneth B. |
| 1LB | Blume, Carl T. | 1NS | Hamilton, Edward P. |
| 1LC | Bowen, Arthur N. | 1NT | Lynch, John P. |
| 1LE | Corney, Chester A. | 1NU | Campbell, Harold G. |
| 1LF | Beverly High School. | 1NV | Mathews, Lloyd F. |
| 1LG | Corey, Frank J. | 1NW | McDermott, Joseph H. |
| 1LH | Dickson, William E. | 1NX | Ward, Talbot. |
| 1LI | Ealoe, Malcolm A. L. | 1NY | Lovis, Donald B. |
| 1LJ | Fitch, Conover. | 1NZ | Leutz, Charles R. |
| 1LK | Haskins, Frederic C. | | |
| 1LM | King, Alexander R. | 1OA | Kenison, Arthur C. |
| 1LN | Newton Technical High School. | 1OB | Kilton, James A., jr. |
| 1LO | Donovan, Arthur B. | 1OC | Hill, Harold F. |
| 1LP | Knight, Hugh C. | 1OD | Miller, Alden W. |
| 1LQ | Perry, Willard H. | 1OE | Porter, Ralph H. |
| 1LR | Rawson, Homer E. | 1OF | Eldredge, Clarence R. |
| 1LS | Runey, Leon C. | 1OG | Florence, William E., jr. |
| 1LT | Scott, Ralph A. | 1OH | Flanders, Fred F. |
| 1LU | Taylor, Frank J. | 1OJ | Howard, Charles S. |
| 1LV | Tufts, J. Warren. | 1OK | Mackenzie, Roy G. |
| 1LW | Van Brocklin, William S. | 1OL | Hinman, George W. |
| 1LY | Moulton, Albert B. | 1OM | Payson, Gilbert R., jr. |
| 1LZ | Murphy, Dudley B. | 1ON | Readio, George U. |
| | | 1OP | Sharpe, Floyd H. |
| 1MA | Anthony, Harvey M. | 1OQ | Struthers, Francis W. |
| 1MB | Boudette, Clayton M. | 1OR | Boyden, Laurance E. |
| 1MC | Baylies, Milton A. | 1OS | Copland, H. Depew. |
| 1MD | Ziegler, Alfred A., jr. | 1OT | Heap, Sheldon S. |
| 1ME | Angell, Otis P. | 1OU | Ryer, Edwin D. |
| 1MH | Herrick, Sumner E. | 1OV | Southwick, Francis B. |
| 1MI | Merrill, Donald F. | 1OW | Stackhouse, Walter T. |
| 1MJ | Burdett, Roland E. | 1OX | Tarr, Melville S. |
| 1MK | Johnson, Thurston A. | 1OY | Zwinge, Conrad J. |
| 1ML | Lyon, William H. | 1OZ | Baer, Louis F. |
| 1MN | Pennell, Leon. | | |
| 1MO | Ostrander, Freeman K., jr. | 1PA | Beckman, Carl W. |
| 1MP | Purssell, Clarence V. | 1PB | Bean, John E., jr. |
| 1MR | Roddin, Thomas. | 1PC | Drake, Ervin T., jr. |
| 1MS | Sabin, G. C. | 1PD | Whittier, Ellerton W. |
| 1MT | Tyler, Samuel F. | 1PE | Hitchcock, Frederick J. |
| 1MU | Byers, John R. | 1PF | Jerauld, Dorrance G. |
| 1MV | Caldwell, George W. | 1PG | Johnson, David E. |
| 1MW | Linn, Harold W. | 1PH | Jones, R. Warren. |
| 1MX | Hathaway, Francis R. | 1PI | Knight, Maurice E. |

AMATEUR RADIO STATIONS—FIRST DISTRICT—ALPHABETICALLY BY CALL SIGNALS—Continued.

| Call signal. | Owner of station. |
|---|---|
| 1PK | Loheed, William J., jr. |
| 1PL | Oudin, C. Folger. |
| 1PM | Wireless Society, Massachusetts Institute of Technology. |
| 1PN | Briggs, Ralph E. |
| 1PO | Reed, Lesley S. |
| 1PQ | Rogers, Wallace B. |
| 1PR | Richards, Fred J. |
| 1PS | Zahn, Edward G. |
| 1PT | Clayton, Henry C. |
| 1PU | Fearing, Sumner E. |
| 1PV | Folsom, Rolfe A. |
| 1PW | Crosby, Carlton. |
| 1PX | Murphy, Harry J. |
| 1PY | Pulley, Lester A. |
| 1PZ | Ranlett, Frederick J., jr. |
| 1QA | Nyquist, Norman A. |
| 1QB | Saunders, George B. |
| 1QC | Wadsworth, Arthur G. |
| 1QD | Therrien, Arthur J. |
| 1QE | Bruce, Edmond. |
| 1QF | Nash, Paul F. |
| 1QG | Edmester, Earle C. |
| 1QH | Melvin, Arthur W. |
| 1QI | St. James, Vincent. |
| 1QJ | O'Brine, Daniel. |
| 1QK | Black, William R. |
| 1QL | Noyes, Russell. |
| 1QM | Proulx, George H. |
| 1QV | Heyman, Harry. |
| 1QW | White, Thomas C. |
| 1QX | Spaulding, Ralph H. |
| 1QY | Linsert, Henry. |
| 1QZ | Danehy, Edward J. |
| 1TC | Aerogram Club of Newport. |
| 1TD | Tilley, Henry H., jr. |
| 1TF | Hodges, Duncan. |
| 1TG | Manchester, Arthur W. |
| 1TH | Manuel, Lloyd. |
| 1TI | Horgan, T. Francis. |
| 1TJ | Johnson, Alexander R. |
| 1TK | Branigan, Hugh S. C. |
| 1TL | Flint, Carl O. |
| 1TM | Mason, Lion G. |
| 1TN | Mahoney, Charles J. |
| 1TO | Newton, Raymond C. |
| 1TP | Jensen, Leonard C. |
| 1TQ | Medbery, Chester H. |
| 1TR | Bazinet, Wilfred J. |
| 1TS | Sampson, Ross D. |
| 1TU | Stackpole, Nelson B. |
| 1TV | Hale, Edward E. |
| 1TW | Watrous, Ralph C. |
| 1UA | Hargraves, Harold T. |
| 1UB | Pease, Reginald M. |
| 1UC | Creaser, Isaiah. |
| 1UD | Donle, Harold P. |
| 1UE | Jette, George E. |
| 1UF | Perkins, Leonard M. |

| Call signal. | Owner of station. |
|---|---|
| 1UG | Bigelow, Fred C. |
| 1UH | Handy, William R. |
| 1UJ | Ashworth, Harry. |
| 1UK | Tutin, Kenneth A. |
| 1UL | Bigelow, Clinton A. |
| 1UM | Miller, Bernard H. |
| 1UN | Henry, William E. |
| 1UO | Doyle, John B. |
| 1UP | Trainor, Francis J. |
| 1UQ | Barth, Karl E. |
| 1UR | Doherty, James E. |
| 1US | Thorndike, Don C. |
| 1UV | Monahan, Edward M. |
| 1UW | Nilson, Arthur R. |
| 1UX | Budlong, Clifton O. |
| 1UY | Lippitt, Gorton T. |
| 1UZ | Homer, Arthur B. |
| 1VA | Lewis, George B. |
| 1VC | Langevin, Carl C. |
| 1VD | McPartland, Frank J. |
| 1VE | Walker, Alva S. |
| 1VF | Mascare, Fred A. |
| 1VG | Tucker, George W. |
| 1VH | Hickmott, William J., jr. |
| 1VI | Slawson, Spencer W. |
| 1VJ | Cowles, George R. |
| 1VK | Barnes, Howard M. |
| 1VL | Belknap, Edward L. |
| 1VM | McGuire, William C. |
| 1VN | Green, Louis S. |
| 1VO | Haskell, Shirley G. |
| 1VP | Weimann, Alfred F. |
| 1VQ | Horsfall, George W. |
| 1VR | Jennings, John W. |
| 1VW | Woodward, Raymond W. |
| 1WA | Bueb, John J., jr. |
| 1WB | Barnum, Roland B. |
| 1WC | Coleman, William F. |
| 1WD | Tuska, Clarence D. |
| 1WE | Baldwin, James P. |
| 1WF | McSweeney, Lawrence P. |
| 1WH | Maxim, Hiram P. |
| 1WI | Rockefeller, Godfrey S. |
| 1WJ | Barrett, John H. |
| 1WK | Moore, David L. |
| 1WL | Hubbard, George F. |
| 1WM | Soules, Norman E. |
| 1WN | Edwin Bancroft Foote Boys' Club. |
| 1WO | Post, Harold D. |
| 1WP | Cummings, Edward H. |
| 1WQ | Seeley, Arthur P. |
| 1WR | Sawtelle, Donald F. |
| 1WS | Buffett, Salathiel. |
| 1WT | Salzgeber, John W. |
| 1WU | Lucas, Orville W. |
| 1WV | Blanke, Donald C. |
| 1WX | Safranek, Jerry. |
| 1WY | Hoggson, Wallace. |
| 1WZ | Davis, Maurice E. |

## SECOND DISTRICT.

[Headquarters: Customhouse, New York, N. Y. The second district comprises the States of New York (county of New York, Staten Island, Long Island, and counties on the Hudson River to and including Schenectady, Albany, and Rensselaer) and New Jersey (counties of Bergen, Passaic, Essex, Union, Middlesex, Monmouth, Hudson, and Ocean).]

ALPHABETICALLY BY OWNERS OF STATIONS.

| Call signal. | Owner of station. | Location of station. | Power. |
|---|---|---|---|
| | | | *Watts.* |
| 2TQ | Adams, E. William, jr | 392 Franklin St., Bloomfield, N. J | 12 |
| 2LX | Adelphi College | St. James and Clifton Pl., Brooklyn, N. Y | 500 |
| 2NA | Adickes, Ernest D | 173 W. Ridgewood St., Ridgewood, N. J | 770 |
| 2VQ | Agnoli, Justus J | 16 Purvis St., Long Island City, N. Y | 36 |
| 2VG | Ahrens, Harry E | 794 Gravesend Ave., Brooklyn, N. Y | 250 |
| 2US | Allstrom, F. Condit | 46 Chestnut St., East Orange, N. J | 9 |
| 2WI | Anderson, Robert N | 353 Warburton Ave., Yonkers, N. Y | 30 |
| 2MM | Apgar, Charles E | 549 Carleton Rd., Westfield, N. J | 450 |
| 2UR | Arany, Leo | 973 Simpson St., New York, N. Y | 500 |
| 2ME | Archibald, John O | 428 Park Hill Ave., Yonkers, N. Y | 440 |
| 2MR | Atwater, Frank G., jr | 1562 E. 15th St., Brooklyn, N. Y | 50 |
| 2CI | Austin, Edward | 576 Pavonia Ave., Jersey City, N. J | 30 |
| 2NY | Austrian, Ralph B | 49 St. Nicholas Ter., New York, N. Y | 450 |
| 2RW | Baily, Hobart W | Summer St., Harrison, N. Y | 220 |
| 2UL | Baker, Alvah L | 153 Manhattan Ave., New York, N. Y | 250 |
| 2LU | Baker, William N | 881 Montgomery St., Jersey City, N. J | 20 |
| 2TG | Balfoort, John M | 4 Regent St., Schenectady, N. Y | 650 |
| 2GM | Ballard, J. Adams | 73 Macon St., Brooklyn, N. Y | 24 |
| 2BD | Banta, Theodore C | 76 Walnut St., Ridgewood, N. J | 16 |
| 2SN | Barnes, C. Everett | 778 1st Ave., Upper Troy, N. Y | 50 |
| 2WO | Barone, Salvatore A | 343 E. 76th St., New York, N. Y | 140 |
| 2BT | Barrett's School of Telegraphy. | 527 Cortlandt Ave., New York, N. Y | 624 |
| 2PC | Barnette, Samuel L | 1483 Bedford Ave., Brooklyn, N. Y | 60 |
| 2GB | Bartlett, Bernard W | 545 Westfield Ave., Westfield, N. J | 500 |
| 2LF | Bartlett, Charles H | 774 Jefferson Ave., Brooklyn, N. Y | 12 |
| 2VP | Bartsch, Henry W | 130 Cedar St., Kingston, N. Y | 15 |
| 2CJ | Bathgate, Walter E | 102 High St., Passaic, N. J | 60 |
| 2EJ | Bechtloff, Claude B | 106 Walnut St., Ridgewood, N. J | 500 |
| 2KJ | Beebe, Lloyd S | 1143 Albany St., Schenectady, N. Y | 225 |
| 2MV | Bell, Arthur E | 92 Elizabeth St., West New Brighton, N. Y | 32 |
| 2WN | Beller, William A. G | 588 Essex St., Brooklyn, N. Y | 50 |
| 2LQ | Belt, Charles B | 145 W. 57th St., New York, N. Y | 100 |
| 2LL | Benedict, Alonzo R | Newburgh, N. Y | 48 |
| 2TE | Bentzig, Victor H | 165 Woodmere Pl., Richmond Hill, N. Y | 20 |
| 2FU | Benzing, Herman | 619 Fulton St., Elizabeth, N. J | 30 |
| 2TO | Benzing, Jacob | 625 Fulton St., Elizabeth, N. J | 20 |
| 2PN | Berger, H. C. V. B | 33 Pennington Ave., Passaic, N. J | 36 |
| 2NU | Berglund, Edward A | 484 45th St., Brooklyn, N. Y | 16 |
| 2QS | Bernard, James L | 1312 Ditmas Ave., Brooklyn, N. Y | 8 |
| 2MS | Berri, Herbert | 497 E. 17th St., Brooklyn, N. Y | 500 |
| 2LB | Bertine, Edwin K | 57 S. 2d Ave., Mt. Vernon, N. Y | 220 |
| 2UK | Biggam, Henry C | 53 W. 94th St., New York, N. Y | 10 |
| 2QW | Birkmire, Harold | 2190 Loring Pl., New York, N. Y | 624 |
| 2FT | Bishop, Mortimer Z | 568 W. 149th St., New York, N. Y | 550 |
| 2PH | Blackburn, Godfrey C | 146 Newburgh Ave., Fishkill-on-Hudson, N. Y. | 200 |
| 2QB | Blackford, Harold W | 237 E. 2d St., Plainfield, N. J | 250 |
| 2CR | Blauvelt, William M | 198 Main St., Nyack, N. Y | 340 |
| 2SP | Bleilevens, Gerhardt | 318 33d St., Woodcliff on Hudson, N. J | 500 |
| 2GI | Bockelmann, Charles F | 1679 42d St., Brooklyn, N. Y | 10 |
| 2JD | Boeder, Arthur R | 3443 Duncomb Ave., New York, N. Y | 1,000 |
| 2PY | Bogardus, Henry L | 427 Bergen Ave., Jersey City, N. J | 250 |
| 2TP | Bohn, William | 1515 2d Ave., New York, N. Y | 12 |
| 2VL | Bond, Arthur M | 274 2d Ave., Newark, N. J | 35 |

AMATEUR RADIO STATIONS—SECOND DISTRICT—ALPHABETICALLY BY OWNERS OF STATIONS—Continued.

| Call signal. | Owner of station. | Location of station. | Power. |
|---|---|---|---|
| | | | Watts. |
| 2UG | Bonduaux, Eugene L | 822 Hewitt Pl., New York, N. Y | 500 |
| 2UH | Boys' Wireless Club of Hackensack High School. | 1st St., Hackensack, N. J | 90 |
| 2UD | Brainard, Edward S | 400 W. Franklin Ave., Ridgewood, N. J | 1,000 |
| 2JH | Brown, David S., jr | 206 W. 86th St., New York, N. Y | 500 |
| 2VM | Brown, Philip T | 1808 Grand Concourse, New York, N. Y | 500 |
| 2KD | Browne, Walram S | 1565 E. 12th St., Brooklyn, N. Y | 1,000 |
| 2VD | Bruell, Joseph P | 69 S. Lexington Ave., White Plains, N. Y | 880 |
| 2AU | Bryan, Chester W | 79 Elm St., Montclair, N. J | 32 |
| 2AF | Bryant, Marquis V | 6 S. Highland Ave., Nyack, N. Y | 580 |
| 2MH | Buchanan, William F | 128 Market St., Perth Amboy, N. J | 24 |
| 2NN | Buck, David E | 42 Grant Ave., Kearney, N. J | 30 |
| 2CT | Bunn, Milo B | 110 Rockland Ave., Yonkers, N. Y | 250 |
| 2NL | Burnett, Walter J | 20 Chestnut St., Ridgewood, N. J | 100 |
| 2HK | Burrows, Henry P | 1415 55th St., Brooklyn, N. Y | 24 |
| 2WK | Caggiano, Carmine J | 245 Pacific St., Brooklyn, N. Y | 12 |
| 2RL | Camp, Victor F | Plymouth Ave., Brightwaters, N. Y | 1,000 |
| 2ES | Campbell, Robert, jr | 117 Marshall St., Elizabeth, N. J | 180 |
| 2SX | Cannon, George C | 183 Drake Ave., New Rochelle, N. Y | 1,000 |
| 2RD | Carey, Stephen W., 3d | Luddington Rd., West Orange, N. J | 72 |
| 2PA | Carman, Newton I | 218 Church St., Hempstead, N. Y | 880 |
| 2TS | Carpenter, Ferris G | 57 Cedar St., Ridgefield Park, N. J | 24 |
| 2MN | Carrougher, Vivian A | 805 Ocean Ave., Brooklyn, N. Y | 3 |
| 2QK | Caskey, Kenneth B | 415 Fort Washington Ave., New York, N. Y. | 250 |
| 2HR | Chandler, Arthur C | 2141 Pacific St., Brooklyn, N. Y | 200 |
| 2VN | Charles, Chester A | 629 Springdale Ave., East Orange, N. J | 40 |
| 2FE | Cheel, Harold W | 35 Corsa Ter., Ridgewood, N. J | 495 |
| 2DS | Clark, Le Roy | Chestnut St., Englewood, N. J | 880 |
| 2FO | Clark, William C | 91 4th Ave., Brooklyn, N. Y | 500 |
| 2SV | Clarke, Frederick D | 558 W. 165th St., New York, N. Y | 250 |
| 2IJ | Cochran, Alexander | 256 Sterling Pl., Brooklyn, N. Y | 25 |
| 2OG | Cockaday, Lawrence M | 227 Audubon Ave., New York, N. Y | 250 |
| 2LO | Coffin, Russell S | 1102 St. Johns Pl., Brooklyn, N. Y | 24 |
| 2PS | Cohen, Samuel | 242 Hinsdale St., Brooklyn, N. Y | 24 |
| 2OS | Cohen, Walter | 2071 5th Ave., New York, N. Y | 440 |
| 2TZ | Collins, Frank J | 22 Cedar St., Yonkers, N. Y | 40 |
| 2RT | Collinson, Jesse G | 65 Cherry St., West Orange, N. J | 24 |
| 2KN | Collison, Percy B | 172 Maple St., Brooklyn, N. Y | 500 |
| 2TM | Collymore, Errold D | 227 W. 63d St., New York, N. Y | 30 |
| 2SC | Constant, S. Victor | Hillside Drive, Yonkers, N. Y | 12 |
| 2DR | Cooper, Telfer C | 260 Garfield Ave., Jersey City, N. J | 440 |
| 2HF | Coote, Charles W | 240 Audubon Ave., New York, N. Y | 250 |
| 2SD | Copersito, Michael | 942 Atlantic Ave., Brooklyn, N. Y | 36 |
| 2AQ | Corson, David N | 51 Berkeley Ave., Newark, N. J | 300 |
| 2LD | Cotter, William F | 68 Oakland Ave., Jersey City, N. J | 24 |
| 2VK | Covert, James D | 40 Glenwood Rd., Upper Montclair, N. J. | 300 |
| 2RI | Cowper, Norman C | Merrick Rd., Lynbrook, N. Y | 1,000 |
| 2MW | Crichton, Arthur M | 139 Washington Ave., Rutherford, N. J | 1,000 |
| 2EM | Crosby, Roy C | 211 W. 148th St., New York, N. Y | 30 |
| 2DN | Cullen, Edward R | 626 45th St., Brooklyn, N. Y | 54 |
| 2DI | Cyriax, Ernest A | 219 E. 71st St., New York, N. Y | 30 |
| 2GG | Dahlgren, Birger A | 1652 41st St., Brooklyn, N. Y | 18 |
| 2AD | Dammers, Albert | 145 Newell Ave., Rutherford, N. J | 1,000 |
| 2QH | Davies, Richard J., jr | 334 4th St., Union Hill, N. J | 1,000 |
| 2KK | Day, Howard B | 555 Mountain Ave., Westfield, N. J | 1,000 |
| 2OD | Debuchy, Edmund A | 591a Summit Ave., West Hoboken, N. J | 15 |
| 2VS | Decker, Ralph W. E | 7 Odell Ave., White Plains, N. Y | 1,000 |

AMATEUR RADIO STATIONS—SECOND DISTRICT—ALPHABETICALLY BY OWNERS OF STATIONS—Continued.

| Call signal. | Owner of station. | Location of station. | Power. |
|---|---|---|---|
| | | | *Watts.* |
| 2JX | De Cortin, Gustav A | 16 Elm St., Mt. Vernon, N. Y | 30 |
| 2HH | Dederick, H. C | 46 N. 5th St., Hudson, N. Y | 72 |
| 2TL | de Forest, Edward L., jr. | Hilton Ave., Garden City, N. Y | 30 |
| 2SY | De Long, Oscar A., jr | 160 N. Mountain Ave., Montclair, N. J | 50 |
| 2AS | De Yoe, Willard L | 689 Broadway St., Paterson, N. J | 250 |
| 2UT | Dick, Benjamin S | Mt. Pleasant Academy, Ossining, N. Y | 75 |
| 2TC | Dickenson, Henry E | 73 Greenridge Ave., White Plains, N. Y | 330 |
| 2CN | Dickey, Edward T | 1649 Amsterdam Ave., New York, N. Y | 220 |
| 2VY | Diehl, John F | 311 3d Ave., New York, N. Y | 30 |
| 2CQ | Dilg, A. Norman | Amboy Rd., Tottenville, N. Y | 30 |
| 2UV | Dimmick, James N | Babylon, N. Y | 12 |
| 2RO | Dodds, Andrew C | 132 S. Swan St., Albany, N. Y | 18 |
| 2EU | Droste, George T | 1309 Pugsley Ave., New York, N. Y | 210 |
| 2OZ | Dufford, John S | 615 S. 20th St., Newark, N. J | 18 |
| 2IY | Dugan, Edward W | 631 Jersey Ave., Jersey City, N. J | 15 |
| 2TX | Dunham, Clarence L | 250 Woodlawn Ave., Jersey City, N. J | 300 |
| 2LM | Dunn, Laurence J | 769 Dawson St., New York, N. Y | 8 |
| 2QN | Dwyer, Martin J., jr | 3800 Broadway, New York, N. Y | 500 |
| 2PR | Dynner, Eugene | 207 26th St., Guttenberg, N. J | 550 |
| 2RG | Earle, William P., jr | Mamaroneck Rd., White Plains, N. Y | 500 |
| 2AI | Eber, John G | 5505 3d Ave., Brooklyn, N. Y | 30 |
| 2QJ | Eckley, Harold J | Beechmont Pk., New Rochelle, N. Y | 27 |
| 2PG | Eckstein, William J | 35 W. 177th St., New York, N. Y | 500 |
| 2JI | Eddy, Leonard E | 295 Hackensack Rd., Ridgefield Park, N. J. | 30 |
| 2AH | Edelman, Abraham | 952 Liggett Ave., New York, N. Y | 500 |
| 2KQ | Edwards, Harry M., jr | 314 Ridgewood Ave., Glen Ridge, N. J | 24 |
| 2LE | Egolf, Richard S | 1052 41st St., Brooklyn, N. Y | 30 |
| 2IQ | Elliott, Paul C | 162 E. 66th St., New York, N. Y | 250 |
| 2UB | Emory, John M. G | 3d St., Garden City, N. Y | 10 |
| 2VH | Engelder, Eberhardt E | 234 Garden St., Hoboken, N. J | 20 |
| 2ET | England, George B | 917 St. Nicholas Ave., New York, N. Y | 432 |
| 2OC | Erasmus Hall High School. | Flatbush Ave., Brooklyn, N. Y | 250 |
| 2UF | Evans, Arthur F | 246 Emerson Pl., Brooklyn, N. Y | 12 |
| 2PI | Evans, Clarence L | 176 S. 11th St., Newark, N. J | 1,000 |
| 2GX | Fallon, Harry A., jr | 555 W. 148th St., New York, N. Y | 48 |
| 2GD | Farquharson, John S | 540 W. 158th St., New York, N. Y | 280 |
| 2AK | Ferris, Howard E | 665 Franklin Ave., Nutley, N. J | 24 |
| 2SS | Fitler, Eugene B., jr | 40 W. 129th St., New York, N. Y | 30 |
| 2DD | Fitzgerald, Gordon P | 611 W. 141st St., New York, N. Y | 250 |
| 2AA | Flagg, John H | 316 Lookout Ave., Hackensack, N. J | 21 |
| 2VU | Flandreaux, Cyrus | 1425 Park St., Peekskill, N. Y | 800 |
| 2WB | Fogetti, Howard J | 7421 Narrows Ave., New York, N. Y | 36 |
| 2OI | Folks, Leslie E | 410 E. 155th St., New York, N. Y | 24 |
| 2TB | Ford, Everett J | 431 Bramhall Ave., Jersey City, N. J | 12 |
| 2QC | Ford, Fullerton | 215 Winthrop St., Brooklyn, N. Y | 18 |
| 2IR | Foulke, J. Brion, jr | Babylon, N. Y | 20 |
| 2WM | Fowler, Jack B | 676 Lincoln Pl., Brooklyn, N. Y | 12 |
| 2OB | Fox, Loyal S | 4706 4th Ave., Brooklyn, N. Y | 64 |
| 2KM | Francis, Charles E | 1662 70th St., Brooklyn, N. Y | 18 |
| 2WS | Francis, Leo A | 102 Maple Ave., Port Richmond, N. Y | 30 |
| 2IZ | Fraser, Frank | 352 Archer St., Freeport, N. Y | 350 |
| 2VZ | Frederick, G. Bentley | 112 Mason St., Schenectady, N. Y | 300 |
| 2JN | Freeland, Wilbur W | 34 Baldwin Ave., Newark, N. J | 550 |
| 2VV | French, Edward | 1216 Lincoln Ter., Peekskill, N. Y | 16 |
| 2JF | Frey, Anthony C | 370 E. 153d St., New York, N. Y | 8 |
| 2KE | Frey, George | 155 W. 80th St., New York, N. Y | 36 |
| 2PE | Fritch, Vincent J | 939 College Ave., New York, N. Y | 15 |

AMATEUR RADIO STATIONS—SECOND DISTRICT—ALPHABETICALLY BY OWNERS OF STATIONS—Continued.

| Call signal. | Owner of station. | Location of station. | Power. |
|---|---|---|---|
| | | | Watts. |
| 2VJ | Furman, Robert S | Park Ave., Bay Shore, N. Y | 60 |
| 2GF | Gabrielson, Henry M | 230 53d St., Brooklyn, N. Y | 60 |
| 2QG | Gale, Rowland A | 540 W. 158th St., New York, N. Y | 156 |
| 2LT | Galvin, Lee R | 193 Fairview Ave., Jersey City, N. J | 18 |
| 2UP | Gannon, J. Kimball | 517 Park St., Upper Montclair, N. J | 30 |
| 2VR | Gassaway, Julian L | Bay 8th St. and Bath Ave., Brooklyn, N.Y | 24 |
| 2VB | Gerlach, Adolph J | 769 E. 218th St., Williams Bridge, N. Y | 12 |
| 2DO | Gerrity, John J | 538 Ocean Ave., Jersey City, N. J | 330 |
| 2AY | Gittelbauer, Frederick | 38 Vreeland St., East Rutherford, N. J | 500 |
| 2TV | Glenn, George | 251 E. 236th St., New York, N. Y | 300 |
| 2JU | Goette, C. J | 1256 Hatch Ave., Woodhaven, N. Y | 500 |
| 2UN | Graham, Malcolm | 4 Overlook Ave., Ridgewood, N. J | 1,000 |
| 2PV | Grebe, Alfred H | 10 Van Wyck Ave., Richmond Hill, N.Y | 1,000 |
| 2BK | Green, Adoniram J | 73 Paterson St., Paterson, N. J | 60 |
| 2QQ | Green, Irving W | 85 Clerk St., Jersey City, N. J | 20 |
| 2LP | Green, Raymond J | 1352 St. Nicholas Ave., New York, N. Y | 18 |
| 2SR | Greenlees, William | 3762 Barnes Ave., Williams Bridge, N. Y | 1,000 |
| 2KL | Gregory, Arthur V | 197 High St., Perth Amboy, N. J | 250 |
| 2BN | Griswold, Edmund J | R. F. D., Slingerlands, N. Y | 30 |
| 2AT | Guild, Baldwin | 495 Mount Prospect Ave., Newark, N. J | 30 |
| 2UH | Hackensack High School (Boys' Wireless Club). | Hackensack, N. J | 90 |
| 2HJ | Hadden, Weston | 1716 Albermarle Rd., Brooklyn, N. Y | 460 |
| 2AM | Haeselbarth, Percy | 54 Catherine St., Nyack, N. Y | 36 |
| 2PB | Haight, Russell P | 31 Overlook Ave., West Orange, N. J | 200 |
| 2MA | Hallenbeck, Charles | 959 55th St., Brooklyn, N. Y | 24 |
| 2UQ | Hallett, E. Douglas | 86 Prospect Pl., Rutherford, N. J | 30 |
| 2EV | Hallock, Charles S | Foot of 57th St., Brooklyn, N. Y | 495 |
| 2PX | Hamilton, Albert G., jr | Beach Ave., Larchmont, N. Y | 250 |
| 2EW | Hamilton, Joseph E | 16 W. Broadway, Port Chester, N. Y | 30 |
| 2FK | Hamilton, Ralph | 358 Willet Ave., Port Chester, N. Y | 30 |
| 2OA | Hammond, Lester | 35 W. 61st St., New York, N. Y | 24 |
| 2AE | Happe, William H | 566 W. 162d St., New York, N. Y | 108 |
| 2FQ | Hardwick, Ambrose H | 224 Oakwood Ave., Orange, N. J | 1,000 |
| 2FZ | Harris, Charles C | Elliott Pl., Freeport, N. Y | 250 |
| 2AC | Hart, Gifford R | 34 Douglas Rd., Glen Ridge, N. J | 30 |
| 2FY | Hartman, Robert | 371 Wadsworth Ave., New York, N. Y | 250 |
| 2DV | Hathaway, Harry C. B | 20 Erie Pl., Nutley, N. J | 72 |
| 2SM | Hatry, William B | 71 Orange St., Brooklyn, N. Y | 30 |
| 2BM | Heermance, Earle | 523 State St., Hudson, N. Y | 200 |
| 2MX | Heffernan, William J | 105 Bay 10th St., Brooklyn, N. Y | 15 |
| 2FJ | Helwig, Herman F | 711 E. 18th St., Brooklyn, N. Y | 250 |
| 2MU | Hengerer, Howard B | 441 Fort Washington Ave., NewYork, N.Y. | 50 |
| 2WE | Heydon, Albert R | 403 Decatur St., Brooklyn, N. Y | 24 |
| 2UO | Heyer, Benjamin W | 45 N. Fullerton Ave., Montclair, N. J | 440 |
| 2DG | Higgs, Harry Y | 30 Irving Pl., Brooklyn, N. Y | 12 |
| 2DK | Hill, William S | 332 Rector St., Perth Amboy, N. J | 48 |
| 2NS | Hoffman, Paul J | 1688 2d Ave., New York, N. Y | 30 |
| 2RA | Hollman, Theodore | 678 Marcy Ave., Brooklyn, N. Y | 25 |
| 2NF | Homan, Eber J | 336 52d St., Brooklyn, N. Y | 30 |
| 2LY | Hoover, Raymond | 171 Ridgewood Ave., Newark, N. J | 250 |
| 2MF | Hoppock, Allen H | 215 Clark St., Westfield, N. J | 500 |
| 2RK | Horle, Lawrence C. F | 142 Fairmount Ave., Newark, N. J | 1,000 |
| 2NH | Horn, Charles W | Broadway, Far Rockaway, N. Y | 250 |
| 2HU | Hotchkiss, Grosvenor | 146 Halsey St., Brooklyn, N. Y | 30 |
| 2II | Howell, Walter J | 135 Edgecombe Ave., New York, N. Y | 60 |
| 2UE | Hoyt, William L | Hilton Ave., Garden City N. Y | 30 |
| 2GK | Hubbard, John W | 327 King St., Port Chester, N. Y | 550 |

AMATEUR RADIO STATIONS—SECOND DISTRICT—ALPHABETICALLY BY OWNERS OF STATIONS—Continued.

| Call signal | Owner of station. | Location of station. | Power. |
|---|---|---|---|
| | | | Watts. |
| 2VA | Huested, William P | Delmar, N. Y | 240 |
| 2EG | Hurd, John B | Tilton Ave., Red Bank, N. J | 250 |
| 2EF | Hurd, Theodore | Tilton Ave., Red Bank, N. J | 24 |
| 2QT | Hynds, Arthur E | 4920 6th Ave., Brooklyn, N. Y | 16 |
| 2UJ | Innes, Richard C | 343 W. 29th St., New York, N. Y | 60 |
| 2GU | Inwright, John A | 400-A Fairmount Ave., Jersey City, N. J | 9 |
| 2NQ | Isaacson, Charles B | 48 W. 89th St., New York, N. Y | 660 |
| 2EX | Jackson, Benjamin B | 188 Montrose Ave., Rutherford, N. J | 165 |
| 2EE | Jacobs, Charles F | 279 Park Pl., Brooklyn, N. Y | 40 |
| 2QY | Jacobson, Walter H | 172 Rector St., Perth Amboy, N. J | 12 |
| 2RR | Johnson, John A | 1026 2d Ave., New York, N. Y | 20 |
| 2VC | Johnson, Theophilus, jr | 17 3d St., Woodside, N. Y | 48 |
| 2RV | Johnson, W. Eugene | Grant Ave., East Rockaway, N. Y | 20 |
| 2SO | Johnston, James E | 1379 Clay Ave., New York, N. Y | 50 |
| 2OY | Jones, Frank | 181½ Brunswick St., Newark, N. J | 24 |
| 2AO | Jones, Robert O | 237 Newark Ave., Bloomfield, N. J | 32 |
| 2RU | Jordon, Fletcher | Ryder Ave., Lynbrook, N. Y | 25 |
| 2DC | Kahn, Walter A | 136 Stuyvesant Pl., New York, N. Y | 24 |
| 2BC | Kaltenbach, Henry J., jr | 150 Alta Ave., Yonkers, N. Y | 65 |
| 2VT | Kayser, Herbert | 41 Convent Ave., New York, N. Y | 800 |
| 2WA | Keers, John K | 224 81st St., Brooklyn, N. Y | 36 |
| 2QX | Keller, George C | 2181 Richmond Turnpike, Port Richmond, N. Y. | 40 |
| 2BY | Keller, Julius F | 36 Ocean Ave., Edgewater, N. Y | 30 |
| 2ON | Kellow, James C | 144 Liberty Ave., Jamaica, N. Y | 550 |
| 2GH | Kelting, Clarence A | 1469 53d St., Brooklyn, N. Y | 27 |
| 2QD | King, Wendell W | 778 1st Ave., Upper Troy, N. Y | 50 |
| 2QA | Kinney, E. M | 212 Parkwood Blvd., Schenectady, N. Y | 200 |
| 2BL | Kirch, George, jr | 364 75th St., Brooklyn, N. Y | 24 |
| 2FI | Kirkpatrick, Louis W | 317 6th Ave., Newark, N. J | 12 |
| 2SZ | Kissick, Robert G | 199 Lincoln Pl., Brooklyn, N. Y | 50 |
| 2TW | Knight, Alexander H | 873 E. 162d St., New York, N. Y | 60 |
| 2VF | Koch, Edward | 168 Willis Ave., New York, N. Y | 20 |
| 2NP | Koenig, George F | 4279 Webster Ave., New York, N. Y | 250 |
| 2SF | Kollock, Alan S | 4197 University Pl., Woodhaven, N. Y | 36 |
| 2QM | Koukol, Edwin P | 436 W. 23d St., New York, N. Y | 28 |
| 2BR | Krech, Karl G | 316 Godwin Ave., Midland Park, N. J | 495 |
| 2SQ | Kreeft, Raymond A | 61 Cherry St., West Orange, N. J | 30 |
| 2KA | Kroener, Christian E | 115 Watchung Ave., Plainfield, N. J | 270 |
| 2PU | Lally, Joseph F | 16 Short St., Coytesville, N. J | 30 |
| 2HX | Lane, David M | 343 9th St., Jersey City, N. J | 24 |
| 2OH | Lang, Ernest | 411 Spring St., West Hoboken, N. J | 30 |
| 2UC | Lange, William H | 280 7th Ave., Brooklyn, N. Y | 300 |
| 2WD | Lasher, Charles E | 253 Decatur St., Brooklyn, N. Y | 24 |
| 2KR | Lebowitz, Samuel | 270 Riverside Drive, New York, N. Y | 450 |
| 2TU | Lee, Robert J. B | 1530 McCormick Ave., Ozone Park, N. Y | 550 |
| 2MT | Leeb, Henry L | 166 Ralston Ave., South Orange, N. J | 660 |
| 2NB | Le Gallez, Clayton B | 974 Madison Ave., Albany, N. Y | 385 |
| 2FL | Lehmann, August, jr | 1520 56th St., Brooklyn, N. Y | 35 |
| 2WG | Lemkie, Harry A | 30 Delaware St., Elizabeth, N. J | 500 |
| 2IE | Lemmon, Walter S | 319 W. 94th St., New York, N. Y | 420 |
| 2SI | Le Queene, C. A., jr | 240 90th St., Brooklyn, N. Y | 48 |
| 2CA | Liedecker, Morris | 40 St. Nicholas Pl., New York, N. Y | 400 |
| 2PL | Lindsay, Daniel E | 501 W. 120th St., New York, N. Y | 36 |
| 2IV | Lindsay, Russell | 39 N. 16th St., East Orange, N. J | 30 |
| 2OV | Littlefield, Charles E | 2662 E. 24th St., Sheepshead Bay, N. Y | 12 |
| 2VI | Loub, Arthur F | 445 E. 88th St., New York, N. Y | 48 |
| 2SA | Lowitz, Donald J | 1307 Union St., Brooklyn, N. Y | 220 |
| 2BZ | Lyman, C. Glenn | George and Cooper Sts., Babylon, N. Y | 10 |

AMATEUR RADIO STATIONS—SECOND DISTRICT—ALPHABETICALLY BY OWNERS OF STATIONS—Continued.

| Call signal. | Owner of station. | Location of station. | Power. |
|---|---|---|---|
| | | | *Watts.* |
| 2HO | Lyons, William B. | Broad St., Bloomfield, N. J. | 820 |
| 2HT | Macartney, George E. | 473 Prospect Pl., Brooklyn, N. Y. | 24 |
| 2FW | MacPherson, Claude V. | 557 W. 144th St., New York, N. Y. | 440 |
| 2OM | Maher, Frank A. | 207 E. 158th St., New York, N. Y. | 6 |
| 2UA | Mann, Samuel | 120 W. 4th St., Plainfield, N. J. | 33 |
| 2QE | Manley, Lee L. | 788 Park Pl., Brooklyn, N. Y. | 50 |
| 2PP | Manvell, Edwin H. | 289 Evergreen Ave., Brooklyn, N. Y. | 18 |
| 2OX | Mardon, F. Herbert. | 1309 West Farms Rd., New York, N. Y. | 20 |
| 2GL | Marshall, Richard E. | 238 Westchester Ave., Port Chester, N.Y. | 550 |
| 2SG | May, Fred | 143 High St., Montclair, N. J. | 12 |
| 2TD | Mayer, Arthur C. | 319 W. 139th St., New York, N. Y. | 220 |
| 2HP | Mayhew, B. Alan, jr. | Laurel Ave., Tenafly, N. J. | 1,000 |
| 2WR | Mayhew, H. Clifford | 346 Main St., New Rochelle, N. Y. | 18 |
| 2VX | McCarthy, George W. | 1012 Sutter Ave., Brooklyn, N. Y. | 24 |
| 2IL | McClintock, George C. | 319 Dudley Ave., Westfield, N. J. | 250 |
| 2KP | McClure, Donald | 11 Rudd Court, Glen Ridge, N. J. | 48 |
| 2HA | McCoy, Daniel | 45 Lee Ave., Yonkers, N. Y. | 1,000 |
| 2DF | McIntire, Meylert A. | 1127 Ave. G, Brooklyn, N. Y. | 250 |
| 2RQ | McKinney, Donald B. | Borthwick Ave., Delmar, N. Y. | 500 |
| 2EY | McKinney, Fred J. | 300 Glenwood Ave., Bloomfield, N. J. | 54 |
| 2LG | McLaughlin, Fred L. | 242 Nostrand Ave., New York, N. Y. | 90 |
| 2KY | McLoughlin, Robert J. | 105 Francisco Ave., Rutherford, N. J. | 190 |
| 2SH | McQuaide, James P. | Larchmont Gardens, Larchmont, N. Y. | 880 |
| 2LI | Meacham, Fredk. C., jr. | 236 Decatur St., Brooklyn, N. Y. | 72 |
| 2EP | Mead, George S. V. | 12 Archer Ave., Mt. Vernon, N. Y. | 330 |
| 2NV | Meder, George C. | 990 1st Ave., New York, N. Y. | 550 |
| 2NX | Mehrbrey, William | 2244 Hughes Ave., New York, N. Y. | 4 |
| 2OF | Meinecke, Ernest | 27 Zabriskie St., Jersey City, N. J. | 20 |
| 2SL | Merrill, J. Stewart. | Roosevelt St., Lynbrook, N. Y. | 1,000 |
| 2NO | Merritt, Frank | 28 Spring St., Red Bank, N. J. | 350 |
| 2QZ | Meyer, Charles A. | Fair Haven, N. J. | 36 |
| 2EL | Meyer, William E. | 181 W. 63d St., New York, N. Y. | 81 |
| 2LA | Miller, Frederick R. | 42 John St., Englewood, N. J. | 24 |
| 2JK | Mitchell, Arthur M. | 299 N. 7th St., Newark, N. J. | 48 |
| 2TI | Mitchell, Everitt. | 7 S. Bayles St., Port Washington, N. Y. | 270 |
| 2NI | Moles, Charles E. | 229 Valentine Lane, Yonkers, N. Y. | 135 |
| 2PQ | Monsen, Hans S. | 583 Riverside Drive, New York, N. Y. | 250 |
| 2WU | Moore, H. Atherton. | 95 Prospect St., Nutley, N. J. | 1,000 |
| 2BI | Morgan, Waller V. | 149 Urban St., Mt. Vernon, N. Y. | 24 |
| 2CO | Morrell, W. Frank. | Broadway and 1st St., Keyport, N. J. | 500 |
| 2MI | Morris, Earle S. | 1192 Dean St., Brooklyn, N. Y. | 500 |
| 2MY | Morris, Robert | 149 W. 88th St., New York, N. Y. | 8 |
| 2LN | Morrison, Clifford P. | 365 Warburton Ave., Yonkers, N. Y. | 400 |
| 2PO | Mott, Harold | 67 Mott Ave., Far Rockaway, N. Y. | 55 |
| 2BG | Mowton, Edward M. | 70 Hillcrest Ave., Yonkers, N. Y. | 275 |
| 2AG | Mulford, Harold C. | 6 Weekes Ave., Oyster Bay, N. Y. | 440 |
| 2SK | Murray, Charles. | Long Hill Rd., Little Falls, N. J. | 250 |
| 2KX | Noble, Kendrick | 441 N. Broadway, Yonkers, N. Y. | 300 |
| 2WF | Nolan, Frank J. | 100 Linden Ave., Bloomfield, N. J. | 18 |
| 2OL | O'Brien, Laurence J. | 285 E. 157th St., New York, N. Y. | 250 |
| 2CK | O'Brien, Thomas | 7 Nassau Ave., Freeport, N. Y. | 250 |
| 2HS | O'Mara, Edward F. | 134 W. 66th St., New York, N. Y. | 12 |
| 2QU | Osborne, J. Spencer. | 45 Broad St., Newark, N. J. | 6 |
| 2MO | Ostman, Frederick B. | 33 Edwards St., Ridgewood, N. J. | 40 |
| 2PK | Otten, G. C. | 58 Chichester Ave., Jamaica, N. Y. | 12 |
| 2RE | Pacent, L. Gerard. | 218 Young St., Blissville, N. Y. | 24 |
| 2NK | Palm, J. Adam. | 18 14th Ave., Mt. Vernon, N. Y. | 30 |
| 2DY | Palmer, Corydon | 48 W. 50th St., New York, N. Y. | 880 |
| 2CU | Palmland, Philip | 1144 St. Johns Pl., Brooklyn, N. Y. | 30 |

AMATEUR RADIO STATIONS—SECOND DISTRICT—ALPHABETICALLY BY OWNERS OF STATIONS—Continued.

| Call signal. | Owner of station. | Location of station. | Power. |
|---|---|---|---|
| | | | Watts. |
| 2FB | Pareis, Robert | 149 Marshall St., Elizabeth, N. J | 12 |
| 2TT | Pattison, Edward H | 21 Locust Ave., Troy, N. Y | 160 |
| 2AZ | Pearl, Eugene S | 307 Gregory Ave., Passaic, N. J | 500 |
| 2WH | Pearsall, Arthur R | 197 Warburton Ave., Yonkers, N. Y | 30 |
| 2MP | Pearsall, William E | 226 Moffat St., Brooklyn, N. Y | 30 |
| 2BS | Pearson, Herbert B | 997 Sterling Pl., Brooklyn, N. Y | 440 |
| 2TF | Pearson, James W | 9 North End Ter., Newark, N. J | 24 |
| 2GO | Peltier, Paul D | 345 W. 70th St., New York, N. Y | 30 |
| 2TY | Pendleton, Archibald F. | 49 Pendleton Pl., New Brighton, N. Y | 1,000 |
| 2MD | Pendleton, Harold A | 799 Quincy St., Brooklyn, N. Y | 16 |
| 2FM | Perkins, William P | 35 Grant Ave., Yonkers, N. Y | 24 |
| 2HG | Peters, Frank J | Broad St., Bloomfield, N. J | 715 |
| 2FA | Pfeifer, Clarence H | 306 Prospect St., Ridgewood, N. J | 250 |
| 2NZ | Pfeil, A. Leslie | 242 Cottage St., Irvington, N. J | 325 |
| 2WJ | Pflomm, George M | 1829 Topping Ave., New York, N. Y | 30 |
| 2UX | Phelan, Charles W | 61 Powell Ave., Rockville Center, N. Y | 60 |
| 2BP | Phipps, Donald A | Oyster Bay, N. Y | 165 |
| 2RX | Picken, James C., jr | 2287 University Ave., New York, N. Y | 500 |
| 2GZ | Plate, Fred W | 91 Van Reypen St., Jersey City, N. J | 36 |
| 2KW | Plummer, James A | 340 Orient Way, Rutherford, N. J | 30 |
| 2CZ | Poe, Vergil C | 862 Sterling Pl., Brooklyn, N. Y | 30 |
| 2UM | Poling, Russell H | Beers St., Keyport, N. J | 500 |
| 2WC | Pollock, J. Millard | 34 Clifton Pl., Brooklyn, N. Y | 30 |
| 2PF | Pope, Frederick B | 24 Carrol St., Yonkers, N. Y | 500 |
| 2RJ | Porter, Charles A | 1700 Ditmas Ave., Brooklyn, N. Y | 25 |
| 2OP | Prendergast, Robert M | 174 4th St., Union Course, N. Y | 500 |
| 2DL | Price, Henry S | 435 Clinton Ave., Brooklyn, N. Y | 500 |
| 2CD | Prosser, Roger D | Chestnut St., Englewood, N. J | 30 |
| 2EI | Quick, Henry C | 471 75th St., Brooklyn, N. Y | 500 |
| 2ML | Quinby, E. Jay | Aqueduct Ave. and Fordham Rd., New York, N. Y. | 250 |
| 2QL | Rabi, Isidor | 481 Hopkinson Ave., New York, N. Y | 24 |
| 2TK | Randolph, Randolph A | 558 W. 165th St., New York, N. Y | 250 |
| 2HC | Raqué, Carl P | 82 Booraem Ave., Jersey City, N. J | 330 |
| 2RH | Reiss, Lester | 580 W. 161st St., New York, N. Y | 250 |
| 2RB | Reuman, William H | 480 9th Ave., New York, N. Y | 525 |
| 2OW | Rextrew, Walter C | 355 Delaware Ave., Albany, N. Y | 40 |
| 2NT | Reyl, George | 309 E. 86th St., New York, N. Y | 50 |
| 2ID | Reyle, Stanley | 42½ Van Reipen Ave., Jersey City, N. J | 24 |
| 2RS | Reymann, Albert E | 752 9th Ave., New York, N. Y | 6 |
| 2IS | Ricketts, Percy E | George St., Babylon, N. Y | 250 |
| 2QF | Ritscher, Hans | 807 Garden St., Hoboken, N. J | 50 |
| 2TX | Robbins, Walter G | Babylon, N. Y | 112 |
| 2LC | Roberts, A. Perry | Tenafly Rd., Tenafly, N. J | 825 |
| 2MC | Roberts, Irven J | 66 E. Baldwin St., Bloomfield, N. J | 24 |
| 2VE | Robertson, Gus | 125 Hunter Ave., Long Island City, N. Y | 36 |
| 2QR | Robertson, William L | 57 Montross Ave., Rutherford N. J | 8 |
| 2TR | Roche, Walter J | 2 Irving Pl., Jamaica, N. Y | 1,000 |
| 2LJ | Rodenburg, Herman | 1626 2d Ave., New York, N. Y | 30 |
| 2SJ | Rodriguez, Joseph, jr | 223 23d St., Brooklyn, N. Y | 24 |
| 2KV | Rogers, Lorlys R | 200 W. 113th St., New York, N. Y | 660 |
| 2TH | Roy, James A. S | 59 Park Ter., West Orange, N. J | 30 |
| 2IA | Royce, Winfred A | 1329 49th St., Brooklyn, N. Y | 500 |
| 2JY | Rupert, S. E. G | 107 2d Ave., Pelham, N. Y | 1,000 |
| 2GP | Rutherford, T. Bruce | 42 Hawthorne St., Brooklyn, N. Y | 24 |
| 2DE | Ruttmann, Ferdinand | 605 W. 141st St., New York, N. Y | 225 |
| 2WL | Ryan, Lester F | 18 Kosciusko St., Brooklyn, N. Y | 15 |
| 2DM | Sach. Harold | 701, Madison Ave., New York, N. Y | 250 |
| 2HN | Sands, Walter H | 178 Anchor Ave., Mt. Vernon, N. Y | 230 |
| 2SB | Sangree, Ernest M | 1807 Ditmas Ave., Brooklyn, N. Y | 18 |

AMATEUR RADIO STATIONS—SECOND DISTRICT—ALPHABETICALLY BY OWNERS OF STATIONS—Continued.

| Call signal. | Owner of station. | Location of station. | Power. |
|---|---|---|---|
| | | | Watts. |
| 2LH | Sayres, Ralph A | 4645 Central Ave., Richmond Hill, N. Y | 36 |
| 2SU | Schabbehar, Edwin A | 412 Village Ave., Rockville Center, N. Y | 770 |
| 2JB | Schaefer, Charles L | 201 Broadway, Port Richmond, N. Y | 500 |
| 2IO | Scharrenbeck, George H. | 126 W. 1st St., Mt. Vernon, N. Y | 220 |
| 2EQ | Schedler, Herbert | 328 Central Ave., Jersey City, N. J | 300 |
| 2BF | Schell, Richard, jr | 35 Grasmere Ave., Grasmere, N. Y | 350 |
| 2BO | Schermerhorn, Howard F. | 211 Orange Rd., Montclair, N. J | 300 |
| 2DJ | Schlitz, Karl W | 28 Jefferson St., Brooklyn, N. Y | 36 |
| 2NC | Schmid, Paul | 110 S. Division St., Peekskill, N. Y | 775 |
| 2EO | Schneider, Alexander | 326 E. 69th St., New York, N. Y | 40 |
| 2VO | Scholerman, Carl | Pleasantville, N. Y | 1,000 |
| 2PD | Schomp, Roy | 76 Undercliff Ave., Edgewater, N. J | 220 |
| 2CB | Schram, John, jr | 21 Locust St., Brooklyn, N. Y | 60 |
| 2BH | Schulte, Carl E | 67 Oak St., Ridgewood, N. J | 250 |
| 2EZ | Schupp, Charles H | Linden Ave., River Edge, N. J | 250 |
| 2UY | Schwartz, Abraham H | 80 2d Ave., New York, N. Y | 350 |
| 2DQ | Schwarzkopf, Irving M | 138 E. 95th St., New York, N. Y | 500 |
| 2ND | Schweizer, Charles L | 710 3d Ave., Brooklyn, N. Y | 50 |
| 2IN | Scofield, Robert W | 87 Macon St., Brooklyn, N. Y | 50 |
| 2AN | Sedlak, Conrad J | 633 Main St., New Durham, N. J | 20 |
| 2PM | Sellars, Millard | 96 N. Bergen Pl., Freeport, N. Y | 30 |
| 2DX | Seyd, Ernest K | 231 Park Pl., Brooklyn, N. Y | 50 |
| 2NM | Sharp, Watkin W | Far Rockaway, N. Y | 1,000 |
| 2PZ | Shaw, Horace S | 2120 Canarsie Lane, Brooklyn, N. Y | 50 |
| 2KS | Shropshire, Lee R | Grand Ave., Palisades Park, N. J | 500 |
| 2OU | Siebert, Walter | 1538 E. 15th St., Brooklyn, N. Y | 45 |
| 2GR | Slagle, E. Lester | 25 S. 2d Ave., Mt. Vernon, N. Y | 18 |
| 2RY | Slosilo, Stephen J | 412 17th St., Brooklyn, N. Y | 48 |
| 2MK | Smith, Daniel W | South St., Oyster Bay, N. Y | 130 |
| 2QV | Smith, Edgar T | 185 Brooklyn Ave., Brooklyn, N. Y | 280 |
| 2DU | Smith, Joseph T | 126 E. 114th St., New York, N. Y | 500 |
| 2JP | Smith, Julius J. R | 807 Lincoln Pl., Brooklyn, N. Y | 12 |
| 2JO | Smith, Nelson V | Lawrence Ave., Lawrence, N. Y | 1,000 |
| 2GW | Snowden, Fred | R. F. D. No. 49, Schenectady, N. Y | 675 |
| 2KH | Solberg, Walter | 620 46th St., Brooklyn, N. Y | 25 |
| 2GC | Sonn, Albert E | 150 2d Ave., Newark, N. J | 550 |
| 2RP | Sorgens, Walter M | 65 Odell St., Schenectady, N. Y | 250 |
| 2IM | Spangenberg, Lester | 25 S. 4th St., Lakeview, N. J | 800 |
| 2WP | Spannaus, Charles O | 660 W. 180th St., New York, N. Y | 500 |
| 2FD | Spiegel, Walter | 1611 1st Ave., New York, N. Y | 30 |
| 2RF | Springer, C. Meredith | 339 Union St., Far Rockaway, N. Y | 24 |
| 2FS | Stanley, Howard L | Main St., Babylon, N. Y | 224 |
| 2AL | Stanley, Walter N | 654 Putnam Ave., Brooklyn, N. Y | 30 |
| 2OK | Stanton, Walter | 46 Smith St., Rockville Center, N. Y | 70 |
| 2VW | Steinkamp, Harold | 89 Hyatt Ave., Yonkers, N. Y | 500 |
| 2UW | Stevens, Herbert H | 4 Elm St., West Orange, N. J | 24 |
| 2UZ | Stewart, G. Edwin | 87 N. Center Ave., Rockville Center, N. Y. | 1,000 |
| 2KO | Stone, Brownell | 1128 Bedford Ave., Brooklyn, N. Y | 100 |
| 2JA | Story, Robert K., jr | 212 Hancock St., Brooklyn, N. Y | 72 |
| 2TA | Stricker, Fred W | 52 6th St., Elizabeth, N. J | 325 |
| 2LV | Stutz, Ernest W | 126 Bainbridge St., Brooklyn, N. Y | 15 |
| 2LR | Taussig, Charles W | 36 W. 85th St., New York, N. Y | 360 |
| 2IH | Tense, William F | 18 Madison Ave., Clifton, N. J | 24 |
| 2EC | Thiede, Ferdinand C | 486 Decatur St., Brooklyn, N. Y | 24 |
| 2PJ | Thomas, Alonzo E., jr | 176-A Union St., Jersey City, N. J | 9 |
| 2PW | Timmins, Walter J | 76 Davis Ave., Kearny, N. J | 10 |
| 2OJ | Tong, Myron A | 148 Housman Ave., Castleton Hill, N. Y | 100 |
| 2CP | Totten, Elmer E | 95 W. 33d St., Bayonne, N. J | 16 |

54773°—14——7

AMATEUR RADIO STATIONS—SECOND DISTRICT—ALPHABETICALLY BY OWNERS OF STATIONS—Continued.

| Call signal. | Owner of station. | Location of station. | Power. |
|---|---|---|---|
| | | | Watts. |
| 2PT | Traver, William F. | Chandler Ave., Far Rockaway, N. Y. | 12 |
| 2RN | Tucker, George C. | Broadway, Upper Nyack, N. Y. | 24 |
| 2KB | Tyrrel, Randolph E. | 677 E. 19th St., Brooklyn, N. Y. | 250 |
| 2ST | Udell, Carlton G. | 130 Lincoln Pl., Brooklyn, N. Y. | 30 |
| 2RM | Underhill, Chester R. | 24 Forest St., Montclair, N. J. | 120 |
| 2HD | Underwood, Kenneth C. | 259 Mt. Prospect Ave., Newark, N. J. | 324 |
| 2KI | Uphoff, Leslie S. | 120 Avenue B, Schenectady, N. Y. | 560 |
| 2OT | Urbain, Ferdinand A. | 1189 44th St., Brooklyn, N. Y. | 180 |
| 2SE | Van Duzer, Charles P. | 172 Fisk Ave., Westerleigh, N. Y. | 50 |
| 2UU | Vanderbilt, Clinton B. | 214 Imwood Ave., Upper Montclair, N. J. | 24 |
| 2MG | Vaughan, George W., jr. | 34 S. 9th Ave., Mt. Vernon, N. Y. | 250 |
| 2RZ | Veneman, Peter. | 36 Watson St., Paterson, N. J. | 12 |
| 2OR | Vermilya, Irving. | 24 Chester St., Mt. Vernon, N. Y. | 250 |
| 2OQ | Wade, J. Melmoth. | 83 Hamilton Ave., Yonkers, N. Y. | 15 |
| 2CV | Waibel, Walter W. | 111 Fabyan Pl., Newark, N. J. | 250 |
| 2OE | Walker, Raymond L. | 49 Roseville Ave., Newark, N. J. | 18 |
| 2QO | Walsh, James L. | 172 Park Ave., East Rutherford, N. J. | 258 |
| 2QP | Ward, John R. | 160 Garfield Pl., Brooklyn, N. Y. | 40 |
| 2RC | Watson, Edmund A. | 78 Van Ness Ave., Rutherford, N. J. | 660 |
| 2DZ | Watters, John J. | Port Richmond, N. Y. | 500 |
| 2FR | Way, John D. | 214 W. 92d St., New York, N. Y. | 280 |
| 2MQ | Weber, Ernest A. | 285 S. 2d St., New York, N. Y. | 18 |
| 2KZ | Weden, Charles. | 97 Myrtle St., Bloomfield, N. J. | 12 |
| 2FH | Weiss, Jacob. | 5 Adams St., Port Washington, N. Y. | 1,000 |
| 2JE | Wendelstadt, Lucius F. | 8 Seymour St., Montclair, N. J. | 1,000 |
| 2KC | Werner, Charles M. | 252 Cambridge Ave., Jersey City, N. J. | 25 |
| 2GE | West, Thomas R. | 256 Grand Ave., Leonia, N. J. | 30 |
| 2NE | Westerhoff, Peter, jr. | Goffle Ave., Midland Park, N. J. | 500 |
| 2TJ | White, Howard E. | Rye, N. Y. | 36 |
| 2BW | Whitson, John H. | Briarcliff Manor, N. Y. | 500 |
| 2EH | Wilmott, George B. | 1138 E. 37th St., Brooklyn, N. Y. | 50 |
| 2WQ | Willets, Gilson V. | 92 Hamilton Ave., Yonkers, N. Y. | 12 |
| 2UI | Williams, Arthur D. | 73 S. Arlington Ave., East Orange, N. J. | 14 |
| 2EA | Williams, Earl C. | 261 Madison Ave., Perth Amboy, N. J. | 330 |
| 2MJ | Williams, Roy D. | 801 Halsey St., Brooklyn, N. Y. | 24 |
| 2QI | Wimpfheimer, Gustave R. | 1218 Wheeler Ave., New York, N. Y. | 250 |
| 2DA | Winn, Arthur H. | 325 Church St., Poughkeepsie, N. Y. | 50 |
| 2FP | Woerner, Charles A. | 247 Union St., Jersey City, N. J. | 30 |
| 2NR | Wohltmann, Henry M. | 168 W. 55th St., Brooklyn, N. Y. | 30 |
| 2LZ | Woodrow, William. | 224 W. 140th St., New York, N. Y. | 880 |
| 2IW | Worth, John B. | Madison St., Cresskill, N. J. | 36 |
| 2BE | Yerbury, George S., jr. | 21 Irving Pl., Passaic, N. J. | 36 |
| 2IT | Young, Henry. | 179 4th St., Jersey City, N. J. | 12 |
| 2HV | Zeitz, Edwin. | 404 Ralph St., Brooklyn, N. Y. | 75 |
| 2OO | Zimmermann, Edwin W. | 106 Magnolia Ave., Arlington, N. J. | 100 |
| 2DB | Zucker, Richard D. | 45 Clinton Pl., Mt. Vernon, N. Y. | 250 |

ALPHABETICALLY BY CALL SIGNALS.

| Call signal. | Owner of station. | Call signal. | Owner of station. |
|---|---|---|---|
| 2AA | Flagg, John H. | 2AG | Mulford, Harold C. |
| 2AC | Hart, Gifford R. | 2AH | Edelman, Abraham. |
| 2AD | Dammers, Albert. | 2AI | Eber, John G. |
| 2AE | Happe, William H. | 2AK | Ferris, Howard E. |
| 2AF | Bryant, Marquis V. | 2AL | Stanley, Walter N. |

AMATEUR RADIO STATIONS—SECOND DISTRICT—ALPHABETICALLY BY CALL SIGNALS—Continued.

| Call signal. | Owner of station. | Call signal. | Owner of station. |
|---|---|---|---|
| 2AM | Haeselbarth, Percy. | 2DO | Gerrity, John J. |
| 2AN | Sedlak, Conrad J. | 2DQ | Schwarzkopf, Irving M. |
| 2AO | Jones, Robert O. | 2DR | Cooper, Telfer C. |
| 2AQ | Corson, David N. | 2DS | Clark, Le Roy. |
| 2AS | De Yoe, Willard L. | 2DU | Smith, Joseph T. |
| 2AT | Guild, Baldwin. | 2DV | Hathaway, Harry C. B. |
| 2AU | Bryan, Chester W. | 2DX | Seyd, Ernest K. |
| 2AY | Gittelbauer, Frederick. | 2DY | Palmer, Corydon. |
| 2AZ | Pearl, Eugene S. | 2DZ | Watters, John J. |
| 2BC | Kaltenbach, Henry J., jr. | 2EA | Williams, Earl C. |
| 2BD | Banta, Theodore C. | 2EC | Thiede, Ferdinand C. |
| 2BE | Yerbury, George S., jr. | 2EE | Jacobs, Charles F. |
| 2BF | Schell, Richard, jr. | 2EF | Hurd, Theodore. |
| 2BG | Mowton, Edward M. | 2EG | Hurd, John B. |
| 2BH | Schulte, Carl E. | 2EH | Wilmott, George B. |
| 2BI | Morgan, Waller V. | 2EI | Quick, Henry C. |
| 2BK | Green, Adoniram J. | 2EJ | Bechtlofft, Claude B. |
| 2BL | Kirch, George, jr. | 2EL | Meyer, William E. |
| 2BM | Heermance, Earle. | 2EM | Crosby, Roy C. |
| 2BN | Griswold, Edmund J. | 2EO | Schneider, Alexander. |
| 2BO | Schermerhorn, Howard F. | 2EP | Mead, George S. V. |
| 2BP | Phipps, Donald A. | 2EQ | Schedler, Herbert. |
| 2BR | Krech, Karl G. | 2ES | Campbell, Robert, jr. |
| 2BS | Pearson, Herbert B. | 2ET | England, George B. |
| 2BT | Barrett's School of Telegraphy. | 2EU | Droste, George T. |
| 2BW | Whitson, John H. | 2EV | Hallock, Charles S. |
| 2BY | Keller, Julius F. | 2EW | Hamilton, Joseph E. |
| 2BZ | Lyman, C. Glenn. | 2EX | Jackson, Benjamin B. |
| | | 2EY | McKinney, Fred J. |
| 2CA | Liedecker, Morris. | 2EZ | Schupp, Charles H. |
| 2CB | Schram, John, jr. | | |
| 2CD | Prosser, Roger D. | 2FA | Pfeifer, Clarence H. |
| 2CI | Austin, Edward. | 2FB | Pareis, Robert. |
| 2CJ | Bathgate, Walter E. | 2FD | Spiegel, Walter. |
| 2CK | O'Brien, Thomas. | 2FE | Checl, Harold W. |
| 2CN | Dickey, Edward T. | 2FH | Weiss, Jacob. |
| 2CO | Morrell, W. Frank. | 2FI | Kirkpatrick, Louis W. |
| 2CP | Totten, Elmer E. | 2FJ | Helwig, Herman F. |
| 2CQ | Dilg, A. Norman. | 2FK | Hamilton, Ralph. |
| 2CR | Blauvelt, William M. | 2FL | Lehmann, August, jr. |
| 2CT | Bunn, Milo B. | 2FM | Perkins, William P. |
| 2CU | Palmland, Philip. | 2FO | Clark, William C. |
| 2CV | Waibel, Walter W. | 2FP | Woerner, Charles A. |
| 2CZ | Poe, Vergil C. | 2FQ | Hardwick, Ambrose H. |
| | | 2FR | Way, John D. |
| 2DA | Winn, Arthur H. | 2FS | Stanley, Howard L. |
| 2DB | Zucker, Richard D. | 2FT | Bishop, Mortimer Z. |
| 2DC | Kahn, Walter A. | 2FU | Benzing, Herman. |
| 2DD | Fitzgerald, Gordon P. | 2FW | MacPherson, Claude V. |
| 2DE | Ruttmann, Ferdinand. | 2FY | Hartman, Robert. |
| 2DF | McIntire, Meylert A. | 2FZ | Harris, Charles C. |
| 2DG | Higgs, Harry Y. | | |
| 2DI | Cyriax, Ernest A. | 2GB | Bartlett, Bernard W. |
| 2DJ | Schlitz, Karl W. | 2GC | Sonn, Albert E. |
| 2DK | Hill, William S. | 2GD | Farquharson, John S. |
| 2DL | Price, Henry S. | 2GE | West, Thomas R. |
| 2DM | Sachs, Harold. | 2GF | Gabrielson, Henry M. |
| 2DN | Cullen, Edward R. | 2GG | Dahlgren, Birger A. |

AMATEUR RADIO STATIONS—SECOND DISTRICT—ALPHABETICALLY BY CALL SIGNALS—Continued.

| Call signal. | Owner of station. |
|---|---|
| 2GH | Kelting, Clarence A. |
| 2GI | Bockelmann, Charles F. |
| 2GK | Hubbard, John W. |
| 2GL | Marshall, Richard E. |
| 2GM | Ballard, J. Adams. |
| 2GO | Peltier, Paul D. |
| 2GP | Rutherford, T. Bruce. |
| 2GR | Slagle, E. Lester. |
| 2GU | Inwright, John A. |
| 2GW | Snowden, Fred. |
| 2GX | Fallon, Harry A., jr. |
| 2GZ | Plate, Fred W. |
| 2HA | McCoy, Daniel. |
| 2HC | Raqué, Carl P. |
| 2HD | Underwood, Kenneth C. |
| 2HF | Coote, Charles W. |
| 2HG | Peters, Frank J. |
| 2HH | Dederick, H. C. |
| 2HJ | Hadden, Weston. |
| 2HK | Burrows, Henry P. |
| 2HN | Sands, Walter H. |
| 2HO | Lyons, William B. |
| 2HP | Mayhew, B. Alan, jr. |
| 2HR | Chandler, Arthur C. |
| 2HS | O'Mara, Edward F. |
| 2HT | Macartney, George E. |
| 2HU | Hotchkiss, Grosvenor. |
| 2HV | Zeitz, Edwin. |
| 2HX | Lane, David M. |
| 2IA | Royce, Winfred A. |
| 2ID | Reyle, Stanley. |
| 2IE | Lemmon, Walter S. |
| 2IH | Tense, William F. |
| 2II | Howell, Walter J. |
| 2IJ | Cochran, Alexander. |
| 2IL | McClintock, George C. |
| 2IM | Spangenberg, Lester. |
| 2IN | Scofield, Robert W. |
| 2IO | Scharrenbeck, George H. |
| 2IQ | Elliott, Paul C. |
| 2IR | Foulke, J. Brion, jr. |
| 2IS | Ricketts, Percy E. |
| 2IT | Young, Henry. |
| 2IV | Lindsay, Russell. |
| 2IW | Worth, John B. |
| 2IY | Dugan, Edward W. |
| 2IZ | Fraser, Frank. |
| 2JA | Story, Robert K., jr. |
| 2JB | Schaefer, Charles L. |
| 2JD | Boeder, Arthur R. |
| 2JE | Wendelstadt, Lucius F. |
| 2JF | Frey, Anthony C. |
| 2JH | Brown, David S., jr. |
| 2JI | Eddy, Leonard E. |
| 2JK | Mitchell, Arthur M. |
| 2JN | Freeland, Wilbur W. |
| 2JO | Smith, Nelson V. |
| 2JP | Smith, Julius J. R. |
| 2JU | Goette, C. J. |
| 2JX | De Cortin, Gustav A. |
| 2JY | Rupert, S. E. G. |
| 2KA | Kroener, Christian E. |
| 2KB | Tyrrel, Randolph E. |
| 2KC | Werner, Charles M. |
| 2KD | Browne, Walram S. |
| 2KE | Frey, George. |
| 2KH | Solberg, Walter. |
| 2KI | Uphoff, Leslie S. |
| 2KJ | Beebe, Lloyd S. |
| 2KK | Day, Howard B. |
| 2KL | Gregory, Arthur V. |
| 2KM | Francis, Charles E. |
| 2KN | Collison, Percy B. |
| 2KO | Stone, Brownell. |
| 2KP | McClure, Donald. |
| 2KQ | Edwards, Harry M., jr. |
| 2KR | Lebowitz, Samuel. |
| 2KS | Shropshire, Lee R. |
| 2KV | Rogers, Lorlys R. |
| 2KW | Plummer, James A. |
| 2KX | Noble, Kendrick. |
| 2KY | McLoughlin, Robert J. |
| 2KZ | Weden, Charles. |
| 2LA | Miller, Frederick R. |
| 2LB | Bertine, Edwin K. |
| 2LC | Roberts, A. Perry. |
| 2LD | Cotter, William F. |
| 2LE | Egolf, Richard S. |
| 2LF | Bartlett, Charles H. |
| 2LG | McLaughlin, Fred L. |
| 2LH | Sayres, Ralph A. |
| 2LI | Meacham, Frederick C., jr. |
| 2LJ | Rodenburg, Herman. |
| 2LL | Benedict, Alonzo R. |
| 2LM | Dunn, Laurence J. |
| 2LN | Morrison, Clifford P. |
| 2LO | Coffin, Russell S. |
| 2LP | Green, Raymond J. |
| 2LQ | Belt, Charles B. |
| 2LR | Taussig, Charles W. |
| 2LT | Galvin, Lee R. |
| 2LU | Baker, William N. |
| 2LV | Stutz, Ernest W. |
| 2LX | Adelphi College. |
| 2LY | Hoover, Raymond. |
| 2LZ | Woodrow, William. |
| 2MA | Hallenbeck, Charles. |
| 2MC | Roberts, Irven J. |
| 2MD | Pendleton, Harold A. |
| 2ME | Archibald, John O. |
| 2MF | Hoppock, Allen H. |
| 2MG | Vaughan, George W., jr. |

AMATEUR RADIO STATIONS—SECOND DISTRICT—ALPHABETICALLY BY CALL SIGNALS—Continued.

| Call signal. | Owner of station. | Call signal. | Owner of station. |
|---|---|---|---|
| 2MH | Buchanan, William F. | 2OP | Prendergast, Robert M.. |
| 2MI | Morris, Earle S. | 2OQ | Wade, J. Melmoth. |
| 2MJ | Williams, Roy D. | 2OR | Vermilya, Irving. |
| 2MK | Smith, Daniel W. | 2OS | Cohen, Walter. |
| 2ML | Quinby, E. J. | 2OT | Urbain, Ferdinand A. |
| 2MM | Apgar, Charles E. | 2OU | Siebert, Walter. |
| 2MN | Carrougher, Vivian A. | 2OV | Littlefield, Charles E. |
| 2MO | Ostman, Frederick B. | 2OW | Rextrew, Walter C. |
| 2MP | Pearsall, William E. | 2OX | Mardon, F. Herbert. |
| 2MQ | Weber, Ernest A. | 2OY | Jones, Frank. |
| 2MR | Atwater, Frank G., jr. | 2OZ | Dufford, John S. |
| 2MS | Berri, Herbert. | | |
| 2MT | Leeb, Henry L. | 2PA | Carman, Newton I. |
| 2MU | Hengerer, Howard B. | 2PB | Haight, Russell P. |
| 2MV | Bell, Arthur E. | 2PC | Barriette, Samuel L. |
| 2MW | Crichton, Arthur M. | 2PD | Schomp, Roy. |
| 2MX | Heffernan, William J. | 2PE | Fritch, Vincent J. |
| 2MY | Morris, Robert. | 2PF | Pope, Frederick B. |
| | | 2PG | Eckstein, William J. |
| 2NA | Adickes, Ernest D. | 2PH | Blackburn, Godfrey C. |
| 2NB | Le Gallez, Clayton B. | 2PI | Evans, Clarence L. |
| 2NC | Schmid, Paul. | 2PJ | Thomas, Alonzo E., jr. |
| 2ND | Schweizer, Charles L. | 2PK | Otten, G. C. |
| 2NE | Westerhoff, Peter, jr. | 2PL | Lindsay, Daniel E. |
| 2NF | Homan, Eber J. | 2PM | Sellars, Millard. |
| 2NH | Horn, Charles W. | 2PN | Berger, H. C. V. B. |
| 2NI | Moles, Charles E. | 2PO | Mott, Harold. |
| 2NK | Palm, J. Adam. | 2PP | Manvell, Edwin H. |
| 2NL | Burnett, Walter J. | 2PQ | Monsen, Hans S. |
| 2NM | Sharp, Watkin W. | 2PR | Dynner, Eugene. |
| 2NN | Buck, David E. | 2PS | Cohen, Samuel. |
| 2NO | Merritt, Frank. | 2PT | Traver, William F. |
| 2NP | Koenig, George F. | 2PU | Lally, Joseph F. |
| 2NQ | Isaacson, Charles B. | 2PV | Grebe, Alfred H. |
| 2NR | Wohltmann, Henry M. | 2PW | Timmins, Walter J. |
| 2NS | Hoffman, Paul J. | 2PX | Hamilton, Albert G., jr. |
| 2NT | Reyl, George. | 2PY | Bogardus, Henry L. |
| 2NU | Berglund, Edward A. | 2PZ | Shaw, Horace S. |
| 2NV | Meder, George C. | | |
| 2NX | Mehrbrey, William. | 2QA | Kinney, E. M. |
| 2NY | Austrian, Ralph B. | 2QB | Blackford, Harold W. |
| 2NZ | Pfeil, A. Leslie. | 2QC | Ford, Fullerton. |
| | | 2QD | King, Wendell W. |
| | | 2QE | Manley, Lee L. |
| 2OA | Hammond, Lester. | 2QF | Ritscher, Hans. |
| 2OB | Fox, Loyal S. | 2QG | Gale, Rowland A. |
| 2OC | Erasmus Hall High School. | 2QH | Davies, Richard J., jr. |
| 2OD | Debuchy, Edmund A. | 2QI | Wimpfheimer, Gustave R. |
| 2OE | Walker, Raymond L. | 2QJ | Eckley, Harold J. |
| 2OF | Meinecke, Ernest. | 2QK | Caskey, Kenneth B. |
| 2OG | Cockaday, Lawrence M. | 2QL | Rabi, Isidor. |
| 2OH | Lang, Ernest. | 2QM | Koukol, Edwin P. |
| 2OI | Folks, Leslie E. | 2QN | Dwyer, Martin J., jr. |
| 2OJ | Tong, Myron A. | 2QO | Walsh, James L. |
| 2OK | Stanton, Walter. | 2QP | Ward, John R. |
| 2OL | O'Brien, Laurence J. | 2QQ | Green, Irving W. |
| 2OM | Maher, Frank A. | 2QR | Robertson, William L. |
| 2ON | Kellow, James C. | 2QS | Bernard, James L. |
| 2OO | Zimmermann, Edwin W. | 2QT | Hynds, Arthur E. |

AMATEUR RADIO STATIONS—SECOND DISTRICT—ALPHABETICALLY BY CALL SIGNALS—Continued.

| Call signal. | Owner of station. | Call signal. | Owner of station. |
|---|---|---|---|
| 2QU | Osborne, J. Spencer. | 2TA | Stricker, Fred W. |
| 2QV | Smith, Edgar T. | 2TB | Ford, Everett J. |
| 2QW | Birkmire, Harold. | 2TC | Dickenson, Henry E. |
| 2QX | Keller, George C. | 2TD | Mayer, Arthur C. |
| 2QY | Jacobsen, Walter H. | 2TE | Bentzig, Victor H. |
| 2QZ | Meyer, Charles A. | 2TF | Pearson, James W. |
| | | 2TG | Balfoort, John M. |
| | | 2TH | Roy, James A. S. |
| 2RA | Hollman, Theodore. | 2TI | Mitchell, Everitt. |
| 2RB | Reuman, William H. | 2TJ | White, Howard E. |
| 2RC | Watson, Edmund A. | 2TK | Randolph, Randolph A. |
| 2RD | Carey, Stephen W., 3d. | 2TL | de Forest, Edward L., jr. |
| 2RE | Pacent, L. Gerard. | 2TM | Collymore, Errold D. |
| 2RF | Springer, C. Meredith. | 2TN | Dunham, Clarence L. |
| 2RG | Earle, William P., jr. | 2TO | Benzing, Jacob. |
| 2RH | Reiss, Lester. | 2TP | Bohn, William. |
| 2RI | Cowper, Norman C. | 2TQ | Adams, E. William, jr. |
| 2RJ | Porter, Charles A. | 2TR | Roche, Walter J. |
| 2RK | Horle, Lawrence C. F. | 2TS | Carpenter, Ferris G. |
| 2RL | Camp, Victor F. | 2TT | Pattison, Edward H. |
| 2RM | Underhill, Chester R. | 2TU | Lee, Robert J. B. |
| 2RN | Tucker, George C. | 2TV | Glenn, George. |
| 2RO | Dodds, Andrew C. | 2TW | Knight, Alexander H. |
| 2RP | Sorgens, Walter M. | 2TX | Robbins, Walter G. |
| 2RQ | McKinney, Donald B. | 2TY | Pendleton, Archibald F. |
| 2RR | Johnson, John A. | 2TZ | Collins, Frank J. |
| 2RS | Reymann, Albert E. | | |
| 2RT | Collinson, Jesse G. | 2UA | Mann, Samuel. |
| 2RU | Jordon, Fletcher. | 2UB | Emory, John M. G. |
| 2RV | Johnson, W. Eugene. | 2UC | Lange, William. |
| 2RW | Baily, Hobart W. | 2UD | Brainard, Edward S. |
| 2RX | Picken, James C., jr. | 2UE | Hoyt, William L. |
| 2RY | Slosilo, Stephen J. | 2UF | Evans, Arthur F. |
| 2RZ | Veneman, Peter. | 2UG | Bonduaux, Eugene L. |
| | | 2UH | Boys' Wireless Club of Hackensack High School. |
| 2SA | Lowitz, Donald J. | | |
| 2SB | Sangree, Ernest M. | 2UI | Williams, Arthur D. |
| 2SC | Constant, S. Victor. | 2UJ | Innes, Richard C. |
| 2SD | Copersito, Michael. | 2UK | Biggam, Henry C. |
| 2SE | Van Duzer, Charles P. | 2UL | Baker, Alvah L. |
| 2SF | Kollock, Alan S. | 2UM | Poling, Russell H. |
| 2SG | May, Fred. | 2UN | Graham, Malcolm. |
| 2SH | McQuaide, James P. | 2UO | Heyer, Benjamin W. |
| 2SI | Le Quesne, C. A., jr. | 2UP | Gannon, J. Kimball. |
| 2SJ | Rodriguez, Joseph, jr. | 2UQ | Hallett, E. Douglas. |
| 2SK | Murray, Charles. | 2UR | Arany, Leo. |
| 2SL | Merrill, J. Stewart. | 2US | Allstrom, F. Condit. |
| 2SM | Hatry, William B. | 2UT | Dick, Benjamin S. |
| 2SN | Barnes, C. Everett. | 2UU | Vanderbilt, Clinton B. |
| 2SO | Johnston, James E. | 2UV | Dimmick, James N. |
| 2SP | Bleilevens, Gerhardt. | 2UW | Stevens, Herbert H. |
| 2SQ | Krecit, Raymond A. | 2UX | Phelan, Charles W. |
| 2SR | Greenlees, William. | 2UY | Schwartz, Abraham H. |
| 2SS | Fitler, Eugene B., jr. | 2UZ | Stewart, G. Edwin. |
| 2ST | Udell, Carlton G. | | |
| 2SU | Schabbehar, Edwin A. | 2VA | Huested, William P. |
| 2SV | Clarke, Frederick D. | 2VB | Gerlach, Adolph J. |
| 2SX | Cannon, George C. | 2VC | Johnson, Theophilus, jr. |
| 2SY | De Long, Oscar A., jr. | 2VD | Bruell, Joseph P. |
| 2SZ | Kissick, Robert G. | 2VE | Robertson, Gus. |

Amateur Radio Stations—Second District—Alphabetically by Call Signals—Continued.

| Call signal. | Owner of station. | Call signal. | Owner of station. |
|---|---|---|---|
| 2VF | Koch, Edward. | 2WA | Keers, John K. |
| 2VG | Ahrens, Harry E. | 2WB | Fogetti, Howard J. |
| 2VH | Engelder, Eberhardt E. | 2WC | Pollock, J. Millard. |
| 2VI | Loub, Arthur F. | 2WD | Lasher, Charles E. |
| 2VJ | Furman, Robert S. | 2WE | Heydon, Albert R. |
| 2VK | Covert, James D. | 2WF | Nolan, Frank J. |
| 2VL | Bond, Arthur M. | 2WG | Lemkie, Harry A. |
| 2VM | Brown, Philip T. | 2WH | Pearsall, Arthur R. |
| 2VN | Charles, Chester A. | 2WI | Anderson, Robert N. |
| 2VO | Scholerman, Carl. | 2WJ | Pflomm, George M. |
| 2VP | Bartsch, Henry W. | 2WK | Caggiano, Carmine J. |
| 2VQ | Agnoli, Justus J. | 2WL | Ryan, Lester F. |
| 2VR | Gassaway, Julian L. | 2WM | Fowler, Jack B. |
| 2VS | Decker, Ralph W. E. | 2WN | Beller, William A. G. |
| 2VT | Kayser, Herbert. | 2WO | Barone, Salvatore A. |
| 2VU | Flandreaux, Cyrus. | 2WP | Spannaus, Charles O. |
| 2VV | French, Edward. | 2WQ | Willets, Gilson V. |
| 2VW | Steinkamp, Harold. | 2WR | Mayhew, H. Clifford. |
| 2VX | McCarthy, George W. | 2WS | Francis, Leo A. |
| 2VY | Diehl, John F. | 2WU | Moore, H. Atherton. |
| 2VZ | Frederick, G. Bentley. | | |

## THIRD DISTRICT.

[Headquarters: Customhouse, Baltimore, Md. The third district comprises the States of New Jersey (all counties not included in second district), Pennsylvania (counties of Philadelphia, Delaware, all counties south of the Blue Mountains, and Franklin County), Delaware, Maryland, Virginia, and the District of Columbia.]

### ALPHABETICALLY BY OWNERS OF STATIONS.

| Call signal. | Owner of station. | Location of station. | Power. |
|---|---|---|---|
| | | | Watts. |
| 3PC | Abbott, E. H. B. | 117 Landis Ave., Vineland, N. J. | 300 |
| 3QK | Adams, Leslie H. | 828 Landis Ave., Vineland, N. J. | 990 |
| 3CA | Adelberger, Adrian J. | W. Wayne Ave., Wayne, Pa. | 500 |
| 3GP | Amig, Edward P. | Highland Park, Pa. | 500 |
| 3KE | Allen, Francis H. | 171 W. Broad St., Burlington, N. J. | 200 |
| 3BM | Allen, George Y. | Bernardsville, N. J. | 312 |
| 3BD | Allen, Percival R. | Haverford, Pa. | 250 |
| 3IP | Anderson, Albert | 313 Chestnut St., Camden, N. J. | 20 |
| 3SR | Anderson, John A. | 612 Cherry St., Camden, N. J. | 18 |
| 3TQ | Andrews, Edward C. | 22d and Morris Sts., Philadelphia, Pa. | 200 |
| 3AX | Arner, Oscar Q. | 56 V St. NW., Washington, D. C. | 24 |
| 3AA | Ashmore, John W. | 3108 Hamilton St., Philadelphia, Pa. | 16 |
| 3CN | Ashton, Leon W. | 106 Washington Ave., Collingswood, N. J. | 30 |
| 3PI | Atlee, Franklin | 2039 Pine St., Philadelphia, Pa. | 18 |
| 3JA | August, Earl W. | 3718 N. Delhi St., Philadelphia, Pa. | 250 |
| 3BU | Austrian, Harry D. | 122 31st St., Newport News, Va. | 36 |
| 3TU | Bach, Earl C. | 413 Cedar St., Allentown, Pa. | 42 |
| 3NN | Bachert, Homer A. | 418 Walnut St., South Bethlehem, Pa. | 18 |
| 3BV | Bacon, Franklin F. | 101 Mansion Ave., Haddonfield, N. J. | 300 |
| 3EN | Bailey, Albert S. | 31 N. 61st St., Philadelphia, Pa. | 120 |
| 3PL | Ballentine, Charles S. | 1810 Germantown Ave., Philadelphia, Pa. | 50 |
| 3MX | Barker, Thomas H., jr. | Gladwyne, Pa. | 11 |
| 3SW | Barnard, Julian W. | Bryn Mawr, Pa. | 33 |
| 3QI | Barnes, Donald K. | 122 N. 61st St., Philadelphia, Pa. | 30 |
| 3MS | Barnhart, Lawrence W. | 1637 N. 6th St., Harrisburg, Pa. | 40 |
| 3KN | Barr, Richard H. | 602 W. Chestnut St., Lancaster, Pa. | 440 |

AMATEUR RADIO STATIONS—THIRD DISTRICT—ALPHABETICALLY BY OWNERS OF STATIONS—Continued.

| Call signal. | Owner of station. | Location of station. | Power. |
|---|---|---|---|
| | | | Watts. |
| 3SY | Barretta, Valroy S. | 518 Elmer St., Vineland, N. J. | 440 |
| 3PE | Bassett, William W. | 205 Mohawk St., Norwood, Pa. | 18 |
| 3DU | Baumann, Frank J. | 160 Carson St., Philadelphia, Pa. | 60 |
| 3AJ | Bausman, George H. | 1228 N. Broadway, Baltimore, Md. | 75 |
| 3SK | Baxley, C. Herbert | 1126 W. North Ave., Baltimore, Md. | 50 |
| 3VM | Baynes, Ralph J. | 812 Vandever Ave., Wilmington, Del. | 36 |
| 3EM | Beaty, Lehman C. | 109 East Ave., Hackettstown, N. J. | 15 |
| 3JS | Beekley, Francis C. | 116 N. Lemon St., Media, Pa. | 72 |
| 3NL | Behm, L. F. F. | 1519 Poplar Grove St., Baltimore, Md. | 250 |
| 3NI | Bell, Albert A., jr. | 8 Catalpha Ave., Hamilton, Md. | 550 |
| 3JQ | Benson, Thomas W. | 252 W. Indiana Ave., Philadelphia, Pa. | 48 |
| 3DC | Bergen, Donald M. | 920 Riverside Ave., Trenton, N. J. | 510 |
| 3JJ | Bergmann, Frederick J. | 1310 Allegheny Ave., Philadelphia, Pa. | 18 |
| 3PJ | Berman, Harry | 315 Central Ave., Staunton, Va. | 495 |
| 3VL | Bernstein, Abe R. | 621 Queen St., Norfolk, Va. | 385 |
| 3MO | Bickel, E. Clifton | 758 High St., Pottstown, Pa. | 550 |
| 3CC | Biddle, Howard L., jr. | 319 Hillside Ave., Jenkintown, Pa. | 12 |
| 3NH | Bierfreund, Max A. | 517 Penn St., Camden, N. J. | 350 |
| 3LQ | Birch, Stanford S. | 45 Washington Ave., Collingswood, N. J. | 100 |
| 3BP | Blackwood, George C. | 5346 Wayne Ave., Philadelphia, Pa. | 120 |
| 3FJ | Blair, Perot E. | 116 W. Lancaster Ave., Ardmore, Pa. | 36 |
| 3SV | Blakeley, George B. | 517 Seneca St., South Bethlehem, Pa. | 330 |
| 3TV | Blanford, Irving | 922 North St., Portsmouth, Va. | 330 |
| 3GF | Blankenship, Elliott E. | 905 5th St. NW., Washington, D. C. | 24 |
| 3TX | Blessing, Joseph M. | 208 Vail St., Hackettstown, N. J. | 10 |
| 3GN | Board of Public Education. | Lehigh Ave. and 8th St., Philadelphia, Pa. | 490 |
| 3SN | Bourgeois, Edmund R. | 901 Central Ave., Ocean City, N. J. | 495 |
| 3KH | Bowen, Albert | 2437 E. Preston St., Baltimore, Md. | 12 |
| 3TL | Bowes, Joseph J. | 2647 Agate St., Philadelphia, Pa. | 18 |
| 3RG | Bowman, Philip W. | 202 E. Montgomery St., Baltimore, Md. | 10 |
| 3BO | Brady, John B. | Somerset, Md. | 330 |
| 3HJ | Bradley, Horace E. | 315 V St. NE., Washington, D. C. | 36 |
| 3UZ | Braidwood, Thomas W. | Anglesea, N. J. | 48 |
| 3NZ | Branin, Manlif L. | 4516 Pacific Ave., Wildwood, N. J. | 18 |
| 3EV | Brannan, Julian L. | 2632 Guilford Ave., Baltimore, Md. | 100 |
| 3SS | Brany, Emil B. | 441 Goepp St., Bethlehem, Pa. | 500 |
| 3EA | Brasheara, Paul B. | Hunter, Va. | 72 |
| 3TP | Brittingham, Otis B. | 1038 North St., Portsmouth, Va. | ...... |
| 3JW | Broadbelt, J. Edward, jr. | 16 Hamilton Ave., Hamilton, Md. | 18 |
| 3JH | Brockman, Francis C. | 3 N. Main St., Nazareth, Pa. | 770 |
| 3BK | Brown, Merritt M. | 2417 N. 16th St., Philadelphia, Pa. | 36 |
| 3OQ | Bryson, Harold E. | Laurel Springs, N. J. | 330 |
| 3BQ | Bugbee, Newton A. | 565 Rutherford Ave., Trenton, N. J. | 330 |
| 3CP | Bunting, George M., jr. | 315 E. Broad St., Chester, Pa. | 500 |
| 3PV | Bunting, Theodore R. | 4202 Granby St., Norfolk, Va. | 440 |
| 3JI | Burdette, Aubrey W. | Adam St., Rockville, Md. | 1,000 |
| 3NW | Burke, Thomas J. | 1750 S. Mole St., Philadelphia, Pa. | 32 |
| 3SM | Burnett, A. Elmo | 418 N. 23d St., Richmond, Va. | 18 |
| 3QB | Butterfield, Harold G. | 6 Burlington St., Bordentown, N. J. | 36 |
| 3UW | Call, J. Richard | 114 Walnut St., Haddonfield, N. J. | 275 |
| 3UJ | Campbell, James D. | 214 Wyncote Rd., Jenkintown, Pa. | 250 |
| 3CO | Campbell, James S. | 1700 S. 60th St., Philadelphia, Pa. | 75 |
| 3BW | Campbell, John W. | 1209 25th St., Philadelphia, Pa. | 30 |
| 3BX | Carpenter, C. E., jr. | 7417 Sprague St., Philadelphia, Pa. | 250 |
| 3RT | Carvin, Frank D. | 1234 S. 53d St., Philadelphia, Pa. | 330 |
| 3UH | Casey, Ellwood R. | 1918 N. 21st St., Philadelphia, Pa. | 18 |
| 3KO | Chalmers, Edwin L. | 125 Burk Ave., Wildwood, N. J. | 36 |
| 3ST | Chappell, Ralph R. | 2112 E. Clay St., Richmond, Va. | 30 |
| 3UT | Cianfrani, Theodore | 1212 Morris St., Philadelphia, Pa. | 45 |

AMATEUR RADIO STATIONS—THIRD DISTRICT—ALPHABETICALLY BY OWNERS OF STATIONS—Continued.

| Call signal. | Owner of station. | Location of station. | Power. |
|---|---|---|---|
| | | | Watts. |
| 3BG | Clark, Edwin T | 1244 Fitzgerald St., Philadelphia, Pa | 12 |
| 3RI | Clough, Thomas A | 2510 W. Thompson St., Philadelphia, Pa. | 12 |
| 3UR | Cohan, William W | 611 Lombard St., Philadelphia, Pa | 24 |
| 3MP | Cohen, Henry | 600 S. 2d St., Philadelphia, Pa | 250 |
| 3II | Coin, Thornley M | Chester Pike and Pine St., Philadelphia, Pa. | 18 |
| 3UB | Colberg, George A | 112 E. Baker Ave., Wildwood, N. J | 500 |
| 3KY | Cole, Jesse James | 1644 N. Felton St., Philadelphia, Pa | 100 |
| 3CL | Coleman, Walter V | 2245 N. 15th St., Philadelphia, Pa | 30 |
| 3AO | Collier, Wilbur H | 820 W. Fayette St., Baltimore, Md | 330 |
| 3OZ | Collins, Benjamin W | 513 Ogden Ave., Swarthmore, Pa | 550 |
| 3FZ | Conley, Charles B | 709 N. 39th St., Philadelphia, Pa | 36 |
| 3IJ | Cooper, James W | 2043 N. College Ave., Philadelphia, Pa | 60 |
| 3LR | Cooper, William F | 14 Ruby St., Lancaster, Pa | 24 |
| 3QT | Corderman, Roy C | R. F. D. No. 6, Hagerstown, Md | 250 |
| 3JZ | Costella, Pietro A | 4313 Baltimore Ave., Philadelphia, Pa | 40 |
| 3PT | Creager, E. Clark | Haverford, Pa | 33 |
| 3BE | Critchlow, Samuel T | 2632 N. 17th St., Philadelphia, Pa | 24 |
| 3BR | Crothers, Harry W | 3033 Susquehanna Ave., Philadelphia, Pa. | 24 |
| 3QJ | Crowley, Robert H | 23 N. Dewey St., Philadelphia, Pa | 30 |
| 3NC | Dalling, Howard | 2942 High St., Camden, N. J | 40 |
| 3FB | Darby, George B., jr | 1 Bala Ave., Bala, Pa | 550 |
| 3TM | Davidson, Delmer S | 2957 N. 7th St., Philadelphia, Pa | 60 |
| 3FA | Davis, Edwin L | 3812 8th St. NW., Washington, D. C | 490 |
| 3VE | Davis, Herbert E | 41 Potter St., Haddonfield, N. J | 10 |
| 3UG | Dearden, Rowland R., 3d. | 11th St. and 69th Ave., Philadelphia, Pa. | 220 |
| 3BI | Deery, Walter J | 5928 Pine St., Philadelphia, Pa | 250 |
| 3QU | Deichman, George L., jr. | Park Heights Ave., Baltimore, Md | 330 |
| 3FN | Deichmiller, Alvin | 1323 S. Carey St., Baltimore, Md | 24 |
| 3FF | Dempster, Warren J | 118 Cleveland Ave., Norwood, Pa | 8 |
| 3LP | Densham, Harry W | 124 Fern Ave., Collingswood, N. J | 220 |
| 3FR | Densten, E. Craig | 2779 W. North Ave., Baltimore, Md | 990 |
| 3JE | Dickerson, E. Stuart, jr | 121 W. Cedar Ave., Merchantville, N. J | 500 |
| 3DJ | Diggins, Edward P. G | 1631 E. Eager St., Baltimore, Md | 18 |
| 3RD | Dimling, Rudolph G. A. | Bancroft Pk., Baltimore, Md | 330 |
| 3EZ | Donovan, Edgar R | 301 W. Norris St., Philadelphia, Pa | 18 |
| 3MA | Downes, Marlboro K | 1002 E. Broad St., Richmond, Va | 40 |
| 3LN | Doyle, John E | 1931 N. Uber St., Philadelphia, Pa | 990 |
| 3FT | Dudley, De Witt C | 3916 Market St., Philadelphia, Pa | 30 |
| 3MD | Dulany, Franklin R | 5 W. Walnut Ave., Merchantville, N. J | 220 |
| 3HP | Duncan, Rodney P | 2039 N. College Ave., Philadelphia, Pa | 100 |
| 3VA | Durham, Wilson N | 316 S. 43d St., Philadelphia, Pa | 60 |
| 3FS | Durkee, Alfred C | 5052 Ludlow St., Philadelphia, Pa | 440 |
| 3AK | Duvall, Edward B | 20 E. Madison St., Baltimore, Md | 250 |
| 3LC | Eberly, Jacob A., jr | 2601 Columbia Ave., Philadelphia, Pa | 250 |
| 3TF | Ebert, Burton E | 194 Atlantic St., Bridgeton, N. J | 28 |
| 3MU | Eckard, Lewis D | 1320 N. Carlisle St., Philadelphia, Pa | 1,000 |
| 3FV | Edwards, Charles | 3345 Ella St., Philadelphia, Pa | 120 |
| 3FO | E. I. du Pont De Nemours Powder Co. | 10th and Market Sts., Wilmington, Del | 448 |
| 3IH | Eisele, Edward. jr | 1116 Glenwood St., Philadelphia, Pa | 66 |
| 3LU | Ellis, J. Elton | 1929 Hoffman St., Philadelphia, Pa | 24 |
| 3CR | Ellis, William G | 2204 N. 15th St., Philadelphia, Pa | 1,000 |
| 3AW | Ely, Harry S | 215 S. Washington St., Baltimore, Md | 275 |
| 3TJ | Emmerson, Frank V | 419 High St., Portsmouth, Va | 36 |
| 3KW | Erickson, Alfred O | Maple Shade, N. J | 20 |
| 3LE | Evans, J. Arthur | 3208 E. Broad St., Richmond, Va | 495 |
| 3DR | Eyster, James A | 317 Washington Ave., Haddonfield, N. J | 540 |
| 3UL | Essick, William W., jr | 520 Franklin St., Reading, Pa | 15 |

AMATEUR RADIO STATIONS—THIRD DISTRICT—ALPHABETICALLY BY OWNERS OF STATIONS—Continued.

| Call signal. | Owner of station. | Location of station. | Power. |
|---|---|---|---|
| | | | *Watts.* |
| 3MJ | Falconer, Norwood B. | 1630 Bolton St., Baltimore, Md. | 60 |
| 3HT | Falkenberg, August E. | 512 Franklin Ter., Baltimore, Md. | 550 |
| 3LM | Faries, Walter R. | Llankerris Rd., Bala, Pa. | 30 |
| 3CT | Farnham, Henry A. | 313 V St. NE., Washington, D. C. | 250 |
| 3IZ | Faunce, B. Warren | 26 Bala Ave., Bala, Pa. | 30 |
| 3OT | Faust, Elmer J. | 728 Hamilton St., Allentown, Pa. | 300 |
| 3TR | Fell, David B. | 19 Park Ave., Ogontz, Pa. | 300 |
| 3GM | Fellows, J. Howard | 5504 Wisconsin Ave., Washington, D. C. | 23 |
| 3JU | Fenimore, Robert S. | 116 Dorchester Ave., Arlington, Md. | 24 |
| 3RC | Fenton, Edward T. | Park Heights Ave., Baltimore, Md. | 330 |
| 3MG | Ferguson, William | 10 Burlington St., Bordentown, N. J. | 80 |
| 3CH | Ferris, Malcolm | 3409 Baring St., Philadelphia, Pa. | 16 |
| 3NR | Ferris, Malcolm | Haverford, Pa. | 154 |
| 3PW | Field, Harry P. | 219 39th St., Norfolk, Va. | 440 |
| 3NM | Finck, Anthony R. | 1120 Girard St., Philadelphia, Pa. | 36 |
| 3AB | Finck, Anthony R. | Port Kennedy, Pa. | 90 |
| 3OP | Fink, Louis, 3d | Laurel Springs, N. J. | 330 |
| 3ET | Fisher, Howes N. | Laurel, Md. | 330 |
| 3DZ | Fisher, Roy S. | 3520 Disston St., Philadelphia, Pa. | 1,000 |
| 3HO | Fithian, William S., jr. | 313 E. Commerce St., Bridgeton, N. J. | 550 |
| 3BH | Flather, Bryan S. | 1358 South Carolina Ave. SE., Washington, D. C. | 16 |
| 3TK | Flather, Bryan S. | Washington, D. C. (portable station) | 12 |
| 3AL | Flentje, George F., jr. | 2023 Eastern Ave., Baltimore, Md. | 12 |
| 3UI | Fletcher, Edward | Parksley, Va. | 120 |
| 3VX | Flounders, Newton | Media, Pa. | 60 |
| 3DN | France, A. Ward | 3544 N. 18th St., Philadelphia, Pa. | 14 |
| 3RE | Frantz, Samuel G. | 64 Morningside St., Princeton, N. J. | 12 |
| 3GW | Frazier, George R. T. | Janvier, N. J. | 30 |
| 3JM | Freedom, Leon | Franklin and 14th Sts., Baltimore, Md. | 500 |
| 3VS | French, Edward R., jr. | 231 9th St. SE., Washington, D. C. | 16 |
| 3EL | Fricke, Henry W. L. | 801 Aisquith St., Baltimore, Md. | 1,000 |
| 3NB | Frye, Marcus, jr. | 616 Elmer St., Vineland, N. J. | 700 |
| 3QH | Fusselman, John | 2436 W. Jefferson St., Philadelphia, Pa. | 18 |
| 3AE | Gaffney, James H. | 1427 E. Hoffman St., Baltimore, Md. | 80 |
| 3RO | Garver, Edwin H. | 118 East Ave., Hagerstown, Md. | 550 |
| 3AY | Gaskins, Richard W. | 931 North St., Portsmouth, Va. | 300 |
| 3CU | Gauss, Harry W. | 221 5th St. SE., Washington, D. C. | 32 |
| 3VJ | Geibel, Henry J. | 1243 N. 30th St., Philadelphia, Pa. | 16 |
| 3EC | Giffin, Sidney H. | 2614 N. Calvert St., Baltimore, Md. | 200 |
| 3UA | Gilbert, Harry P., jr. | 401 Washington St., Portsmouth, Va. | 220 |
| 3AZ | Gillingham, Geo. L., jr. | 4508 Richmond St., Bridesburg, Pa. | 440 |
| 3AR | Gilpin, Levering H. | 2702 N. Calvert St., Baltimore, Md. | 770 |
| 3AV | Glasshoff, H. Irving | 126 N. East Ave., Baltimore, Md. | 9 |
| 3SJ | Glenn, Charles R. | 1919 Penrose Ave., Baltimore, Md. | 24 |
| 3LO | Godfrey, Clarence M. | 915 14th St. SE., Washington, D. C. | 36 |
| 3IF | Godfrey, Earle | 145 St. Charles Pl., Atlantic City, N. J. | 550 |
| 3NK | Godfrey, Howard L. | 2150 N. Corlies St., Philadelphia, Pa. | 30 |
| 3FG | Godfrey, James M. | 49th St. and Florence Ave., Philadelphia, Pa. | 500 |
| 3OY | Gompf, August P. | Howardville, Md. | 64 |
| 3IB | Good, Horace D. | 419 Gordon St., Reading, Pa. | 24 |
| 3KB | Goodall, Alfred B. | 518 Rhode Island Ave. NE., Washington, D. C. | 60 |
| 3OL | Grant, Arthur F. | 2112 Venango St., Philadelphia, Pa. | 100 |
| 3CB | Grant, Ulysses S. | 28 Church St., Newton, N. J. | 90 |
| 3UO | Graves, Edwin D., jr. | Marietta, Pa. | 330 |
| 3KM | Gray, Gerald | 92 Main St., Newton, N. J. | 21 |
| 3OE | Gray, Harry L. | 329 Parker St., Chester, Pa. | 18 |
| 3KF | Green, Anthony J. | 1112 S. Lakewood Ave., Baltimore, Md. | 10 |

AMATEUR RADIO STATIONS—THIRD DISTRICT—ALPHABETICALLY BY OWNERS OF STATIONS—Continued.

| Call signal. | Owner of station. | Location of station. | Power. |
|---|---|---|---|
| | | | Watts. |
| 3LV | Griffin, Aloysius | 706 Pine St., Bristol, Pa | 36 |
| 3VK | Griffith, Dorsey J | 3104 R St. NW., Washington, D. C | 50 |
| 3PZ | Griffith, Elmer G | 1824 Cayuga St., Philadelphia, Pa | 50 |
| 3OC | Grover, H. Marshall | R. F. D. No. 9, West Chester, Pa | 32 |
| 3PR | Hahn, Clarence LeRoy | 200 N. Pulaski St., Baltimore, Md | 12 |
| 3QF | Haig, J. Donald | 118 E. Maple Ave., Merchantville, N. J | 20 |
| 3QO | Hake, Elias G | 614 Goepp St., Bethlehem, Pa | 18 |
| 3QV | Hall, Robert S | Clarke's Lane, Arlington, Md | 48 |
| 3RV | Hamill, McClintock, jr | 1822 Spruce St., Philadelphia, Pa | 18 |
| 3JT | Hampson, George M | 731 Newington Ave., Baltimore, Md | 100 |
| 3JY | Hann, Charles B | 206 E. Preston St., Baltimore, Md | 250 |
| 3HQ | Happold, Harold H | Union Ave., Bala, Pa | 600 |
| 3PH | Harris, Edwin R | 61 N. 61st St., Philadelphia, Pa | 60 |
| 3LY | Harris, William J | 23d and Howard Sts., Chester, Pa | 25 |
| 3QW | Harsch, Lawrence P | Mt. Rainier, Md | 480 |
| 3FM | Hartley, Milton E | 635 E St. NE., Washington, D. C | 18 |
| 3ID | Hasenfus, Joseph F | 2328 N. Fairhill St., Philadelphia, Pa | 75 |
| 3TG | Hatch, William B | 1926 Corlies St., Philadelphia, Pa | 36 |
| 3UN | Hayes, William F | Robbins Nest, Pa | 64 |
| 3BN | Heisley, George E | 1114 Monroe St. NW., Washington, D. C | 500 |
| 3OD | Hemmann, William C | 176 Hampton St., Bridgeton, N. J | 500 |
| 3BJ | Henderson, Frank | 813 Highland Ave., Philadelphia, Pa | 275 |
| 3RK | Hepler, Walter R | 31 E. James St., Lancaster, Pa | 48 |
| 3SZ | Herndon, Landon C | 409 Middle St., Portsmouth, Va | 25 |
| 3HM | Hickman, Paul W | 1917 Green St., Philadelphia, Pa | 330 |
| 3JO | Hicks, A. Willet, jr | 1275 S. Madison St., Allentown, Pa | 60 |
| 3CI | Hillers, John K | 238 1st St. SE., Washington, D. C | 72 |
| 3OO | Hindin, Louis M | 1615 S. 5th St., Philadelphia, Pa | 18 |
| 3ND | Hirst, Arthur C | Haverford, Pa | 400 |
| 3MF | Hitchner, Clyde G | 405 8th St., Vineland, N. J | 32 |
| 3JX | Hoagland, Donald | 43 Lake St., Bridgeton, N. J | 180 |
| 3RU | Hoff, J. Marshall | 4909 Knox St., Philadelphia, Pa | 36 |
| 3BT | Hoffman, W. Hollis | Cold Spring, N. J | 18 |
| 3KK | Hofmann, George A | Engle Ave., Burlington, N. J | 60 |
| 3AQ | Hogan, Harold O | 2630 Guilford Ave., Baltimore, Md | 225 |
| 3MN | Hollinshead, Norman B | 800 White Horse Pike, Oaklyn, N. J | 12 |
| 3PS | Holt, Clarence J | 136 D St. SE., Washington, D. C | 36 |
| 3KT | Holtzinger, Horace K | 5th and Spring Garden Sts., Philadelphia, Pa. | 9 |
| 3SF | Hookey, Anthony C | 1727 Girard Ave., Philadelphia, Pa | 125 |
| 3US | Hopkins, James R | 122 32d St., Newport News, Va | 600 |
| 3GU | Hopkins, Robert E | 2428 Nicholas St., Philadelphia, Pa | 36 |
| 3SC | Hopper, Sterling A | 5909 Green St., Philadelphia, Pa | 30 |
| 3PX | Howard, H. Trumbull | 221 Park Ave., Swarthmore, Pa | 50 |
| 3UP | Howlett, Joseph T. F | 2303 N. Broad St., Philadelphia, Pa. (portable station). | 100 |
| 3UQ | Howlett, Joseph T. F | Mt. Pocono, Pa | 1,000 |
| 3UF | Howlett, Joseph T. F | 2303 N. Broad St., Philadelphia, Pa | 330 |
| 3CY | Hubbs, Edwin E | 145 E. Washington Lane, Philadelphia, Pa. | 130 |
| 3FW | Hunter, Edwin J | 2429 E. Cumberland St., Philadelphia, Pa. | 385 |
| 3QQ | Husk, Dayton E | 34 John St., Dorranceton, Pa | 425 |
| 3MZ | Husted, Mortimer I | 9 Dorchester Rd., Baltimore, Md | 40 |
| 3FX | Hutchinson, Samuel J | 944 Maple Ave., Collingswood, N. J | 440 |
| 3SE | Hyatt, C. Brown | 310 Carlisle Ave., York, Pa | 330 |
| 3LB | Iddings, Frederick T | 1608 Linden Ave., Baltimore, Md | 990 |
| 3CJ | Imfield, Fred H | 117 N. 6th St., Philadelphia, Pa | 330 |
| 3IE | Jacobson, Bernard H | 3803 Park Heights Ave., Baltimore, Md | 550 |
| 3HW | James, Herman | 239 Kaighn Ave., Camden, N. J | 15 |

AMATEUR RADIO STATIONS—THIRD DISTRICT—ALPHABETICALLY BY OWNERS OF STATIONS—Continued.

| Call signal. | Owner of station. | Location of station. | Power. |
|---|---|---|---|
| | | | Watts. |
| 3BL | Jaquett, Maurice J. | 3156 N. Carlisle St., Philadelphia, Pa. | 18 |
| 3RY | Jarvis, Thomas R. | 508 Cedar Lane, Swarthmore, Pa. | 40 |
| 3CS | Johnson, Burch R. | Oak Lane, Pa. | 330 |
| 3IG | Johnson, Earle K. | 127 North Carolina Ave., South, Atlantic City, N. J. | 150 |
| 3OG | Jones, John W. | 328 Cooper St., Camden, N. J. | 30 |
| 3NP | Jones, La Frantz. | 923 French St., Wilmington, Del. | 24 |
| 3GG | Jones, Winters. | 728 N. Monroe St., Baltimore, Md. | 12 |
| 3TZ | Kellert, Charles. | 1208 St. Matthew St., Baltimore, Md. | 24 |
| 3CV | Kelley, George W., jr. | 1738 N. 16th St., Philadelphia, Pa. | 275 |
| 3KC | Kendall, Raymond V. | 1813 N. Milton Ave., Baltimore, Md. | 20 |
| 3OB | Kennedy, Ignatius L. | 28 S. Market St., Frederick, Md. | 24 |
| 3EP | Kennedy, Joseph H. | 2052 E. Fletcher St., Philadelphia, Pa. | 275 |
| 3SH | Kenyon, Walter R. | 1838 Columbia Ave., Philadelphia, Pa. | 511 |
| 3OK | Kerr, William C. | Frederick Rd., Catonsville, Md. | 24 |
| 3TT | Kindt, Charles F., jr. | 301 Washington Lane, Jenkintown, Pa. | 275 |
| 3MM | King, Albert. | 209 St. Mary St., Burlington, N. J. | 250 |
| 3RP | Kirby, Elmer S. | 5300 Glenmore Ave., Philadelphia, Pa. | 20 |
| 3RH | Kline, H. N. Gay. | Central Ave., Sea Isle City, N. J. | 550 |
| 3LX | Knight, A. Stanley. | 311 N. 11th St., Richmond, Va. | 18 |
| 3KX | Knight, G. Webber, jr. | 1545 Walnut St., Harrisburg, Pa. | 1000 |
| 3IQ | Knoll, Lloyd M. | 3260 Chestnut St., Philadelphia, Pa. | 40 |
| 3VB | Knowles, Edward P., jr. | 648 Princeton Ave., Trenton, N. J. | 18 |
| 3JN | Korab, Harry E. | 418 W. Clay St., Richmond, Va. | 490 |
| 3FQ | Krainer, John B. | Washington St., Laurel, Md. | 330 |
| 3BB | Kralovec, Dalibor. | 3535 N. Water St., Philadelphia, Pa. | 32 |
| 3HX | Kratz, Herman A. | 2001 W. Pratt St., Baltimore, Md. | 173 |
| 3TY | Krone, Julian E. | 2908 West Ave., Newport News, Va. | 24 |
| 3EI | Kumler, Kelvin C. | Kensington, Md. | 330 |
| 3ML | Kutz, Charles E. | 1804 Green St., Harrisburg, Pa. | 1,000 |
| 3CF | Laager, Creston F. | 1029 Belmont Ave., West Philadelphia, Pa. | 18 |
| 3GV | Laber, Joseph M. | 2422 N. Gratz St., Philadelphia, Pa. | 18 |
| 3OS | Lafferty, Francis A. | 1717 Ingersoll St., Philadelphia, Pa. | 18 |
| 3GZ | Laird, J. Ira. | 25 Strode Ave., Coatesville, Pa. | 30 |
| 3VD | Lamb, Franklin. | 623 Elmer St., Vineland, N. J. | 200 |
| 3ME | Lamdin, Charles R. | 4016 Edmondson Ave., Baltimore, Md. | 500 |
| 3QG | Landis, Harold O. | 341 N. Front St., Reading, Pa. | 36 |
| 3TC | Landis, Harry. | 2436 Corlies St., Philadelphia, Pa. | 36 |
| 3CW | Lange, J. Robert. | 1938 Lemmon St., Baltimore, Md. | 16 |
| 3QC | Lanning, John M. | 77 E. Commerce St., Bridgeton, N. J. | 550 |
| 3ER | Larrimore, James F. | 1814 N. Calvert St., Baltimore, Md. | 550 |
| 3RZ | La Rue, Lester J. | 701 Washington St., Hackettstown, N. J. | 15 |
| 3RJ | La Rue, Robert G. | 264 Main St., Hackettstown, N. J. | 7 |
| 3EB | La Salle College. | 1240 N. Broad St., Philadelphia, Pa. | 715 |
| 3SO | Law, Bartley H. | 301-A S. 17½ St., Reading, Pa. | 30 |
| 3VI | Laws, J. Waltham, jr. | 230 Park Ave., Swarthmore, Pa. | 36 |
| 3VO | Leayman, Charles S. | Girard College, Philadelphia, Pa. | 306 |
| 3JV | Lehr, William. | 3912 Maine Ave., Baltimore, Md. | 36 |
| 3BZ | Leister, Fayette. | 68th and Jefferson Sts., Philadelphia, Pa. | 36 |
| 3TW | Leslie, Malcolm C. | 749 Asbury Ave., Ocean City, N. J. | 18 |
| 3LA | Levin, Davis. | 44 S. Bond St., Baltimore, Md. | 30 |
| 3OH | Levy, Lewis. | 243 E. Pearl St., Burlington, N. J. | 20 |
| 3RB | Lewis, Ellis. | 658 Linden Ave., York, Pa. | 880 |
| 3UU | Lewis, Joseph W. | 26th and Master Sts., Philadelphia, Pa. | 880 |
| 3DW | Lowery, Norman S. | 1406 3d St. NW., Washington, D. C. | 45 |
| 3UX | Loughlin, John K. | 2215 Hunting Park Ave., Philadelphia, Pa. | 16 |
| 3DI | Lowell, Percival D. | 2838 27th St. NW., Washington, D. C. | 330 |
| 3DX | Lukens, Wilfred P. | 527 Spring Mill Ave., Conshohocken, Pa. | 605 |
| 3PM | Lusse, Richard N. | 2855 N. 8th St., Philadelphia, Pa. | 60 |

AMATEUR RADIO STATIONS—THIRD DISTRICT—ALPHABETICALLY BY OWNERS OF STATIONS—Continued.

| Call signal. | Owner of station. | Location of station. | Power. |
|---|---|---|---|
| | | | *Watts.* |
| 3LG | Lyon, Harry H | Hyattsville, Md | 500 |
| 3GH | MacDonald, Stuart | 209 N. 53d St., Philadelphia, Pa | 330 |
| 3DM | MacFeeters, John | 1538 N. Gratz St., Philadelphia, Pa | 32 |
| 3EQ | MacKendrick, Robert G | 307 Amos Land Rd., Holmes, Pa | 1,000 |
| 3SG | Maris, Carroll B | 47 W. Stratford Ave., Lansdowne, Pa | 18 |
| 3ES | Martin, E. Linton | 315 Radcliffe St., Bristol, Pa | 64 |
| 3LK | Martin, Robert C | 2500 N. 19th St., Philadelphia, Pa | 25 |
| 3ON | Matos, Walter A | 309 College Ave., Swarthmore, Pa | 120 |
| 3DO | Maxson, Donald L | Kensington, Md | 330 |
| 3GS | McCafferty, Rea B | 750 S. 60th St., Philadelphia, Pa | 72 |
| 3JL | McCaskey, Edward R | 1029 Main St., Darby, Pa | 500 |
| 3RL | McClellan, Frederick W | 180 Main St., Hackettstown, N. J | 6 |
| 3LZ | McCullough, Earl N | 125 N. Gross St., Philadelphia, Pa | 10 |
| 3DP | McDonald, Lester B | 36 E. Tulpehocken St., Philadelphia, Pa | 330 |
| 3KA | McEuen, Earl W | 705 Bath St., Bristol, Pa | 100 |
| 3PK | McGear, Herbert K | 3014 W. York St., Philadelphia, Pa | 18 |
| 3EY | McIntyre, William | Oak Lane, Pa | 440 |
| 3MB | McKee, W. Wesley | 1411 W. Ontario St., Philadelphia, Pa | 18 |
| 3VR | McVicker, W. Patton | 635 Mohawk Ave., Norwood, Pa | 1,000 |
| 3GL | Meck, Michael | 1550 N. Allison St., Philadelphia, Pa | 36 |
| 3IM | Mellon, Charles E | 116 Pennsylvania Ave., Coatesville, Pa | 950 |
| 3RA | Messinger, Miles B | 309 N. Linden St., Bethlehem, Pa | 24 |
| 3PD | Meyer, Emil J | 1919 Green St., Philadelphia, Pa | 36 |
| 3AC | Miller, Alfred H | 6358 McCallum St., Philadelphia, Pa | 18 |
| 3DY | Miller, Frederick E | 3134 N. Rosewood St., Philadelphia, Pa | 18 |
| 3GQ | Miller, Kelly, jr | 430 College St. NW., Washington, D. C | 15 |
| 3TD | Miller, Harry G | 1526 2d Ave., York, Pa | 500 |
| 3NU | Mitchener, Frederick D | 119 Pond St., Bristol, Pa | 100 |
| 3IW | Mitchener, Harold G | 528 Swain St., Bristol, Pa | 18 |
| 3AI | Mohr, Paul D | 537 Chestnut St., Emaus, Pa | 15 |
| 3CK | Moody, Matthew C | 2511 S. 7th St., Philadelphia, Pa | 12 |
| 3OM | Mooney, John, jr | 2903 Girard Ave., Philadelphia, Pa | 36 |
| 3EK | Moore, Daniel D | 2308 N. Charles St., Baltimore, Md | 250 |
| 3NQ | Morley, Augustin H | 1008 McKean St., Philadelphia, Pa | 27 |
| 3IC | Morris, Edward P | 3114 D St., Philadelphia, Pa | 18 |
| 3UD | Mundy, Elmer | 21 W. Airy St., Norristown, Pa | 275 |
| 3HS | Murray, Eugene M | Grays Lane, Haverford, Pa | 990 |
| 3DL | Muth, Gerard J | 16 Melvin Ave., Catonsville, Md | 330 |
| 3KP | Myers, Roy R | Main St., South Perkasie, Pa | 72 |
| 3MI | Nash, Clifford S | 3615 N. 19th St., Philadelphia, Pa | 18 |
| 3QY | Nees, Milton | 500 Chester Ave., Norwood, Pa | 36 |
| 3TI | Nichols, Crawford V | 218 Crawford St., Portsmouth, Va | 30 |
| 3HL | Nielsen, Harold, jr | 8751 Frankford Ave., Holmesburg, Pa | 18 |
| 3VU | Nikirk, Thomas E | 411 12th St. SE., Washington, D. C | 20 |
| 3RX | Nisley, Paul H | 2406 6th St., Harrisburg, Pa | 40 |
| 3KD | Noel, James F | 228 2d St. NE., Washington, D. C | 72 |
| 3GO | Norcross, Earl L | 216 Roberts Ave., Glenside, Pa | 250 |
| 3QA | O'Brien, Francis J | 2226 N. Carlisle St., Philadelphia, Pa | 500 |
| 3VZ | Orlando, Frank | 1948 S. 11th St., Philadelphia, Pa | 16 |
| 3UY | Parker, Herbert H | Rockford, Wilmington, Del | 72 |
| 3HE | Parks, Laurence W | 3812 Hamilton St., Philadelphia, Pa | 12 |
| 3DS | Parks, Walther A | 901 Lawrence St. NE., Washington, D. C | 500 |
| 3AT | Parsons, Harry S | 13 N. Carey St., Baltimore, Md | 9 |
| 3NE | Passano, Leonard W | 2504 Maryland Ave., Baltimore, Md | 330 |
| 3OW | Patchel, Robert E | 532 S. 15th St., Philadelphia, Pa | 40 |
| 3AP | Patzschke, August | Old Harford Rd., Hamilton, Md | 990 |
| 3CG | Pauly, Robert | 204 N. New St., Nazareth, Pa | 18 |
| 3IL | Pawson, James M | 336 W. Logan St., Philadelphia, Pa | 24 |
| 3MT | Peck, G. Warren | 2531 Shirley Ave., Baltimore, Md | 300 |

AMATEUR RADIO STATIONS—THIRD DISTRICT—ALPHABETICALLY BY OWNERS OF STATIONS—Continued.

| Call signal. | Owner of station. | Location of station. | Power. |
|---|---|---|---|
| | | | Watts. |
| 3GI | Pelham, Fred B | 603 Howard Pl. NW., Washington, D. C. | 74 |
| 3PN | Pemberton, Henry R | 1008 Clinton St., Philadelphia, Pa | 36 |
| 3TO | Pent, Robert E | 305 Wyncote Rd., Jenkintown, Pa | 36 |
| 3DB | Perry, Willard P., jr | Titusville, N. J | 48 |
| 3DA | Peterson, Raymond E | 1602 S. Frazier St., Philadelphia, Pa | 16 |
| 3UK | Peyser, Philip S | 3208 West Ave., Newport News, Va | 24 |
| 3IX | Philadelphia School of Wireless Telegraphy. | Park Building, Broad and Cherry Sts., Philadelphia, Pa. | 495 |
| 3RM | Phillips, Albert L | 612 N. 2d St., Reading, Pa | 128 |
| 3AD | Phillips, William J | 1530 Orleans St., Baltimore, Md | 250 |
| 3TA | Piper, S. Webster | 133 E. Antietam St., Hagerstown, Md | 200 |
| 3LD | Pisani, Sylvester | 226 N. Calhoun St., Baltimore, Md | 36 |
| 3HH | Place, Samuel W | 662 Stanbridge St., Norristown, Pa | 660 |
| 3MW | Poalk, James L., jr | 325 Summit Ave., Jenkintown, Pa | 60 |
| 3NF | Pohlig, William T | Bala, Pa | 275 |
| 3SP | Polk, Charles P | 33 E. Walnut Ave., Merchantville, N. J | 20 |
| 3OJ | Pool, J. Alexander | 114 E. Montgomery Ave., Ardmore, Pa | 33 |
| 3TE | Poorman, Arthur E | Second St., Highspire, Pa | 275 |
| 3PF | Postpichal, Otto I | 1617 S. 16th St., Philadelphia, Pa | 26 |
| 3EH | Powell, Edwin H | 1206 E. Capitol St., Washington, D. C | 36 |
| 3EJ | Primrose, Donald L | 2814 St. Paul St., Baltimore, Md | 440 |
| 3PG | Proudley, Charles E | 21 R St. NW., Washington, D. C | 32 |
| 3IA | Puff, Stephen F | 222 Wildwood Ave., Wildwood, N. J | 60 |
| 3FE | Rabl, Samuel | 419 3d St., Baltimore, Md | 30 |
| 3NS | Radio Apparatus Co | 258 Beech St., Pottstown, Pa | 1,000 |
| 3NT | Rafferty, John A | 642 Pine St., Bristol, Pa | 24 |
| 3KU | Rakestraw, Charles E., jr | 110 E. Pine Ave., Wildwood, N. J | 440 |
| 3RN | Ramsey, Howard N | 96 W. Sharpnack St., Philadelphia, Pa | 30 |
| 3VC | Rancetelli, Ernani | 1151 S. 9th St., Philadelphia, Pa | 66 |
| 3KR | Rede, G. Ross | 210 W. Madison St., Baltimore, Md | 100 |
| 3RW | Redgrave, De Witt C | 1505 Bolton St., Baltimore, Md | 250 |
| 3EF | Reiff, W. Norman | 916 Fayette St., Conshohocken, Pa | 330 |
| 3SA | Requa, Fred A | 4112 Frederick Ave., Baltimore, Md | 272 |
| 3QE | Richards, Clift R., jr | 9 W. Irving St., Chevy Chase, Md | 330 |
| 3DK | Richardson, Thomas L | Quarantine, Curtis Bay, Md | 30 |
| 3BF | Richter, Harry A | 2733 N. Fairhill St., Philadelphia, Pa | 60 |
| 3HY | Richwien, Louis C | 2014 W. Pratt St., Baltimore, Md | 24 |
| 3JC | Riley, Arthur S | 147 Bank St., Bridgeton, N. J | 385 |
| 3KZ | Roberts, Harold A | Kromer Ave., Berwyn, Pa | 250 |
| 3NV | Robey, V. C. K | 117 Commerce St., Rockville, Md | 1,000 |
| 3GX | Robinson, George C | 607 N. 10th St., Richmond, Va | 108 |
| 3QS | Roekens, Noel H | Glenside, Pa | 330 |
| 3RR | Roeller, Harold C | 66 Chestnut St., Pottstown, Pa | 280 |
| 3GB | Rohrich, George J | Bethesda, Md | 440 |
| 3VV | Rose, Harold W | 2602 Connecticut Ave., Washington D. C. | 330 |
| 3UV | Ross, John W | 1314 Lewellyn Ave., Norfolk, Va | 440 |
| 3VP | Rothman, Charles | 1837 Wilhelm St., Baltimore, Md | 18 |
| 3QD | Rynick, George M., jr | Catonsville, Md | 460 |
| 3EW | Scheffey, Ralph B | 346 Lafayette St., Bristol, Pa | 250 |
| 3FK | Schleher, Paul H | 1912 N. Marvine St., Philadelphia, Pa | 42 |
| 3PA | Schlichting, E. N. E | 224 E. Burk Ave., Wildwood, N. J | 30 |
| 3JG | Scholl, Warren | 179 Kalos St., Wissahickon, Pa | 54 |
| 3IU | Schramm, Carl | 721 Peach St., Vineland, N. J | 330 |
| 3HN | Schuck, Leon H | 2441 N. 8th St., Philadelphia, Pa | 550 |
| 3AU | Schultz, Henry | 14 S. Arlington Ave., Baltimore, Md | 275 |
| 3OU | Schwering, Harry C., jr | 1533 S. 16th St., Philadelphia, Pa | 26 |
| 3GT | Searle, William J., jr | 164 Harrison Ave., Glenside, Pa | 300 |
| 3SU | Seeley, Alfred J | 241 N. Wilton St., Philadelphia, Pa | 18 |
| 3VT | Seidenberg, Frank | 4219 Parrish St., Philadelphia, Pa | 72 |

AMATEUR RADIO STATIONS—THIRD DISTRICT—ALPHABETICALLY BY OWNERS OF STATIONS—Continued.

| Call signal. | Owner of station. | Location of station. | Power. |
|---|---|---|---|
| | | | *Watts.* |
| 3SQ | Sellers, William, jr. | 115 Glenn Rd., Ardmore, Pa. | 250 |
| 3QZ | Service, Charles A., jr. | Bala, Pa. | 550 |
| 3SD | Shafer, Albert G. | 201 Sylvan St., Rutledge, Pa. | 15 |
| 3SL | Shaw, Lemuel A. | 514 D St. SE., Washington, D. C. | 24 |
| 3EU | Shelley, F. Cheston | 2612 Hampden St., Baltimore, Md. | 40 |
| 3LF | Shreiner, Carl H. | 37 E. James St., Lancaster, Pa. | 50 |
| 3OR | Signor, Frederick H. | 717 7th St. SE., Washington, D. C. | 36 |
| 3FD | Simon, Walter | 1234 Carroll St., Baltimore, Md. | 36 |
| 3SX | Simons, Joseph M. | 4553 Pulaski Ave., Philadelphia, Pa. | 36 |
| 3RQ | Skene, Andrew A. | 4717 Northwood Ave., Philadelphia, Pa. | 24 |
| 3PP | Skinner, William H. | 117 Glenn Rd., Ardmore, Pa. | 12 |
| 3NO | Sleath, Robert W. | 305 Schuylkill Ave., Reading, Pa. | 6 |
| 3DQ | Smith, G. Victor | 300 Mill St., Bristol, Pa. | 800 |
| 3PU | Smith, Hubert B. | 1721 N. 17th St., Philadelphia, Pa. | 330 |
| 3DF | Smith, Randolph | 2647 N. Calvert St., Baltimore, Md. | 360 |
| 3FH | Smith, Sewall P. | Wyndcrest Ave., Catonsville, Md. | 440 |
| 3UE | Smith, William M., jr. | 433 King St., Portsmouth, Va. | 54 |
| 3HG | Smith, W. P. | 715 N. 49th St., Philadelphia, Pa. | 250 |
| 3JR | Snow, Harold A. | 4715 Wisconsin Ave., Washington, D. C. | 30 |
| 3IK | Snyder, Harry H. | Cold Spring, N. J. | 60 |
| 3EG | Snyder, James R. | 319 Vassar Ave., Swarthmore, Pa. | 550 |
| 3DH | Stahl, Harry E., jr. | 275 Bellevue Ave., Trenton, N. J. | 200 |
| 3KI | Stanley, John S. | Laurel, Md. | 500 |
| 3VY | Stannard, Charles F., jr. | 800 N. 63d St., Philadelphia, Pa. | 24 |
| 3BY | Statz, Henry M. | 709 Euclid St. NW., Washington, D. C. | 48 |
| 3GY | Staub, James | Sluice Rd., Burlington Township, N. J. | 60 |
| 3NY | Steele, Sherman E. | 122 S. Queen St., Lancaster, Pa. | 200 |
| 3BC | Stephen C. Chester | Laurel Springs, N. J. | 72 |
| 3HI | Stepp, John W. | 630 Morton St. NW., Washington, D. C. | 48 |
| 3JP | Sterns, Morton W. | 29 N. Main St., Bethlehem, Pa. | 1,000 |
| 3VH | Stickell, Daniel R. | 449 Potomac Ave., Hagerstown, Md. | 550 |
| 3HK | Stokes, Josiah T. | 15 W. Stiles Ave., Collingswood, N. J. | 24 |
| 3UM | Strailman, Gilbert T. | 649 29th St., Newport News, Va. | 18 |
| 3PQ | Strieby, Malcolm | 112 Rutgers Ave., Swarthmore, Pa. | 1,000 |
| 3IT | Stritzel, Alfred H. | 12 North Carolina Ave., South, Atlantic City, N. J. | 250 |
| 3AS | Stumptner, Albert G. | Old Harford Rd., Hamilton, Md. | 440 |
| 3QR | Sullivan, Frank J. | 2233 S. Carlisle St., Philadelphia, Pa. | 60 |
| 3TH | Tabb, Vincent W. | 26 Court St., Portsmouth, Va. | 30 |
| 3OF | Talbot, George L. | 506 14th St., Highlandtown, Md. | 165 |
| 3DE | Tallman, Frank G., jr. | 1102 Broome St., Wilmington, Del. | 550 |
| 3QL | Tapley, Robert E. | Hampton Court, Norfolk, Va. | 18 |
| 3GC | Taylor, B. Irving | 300 Hillside Ave., Jenkintown, Pa. | 20 |
| 3HB | Taylor, Sidney L. M. | 321 Mohawk Ave., Norwood, Pa. | 120 |
| 3UC | Teller, Leslie W. | 4012 7th St. NW., Washington, D. C. | 210 |
| 3HC | Thackery, Samuel J. | 4232 Paul St., Philadelphia, Pa. | 18 |
| 3HR | Thornton, Earl H. | 131 E. Durham St., Philadelphia, Pa. | 550 |
| 3NG | Tichenor, George C. | 123 S. Chester Rd., Swarthmore, Pa. | 15 |
| 3CX | Toboldt, William K. | 2412 N. 16th St., Philadelphia, Pa. | 72 |
| 3IY | Tolbert, Warren | 7037 Hegerman St., Philadelphia, Pa. | 24 |
| 3VF | Tompkins, E. Randolph | 526 9th Ave. SW., Roanoke, Va. | 350 |
| 3PY | Torrisi, Salvatore | 1710 S. 11th St., Philadelphia, Pa. | 32 |
| 3AH | Treide, Carl L. | 2402 E. Baltimore St., Baltimore, Md. | 315 |
| 3RS | Tripp, George B., jr. | 113 S. Front St., Harrisburg, Pa. | 300 |
| 3GK | Troth, Raymond H. | 3350 N. 18th St., Philadelphia, Pa. | 36 |
| 3MQ | Trumbower, Raymond | 24 Collingswood Ave., Oaklyn, N. J. | 18 |
| 3TS | Turner, Alfred W. | 61 Hampton St., Bridgeton, N. J. | 18 |
| 3DV | Uphoff, Frank B. | 3649 York Rd., Philadelphia, Pa. | 18 |
| 3VQ | Uphoff, Frank B. | 87-89 Thorofare Ave., Margate City, N. J. | 80 |

AMATEUR RADIO STATIONS—THIRD DISTRICT—ALPHABETICALLY BY OWNERS OF STATIONS—Continued.

| Call signal. | Owner of station. | Location of station. | Power. |
|---|---|---|---|
| | | | *Watts.* |
| 3VW | Uphoff, Frank B | Philadelphia, Pa. (portable station) | 8 |
| 3OA | Urner, Joseph W | 215 E. 2d St., Frederick, Md | 24 |
| 3KV | Van Duyne, Carlton | 163 Lake Ave., Boonton, N. J | 250 |
| 3CM | Van Horn, J. Clunn | 5127 Arch St., Philadelphia, Pa | 500 |
| 3LL | Van Horn, J. Orville | 1427 N. 17th St., Philadelphia, Pa | 12 |
| 3SB | Van Hulsteyn, J. M. C | Cockeysville, Md | 250 |
| 3QM | Varnes, Earl W | 8 Race St., Cambridge, Md | 48 |
| 3RF | Vaughan, Charles A | 118 Pastorius St., Philadelphia, Pa | 36 |
| 3TN | Venn, Silas N | 900 Vandever Ave., Wilmington, Del | 250 |
| 3IN | Vogel, Charles C | 1244 N. Taney St., Philadelphia, Pa | 18 |
| 3KL | Wagner, William H | 121 Obold St., West Reading, Pa | 18 |
| 3LW | Waite, John W | 2938 N. 3d St., Philadelphia, Pa | 55 |
| 3IR | Wallace, Lewis J | 2728 Poplar St., Philadelphia, Pa | 18 |
| 3AN | Walsh, Maurice L | 819 W. Lexington St., Baltimore, Md | 1,000 |
| 3PO | Watson, James B | 2412 S. Rosewood St., Philadelphia, Pa | 54 |
| 3VN | Ways, Clarence I | 10 Hanover St., Cumberland, Md | 550 |
| 3AG | Weant, Clarence H | 1546 Aisquith St., Baltimore, Md | 275 |
| 3IS | Weaver, Howard A | 5545 Webster Ter., Philadelphia, Pa | 24 |
| 3QP | Weber, Henry M | Mt. Rainier, Md | 18 |
| 3FC | Weik, Charles F | 7148 Vandyke St., Philadelphia, Pa | 24 |
| 3LH | Weiss, Leonard | 1608 South St., Philadelphia, Pa | 40 |
| 3NX | Wells, John M | 6118 Boynton St., Philadelphia, Pa | 42 |
| 3DT | Wells, William C., jr | 124 S. 66th St., Philadelphia, Pa | 495 |
| 3AF | West, William M | 1407 N. Central Ave., Baltimore, Md | 105 |
| 3FI | Wever, John A | 238 S. Patterson Park Ave., Baltimore, Md | 21 |
| 3KQ | Wexler, Bernard | 431 Dickinson St., Philadelphia, Pa | 495 |
| 3CZ | Wheatley, Douglas N | 405 N. 32d St., Philadelphia, Pa | 48 |
| 3MY | Wheeler, William A | 208 9th St. NE., Washington, D. C | 500 |
| 3MV | Whitaker, Lorenzo D | 937 14th St. SE., Washington, D. C | 36 |
| 3DG | White, Norman P | 19 General Greene Ave., Trenton, N. J | 18 |
| 3OX | Wick, Arthur | 2406 S. Percy St., Philadelphia, Pa | 12 |
| 3NJ | Wicks, Preston S | 2206 Ruskin Ave., Baltimore, Md | 550 |
| 3CD | Widmyer, John H | 1 S. Duke St., Lancaster, Pa | 16 |
| 3FL | Wiler, William L | 1735 Arch St., Philadelphia, Pa | 15 |
| 3SI | Williams, Harvey | 3523 N. 18th St., Philadelphia, Pa | 1,000 |
| 3KS | Williams, John McC | Elkridge, Md | 16 |
| 3IV | Wilson, Willard S | 705 Adams St., Wilmington, Del | 490 |
| 3MK | Wilson, William P | 2400 Barclay St., Baltimore, Md | 60 |
| 3AM | Wise, Leonard J | 419 N. Patterson Park Ave., Baltimore, Md | 80 |
| 3HA | Wiseman, Luther B | 330 W St. NW., Washington, D. C | 16 |
| 3HU | Witmer, Charles T | 133 W. Buttonwood St., Phildelphia, Pa | 330 |
| 3JD | Wolcott, Roger G | 224 41st St., Norfolk, Va | 440 |
| 3MC | Wolf, Henry S | 2405 E. Fairmount Ave., Baltimore, Md | 550 |
| 3BS | Wolff, William J | 2422 S. Iseminger St., Philadelphia, Pa | 24 |
| 3OI | Wolle, Aubrey B | 906 Prospect Ave., Bethlehem, Pa | 330 |
| 3VG | Wood, Frederick B | Bryn Mawr, Pa | 330 |
| 3GR | Wood, Richard M | Keyworth Ave., Baltimore, Md | 330 |
| 3QX | Worcester, Paul S | 1911 Green St., Harrisburg, Pa | 40 |
| 3DD | Work, Ashton G | 807 St. Charles Pl., Ocean City, N. J | 250 |
| 3KJ | Worrest, Howard A | 629 N. Duke St., Lancaster, Pa | 130 |
| 3FU | Wunder, William F | 6211 Germantown St., Philadelphia, Pa | 80 |
| 3CQ | Yeager, George R | 718 S. American St., Philadelphia, Pa | 50 |
| 3TB | Young Men's Christian Association. | 10th and Orange Sts., Wilmington, Del | 330 |
| 3NA | Zang, Joseph A., jr | 700 N. 37th St., Philadelphia, Pa | 440 |
| 3QN | Zinszer, Harvey A | 920 S. 6th St., Allentown, Pa | 120 |
| 3PB | Zorger, Daniel H | 409 Kelker St., Harrisburg, Pa | 1,000 |

## Amateur Radio Stations—Third District—Continued.

ALPHABETICALLY BY CALL SIGNALS.

| Call signal. | Owner of station. |
|---|---|
| 3AA | Ashmore, John W. |
| 3AB | Finck, Anthony R. |
| 3AC | Miller, Alfred H. |
| 3AD | Phillips, William J. |
| 3AE | Gaffney, James H. |
| 3AF | West, William M. |
| 3AG | Weant, Clarence H. |
| 3AH | Treide, Carl L. |
| 3AI | Mohr, Paul D. |
| 3AJ | Bausman, George H. |
| 3AK | Duvall, Edward B. |
| 3AL | Flentje, George F., jr. |
| 3AM | Wise, Leonard J. |
| 3AN | Walsh, Maurice L. |
| 3AO | Collier, Wilbur H. |
| 3AP | Patzschke, August. |
| 3AQ | Hogan, Harold O. |
| 3AR | Gilpin, Levering H. |
| 3AS | Stumptner, Albert G. |
| 3AT | Parsons, Harry S. |
| 3AU | Schultz, Henry. |
| 3AV | Glashoff, H. Irving. |
| 3AW | Ely, Harry S. |
| 3AX | Arner, Oscar Q. |
| 3AY | Gaskins, Richard W. |
| 3AZ | Gillingham, George L., jr. |
| 3BB | Kralovec, Dalibor. |
| 3BC | Stephen, C. Chester. |
| 3BD | Allen, Percival R. |
| 3BE | Critchlow, Samuel T. |
| 3BF | Richter, Harry A. |
| 3BG | Clark, Edwin T. |
| 3BH | Flather, Bryan S. |
| 3BI | Deery, Walter J. |
| 3BJ | Henderson, Frank. |
| 3BK | Brown, Merritt M. |
| 3BL | Jaquett, Maurice J. |
| 3BM | Allen, George Y. |
| 3BN | Heisley, George E. |
| 3BO | Brady, John B. |
| 3BP | Blackwood, George C. |
| 3BQ | Bugbee, Newton A. |
| 3BR | Crothers, Harry W. |
| 3BS | Wolff, William J. |
| 3BT | Hoffman, W. Hollis. |
| 3BU | Austrian, Harry D. |
| 3BV | Bacon, Franklin F. |
| 3BW | Campbell, John W. |
| 3BX | Carpenter, C. E., jr. |
| 3BY | Statz, Henry M. |
| 3BZ | Leister, Fayette. |
| 3CA | Adelberger, Adrian J. |
| 3CB | Grant, Ulysses S. |
| 3CC | Biddle, Howard L., jr. |
| 3CD | Widmyer, John H. |
| 3CF | Laager, Creston F. |
| 3CG | Pauly, Robert. |
| 3CH | Ferris, Malcolm. |
| 3CI | Hillers, John K. |
| 3CJ | Imfield, Fred H. |
| 3CK | Moody, Matthew C. |
| 3CL | Coleman, Walter V. |
| 3CM | Van Horn, J. Clunn. |
| 3CN | Ashton, Leon W. |
| 3CO | Campbell, James S. |
| 3CP | Bunting, George M., jr. |
| 3CQ | Yeager, George R. |
| 3CR | Ellis, William G. |
| 3CS | Johnson, Burch R. |
| 3CT | Farnham, Henry A. |
| 3CU | Gauss, Harry W. |
| 3CV | Kelley, George W., jr. |
| 3CW | Lange, J. Robert. |
| 3CX | Toboldt, William K. |
| 3CY | Hubbs, Edwin E. |
| 3CZ | Wheatley, Douglas M. |
| 3DA | Peterson, Raymond E. |
| 3DB | Perry, Willard P., jr. |
| 3DC | Bergen, Donald M. |
| 3DD | Work, Ashton G. |
| 3DE | Tallman, Frank G., jr. |
| 3DF | Smith, Randolph. |
| 3DG | White, Norman P. |
| 3DH | Stahl, Harry E., jr. |
| 3DI | Lowell, Percival D. |
| 3DJ | Diggins, Edward P. G. |
| 3DK | Richardson, Thomas L. |
| 3DL | Muth, Gerard J. |
| 3DM | MacFeeters, John. |
| 3DN | France, A. Ward. |
| 3DO | Maxson, Donald L. |
| 3DP | McDonald, Lester B. |
| 3DQ | Smith, G. Victor. |
| 3DR | Eyster, James A. |
| 3DS | Parks, Walther A. |
| 3DT | Wells, William C., jr. |
| 3DU | Baumann, Frank J. |
| 3DV | Uphoff, Frank B. |
| 3DW | Lowery, Norman S. |
| 3DX | Lukens, Wilfred P. |
| 3DY | Miller, Frederick E. |
| 3DZ | Fisher, Roy S. |
| 3EA | Brashears, Paul B. |
| 3EB | La Salle College. |
| 3EC | Giffin, Sidney H. |
| 3EF | Reiff, W. Norman. |
| 3EG | Snyder, James R. |
| 3EH | Powell, Edwin H. |
| 3EI | Kumler, Kelvin C. |
| 3EJ | Primrose, Donald L. |
| 3EK | Moore, Daniel D. |
| 3EL | Fricke, Henry W. L. |
| 3EM | Beaty, Lehman C. |
| 3EN | Bailey, Albert S. |

54773°—14——8

AMATEUR RADIO STATIONS—THIRD DISTRICT—ALPHABETICALLY BY CALL SIGNALS—Continued.

| Call signal. | Owner of station. |
|---|---|
| 3EP | Kennedy, Joseph H. |
| 3EQ | MacKendrick, Robert G. |
| 3ER | Larrimore, James F. |
| 3ES | Martin, E. Linton. |
| 3ET | Fisher, Howes N. |
| 3EU | Shelley, F. Cheston. |
| 3EV | Brannan, Julian L. |
| 3EW | Scheffey, Ralph B. |
| 3EY | McIntyre, William. |
| 3EZ | Donovan, Edgar R. |
| 3FA | Davis, Edwin L. |
| 3FB | Darby, George B., jr. |
| 3FC | Weik, Charles F. |
| 3FD | Simon, Walter. |
| 3FE | Rabl, Samuel. |
| 3FF | Dempster, Warren J. |
| 3FG | Godfrey, James M. |
| 3FH | Smith, Sewall P. |
| 3FI | Wever, John A. |
| 3FJ | Blair, Perot E. |
| 3FK | Schleher, Paul H. |
| 3FL | Wiler, William L. |
| 3FM | Hartley, Milton E. |
| 3FN | Deichmiller, Alvin. |
| 3FO | E. I. du Pont De Nemours Powder Co. |
| 3FQ | Krainer, John B. |
| 3FR | Denston, E. Craig. |
| 3FS | Durkee, Alfred C. |
| 3FT | Dudley, De Witt C. |
| 3FU | Wunder, William F. |
| 3FV | Edwards, Charles. |
| 3FW | Hunter, Edwin J. |
| 3FX | Hutchinson, Samuel J. |
| 3FZ | Conley, Charles B. |
| 3GB | Rohrich, George J. |
| 3GC | Taylor, B. Irving. |
| 3GF | Blankenship, Elliott E. |
| 3GG | Jones, Winters. |
| 3GH | MacDonald, Stuart. |
| 3GI | Pelham, Fred B. |
| 3GK | Troth, Raymond H. |
| 3GL | Meck, Michael. |
| 3GM | Fellows, J. Howard. |
| 3GN | Board of Public Education, Philadelphia, Pa. |
| 3GO | Norcross, Earl L. |
| 3GP | Amig, Edward P. |
| 3GQ | Miller, Kelly, jr. |
| 3GR | Wood, Richard, M. |
| 3GS | McCafferty, Rea B. |
| 3GT | Searle, William J., jr. |
| 3GU | Hopkins, Robert E. |
| 3GV | Laber, Joseph M. |
| 3GW | Frazier, George R. T. |
| 3GX | Robinson, George O. |
| 3GY | Staub, James. |
| 3GZ | Laird, J. Ira. |
| 3HA | Wiseman, Luther B. |
| 3HB | Taylor, Sidney L. M. |
| 3HC | Thackeray, Samuel J. |
| 3HE | Parks, Laurence W. |
| 3HG | Smith, W. P. |
| 3HH | Place, Samuel W. |
| 3HI | Stepp, John W. |
| 3HJ | Bradley, Horace E. |
| 3HK | Stokes, Josiah T. |
| 3HL | Nielsen, Harold, jr. |
| 3HM | Hickman, Paul W. |
| 3HN | Schuck, Leon H. |
| 3HO | Fithian, William S., jr. |
| 3HP | Duncan, Rodney P. |
| 3HQ | Happold, Harold H. |
| 3HR | Thornton, Earl H. |
| 3HS | Murray, Eugene M. |
| 3HT | Falkenberg, August E. |
| 3HU | Witmer, Charles T. |
| 3HW | James, Herman. |
| 3HX | Kratz, Herman A. |
| 3HY | Richwein, Louis C. |
| 3IA | Puff, Stephen F. |
| 3IB | Good, Horace D. |
| 3IC | Morris, Edward P. |
| 3ID | Hasenfus, Joseph F. |
| 3IE | Jacobson, Bernard H. |
| 3IF | Godfrey, Earle. |
| 3IG | Johnson, Earle K. |
| 3IH | Eisele, Edward, jr. |
| 3II | Coin, Thornley M. |
| 3IJ | Cooper, James W. |
| 3IK | Snyder, Harry H. |
| 3IL | Pawson, James M. |
| 3IM | Mellon, Charles E. |
| 3IN | Vogel, Charles C. |
| 3IP | Anderson, Albert. |
| 3IQ | Knoll, Lloyd M. |
| 3IR | Wallace, Lewis J. |
| 3IS | Weaver, Howard A. |
| 3IT | Stritzel, Alfred H. |
| 3IU | Schramm, Carl. |
| 3IV | Wilson, Willard S. |
| 3IW | Mitchener, Harold G. |
| 3IX | Philadelphia School of Wireless Telegraphy. |
| 3IY | Tolbert, Warren. |
| 3IZ | Faunce, B. Warren. |
| 3JA | August, Earl W. |
| 3JC | Riley, Arthur S. |
| 3JD | Wolcott, Roger G. |
| 3JE | Dickerson, E. Stuart, jr. |
| 3JG | Scholl, Warren. |
| 3JH | Brockman, Francis C. |
| 3JI | Burdette, Aubrey W. |
| 3JJ | Bergmann, Frederick J. |
| 3JL | McCaskey, Edward R. |
| 3JM | Freedom, Leon. |
| 3JN | Korab, Harry E. |

AMATEUR RADIO STATIONS—THIRD DISTRICT—ALPHABETICALLY BY CALL SIGNALS—Continued.

| Call signal. | Owner of station. | Call signal. | Owner of station. |
|---|---|---|---|
| 3JO | Hicks, A. Willet, jr. | 3MA | Downes, Marlboro K. |
| 3JP | Sterns, Morton W. | 3MB | McKee, W. Wesley. |
| 3JQ | Benson, Thomas W. | 3MC | Wolf, Henry S. |
| 3JR | Snow, Harold A. | 3MD | Dulany, Franklin R. |
| 3JS | Beekley, Francis C. | 3ME | Lamdin, Charles R. |
| 3JT | Hampson, George M. | 3MF | Hitchner, Clyde G. |
| 3JU | Fenimore, Robert S. | 3MG | Ferguson, William. |
| 3JV | Lehr, William. | 3MI | Nash, Clifford S. |
| 3JW | Broadbelt, J. Edward, jr. | 3MK | Wilson, William P. |
| 3JX | Hoagland, Donald. | 3ML | Kutz, Charles E. |
| 3JY | Hann, Charles B. | 3MM | King, Albert. |
| 3JZ | Costella, Pietro A. | 3MN | Hollinshead, Norman B. |
| | | 3MO | Bickel, E. Clifton. |
| 3KA | McEuen, Earl W. | 3MP | Cohen, Henry. |
| 3KB | Goodall, Alfred B. | 3MQ | Trumbower, Raymond. |
| 3KC | Kendall, Raymond V. | 3MS | Barnhart, Lawrence W. |
| 3KD | Noel, James F. | 3MT | Peck, G. Warren. |
| 3KE | Allen, Francis H. | 3MU | Eckard, Lewis D. |
| 3KF | Green, Anthony J. | 3MV | Whitaker, Lorenzo D. |
| 3KH | Bowen, Albert. | 3MW | Poalk, James L., jr. |
| 3KI | Stanley, John S. | 3MX | Barker, Thomas H., jr. |
| 3KJ | Worrest, Howard A. | 3MY | Wheeler, William A. |
| 3KK | Hofmann, George A. | 3MZ | Husted, Mortimer I. |
| 3KL | Wagner, William H. | | |
| 3KM | Gray, Gerald. | 3NA | Zang, Joseph A., jr. |
| 3KN | Barr, Richard H. | 3NB | Frye, Marcus, jr. |
| 3KO | Chalmers, Edwin L. | 3NC | Dalling, Howard. |
| 3KP | Myers, Roy R. | 3ND | Hirst, Arthur C. |
| 3KQ | Wexler, Bernard. | 3NE | Passano, Leonard W. |
| 3KR | Rede, G. Ross. | 3NF | Pohlig, William T. |
| 3KS | Williams, John McC. | 3NG | Tichenor, George C. |
| 3KT | Holtzinger, Horace K. | 3NH | Bierfreund, Max A. |
| 3KU | Rakestraw, Charles E., jr. | 3NI | Bell, Albert A., jr. |
| 3KV | Van Duyne, Carlton. | 3NJ | Wicks, Preston S. |
| 3KW | Erickson, Alfred O. | 3NK | Godfrey, Howard L. |
| 3KX | Knight, G. Webber, jr. | 3NL | Behm, L. F. F. |
| 3KY | Cole, Jesse James. | 3NM | Finck, Anthony R. |
| 3KZ | Roberts, Harold A. | 3NN | Bachert, Homer A. |
| | | 3NO | Sleath, Robert W. |
| 3LA | Levin, Davis. | 3NP | Jones, La Frantz. |
| 3LB | Iddings, Frederick T. | 3NQ | Morley, Augustin H. |
| 3LC | Eberly, Jacob A., jr. | 3NR | Ferris, Malcolm. |
| 3LD | Pisani, Sylvester. | 3NS | Radio Apparatus Co. |
| 3LE | Evans, J. Arthur. | 3NT | Rafferty, John A. |
| 3LF | Shreiner, Carl H. | 3NU | Mitchener, Frederick D. |
| 3LG | Lyon, Harry H. | 3NV | Robey, V. C. K. |
| 3LH | Weiss, Leonard. | 3NW | Burke, Thomas J. |
| 3LK | Martin, Robert C. | 3NX | Wells, John M. |
| 3LL | Van Horn, J. Orville. | 3NY | Steele, Sherman E. |
| 3LM | Faries, Walter R. | 3NZ | Branin, Manlif L. |
| 3LN | Doyle, John E. | | |
| 3LO | Godfrey, Clarence M. | 3OA | Urner, Joseph W. |
| 3LP | Densham, Harry W. | 3OB | Kennedy, Ignatius L. |
| 3LQ | Birch, Stanford S. | 3OC | Grover, H. Marshall. |
| 3LR | Cooper, William F. | 3OD | Hemmann, William C. |
| 3LU | Ellis, J. Elton. | 3OE | Gray, Harry L. |
| 3LV | Griffin, Aloysius. | 3OF | Talbot, George L. |
| 3LW | Waite, John W. | 3OG | Jones, John W. |
| 3LX | Knight, A. Stanley. | 3OH | Levy, Lewis. |
| 3LY | Harris, William J. | 3OI | Wolle, Aubrey B. |
| 3LZ | McCullough, Earl N. | 3OJ | Pool, J. Alexander. |

AMATEUR RADIO STATIONS—THIRD DISTRICT—ALPHABETICALLY BY CALL SIGNALS—Continued.

| Call signal. | Owner of station. |
|---|---|
| 3OK | Kerr, William C. |
| 3OL | Grant, Arthur F. |
| 3OM | Mooney, John, jr. |
| 3ON | Matos, Walter A. |
| 3OO | Hindin, Louis M. |
| 3OP | Fink, Louis, 3d. |
| 3OQ | Bryson, Harold E. |
| 3OR | Signor, Frederick H. |
| 3OS | Lafferty, Francis A. |
| 3OT | Faust, Elmer J. |
| 3OU | Schwering, Harry C., jr. |
| 3OW | Patchel, Robert E. |
| 3OX | Wick, Arthur. |
| 3OY | Gompf, August P. |
| 3OZ | Collins, Benjamin W. |
| | |
| 3PA | Schlichting, E. N. E. |
| 3PB | Zorger, Daniel H. |
| 3PC | Abbott, E. H. B. |
| 3PD | Meyer, Emil J. |
| 3PE | Bassett, William W. |
| 3PF | Postpichal, Otto I. |
| 3PG | Proudley, Charles E. |
| 3PH | Harris, Edwin R. |
| 3PI | Atlee, Franklin. |
| 3PJ | Berman, Harry. |
| 3PK | McGear, Herbert K. |
| 3PL | Ballantine, Charles S. |
| 3PM | Lusse, Richard N. |
| 3PN | Pemberton, Henry R. |
| 3PO | Watson, James B. |
| 3PP | Skinner, William H. |
| 3PQ | Strieby, Malcolm. |
| 3PR | Hahn, Clarence Le Roy. |
| 3PS | Holt, Clarence J. |
| 3PT | Creager, E. Clark. |
| 3PU | Smith, Hubert B. |
| 3PV | Bunting, Theodore R. |
| 3PW | Field, Harry P. |
| 3PX | Howard, H. Trumbull. |
| 3PY | Torrisi, Salvatore. |
| 3PZ | Griffith, Elmer G. |
| | |
| 3QA | O'Brien, Francis J. |
| 3QB | Butterfield, Harold G. |
| 3QC | Lanning, John M. |
| 3QD | Rynick, George M., jr. |
| 3QE | Richards, Clift R., jr. |
| 3QF | Haig, J. Donald. |
| 3QG | Landis, Harold O. |
| 3QH | Fusselman, John. |
| 3QI | Barnes, Donald K. |
| 3QJ | Crowley, Robert H. |
| 3QK | Adams, Leslie H. |
| 3QL | Tapley, Robert E. |
| 3QM | Varnes, Earl W. |
| 3QN | Zinazer, Harvey A. |
| 3QO | Hake, Elias G. |
| 3QP | Weber, Henry M. |
| 3QQ | Husk, Dayton E. |
| 3QR | Sullivan, Frank J. |
| 3QS | Roekens, Noel H. |
| 3QT | Corderman, Roy C. |
| 3QU | Deichmann, George L., jr. |
| 3QV | Hall, Robert S. |
| 3QW | Harsch, Lawrence P. |
| 3QX | Worcester, Paul S. |
| 3QY | Nees, Milton. |
| 3QZ | Service, Charles A., jr. |
| | |
| 3RA | Messinger, Miles B. |
| 3RB | Lewis, Ellis. |
| 3RC | Fenton, Edward T. |
| 3RD | Dimling, Rudolph G. A. |
| 3RE | Frantz, Samuel G. |
| 3RF | Vaughan, Charles A. |
| 3RG | Bowman, Philip W. |
| 3RH | Kline, H. N. Gay. |
| 3RI | Clough, Thomas A. |
| 3RJ | La Rue, Robert G. |
| 3RK | Hepler, Walter R. |
| 3RL | McClellan, Frederick W. |
| 3RM | Phillips, Albert L. |
| 3RN | Ramsey, Howard N. |
| 3RO | Garver, Edwin H. |
| 3RP | Kirby, Elmer S. |
| 3RQ | Skene, Andrew A. |
| 3RR | Roeller, Harold C. |
| 3RS | Tripp, George B., jr. |
| 3RT | Carvin, Frank D. |
| 3RU | Hoff, J. Marshall. |
| 3RV | Hamill, McClintock, jr. |
| 3RW | Redgrave, De Witt C. |
| 3RX | Nisley, Paul H. |
| 3RY | Jarvis, Thomas R. |
| 3RZ | La Rue, Lester J. |
| | |
| 3SA | Requa, Fred A. |
| 3SB | Van Hulsteyn, J. M. C. |
| 3SC | Hopper, Sterling A. |
| 3SD | Shafer, Albert G. |
| 3SE | Hyatt, C. Brown. |
| 3SF | Hookey, Anthony C. |
| 3SG | Maris, Carroll B. |
| 3SH | Kenyon, Walter R. |
| 3SI | Williams, Harvey. |
| 3SJ | Glenn, Charles R. |
| 3SK | Baxley, C. Herbert. |
| 3SL | Shaw, Lemuel A. |
| 3SM | Burnett, A. Elmo. |
| 3SN | Bourgeois, Edmund R. |
| 3SO | Law, Bartley H. |
| 3SP | Polk, Charles P. |
| 3SQ | Sellers, William, jr. |
| 3SR | Anderson, John A. |
| 3SS | Brany, Emil B. |
| 3ST | Chappell, Ralph R. |
| 3SU | Seeley, Alfred J. |

AMATEUR RADIO STATIONS—THIRD DISTRICT—ALPHABETICALLY BY CALL SIGNALS—Continued.

| Call signal. | Owner of station. | Call signal. | Owner of station. |
|---|---|---|---|
| 3SV | Blakeley, George B. | 3UK | Peyser, Philip S. |
| 3SW | Barnard, Julian W. | 3UL | Essick, William W., jr. |
| 3SX | Simons, Joseph M. | 3UM | Strailman, Gilbert T. |
| 3SY | Barretta, Valroy S. | 3UN | Hayes, William F. |
| 3SZ | Herndon, Landon C. | 3UO | Graves, Edwin D., jr. |
| | | 3UP | Howlett, Joseph T. F. |
| 3TA | Piper, S. Webster. | 3UQ | Howlett, Joseph T. F. |
| 3TB | Y. M. C. A., Wilmington, Del. | 3UR | Cohan, William W. |
| 3TC | Landis, Harry. | 3US | Hopkins, James R. |
| 3TD | Miller, Harry G. | 3UT | Cianfrani, Theodore. |
| 3TE | Poorman, Arthur E. | 3UU | Lewis, Joseph W. |
| 3TF | Ebert, Burton E. | 3UV | Ross, John W. |
| 3TG | Hatch, William B. | 3UW | Call, J. Richardson. |
| 3TH | Tabb, Vincent W. | 3UX | Loughlin, John K. |
| 3TI | Nichols, Crawford V. | 3UY | Parker, Herbert H. |
| 3TJ | Emmerson, Frank V. | 3UZ | Braidwood, Thomas W. |
| 3TK | Flather, Bryan S. | | |
| 3TL | Bowes, Joseph J. | 3VA | Durham, Wilson N. |
| 3TM | Davidson, Delmer S. | 3VB | Knowles, Edward P., jr. |
| 3TN | Venn, Silas N. | 3VC | Rancetelli, Ernain. |
| 3TO | Pent, Robert E. | 3VD | Lamb, Franklin. |
| 3TP | Brittingham, Otis B. | 3VE | Davis, Herbert E. |
| 3TQ | Andrews, Edward C. | 3VF | Tompkins, Eugene R. |
| 3TR | Fell, David B. | 3VG | Wood, Frederick B. |
| 3TS | Turner, Alfred W. | 3VH | Stickell, Daniel R. |
| 3TT | Kindt, Charles F., jr. | 3VI | Laws, J. Waltham, jr. |
| 3TU | Bach, Earl C. | 3VJ | Geibel, Henry J. |
| 3TV | Blanford, Irving. | 3VK | Griffith, Dorsey J. |
| 3TW | Leslie, Malcolm C. | 3VL | Bernstein, Abraham R. |
| 3TX | Blessing, Joseph M. | 3VM | Baynes, Ralph J. |
| 3TY | Krone, Julian E. | 3VN | Ways, Clarence I. |
| 3TZ | Kellert, Charles. | 3VO | Leayman, Charles S. |
| | | 3VP | Rothman, Charles. |
| 3UA | Gilbert, Harry P., jr. | 3VQ | Uphoff, Frank B. |
| 3UB | Colberg, George A. | 3VR | McVickar, W. Patton. |
| 3UC | Teller, Leslie W. | 3VS | French, Edward R., jr. |
| 3UD | Mundy, Elmer. | 3VT | Seidenberg, Frank. |
| 3UE | Smith, William M., jr. | 3VU | Nikirk, Thomas E. |
| 3UF | Howlett, Joseph T. F. | 3VV | Rose, Harold W. |
| 3UG | Dearden, Rowland R., 3d. | 3VW | Uphoff, Frank B. |
| 3UH | Casey, Elwood R. | 3VX | Flounders, Newton. |
| 3UI | Fletcher, Edward. | 3VY | Stannard, Charles F., jr. |
| 3UJ | Campbell, James D. | 3VZ | Orlando, Frank. |

## FOURTH DISTRICT.

[Headquarters: Customhouse, Savannah, Ga. The fourth district comprises the States of North Carolina, South Carolina, Georgia, Florida, and the Territory of Porto Rico.]

ALPHABETICALLY BY OWNERS OF STATIONS.

| Call signal. | Owner of station. | Location of station. | Power. |
|---|---|---|---|
| | | | *Watts.* |
| 4AN | Adams, George G. | 45 Whitaker St., Savannah, Ga. | 20 |
| 4BA | Avant, Marion C. | 806 N. 4th St., Wilmington, N. C. | 200 |
| 4AU | Avera, William W. | Watkinsville, Ga. | 30 |
| 4AL | Bangs, Philip C. | 918 E. Duffy St., Savannah, Ga. | 350 |
| 4AS | Brandon, Beverly A. | 322 E. 6th St., Jacksonville, Fla. | 330 |
| 4AW | Crevasse, Joe N. | 1605 Blvd., Jacksonville, Fla. | 165 |

AMATEUR RADIO STATIONS—FOURTH DISTRICT—ALPHABETICALLY BY OWNERS OF STATIONS—Continued.

| Call signal. | Owner of station. | Location of station. | Power. |
|---|---|---|---|
| | | | Watts. |
| 4BN | Cross, K. E. | Port Tampa, Fla. | 50 |
| 4AE | Davis, Loren V. | St. Petersburg, Fla. | 60 |
| 4AZ | Dunk, Thomas R. | 1424 Laura St., Jacksonville, Fla. | 550 |
| 4AT | Ehle, Frank R. | 1337 Liberty St., Jacksonville, Fla. | 330 |
| 4AQ | Fisher, C. C. | 711 Whaley St., Columbia, S. C. | 30 |
| 4BE | Fowler, Carl A. | S. N. S. Station, Athens, Ga. | 500 |
| 4AX | Gordon, Clarence M. | Helena, Ga. | 990 |
| 4AF | Humphrey, Arthur L. | 1105 Market St., Wilmington, N. C. | 18 |
| 4BI | Kreis, Joseph W., jr. | 655 S. Pryor St., Atlanta, Ga. | 36 |
| 4AR | Marbury, Ralph E. | 26 Wesley St., Newnan, Ga. | 500 |
| 4AD | McQuade, James H. | 1 25th St., Miami, Fla. | 175 |
| 4AB | Meltzer, Isador. | 627 Margaret St., Key West, Fla. | 225 |
| 4BJ | Milam, Ralph L. | 1039 Highway Ave., Jacksonville, Fla. | 150 |
| 4AJ | Moore, Victor W. | 147 Nacoochee Ave., Athens, Ga. | 250 |
| 4BC | Morgan, Sidney. | 208 W. Gaston St., Savannah, Ga. | 88 |
| 4AY | Moseley, Charles W. | 815 Mulberry St., Columbia, S. C. | 20 |
| 4AP | Peer, Emmitt E. | 419 W. Duval St., Jacksonville, Fla. | 800 |
| 4AA | Pope, Wilbur B. | 197 Dearing St., Athens, Ga. | 432 |
| 4BB | Rankin, Robert G., jr. | 3 N. 9th St., Wilmington, N. C. | 16 |
| 4AC | Rice, Elmer L. | 1702 E. Duval St., Jacksonville, Fla. | 880 |
| 4BL | Schoenwald, Byron B. | 116 Nun St., Wilmington, N. C. | 30 |
| 4AM | Sebastian, Lawrence F. | 336 Myrtle Ave., South Jacksonville, Fla. | 250 |
| 4BK | Simons, Mayrant. | Summerville, S. C. | 1,000 |
| 4BD | Speight, Marshall C. | 5 Johnson St., Newbern, N. C. | 100 |
| 4AO | Swearingen, Thos. J., jr. | 403 Prairie Ave., Gainesville, Fla. | 990 |
| 4AV | Treisback, Robert T. | 2228 Riverside Ave., Jacksonville, Fla. | 500 |
| 4BM | Villareal, Dewey R. | 412 William St., Key West, Fla. | 100 |
| 4AK | Whiting, Charles T. | R. F. D. No. 6, Gainesville, Fla. | 770 |
| 4BH | Wikle, James R. | 619 S. Pryor St., Atlanta, Ga. | 300 |
| 4BS | Wilmington High School | 4th and Ann Sts., Wilmington, N. C. | 220 |

ALPHABETICALLY BY CALL SIGNALS.

| Call signal. | Owner of station. | Call signal. | Owner of station. |
|---|---|---|---|
| 4AA | Pope, Wilbur B. | 4AW | Crevasse, Joe N. |
| 4AB | Meltzer, Isador. | 4AX | Gordon, Clarence M. |
| 4AC | Rice, Elmer L. | 4AY | Moseley, Charles W. |
| 4AD | McQuade, James H. | 4AZ | Dunk, Thomas R. |
| 4AE | Davis, Loren V. | | |
| 4AF | Humphrey, Arthur L. | 4BA | Avant, Marion C. |
| 4AJ | Moore, Victor W. | 4BB | Rankin, Robert G., jr. |
| 4AK | Whiting, Charles T. | 4BC | Morgan, Sidney. |
| 4AL | Bangs, Philip C. | 4BD | Speight, Marshall C. |
| 4AM | Sebastian, Lawrence F. | 4BE | Fowler, Carl A. |
| 4AN | Adams, George G. | 4BH | Wikle, James R. |
| 4AO | Swearingen, Thos. J., jr. | 4BI | Kreis, Joseph W., jr. |
| 4AP | Peer, Emmitt E. | 4BJ | Milam, Ralph L. |
| 4AQ | Fisher, C. C. | 4BK | Simons, Mayrant. |
| 4AR | Marbury, Ralph E. | 4BL | Schoenwald, Byron B. |
| 4AS | Brandon, Beverly A. | 4BM | Villareal, Dewey R. |
| 4AT | Ehle, Frank R. | 4BN | Cross, K. E. |
| 4AU | Avera, William W. | 4BS | Wilmington High School. |
| 4AV | Treisback, Robert T. | | |

AMATEUR RADIO STATIONS—Continued.

## FIFTH DISTRICT.

[Headquarters: Customhouse, New Orleans, La. The fifth district comprises the States of Alabama, Mississippi, Louisiana, Texas, Tennessee, Arkansas, Oklahoma, New Mexico.]

### ALPHABETICALLY BY OWNERS OF STATIONS.

| Call signal. | Owner of station. | Location of station. | Power. |
|---|---|---|---|
| | | | *Watts.* |
| 5AC | A. & M. College of Texas. | College Station, Tex. | 300 |
| 5BC | Amerine, William H. | 435 S. Court St., Montgomery, Ala. | 495 |
| 5AR | Beynon, Eugene T. | 604 Artesian St., Corpus Christi, Tex. | 496 |
| 5AX | Bonnecaze, Leonce, jr. | 1428 Kerlerec St., New Orleans, La. | 225 |
| 5BW | Brown, Max T. | 1017 Cumberland St., Little Rock, Ark. | 60 |
| 5AM | Brownell, Harold S. | 1512 Phelan St., Birmingham, Ala. | 500 |
| 5BD | Casey, Robert H., jr. | 313 N. Main St., Cleburne, Tex. | 770 |
| 5BV | Clayton, John M. | 1301 Welch St., Little Rock, Ark. | 15 |
| 5BR | Curtis, Earnest M. | 350 Selma St., Mobile, Ala. | 440 |
| 5AU | Gallo, Louis. | 821 Royal St., New Orleans, La. | 10 |
| 5AQ | Goldstein, Henry R. | 1819 Octavia St., New Orleans, La. | 75 |
| 5AS | Goodman, Louis N. | 300 Main St., Starkville, Miss. | 1,000 |
| 5BP | Glover, Charles W. | 327 Sayre St., Montgomery, Ala. | 506 |
| 5EK | Hamby, Otis. | 514 S. 5th St., Temple, Tex. | 50 |
| 5BJ | Hanz, Harry W. | 310 Bridge St., New Braunfels, Tex. | 500 |
| 5AY | Harris, Russell S. | 1240 Esplanade St., New Orleans, La. | 30 |
| 5BI | Harrison, Jackson W. | 800 Highland Ave., Montgomery, Ala. | 550 |
| 5BM | Hayes, James J., jr. | 106 Brown St., Brownwood, Tex. | 750 |
| 5AG | Johannsen, John, jr. | Lafayette Ave. and Miro St., New Orleans, La. | ...... |
| 5BK | Leroy, Louis. | 1005 Rayner Ave., Memphis, Tenn. | 1,000 |
| 5BQ | Lockland, Scott B. | 807 Bois d'Arc St., Fort Worth, Tex. | 250 |
| 5AV | Macke, William. | 2414 Painter St., New Orleans, La. | 250 |
| 5BL | Marks, George M., jr. | 615 S. Perry St., Montgomery, Ala. | 220 |
| 5AH | Martin, Ben W. | 438 Spring Hill Ave., Mobile, Ala. | 275 |
| 5BS | McLain, Robert M. | 513 W. Clinton St., Huntsville, Ala. | 770 |
| 5AW | McNeil, Ernest W. | 1039 Robert St., New Orleans, La. | 30 |
| 5BT | Medlen, Charles C. | 114 E. 3d St., Okmulgee, Okla. | 1,000 |
| 5BE | Mollenhauer, Arthur E. | 812 Castell St., New Braunfels, Tex. | 100 |
| 5AL | Reboul, Theophile, jr. | 2106 Chartres St., New Orleans, La. | 500 |
| 5AD | Rorshach, Harold E. | 619 N. E St., Muskogee, Okla. | 870 |
| 5BN | Salzer, Harry S. | 2322 N. Villere St., New Orleans, La. | 450 |
| 5AT | Stone, Frank M. | 7919 Jeannette St., New Orleans, La. | 1,000 |
| 5AP | Thompson, Vance M. | 267 Pasadena Pl., Memphis, Tenn. | 880 |
| 5BA | Toupe, Roy N. | 1512 Ursuline St., New Orleans, La. | 125 |
| 5BH | Vogler, Robert L. | Lee St. and Bringhurst Ave., Alexandria, La. | 100 |
| 5BU | Ward, Robert P. | 233 Orchard St., Georgetown, Tex. | 550 |

### ALPHABETICALLY BY CALL SIGNALS.

| Call signal. | Owner of station. | Call signal. | Owner of station. |
|---|---|---|---|
| 5AC | A. & M. College of Texas. | 5AR | Beynon, Eugene T. |
| 5AD | Rorshach, Harold E. | 5AS | Goodman, Louis N. |
| 5AG | Johannsen, John, jr. | 5AT | Stone, Frank M. |
| 5AH | Martin, Ben W. | 5AU | Gallo, Louis. |
| 5AL | Reboul, Theophile, jr. | 5AV | Macke, William. |
| 5AM | Brownell, Harold S. | 5AW | McNeil, Ernest W. |
| 5AP | Thompson, Vance M. | 5AX | Bonnecaze, Leonce, jr. |
| 5AQ | Goldstein, Henry R. | 5AY | Harris, Russell S. |

AMATEUR RADIO STATIONS—FIFTH DISTRICT—ALPHABETICALLY BY CALL SIGNALS—Continued.

| Call signal. | Owner of station. | Call signal. | Owner of station. |
|---|---|---|---|
| 5BA | Toupe, Roy N. | 5BP | Glover, Charles W. |
| 5BC | Amerine, William H. | 5BQ | Lockland, Scott B. |
| 5BD | Casey, Robert H., jr. | 5BR | Curtis, Earnest M. |
| 5BE | Mollenhauer, Arthur E. | 5BS | McLain, Robert M. |
| 5BH | Vogler, Robert L. | 5BT | Medlen, Charles C. |
| 5BI | Harrison, Jackson W. | 5BU | Ward, Robert P. |
| 5BJ | Hanz, Harry W. | 5BV | Clayton, John M. |
| 5BK | Leroy, Louis. | 5BW | Brown, Max T. |
| 5BL | Marks, George M., jr. | | |
| 5BM | Hayes, James J., jr. | 5EK | Hamby, Otis. |
| 5BN | Salzer, Harry S. | | |

## SIXTH DISTRICT.

Headquarters: Customhouse, San Francisco, Cal. The sixth district comprises the States of California, Nevada, Utah, Arizona, and the Territory of Hawaii.]

### ALPHABETICALLY BY OWNERS OF STATIONS.

| Call signal. | Owner of station. | Location of station. | Power. |
|---|---|---|---|
| | | | *Watts.* |
| 6QN | Abbott, Raymond B. | 1803 Cedar St., Berkeley, Cal. | 250 |
| 6QD | Adam, Carl F., jr. | 2830 Garber St., Berkeley, Cal. | 550 |
| 6DS | Adams, Charles C. | 704 E. 21st St., Los Angeles, Cal. | 750 |
| 6NU | Adkins, Edward S. | 143 N. Pasadena Ave., Pasadena, Cal. | 500 |
| 6LF | Alexander, Lee. | 182 Flora St., Bell, Cal. | 35 |
| 6AAO | Alexander, Willard B. | 219 W. 24th St., Los Angeles, Cal. | 440 |
| 6PF | Allen, Preston D. | 1410 West St., Oakland, Cal. | 1,000 |
| 6LD | Anderlini, Louis J. | 2012 Keith St., San Francisco, Cal. | 32 |
| 6SW | Anderson, Elroy E. | 80 Barson St., Santa Cruz, Cal. | 550 |
| 6VM | Anderson, Herbert E. | Lindsay, Cal. | 220 |
| 6KY | Andrews, Harold S. | 2171 W. 29th Pl., Los Angeles, Cal. | 300 |
| 6WA | Anthes, William F., jr. | 230 S. 7th St., San Jose, Cal. | 20 |
| 6DM | Archer, Robert P. | 2912 S. Flower St., Los Angeles, Cal. | 30 |
| 6FA | Arnberger, Frank, jr. | 3230 Garfield Ave., Alameda, Cal. | 1,000 |
| 6UA | Asadoorian, Theodore N. | 1205 Garfield Ave., Pasadena, Cal. | 150 |
| 6AA | Aster, Alvin K. | 1814 Alameda Ave., Alameda, Cal. | 1,000 |
| 6EG | Aten, Arthur B. | 428 Clark St., Sherman, Cal. | 250 |
| 6IC | Austin, Russell F. | 210 3d St., Riverside, Cal. | 250 |
| 6MF | Aymar, Clarence A. | 1525 6th Ave., Oakland, Cal. | 450 |
| 6MB | Baden, Merle L. | 2637½ Piedmont Ave., Berkeley, Cal. | 1,000 |
| 6BQ | Baer, Charles M. | Cupertino, Cal. | 15 |
| 6ER | Bailey, Cecil. | R. F. D. No. 18, Los Altos, Cal. | 4 |
| 6QX | Baird, Maxfield A. | 913 S. Main St., Corona, Cal. | 250 |
| 6HB | Baker, Harry G. | 643 W. 42d Pl., Los Angeles, Cal. | 900 |
| 6VJ | Barbour, Joseph L. | 217 W. 8th St., Hermosa Beach, Cal. | 1,000 |
| 6QL | Barker, Waldo W. | 331 Lighthouse Ave., Pacific Grove, Cal. | 25 |
| 6FJ | Barnum, Coit L. | 9034 Hillside Ave., Oakland, Cal. | 990 |
| 6BX | Barrett, Eldridge D. | 729 Capp St., San Francisco, Cal. | 7 |
| 6LB | Barton, Larry J. | 19 Crystal Springs Rd., San Mateo, Cal. | 1,000 |
| 6BP | Bauer, Roy M. | 402 S. Jefferson St., Napa, Cal. | 35 |
| 6VS | Bauman, Warren C. | Newcastle, Cal. | 495 |
| 6QP | Beament, Thomas. | 841 14th St., San Francisco, Cal. | 100 |
| 6EJ | Bean, Arthur E. | 1450 Washington St., San Francisco, Cal. | 440 |
| 6AJ | Bean, James. | 1775 Alameda Ave., San Jose, Cal. | 40 |
| 6KZ | Beaver, Gerald A. | 1533 Court St., Alameda, Cal. | 500 |
| 6WJ | Bechtel, Warren, jr. | 302 Perry St., Oakland, Cal. | 500 |
| 6TN | Beckman, Philip E. | 821 14th St., San Francisco, Cal. | 150 |

AMATEUR RADIO STATIONS—SIXTH DISTRICT—ALPHABETICALLY BY OWNERS OF STATIONS—Continued.

| Call signal. | Owner of station. | Location of station. | Power. |
|---|---|---|---|
| | | | *Watts.* |
| 6VQ | Benner, Bryan | 253 N. Lake Ave., Pasadena, Cal | 250 |
| 6VW | Beraldo, Dewey | 511 S. Chapel St., Alhambra, Cal | ..... |
| 6QT | Bennett, George S | 3000 Grove St., Berkeley, Cal | 500 |
| 6FU | Bergstrom, R. Bernard | Turlock, Cal | ..... |
| 6LX | Berlin, Latham | 1525 Chestnut St., Alameda, Cal | 110 |
| 6MT | Berringer, Hall | 6 Arundel Rd., Burlingame, Cal | 1,000 |
| 6JH | Berry, Charles A | 1st St., Los Altos, Cal | 12 |
| 6QF | Biber, Albert L | 1731 Noe St., San Francisco, Cal | 250 |
| 6WR | Bilger, Anson S | 407 Vernon St., Oakland, Cal | 550 |
| 6SB | Bisson, Charles S | 1734 Channing Way, Berkeley, Cal | 330 |
| 6EO | Blake, Albert W | 1055 Lincoln Ave., Pasadena, Cal | 60 |
| 6LA | Blochman, Lawrence G | 3260 1st St., San Diego, Cal | 500 |
| 6IJ | Boehme, Herbert L | 1437 6th St., Santa Monica, Cal | 500 |
| 6PM | Bolton, Harold B | 4300 Judah St., San Francisco, Cal | 250 |
| 6WB | Booth, Wilber C | 2229 Ashby Ave., Berkeley, Cal | 770 |
| 6TB | Boudinot, Truman E | 33 Navy St., Ocean Park, Cal | 500 |
| 6GB | Bowlus, Glen H | Paxton Ave, San Fernando, Cal | 120 |
| 6PB | Bradley, Philip L | 523 19th Ave., San Francisco, Cal | ..... |
| 6AL | Brandis, Fred A | 214 W. San Carlos St., San Jose, Cal | 30 |
| 6RA | Brandt, Robert L | 322 Grand Blvd., San Mateo, Cal | 1,000 |
| 6ND | Breck, F. Bon | 285 Mather St., Oakland, Cal | 550 |
| 6FV | Brockett, Charles | 248 Olive St., Los Angeles, Cal | 250 |
| 6JB | Brown, Julian T | 2604 E. 2d St., Los Angeles, Cal | 500 |
| 6DA | Brown, Ralph E | 838 E. 22d St., Los Angeles, Cal | 275 |
| 6PZ | Brown, Robert L | 634 Franklin St., Maple, Cal | 1,000 |
| 6AP | Brown, Victor | 520 2d St., San Jose, Cal | 500 |
| 6JY | Browne, G. R. A., jr | Los Altos, Cal | 250 |
| 6RB | Brumter, Ralph | 1214 E St., San Diego, Cal | 218 |
| 6IO | Buchanan, Roy J | 953 E. 22d St., Los Angeles, Cal | 550 |
| 6AM | Buckley, Ernest V | 327 Martin Ave., San Jose, Cal | 30 |
| 6FY | Buell, Clarence R | 732 56th St., Oakland, Cal | 110 |
| 6OH | Bull, Harold F | 208 S. 2d St., Sawtelle, Cal | 1,000 |
| 6RY | Bullard, Orlan K | 1655 10th St., San Diego, Cal | 550 |
| 6SO | Bunting, Howard S | 109 Forest Ave., Pacific Grove, Cal | 1,000 |
| 6OZ | Burge, Walter M | 33 Hester Ave., San Jose, Cal | 35 |
| 6DZ | Caldwell, Duncan K | 427 Crane Ave., Turlock, Cal | 330 |
| 6NX | Calvert, Paul P | Inglewood, Cal | 1,000 |
| 6WZ | Capps, Delphin | 710 Peninsula St., Burlingame, Cal | 1,000 |
| 6AC | Capwell, Cebert | Hillside Ave. and Kelton Court, Oakland, Cal. | 270 |
| 6FC | Carey, Francis K | 2116 Thompson St., Los Angeles, Cal | 235 |
| 6NY | Carroll, Elvin K | Capitola, Cal | 250 |
| 6SY | Carroll, Russell W | 354 Perry St., Oakland, Cal | 440 |
| 6MS | Carson, E. A | Dominguez Station, Cal | 1,000 |
| 6KR | Center, Hugh | Race St., San Jose, Cal | 250 |
| 6QJ | Chamberlain, George E | 121 N. 6th St., Sawtelle, Cal | 250 |
| 6AG | Chamberlain, Leon H | 553 27th St., Oakland, Cal | 550 |
| 6IE | Chambers, James | 427 Banks St., San Francisco, Cal | 500 |
| 6JZ | Charters, John R | 2606 E. 1st St., Los Angeles, Cal | 250 |
| 6JC | Chase, John H | 1323 Lemon St., Riverside, Cal | 300 |
| 6AD | Childs, Ralph S | 3050 Hopkins St., Oakland, Cal | 500 |
| 6EZ | Christie, A. Edwin | 1052 Cole St., San Francisco, Cal | ..... |
| 6QC | Christensen, V. H | 72 Lundy's Lane, San Francisco, Cal | 100 |
| 6AU | Clark, Paul U | 898 S. 8th St., San Jose, Cal | 18 |
| 6DD | Clark, Victor M | 1336 E. Colorado St., Pasadena, Cal | 600 |
| 6AAF | Collins, Wayne A | 788 19th St., Oakland, Cal | 250 |
| 6LC | Comins, Frank L | Niles, Cal | 500 |
| 6OD | Cook, John A | 1504 Locust St., Long Beach, Cal | 250 |
| 6RC | Cook, J. Ralph | 1221 Oxford St., Berkeley, Cal | 357 |
| 6DI | Cookson, Howard A | 465 University Ave., Palo Alto, Cal | 1,000 |

AMATEUR RADIO STATIONS—SIXTH DISTRICT—ALPHABETICALLY BY OWNERS OF STATIONS—Continued.

| Call signal. | Owner of station. | Location of station. | Power. |
|---|---|---|---|
| | | | *Watts.* |
| 6CY | Cooper, Charles P | 66 Linda Ave., Oakland, Cal | 330 |
| 6CA | Corby, Grant W | 1129 W. 6th St., Los Angeles, Cal | 330 |
| 6IQ | Cornell, Ezra B | 18 Culloden Park, San Rafael, Cal | 500 |
| 6RT | Cornish, Lester R | 107 3d St., Pacific Grove, Cal | ..... |
| 6WC | Cornish, Warren D | 107 3d St., Pacific Grove, Cal | 750 |
| 6WQ | Cowles, John | 28 Butler Ave., San Francisco, Cal | 500 |
| 6HC | Craig, Harold F | 696 2d St., San Pedro, Cal | 330 |
| 6UP | Creswell, Frank, jr | 833 W. 58th St., Los Angeles, Cal | 300 |
| 6FX | Cross, Fred M | 144 N. Beaudry St., Los Angeles, Cal | 500 |
| 6NJ | Cunningham, Edward J | Santa Clara, Cal | 660 |
| 6DE | Curtis, Burbank | 832 Linden St., Long Beach, Cal | 250 |
| 6WI | Cusick, William J | 2595 Folsom St., San Francisco, Cal | 250 |
| 6PV | Czapkay, Edward | Albany, Cal | 250 |
| 6BS | Davidson, G. Edward | 419 6th St., Richmond, Cal | 250 |
| 6TW | Davidson, Stanley E | 617 Fallon St., Oakland, Cal | 250 |
| 6EP | Davis, Elwood | 876 N. Orange Grove Ave., Pasadena, Cal | 500 |
| 6OI | Dawson, J. Percy | 763 Oakland Ave., Pasadena, Cal | 500 |
| 6GD | Day, Elwin C | 4304 19th St., San Francisco, Cal | 500 |
| 6FD | Deardorf, Francis H | Los Altos, Cal | 12 |
| 6AQ | De La Cruz, George | 706 W. San Carlos St., San Jose, Cal | 12 |
| 6UJ | Delius, Herbert A | 2057 Alameda Ave., Alameda, Cal | 500 |
| 6EN | de Neuf, Emil A | 1538 Russell St., Berkeley, Cal | 500 |
| 6DW | De Wald, Alfred S | Felton, Cal | 80 |
| 6HD | Dickow, Henry | 413 26th Ave., San Francisco, Cal | 500 |
| 6OK | Dillon, Lyle | 757 Carondelet St., Los Angeles, Cal | 1,000 |
| 6KC | Dinley, Laurence J | 850 E. 49th Pl., Los Angeles, Cal | 125 |
| 6QE | Dodge, Earl E | 170 Athol Ave., Oakland, Cal | 250 |
| 6KE | Dogan, Kenneth D | 1115 Cole St., San Francisco, Cal | ..... |
| 6OV | Doig, John H., jr | 1029 Washington St., San Diego, Cal | 300 |
| 6NO | Donaldson, Ernest S | Pearl and 14th Sts., Santa Monica, Cal | 1,000 |
| 6WP | Donelson, William E., jr | 1215 West Ave., Eureka, Cal | 575 |
| 6VN | Dorcy, Ben H., jr | 190 Ocean View Ave., Santa Cruz, Cal | 250 |
| 6OF | Doty, Arthur H | 2135 California St., Eureka, Cal | 25 |
| 6AZ | Downing, Alan S | 2510 Fruitvale Ave., Oakland, Cal | 1,000 |
| 6LT | Downs, LaRoy | 108 N. Pasadena Ave., Pasadena, Cal | 275 |
| 6RG | Downs, Robert | 1062 10th St., San Diego, Cal | 500 |
| 6BV | Drake, Charles | 422 22d St., Richmond, Cal | 300 |
| 6PO | Drath, Walter J | 682 34th St., Oakland, Cal | 250 |
| 6KD | Dutton, Kingsley | 1447 Salem St., Glendale, Cal | 250 |
| 6HE | Eastling, Harvey | 2659 Folsom St., San Francisco, Cal | 50 |
| 6HY | Ebeling, Hyde S | 444 Delmas Ave., San Jose, Cal | 18 |
| 6WX | Ebert, Howard W | 455 Orchard St., San Jose, Cal | 15 |
| 6QV | Echlin, Jack E | 460 Vernon St., Oakland, Cal | 500 |
| 6GZ | Edgar, George P | Broadmoor Blvd., San Leandro, Cal | 500 |
| 6BJ | Edwards, Lewis W | 903 Wilshire St., Sawtelle, Cal | 250 |
| 6NM | Eidemiller, Charles H | 1110 Summit Ave., Pasadena, Cal | 550 |
| 6EK | Eiferle, Chrissie | 3018 Boulevard Ave., Fruitvale, Cal | 15 |
| 6TE | Eisenhuth, Thomas V | 2138 McKinley St., Berkeley, Cal | 500 |
| 6OU | Eldredge, George E | 2731 Benvenue Ave., Berkeley, Cal | 250 |
| 6NZ | Emmerling, Herbert J | 439 3d Ave., San Francisco, Cal | 1,000 |
| 6QM | Ensign, Millard J | 4420 Falcon St., San Diego, Cal | 250 |
| 6DL | Espe, Oliver E | 4425 S. Main St., Los Angeles, Cal | 500 |
| 6RE | Esplen, Elmer R | 425 Hawthorne St., Stockton, Cal | 1,000 |
| 6ST | Evans, Bryan | Presidio of Monterey, Cal | 100 |
| 6FI | Eveleth, Harlan A | 2805 Russell St., Berkeley, Cal | 1,000 |
| 6UT | Everard, Charles E | 895 E. 56th St., Los Angeles, Cal | 440 |
| 6CZ | Everard, Charles E | 158 Bruce Ave., Pasadena, Cal | 400 |
| 6KM | Everett, J. Victor | Huntington Beach, Cal | ..... |
| 6UY | Everharty, Laurence | 2320 E. 3d St., Los Angeles, Cal | ..... |
| 6VF | Falk, Victor H | 64 S. 10th St., San Jose, Cal | 20 |

AMATEUR RADIO STATIONS—SIXTH DISTRICT—ALPHABETICALLY BY OWNERS OF STATIONS—Continued.

| Call signal. | Owner of station. | Location of station. | Power. |
|---|---|---|---|
| | | | *Watts.* |
| 6FL | Faneuf, Forrest E. | 153 Water St., Santa Cruz, Cal. | 250 |
| 6FB | Farlinger, Ernest | 227 2d St., Richmond, Cal. | 495 |
| 6GF | Farmer, Gordon | Clearwater, Cal. | 50 |
| 6TR | Farrell, Raymond | 2326 Pacific Ave., Alameda, Cal. | ..... |
| 6IF | Farwell, Ivyn | 2230 9th St., Berkeley, Cal. | 250 |
| 6FE | Felt, Clarence J. | 1732 Channing Way, Berkeley, Cal. | 330 |
| 6ET | Fenner, Paul R. | 1338 Masonic Ave., San Francisco, Cal. | 42 |
| 6II | Ferguson, E. Franklin | 596 Newton Ave., San Diego, Cal. | 25 |
| 6HV | Ferrill, Herbert E. | Bostonia, Cal. | ..... |
| 6KF | Filben, Frank | 37 Hester Ave., San Jose, Cal. | 679 |
| 6QQ | Finnell, Phillip S. | 2251 Green St., San Francisco, Cal. | 500 |
| 6CB | Fisher, Frank L | 661 Buchon St., San Luis Obispo, Cal. | 40 |
| 6JU | Fisher, Jules | 2214 Carlton St., Berkeley, Cal. | 38 |
| 6TC | Fisher, Thomas A. | Perry, Cal. | 900 |
| 6KW | Fisk, Alfred C. | 524 Almond Ave., Long Beach, Cal. | 250 |
| 6HF | Flenner, Harry A. | 1695 Granada Ave., San Diego, Cal. | 500 |
| 6ED | Flinspach, J. Henry | 403 E. Citrus Ave., Redlands, Cal. | 250 |
| 6QU | Floud, J. Harold | 260 3d Ave., San Francisco, Cal. | 250 |
| 6FO | Fones, Robert | 832 Cleveland St., Oakland, Cal. | 1,000 |
| 6SQ | Fonseca, Arthur | 2610 Valdez St., Oakland, Cal. | 100 |
| 6WF | Ford, Walter B. | 3653 Arnold St., San Diego, Cal. | 500 |
| 6JF | Forsburg, Joe A. | 1616 Josephine St., Berkeley, Cal. | 250 |
| 6NQ | Francis, Ernest R. | Mountain View, Cal. | 50 |
| 6FK | Frank, Walter | 465 18th St., San Diego, Cal. | 450 |
| 6UM | Freeman, Elmer D. | Nordhoff, Cal. | 120 |
| 6FH | French, Donald K. | 3027 Capp St., Fruitvale, Cal. | 250 |
| 6RF | Frier, Robert L. | 1017 W. 17th St., Los Angeles, Cal. | 250 |
| 6BK | Frost, William H. | 473 Minor Ave., San Jose, Cal. | 20 |
| 6CX | Frunk, Carl G. | 1345 Northside Ave., Berkeley, Cal. | 250 |
| 6AAE | Garcia, David | 3434 Hollis St., Oakland, Cal. | 500 |
| 6GA | Garratt, Edward D. | 1308 Crown Hill Ave., Los Angeles, Cal | 300 |
| 6JW | Gastman, Henry | 2530 Eunice St., Berkeley, Cal. | 990 |
| 6UH | Gates, Howard C. | E. Kingsley Ave., Pomona, Cal. | ..... |
| 6GJ | Gaugh, H. E. F. | 1379 Boston Ave., San Diego, Cal. | 400 |
| 6NG | Gerlach, Leonard | Point Richmond, Cal | 100 |
| 6GE | Gerlach, William G. | 512 Crofton Ave., Oakland, Cal. | 470 |
| 6ON | Germain, H. | 1450 Pacific Ave., San Francisco, Cal. | 500 |
| 6LG | Gianini, Leo G. | 535 5th Ave., San Francisco, Cal. | 60 |
| 6US | Gibson, Walter L. | 2324 Dennison St., East Oakland, Cal. | 25 |
| 6AAG | Gilbert, Phillip H. | 387 W. 8th St., Pomona, Cal. | 1,000 |
| 6GG | Gildersleeve, Given | 506 Calistoga Ave., Napa, Cal. | 50 |
| 6QK | Gill, Fred M. | 2715 4th St., Ocean Park, Cal. | 750 |
| 6PG | Gillmore, Purcell | 375 N. Fair Oaks Ave., Pasadena, Cal. | 200 |
| 6AAH | Gilstrap, L. Frederick | 517 N. Curtis Ave., Alhambra, Cal. | 160 |
| 6MG | Glindemann, Melvern | 825 Fillmore St., San Francisco, Cal. | 495 |
| 6BM | Godwin, Merle H. | 19 Grigsby Court, Napa, Cal. | 300 |
| 6UZ | Goemann, Jack L. | 2389 W. 31st St., Los Angeles, Cal. | 250 |
| 6GO | Goss, William M | 516 Bath St., Santa Barbara, Cal. | 500 |
| 6VC | Gottwald, Eugene A. | 404 S St., Eureka, Cal. | 250 |
| 6JG | Gould, Gordon | 2265 Clinton Ave., Alameda, Cal. | 24 |
| 6FG | Granger, Floyd | 305 Phelps St., Redwood, Cal. | ..... |
| 6BG | Grates, John | 634 Citrus Ave., Redlands, Cal. | 30 |
| 6LP | Gray, Clifford | Stevens Creek Rd., San Jose, Cal. | 120 |
| 6RX | Gray, Harold G. | 2604 9th Ave., Oakland, Cal. | 420 |
| 6AAK | Green, Carl V., jr. | 317 E. 49th St., Los Angeles, Cal. | 495 |
| 6AR | Greenquist, Elmer A. | 516 W. San Carlos St., San Jose, Cal. | 225 |
| 6AAI | Gregory, Merle M. | 1011 Orchard St., Santa Rosa, Cal. | 40 |
| 6EE | Griffin, Clyde S. | Stevinson, Cal. | ..... |
| 6LL | Griffith, William M. | 139 Pierce St., San Francisco, Cal. | 25 |
| 6DH | Grimes, W. Frank | 103 N. Pasadena Ave., Pasadena, Cal. | 1,000 |

AMATEUR RADIO STATIONS—SIXTH DISTRICT—ALPHABETICALLY BY OWNERS OF STATIONS—Continued.

| Call signal. | Owner of station. | Location of station. | Power. |
|---|---|---|---|
| | | | Watts. |
| 6DP | Grundell, Hubert | 285 11th St., San Pedro, Cal | 20 |
| 6LR | Guenther, Leo H | 309 W. Ortega St., Santa Barbara, Cal | 500 |
| 6AN | Guidotti, W. F | 745 W. San Fernando St., San Jose, Cal | 115 |
| 6GU | Gurnette, Bernard A | 51 Beaver St., San Francisco, Cal | 330 |
| 6GC | Hall, Gordon V | 1446 National Ave., San Diego, Cal | 500 |
| 6TH | Hall, Thomas C | 1278 Market St., San Francisco, Cal | 500 |
| 6VP | Hancock, Hadys D | Venice Pier, Venice, Cal | 1,000 |
| 6CQ | Hanson, Earl C | 2534 4th Ave., Los Angeles, Cal | 330 |
| 6RH | Hare, Ralph M | 74 Castro St., San Francisco, Cal | 95 |
| 6TZ | Harmon, Orville A | 2742 35th Ave., Oakland, Cal | 500 |
| 6CG | Harty, Courtenay E | 5167 Wilton Pl., Los Angeles, Cal | 200 |
| 6PQ | Harvey, George C | San Fernando, Cal | 250 |
| 6CH | Haun, John K | 152 E. 36th Pl., Los Angeles, Cal | 330 |
| 6IH | Hazleton, Ralph L | 53 Bryce St., Santa Cruz, Cal | 220 |
| 6KP | Heagney, Elmer D | 901 S. Center St., Stockton, Cal | 250 |
| 6UK | Heald's Business College | San Francisco, Cal | 1,000 |
| 6AAC | Heaney, Clarence M | 374 22d Ave., San Francisco, Cal | 500 |
| 6HN | Heinz, Albert | 127 N. F St., San Mateo, Cal | 330 |
| 6WD | Hemsley, Will | 430 20th St., San Diego, Cal | 450 |
| 6AAB | Hemenway, Clyde C | 1407 Vermont St., San Francisco, Cal | 50 |
| 6PS | Henn, Charles W | 1468 47th Ave., San Francisco, Cal | 250 |
| 6UL | Herzog, Aurelius | 1468 La Playa St., San Francisco, Cal | 125 |
| 6DC | Hibbard, Charles H., jr | 156 Bellefontaine St., Pasadena, Cal | 500 |
| 6WH | Hill, William F | 2348 G St., San Diego, Cal | 500 |
| 6CC | Hilleary, Frank J | 2600 E. 2d St., Los Angeles, Cal | 400 |
| 6NF | Hillier, H. H | 337 Rosemont Ave., Pasadena, Cal | 200 |
| 6HZ | Hoffman, Harold H | 625 Forest Ave., Pacific Grove, Cal | ...... |
| 6LU | Hoffman, Lucien C | 315 3d Ave., San Francisco, Cal | 500 |
| 6RD | Hogaboom, Raymond | 4924 Guizot St., San Diego, Cal | 55 |
| 6DQ | Holmes, Joseph J | 135 Ripley Ave., Richmond, Cal | 250 |
| 6FQ | Holt, Felix | 2042 Albatross St., San Diego, Cal | 500 |
| 6NL | Horton, Stephen E | 235 N. Mentor St., Pasadena, Cal | 600 |
| 6SI | Hoyt, Leander L | Hayward, Cal | 250 |
| 6LH | Hunt, Lloyd F | Inglewood, Cal | 770 |
| 6BW | Hyde, Stanley E | 403½ S. Bonnie Brae St., Los Angeles, Cal | 330 |
| 6PI | Hyndman, Elmore | 638 E. 23d St., Los Angeles, Cal | 250 |
| 6SJ | Indart, Carl A | 170 S. Rowan Ave., Los Angeles, Cal | 500 |
| 6IR | Irey, Earl R | 3667 3d St., San Diego, Cal | 500 |
| 6LI | Isaacs, Louis R | 1200 Regent St., Alameda, Cal | 648 |
| 6JI | Jackson, Chester M | 4025 Brookdale Ave., Oakland, Cal | 1,000 |
| 6JA | Janes, Charles V | 38 Jupiter St., San Francisco, Cal | 32 |
| 6JJ | Jessup, John H | 2620 Cedar St., Berkeley, Cal | 250 |
| 6JO | Johnson, Clarence N | 730 Julian Ave., San Diego, Cal | 500 |
| 6SA | Johnson, F. Kenneth | 715 E. 43d Ave., Los Angeles, Cal | 1,000 |
| 6TP | Johnson, Harold M | 15 King St., San Jose, Cal | 27 |
| 6NR | Johnson, J. William | 1716 Toberman St., Los Angeles, Cal | 440 |
| 6TI | Johnson, Melvern L | 720 52d St., Oakland, Cal | 250 |
| 6MY | Johnston, Robert | 734 K St., Eureka, Cal | 250 |
| 6MJ | Jones, Myron A | 4190 41st St., San Diego, Cal | 500 |
| 6RJ | Jones, Russell B | 1041 Stanyan St., San Francisco, Cal | 250 |
| 6KX | Jones, Walter | 615 L St., Eureka, Cal | 250 |
| 6VL | Kaiser, Erlin | 1665 9th St., San Diego, Cal | 45 |
| 6BL | Kather, Karl E | 104 Wilson St., Napa, Cal | 250 |
| 6OM | Kaufmann, Irwin | 56 20th Ave., San Francisco, Cal | 500 |
| 6WN | Kelly, Wallace N | Redondo, Cal | 1,000 |
| 6UF | Kemp, Thomas J | 950 Atlantic Ave., Long Beach, Cal | 500 |
| 6RK | Kerns, Roy | 219 Russell St., Berkeley, Cal | 250 |
| 6AH | Kessell, James H | 551 Willis Ave., San Jose, Cal | 20 |
| 6CE | Kilto, Carl | 506 Fremont Ave., Los Angeles, Cal | 400 |
| 6KK | Kincaid, Kenneth | 1604 S. Hope St., Los Angeles, Cal | 250 |

AMATEUR RADIO STATIONS—SIXTH DISTRICT—ALPHABETICALLY BY OWNERS OF STATIONS—Continued.

| Call signal. | Owner of station. | Location of station. | Power. |
|---|---|---|---|
| | | | Watts. |
| 6OQ | King, Clarance A | 1141 Garfield Ave., Pasadena, Cal | 500 |
| 6EX | King, William E | 80 Elgin Park, San Francisco, Cal | 250 |
| 6CK | Kinsel, Charles M | 396 Oakland Ave., Oakland, Cal | 550 |
| 6KI | Kispert, Charles H | 1748 Quesada Ave., San Francisco, Cal | ...... |
| 6JK | Klemgard, James G | 947 Cedar Ave., Long Beach, Cal | 345 |
| 6WK | Koerber, Walter A | 1099 N. Wilson Ave., Pasadena, Cal | 660 |
| 6UE | Kramer, Augustus A | 6th St. and Margarita Ave., Coronado, Cal | 500 |
| 6HK | Krauter, Howard R | 850 W. 43d Pl., Los Angeles, Cal | 990 |
| 6IW | Kreiss, Rudolph L | 1062 Stannage Ave., Berkeley, Cal | 440 |
| 6PK | Kyes, Percy L | 617 Eucalyptus Ave., Riverside, Cal | 500 |
| 6HW | La Barre, Harold J | 64 W. Colorado St., Pasadena, Cal | 280 |
| 6LY | Ladley, William A | Yohoma St., Napa, Cal | 250 |
| 6VI | Lambert, Tom | 1077 16th St., Oakland, Cal | 750 |
| 6KB | Lankston, Jesse M | 152 Ohio Ave., Sawtelle, Cal | 1,000 |
| 6SL | Leach, Stanley P | 2049 10th Ave., Oakland, Cal | 495 |
| 6LE | Lee, Daniel | 2259 Green St., San Francisco, Cal | 250 |
| 6TM | Lee, Howard R | 1580 Grove St., San Francisco, Cal | 500 |
| 6VO | Lee, John A | 134 N. Johnston St., Los Angeles, Cal | 1,000 |
| 6IZ | Leeper, Ernest W | 648 4th St., San Bernardino, Cal | 1,000 |
| 6EL | Le Fevre, Eugene | 243 Boniview Ave., San Francisco, Cal | 100 |
| 6WL | Leland, Wallace H | 912 Indian Rock Ave., Berkeley, Cal | 1,000 |
| 6HL | Linhoff, Harold R | 416 Winona Ave., Pasadena, Cal | 250 |
| 6UI | Lindsay, Edward G | 1145 Brunswick St., San Francisco, Cal | 500 |
| 6AAJ | Linville, Charles R | 307 N. Curtis Ave., Alhambra, Cal | 50 |
| 6VX | Loos, William V | 3012 Western Ave., Los Angeles, Cal | 220 |
| 6PU | Lordge, Albert | 931 Jefferson St., San Jose, Cal | 250 |
| 6LO | Lory, C. S | 3839 7th St., San Diego, Cal | 25 |
| 6VD | Loudon, Donald F | 2272 4th St., San Diego, Cal | 45 |
| 6LQ | Lowe, Sam K | 6433 Benvenue Ave., Oakland, Cal | 1,000 |
| 6CP | Lowe, William E | 1300 Garfield Ave., South Pasadena, Cal | 500 |
| 6AAL | Lyon, John D | Altadena, Cal | 500 |
| 6SF | Mack, S. Franklin | 541 Pine Ave., Pacific Grove, Cal | 500 |
| 6MV | MacMullen, Gerald | 2231 1st St., San Diego, Cal | 200 |
| 6GQ | Magee, Clark | 854 E. 47th St., Los Angeles, Cal | 330 |
| 6MX | Magill, Clyde E | E. 6th St., Ontario, Cal | 200 |
| 6MN | Maher, Edward T | 3109 Grove St., Oakland, Cal | 250 |
| 6EQ | Maher, Zacheus J | 2211 Hayes St., San Francisco, Cal | 476 |
| 6AAD | Mahn, Erich G | 29 Saturn St., San Francisco, Cal | 30 |
| 6BR | Manasse, Mervyn H | 618 Franklin St., Napa, Cal | 30 |
| 6WT | Mann, Frank W | Saratoga, Cal | 18 |
| 6HM | Mansfelt, J. Harold | 2590 Pine St., San Francisco, Cal | ...... |
| 6EM | Marlin, Evan S | Capitola, Cal | ...... |
| 6OX | Martin, Andrew W., jr | 894 Waller St., San Francisco, Cal | 500 |
| 6KS | Martin, Neal D | 2018 Delaware St., Berkeley, Cal | ...... |
| 6LM | Martinelli, Lloyd A | 1512 Shrader St., San Francisco, Cal | 50 |
| 6CU | Maskey, Franklin E | 822 E. 33d St., Los Angeles, Cal | 30 |
| 6BO | Mattoon, Stanley F | San Carlos, Cal | 30 |
| 6IM | Matsuda, Fukuzo | 2921 Pine St., San Francisco, Cal | 500 |
| 6MA | Max, Charles A | Morrill Road, San Jose, Cal | 500 |
| 6UW | Maynes, Walter W | 207 Hugo St., San Francisco, Cal | 225 |
| 6LK | McCargar, Lincoln | 1413 16th St., Oakland, Cal | 1,000 |
| 6OA | McCartney, George | 4226 Brighton Ave., Los Angeles, Cal | 250 |
| 6CF | McClatchy, Keith | Hawthorne and Ivy Sts., Inglewood, Cal | 1,000 |
| 6IU | McCleery, Ralph A | 3435 Eagle St., Los Angeles, Cal | 1,000 |
| 6IX | McCreery, Maurice E | 700 W. 32d St., Los Angeles, Cal | 440 |
| 6PY | McCullough, Harold | San Fernando, Cal | 250 |
| 6PJ | McDonald, Byron C | 85 S. El Molino St., Pasadena, Cal | 1,000 |
| 6TO | McFern, Arthur L | 1652 Berendo St., Los Angeles, Cal | 500 |
| 6JL | McGiffin, James | 2835 Vallecito Pl., Oakland, Cal | 220 |
| 6MC | McGown, Dudley B | 1247 47th Ave., San Francisco, Cal | 500 |

AMATEUR RADIO STATIONS—SIXTH DISTRICT—ALPHABETICALLY BY OWNERS OF STATIONS—Continued.

| Call signal. | Owner of station. | Location of station. | Power. |
|---|---|---|---|
| | | | *Watts.* |
| 6HJ | McIntosh, Harold St. J. | 249 Bixel St., Los Angeles, Cal. | 500 |
| 6MM | McKay, Malcolm D. | 1635 Grant St., Berkeley, Cal. | 50 |
| 6MZ | McKimmins, Mark. | 849 Laurel St., Alameda, Cal. | 500 |
| 6RM | McLaughlin, Richard A. | 420 5th Ave., San Francisco, Cal. | 50 |
| 6FM | McNabb, Floyd R. | 1886 Harmon St., Berkeley, Cal. | 880 |
| 6MR | McRoberts, Lewis H. | 3960 Elm St., San Diego, Cal. | 50 |
| 6DJ | Merritt, Lawrence G. | 252 Clinton St., Pasadena, Cal. | 600 |
| 6JM | Michaels, Joe G. | 327 7th St., Richmond, Cal. | 50 |
| 6NV | Midgley, Roland. | Menlo Park, Cal. | 50 |
| 6IA | Miles, Frederick F. | 1811 Encinal Ave., Alameda, Cal. | 250 |
| 6QY | Miley, Jerome. | 685 Bellefontaine Ave., Pasadena, Cal. | 250 |
| 6KT | Miller, Walter G. | 18 Hester Ave., San Jose, Cal. | ...... |
| 6KJ | Mills, Eldon C. | 425 Orchard St., San Jose, Cal. | 15 |
| 6MI | Mirsky, Sylvian S. | 1834 McAllister St., San Francisco, Cal. | 500 |
| 6BE | Mitchell, John C. | Mark West, Cal. | 42 |
| 6AI | Mooers, Ernest. | 155 N. 9th St., San Jose, Cal. | 1,000 |
| 6BI | Moore, Ezra. | 108 11th St., Redlands, Cal. | 500 |
| 6MO | Moore, Leon A. | 3961 Juniper St., San Diego, Cal. | 100 |
| 6CM | Moore, Paul. | 116 Berkeley Way, Whittier, Cal. | 500 |
| 6PP | Mora, Frank S. | 306 12th St., Oakland, Cal. | 1,000 |
| 6SS | Morrow, James W. | 389 63d St., Oakland, Cal. | 1,000 |
| 6WM | Morse, Willard A. | 416 E. 7th St., Oakland, Cal. | 500 |
| 6VY | Morton, J. Walter. | 610 Bellefontaine Ave., Pasadena, Cal. | 220 |
| 6WO | Mulford, Walter F. | 3900 Geary St., San Francisco, Cal. | 375 |
| 6MU | Murray, Donald W. | 70 Eureka St., Pasadena, Cal. | 120 |
| 6QG | Nelson, Martin A. | 65 Alverado St., San Leandro, Cal. | 1,000 |
| 6NB | Neumann, Edward R. | 2 Mastick Ter., Alameda, Cal. | 500 |
| 6NE | Newbould, C. Percy. | 351 26th St., San Diego, Cal. | ...... |
| 6HQ | Newton, Henry G. | 5th St. and Bay Blvd., Coronado, Cal. | 80 |
| 6KN | Nicholson, Knox W. | 721 17th St., Oakland, Cal. | ...... |
| 6NA | Nielsen, Anders. | 849 Athens Ave., Oakland, Cal. | 200 |
| 6OR | Nielsen, Fred. | 136 Caine Ave., San Francisco, Cal. | 354 |
| 6NI | Nilli, Emil. | 34 Hester Ave., San Jose, Cal. | 60 |
| 6HA | Niver, Henry A. | 618 E. Center St., Anaheim, Cal. | 660 |
| 6SD | Northon, Selden. | 385 61st St., Oakland, Cal. | 1,000 |
| 6RN | Norton, Russell. | 825 1st St., Napa, Cal. | ...... |
| 6AW | Nosler, Claud E. | 228 University St., Healdsburg, Cal. | 500 |
| 6PT | Nulsen, William B. | 545 San Benito St., Los Angeles, Cal. | 40 |
| 6BC | Oldham, William G., jr. | 720 Mendocino Ave., Santa Rosa, Cal. | 125 |
| 6OB | Oliver, Leslie R. | 1116 N. Catalina Ave., Pasadena, Cal. | 275 |
| 6LJ | Olmstead, William H. | 1433 J St., Eureka, Cal. | 1,000 |
| 6HO | Olschefsky, Henry H. | 283 Ney St., San Francisco, Cal. | 80 |
| 6BZ | O'Neill, Frank J. M. | 1423 Oxford St., Berkeley, Cal. | 1,000 |
| 6UQ | Osborne, Butler D. | 153 6th Ave., San Francisco, Cal. | 500 |
| 6OY | Oyarzo, Ben. | 343 49th St., Oakland, Cal. | 220 |
| 6HP | Pampinella, Harold. | 1755 Hayes St., San Francisco, Cal. | 50 |
| 6TK | Parker, Paul V. | 490 Geary St., San Francisco, Cal. | 500 |
| 6GK | Parkin, Gladys K. | 22 Terradillo Ave., San Rafael, Cal. | ...... |
| 6LV | Passage, Raye L. | 1966 Bonita Ave., Los Angeles, Cal. | 1,000 |
| 6PA | Pattison, Alexander. | 3881 Telegraph Ave., Oakland, Cal. | 15 |
| 6VG | Patton, Claude W. | 195 Hill Ave., Pasadena, Cal. | 1,000 |
| 6DG | Patton, Nelson. | 194 N. El Molino Ave., Pasadena, Cal. | 330 |
| 6JV | Paul, Jack. | 184 Edgewood Ave., San Francisco, Cal. | 25 |
| 6PN | Pearson, Harry. | 1015 W. 78th St., Los Angeles, Cal. | 250 |
| 6SP | Peck, C. Sherman. | 1033 Cole St., San Francisco, Cal. | 20 |
| 6OL | Petersen, Odin T. | 490 E. 48th St., Los Angeles, Cal. | 220 |
| 6FP | Peterson, Frank E. | 2615 Virginia St., Berkeley, Cal. | 250 |
| 6CD | Peterson, Walter. | 2177 W. 29th Pl., Los Angeles, Cal. | 440 |
| 6LW | Phelps, Allen G. | 611 E. 17th St., Santa Ana, Cal. | 150 |
| 6TD | Phelps, Carl A. | 810 Petaluma Ave., San Rafael, Cal. | 1,000 |

AMATEUR RADIO STATIONS—SIXTH DISTRICT—ALPHABETICALLY BY OWNERS OF STATIONS—Continued.

| Call signal. | Owner of station. | Location of station. | Power. |
|---|---|---|---|
| | | | Watts. |
| 6KH | Philippi, Charles E | 3467 E. 5th St., Los Angeles, Cal | 250 |
| 6MK | Phillips, Manuel | 1050 Cotton St., East Oakland, Cal | 1,000 |
| 6IV | Pierson, Walter | Walnut Creek, Cal | 500 |
| 6AE | Pinard, Vivian E | 505 San Salvador St., San Jose, Cal | 20 |
| 6RP | Pittman, Roy F | 1001 N. Pacific Ave., Glendale, Cal | 1,000 |
| 6UO | Polkinghorn, Frank A | 180 W. Date St., Riverside, Cal | 150 |
| 6AO | Portal, Emile A | 142 Vine St., San Jose, Cal | 32 |
| 6GP | Post, George W | 715½ Lyon St., San Francisco, Cal | 15 |
| 6CR | Potter, Lee Roy | Maple and Spadra Sts., Fullerton, Cal | 990 |
| 6BF | Powell, Meade W | Cole Bldg., Warren, Ariz | 263 |
| 6NW | Pressley, Jackson H | 1003 Mariposa Ave., Berkeley, Cal | 275 |
| 6PR | Preston, Alva W | Euclid Ave., Garden Grove, Cal | ..... |
| 6QO | Preston, Harold | Hayward, Cal | 250 |
| 6PD | Pridham, Bertrand | 885 Randolph St., Pomona, Cal | 1,000 |
| 6DV | Prosser, Norman I | R. F. D. No. 2, Pasadena, Cal | 990 |
| 6RV | Querolo, Louis | 892 Isabella St., Oakland, Cal | 250 |
| 6TQ | Quitsow, Chauncey M | 2871 Logan Ave., San Diego, Cal | 500 |
| 6UB | Ray, George | 318 7th St., San Pedro, Cal | 330 |
| 6UV | Reed, Carroll F | 683 7th Ave., San Francisco, Cal | 495 |
| 6PL | Reilly, John F | 2425 94th Ave., Oakland, Cal | 240 |
| 6SG | Reiner, Rudolf | 155 Front St., Santa Cruz, Cal | 1,000 |
| 6UR | Richards, Hugh F | Hughson, Cal | 250 |
| 6RQ | Richardson, Charles, jr | 406 W. 28th St., Los Angeles, Cal | 20 |
| 6EB | Richardson, Charles, jr | 929 W. 50th Pl., Los Angeles, Cal | 330 |
| 6JP | Richardson, Leslie | 558 Chenery St., San Francisco, Cal | 384 |
| 6RI | Richman, Clinton | 541 W. Commonwealth St., Fullerton, Cal | 1,000 |
| 6RZ | Riese, Paul E | 302 San Jose Ave., Los Gatos, Cal | 300 |
| 6JX | Riley, William M | 115 E. Haley St., Santa Barbara, Cal | 330 |
| 6FR | Rodgers, Frank | 82 Echo Ave., Oakland, Cal | ..... |
| 6NK | Roehrig, Russell S | 501 S. Oakland Ave., Pasadena, Cal | 500 |
| 6PE | Rogatsky, Carl H | 526 16th St., San Diego, Cal | 250 |
| 6BT | Rogers, Henry J | Vacaville, Cal | 30 |
| 6BD | Rogers, Stuart De Witt | 312 Orange St., Santa Rosa, Cal | 200 |
| 6VH | Root, John | 710 Pacific Ave., San Pedro, Cal | 330 |
| 6GN | Rose, George E | 105 Grattan St., San Francisco, Cal | 250 |
| 6RO | Roussin, Cecil J | 364 Lincoln Ave., Pasadena, Cal | ..... |
| 6RU | Rowley, Burton H | 202 Cypress Ave., Santa Ana, Cal | 1,000 |
| 6HR | Royden, Herbert N., jr | 311 Ellsworth Ave., San Mateo, Cal | 1,000 |
| 6GR | Rucker, George A | 2639 Grant St., Berkeley, Cal | 500 |
| 6EU | Rumble, Ernest | 114 G St., Napa Cal | 250 |
| 6DR | Sandham, Bert E | 1122 W. 55th St., Los Angeles, Cal | 300 |
| 6MP | Saveker, William T | 1156 Park Ave., San Jose, Cal | 25 |
| 6IS | Sawyer, Irving W | Capitola, Cal | ..... |
| 6HS | Schade, Henry | 15 Bennington St., San Francisco, Cal | 180 |
| 6ES | Schaefer, Carl | 3118 Stillson Ave., Sacramento, Cal | 550 |
| 6QS | Schafer, Frank | 336 Forrest St., Oakland, Cal | 250 |
| 6OS | Scheidemantel, Oscar A | 823 E. 28th St., Los Angeles, Cal | 550 |
| 6VT | Schleicher, Lorenz D | 2728 E. 2d St., Los Angeles, Cal | 500 |
| 6TS | Schneider, Tony | 424 20th Ave., San Francisco, Cal | 24 |
| 6WS | Schneider, William P | 2716 22d St., Fruitvale, Cal | 15 |
| 6SC | Schroder, Harold L | 666 53d St., Oakland, Cal | 250 |
| 6QZ | Schwartz, Sylvain A | 1726 Sutter St., San Franciso, Cal | 1,000 |
| 6EA | Seefred, Howard C. and Lyndon F. | 339 S. Fremont Ave., Los Angeles, Cal | 250 |
| 6TF | Seely, Frank | 2615 Etna St., Berkeley, Cal | 500 |
| 6CT | Seidel, William E | 2717 Brighton Ave., Los Angeles, Cal | 500 |
| 6QI | Seidl, Alexander | 3252 Prentiss St., Oakland, Cal | 60 |
| 6NT | Selby, Charles J | 3316 Market St., Oakland, Cal | 500 |
| 6SE | Serex, John F | 1820 Central Ave., Alameda, Cal | 100 |
| 6UU | Shaffner, Lucius | 1320 Illinois St., Los Angeles, Cal | 500 |

AMATEUR RADIO STATIONS—SIXTH DISTRICT—ALPHABETICALLY BY OWNERS OF STATIONS—Continued.

| Call signal. | Owner of station. | Location of station. | Power. |
|---|---|---|---|
| | | | Watts. |
| 6UN | Shaw, William A | 924 26th St., San Diego, Cal | 550 |
| 6SH | Shippam, Cecil H | 3939 I St., San Diego, Cal | 330 |
| 6FS | Short, Frank A | 846 Walnut St., Riverside, Cal | 270 |
| 6KO | Short, Ralph R | 160 Dearborn St., Pasadena, Cal | 1,000 |
| 6JS | Silvershield, Bernhard J | 832 W. 92d St., Los Angeles, Cal | 36 |
| 6AX | Simney, Albert W | 300 Joaquin Ave., San Leandro, Cal | 275 |
| 6VR | Sisson, Waldo L | 229 S. Cummings St., Los Angeles, Cal | 550 |
| 6SK | Skaalo, Arthur J | 2937 Martinez Ave., Berkeley, Cal | 250 |
| 6LZ | Slaght, Edward L | 752 S. 9th St., San Jose, Cal | 180 |
| 6LS | Smelser, Laurel J | 318 2d St., Napa, Cal | 500 |
| 6SM | Smith, Hazel P | 138 Wilshire St., Fullerton, Cal | 250 |
| 6SX | Smith, Jesse A | 1853 E. 53d St., Los Angeles, Cal | 100 |
| 6QH | Smith, Marion R | Calaveras St., Pasadena, Cal | 500 |
| 6NC | Smith, Norman E | 115 I Ave., Coronado, Cal | ..... |
| 6TV | Soprano, Anthony | 245 Clement St., San Francisco, Cal | 250 |
| 6AS | Soules, Ernest H | 75 Bush St., San Jose, Cal | 18 |
| 6TG | Speir, Godfrey B | 2731 Dwight Way, Berkeley, Cal | 500 |
| 6GI | Spelt, George S | 539 Day St., San Francisco, Cal | 500 |
| 6OE | Spence, Victor J | 415 Bartlett St., San Francisco, Cal | 50 |
| 6OJ | Spencer, Oscar J | 35 Douglass St., San Francisco, Cal | 90 |
| 6QA | St. Sure, Pettes | 1209 La Fayette St., Alameda, Cal | 300 |
| 6TY | Standiford, Vaughn H | 382 Central Ave., Pacific Grove, Cal | 550 |
| 6JR | Stauffer, John | 601 Broderick St., San Francisco, Cal | 250 |
| 6CO | Storm, Hans O | 707 W. Broadway, Anaheim, Cal | 495 |
| 6CJ | Stowe, Theodore E | 41st Ave., Capitola, Cal | 60 |
| 6GH | Stricker, George H., jr | 1411 Oxford St., Berkeley, Cal | 500 |
| 6SZ | Strong, Stuart E | 268 Jayne St., Oakland, Cal | 1,000 |
| 6WG | Strong, William A | 721 Petaluma St., San Rafael, Cal | 1,000 |
| 6SN | Sunderland, Arthur G | 92 Mary St., Pasadena, Cal | 990 |
| 6VB | Sundquist, Fred | 2153 Albee St., Eureka, Cal | 500 |
| 6SU | Sutherland, Clarence | 2334 94th Ave., Oakland, Cal | 990 |
| 6GS | Swartout, Glenn | 1044 77th St., Los Angeles, Cal | 500 |
| 6CV | Swinnerton, Kenneth | 1242 W. 51st St., Los Angeles, Cal | 275 |
| 6AAN | Sykes, Joseph | 453 S. Hope St., Los Angeles, Cal | 110 |
| 6EH | Taylor, Frank G | 512 Oak St., San Francisco, Cal | 100 |
| 6HX | Taylor, Howard L | 394 15th St., San Pedro, Cal | 330 |
| 6HI | Tessien, Henry | 2929 Octavia St., Oakland Cal | 220 |
| 6TX | Thacker, Roy M | 931 Concord St., Los Angeles, Cal | 800 |
| 6HT | Thayer, Halsey | 2123 Oak St., Los Angeles, Cal | 440 |
| 6TA | Thompson, Harold P | 101 Rivoli St., San Francisco, Cal | 500 |
| 6JT | Tibbitts, Jonathan C | 1246 St. Charles St., Alameda, Cal | 1,000 |
| 6GT | Timmermann, Gustave | 256 California Ave., San Francisco, Cal | 160 |
| 6TT | Tournat, Thomas | Garden Grove, Cal | 250 |
| 6KG | Tripp, Dwight K | 933 Gramercy Drive, Los Angeles, Cal | 250 |
| 6AY | Tuggy, Arthur W | 1289 Lemon St., Riverside, Cal | 185 |
| 6FZ | Uhl, Fred, jr | 436 S. Church St., Visalia, Cal | 1,000 |
| 6DT | Underwood, Ernest G | Commercial St., Inglewood, Cal | 250 |
| 6HU | Unger, Harry J | 228 Grattan St., San Francisco, Cal | 50 |
| 6JQ | Valentin, H | Fort St., Honolulu, Hawaii | 500 |
| 6KA | Valentin, H | Kaimuki St., Honolulu, Hawaii | 250 |
| 6AB | Valentine, Philip C | 246 Perry St., Oakland, Cal | 425 |
| 6GL | Van Auken, George L | McKee and Jackson Sts., San Jose, Cal | ..... |
| 6LN | Van Cleave, Louis V | 325 S. Flower St., Los Angeles, Cal | 250 |
| 6OP | Van Horn, Kenneth | 1457 E. 50th St., Los Angeles, Cal | 60 |
| 6NH | Van Liew, Samuel C | 825 Main St., Long Beach, Cal | 100 |
| 6GV | Van Wagner, George | 22 Franklin St., Santa Cruz, Cal | 990 |
| 6KU | Vaughan, J. H | 2325 Broadway, Oakland, Cal | 800 |
| 6SV | Verney, Stanley S | 406 Grand Blvd., San Mateo, Cal | 216 |
| 6DF | Vogeley, Herbert H | 341 Chestnut Ave., Long Beach, Cal | 20 |
| 6VU | Vonderheide, Harold H | Carson City, Nev | 220 |

AMATEUR RADIO STATIONS—SIXTH DISTRICT—ALPHABETICALLY BY OWNERS OF STATIONS—Continued.

| Call signal. | Owner of station. | Location of station. | Power. |
|---|---|---|---|
| | | | *Watts.* |
| 6VK | von Konigsberg, Charles | 1044 E. 15th St., Oakland, Cal | 25 |
| 6BA | Wadsworth, Claude E | 468 Matheson St., Healdsburg, Cal | 250 |
| 6OO | Walden, Myran | 1050 48th St., Oakland, Cal | 600 |
| 6OC | Wallace, Donald C | 1431 Linden Ave., Long Beach, Cal | 150 |
| 6IG | Wallace, Edward A | 156 Water St., Santa Cruz, Cal | 1,000 |
| 6VV | Wallace, Forrest P | 120 S. Monterey St., Alhambra, Cal | 220 |
| 6CL | Walters, Clarence O | 4326 Grand Ave., Los Angeles, Cal | 350 |
| 6KQ | Ward, Charles D | 2026 Center St., Berkeley, Cal | 250 |
| 6TJ | Warner, Stafford W | 1829 West St., Oakland, Cal | 250 |
| 6RR | Waterman, Russell R | 4561 38th St., San Diego, Cal | 80 |
| 6QW | Waters, John E | 2642 Baycroft Way, Berkeley, Cal | 1,000 |
| 6WW | Webb, Walter R | 700 E. 47th St., Los Angeles, Cal | 50 |
| 6CS | Webber, Franklin C | 632 N. Bunker Hill Ave., Los Angeles, Cal | 750 |
| 6CI | Weber, Anton M | 252 W. 43d St., Los Angeles, Cal | 350 |
| 6WE | Weddell, Clarence C | 553 Willis Ave., San Jose, Cal | ..... |
| 6RW | Weisbrod, Raymond H | 314 Lucas Ave., Los Angeles, Cal | 250 |
| 6OW | Welling, Orville E | 582 58th St., Oakland, Cal | 550 |
| 6PX | Welsch, Louie | R. F. D. No. 1, Visalia, Cal | 1,000 |
| 6JE | Welsh, Joseph E | 55 Eureka St., Pasadena, Cal | 60 |
| 6EY | Werner, Edward A | 2313 9th St., West Berkeley, Cal | 1,000 |
| 6GW | Werner, George W., jr | 3039 Adeline St., Berkeley, Cal | 250 |
| 6DK | Wescott, Laurence M | Ocean Beach, Cal | 50 |
| 6PW | Weymouth, Percy E | 1916 Woolsey St., Berkeley, Cal | 1,000 |
| 6DX | Wheelock, Charles D | 1235 Lemon St., Riverside, Cal | 65 |
| 6UX | Whidden, Ira P | 47-A Homestead Rd., Santa Clara, Cal | 150 |
| 6AF | White, Clarence E | 3024 Blossom St., Fruitvale, Cal | 1,000 |
| 6VA | White, G. Richard | 435 Oakland Ave., Pasadena, Cal | 250 |
| 6FT | Wiese, Fred T | 4174 17th St., San Francisco, Cal | 500 |
| 6RL | Wiley, Ralph W | 1250 26th Ave., San Francisco, Cal | 500 |
| 6AAM | Willey, Oscar F | 292 King St., Santa Cruz, Cal | 250 |
| 6WV | Williams, Creah | 228 E. San Carlos St., San Jose, Cal | 30 |
| 6GX | Williams, George F | 2700 High St., Oakland, Cal | 500 |
| 6UG | Williams, Tom A | 421 7th St., San Pedro, Cal | 330 |
| 6BH | Williamson, Harry | 10 S. Church St., Redlands, Cal | 30 |
| 6OG | Willis, Fred S | 2140 California St., Eureka, Cal | 25 |
| 6QB | Wilmot, Allen G | 2114 3d Ave., Los Angeles, Cal | 500 |
| 6NP | Wilson, J. Vernon | 3847 6th St., San Diego, Cal | 25 |
| 6ME | Wilson, Maurice E | 431 E. Victoria St., Santa Barbara, Cal | 1,000 |
| 6VZ | Winser, Lindley | 200 22d St., Bakersfield, Cal | 440 |
| 6IT | Winship, Leslie W | 4820 Jackdaw St., San Diego, Cal | 6 |
| 6MW | Wood, Melvin S | 5101 S. Main St., Los Angeles, Cal | 1,000 |
| 6AK | Wright, John W | 657 Asbury St., San Jose, Cal | 30 |
| 6QR | Wright, Melvin H | 241 18th St., Richmond, Cal | 125 |
| 6WU | Wulbern, Henry | 1720 Nason St., Alameda, Cal | 660 |
| 6EI | Young, Bert C | 1401 W. 9th St., Los Angeles, Cal | 550 |
| 6WY | Young, William H | 829 E. 18th St., Oakland, Cal | 250 |
| 6EW | Zahniser, Charles L | 320 Lexington Ave., Rust, Cal | ..... |
| 6MQ | Zangraft, Thomas J | 479 Cypress St., Pasadena, Cal | 990 |

ALPHABETICALLY BY CALL SIGNALS.

| Call signal. | Owner of station. | Call signal. | Owner of station. |
|---|---|---|---|
| 6AA | Aster, Alvin K. | 6AAE | Garcia, David. |
| 6AAB | Hemenway, Clyde C. | 6AAF | Collins, Wayne A. |
| 6AAC | Heaney, Clarence M. | 6AAG | Gilbert, Phillip H. |
| 6AAD | Mahn, Erich G. | 6AAH | Gilstrap, L. Frederick. |

54773°—14——9

AMATEUR RADIO STATIONS—SIXTH DISTRICT—ALPHABETICALLY BY CALL SIGNALS—Continued.

| Call signal. | Owner of station. |
|---|---|
| 6AAI | Gregory, Merle M. |
| 6AAJ | Linville, Charles R. |
| 6AAK | Green, Carl B., jr. |
| 6AAL | Lyon, John D. |
| 6AAM | Willey, Oscar F. |
| 6AAN | Sykes, Joseph. |
| 6AAO | Alexander, Willard B. |
| 6AB | Valentine, Philip C. |
| 6AC | Capwell, Cebert. |
| 6AD | Childs, Ralph S. |
| 6AE | Pinard, Vivian E. |
| 6AF | White, Clarence E. |
| 6AG | Chamberlain, Leon H. |
| 6AH | Kessel, James H. |
| 6AI | Mooers, Ernest. |
| 6AJ | Bean, James. |
| 6AK | Wright, John W. |
| 6AL | Brandis, Fred A. |
| 6AM | Buckley, Ernest V. |
| 6AN | Guidotti, W. F. |
| 6AO | Portal, Emile A. |
| 6AP | Brown, Victor. |
| 6AQ | De La Cruz, George. |
| 6AR | Greenquist, Elmer A. |
| 6AS | Soules, Ernest H. |
| 6AU | Clark, Paul U. |
| 6AW | Nosler, Claud E. |
| 6AX | Simney, Albert W. |
| 6AY | Tuggy, Arthur W. |
| 6AZ | Downing, Alan S. |
| 6BA | Wadsworth, Claude E. |
| 6BC | Oldham, William G., jr. |
| 6BD | Rogers, Stuart De Witt. |
| 6BE | Mitchell, John C. |
| 6BF | Powell, Meade W. |
| 6BG | Grates, John. |
| 6BH | Williamson, Harry. |
| 6BI | Moore, Ezra. |
| 6BJ | Edwards, Lewis W. |
| 6BK | Frost, William H. |
| 6BL | Kather, Karl E. |
| 6BM | Godwin, Merle H. |
| 6BO | Mattoon, Stanley F. |
| 6BP | Bauer, Roy M. |
| 6BQ | Baer, Charles M. |
| 6BR | Manasse, Mervyn H. |
| 6BS | Davidson, G. Edward. |
| 6BT | Rogers, Henry J. |
| 6BV | Drake, Charles. |
| 6BW | Hyde, Stanley E. |
| 6BX | Barrett, Eldridge D. |
| 6BZ | O'Neill, Frank J. M. |
| 6CA | Corby, Grant W. |
| 6CB | Fisher, Frank L. |
| 6CC | Hilleary, Frank J. |
| 6CD | Peterson, Walter. |
| 6CE | Kilto, Carl. |
| 6CF | McClatchy, Keith. |
| 6CG | Harty, Courtenay E. |
| 6CH | Haun, John K. |
| 6CI | Weber, Anton M. |
| 6CJ | Stowe, Theodore E. |
| 6CK | Kinsel, Charles M. |
| 6CL | Walters, Clarence O. |
| 6CM | Moore, Paul. |
| 6CO | Storm, Hans O. |
| 6CP | Lowe, William E. |
| 6CQ | Hanson, Earl C. |
| 6CR | Potter, Lee Roy. |
| 6CS | Webber, Franklin C. |
| 6CT | Seidel, William E. |
| 6CU | Maskey, Franklin E. |
| 6CV | Swinnerton, Kenneth. |
| 6CX | Frunk, Carl G. |
| 6CY | Cooper, Charles P. |
| 6CZ | Everard, Charles E. |
| 6DA | Brown, Ralph E. |
| 6DC | Hibbard, Charles H., jr. |
| 6DD | Clark, Victor M. |
| 6DE | Curtis, Burbank. |
| 6DF | Vogeley, Herbert H. |
| 6DG | Patton, Nelson. |
| 6DH | Grimes, W. Frank. |
| 6DI | Cookson, Howard A. |
| 6DJ | Merritt, Lawrence G. |
| 6DK | Wescott, Laurence M. |
| 6DL | Espe, Oliver E. |
| 6DM | Archer, Robert P. |
| 6DP | Grundell, Hubert. |
| 6DQ | Holmes, Joseph J. |
| 6DR | Sandham, Bert E. |
| 6DS | Adams, Charles C. |
| 6DT | Underwood, Ernest G. |
| 6DV | Prosser, Norman I. |
| 6DW | De Wald, Alfred S. |
| 6DX | Wheelock, Charles D. |
| 6DZ | Caldwell, Duncan K. |
| 6EA | Seefred, Howard C. and Lyndon F. |
| 6EB | Richardson, Charles, jr. |
| 6ED | Flinspach, J. Henry. |
| 6EE | Griffin, Clyde S. |
| 6EG | Aten, Arthur B. |
| 6EH | Taylor, Frank G. |
| 6EI | Young, Bert C. |
| 6EJ | Bean, Arthur E. |
| 6EK | Eiferle, Chrissie. |
| 6EL | Le Fevre, Eugene. |
| 6EM | Marlin, Evan S. |
| 6EN | de Neuf, Emil A. |
| 6EO | Blake, Albert W. |
| 6EP | Davis, Elwood. |
| 6EQ | Maher, Zacheus J. |
| 6ER | Bailey, Cecil. |
| 6ES | Schaefer, Carl. |
| 6ET | Fenner, Paul R. |

Amateur Radio Stations—Sixth District—Alphabetically by Call Signals—Continued.

| Call signal. | Owner of station. |
|---|---|
| 6EU | Rumble, Ernest. |
| 6EW | Zahniser, Charles L. |
| 6EX | King, William E. |
| 6EY | Werner, Edward A. |
| 6EZ | Christie, A. Edwin. |
| 6FA | Arnberger, Frank, jr. |
| 6FB | Farlinger, Ernest. |
| 6FC | Carey, Francis K. |
| 6FD | Deardorf, Francis H. |
| 6FE | Felt, Clarence J. |
| 6FG | Granger, Floyd. |
| 6FH | French, Donald K. |
| 6FI | Eveleth, Harlan A. |
| 6FJ | Barnum, Coit L. |
| 6FK | Frank, Walter. |
| 6FL | Faneuf, Forrest E. |
| 6FM | McNabb, Floyd R. |
| 6FO | Fones, Robert. |
| 6FP | Peterson, Frank E. |
| 6FQ | Holt, Felix. |
| 6FR | Rodgers, Frank. |
| 6FS | Short, Frank A. |
| 6FT | Wiese, Fred T. |
| 6FU | Bergstrom, R. Bernard. |
| 6FV | Brockett, Charles. |
| 6FX | Cross, Fred M. |
| 6FY | Buell, Clarence R. |
| 6FZ | Uhl, Fred, jr. |
| 6GA | Garratt, Edward D. |
| 6GB | Bowlus, Glen H. |
| 6GC | Hall, Gordon V. |
| 6GD | Day, Elwin C. |
| 6GE | Gerlach, William G. |
| 6GF | Farmer, Gordon. |
| 6GG | Gildersleeve, Given. |
| 6GH | Stricker, George H., jr. |
| 6GI | Spelt, George S. |
| 6GJ | Gaugh, H. E. F. |
| 6GK | Parkin, Gladys K. |
| 6GL | Van Auken, George L. |
| 6GN | Rose, George E. |
| 6GO | Goss, William M. |
| 6GP | Post, George W. |
| 6GQ | Magee, Clark. |
| 6GR | Rucker, George A. |
| 6GS | Swartout, Glenn. |
| 6GT | Timmermann, Gustave. |
| 6GU | Gurnette, Bernard A. |
| 6GV | Van Wagner, George. |
| 6GW | Werner, George W., jr. |
| 6GX | Williams, George F. |
| 6GZ | Edgar, George P. |
| 6HA | Niver, Henry A. |
| 6HB | Baker, Harry G. |
| 6HC | Craig, Harold F. |
| 6HD | Dickow, Henry. |
| 6HE | Eastling, Harvey. |
| 6HF | Flenner, Harry A. |
| 6HI | Tession, Henry. |
| 6HJ | McIntosh, Harold St. J. |
| 6HK | Krauter, Howard R. |
| 6HL | Linhoff, Harold R. |
| 6HM | Mansfelt, J. Harold. |
| 6HN | Heinz, Albert. |
| 6HO | Olschefsky, Henry H. |
| 6HP | Pampinella, Harold. |
| 6HQ | Newton, Henry G. |
| 6HR | Royden, Herbert N., jr. |
| 6HS | Schade, Henry. |
| 6HT | Thayer, Halsey. |
| 6HU | Unger, Harry J. |
| 6HV | Ferrill, Herbert E. |
| 6HW | La Barre, Harold J. |
| 6HX | Taylor, Howard L. |
| 6HY | Ebeling, Hyde S. |
| 6HZ | Hoffman, Harold H. |
| 6IA | Miles, Frederick F. |
| 6IC | Austin, Russell F. |
| 6IE | Chambers, James. |
| 6IF | Farwell, Ivyn. |
| 6IG | Wallace, Edward A. |
| 6IH | Hazleton, Ralph L. |
| 6II | Ferguson, E. Franklin. |
| 6IJ | Boehme, Herbert L. |
| 6IM | Matsuda, Fukuzo. |
| 6IO | Buchanan, Roy J. |
| 6IQ | Cornell, Ezra B. |
| 6IR | Irey, Earl R. |
| 6IS | Sawyer, Irving W. |
| 6IT | Winship, Leslie W. |
| 6IU | McCleery, Ralph A. |
| 6IV | Pierson, Walter. |
| 6IW | Kreiss, Rudolph L. |
| 6IX | McCreery, Maurice E. |
| 6IZ | Leeper, Ernest W. |
| 6JA | Janes, Charles V. |
| 6JB | Brown, Julian T. |
| 6JC | Chase, John H. |
| 6JE | Welsh, Joseph E. |
| 6JF | Forsburg, Joe A. |
| 6JG | Gould, Gordon. |
| 6JH | Berry, Charles A. |
| 6JI | Jackson, Chester M. |
| 6JJ | Jessup, John H. |
| 6JK | Klemgard, James G. |
| 6JL | McGiffin, James. |
| 6JM | Michaels, Joe G. |
| 6JO | Johnson, Clarence N. |
| 6JP | Richardson, Leslie. |
| 6JQ | Valentin, H. |
| 6JR | Stauffer, John. |
| 6JS | Silvershield, Bernhard J. |
| 6JT | Tibbitts, Jonathan C. |
| 6JU | Fisher, Jules. |
| 6JV | Paul, Jack. |

AMATEUR RADIO STATIONS—SIXTH DISTRICT—ALPHABETICALLY BY CALL SIGNALS—Continued.

| Call signal. | Owner of station. | Call signal. | Owner of station. |
|---|---|---|---|
| 6JW | Gastman, Henry. | 6ME | Wilson, Maurice E. |
| 6JX | Riley, William M. | 6MF | Aymar, Clarence A. |
| 6JY | Browne, G. R. A., jr. | 6MG | Glindemann, Melvern. |
| 6JZ | Charters, John R. | 6MI | Mirsky, Sylvian S. |
| | | 6MJ | Jones, Myron A. |
| 6KA | Valentin, H. | 6MK | Phillips, Manuel. |
| 6KB | Lankston, Jesse M. | 6MM | McKay, Malcom D. |
| 6KC | Dinley, Laurence J. | 6MN | Maher, Edward T. |
| 6KD | Dutton, Kingsley. | 6MO | Moore, Leon A. |
| 6KE | Dogan, Kenneth D. | 6MP | Saveker, William T. |
| 6KF | Filben, Frank. | 6MQ | Zangraft, Thomas J. |
| 6KG | Tripp, Dwight K. | 6MR | McRoberts, Lewis H. |
| 6KH | Philippi, Charles E. | 6MS | Carson, E. A. |
| 6KI | Kispert, Charles H. | 6MT | Berringer, Hall. |
| 6KJ | Mills, Eldon C. | 6MU | Murray, Donald W. |
| 6KK | Kincaid, Kenneth. | 6MV | MacMullen, Gerald. |
| 6KM | Everett, J. Victor. | 6MW | Wood, Melvin S. |
| 6KN | Nicholson, Knox W. | 6MX | Magill, Clyde E. |
| 6KO | Short, Ralph R. | 6MY | Johnston, Robert. |
| 6KP | Heagney, Elmer D. | 6MZ | McKimmins, Mark. |
| 6KQ | Ward, Charles D. | | |
| 6KR | Center, Hugh. | 6NA | Nielsen, Anders. |
| 6KS | Martin, Neal D. | 6NB | Neumann, Edward R. |
| 6KT | Miller, Walter G. | 6NC | Smith, Norman E. |
| 6KU | Vaughan, J. H. | 6ND | Breck, F. Bon. |
| 6KW | Fisk, Alfred C. | 6NE | Newbould, C. Percy. |
| 6KX | Jones, Walter. | 6NF | Hillier, H. H. |
| 6KY | Andrews, Harold S. | 6NG | Gerlach, Leonard. |
| 6KZ | Beaver, Gerald A. | 6NH | Van Liew, Samuel C. |
| | | 6NI | Nilli, Emil. |
| 6LA | Blochman, Lawrence G. | 6NJ | Cunningham, Edward J. |
| 6LB | Barton, Larry J. | 6NK | Roehrig, Russell S. |
| 6LC | Comins, Frank L. | 6NL | Horton, Stephen E. |
| 6LD | Anderlini, Louis J. | 6NM | Eidemiller, Charles H. |
| 6LE | Lee, Daniel. | 6NO | Donaldson, Ernest S. |
| 6LF | Alexander, Lee. | 6NP | Wilson, J. Vernon. |
| 6LG | Gianini, Leo G. | 6NQ | Francis, Ernest R. |
| 6LH | Hunt, Lloyd F. | 6NR | Johnson, J. William. |
| 6LI | Isaacs, Louis R. | 6NT | Selby, Charles J. |
| 6LJ | Olmstead, William H. | 6NU | Adkins, Edward S. |
| 6LK | McCargar, Lincoln. | 6NV | Midgley, Roland. |
| 6LL | Griffith, William M. | 6NW | Pressley, Jackson H. |
| 6LM | Martinelli, Lloyd A. | 6NX | Calvert, Paul P. |
| 6LN | Van Cleave, Louis V. | 6NY | Carroll, Elvin K. |
| 6LO | Lory, C. S. | 6NZ | Emmerling, Herbert J. |
| 6LP | Gray, Clifford. | | |
| 6LQ | Lowe, Sam K. | 6OA | McCartney, George. |
| 6LR | Guenther, Leo H. | 6OB | Oliver, Leslie R. |
| 6LS | Smelser, Laurel J. | 6OC | Wallace, Donald C. |
| 6LT | Downs, La Roy. | 6OD | Cook, John A. |
| 6LU | Hoffman, Lucien C. | 6OE | Spence, Victor J. |
| 6LV | Passage, Raye L. | 6OF | Doty, Arthur H. |
| 6LW | Phelps, Allen G. | 6OG | Willis, Fred S. |
| 6LX | Berlin, Latham. | 6OH | Bull, Harold F. |
| 6LY | Ladley, William A. | 6OI | Dawson, J. Percy. |
| 6LZ | Slaght, Edward L. | 6OJ | Spencer, Oscar J. |
| | | 6OK | Dillon, Lyle. |
| 6MA | Max, Charles A. | 6OL | Petersen, Odin T. |
| 6MB | Baden, Merle L. | 6OM | Kaufmann, Irwin. |
| 6MC | McGown, Dudley B. | 6ON | Germain, H. |

AMATEUR RADIO STATIONS—SIXTH DISTRICT—ALPHABETICALLY BY CALL SIGNALS—Continued.

| Call signal. | Owner of station. | Call signal. | Owner of station. |
|---|---|---|---|
| 6OO | Walden, Myran. | 6QX | Baird, Maxfield A. |
| 6OP | Van Horn, Kenneth. | 6QY | Miley, Jerome. |
| 6OQ | King, Clarance A. | 6QZ | Schwartz, Silvain A. |
| 6OR | Nielsen, Fred. | | |
| 6OS | Scheidemantel, Oscar A. | 6RA | Brandt, Robert L. |
| 6OU | Eldredge, George E. | 6RB | Brumter, Ralph. |
| 6OV | Doig, John H., jr. | 6RC | Cook, J. Ralph. |
| 6OW | Welling, Orville E. | 6RD | Hogaboom, Raymond. |
| 6OX | Martin, Andrew W., jr. | 6RE | Esplen, Elmer R. |
| 6OY | Oyarzo, Ben. | 6RF | Frier, Robert L. |
| 6OZ | Burge, Walter M. | 6RG | Downs, Robert. |
| | | 6RH | Hare, Ralph M. |
| 6PA | Pattison, Alexander. | 6RI | Richman, Clinton. |
| 6PB | Bradley, Philip L. | 6RJ | Jones, Russell B. |
| 6PD | Pridham, Bertrand. | 6RK | Kerns, Roy. |
| 6PE | Rogatsky, Carl H. | 6RL | Wiley, Ralph W. |
| 6PF | Allen, Preston D. | 6RM | McLaughlin, Richard A. |
| 6PG | Gillmore, Purcell. | 6RN | Norton, Russell. |
| 6PI | Hyndman, Elmore. | 6RO | Roussin, Cecil J. |
| 6PJ | McDonald, Byron C. | 6RP | Pittman, Roy F. |
| 6PK | Kyes, Percy L. | 6RQ | Richardson, Charles, jr. |
| 6PL | Reilly, John F. | 6RR | Waterman, Russell R. |
| 6PM | Bolton, Harold B. | 6RT | Cornish, Lester R. |
| 6PN | Pearson, Harry. | 6RU | Rowley, Burton H. |
| 6PO | Drath, Walter J. | 6RV | Querolo, Louis. |
| 6PP | Mora, Frank S. | 6RW | Weisbrod, Raymond H. |
| 6PQ | Harvey, George C. | 6RX | Gray, Harold G. |
| 6PR | Preston, Alva W. | 6RY | Bullard, Orlan K. |
| 6PS | Henn, Charles W. | 6RZ | Riese, Paul E. |
| 6PT | Nulsen, William B. | | |
| 6PU | Lordge, Albert. | 6SA | Johnson, F. Kenneth. |
| 6PV | Czapkay, Edward. | 6SB | Bisson, Charles S. |
| 6PW | Weymouth, Percy E. | 6SC | Schroder, Harold L. |
| 6PX | Welsch, Louie. | 6SD | Northon, Selden. |
| 6PY | McCullough, Harold. | 6SE | Serex, John F. |
| 6PZ | Brown, Robert L. | 6SF | Mack, S. Franklin. |
| | | 6SG | Reiner, Rudolf. |
| 6QA | St. Sure, Pettes. | 6SH | Shippam, Cecil H. |
| 6QB | Wilmot, Allen G. | 6SI | Hoyt, Leander L. |
| 6QC | Christensen, V. H. | 6SJ | Indart, Carl A. |
| 6QD | Adam, Carl F., jr. | 6SK | Skaale, Arthur J. |
| 6QE | Dodge, Earl E. | 6SL | Leach, Stanley P. |
| 6QF | Biber, Albert L. | 6SM | Smith, Hazel P. |
| 6QG | Nelson, Martin A. | 6SN | Sunderland, Arthur G. |
| 6QH | Smith, Marion R. | 6SO | Bunting, Howard S. |
| 6QI | Seidl, Alexander. | 6SP | Peck, C. Sherman. |
| 6QJ | Chamberlain, George E. | 6SQ | Fonseca, Arthur. |
| 6QK | Gill, Fred M. | 6SS | Morrow, James W. |
| 6QL | Barker, Waldo W. | 6ST | Evans, Bryan. |
| 6QM | Ensign, Millard J. | 6SU | Sutherland, Clarence. |
| 6QN | Abbott, Raymond B. | 6SV | Verney, Stanley S. |
| 6QO | Preston, Harold. | 6SW | Anderson, Elroy E. |
| 6QP | Beament, Thomas. | 6SX | Smith, Jesse A. |
| 6QQ | Finnell, Phillip S. | 6SY | Carroll, Russell W. |
| 6QR | Wright, Melvin H. | 6SZ | Strong, Stuart E. |
| 6QS | Schafer, Frank. | | |
| 6QT | Bennett, George S. | 6TA | Thompson, Harold P. |
| 6QU | Floud, J. Harold. | 6TB | Boudinot, Truman E. |
| 6QV | Echlin, Jack E. | 6TC | Fisher, Thomas A. |
| 6QW | Waters, John E. | 6TD | Phelps, Carl A. |

AMATEUR RADIO STATIONS—SIXTH DISTRICT—ALPHABETICALLY BY CALL SIGNALS—Continued.

| Call signal. | Owner of station. | Call signal. | Owner of station. |
|---|---|---|---|
| 6TE | Eisenhuth, Thomas V. | 6VD | Loudon, Donald F. |
| 6TF | Seely, Frank. | 6VF | Falk, Victor H. |
| 6TG | Speir, Godfrey B. | 6VG | Patton, Claude W. |
| 6TH | Hall, Thomas C. | 6VH | Root, John. |
| 6TI | Johnson, Melvern L. | 6VI | Lambert, Tom. |
| 6TJ | Warner, Stafford W. | 6VJ | Barbour, Joseph L. |
| 6TK | Parker, Paul V. | 6VK | von Konigsberg, Charles. |
| 6TM | Lee, Howard R. | 6VL | Kaiser, Erlin. |
| 6TN | Beckman, Philip E. | 6VM | Anderson, Herbert E. |
| 6TO | McFern, Arthur L. | 6VN | Dorcy, Ben H., jr. |
| 6TP | Johnson, Harold M. | 6VO | Lee, John A. |
| 6TQ | Quitsow, Chauncey M. | 6VP | Hancock, Hadys D. |
| 6TR | Farrell, Raymond. | 6VQ | Benner, Bryan. |
| 6TS | Schneider, Tony. | 6VR | Sisson, Waldo L. |
| 6TT | Tournat, Thomas. | 6VS | Bauman, Warren C. |
| 6TV | Soprano, Anthony. | 6VT | Schleicher, Lorenz D. |
| 6TW | Davidson, Stanley E. | 6VU | Vonderheide, Harold H. |
| 6TX | Thacker, Roy M. | 6VV | Wallace, Forrest P. |
| 6TY | Standiford, Vaughn H. | 6VW | Beraldo, Dewey. |
| 6TZ | Harmon, Orville A. | 6VX | Loos, William V. |
| | | 6VY | Morton, J. Walter. |
| 6UA | Asadoorian, Theodore N. | 6VZ | Winser, Lindley. |
| 6UB | Ray, George. | | |
| 6UE | Kramer, Augustus A. | 6WA | Anthes, William F., jr. |
| 6UF | Kemp, Thomas J. | 6WB | Booth, Wilber C. |
| 6UG | Williams, Tom A. | 6WC | Cornish, Warren D. |
| 6UH | Gates, Howard C. | 6WD | Hemsley, Will. |
| 6UI | Lindsay, Edward G. | 6WE | Weddell, Clarence C. |
| 6UJ | Delius, Herbert A. | 6WF | Ford, Walter B. |
| 6UK | Heald's Business College. | 6WG | Strong, William A. |
| 6UL | Herzog, Aurelius. | 6WH | Hill, William F. |
| 6UM | Freeman, Elmer D. | 6WI | Cusick, William J. |
| 6UN | Shaw, William A. | 6WJ | Bechtel, Warren, jr. |
| 6UO | Polkinghorn, Frank A. | 6WK | Koerber, Walter A. |
| 6UP | Creswell, Frank, jr. | 6WL | Leland, Wallace H. |
| 6UQ | Osborne, Butler D. | 6WM | Morse, Willard A. |
| 6UR | Richards, Hugh F. | 6WN | Kelly, Wallace N. |
| 6US | Gibson, Walter L. | 6WO | Mulford, Walter F. |
| 6UT | Everard, Charles E. | 6WP | Donelson, William E., jr. |
| 6UU | Shaffner, Lucius. | 6WQ | Cowles, John. |
| 6UV | Reed, Carroll F. | 6WR | Bigler, Anson S. |
| 6UW | Maynes, Walter W. | 6WS | Schneider, William P. |
| 6UX | Whidden, Ira P. | 6WT | Mann, Frank W. |
| 6UY | Everharty, Laurence. | 6WU | Wulbern, Henry. |
| 6UZ | Gosmann, Jack L. | 6WV | Williams, Creah. |
| | | 6WW | Webb, Walter R. |
| 6VA | White, G. Richard. | 6WX | Ebert, Howard W. |
| 6VB | Sundquist, Fred. | 6WY | Young, William H. |
| 6VC | Gottwald, Eugene A. | 6WZ | Capps, Delphin. |

## AMATEUR RADIO STATIONS—Continued.

### SEVENTH DISTRICT.

[Headquarters: Customhouse, Seattle, Wash. The seventh district comprises the States of Oregon, Washington, Idaho, Montana, Wyoming, and the Territory of Alaska.]

ALPHABETICALLY BY OWNERS OF STATIONS.

| Call signal. | Owner of station. | Location of station. | Power. |
|---|---|---|---|
| | | | Watts. |
| 7EA | Adams, Edison | 1020½ Tacoma Ave., Tacoma, Wash | 50 |
| 7AB | Anderson, Alfred S | 1253 Grand Ave., Astoria, Oreg | 100 |
| 7CB | Bennett, Cecil H | Rainier, Oreg | 500 |
| 7AT | Bennett, Henry | 3125 Oakes Ave., Everett, Wash | 660 |
| 7AS | Bird, Lester F | 909 Blewett St., Seattle, Wash | 470 |
| 7DB | Bolstad, Archie L | 1832 4th Ave. W., Seattle, Wash | 16 |
| 7FB | Boswell, George | 3887 16th St. SW., Seattle, Wash | 440 |
| 7HB | Breum, Helmer O | 3416 S. Madison St., Tacoma, Wash | 200 |
| 7BB | Brown, David M | 4943 73d St. SE., Portland, Oreg | 100 |
| 7GB | Butterfield, George H | 815 Kearney St., Portland, Oreg | 960 |
| 7WC | Cates, Walter C | 1704 Franklin St., Vancouver, Wash | 1,000 |
| 7VC | Coburn, William D | Ashland, Oreg | 550 |
| 7EC | Covey, E. Channing | 2429 Baker Ave., Everett, Wash | 1,000 |
| 7DC | Crockett, George D | 1420 Hawthorne Ave., Portland, Oreg | 240 |
| 7AP | Crossley, Jack | 1053 Vaughn St., Portland, Oreg | 500 |
| 7HC | Cutting, H. Everett | 231 W. Main St., Bozeman, Mont | 500 |
| 7AC | Dailey, Arthur C | 3915 Colby Ave., Everett, Wash | 550 |
| 7HD | Davis, Hubert A | 1904 Canoe Pl., Seattle, Wash | 500 |
| 7PD | Davis, Percy E | 28 E. 60th St., Portland, Oreg | 450 |
| 7AN | Dolloff, Ralph E | 3724 Colby Ave., Everett, Wash | 660 |
| 7AD | Douglas, Alfred E | 824 East E St., Grants Pass, Oreg | 1,000 |
| 7MD | Durkee, Mealon | 713 St. Helens Ave., Tacoma, Wash | 500 |
| 7CE | Eichelberger, H. Carl | 715 N. 9th St., Boise, Idaho | 770 |
| 7BA | Elbon, Jennings | 2122 Commercial St., Astoria, Oreg | 500 |
| 7ME | Elliott, Morton W | 635 S. Atlantic St., Dillon, Mont | 300 |
| 7CF | Farrar, Clyde L | 311 Wimer St., Ashland, Oreg | 55 |
| 7FF | Farris, Frank E | 1604 Spring St., Olympia, Wash | 250 |
| 7EF | Ford, Edwin D., jr | Weiser, Idaho | 150 |
| 7GF | Gibbs, Floyd F | 512 E. 4th St., Hood River, Oreg | 275 |
| 7CG | Gillespie, Charles R | Kalama, Wash | 75 |
| 7RO | Grant, Robert E | 1317 Fort St., Boise, Idaho | 500 |
| 7FG | Gruwell, Fred N | 616 Concord St., Bremerton, Wash | 500 |
| 7CH | Hansen, Carl L | 5415 6th Ave. NW., Seattle, Wash | 400 |
| 7BD | Hapner, Harry | 1213 Harris St., South Bellingham, Wash | 50 |
| 7AH | Hardesty, Adolph | 195 3d St., Astoria, Oreg | ..... |
| 7EE | Hawkins, Edward K | 1800 27th Ave. S., Seattle, Wash | 250 |
| 7HH | Hayden, Harold L | 560 Balm St., Walla Walla, Wash | 275 |
| 7GC | Henny, George C | 530 Heights Ter., Portland, Oreg | 32 |
| 7GH | Hess, George F | 1604 Van Buren St., Corvallis, Oreg | 330 |
| 7HI | Hignan, Harry H | Hamilton, Mont | 200 |
| 7PH | Hoffmann, Philip | 621 S. 1st St., Walla Walla, Wash | 220 |
| 7AQ | Holm, Paul E | 422 Blackstone St., Portland, Oreg | 100 |
| 7HU | Hursh, Harold H | Medical Springs, Oreg | 600 |
| 7EJ | Jackson, Edgar F | 1135 Thurman St., Portland, Oreg | 150 |
| 7DJ | John, D. Morris | 745 N. 9th St., Corvallis, Oreg | ..... |
| 7AI | Johnson, Clifford E | 1004 N. Adams St., Tacoma, Wash | 450 |
| 7GJ | Johnson, Gale H | 124 Queen Anne Ave., Seattle, Wash | 660 |
| 7JJ | Johnson, Joseph E | 2716 Grand Ave., Everett, Wash | 495 |
| 7HJ | Jones, Henry L | 1111 E. Cherry St., Seattle, Wash | 250 |
| 7AK | Koester, Alpha M | Near North Powder, Oreg | 450 |
| 7EL | La Pine, Earl | 1747 26th Ave. N., Seattle, Wash | 550 |
| 7LA | Larson, Walter L | 1700 W. 57th St., Seattle, Wash | 500 |
| 7CL | Law, Charles J | Union, Oreg | 1,000 |
| 7FW | Lee, Emery H. I | 1412 Summit Ave., Seattle, Wash | 550 |
| 7FL | Ling, Frank Moy | 506 Mill St., Portland, Oreg | 50 |
| 7HL | Longmire, Harold D | 408 S. 32d St., Tacoma, Wash | 125 |

AMATEUR RADIO STATIONS—SEVENTH DISTRICT—ALPHABETICALLY BY OWNERS OF STATIONS—Continued.

| Call signal. | Owner of station. | Location of station. | Power. |
|---|---|---|---|
| | | | *Watts.* |
| 7MM | Mathison, Martin J | 4102 N. 13th St., Tacoma, Wash | 220 |
| 7HM | McCandless, Howard F | 204 S. Tacoma Ave., Tacoma, Wash | 1,000 |
| 7MC | McClelland, Joseph S | 1128 15th St., Seattle, Wash | 500 |
| 7AW | Meals, Owen E | Valdez, Alaska | 250 |
| 7JO | Methven, John H | Ronald-by-Roslyn, Wash | 12 |
| 7MH | Middlekauff, Mark H | N. 27th St., Corvallis, Oreg | ..... |
| 7EM | Miller, E. Clarence | 504 E. Republican St., Seattle, Wash | 130 |
| 7DM | Minkler, Darrell | 240 C St., Ashland, Oreg | 550 |
| 7MI | Minter, John W | 610 E. 19th St., Cheyenne, Wyo | 1,000 |
| 7AG | Moe, George | 4118 N. 16th St., Tacoma, Wash | 320 |
| 7RD | Montgomery, Jack H | 5006 52d St. SE., Portland, Oreg | 100 |
| 7RC | Mood, George T | Clarkston, Wash | 100 |
| 7GM | Moore, Gale L | 4735 58th St. SE., Portland, Oreg | 1,000 |
| 7LN | Nagle, Leo W | 1109 Washington St., Vancouver, Wash | 1,000 |
| 7IN | Nelson, Ivan L | 1003 N. 12th St., Boise, Idaho | 495 |
| 7ON | Nicholson, W. Otto | 3115 S. 7th St., Tacoma, Wash | 1,000 |
| 7RE | Nitschke, Erville W | 346 E. 34th St., Portland, Oreg | 100 |
| 7SN | Norman, Stacy W | 137 N. 79th St., Seattle, Wash | 500 |
| 7IO | O'Donoughue, Ivan | 355 Almond St., Ashland, Oreg | 50 |
| 7KP | Pennebaker, Kenneth T | R. F. D. No. 1, Tangent, Wash | 250 |
| 7CP | Peterson, C. Edward | 1008 Raleigh St., Portland, Oreg | 375 |
| 7CW | Peterson, Charles W | 2922 3d Ave. W., Seattle, Wash | 500 |
| 7EP | Peterson, Edward T | 718 E. Ash St., Portland, Oreg | 45 |
| 7AO | Piercy, Russell H | 313 Tillamook St., Portland, Oreg | 100 |
| 7HP | Pyle, Howard S | 3311 S. 37th Ave., Seattle, Wash | ..... |
| 7WR | Rogers, Wilber L | 2304 Monroe St., Corvallis, Oreg | ..... |
| 7AV | Root, Charles W | 905 Jersey St., St. Johns, Oreg | 150 |
| 7AR | Root, Dellmar A | 631 Buchanen St., St. Johns, Oreg | 475 |
| 7LR | Ross, Lindsley W | 590 Main St., Portland, Oreg | 936 |
| 7JQ | Roy, James | 2028 6th Ave., Seattle, Wash | 50 |
| 7BC | Ruth, Orin S | 622 W. G St., Grants Pass, Oreg | 500 |
| 7AF | Scrutton, Gerald | 330 E. 35th St., Portland, Oreg | 300 |
| 7DS | Shingler, Don G | 208 W. 19th St., Cheyenne, Wyo | 150 |
| 7AA | Skyles, Theron G | 522 11th St., Astoria, Oreg | 75 |
| 7US | Slewing, Vere T | 531 W. Palm St., Medford, Oreg | 1,000 |
| 7HS | Slocum, Herbert R | 47 E. 9th St. South, Portland, Oreg | 300 |
| 7VS | Small, Vincent | 2322 Wetmore Ave., Everett, Wash | 935 |
| 7LS | Smith, Lloyd T | 468 Oak St., Ashland, Oreg | 250 |
| 7AJ | Sorensen, Chester J | 4031 Quimby St., Portland, Oreg | 100 |
| 7WS | Sparrow, William T | 932 W. 63d St., Seattle, Wash | 550 |
| 7BS | Spencer, Arthur | 2519 Fulton St., Everett, Wash | 990 |
| 7WQ | Stedman, William | Kake, Alaska | 25 |
| 7SW | Swan, Emil | 1461 Portsmouth Ave., Portland, Oreg | 1,000 |
| 7AE | Thomas, Edward J | Cœur d'Alene, Idaho | 24 |
| 7LT | Thompson, Lloyd S | 109 5th St., Hamilton, Mont | 170 |
| 7JR | Tolmie, Jack R | 1213 Columbia St., Seattle, Wash | 10 |
| 7JT | Tyler, John L | 505 S. 4th St., Hamilton, Mont | 250 |
| 7AZ | Warner, Archie | Deer Park, Wash | 500 |
| 7KW | Warrens, C. Kenneth | 848 Melinda Ave., Portland, Oreg | 220 |
| 7RV | Westcott, Roy | 1607 N. 19th St., Boise, Idaho | 1,000 |
| 7HT | Whelan, Harold J | 612 W. 27th St., Vancouver, Wash | 50 |
| 7BW | Williams, Charles E | 8326 13th Ave. NW., Seattle, Wash | 50 |
| 7DW | Willis, Cecil D | 1316 Columbia St., Seattle, Wash | 10 |
| 7GW | Wilson, George D | 1022 E. Heron St., Aberdeen, Wash | 1,000 |
| 7JW | Wilson, John C | 295 N. 24th St., Portland, Oreg | 700 |
| 7HW | Winningham, Harold | 3701 N. 18th St., Tacoma, Wash | ..... |
| 7LW | Wollaston, Arthur L | 541 19th Ave., Seattle, Wash | 90 |
| 7RB | Wormington, Ralph V | 104 Park St., Milton, Oreg | 330 |
| 7RW | Wright, Raymond F | R. F. D., Port Orchard, Wash | 440 |
| 7GA | Wurtz, George A | Hanford, Wash | 990 |

AMATEUR RADIO STATIONS—SEVENTH DISTRICT—ALPHABETICALLY BY OWNERS OF STATIONS—Continued.

ALPHABETICALLY BY CALL SIGNALS.

| Call signal. | Owner of station. |
|---|---|
| 7AA | Skyles, Theron G. |
| 7AB | Anderson, Alfred S. |
| 7AC | Dailey, Arthur C. |
| 7AD | Douglas, Alfred E. |
| 7AE | Thomas, Edward J. |
| 7AF | Scrutton, Gerald. |
| 7AG | Moe, George. |
| 7AH | Hardesty, Adolph. |
| 7AI | Johnson, Clifford E. |
| 7AJ | Sorenson, Chester J. |
| 7AK | Koester, Alpha M. |
| 7AN | Dolloff, Ralph E. |
| 7AO | Piercy, Russell H. |
| 7AP | Crossley, Jack. |
| 7AQ | Holm, Paul E. |
| 7AR | Root, Dellmar A. |
| 7AS | Bird, Lester F. |
| 7AT | Bennett, Henry. |
| 7AV | Root, Charles W. |
| 7AW | Meals, Owen E. |
| 7AZ | Warner, Archie E. |
| 7BA | Elbon, Jennings. |
| 7BB | Brown, David M. |
| 7BC | Ruth, Orin S. |
| 7BD | Hapner, Harry. |
| 7BS | Spencer, Arthur. |
| 7BW | Williams, Charles E. |
| 7CB | Bennett, Cecil H. |
| 7CE | Eichelberger, H. Carl. |
| 7CF | Farrar, Clyde L. |
| 7CG | Gillespie, Charles R. |
| 7CH | Hansen, Carl L. |
| 7CL | Law, Charles J. |
| 7CP | Peterson, C. Edward. |
| 7CW | Peterson, Charles W. |
| 7DB | Bolstad, Archie L. |
| 7DC | Crockett, George D. |
| 7DJ | John, D. Morris. |
| 7DM | Minkler, Darrell. |
| 7DS | Shingler, Don G. |
| 7DW | Willis, Cecil D. |
| 7EA | Adams, Edison. |
| 7EC | Covey, E. Channing. |
| 7EE | Hawkins, Edward K. |
| 7EF | Ford, Edwin D., jr. |
| 7EJ | Jackson, Edgar F. |
| 7EL | La Pine, Earl. |
| 7EM | Miller, E. Clarence. |
| 7EP | Peterson, Edward T. |
| 7FB | Boswell, George. |
| 7FF | Farris, Frank E. |
| 7FG | Gruwell, Fred N. |
| 7FL | Ling, Frank Moy. |
| 7FW | Lee, Emery H. I. |
| 7GA | Wurtz, George A. |
| 7GB | Butterfield, George H. |
| 7GC | Henny, George C. |
| 7GF | Gibbs, Floyd F. |
| 7GH | Hess, George F. |
| 7GJ | Johnson, Gale H. |
| 7GM | Moore, Gale L. |
| 7GW | Wilson, George D. |
| 7HB | Breum, Helmer O. |
| 7HC | Cutting, H. Everett. |
| 7HD | Davis, Hubert A. |
| 7HH | Hayden, Harold. |
| 7HI | Higman, Harry H. |
| 7HJ | Jones, Henry L. |
| 7HL | Longmire, Harold D. |
| 7HM | McCandless, Howard F. |
| 7HP | Pyle, Howard S. |
| 7HS | Slocum, Herbert R. |
| 7HT | Whelan, Harold J. |
| 7HU | Hursh, Harold H. |
| 7HW | Winningham, Harold. |
| 7IN | Nelson, Ivan L. |
| 7IO | O'Donoughue, Ivan. |
| 7JJ | Johnson, Joseph E. |
| 7JO | Methven, John H. |
| 7JQ | Roy, James. |
| 7JR | Tolmie, Jack R. |
| 7JT | Tyler, John L. |
| 7JW | Wilson, John C. |
| 7KP | Pennebaker, Kenneth T. |
| 7KW | Warrens, C. Kenneth. |
| 7LA | Larson, Walter L. |
| 7LN | Nagle, Leo W. |
| 7LR | Ross, Lindsley W. |
| 7LS | Smith, Lloyd T. |
| 7LT | Thompson, Lloyd S. |
| 7LW | Wollaston, Arthur L. |
| 7MC | McClelland, Joseph S. |
| 7MD | Durkee, Mealon. |
| 7ME | Elliott, Morton W. |
| 7MH | Middlekauff, Mark H. |
| 7MI | Minter, John W. |
| 7MM | Mathison, Martin J. |
| 7ON | Nicholson, W. Otto. |
| 7PD | Davis, Percy E. |
| 7PH | Hoffmann, Philip. |
| 7RB | Wormington, Ralph V. |
| 7RC | Mood, George T. |
| 7RD | Montgomery, Jack H. |

AMATEUR RADIO STATIONS—SEVENTH DISTRICT—ALPHABETICALLY BY CALL SIGNALS—Continued.

| Call signal. | Owner of station. | Call signal. | Owner of station. |
|---|---|---|---|
| 7RE | Nitschke, Erville W. | 7VC | Coburn, William D. |
| 7RO | Grant, Robert E. | 7VS | Small, Vincent. |
| 7RV | Wescott, Roy. | | |
| 7RW | Wright, Raymond F. | 7WC | Cates, Walter C. |
| | | 7WR | Rogers, Wilber L. |
| 7SN | Norman, Stacy W. | 7WQ | Stedman, William. |
| 7SW | Swan, Emil. | 7WS | Sparrow, William T. |
| 7US | Slewing, Vere T. | | |

## EIGHTH DISTRICT.

[Headquarters: Customhouse, Cleveland, Ohio. The eighth district comprises the States of New York (all counties not included in second district), Pennsylvania (all counties not included in third district), West Virginia, Ohio, Michigan (Lower Peninsula).]

### ALPHABETICALLY BY OWNERS OF STATIONS.

| Call signal. | Owner of station. | Location of station. | Power. |
|---|---|---|---|
| | | | *Watts.* |
| 8GM | Adams, Ralph F. | 327 17th St., Toledo, Ohio | 48 |
| 8CE | Adler, Jerome | 5550 Avondale St., Pittsburgh, Pa | 275 |
| 8JT | Albrecht, Harvey O. | 10608 Dupont Ave. NE., Cleveland, Ohio | 21 |
| 8JU | Aldridge, George P. | 12702 Penobscot Ave., Cleveland, Ohio | 500 |
| 8RP | Amos, Clyde O. | 514 W. Pitt St., Bedford, Pa | 160 |
| 8GE | Anderson, John M., jr. | 2215 Auburn Ave., Cincinnati, Ohio | 115 |
| 8JW | Anderson, Joseph D. | 719 E. 127th St., Cleveland, Ohio | 330 |
| 8AA | Anderson, Sidney E. | 1320 14th Ave., Detroit, Mich | 250 |
| 8CJ | Andrews, William S. | 907 Mellon St., Pittsburgh, Pa | 250 |
| 8KA | Ankerman, Roy E. | 403 E. Lima St., Wapakoneta, Ohio | 30 |
| 8DW | Apger, Charles O. | 555 18th St., Detroit, Mich | 400 |
| 8JL | Appleton, Francis W. | 12 Kanada St., Highland Park, Mich | 220 |
| 8RQ | Ashtabula High School | Ashtabula, Ohio | 500 |
| 8FV | Backus, Harry F. | 1740 E. 31st St., Cleveland, Ohio | 400 |
| 8CP | Baker, Norman E. | 638 Junction Ave., Detroit, Mich | 36 |
| 8FF | Baker, Raymond S. | 39 Steele Ave., Gloversville, N. Y | 330 |
| 8OM | Balsley, James I. | 109 S. Cottage Ave., Connellsville, Pa | 125 |
| 8HI | Barber, Nelson J. | 77 Cleveland St., Amherst, Ohio | 500 |
| 8AB | Barr, Forrest L. | R. F. D. No. 1, Vickery, Ohio | 440 |
| 8RX | Barringer, Russ | 418 N. Wood St., Fremont, Ohio | 14 |
| 8NJ | Bartholomew, William F. | 234 N. Tod Ave., Warren, Ohio | 110 |
| 8DI | Barton, Charles E. | 155 Harmon Ave., Detroit, Mich | 440 |
| 8LJ | Baxter, Raymond L. | 2745 Woodward Ave., Highland Park, Mich. | 220 |
| 8SI | Beach, Walter R. | 2180 E. 90th St., Cleveland, Ohio | 550 |
| 8JB | Beare, George L. | Columbus Ave. and Washington Row, Sandusky, Ohio. | 990 |
| 8AC | Beeclaere, Lawrence H. | 400 Dix Ave., Detroit, Mich | 250 |
| 8NS | Beck, Frank G. | 119 N. Pennsylvania Ave., Greensburg, Pa. | 800 |
| 8JP | Becker, Freeman A. | 108 9th St., Buffalo, N. Y | 20 |
| 8RI | Beeler, Hughes | 379 S. D St., Hamilton, Ohio | 18 |
| 8KD | Benjamin, Carlisle | 174 Glasgow St., Clyde, N. Y | 30 |
| 8FZ | Bennett, Edward J. | 1923 W. 75th St. NW., Cleveland, Ohio | 26 |
| 8MM | Benzee, Arthur H., jr. | 701 Walden Ave., Buffalo, N. Y | 20 |
| 8KT | Benzee, Joseph M. | 93 Wex Ave., Buffalo, N. Y | 32 |
| 8AE | Berndt, William F. | 608 Clark Ave., Detroit, Mich | 250 |
| 8HS | Berry, L. Mack | 131 W. Walnut St., Galion, Ohio | 990 |

AMATEUR RADIO STATIONS—EIGHTH DISTRICT—ALPHABETICALLY BY OWNERS OF STATIONS—Continued.

| Call signal. | Owner of station. | Location of station. | Power. |
|---|---|---|---|
| | | | *Watts.* |
| 8SC | Bidwell, Paul | 8903 Cedar St., Cleveland, Ohio | 21 |
| 8OO | Bird, Harold C | 92 S. Johnson Ave., Pontiac, Mich | 500 |
| 8PZ | Bishop, Carryl L | 1 North Ave., Binghamton, N. Y | 24 |
| 8EY | Blackmore, Andrew H | 3351 Reading Rd., Cincinnati, Ohio | 250 |
| 8FU | Blattner, E. Herman | 73 Pardee St., Rochester, N. Y | 25 |
| 8RH | Blum, Robert A | 157 High St., Buffalo, N. Y | 18 |
| 8LP | Bly, Ralph | 1358 Michigan Ave., Niagara Falls, N. Y | 30 |
| 8PA | Boekeloo, Ross M | 813 Washington Ave., Kalamazoo, Mich | 24 |
| 8IA | Bolton, Frederick R | 531 E. Grand Blvd., Detroit, Mich | 250 |
| 8QJ | Bornman, Frederick D | 134 Delaware Ave., Detroit, Mich | 440 |
| 8OU | Boyer, Harry | 89 Kibbie St., Mt. Clemens, Mich | 440 |
| 8LO | Breckel, Harry F | 4318 Virginia Ave., Cincinnati, Ohio | 495 |
| 8CQ | Brede, Erwin F | 55 Melbourne Ave., Detroit, Mich | 333 |
| 8DG | Bremer, Edmund H | 301 W. Forest Ave., Detroit, Mich | 1,000 |
| 8AF | Brewer, George S | 112 E. Main St., Westfield, N. Y | 1,000 |
| 8OG | Brink, Frank J | Galen, N. Y | 30 |
| 8FB | Britney, Dudley R | Winton Rd., Cincinnati, Ohio | 36 |
| 8AG | Broome, Donald W | 100 Grand Ave., Mt. Clemens, Mich | 1,000 |
| 8KF | Broughton, Harry J | 702 N. George St., Rome, N. Y | 250 |
| 8QS | Brow, Robert | Rose Hill, N. Y | 500 |
| 8AH | Brown, Edward H | 2208 Harcourt Drive, Cleveland, Ohio | 550 |
| 8NU | Brown, Willard S | 2134 E. 77th St., Cleveland, Ohio | 500 |
| 8FR | Brownell, Elmer | 1300 Steuben St., Utica, N. Y | 18 |
| 8DM | Bruns, Carl H | 1316 Ontario St., Toledo, Ohio | 30 |
| 8NL | Budwig, Gilbert G | 1017 Ansel Rd., Cleveland, Ohio | 1,000 |
| 8FI | Burger, Richard W | 822 S. McDonel St., Lima, Ohio | 495 |
| 8GA | Burr, Gordon | 7209 Clinton Ave., Cleveland, Ohio | 20 |
| 8RD | Burr, Roy C | 68 E. Elm St., Norwalk, Ohio | 880 |
| 8MH | Bushnell, Clarence E | 645 W. Ferry St., Buffalo, N. Y | 48 |
| 8PP | Butcher, W. Byron | Waynesfield, Ohio | 990 |
| 8OQ | Butzler, Harry | 196 Robertson St., Mt. Clemens, Mich | 770 |
| 8MJ | Cahow, Paul D | Reading, Mich | 385 |
| 8KG | Camp, John D | 1001 La Fayette Ave., Buffalo, N. Y | 120 |
| 8MV | Carson, William H | 1140 James St., Kalamazoo, Mich | 550 |
| 8EU | Carson, William J | 5558 Black St., Pittsburgh, Pa | 30 |
| 8ED | Carver, Alfred J | 4 Warring Ave., Buffalo, N. Y | 9 |
| 8NB | Chafee, C. Lloyd | Davis, W. Va | 48 |
| 8IU | Clarke, Andrew W | Glenshaw, Pa | 24 |
| 8SQ | Clarke, John H | 1010 Central Ave., Dunkirk, N. Y | 1,000 |
| 8AJ | Clough, Bert E | 186 N. Washington Ave., Battle Creek, Mich. | 1,000 |
| 8FJ | Clausing, Leroy M. E | 406 Nye St., Lima, Ohio | 770 |
| 8DV | Cobb, Rupert G | 17 E. Alexandrine Ave., Detroit, Mich | 50 |
| 8EE | Coleman, Clarence E | 47 Yale Pl., Buffalo, N. Y | 770 |
| 8SM | Coleman, H. Burr | Savannah, N. Y | 120 |
| 8KO | Combs, Frayne | 601 W. Anglaize St., Wapakoneta, Ohio | 31 |
| 8NC | Coolidge, James H., 3d | 34 Chapman Ave., East Cleveland, Ohio | 280 |
| 8KB | Core, Eugene D | 53 E. High St., Columbus Grove, Ohio | 1,000 |
| 8MO | Corts, Raymond E | 243 May St., Buffalo, N. Y | 20 |
| 8CR | Coven, Allen W | 446 Earl Court, Elyria, Ohio | 35 |
| 8IE | Cross, Gorham L | Cape Vincent, N. Y | 30 |
| 8IT | Cross, Gorham L | 340 Genesee St., Utica, N. Y | 165 |
| 8KX | Cuff, Harold C | 79 Walnut St., Buffalo, N. Y | 16 |
| 8RK | Dalrymple, Clarence F | Sheridan, N. Y | 24 |
| 8NI | Daniels, Worth D | 1233 W. State St., Fremont, Ohio | 24 |
| 8LR | Davis, Charles W | 98 Sumner Pl., Buffalo, N. Y | 30 |
| 8AN | Davis, Frank | 73 Dakota Ave., Columbus, Ohio | 500 |
| 8MZ | Davison, John | 400 W. High St., Lima, Ohio | 1,000 |
| 8PI | Day, James M | Waynesfield, Ohio | 990 |
| 8MQ | Dear, Harry D | 636 Preble Ave., Pittsburgh, Pa | 20 |

AMATEUR RADIO STATIONS—EIGHTH DISTRICT—ALPHABETICALLY BY OWNERS OF STATIONS—Continued.

| Call signal. | Owner of station. | Location of station. | Power. |
|---|---|---|---|
| | | | Watts. |
| 8AO | Deighan, Edward I. | 5415 Herman Ave., Cleveland, Ohio | 40 |
| 8HV | Denniston, Harry J. | 118 Fulton Ave., Rochester, N. Y. | 24 |
| 8MX | De Rose, Ralph | 69 S. Judson St., Gloversville, N. Y. | 250 |
| 8KJ | Des Jardins, Gregory T. | 2019 Main St., Cincinnati, Ohio | 6 |
| 8KK | Devaney, Richard G. | 196 Murray St., Binghamton, N. Y. | 20 |
| 8IJ | Diederich, Paul E. | 915 E. Grand Blvd., Detroit, Mich. | 1,000 |
| 8KV | Dobbie, John, jr. | 700 Buffalo Ave., Niagara Falls, N. Y. | 500 |
| 8FK | Donehoo, Gray G. | 823 Heberton Ave., Pittsburgh, Pa. | 100 |
| 8GD | Donnelly, John J. | 3614 W. 32d St. SW., Cleveland, Ohio | 550 |
| 8AP | Dorsch, George | 1338 Walnut St., Cincinnati, Ohio | 550 |
| 8EF | Dorst, Edward | 39 Eaton St., Buffalo, N. Y. | 18 |
| 8OW | Dotterweich, Joseph H. | 379 Genesee St., Buffalo, N. Y. | 500 |
| 8DU | Downing, Harry E. | 2308 E. 57th St., Cleveland, Ohio | 440 |
| 8OX | Dreux, Alexander J. | 48 Garner Ave., Buffalo, N. Y. | 9 |
| 8KL | Dreifus, Fred B. | 5621 Hays St., Pittsburgh, Pa. | 24 |
| 8LQ | Dunlap, Orrin E., jr. | 1029 Cleveland Ave., Niagara Falls, N. Y. | 250 |
| 8KM | Eden, Henley S. | 112 Ivy St., Edgewood Park, Pa. | 220 |
| 8JH | Edwards, C. Beaver | 120 Green Ave., Detroit, Mich. | 30 |
| 8PJ | Ehrich, William F. | 300 Warren St., Bucyrus, Ohio | 1,000 |
| 8AQ | Ela, Edward C. and William C. | 1320 Woodland Ave., Pittsburgh, Pa. | 400 |
| 8QL | Emmert, Herman C. | 1063 23d St., Detroit, Mich. | 250 |
| 8GF | Erney, J. Clarence | 7417 Myron Ave., Cleveland, Ohio | 24 |
| 8GG | Eucher, Clarence J. | 7427 Detroit Ave., Cleveland, Ohio | 550 |
| 8SE | Falck, Norman B. | 1529 Davis Ave., Pittsburgh, Pa. | 400 |
| 8HU | Faroo, Glenn | 269 Grand Ave., Rochester, N. Y. | 30 |
| 8AS | Feightner, Amos E. | 715 S. Broadway, Lima, Ohio | 220 |
| 8DB | Fellows, Bernard D. | 67 Parke St., Pontiac, Mich. | 250 |
| 8FA | Fender, Clinton H. | 28 W. 13th St., Cincinnati, Ohio | 495 |
| 8QA | Ferguson, James G. | 671 W. Ferry St., Buffalo, N. Y. | 75 |
| 8LS | Ferris, Warren O. | 514 Elizabeth St., Petoskey, Mich. | 250 |
| 8FE | Finch, Brent S. | 1727 E. McMillan St., Cincinnati, Ohio | 385 |
| 8MK | Finch, William G. H. | 9–15 E. 3d St., Cincinnati, Ohio | 500 |
| 8MG | Fish, J. Mulford | 307 Collins Ave., Pittsburgh, Pa. | 20 |
| 8MY | Fisher, Harold W. | 906 W. Wayne St., Lima, Ohio | 27 |
| 8KQ | Fisher, Earl U. | 1505 5th Ave., Pittsburgh, Pa. | 20 |
| 8OZ | Fleming, James J. | Kane, Pa. | 1,000 |
| 8QZ | Fletcher, Vernon | 209 Spring St., Bedford, Pa. | 21 |
| 8KI | Flint High School | Flint, Mich. | 770 |
| 8MW | Follet, Louis, jr. | Crafton, Pa. | 60 |
| 8OT | Foster, Frank, jr. | 202 Madison St., Wilkes-Barre, Pa. | 880 |
| 8SF | Fowler, Robert J. | 324 Walnut St., Flint, Mich. | 600 |
| 8AT | France, William | 829 Western Ave., N. S., Pittsburgh, Pa. | 500 |
| 8RE | Frank, Alfred | 2226 W. Jefferson Ave., Detroit, Mich. | 16 |
| 8HZ | Fraser, John W. | 102 Garner Ave., Buffalo, N. Y. | 23 |
| 8RZ | Fritz, Rudolph A. | 1242 Dewey Ave., Cincinnati, Ohio | 250 |
| 8AU | Frost, Harry E. | 552 Glenwood Ave., Buffalo, N. Y. | 330 |
| 8LT | Fryman, Zalman B. | 218 Michigan St., Petoskey, Mich. | 125 |
| 8AV | Fullwood, William R. | 1017 Pollock Ave., New Castle, Pa. | 660 |
| 8OJ | Furlong, Marcie J. | 711 N. Main St., Clyde, Ohio | 250 |
| 8KP | Fuss, Chester G. | Little Valley, N. Y. | 770 |
| 8BV | Gale, Roy H. | 1806 Brewster Ave., Cincinnati, Ohio | 50 |
| 8PK | Gamble, Frederick D. | 2412 Putnam St., Toledo, Ohio | 500 |
| 8EG | Gebhard, Louis A. | 1127 Ellicott St., Buffalo, N. Y. | 550 |
| 8AX | Gentzsch, Leonard H. | 102 Northampton St., Buffalo, N. Y. | 18 |
| 8QN | Given, Everett J. | 908 E. Ann St., Ann Arbor, Mich. | 60 |
| 8SN | Glatzell, Earle D. | 418 S. First St., Ann Arbor, Mich. | 16 |
| 8GH | Glekler, Truman J. | 3015 Marvin Ave., Cleveland, Ohio | 550 |
| 8ET | Goettel, Edward V. | 1773 Crawford Rd., Cleveland, Ohio | 600 |
| 8RY | Goetz, Carl P. | 1518 Knowlton St., Cincinnati, Ohio | 500 |

AMATEUR RADIO STATIONS—EIGHTH DISTRICT—ALPHABETICALLY BY OWNERS OF STATIONS—Continued.

| Call signal. | Owner of station. | Location of station. | Power. |
|---|---|---|---|
| | | | *Watts.* |
| 8AW | Gogel, Adelbert J | 628 S. Erie St., Toledo, Ohio | 440 |
| 8OF | Goodwin, Seth A | 6032 St. Marie St., Pittsburgh, Pa | 1,000 |
| 8EI | Gray, Clarence N | 32 Duerstein Ave., Buffalo, N. Y | 330 |
| 8GJ | Green, Harold L | 1650 82d St., Cleveland, Ohio | 440 |
| 8ND | Grigg, Arthur | 741 Clinton St., Cincinnati, Ohio | 495 |
| 8AY | Grosse, Frederick W | 1326 Walnut St., Cincinanti, Ohio | 500 |
| 8QR | Grostick, George E | 1605 Wagar Ave., Lakewood, Ohio | 15 |
| 8EH | Grove, Nelson B | 242 Ashland Ave., Buffalo, N. Y | 60 |
| 8JA | Gunn, Ross | 369 W. Lorain St., Oberlin, Ohio | 500 |
| 8RO | Gwinner, Frederick, 3d | 5th and Amberson Sts., Pittsburgh, Pa | 36 |
| 8QB | Haderer, John | 330 Fox St., Buffalo, N. Y | 18 |
| 8NN | Hahn, Ralph H | 423 Fox St., Buffalo, N. Y | 250 |
| 8MD | Hall, Eldred R | 1613 Milton Ave., Solvay, N. Y | 495 |
| 8GT | Hamel, Arthur | 29 Martin St., Amherst, Ohio | 550 |
| 8NW | Hankin, John H | 30 Schutz Ave., Buffalo, N. Y | 6 |
| 8AZ | Hansen, Edmund H | 31 Deer St., Plymouth, Mich | 750 |
| 8NO | Hansen, Torvald | 7325 Clinton Ave., Cleveland, Ohio | 220 |
| 8NV | Harrison, P. William, jr | 125 Medbury Blvd., Detroit, Mich | 6 |
| 8PS | Hart, John R | Duncannon, Pa | 550 |
| 8QC | Hauck, Roland E | 850 Walden Ave., Buffalo, N. Y | 20 |
| 8FH | Haynes, William | 102 N. Florence St., Springfield, Ohio | 880 |
| 8JD | Heiser, Ernest J | 819 Dayton St., Hamilton, Ohio | 990 |
| 8NP | Henderson, Earl G | 457 Orchard Ave., Bellevue, Pa | 500 |
| 8PB | Henika, Charles F | 441 State St., Petoskey, Mich | 550 |
| 8EX | Henlein, Carl A | 1855 Hewitt Ave., Cincinnati, Ohio | 24 |
| 8GN | Henninger, Alan E | 2038 W. 100th St., Cleveland, Ohio | 440 |
| 8BW | Hermann, Harold N | 2237 Frances Lane, Cincinnati, Ohio | 35 |
| 8FG | Hewitt, Charles P | R. F. D. No. 1, Oak Harbor, Ohio | 36 |
| 8LU | Hewitt, James F | 405 Portland Ave., Rochester, N. Y | 24 |
| 8PM | Higgey, Robert C | 1072 W. Market St., Lima, Ohio | 250 |
| 8PL | Higgins, Robert R | 11408 Bell Flower Rd., Cleveland, Ohio | 225 |
| 8IC | Hill, Charles C., jr | 1134 Mellon St., Pittsburgh, Pa | 1,000 |
| 8GB | Hill Top Y. M. C. A | Pittsburgh, Pa | 270 |
| 8BA | Hiller, Herbert A | 117 Hanover St., Silver Creek, N. Y | 240 |
| 8KR | Hills, Virgil A | 2066 E. 100th St., Cleveland, Ohio | 220 |
| 8BD | Hoch, Ellery T | R. F. D. No. 33, Barberton, Ohio | 48 |
| 8GP | Hoffman, Edward H | 1617 Buhrer Ave., Cleveland, Ohio | 20 |
| 8QV | Hogan, James E | 26 Lincoln Ave., Crafton, Pa | 60 |
| 8FC | Holden, Ira S | 2920 Vernon Pl., Cincinnati, Ohio | 900 |
| 8MC | Holmes, Charles A | New Berlin, N. Y | 1,000 |
| 8DR | Holmes, Charles E | 310 W. Brown St., Grand Rapids, Mich | 495 |
| 8HO | Holt, George W | 789 Prospect Ave., Buffalo, N. Y | 49 |
| 8BC | Holt, Nelson E | 185 Congress St., Buffalo, N. Y | 715 |
| 8GQ | Horn, Herbert E | 557 E. 117th St., Cleveland, Ohio | 500 |
| 8PT | Hornung, Romey W | Lavelle, Pa | 450 |
| 8NF | House, Elra E | 11 Taft St., Battle Creek, Mich | 880 |
| 8BB | Howes, Stanley L | 515 Eleanor St., Kalamazoo, Mich | 330 |
| 8CS | Howland, Dean W | 1081 Cass Ave., Detroit, Mich | 330 |
| 8BX | Hubbell, Aaron W | 3458 Hallwood Pl., Cincinnati, Ohio | 600 |
| 8RR | Hull, Earl C | 763½ 15th St., Niagara Falls, N. Y | 550 |
| 8CF | Hull, Guy McC | 123 S. Whitfield St., Pittsburgh, Pa | 50 |
| 8CG | Hull, Ralph S | 5819 Rural St., Pittsburgh, Pa | 550 |
| 8NH | Hyatt, Bunyan, J | 202 Rogers St., Mt. Vernon, Ohio | 1,000 |
| 8PU | Imbt, Russell | 324 Braeside Ave., East Stroudsburg, Pa | 660 |
| 8ON | Ilgenfritz, Lester M | 2 E. Forest Ave., Detroit, Mich | 30 |
| 8RJ | Irvine, Robert P | 3380 Fulton Rd., Cleveland, Ohio | 330 |
| 8JK | Jackson, Cotesworth M | St. Clair Rd., Pottsville, Pa | 300 |
| 8BF | Jarvis, Roy B | 647 Main St., Wheeling, W. Va | 1,000 |
| 8FL | Jenkins, William E | 2108 Potomac St., Banksville, Pa | 30 |
| 8GR | Joecken, George I | 10310 Joan Ave., Cleveland, Ohio | 55 |

AMATEUR RADIO STATIONS—EIGHTH DISTRICT—ALPHABETICALLY BY OWNERS OF STATIONS—Continued.

| Call signal. | Owner of station. | Location of station. | Power. |
|---|---|---|---|
| | | | Watts. |
| 8HC | Johnston, S. Paul | 201 S. Craig St., Pittsburgh, Pa. | 275 |
| 8QK | Jones, Edwin P | 1114 Middle Ave., Elyria, Ohio | 30 |
| 8QM | Jones, Jesse K | 200 W. Market St., Pottsville, Pa. | 24 |
| 8KU | Jones, Miller | Grafton, Ohio | 500 |
| 8QQ | Kampfe, Lorbert J | 1241 E. 103d St., Cleveland, Ohio | 1,000 |
| 8BG | Kastenberg, Paul G | 298 Hurlbut Ave., Detroit, Mich. | 30 |
| 8NM | Keen, William L | 608 Broadway, Cincinnati, Ohio | 24 |
| 8PC | Kersting, Ferdinand | 165 S. Gratiot Ave., Mt. Clemons, Mich. | 440 |
| 8CC | Kesel, George | 2704 Wylie Ave., Pittsburgh, Pa. | 440 |
| 8QE | Kester, Harold P | 626 University Ave., Rochester, N. Y. | 36 |
| 8BH | Kingsbury, Kenneth | 24 Chestnut St., Binghamton, N. Y. | 495 |
| 8QO | Kirly, H. Howard | 863 E. 73d St., Cleveland, Ohio | 250 |
| 8RA | Klager, Oscar C | 611 S. Main St., Ann Arbor, Mich. | 16 |
| 8GV | Kleber, Jackson O | 1135 Murray Hill Ave., Pittsburgh, Pa. | 275 |
| 8QF | Klinck, Charles C., jr. | 38 W. Parade Ave., Buffalo, N. Y. | 250 |
| 8RB | Knapp, Harold | 224 Elm St., Edgewood Park, Pa. | 550 |
| 8DN | Knappen, Bert | 4 Trankla Ave., Grand Rapids, Mich. | 25 |
| 8GS | Kneale, C. Kewley | 1337 W. 114th St., Cleveland, Ohio | 100 |
| 8KW | Kohler, Harry W | 605 E. Middle St., Wapakoneta, Ohio | 36 |
| 8EJ | Kolb, Edwin H | 18 Camp St., Buffalo, N. Y. | 660 |
| 8GL | Konrad, Henry | 750 Ross Ave., Hamilton, Ohio | 550 |
| 8BJ | Kraus, Norman M | 4121 Henritze Ave., Cleveland, Ohio | 990 |
| 8PD | Krause, Karl A | 244 S. Front St., Mt. Clemens, Mich. | 225 |
| 8JV | Kreighbaum, Cyril H | 12414 Ingomar Ave., Cleveland, Ohio | 600 |
| 8BI | Kroeger, Gustav H | 1837 Clarion Ave., Cincinnati, Ohio | 990 |
| 8EK | Kumpf, Elmer H | Crittenden, N. Y. | 675 |
| 8OC | Kuehnle, George J | 156 Woolper Ave., Cincinnati, Ohio | 120 |
| 8KY | Kunnar, William | R. F. D. No. 4, Ashtabula, Ohio | 48 |
| 8KZ | Landgraff, William J | 3718 Parviss St., Pittsburgh, Pa. | 250 |
| 8EL | Langenbach, Leo | 186 Riley St., Buffalo, N. Y. | 24 |
| 8BK | Lappe, E. Robert | 5520 Baywood St., Pittsburgh, Pa. | 275 |
| 8RL | Last, George | 107 E. Buckeye St., Clyde, Ohio | 550 |
| 8EQ | Leighton, Clifford R | 128 Eagle St., Utica, N. Y. | 1,000 |
| 8QG | Lewis, Walter E | 128 Denver St., Rochester, N. Y. | 500 |
| 8BL | Leyh, Edward L | 10 Overhill St., Pittsburgh, Pa. | 60 |
| 8MT | Liller, William P | Keyser, W. Va. | 18 |
| | Lima High School. *See* Davison, John. | | |
| 8LV | Lindow, Daniel A | 625 Field Ave., Detroit, Mich. | 275 |
| 8BE | Lippert, John P | 41 Stanwood Rd., East Cleveland, Ohio | 275 |
| 8JO | Little, Donald G | 415 Woodward Ave., Kalamazoo, Mich. | 540 |
| 8MR | Livinggood, Hubert W | 1825 Michigan Ave., Detroit, Mich. | 880 |
| 8GU | Loehr, George R | 11444 Euclid Ave., Cleveland, Ohio | 500 |
| 8CZ | London, Henry J | 267 Palmer St., Grand Rapids, Mich. | 90 |
| 8JG | Lord, Donald M | 531 Beach Ave., Cambridge Springs, Pa. | 30 |
| 8BN | Lovejoy, Julian | 3325 Perkins Ave., Cincinnati, Ohio | 40 |
| 8ML | Lovell, Charles L | 540 Prospect Pl., Cincinnati, Ohio | 550 |
| 8PE | Lucas, Clarence E | 119 24th St., Detroit, Mich. | 16 |
| 8HM | Lucas, Howard E | 5005 Dearborn St., Pittsburgh, Pa. | 990 |
| 8OD | Luedeke, William P., jr. | 40 Hodge Ave., Buffalo, N. Y. | 18 |
| 8JQ | Lusink, C. Irving | 642 North St., Rochester, N. Y. | 18 |
| 8BO | Lyons, Henry E | Ripley, N. Y. | 60 |
| 8JX | MacCandless, Lyon H | 351 Jefferson St., Rochester, Pa. | 440 |
| 8BP | Macer, Arthur J | 37 Jefferson St., Westfield, N. Y. | 1,000 |
| 8EA | Mack, Clifford J | 49 McGovern Ave., Ashtabula, Ohio | 770 |
| 8SO | Maggs, H. Carrol | Girard, Ohio | 312 |
| 8PF | Malbin, Samuel | 14 S. Gratiot Ave., Mt. Clemens, Mich. | 117 |
| 8JZ | Manning, Alfred J | 6914 Woodland Ave., Cleveland, Ohio | 36 |
| 8MI | Manning, Howard H | 298 Prospect St., Meadville, Pa. | 330 |
| 8KC | Manning, Jerry J | 12 Parson St., Ashtabula, Ohio | 385 |

AMATEUR RADIO STATIONS—EIGHTH DISTRICT—ALPHABETICALLY BY OWNERS OF STATIONS—Continued.

| Call signal. | Owner of station. | Location of station. | Power. |
|---|---|---|---|
| | | | Watts. |
| 8OV | Marcum, Richard | Britain Ave., Benton Harbor, Mich | 1,000 |
| 8PX | Marsh, Harry H., jr | Park View, W. Va | 24 |
| 8HY | Marshall, Floyd W | Avery Ter., Detroit, Mich | 1,000 |
| 8RV | Marshall, Frank J | 517 W. Delaware Ave., Toledo, Ohio | 500 |
| 8QY | Martin, Cecil E | Depew, N. Y | 24 |
| 8EV | Mason, Carl D | R. F. D. No. 3, Oak Grove, Mich | 25 |
| 8LA | Mason, George S | 119 Temple St., Fredonia, N. Y | 1,000 |
| 8MB | Maxon, Harry L | 267 Brinkman St., Buffalo, N. Y | 16 |
| 8NT | Maue, Leon G | Y. M. C. A. Bldg., Hazleton, Pa | 330 |
| 8HL | McCamon, Aurel | R. F. D. No. 4, Lisbon, Ohio | 36 |
| 8EZ | McConaughy, Mary Alice | 6112 Navarre Pl., Cincinnati, Ohio | 48 |
| 8QI | McEniry, Clifford U | 875 Michigan St., Buffalo, N. Y | 18 |
| 8OY | McElhinny, J. Schubert | 103 Sumner Pl., Buffalo, N. Y | 24 |
| 8IK | Mellon, J. H | Patton, Pa | 45 |
| 8BQ | Menges, William E | 6428 Aurelia St., Pittsburgh, Pa | 275 |
| 8IS | Middleton, Charles | Vernon, Ohio | 94 |
| 8IB | Mielke, Carl E | 3619 Grenada St., Pittsburgh, Pa | 1,000 |
| 8IR | Miller, Arthur P | 14 Beuland Ave., Mt. Clemens, Mich | 200 |
| 8IN | Miller, Kenneth | 1086 Shady Ave., Pittsburgh, Pa | 500 |
| 8BR | Miner, Simeon J | 2253 E. Jefferson Ave., Detroit, Mich | 50 |
| 8GW | Moffet, Floyd E | 5408 Euclid Ave., Cleveland, Ohio | 500 |
| 8BS | Mogridge, Clarence J | 463 16th St., Detroit, Mich | 1,000 |
| 8DS | Moynahan, Roy D | 355 E. Warren Ave., Detroit, Mich | 240 |
| 8EB | Munsell, Robert S | 191 Center St., Ashtabula, Ohio | 260 |
| 8EM | Murphy, John V | 98 St. James Pl., Buffalo, N. Y | 24 |
| 8HD | Myers, Homer B | 1600 Euclid Ave., Cleveland, Ohio | 20 |
| 8CT | Myers, Raymond W | 166 E. Perry St., Tiffin, Ohio | 275 |
| 8IG | Neumann, Allen J | 1033 Ellicott St., Buffalo, N. Y | 20 |
| 8MP | Neupert, Robert E | 500 Chartiers Ave., McKees Rocks, Pa | 550 |
| 8IX | Newman, Arthur J | 1415 Newman Ave., Cleveland, Ohio | 500 |
| 8IM | Nichols, D. A | Wapakoneta, Ohio | 720 |
| 8ID | Norris, George H | 77 Melbourne Ave., Detroit, Mich | 960 |
| 8BT | Ogle, Harry B | 2636 East Blvd., Cleveland, Ohio | 440 |
| 8FM | Olson, Milton E | 6357 Luther St., Pittsburgh, Pa | 250 |
| 8DF | Orrell, Robert W | 87 Frederick Ave., Detroit, Mich | 500 |
| 8SJ | Ottney, James N | R. F. D. No. 4, Gilsonburg, Ohio | 22 |
| 8DY | Pancoast, Donald F | 107 Prospect St., Ashtabula, Ohio | 1,000 |
| 8OI | Patterson, Grant, jr | 35 E. State St., Gloversville, N. Y | 250 |
| 8CH | Paul, James T | 628 N. Euclid Ave., Pittsburgh., Pa | 60 |
| 8CY | Payne, Arthur E | Birmingham, Mich | 990 |
| 8NZ | Payne, William H | 12½ Clarke St., Binghamton, N. Y | 20 |
| 8PV | Pearson, Harry | 4 W. North Ave., Pittsburgh, Pa | 36 |
| 8GX | Pentland, Henry B | 2053 E. 105th St., Cleveland, Ohio | 495 |
| 8SG | Pesek, Miro R | 3288 Fulton Rd. SW., Cleveland, Ohio | 56 |
| 8LW | Philepp, Lawrence A | Concord, Mich | 660 |
| 8DJ | Phillips, Glenn E | 551 McKinstry Ave., Detroit, Mich | 100 |
| 8CX | Phippeny, Forrest I | R. F. D. No. 4, Battle Creek, Mich | 1,000 |
| 8JF | Plekenpol, Ernest | 7804 W. Madison Ave. NW., Cleveland, Ohio. | 30 |
| 8DX | Porter, Harry T | 714 Main St., Conneaut, Ohio | 900 |
| 8QW | Potts, Charles G | 726 W. Norwegian St., Pottsville, Pa | 52 |
| 8HQ | Poux, Noel J | 432 Pine St., Meadville, Pa | 440 |
| 8QP | Powell, Ralph C | 5236 Westminster Pl., Pittsburgh, Pa | 42 |
| 8GZ | Probeck, John | 2489 E. 59th St., Cleveland, Ohio | 30 |
| 8LB | Purves, Stuart S | 3461 Brookline Ave., Cincinnati, Ohio | 20 |
| 8LC | Ramge, Edwin H | R. F. D. No. 7, Wapakoneta, Ohio | 30 |
| 8DA | Rathbun, Hugh T | 112 Colfax St., Grand Rapids, Mich | 50 |
| 8DC | Reb, Frank | 1635 Gratiot Ave., Detroit, Mich | 1,000 |
| 8LX | Reitt, Arthur A | 1100 Washington Ave., Monaca, Pa | 40 |
| 8FQ | Remorino, L., jr | 97 Washington St., Gloversville, N. Y | 490 |

AMATEUR RADIO STATIONS—EIGHTH DISTRICT—ALPHABETICALLY BY OWNERS OF STATIONS—Continued.

| Call signal. | Owner of station. | Location of station. | Power. |
|---|---|---|---|
| | | | *Watts.* |
| 8OP | Reynolds, Charles L. | 25 Sturges St., Binghamton, N. Y. | 24 |
| 8LD | Rice, Homer D. | 150 Livingston St., Buffalo, N. Y. | 12 |
| 8SP | Rich, Harland E. | 228 N. Limestone St., Springfied, Ohio. | 770 |
| 8IQ | Richard, Roy H. | 68 Lincoln Ave., Meadville, Pa. | 30 |
| 8CI | Richards, Theodore D. and George B. | 934 W. North Ave., Pittsburgh, Pa. | 380 |
| 8PN | Ritchie, Burrus L. | 2216 E. 100th St., Cleveland, Ohio. | 330 |
| 8RF | Ritchie, Carl L. | 305½ Minton St., Pittsburgh, Pa. | 24 |
| 8MS | Ritchey, Ole B. | Reading, Mich. | 440 |
| 8NQ | Robbins, Melvin G. | 219 Reynolds St., Kingston, Pa. | 1,000 |
| 8HB | Roberts, Hayden P. | 11215 Clifton Blvd., Cleveland, Ohio. | 220 |
| 8MF | Robin, Milo H. | 7 Lake Ave., Williamson, N. Y. | 24 |
| 8HA | Roblee, Judson. | 59 Idlewood Ave., Cleveland, Ohio. | 220 |
| 8IO | Roe, Howard L. | 723 Homewood Ave., Pittsburgh, Pa. | 250 |
| 8DQ | Roener, Hubert J. | 115 Floyd St., Toledo, Ohio. | 30 |
| 8DT | Rogers, Grant. | 2065 McKinley Ave., Lakewood, Ohio. | 880 |
| 8HT | Romzick, Lawrence. | R. F. D. No. 2, Ruth, Mich. | 28 |
| 8LY | Rose, Herman. | 77 Johnson St., Buffalo, N. Y. | 18 |
| 8EW | Rubel, Henry M., jr. | 920 Burton Ave., Cincinnati, Ohio. | 1,000 |
| 8CD | Sachs, Gus. | 1522 Center Ave., Pittsburgh, Pa. | 275 |
| 8LF | Saunders, Ezra L. | 141 4th Ave., Gallipolis, Ohio. | 750 |
| 8PO | Schaaf, John M. | 300 Warren St., Bucyrus, Ohio. | 1,000 |
| 8HG | Schardt, Earl M. | 12813 Marston Ave., Cleveland, Ohio. | 24 |
| 8OK | Scheib, Joseph. | 6243 Station St., Pittsburgh, Pa. | 20 |
| 8SD | Schindler, Louis J. | 2103 Robinwood Ave., Toledo, Ohio. | 500 |
| 8RW | Schmidle, Claude. | 553 E. North St., Buffalo, N. Y. | 18 |
| 8SB | Schmidt, Norman F. | 5600 Forbes St., Pittsburgh, Pa. | 250 |
| 8JC | Schoenhen, Edwin B. | 1201 Middle Ave., Elyria, Ohio. | 120 |
| 8HH | Schoren, William E. | 2954 W. 25th St., Cleveland, Ohio. | 480 |
| 8HR | Schouman, Hazen. | 210 Riverside Ave., St. Clair, Mich. | 30 |
| 8MA | Schulz, Edward G. | 329 Arndt St., Detroit, Mich. | 330 |
| 8QU | Schunck, Robert F. | 407 W. Anglaize St., Wapakoneta, Ohio. | ...... |
| 8FY | Schwalb, Walter J. | 715 Main St., Wheeling, W. Va. | 880 |
| 8LL | Schwanecamp, Raymond | 207 Lemon St., Buffalo, N. Y. | 30 |
| 8BY | Schwindt, Herman J. | 3517 Bevis Ave., Cincinnati, Ohio. | 60 |
| 8IV | Scott, Gail. | Degraff, Ohio. | 100 |
| 8LE | Scott, Hoyt S. | North Fairfield, Ohio. | 36 |
| 8EP | Scovill, Edward H. | 10528 Park Lane, Cleveland, Ohio. | 750 |
| 8HN | Selinske, Louis. | 510 15th St., Detroit, Mich. | 30 |
| 8HF | Shaney, Aubrey A. | 5713 Curtiss Ave., Cleveland, Ohio. | 440 |
| 8LZ | Sharbaugh, Wilbur. | 2109 Eoff St., Wheeling, W. Va. | 550 |
| 8PQ | Shaw, Eurcile L. | 205½ E. Anglaize St., Wapakoneta, Ohio. | 19 |
| 8EN | Shepard, Charles A. | 186 Grant St., Buffalo, N. Y. | 12 |
| 8CN | Sheppard, Hamilton W. | 6420 Darlington Rd., Pittsburgh, Pa. | 250 |
| 8PG | Sherman, Fred. | Britain Ave., Benton Harbor, Mich. | 1,000 |
| 8JR | Sherrill, Alvan C. | 326 S. Highland Ave., Pittsburgh, Pa. | 750 |
| 8BZ | Shumard, Asbury. | 5609 Tompkins Ave., Cincinnati, Ohio. | 660 |
| 8LG | Sibert, Richard E. | 111 E. Benton St., Wapakoneta, Ohio. | 30 |
| 8KS | Sidnell, Robert G. | 1268 W. 115th St., Cleveland, Ohio. | 30 |
| 8DL | Sisson, William A. | 1024 Erie St., Toledo, Ohio. | 30 |
| 8QT | Sly, Edward E. | 1820 Myrtle St., Erie, Pa. | 144 |
| 8PH | Slyfield, Charles O. | Frankfort, Mich. | 24 |
| 8CL | Smith, G. C. | 335 Atwood St., Pittsburgh, Pa. | 250 |
| 8RM | Smith, Harold M. | Highland Ave., Monticello, N. Y. | 24 |
| 8CV | Smith, Lewis A. | 55 Brandon Ave., Detroit, Mich. | 35 |
| 8CK | Smith, Roland C. | 5814 Hays St., Pittsburgh, Pa. | 302 |
| 8OE | Smith, Verne E. | Knox, Pa. | 12 |
| 8FO | Snyder, Norman G. | 7 Central Ave., Ithaca, N. Y. | 36 |
| 8FT | Spargo, James A., jr. | 403 N. George St., Rome, N. Y. | 1,000 |
| 8LN | Spaulding, Ray F. | Ripley, N. Y. | 20 |

AMATEUR RADIO STATIONS—EIGHTH DISTRICT—ALPHABETICALLY BY OWNERS OF STATIONS—Continued.

| Call signal. | Owner of station. | Location of station. | Power. |
|---|---|---|---|
| | | | *Watts.* |
| 8HK | Spiller, Archibald G | 603 Missouri Ave., East Cleveland, Ohio | 550 |
| 8SH | Spotts, Ralph T | 2179 E. 87th St., Cleveland, Ohio | 700 |
| 8RU | Staaf, Werner | 5638 Weldin St., Pittsburgh, Pa | 60 |
| 8LH | Stauft, Jacob L | 347 Oakland Ave., Pittsburgh, Pa | 250 |
| 8II | Steim, L. Harold | R. F. D. No. 2, Kittanning, Pa | 270 |
| 8NK | Steinhoff, Charles F | 224 E. Lorain St., Oberlin, Ohio | 36 |
| 8IZ | Steinman, Dwight H | 416 Pine St., Lima, Ohio | 825 |
| 8NR | Stenger, John H | 66 Gildersleeve St., Wilkes-Barre, Pa | 1,000 |
| 8SL | Stenzel, Arthur W | 125 Geary St., Buffalo, N. Y | 550 |
| 8OL | Stern, Fred W | 835 Glenwood Ave., Cincinnati, Ohio | 165 |
| 8HE | Stevenson, George L | Durand, Mich | 1,000 |
| 8EO | Stickney, Richard W | 94 Normal Ave., Buffalo, N. Y | 25 |
| 8PR | Stiveson, Andrew | 4 North Ave., Pittsburgh, Pa | 24 |
| 8NY | Straub, John O | 1724 Wightman St., Pittsburgh, Pa | 250 |
| 8CA | Stueve, Everett S | 3540 Wabash Ave., Cincinnati, Ohio | 330 |
| 8IY | Swain, Herbert N | 405 Franklin St., Hamilton, Ohio | 990 |
| 8OH | Swisher, Oka V | 221 Spring St., Fairmont, W. Va | 80 |
| 8HJ | Terry, James E., jr | 1877 E. 90th St. NE., Cleveland, Ohio | 330 |
| 8CB | Thiessen, H. F. W | 161 E. McMicken Ave., Cincinnati, Ohio | 500 |
| 8DE | Thomas, William K | 400 Minton St., Pittsburgh, Pa | 250 |
| 8CM | Thorn, Thomas H | 1217 Chislett St., Pittsburgh, Pa | 225 |
| 8FN | Toland, Gerald H | R. F. D. No. 3, Geneseo, N. Y | 100 |
| 8IP | Trotter, Robert J | 214 Amanda Ave., Mt. Oliver, Pa | 30 |
| 8JE | Twitchell, Herbert D | 4th and Wood Sts., Hamilton, Ohio | 990 |
| 8KN | Tyne, Gerald F | 36 Walnut St., Binghamton, N. Y | 20 |
| 8RT | Ubersax, Delmar G | 2248 E. 100th St., Cleveland, Ohio | 18 |
| 8IF | Urban, Raymond G | Pine Ridge Rd., Buffalo, N. Y | 660 |
| 8ES | Van Hoesen, Claude L | 206 Frank St., Rochester, N. Y | 60 |
| 8LI | Vanselow, Waldemar | 206 W. 9th St., Holland, Mich | 24 |
| 8GI | Wahl, Edward C | 60 Stewart Ave., Buffalo, N. Y | 24 |
| 8OB | Waldrip, Laurence H | 233 Delavan St., Buffalo, N. Y | 36 |
| 8FD | Walker, Carl | 1626 Potter Pl., Cincinnati, Ohio | 27 |
| 8OS | Walker, Harlan N | 49 Rhode Island Ave., Detroit, Mich | 440 |
| 8QH | Washington, Booker | 724 Delaware Ave., Buffalo, N. Y | 48 |
| 8ME | Washington, George F | 37 Erie St., Washington, Pa | 24 |
| 8NA | Waterman, Fred W | 116 Broad St., Elyria, Ohio | 936 |
| 8MU | Watson, Martin L | 116 Alice St., Keyser, W. Va | 18 |
| 8DD | Watts, Felix J | 1118 Pearl St., Port Huron, Mich | 900 |
| 8PW | Weaver, Frank M | 2706 Toledo St., Pittsburgh, Pa | 1,000 |
| 8RC | Weil, Norman C | 231 Riley St., Buffalo, N. Y | 300 |
| 8NX | Weiser, Elmer P | 284 Brinkman St., Buffalo, N. Y | 30 |
| 8HW | Wellington, Vernon D | 511 Gibbs Ave., Wapakoneta, Ohio | 32 |
| 8OR | Weny, Joseph C | 58 Katherine Court, Allegan, Mich | 550 |
| 8JS | West Tech Wireless Club | W. 93d St. and Willard Ave., Cleveland, Ohio. | 1,000 |
| 8FS | Wheat, G. F. Roy | 605 Floyd Ave., Rome, N. Y | 54 |
| 8HX | White, Chester A | 18 Kamper Ave., Buffalo, N. Y | 220 |
| 8FW | Whitehead, D. R | 3349 Webster Ave., Pittsburgh, Pa | 24 |
| 8DK | Whitmoyer, Ralph E | 190 Frederick Ave., Detroit, Mich | 24 |
| 8LK | Wieneke, Edward | 128 Peterboro St., Detroit, Mich | 20 |
| 8HP | Wilder, John H | 194 Temple St., Fredonia, N. Y | 20 |
| 8IL | Williams, Burton P | 2321 Perrysville Ave. NS., Pittsburgh, Pa | 500 |
| 8KE | Williams, Edward R | 2106 E. 83d St., Cleveland, Ohio | 60 |
| 8DZ | Williams, Homer | 28 Auburn St., Ashtabula, Ohio | 12 |
| 8NG | Williams, Joseph H | 195 Bird Ave., Buffalo, N. Y | 36 |
| 8PY | Williams, Roy J | 499 Parsells Ave., Rochester, N. Y | 24 |
| 8IW | Wilson, Mark E | 323 12th St., Elyria, Ohio | 500 |
| 8NE | Winglemire, Maurice | Saginaw St., Holly, Mich | 1,000 |
| 8KH | Winston, Norman E | 276 Federal St., Rochester, N. Y | 30 |

54773°—14——10

AMATEUR RADIO STATIONS—EIGHTH DISTRICT—ALPHABETICALLY BY OWNERS OF STATIONS—Continued.

| Call signal. | Owner of station. | Location of station. | Power. |
|---|---|---|---|
| | | | Watts. |
| 8SA | Wood, Dewey H. | 402 E. Dutton St., Kalamazoo, Mich. | 20 |
| 8LM | Wood, John P. | Glenwood, N. Y. | 18 |
| 8SK | Woodcock, William D. | 496 W. Ferry St., Buffalo, N. Y. | 385 |
| 8OA | Worbass, Raymond K. | 7410 Carnegie Ave., Cleveland, Ohio. | 250 |
| 8DO | Wright, Claude B. | 822 Michigan St., Petoskey, Mich. | 550 |
| 8QX | Young, Charles A. | 427 Glenwood Ave., Buffalo, N. Y. | 15 |
| 8GB | Young Men's Christian Association. | Zara and Virginia Sts., Pittsburgh, Pa. | 270 |
| 8GK | Young, Montgomery K. | 19 Darien St., Rochester, N. Y. | 16 |
| 8RG | Zittel, Harold E. | 672 Elm St., Buffalo, N. Y. | 18 |

ALPHABETICALLY BY CALL SIGNALS.

| Call signal. | Owner of station. |
|---|---|
| 8AA | Anderson, Sidney E. |
| 8AB | Barr, Forrest L. |
| 8AC | Becelaere, Lawrence H. |
| 8AE | Berndt, William F. |
| 8AF | Brewer, George S. |
| 8AG | Broome, Donald W. |
| 8AH | Brown, Edward H. |
| 8AJ | Clough, Bert E. |
| 8AN | Davis, Frank. |
| 8AO | Deighan, Edward I. |
| 8AP | Dorsch, George. |
| 8AQ | Ela, Edward C. and Willard C. |
| 8AS | Feightner, Amos E. |
| 8AT | France, William. |
| 8AU | Frost, Harry E. |
| 8AV | Fullwood, William R. |
| 8AW | Gogel, Adelbert J. |
| 8AX | Gentzsch, Leonard H. |
| 8AY | Grosse, Frederick W. |
| 8AZ | Hansen, Edmund H. |
| 8BA | Hiller, Herbert A. |
| 8BB | Howes, Stanley L. |
| 8BC | Holt, Nelson E. |
| 8BD | Hoch, Ellery T. |
| 8BE | Lippert, John P. |
| 8BF | Jarvis, Roy B. |
| 8BG | Kastenberg, Paul G. |
| 8BH | Kingsbury, Kenneth. |
| 8BI | Kroeger, Gustav H. |
| 8BJ | Kraus, Norman M. |
| 8BK | Lappe, E. Robert. |
| 8BL | Leyh, Edward L. |
| 8BN | Lovejoy, Julian. |
| 8BO | Lyons, Henry E. |
| 8BP | Macer, Arthur J. |
| 8BQ | Menges, William E. |
| 8BR | Miner, Simeon J. |
| 8BS | Mogridge, Clarence J. |
| 8BT | Ogle, Harry B. |
| 8BV | Gale, Roy H. |
| 8BW | Hermann, Harold N. |
| 8BX | Hubbell, Aaron W. |
| 8BY | Schwindt, Herman J. |
| 8BZ | Shumard, Asbury. |
| 8CA | Stueve, Everett S. |
| 8CB | Thiessen, H. F. W. |
| 8CC | Kesel, George. |
| 8CD | Sachs, Gus. |
| 8CE | Adler, Jerome. |
| 8CF | Hull, Guy McC. |
| 8CG | Hull, Ralph S. |
| 8CH | Paul, James T. |
| 8CI | Richards, Theodore D. and George B. |
| 8CJ | Andrews, William S. |
| 8CK | Smith, Roland C. |
| 8CL | Smith, G. C. |
| 8CM | Thorn, Thomas H. |
| 8CN | Sheppard, Hamilton W. |
| 8CP | Baker, Norman E. |
| 8CQ | Brede, Erwin F. |
| 8CR | Coven, Allen W. |
| 8CS | Howland, Dean W. |
| 8CT | Myers, Raymond W. |
| 8CV | Smith, Lewis A. |
| 8CX | Phippeny, Forrest I. |
| 8CY | Payne, Arthur F. |
| 8CZ | London, Henry J. |
| 8DA | Rathbun, Hugh T. |
| 8DB | Fellows, Bernard D. |
| 8DC | Reb, Frank. |
| 8DD | Watts, Felix J. |
| 8DE | Thomas, William K. |
| 8DF | Orrell, Robert W. |
| 8DG | Bremer, Edmund H. |
| 8DI | Barton, Charles E. |
| 8DJ | Phillips, Glenn E. |
| 8DK | Whitmoyer, Ralph E. |
| 8DL | Sisson, William A. |
| 8DM | Bruns, Carl H. |
| 8DN | Knappen, Bert. |

AMATEUR RADIO STATIONS—EIGHTH DISTRICT—ALPHABETICALLY BY CALL SIGNALS—Continued.

| Call signal. | Owner of station. | Call signal. | Owner of station. |
|---|---|---|---|
| 8DO | Wright, Claude B. | 8GA | Burr, Gordon. |
| 8DQ | Roemer, Hubert J. | 8GB | Hill Top Y. M. C. A. |
| 8DR | Holmes, Charles E. | 8GD | Donnelly, John J. |
| 8DS | Moynahan, Roy D. | 8GE | Anderson, John M., jr. |
| 8DT | Rogers, Grant. | 8GF | Erney, J. Clarence. |
| 8DU | Downing, Harry E. | 8GG | Eucher, Clarence J. |
| 8DV | Cobb, Rupert G. | 8GH | Glekler, Truman J. |
| 8DW | Apger, Charles O. | 8GI | Wahl, Edward C. |
| 8DX | Porter, Harry T. | 8GJ | Green, Harold L. |
| 8DY | Pancoast, Donald F. | 8GK | Young, Montgomery K. |
| 8DZ | Williams, Homer. | 8GL | Konrad, Henry. |
| | | 8GM | Adams, Ralph F. |
| 8EA | Mack, Clifford J. | 8GN | Henninger, Alan E. |
| 8EB | Munsell, Robert S. | 8GP | Hoffman, Edward H. |
| 8ED | Carver, Alfred J. | 8GQ | Horn, Herbert E. |
| 8EE | Coleman, Clarence E. | 8GR | Joecken, George I. |
| 8EF | Dorst, Edward. | 8GS | Kneale, C. Kewley. |
| 8EG | Gebhard, Louis A. | 8GT | Hamel, Arthur. |
| 8EH | Grove, Nelson B. | 8GU | Loehr, George R. |
| 8EI | Gray, Clarence N. | 8GV | Kleber, Jackson O. |
| 8EJ | Kolb, Edwin H. | 8GW | Moffet, Floyd E. |
| 8EK | Kumpf, Elmer H. | 8GX | Pentland, Henry B. |
| 8EL | Langenbach, Leo. | 8GZ | Probeck, John. |
| 8EM | Murphy, John V. | | |
| 8EN | Shepard, Charles A. | 8HA | Roblee, Judson. |
| 8EO | Stickney, Richard W. | 8HB | Roberts, Hayden P. |
| 8EP | Scovill, Edward H. | 8HC | Johnston, S. Paul. |
| 8EQ | Leighton, Clifford R. | 8HD | Myers, Homer B. |
| 8ES | Van Hoesen, Claude L. | 8HE | Stevenson, George L. |
| 8ET | Goettel, Edward V. | 8HF | Shaney, Aubrey A. |
| 8EU | Carson, William J. | 8HG | Schardt, Earl M. |
| 8EV | Mason, Carl D. | 8HH | Schoren, William E. |
| 8EW | Rubel, Henry M., jr. | 8HI | Barber, Nelson J. |
| 8EX | Henlein, Carl A. | 8HJ | Terry, James E., jr. |
| 8EY | Blackmore, Andrew H. | 8HK | Spiller, Archibald G. |
| 8EZ | McConaughy, Mary Alice. | 8HL | McCamon, Aurel. |
| | | 8HM | Lucas, Howard E. |
| 8FA | Fender, Clinton H. | 8HN | Selinske, Louis. |
| 8FB | Britney, Dudley R. | 8HO | Holt, George W. |
| 8FC | Holden, Ira S. | 8HP | Wilder, John H. |
| 8FD | Walker, Carl. | 8HQ | Poux, Noel J. |
| 8FE | Finch, Brent S. | 8HR | Schouman, Hazen. |
| 8FF | Baker, Raymond S. | 8HS | Berry, L. Mack. |
| 8FG | Hewitt, Charles P. | 8HT | Romzick, Lawrence. |
| 8FH | Haynes, William. | 8HU | Faroo, Glenn. |
| 8FI | Burger, Richard W. | 8HV | Denniston, Harry J. |
| 8FJ | Clausing, Leroy M. E. | 8HW | Wellington, Vernon D. |
| 8FK | Donehoo, Gray G. | 8HX | White, Chester A. |
| 8FL | Jenkins, William E. | 8HY | Marshall, Floyd W. |
| 8FM | Olson, Milton E. | 8HZ | Fraser, John W. |
| 8FN | Toland, Gerald H. | | |
| 8FO | Snyder, Norman G. | 8IA | Bolton, Frederick R. |
| 8FQ | Remorino, L., jr. | 8IB | Mielke, Carl E. |
| 8FR | Brownell, Elmer. | 8IC | Hill, Charles C., jr. |
| 8FS | Wheat, G. F. Roy. | 8ID | Norris, George H. |
| 8FT | Spargo, James A., jr. | 8IE | Cross, Gorham L. |
| 8FU | Blattner, E. Herman. | 8IF | Urban, Raymond G. |
| 8FV | Backus, Harry F. | 8IG | Neumann, Allen J. |
| 8FW | Whitehead, D. R. | 8II | Steim, L. Harold. |
| 8FY | Schwalb, Walter J. | 8IJ | Diederich, Paul E. |
| 8FZ | Bennett, Edward J. | 8IK | Mellon, J. H. |

AMATEUR RADIO STATIONS—EIGHTH DISTRICT—ALPHABETICALLY BY CALL SIGNALS—Continued.

| Call signal. | Owner of station. | Call signal. | Owner of station. |
|---|---|---|---|
| 8IL | Williams, Burton P. | 8KW | Kohler, Harry W. |
| 8IM | Nichols, D. A. | 8KX | Cuff, Harold C. |
| 8IN | Miller, Kenneth. | 8KY | Kunnar, William. |
| 8IO | Roe, Howard L. | 8KZ | Landgraff, William J. |
| 8IP | Trotter, Robert J. | | |
| 8IQ | Richard, Roy H. | 8LA | Mason, George S. |
| 8IR | Miller, Arthur P. | 8LB | Purves, Stuart S. |
| 8IS | Middleton, Charles. | 8LC | Ramge, Edwin H. |
| 8IT | Cross, Gorham L. | 8LD | Rice, Homer D. |
| 8IU | Clarke, Andrew W. | 8LE | Scott, Hoyt S. |
| 8IV | Scott, Gail. | 8LF | Saunders, Ezra L. |
| 8IW | Wilson, Mark E. | 8LG | Sibert, Richard E. |
| 8IX | Newman, Arthur J. | 8LH | Stauft, Jacob L. |
| 8IY | Swain, Herbert N | 8LI | Vanselow, Waldemar |
| 8IZ | Steinman, Dwight H. | 8LJ | Baxter, Raymond L. |
| | | 8LK | Wieneke, Edward. |
| 8JA | Gunn, Ross. | 8LL | Schwanecamp, Raymond. |
| 8JB | Beare, George L. | 8LM | Wood, John P. |
| 8JC | Schoenhen, Edwin B. | 8LN | Spaulding, Ray F. |
| 8JD | Heiser, Ernest J. | 8LO | Breckel, Harry F. |
| 8JE | Twitchell, Herbert D. | 8LP | Bly, Ralph. |
| 8JF | Pleckenpol, Ernest. | 8LQ | Dunlap, Orrin E., jr. |
| 8JG | Lord, Donald M. | 8LR | Davis, Charles W. |
| 8JH | Edwards, C. Beaver. | 8LS | Ferris, Warren O. |
| 8JK | Jackson, Cotesworth M. | 8LT | Fryman, Zalman B. |
| 8JL | Appleton, Francis W. | 8LU | Hewitt, James F. |
| 8JO | Little, Donald G. | 8LV | Lindow, Daniel A. |
| 8JP | Becker, Freeman A. | 8LW | Philepp, Lawrence A. |
| 8JQ | Lusink, C. Irving | 8LX | Reitt, Arthur A. |
| 8JR | Sherrill, Alvan C. | 8LY | Rose, Herman |
| 8JS | West Tech Wireless Club. | 8LZ | Sharbaugh, Wilbur. |
| 8JT | Albrecht, Harvey O. | | |
| 8JU | Aldridge, George P. | 8MA | Schulz, Edward G. |
| 8JV | Kreighbaum, Cyril H. | 8MB | Maxon, Harry L. |
| 8JW | Anderson, Joseph D. | 8MC | Holmes, Charles A. |
| 8JX | MacCandless, Lyon H. | 8MD | Hall, Eldred R. |
| 8JZ | Manning, Alfred J. | 8ME | Washington, George F. |
| | | 8MF | Robbin, Milo H. |
| 8KA | Ankerman, Roy E. | 8MG | Fish, J. Mulford. |
| 8KB | Core, Eugene D. | 8MH | Bushnell, Clarence E. |
| 8KC | Manning, Jerry J. | 8MI | Manning, Howard H. |
| 8KD | Benjamin, Carlisle. | 8MJ | Cahow, Paul D. |
| 8KE | Williams, Edward R. | 8MK | Finch, William G. H. |
| 8KF | Broughton, Harry J. | 8ML | Lovell, Charles L. |
| 8KG | Camp, John D. | 8MM | Benzee, Arthur H., jr. |
| 8KH | Winston, Norman E. | 8MO | Corts, Raymond E. |
| 8KI | Flint High School. | 8MP | Neupert, Robert E. |
| 8KJ | Des Jardins, Gregory T. | 8MQ | Dear, Harry D. |
| 8KK | Devaney, Richard G. | 8MR | Livinggood, Hubert W. |
| 8KL | Dreifus, Fred B. | 8MS | Ritchie, Ole B. |
| 8KM | Eden, Henley S. | 8MT | Liller, William P. |
| 8KN | Tyne, Gerald F. | 8MU | Watson, Martin L. |
| 8KO | Combs, Frayne. | 8MV | Carson, William H. |
| 8KP | Fuss, Chester G. | 8MW | Follet, Louis, jr. |
| 8KQ | Fisher, Earl U. | 8MX | De Rose, Ralph. |
| 8KR | Hills, Virgil A. | 8MY | Fisher, Harold W. |
| 8KS | Sidnell, Robert G. | 8MZ | Davison, John. |
| 8KT | Benzee, Joseph M. | | |
| 8KU | Jones, Miller. | 8NA | Waterman, Fred W. |
| 8KV | Dobbie, John, jr. | 8NB | Chaffee, C. Lloyd. |

AMATEUR RADIO STATIONS—EIGHTH DISTRICT—ALPHABETICALLY BY CALL SIGNALS—Continued.

| Call signal. | Owner of station. |
|---|---|
| 8NC | Coolidge, James H., 3d. |
| 8ND | Grigg, Arthur. |
| 8NE | Winglemire, Maurice. |
| 8NF | House, Elra E. |
| 8NG | Williams, Joseph H. |
| 8NH | Hyatt, Bunyan J. |
| 8NI | Daniels, Worth D. |
| 8NJ | Bartholomew, William F. |
| 8NK | Steinhoff, Charles F. |
| 8NL | Budwig, Gilbert G. |
| 8NM | Keen, William L. |
| 8NN | Hahn, Ralph H. |
| 8NO | Hansen, Torvald. |
| 8NP | Henderson, Earl G. |
| 8NQ | Robbins, Melvin G. |
| 8NR | Stenger, John H. |
| 8NS | Beck, Frank G. |
| 8NT | Maue, Leon G. |
| 8NU | Brown, Willard S. |
| 8NV | Harrison, P. William, jr. |
| 8NW | Hankin, John H. |
| 8NX | Weiser, Elmer P. |
| 8NY | Straub, John O. |
| 8NZ | Payne, William H. |
| 8OA | Worbass, Raymond K. |
| 8OB | Waldrip, Laurence H. |
| 8OC | Kuehnlo, George J. |
| 8OD | Luedeke, William P., jr. |
| 8OE | Smith, Verne E. |
| 8OF | Goodwin, Seth A. |
| 8OG | Brink, Frank J. |
| 8OH | Swisher, Oka V. |
| 8OI | Patterson, Grant, jr. |
| 8OJ | Furlong, Marcie J. |
| 8OK | Scheib, Joseph. |
| 8OL | Stern, Fred W. |
| 8OM | Balsley, James I. |
| 8ON | Ilgenfritz, Lester M. |
| 8OO | Bird, Harold C. |
| 8OP | Reynolds, Charles L. |
| 8OQ | Butzler, Harry. |
| 8OR | Weny, Joseph C. |
| 8OS | Walker, Harlan N. |
| 8OT | Foster, Frank, jr. |
| 8OU | Boyer, Harry. |
| 8OV | Marcum, Richard. |
| 8OW | Dotterweich, Joseph H. |
| 8OX | Dreux, Alexander J. |
| 8OY | McElhinny, J. Schubert. |
| 8OZ | Fleming, James J. |
| 8PA | Boekeloo, Ross M. |
| 8PB | Henika, Charles F. |
| 8PC | Kersting, Ferdinand. |
| 8PD | Krause, Karl A. |
| 8PE | Lucas, Clarence E. |
| 8PF | Malbin, Samuel. |
| 8PG | Sherman, Fred. |
| 8PH | Slyfield, Charles O. |

| Call signal. | Owner of station. |
|---|---|
| 8PI | Day, James M. |
| 8PJ | Ehrick, William F. |
| 8PK | Gamble, Frederick D. |
| 8PL | Higgins, Robert R. |
| 8PM | Higgy, Robert C. |
| 8PN | Ritchie, Burrus L. |
| 8PO | Schaaf, John M. |
| 8PP | Butcher, W. Byron. |
| 8PQ | Shaw, Eurcile L. |
| 8PR | Stiveson, Andrew. |
| 8PS | Hart, John R. |
| 8PT | Hornung, Romey W. |
| 8PU | Imbt, Russell. |
| 8PV | Pearson, Harry. |
| 8PW | Weaver, Frank M. |
| 8PX | Marsh, Harry H., jr. |
| 8PY | Williams, Roy J. |
| 8PZ | Bishop, Carryl L. |
| 8QA | Ferguson, James G. |
| 8QB | Haderer, John. |
| 8QC | Hauck, Roland E. |
| 8QE | Kester, Harold P. |
| 8QF | Klinck, Charles C., jr. |
| 8QG | Lewis, Walter E. |
| 8QH | Washington, Booker. |
| 8QI | McEniry, Clifford U. |
| 8QJ | Bornman, Frederick D. |
| 8QK | Jones, Edwin P. |
| 8QL | Emmert, Herman C. |
| 8QM | Jones, Jesse K. |
| 8QN | Given, Everett J. |
| 8QO | Kirly, H. Howard. |
| 8QP | Powell, Ralph C. |
| 8QQ | Kampfe, Norbert J. |
| 8QR | Grostick, George E. |
| 8QS | Brow, Robert. |
| 8QT | Sly, Edward E. |
| 8QU | Schunck, Robert F. |
| 8QV | Hogan, James E. |
| 8QW | Potts, Charles G. |
| 8QX | Young, Charles A. |
| 8QY | Martin, Cecil E. |
| 8QZ | Fletcher, Vernon. |
| 8RA | Klager, Oscar C. |
| 8RB | Knapp, Harold. |
| 8RC | Weil, Norman C. |
| 8RD | Burr, Roy C. |
| 8RE | Frank, Alfred. |
| 8RF | Ritchie, Carl L. |
| 8RG | Zittel, Howell E. |
| 8RH | Blum, Robert A. |
| 8RI | Beeler, Hughes. |
| 8RJ | Irvine, Robert P. |
| 8RK | Dalrymple, Clarence F. |
| 8RL | Last, George. |
| 8RM | Smith, Harold M. |
| 8RO | Gwinner, Frederick, 3d. |
| 8RP | Amos, Clyde O. |

AMATEUR RADIO STATIONS—EIGHTH DISTRICT—ALPHABETICALLY BY OWNERS OF STATIONS—Continued.

| Call signal. | Owner of station. | Call signal. | Owner of station. |
|---|---|---|---|
| 8RQ | Ashtabula High School. | 8SE | Falck, Norman B. |
| 8RR | Hull, Earl C. | 8SF | Fowler, Robert J. |
| 8RT | Ubersax, Delmar G. | 8SG | Pesek, Miro R. |
| 8RU | Staaf, Werner. | 8SH | Spotts, Ralph T. |
| 8RV | Marshall, Frank J. | 8SI | Beach, Walter R. |
| 8RW | Schmidle, Claude. | 8SJ | Ottney, James N. |
| 8RX | Barringer, Russ. | 8SK | Woodcock, William D. |
| 8RY | Goetz, Carl P. | 8SL | Stenzel, Arthur W. |
| 8RZ | Fritz, Rudolph A. | 8SM | Coleman, H. Burr. |
| | | 8SN | Glatzel, Earle D. |
| 8SA | Wood, Dewey H. | 8SO | Maggs, H. Carrol. |
| 8SB | Schmidt, Norman F. | 8SP | Rich, Harland E. |
| 8SC | Bidwell, Paul. | 8SQ | Clarke, John H. |
| 8SD | Schindler, Louis J. | | |

## NINTH DISTRICT.

[Headquarters: Customhouse, Chicago, Ill. The ninth district comprises the States of Indiana, Illinois, Wisconsin, Michigan (Upper Peninsula), Minnesota, Kentucky, Missouri, Kansas, Colorado, Iowa, Nebraska, South Dakota, and North Dakota.]

### ALPHABETICALLY BY OWNERS OF STATIONS.

| Call signal. | Owner of station. | Location of station. | Power. |
|---|---|---|---|
| | | | Watts. |
| 9FN | Abraham, Walter H. | 1204½ W. 5th St., Davenport, Iowa | 16 |
| 9EX | Adolfson, George S. | 5229 Colorado St., Duluth, Minn. | 770 |
| 9BF | Afanasiew, Nick | 1265 S. Bannock St., Denver, Colo. | 30 |
| 9FC | Anders, Harry R. | 4811 West End Ave., Chicago, Ill. | 495 |
| 9CF | Anderson, Adolf G. | 502 St. Lawrence Ave., Beloit, Wis. | 500 |
| 9GW | Arnold, Ercil | Chapman, Kans. | 250 |
| 9CO | Bantz, Russell | 414 22d Ave., Milwaukee, Wis. | 50 |
| 9DA | Berger, Frank G. | 1425 Edgemont Ave., Chicago, Ill. | 225 |
| 9HE | Bergvall, Royal C. and Wesley E. | Stephenson, Wis. | 20 |
| 9AS | Billiter, Earle D. | 2610 S. Dupont Ave., Minneapolis, Minn. | 1,000 |
| 9DJ | Biltonen, William A. | Houghton, Mich. | 50 |
| 9GB | Boess, Murray R. | Lake Bluff, Ill. | 24 |
| 9BU | Brown, Clarence L. | 1022 E. Tabor St., Indianapolis, Ind. | 500 |
| 9AD | Bryant, Stanley C. | 2439 Mozart St., Chicago, Ill. | 150 |
| 9CR | Buehner, Howard | 381 19th Ave., Milwaukee, Wis. | ..... |
| 9GY | Bullock, Asa C. | Hobart, Ind. | 1,000 |
| 9ED | Burgess, Charles M. | Geneva, Ill. | ..... |
| 9GX | Capper, Earl W. | Letts Corner, Ind. | 24 |
| 9BJ | Chapin, Edwin C. | 79 Washington St., Denver, Colo. | 500 |
| 9FI | Chaudet, William J. | 4176-A Delmar Blvd., St. Louis, Mo. | 500 |
| 9DP | Clark, Bayard H. | 205 Augusta Ave., De Kalb, Ill. | 1,000 |
| 9GU | Clayton, Homer E. | 680 Arch St., Indianaoplis, Ind. | 770 |
| 9BK | Clemons, G. H. | Storm Lake, Iowa | 50 |
| 9CN | Cobb, Merle | Elkhorn, Wis. | 50 |
| 9GV | Coles, James A. | 1500 Park Ave., Minneapolis, Minn. | 63 |
| 9BG | Connell, John F. | 205 E. Jackson St., Attica, Ind. | 50 |
| 9ET | Conzelman, J. Wilson | 5207 Ridge Ave., St. Louis, Mo. | 770 |
| 9DI | Cottrell, W. Roscoe | Prairie City, Iowa | 50 |
| 9EQ | Cruikshank, Charles A., jr. | 1000 Bird St., Hannibal, Mo. | 660 |
| 9GN | Curtis, Charles D. | High School Bldg., Pembina, N. Dak. | 100 |
| 9AI | Cutting, Irving E. | 3611 Galena St., Milwaukee, Wis. | 700 |
| 9FH | Dahm, Henry L. | 5932 Plymouth Ave., St. Louis, Mo. | 950 |

AMATEUR RADIO STATIONS—NINTH DISTRICT—ALPHABETICALLY BY OWNERS OF STATIONS—Continued.

| Call signal. | Owner of station. | Location of station. | Power. |
|---|---|---|---|
| | | | *Watts.* |
| 9DF | Dangerfield, Alfred H | 405 Moffett Ave., Joplin, Mo | 275 |
| 9EZ | Davis, Richard M | 1065 Yuma St., Denver, Colo | 40 |
| 9EG | Dean, Carl W | 3115 N. Capitol Ave., Indianapolis, Ind | 460 |
| 9GP | Denny, L. Erle | Sorento, Ill | 24 |
| 9FE | Dunklan, George | 2634 Cottage Grove Ave., Chicago, Ill | 250 |
| 9BT | Duquette, Herbert E | 500 Glen Ave., Council Bluffs, Iowa | 250 |
| 9CW | Egloff, Martin F | 2729 W. Noble Ave., Chicago, Ill | 400 |
| 9EN | Fisher, Ralph | 918 S. 7th St., Fargo, N. Dak | 330 |
| 9BN | Flynn, John H., jr | 228 E. 5th St., Newport, Ky | 1,000 |
| 9AM | Foster, Edwin J | 925 Winchester St., Milwaukee, Wis | 750 |
| 9AX | Fowler, Harry A | 3 E. Armour Blvd., Kansas City, Mo | 1,000 |
| 9EK | French, Newell E | 1722 Maple St., Racine, Wis | 250 |
| 9BO | Fry, Claud | 833 W. 12th St., Des Moines, Iowa | 50 |
| 9BP | Gatzek, Richard | 317 S. 5th St., Richmond, Ind | 450 |
| 9AZ | Gerhard, George J | 1710 Dorcas St., Omaha, Nebr | 250 |
| 9DL | Goodell, Myron L | 613 N. Broadway, Abilene, Kans | 250 |
| 9ES | Graham, Walter N., jr | 4842 Maffitt Ave., St. Louis, Mo | 110 |
| 9FT | Graves, G. G | Woodstock, Ill | 60 |
| 9GT | Grecian, Everett | Hill City, Kans | 1,000 |
| 9AB | Groskopf, William L | 4816 W. Berteau Ave., Chicago, Ill | 250 |
| 9AE | Gundlach, Waldo L | 1837 Pratt Ave., Chicago, Ill | 20 |
| 9GG | Hagen, Edwin | 2330 Banks Ave., Superior, Wis | 220 |
| 9AV | Hamel, Walter H | 1006 S. 14th St., Lafayette, Ind | ...... |
| 9CV | Hamilton, Leo L | 111 Brainard St., Harvard, Ill | 500 |
| 9CE | Hansen, Leland H | 1123 Herrick Ave., Racine, Wis | 500 |
| 9GI | Hanson, Frederick R. A | 477 31st Ave., Milwaukee, Wis | 24 |
| 9BX | Hantzsch, Ralph E | 1161 Island Ave., Milwaukee, Wis | 275 |
| 9CJ | Harry, Charles | Quincy and Douglas Sts., Houghton, Mich | 660 |
| 9FL | Hauck, George | 218 Chestnut St., Newport, Ky | 16 |
| 9CX | Haynes, Roy | 6939 May St., Chicago, Ill | 420 |
| 9FR | Heckenkamp, Emile B | 300 E St., Belleville, Ill | 770 |
| 9CP | Held, William J | 770 Washington St., Milwaukee, Wis | 50 |
| 9CU | Hieronymus, Thomas G | 3512 Independence Ave., Kansas City, Mo | 50 |
| 9DG | Hilgenberg, Noble C | 827 N. Capitol Ave., Indianapolis, Ind | 50 |
| 9AR | Hines, Gene | 1209 W. 25th St., Minneapolis, Minn | 250 |
| 9AF | Hollister, Harold A | 370 18th Ave., Milwaukee, Wis | ...... |
| 9FQ | Hood, Norman R | Y. M. C. A. Bldg., Burlington, Iowa | 20 |
| 9FF | Hughes, Walter J | 4100 State St., Chicago, Ill | 25 |
| 9GZ | Ihl, G. Sheridan | 3834 N. 25th St., St. Louis, Mo | 330 |
| 9EW | Jackson, Arved C | 910 N. Girard Ave., Minneapolis, Minn | 30 |
| 9BI | Jens, Elmer | 1401 3d St., Davenport, Iowa | 50 |
| 9DE | Jensen, Arnold L | 334 High School Ave., Council Bluffs, Iowa. | 450 |
| 9CI | Johnson, August R | Houghton, Mich | 50 |
| 9BS | Jorgenson, Harold | 941 Herrick Ave., Racine, Wis | 50 |
| 9CZ | Joyce, Raymond A | 516 E. 41st St., Chicago, Ill | 500 |
| 9BD | Keeler, Fayette W | 1807 Cumming Ave., Superior, Wis | 1,000 |
| 9EH | Kegley, William F | 2430 Kenwood Ave., Indianapolis, Ind | 1,000 |
| 9BY | Kennan, Richard C | 3170 N. Illinois St., Indianapolis, Ind | 250 |
| 9FA | King, Lawrence | 416 W. Michigan St., New Carlisle, Ind | 495 |
| 9AA | Klentz, Clarence | 3809 Vincennes Ave., Chicago, Ill | 500 |
| 9CM | Klicpera, Milhart F | 1705 Douglas Ave., Racine, Wis | 500 |
| 9DH | Knehans, Irwin N | 7 S. Sprigg St., Cape Girardeau, Mo | 250 |
| 9DB | Knotts, H. J. E | Illiopolis, Ill | 60 |
| 9AK | Kottler, Carl F | 1035 2d St., Milwaukee, Wis | ...... |
| 9EJ | Kreis, Erwin | 542 35th St., Milwaukee, Wis | 18 |
| 9FU | La Duke, Earl R | 1100 S. Josephine St., Denver, Colo | 250 |
| 9EU | Landis, Clyde L | 3020 S. Bryant Ave., Minneapolis, Minn | 250 |
| 9EC | Lebo, Robert B | 1306 Main St., Richmond, Ind | 700 |
| 9AO | Lipman, Theodore E. K | 136 W. Grand Ave., Beloit, Wis | 1,000 |

AMATEUR RADIO STATIONS—NINTH DISTRICT—ALPHABETICALLY BY OWNERS OF STATIONS—Continued.

| Call signal. | Owner of station. | Location of station. | Power. |
|---|---|---|---|
| | | | Watts. |
| 9GK | Lobas, John | 635 31st St., Milwaukee, Wis | 24 |
| 9GL | Long, Frank A | 6046 Woodlawn Ave., Chicago, Ill | 440 |
| 9EM | Love, Andrew A., jr | 812 S. 7th St., Fargo, N. Dak | 110 |
| 9CK | Lowe, Meredith B | 237½ E. Pratt St., Indianapolis, Ind | 50 |
| 9CG | Mahan, Joe R | 214 S. 6th St., Independence, Kans | 280 |
| 9FB | Martin, John J | 2107 Adams St., Chicago, Ill | 220 |
| 9AG | Marx, Gustav A | 334½ 15th St., Milwaukee, Wis | ..... |
| 9BB | Mattenheimer, Ervin B | 559 Lexington Ave., Newport, Ky | 85 |
| 9AC | McGuffage, William J | 4418 Wabash Ave., Chicago, Ill | 500 |
| 9ER | McLoad, Kenneth | 3962-A Blaine Ave., St. Louis, Mo | 550 |
| 9FZ | McManus, John C | 1001 Morgan St., Keokuk, Iowa | 150 |
| 9BH | Miller, R. Boyce | 400 S. 16th St., Independence, Kans | 500 |
| 9CD | Moen, Vere | 216 Cedar St., Boone, Iowa | 50 |
| 9BR | Moore, Robert R | 200 E. Armour Blvd., Kansas City, Mo | 1,000 |
| 9FW | Moreland, Henry F | 1009 Washington Ave., Cairo, Ill | 400 |
| 9AP | Morgan, Hiram | R. F. D. No. 30, Beloit, Wis | 1,000 |
| 9GF | Mueller, Carl E | 1010 S. Pierce St., Milwaukee, Wis | 24 |
| 9EL | Murphy, James P | Broadland, S. Dak | 30 |
| 9BE | Myers, Delbert | Amboy, Ind | 45 |
| 9BQ | Nelson, Eddie | 731 N. 3d St., Fargo, N. Dak | 550 |
| 9CA | Norene, Raymond E | 2558 Avenue A, Council Bluffs, Iowa | 220 |
| 9FK | Oetjen, Richard J | Williams Bay, Wis | 500 |
| 9DK | O'Neil, Donald H. C | 5740 Bartmer Ave., St. Louis, Mo | 600 |
| 9FY | Pagett, Harry L | 1027 Fulton St., Keokuk, Iowa | 18 |
| 9BL | Perine, W. B | 1728 Hall Pl., Indianapolis, Ind | 500 |
| 9CC | Pierson, Oscar E | Williams Bay, Wis | 60 |
| 9HD | Prahl, Louis | 463 10th Ave., Milwaukee, Wis | 24 |
| 9FM | Preuss, Arthur C | 212 E. 9th St., Newport, Ky | 10 |
| 9AY | Quinby, Porter H | 114 S. 19th St., Omaha, Nebr | 20 |
| 9GA | Racke, Arthur L | 31 18th St., Newport, Ky | 490 |
| 9CS | Ragan, Tate V | 523 Garfield Ave., Kansas City, Mo | ..... |
| 9FO | Rehm, Ralph E | 1102 N. 3d St., Kansas City, Kans | 160 |
| 9BW | Reinhardt, William | 3437 Taylor St., Omaha, Nebr | 250 |
| 9FS | Reineke, Earl C | 1019 S. 5th Ave., Fargo, N. Dak | 1,000 |
| 9CH | Riggin, Benjamin F | 2112 Ammie Ave., Kansas City, Mo | 50 |
| 9AQ | Riner, John A | High School, Beloit, Wis | 1,000 |
| 9EO | Rivett, Ralph | 1934 Garfield Ave., Lincoln, Nebr | 400 |
| 9GS | Robbins, Donald T | 15 W. 58th St., Kansas City, Mo | 24 |
| 9EV | Sandquist, Reuben G | 1122 W. Erie St., Chicago, Ill | 20 |
| 9FV | Saunders, P. Bushnell | 700 E. 4th St., Delta, Colo | 550 |
| 9AL | Schroeder, Walter | 647 Washington St., Milwaukee, Wis | ..... |
| 9DN | Sears, Charles L | 1322 Bayard Ave., St. Louis, Mo | 185 |
| 9GH | Sever, Harold C | 303 E. Broadway, Pleasant Plains, Ill | 40 |
| 9BM | Shively, Roy J | 827 S. 29th St., Omaha, Nebr | 500 |
| 9EF | Shotwell, Harold H | 446 W. 61st Pl., Chicago, Ill | 770 |
| 9AJ | Siegel, Robert C | 478 Potter Ave., Milwaukee, Wis | 800 |
| 9EE | Silcox, Harry | 1526 S. New Jersey St., Indianapolis, Ind | 550 |
| 9GJ | Simpson, Virgil S | 1380 Union Ave., St. Louis, Mo | 550 |
| 9GE | Smith, Hubert A | 301 W. Illinois St., Urbana, Ill | 1,000 |
| 9BA | Smith, Paul C | Mulberry, Ind | 60 |
| 9FX | Smith, Wilson | 219 Rome Ave., Rockford, Ill | 450 |
| 9DO | Snyder, W. Roy | 5356 Easton Ave., St. Louis, Mo | 275 |
| 9EI | Spaniol, John T | 1324 Harrison St., Superior, Wis | 250 |
| 9GM | Sproehnle, John R | 5809 Blackstone Ave., Chicago, Ill | 250 |
| 9AT | Stetson, Donald T | 2162 Carrol Ave., St. Paul, Minn | 400 |
| 9AW | Stewart, Albert H | 522 Ann St., Frankfort, Ky | 250 |
| 9EA | Stribley, Orris J | 511 S. 4th St., Moorhead, Minn | 220 |
| 9FP | Tawkes, Charles E | 503 Hill St., Dubuque, Iowa | 85 |
| 9AU | Taylor, Thomas J | 1846 Lincoln Ave., St. Paul, Minn | 280 |
| 9BC | Thesing, Herman | 216 N. 16th St., Richmond, Ind | 500 |

**Amateur Radio Stations—Ninth District—Alphabetically by Owners of Stations—Continued.**

| Call signal. | Owner of station. | Location of station. | Power. |
|---|---|---|---|
| | | | Watts. |
| 9AH | Thomas, Carroll W. | 266 17th St., Milwaukee, Wis. | 12 |
| 9GO | Thompson, Harry E. | 712 E. Madison St., Belvidere, Ill | 100 |
| 9GD | Thompson, Hugh L. | 3810 Walnut St., Kansas City, Mo | 24 |
| 9EB | Tomann, Orville R. | R. F. D. No. 1, Ellsworth, Wis. | 21 |
| 9DD | Tschernitz, Frank | 315 Chestnut St., Milwaukee, Wi | 250 |
| 9EY | Urquhart, David G. | 110 S. Irving Ave., Chicago, Ill | 32 |
| 9BZ | Van Deusen, Arthur S., jr. | 1613 Wesley Ave., Evanston, Ill. | 200 |
| 9BV | Van Slyck, Wellington | 836 Main St., Lake Geneva, Wi | 250 |
| 9DC | Wanner, Theodore L. | Fargo, N. Dak. | 1,000 |
| 9CT | Wember, Anthony A. | 89 13th St., North Chicago, Ill. | 550 |
| 9CQ | Weyant, James E. | Shortridge High School, Indianapolis, Ind | 250 |
| 9CL | Whitaker, Harold P. | 1004 10th St., Racine, Wis. | 50 |
| 9GQ | Wiggin, Parker E. | 737 Waverly Ave., Kansas City, Kans. | 550 |
| 9AN | Willett, Charles J. | 425 Clement Ave., Milwaukee, Wis. | 110 |
| 9FG | Wilson, Gilbert M. | 718 S. 10th St., La Fayette, Ind | 495 |
| 9EP | Wilson, Guy E. | 3922 Flora Ave., Kansas City, Mo | 40 |
| 9HA | Woods, William L. | 4536 A Laclede Ave., St. Louis, Mo | 500 |
| 9CY | Wooster, Stanley W. | 5731 Lowe Ave., Chicago, Ill | 420 |
| 9FJ | Wyckoff, Ralph R. | 167 Diamond St., Houghton, Mich | 27 |
| 9HB | Yoaker, J. Clayton | Lake Bluff, Ill. | 24 |
| 9DM | Ziesenis, Harry | 700 Mississippi St., Lawrence, Kans. | [illegible] |

**ALPHABETICALLY BY CALL SIGNALS.**

| Call signal. | Owner of station. | Call signal. | Owner of station. |
|---|---|---|---|
| 9AA | Klentz, Clarence. | 9BF | Afanasiew, Nick. |
| 9AB | Groskopf, William L. | 9BG | Connell, John F. |
| 9AC | McGuffage, William J. | 9BH | Miller, R. Boyce. |
| 9AD | Bryant, Stanley C. | 9BI | Jens, Elmer. |
| 9AE | Gundlach, Waldo L. | 9BJ | Chapin, Edwin C. |
| 9AF | Hollister, Harold A. | 9BK | Clemons, G. H. |
| 9AG | Marx, Gustav A. | 9BL | Perine, W. B. |
| 9AH | Thomas, Carroll W. | 9BM | Shively, Roy J. |
| 9AI | Cutting, Irving E. | 9BN | Flynn, John H., jr. |
| 9AJ | Siegel, Robert C. | 9BO | Fry, Claud. |
| 9AK | Kottler, Carl F. | 9BP | Gatzek, Richard. |
| 9AL | Schroeder, Walter. | 9BQ | Nelson, Eddie. |
| 9AM | Foster, Edwin J. | 9BR | Moore, Robert R. |
| 9AN | Willett, Charles J. | 9BS | Jorgenson, Harold. |
| 9AO | Lipman, Theodore E. K. | 9BT | Duquette, Herbert E. |
| 9AP | Morgan, Hiram. | 9BU | Brown, Clarence L. |
| 9AQ | Riner, John A. | 9BV | Van Slyck, Wellington. |
| 9AR | Hines, Gene. | 9BW | Reinhardt, William. |
| 9AS | Billiter, Earle D. | 9BX | Hantzsch, Ralph E. |
| 9AT | Stetson, Donald T. | 9BY | Kennan, Richard C. |
| 9AU | Taylor, Thomas J. | 9BZ | Van Deusen, Arthur S., jr. |
| 9AV | Hamel, Walter H. | | |
| 9AW | Stewart, Albert H. | 9CA | Norene, Raymond E. |
| 9AX | Fowler, Harry A. | 9CC | Pierson, Oscar E. |
| 9AY | Quinby, Porter H. | 9CD | Moen, Vere. |
| 9AZ | Gerhard, George J. | 9CE | Hansen, Leland H. |
| | | 9CF | Anderson, Adolf G. |
| 9BA | Smith, Paul C. | 9CG | Mahan, Joe R. |
| 9BB | Mattenheimer, Ervin B. | 9CH | Riggin, Benjamin F. |
| 9BC | Thesing, Herman. | 9CI | Johnson, August R. |
| 9BD | Keeler, Fayette W. | 9CJ | Harry, Charles. |
| 9BE | Myers, Delbert. | 9CK | Lowe, Meredith B. |

AMATEUR RADIO STATIONS—NINTH DISTRICT—ALPHABETICALLY BY CALL SIGNALS—Continued.

| Call signal. | Owner of station. |
|---|---|
| 9CL | Whitaker, Harold P. |
| 9CM | Klicpera, Milhart F. |
| 9CN | Cobb, Merle. |
| 9CO | Bantz, Russell. |
| 9CP | Held, William J. |
| 9CQ | Weyant, James E. |
| 9CR | Buehner, Howard. |
| 9CS | Ragan, Tate V. |
| 9CT | Wember, Anthony A. |
| 9CU | Hieronymus, Thomas G. |
| 9CV | Hamilton, Leo L. |
| 9CW | Egloff, Martin F. |
| 9CX | Haynes, Roy. |
| 9CY | Wooster, Stanley W. |
| 9CZ | Joyce, Raymond A. |
| 9DA | Berger, Frank G. |
| 9DB | Knotts, H. J. E. |
| 9DC | Wanner, Theodore L. |
| 9DD | Tschernitz, Frank. |
| 9DE | Jensen, Arnold L. |
| 9DF | Dangerfield, Alfred H. |
| 9DG | Hilgenberg, Noble C. |
| 9DH | Knehans, Irwin N. |
| 9DI | Cottrell, W. Roscoe. |
| 9DJ | Biltonen, William A. |
| 9DK | O'Neil, Donald H. C. |
| 9DL | Goodell, Myron L. |
| 9DM | Ziesenis, Harry. |
| 9DN | Sears, Charles L. |
| 9DO | Snyder, W. Roy. |
| 9DP | Clark, Bayard H. |
| 9EA | Stribley, Orris J. |
| 9EB | Tomann, Orville R. |
| 9EC | Lebo, Robert B. |
| 9ED | Burgess, Charles M. |
| 9EE | Silcox, Harry. |
| 9EF | Shotwell, Harold H. |
| 9EG | Dean, Carl W. |
| 9EH | Kegley, William F. |
| 9EI | Spaniol, John T. |
| 9EJ | Kreis, Erwin. |
| 9EK | French, Newell E. |
| 9EL | Murphy, James P. |
| 9EM | Love, Andrew A., jr. |
| 9EN | Fisher, Ralph. |
| 9EO | Rivett, Ralph. |
| 9EP | Wilson, Guy E. |
| 9EQ | Cruikshank, Charles A., jr. |
| 9ER | McLoad, Kenneth. |
| 9ES | Graham, Walter N., jr. |
| 9ET | Conzelman, J. Wilson. |
| 9EU | Landis, Clyde L. |
| 9EV | Sandquist, Reuben G. |
| 9EW | Jackson, Arved C. |
| 9EX | Adolfson, George S. |
| 9EY | Urquhart, David G. |
| 9EZ | Davis, Richard M. |
| 9FA | King, Lawrence |
| 9FB | Martin, John J. |
| 9FC | Anders, Harry R. |
| 9FE | Dunklan, George. |
| 9FF | Hughes, Walter J. |
| 9FG | Wilson, Gilbert M. |
| 9FH | Dahm, Henry L. |
| 9FI | Chaudet, William J. |
| 9FJ | Wyckoff, Ralph R. |
| 9FK | Oetjen, Richard J. |
| 9FL | Hauck, George. |
| 9FM | Preuss, Arthur C. |
| 9FN | Abraham, Walter H. |
| 9FO | Rehm, Ralph E. |
| 9FP | Tawkes, Charles E. |
| 9FQ | Hood, Norman R. |
| 9FR | Heckencamp, Emile B. |
| 9FS | Reineke, Earl C. |
| 9FT | Graves, G. G. |
| 9FU | La Duke, Earl R. |
| 9FV | Saunders, P. Bushnell. |
| 9FW | Moreland, Henry F. |
| 9FX | Smith, Wilson. |
| 9FY | Pagett, Harry L. |
| 9FZ | McManus, John C. |
| 9GA | Racke, Arthur L. |
| 9GB | Boess, Murray R. |
| 9GD | Thompson, Hugh L. |
| 9GE | Smith, Hubert A. |
| 9GF | Mueller, Carl E. |
| 9GG | Hagen, Edwin. |
| 9GH | Sever, Harold C. |
| 9GI | Hanson, Frederick R. A. |
| 9GJ | Simpson, Virgil S. |
| 9GK | Lobas, John. |
| 9GL | Long, Frank A. |
| 9GM | Sproehnle, John R. |
| 9GN | Curtis, Charles D. |
| 9GO | Thompson, Harry E. |
| 9GP | Denny, L. Erle. |
| 9GQ | Wiggin, Parker E. |
| 9GS | Robbins, Donald T. |
| 9GT | Grecian, Everett. |
| 9GU | Clayton, Homer E. |
| 9GV | Coles, James A. |
| 9GW | Arnold, Ercil. |
| 9GX | Capper, Earl W. |
| 9GY | Bullock, Asa C. |
| 9GZ | Ihl, G. Sheridan. |
| 9HA | Woods, William E. |
| 9HB | Youker, J. Clayton. |
| 9HD | Prahl, Louis. |
| 9HE | Bergvall, Royal C. and Wesley E. |

Zeitfracht Medien GmbH
Ferdinand-Jühlke-Straße 7
99095 Erfurt, Deutschland
produktsicherheit@kolibri360.de